Richmond upon Thames Libraries

Renew online at www.richmond.gov.uk/libraries

LONDON B(
RICHMOND

D1380117

90710 000 243 024

Guides

Time Out Digital Ltd
4th Floor
125 Shaftesbury Avenue
London WC2H 8AD
United Kingdom
Tel: +44 (0)20 7813 3000
Fax: +44 (0)20 7813 6001
Email: guides@timeout.com
www.timeout.com

Published by Time Out Digital Ltd, a wholly owned subsidiary
of Time Out Group Ltd. Time Out and the Time Out logo are
trademarks of Time Out Group Ltd.

© Time Out Group Ltd 2015

10 9 8 7 6 5 4 3 2 1

This edition first published in Great Britain in 2015 by Ebury Publishing
20 Vauxhall Bridge Road, London SW1V 2SA

Ebury Publishing is part of the Penguin Random House group of companies
whose addresses can be found at global.penguinrandomhouse.com

Distributed in the US and Latin America by Publishers Group West
(1-510-809-3700)

For further distribution details, see www.timeout.com

ISBN: 978-1-84670-356-0

A CIP catalogue record for this book is available from the British Library.

Printed and bound in China by Leo Paper Products Ltd.

Penguin Random House is committed to a sustainable future for our
business, our readers and our planet. This book is made from Forest
Stewardship Council® certified paper.

MIX
Paper from
responsible sources
FSC® C018179
www.fsc.org

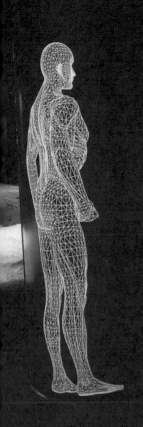

Free entry

Get beneath the surface of the City.

Discover 2,000 years of London's history.

Guildhall Galleries.

Where London began.

Download the Guildhall Galleries app

What to see

The Guildhall Galleries form a fascinating part of the historic Guildhall complex. From a Roman amphitheatre to one of England's oldest public libraries, explore the art, treasures and curiosities gathered together in the heart of the capital.

Getting there

Nearest tubes: Bank, Mansion House & Moorgate.

Find out more

www.cityoflondon.gov.uk/ guildhallgalleries

CITY OF LONDON

London for Londoners

Editorial
Editor Jessica Cargill Thompson
Copy Editors Dominic Earle, Keith Davidson
Editorial Assistants Carol Baker, Annie Bishop,
William Crow, Sophie Gledhill, Anna Stringer
Proofreader John Shandy Watson
Indexer Annie Bishop

Editorial Director Sarah Guy
Group Finance Manager Margaret Wright

Design
Art Editor Christie Webster
Group Commercial Senior Designer Jason Tansley

Picture Desk
Picture Editor Jael Marschner
Deputy Picture Editor Ben Rowe
Picture Researcher Lizzy Owen

Advertising
Managing Director St John Betteridge
Advertising Sales Deborah Maclaren, Helen
Debenham at The Media Sales House

Marketing
Senior Publishing Brand Manager Luthfa Begum
Head of Circulation Dan Collins

Production
Production Controller Katie Mulhern-Bhudia

Time Out Group
Founder Tony Elliott
Chief Executive Officer Tim Arthur
Managing Director Europe Noel Penzer
Publisher Alex Batho

Written by
Saffraz Ali, Ashleigh Arnott, Conori Blue, Jaclyn Bradshaw, Jessica Cargill Thompson, Amirah Chaudry,
Carly-Ann Clements, Simon Coppock, Alexander Corona, Annie Darling, Laura Lee Davies, Dominic Earle,
Georgia Edkins Audrey Fiodorenko, Nicola Foxwell, Gareth Gardner, Sophie Gledhill, Nadia Gonzalez,
Sarah Guy, Roxanne Haouet, Ronnie Haydon, Rebecca Hearn, Tomas Howells, Paul Ireson, Tiffany Lo,
James Manning, Justin McDonnell, Anna Norman, Lucy Palmer, Ben Rowe, Ros Sales, Gabriel Tate,
Tamsin Vincent, Katrina Wales, Peter Watts, Maggie Westhead, Jack Woodcock

Maps JS Graphics Ltd (john@jsgraphics.co.uk)

Cover Photography The Bell, Walthamstow by Ben Rowe

Back Cover Photography Clapham terrace by Amos Chapple/Getty Images

Photography Pages 2/3, 15 (bottom), 20/21, 192/193, 216 Ed Marshall; 9, 24/25, 38/39,
114 Jael Marschner; 12 (top), 243, 263, 264, 273, 277, 296, 298, 305, 314/315 Charlotte
Mayhew; 12 (bottom), 30/31, 190/191, 212/213, 220/221, 255, 316 Michelle Grant; 13 (middle)
Хомелка/Wikimedia Commons; 13 (bottom), 97, 99, 108, 161, 210, 230, 252, 293, 322/323, 328/
329 Ben Rowe; 15 (top), 92/93, 128/129, 317 Scott Wishart; 26/27 Oliver Knight; 34/35 Will
Rodrigues/Shutterstock.com; 40, 52/53, 82, 89, 109, 144/145, 176, 238/239, 304, 326 Rob
Greig; 45 Travis Hodges; 47 Nigel Tradewell; 48/49 Morley von Sternberg; 55, 60/61, 74 (right),
117, 196/197, 217, 248, 269, 280 Jonathan Perugia; 58/59 Tony Watson/Alamy; 64/65, 300/301,
310/311, 331, 338/339 Heloise Bergman; 68/69, 72/73 Olivia Rutherford; 74 (left) Christina Theisen;
75 Will Robson Scott; 76/77 RIDLEY; 85 Charlie Pinder; 98, 306 Celia Topping; 104/105 mikecphoto/
Shutterstock.com ; 113, 158, 198/199 Alys Tomlinson; 115, 130 Jamie Lau; 122 Claudio Divizia/
Shutterstock.com; 125 Eleonore de Bonneval; 134/135 www.simonleigh.com; 136 Jonas Rodin;
140, 141, 291 Tricia de Courcy Ling; 146/147 Scott Chasserot; 155 Jack Latimer; 159 Andrew
Brackenbury; 167 Lisa Payne; 180 Tove K Breitstein; 181 David Mackenzie ; 186/187, 309 Ming
Tang-Evans; 201 Jitka Hynkova; 202/203, 231 IR/Stone/Shutterstock.com; 204/205 © incamerastock/
Alamy; 218/219 Gemma Day; 224/225 pcruciatti/Shutterstock.com; 232/233 Adam Lawrence; 257
Greg Balfour Evans/Alamy; 284/285 Britta Jaschinski; 334/335 Robert Harding/REX Shutterstock

" ONE OF THE BEST THINGS I HAVE EVER DONE "

★★★★★ TripAdvisor Review

Photo: Jason Hawkes

BOOK NOW

📞 020 7887 2626

🖥 thelondonhelicopter.com

The
LONDON
HELICOPTER

Contents

THIS IS **Hard Rock** CAFE

THERE'S NO GREATER SALUTE TO ROCK 'N' ROLL HISTORY THAN A HARD ROCK CLASSIC TEE.

Present this ad and receive a complimentary gift with a £25 retail spend in the Rock Shop

Valid in London only. Expires 30/12/15

Rock Shop: Mon – Sat: 09.30 – 23.30 Sun: 09.30 – 23.00
Nearest Tube: Hyde Park Corner (Piccadilly Line) Green Park (Jubilee/Piccadilly/Victoria Line)
Bus: 9, 14, 19, 22, 38, C2

LONDON | 150 OLD PARK LANE | +44 0207 514 1700
HARDROCK.COM 　f 🐦 📷 You Tube #THISISHARDROCK

About this guide

London is big. Roughly 162,300 hectares, with more than 8.5 million residents, monumental architecture, internationally renowned arts, world-famous museums and top-flight restaurants. But it's also a city of villages and high streets, commuters, families, freelancers, local shops and restaurants, quirky galleries, pleasant parks and pub theatres. This is a guide to that London, the one Londoners live in: expanded to include all 33 administrative districts (32 boroughs plus the City of London) and more than 150 neighbourhoods. There's information on property and rental prices, schools and leisure facilities for those looking for a new place to call home; and tips on where to eat, drink, shop or explore for those just dropping by.

Ever-changing capital

As central London property prices soar, Londoners have started looking to the outer zones – Palmers Green, Wood Green, Penge and Ealing – for cheaper rents and house prices or a larger family home, and being pleasantly surprised with what they've found. And for entertainment, many are swapping the bright lights of the city centre for local attractions – streetfood pop ups and rooftop bars, community gardens and comedy nights. High streets that used to be a bit shabby have experienced rampant gentrification (Peckham, Leyton, Walthamstow, Acton central, Shepherd's Bush) and places that used to be considered 'cheap' no longer are.

The last edition of this guide was published in 2012, just as London was hosting the Olympic Games. Since then, regeneration has left its legacy across East London, beginning with Stratford, Clapton, Leyton and Forest Gate, but now rapidly spreading out even further east and up the Lee Valley, with great things planned for perpetually troubled Tottenham.

Meanwhile, Transport for London's steady expansion of the Overground network has significantly changed the geography of the capital, linking new neighbourhoods. Places such as Forest Hill, Sydenham and Crystal Palace are no longer adrift in south east London but have swift connections to east and central London, inviting a cultural exchange between the two.

With the regneration spotlight on east London, the west has been neglected. This will change as Crossrail – the commuter rail service that shoots under London from Essex to Berkshire and Buckinghamshire – gets ready to start operating in 2018. Major mixed-use developments are planned around stations in Hounslow and Ealing.

London boroughs

The current borough map dates back to 1965 when the London Government Act came into force, absorbing outer areas previously part of the home counties (some of which still think they are). We've divided the book between Inner London boroughs (in the first section) and Outer, tackled in varying degrees of depth.

Annoyingly, London's borough boundaries weren't drawn up neatly around neighbourhood centres and as a result, several areas fall messily across a boundary. Where this happens, we've only covered them once; for the full list of which neighbourhoods you'll find where, see Contents (p7).

Local listings

Unfortunately, we can only offer a flavour of each neighbourhood and a taste of their many shops, bars and restaurants, so apologies to the hundreds of other great places we've had to leave out. Details were checked at the time of going to press but new places open up (and, sadly, close down) all the time; keep up with the latest openings on www.timeout.com. For more detailed information on the practicalities of living in a particular borough, see the local council website.

Statistics

With each borough is a handful of basic facts and figures. House prices have come from the Land Registry house price index and rental prices from the GLA's London Rents Map. Both are averages for the borough so may vary wildly from area to area. Council tax rates come from the local councils. Borough size and estimated 2015 population have been taken from the GLA's London Borough Profiles, a fabulous, information-rich resource collating a wealth of borough statistics, downloadable from http://data.london.gov.uk/dataset/london.

Neighbourhoods by numbers

HIGHEST EARNERS

Kensington & Chelsea	£45,263pa	Wandsworth	£39,014pa
Westminster	£40,389pa	Camden	£37,014pa
Richmond	£39,868pa		

BUSIEST TUBE LINES

1. CENTRAL
2. NORTHERN
3. JUBILEE

HAPPIEST BOROUGHS

1. Kensington & Chelsea
2. Bromley
3. Richmond
4. Barnet
5. Hounslow

SAFEST PLACES TO LIVE

1. Bexley
2. Harrow
3. Sutton
4. Richmond
5. Kingston

UNHEALTHIEST HIGH STREETS

1. Whitechapel
2. New Addington
3. Camberwell
4. Chrisp Street
5. West Green Road/Seven Sisters
6. Plumstead
7. New Cross
8. Finsbury Park
9. Bakers Arms
10. East Beckton

MOST BURGLED POSTCODES

RM8	Dagenham & Becontree
IG2	Gants Hill, Newbury Park & Aldborough Hatch
E18	Woodford
RM11	Hornchurch
TW 11	Teddington & Bushy Park
EN4	Cockfosters
IG3	Hainault
W4	Chiswick
TW5	Heston
UB6	Greenford & Perivale

PRICIEST STREETS

Grosvenor Crescent	£16.9m
Eaton Square	£15.5m
Trevor Square	£10.2m
Cadogan Square	£8.6m
Montpelier Square	£8.5m

OLDEST DENIZENS ▲		HIGHEST LIFE EXPECTANCY FOR MEN	
City of London	41.9 years	Kensington & Chelsea	82.6 years
Havering	40.3 years	Harrow	82.4 years
Bromley	40.1 years	Richmond	81.9 years
Bexley	38.9 years	Barnet	81.9 years
Kensington & Chelsea	38.9 years	Westminster	81.7 years
...AND YOUNGEST ▼		HIGHEST LIFE EXPECTANCY FOR WOMEN	
Tower Hamlets	31.2 years	Kensington & Chelsea	86.2 years
Newham	31.7 years	Camden	86.0 years
Hackney	32.8 years	Harrow	85.9 years
Barking & Dagenham	32.9 years	Richmond	85.9 years
Southwark	34.1 years	Westminster	85.9 years

BUSIEST BUS ROUTES

25	Ilford to Oxford Circus
18	Sudbury to Euston
29	Wood Green to Trafalgar Square
149	Edmonton Green to London Bridge
38	Clapton Pond to Victoria

THE NATIONAL GALLERY

Located in Trafalgar Square, the National Gallery houses one of the greatest collections of European paintings in the world. These pictures belong to the British public and admission to see them is free.

The collection contains over 2,300 works, dating from the Middle Ages to the early 20th century. All major traditions of Western European painting are represented, with artists including Titian, Monet, Velázquez, Rembrandt and Van Gogh.

Every day you can learn more about the paintings by joining a free guided tour, lunchtime talk, or use an audio guide. On Fridays you can also visit the gallery after hours for special events and activities.

THE NATIONAL GALLERY
TRAFALGAR SQUARE
LONDON
WC2N 5DN

W: www.nationalgallery.org.uk
T: 020 7747 2885
E: information@ng-london.org.uk

OPENING HOURS
Daily 10am - 6pm
Fridays 10am - 9pm

NEAREST TUBE
Charing Cross/ Leicester Square

BUSES
3, 6, 9, 11, 12, 13, 15, 23, 24, 29, 87, 88, 91, 139, 159, 176, 453

BIKE STANDS
Leicester Square, St Martin's Place, Duncannon Street, Orange Street

DESIGNATED PARKING BAYS
St Martin's Street: Phone Westminster Parking Information Service on 020 7823 4567

CAR PARK:
Q-Park Trafalgar,
Leicester Square car park

EAT AND DRINK
Visit the National Café for brunch, lunch and afternoon tea, or plan your route around the gallery over a coffee in the Espresso Bar. For the ultimate dining experience, visit the award-winning restaurant, the National Dining Rooms, offering a classic menu of delicious regional dishes.

SHOP
The National Gallery has three shops selling books and high quality gifts; from stationary to jewellery and t-shirts. The shops are located near the Portico entrance, the Getty entrance and in the Sainsbury Wing.

DISABLED ACCESS
There is level access to the Sainsbury Wing and wheelchairs are available at the Sainsbury Wing cloakroom, on Level 0. Call 020 7747 2885 or email information@ng-london.org.uk for more details on access across the National Gallery.

RECYCLING HEROES ▲		AND RECYCLING VILLAINS ▼	
Bexley	55.2%	Lewisham	17.7%
Bromley	49.6%	Newham	17.7%
Harrow	49.2%	Wandsworth	20.4%
Kingston	46.3%	Hammersmith	20.5%
Richmond	43.5%	Lambeth	21.1%
Hillingdon	43.1%	Westminster	21.1%

KEENEST CYCLISTS

1. Richmond
2. Hammersmith & Fulham
3. Wandsworth
4. Hackney
5. Kingston

MOST POLLUTED ROADS	MAIN LANGUAGE NOT ENGLISH	
1. Marylebone Road	Newham	41.4%
2. Park Lane	Brent	37.2%
3. Knightsbridge	Tower Hamlets	34.2%
4. Hammersmith Flyover	Ealing	33.9%
5. Alfred's Way, A13	Westminster	30.8%

NUMBER OF MICROBREWERIES

Southwark	9
Wandsworth	6
Lambeth	6
Hackney	6

Highest earners Gross annual pay 2014. Source: ONS Annual Survey of Hours and Earnings. **Busiest tube lines** Annual passenger figures across the network, 2011/2012. Source: www.citymetric.com. **Happiest boroughs** Source: Sport England Active People Survey, 2013-14. **Safest places to live** Lowest crime rates 2013/14. Source: Metropolitan Police Service. **Unhealthiest high streets** Based on concentration of businesses deemed to have a negative impact on health. Source: Royal Society for Public Health, 2015. **Most burgled postcodes** Burglary Claims Tracker data on 2.86m burglary claims made. Source: MoneySupermarket 2014. **Priciest streets** Average house price. Source: Lloyds Bank, 2014. **Oldest denizens** Average age, 2015. Source: GLA DataStore http://data.london.gov.uk. **Highest life expectancy** Source: Office of National Statistics, 2011-13. **Busiest bus routes** Source: TfL, 2013. **Recycling heroes** Proportion of collected household waste recycled or composted. Source: DEFRA 2013/14. **Keenest cyclists** Percentage of adults who cycle at least once per month. Source: GLA DataStore 2012/13. **Most polluted roads** Source: www.gov.uk. **Main language not English** Percentage of residents with a mother tongue other than English Source: 2011 Census. **Number of microbreweries** See www.londonbrewers.org for up-to-date membership. In some of these statistics, City of London is not included in calculations.

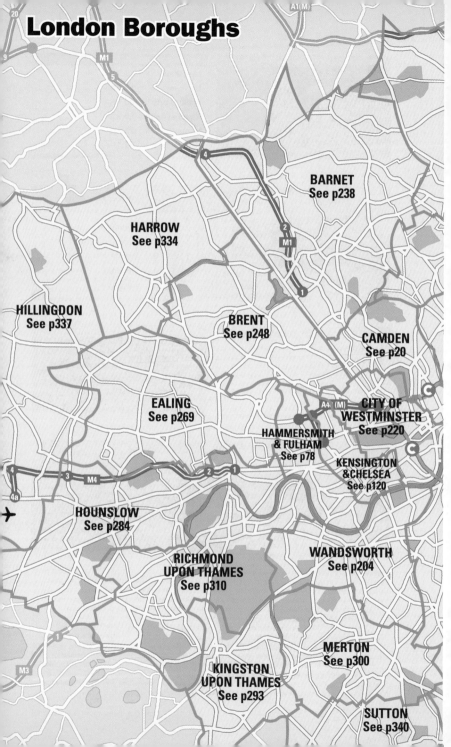

London Boroughs

BARNET
See p238

HARROW
See p334

HILLINGDON
See p337

BRENT
See p248

CAMDEN
See p20

EALING
See p269

CITY OF
WESTMINSTER
See p220

HAMMERSMITH
& FULHAM
See p78

KENSINGTON
&CHELSEA
See p120

HOUNSLOW
See p284

RICHMOND
UPON THAMES
See p310

WANDSWORTH
See p204

MERTON
See p300

KINGSTON
UPON THAMES
See p293

SUTTON
See p340

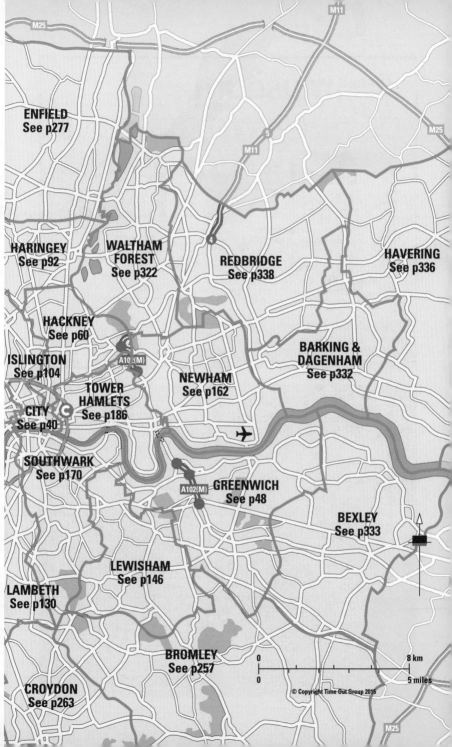

Inner Boroughs

Granary Square, King's Cross

Camden

This central borough begins in the learned Georgian squares of Bloomsbury before hitting Europe's biggest regeneration project at King's Cross. Beyond, Camden Town continues to get busier and brasher, but further north – in Hampstead, Highgate and Primrose Hill – it's leafy business as usual.

AVERAGE PROPERTY PRICE		AVERAGE RENTAL PRICE PER WEEK	
Detached £2,365,925	**Terraced** £1,327,778	**Studio** £250	**2 bed** £450
Semi-detached £1,751,450	**Flat** £729,675	**1 bed** £350	**3 bed** £650

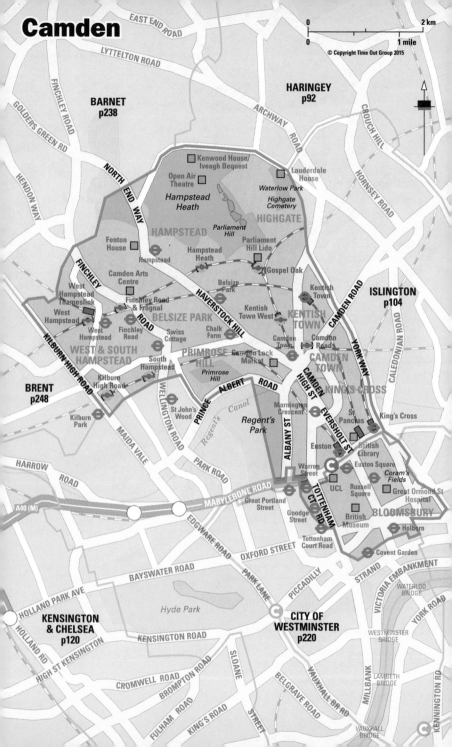

Neighbourhoods

Bloomsbury WC1

The neighbourhood's well-ordered streets have long been a retreat for the literati, and there's a blue plaque at every turn. Yeats, Eliot and Dickens are among its illustrious former residents – though it was Virginia Woolf's gatherings in the drawing room at 46 Gordon Square that assured its literary immortality.

It's still a proudly cultural area – celebrated in October's arty Bloomsbury Festival – and dominated by scholarly establishments. The grand modern buildings of UCL, SOAS, RADA and, down by Lincoln's Inn Fields in Westminster, the LSE, fill blocks between squares and streets of Georgian townhouses (often also occupied by university departments). Here, too, is the brooding art deco Senate House: the University of London's library and George Orwell's inspiration for the Ministry of Truth in *Nineteen Eighty-Four*.

Up on Euston Road are two further major cultural establishments. The British Library has an aura of exclusivity but hosts interesting exhibitions that are open to all. The Wellcome Trust has a knack for staging medical exhibitions in original and engaging ways. Down towards Holborn is the British Museum, with its great glass-domed courtyard, filled with visitors and antiquities from around the world.

The streets around the British Museum cater to the collector's mindset with a number of specialist shops: the London Review of Books bookshop and café, Blade Rubber Stamps, Royal Mile Whiskies, James Smith umbrellas, Bookmarks socialist bookshop and the Contemporary Ceramics Centre.

To the west, busy Tottenham Court Road marks Bloomsbury's border with Fitzrovia. Best known for its cut-price electrical shops, it has also been home to design-forward furniture store Heal's for the past 100 years. Much of this area has been dominated by major Crossrail works around the foot of Centre Point (itself finally getting some attention). Several old landmarks have been bulldozed, and the axe hovers over the much-loved music shops of Denmark Street. The most prominent newcomer is Renzo Piano's multicoloured Central St Giles mid-rise development of offices and apartments, with restaurants at their base. The Korean community is moving out, but there are two superb new ramen places: Kanada Ya and Ippudo.

To the east, on the other side of Kingsway, big institutional buildings make way for a more residential neighbourhood, with a mix of period streets, council housing and mansion blocks. At its heart is the Brunswick Centre. Once a neglected 1960s concrete eyesore, it's now fixed up and its flats are much sought after by an architecture-loving crowd. The central plaza offers chain boutiques, a Waitrose and a Curzon cinema. Local families have charming Coram's Fields on their doorstep – a playground and animal centre where adults are allowed in only if accompanied by a child.

Heading north towards the Euston Road, Marchmont Street and surrounding streets (many with local authority and Guinness Trust blocks) provide another neighbourhood hub with sociable cafés and the North Sea Fish Restaurant. Bibliophiles head here for Judd Books, Skoob Books (in the Brunswick Centre) and Gay's the Word, while those of a philosophical leaning broaden their minds at the School of Life.

Holborn WC1

Cunning marketers have attempted to bring cohesion to this largely commercial area – not quite the City, and not quite the West End – by rebranding it 'Midtown'. The ploy is working to an extent, with several hotels opening and companies moving their headquarters into the area. Eventually they'll all benefit from Crossrail; right now they're stuck with building works and a gyratory system.

High Holborn, heading to the City, is fairly dull and commercial. But Theobald's Road, leading to Clerkenwell, has more of residential interest, passing one of London's best chippies, the Fryer's Delight, and the barristers' chambers of Gray's Inn, before reaching the visibly Italian community of Clerkenwell Road.

To the north of Theobald's Road is one of London's loveliest streets, Lamb's Conduit Street, peaceful and flanked by all one might need for a tasteful urban existence. There's clean-lined mens- and womenswear at Oliver Spencer, Universal Works, Folk and Content; Aesop lotions; Bikefix; Albion Wine Shippers; and Persephone Books (an independent publisher specialising in exquisitely produced 20th-century works by women). Eat out at Cigala (tapas), stock up on groceries at the socially responsible People's Supermarket, and drink in well-preserved Victorian pub the Lamb.

Hatton Garden is London's jewellery quarter and diamond centre, home to more than 50 traders. It also hides the quirky Ely Place – for a long time outside the jurisdiction of London police and therefore a refuge for robbers on the run – and the fantastic Ye Olde Mitre pub. Leather Lane still has its traditional market, but it's expanding and becoming ever more popular with the addition of street-food stalls and permanent cafés such as Prufrock.

King's Cross WC1

This area is finally emerging from decades of regeneration – and who knew how handsome grotty old King's Cross could look? The mainline station has been scrubbed clean of superfluous additions and years of grime, new public spaces have been opened up, the Regent's Canal has been spruced up and the long-empty Midland Grand hotel (now the St Pancras Renaissance) has been returned to its five-star Gothic Revival glory.

The first tranche of regeneration along York Way brought Kings Place (home to the *Guardian* newspaper, a concert space, theatre and galleries), canalside drinking, pleasant moorings and the Regent Quarter complex, housing the Camino tapas bar and tiny Bar Pepito for hams and sherry.

The relocation of art school Central Saint Martins to the Granary Building has brought a creative edge to the area north of Regent's Canal, centred on Granary Square. There's a community skip garden, street-food market Kerb at Lewis Cubitt Square, specialist gallery the House of Illustration, and fun pop-ups such as swimming ponds and viewing towers. Restaurants such as Yum Chaa, Caravan and Bruno Loubet's vegetarian-friendly Grain Store spill out on to the square, with higher-end offerings in the pipeline. Beside the canal, Camley Street Natural Park offers a two-acre oasis of water and woodland.

Building continues apace north of the canal, with selected industrial features preserved: the arches of the coal drops are being transformed into a shopping street, while the gasholder frames will form the backdrop to new apartments and a playground. Once the diggers have gone, this could become a very pleasant place to live, work or just wander.

King's Cross and St Pancras stations have become mini-shopping malls – St Pancras winning on account of the St Pancras Grand restaurant and Europe's longest champagne bar (though minus points for some terrible sculpture). The Renaissance hotel, meanwhile, has brought back fine dining in the shape of Marcus Wareing's Gilbert Scott bar and restaurant; a drink at the Booking Office Bar & Restaurant is another pleasant way to enjoy the beautiful surroundings.

Waterlow Park, Highgate

Many of the area's old Victorian tenement buildings have been swept aside by the glass and steel mid-rise revolution, but there are still pockets of traditional streets. The bottom of Caledonian Road has a neighbourhood feel, with advice centres for local residents and some pleasant shops and eateries: VX vegan boutique, Pattern Coffee, Ted restaurant (seasonal British food), craft shop/café Drink Shop Do, and much-loved old deli KC Continental Stores. There are also still nooks and crannies such as Keystone Crescent, which has the smallest radius of any crescent in Europe and is unique in having matching inner and outer faces.

Pentonville Road is still home to plenty of hostels and cheap hotels, as well as people drinking cans of Special Brew at 11am. Raising the tone, the old municipal garages on Britannia Street are now the Gagosian Gallery – a vast, starkly impressive showcase for contemporary art. A handful of venues such as the Scala and the Water Rats host bands, but the new generation of clubs such as Egg and the Big Chill House are tame compared to the area's legendary raving days.

Camden Town NW1

Camden is all about the two Ms: market and music. It may not be as cool as in its Britpop heyday, but the area can still be fun. These

days, the Hawley Arms (once the Britpop hangout) plays host to thirtysomething men in fedoras and Chelsea boots, the kind who've been there since it was actually cool and never quite moved on. Nevertheless, Camden remains the best area in town for mid-sized venues (Koko, Roundhouse, Electric Ballroom) and small ones (Barfly, Black Heart, Jazz Café, Purple Turtle, Monarch, Underworld, Stillery). Many – such as the Lock Tavern with its lovely roof terrace – are also good pubs in their own right.

Camden's sprawling collection of markets offers a smörgåsbord of street styles and shopping possibilities. Camden Market proper (on the junction with Buck Street) and Canal Market are the places for cheap jeans, T-shirts and accessories. Stables Market is a bit more boho vintage and arts-and-crafts. At waterside Camden Lock, there's an eclectic jumble of clothes, gifts and street food.

On Chalk Farm Road and Camden High Street, colourful shopfronts sport huge sculptures of their wares (Dr Martens boots, leather jackets), while scowling teenagers shop for stripy tights and vintage T-shirts. But there's always been another side to the Camden of 'Tapas, fracas, alcohol, tobaccos/Bongs, bongo bingo, Portuguese maracas' that Suggs sang about in 'Camden Town'. Local residents aged over 30 tend to give the market a wide berth: unless you live on Chalk Farm Road, it's easy to avoid getting entangled. Older, more discerning Camdenites prefer to stroll across the bridge to serene Primrose Hill, meander along the canal to Regent's Park, or take in a concert at the Roundhouse.

There are also plenty of good places to eat, though generally of the upscale fast-food variety: Haché (burgers), Hook (fish and chips), Q Grill (US-style grill), Porkys (ribs) and innovative ice-cream at Chin Chin Labs.

Kentish Town NW5

Often overshadowed by raucous neighbour Camden, Kentish Town has an appeal all of its own. Gentrification has crept in as property prices have risen, but it's still endearingly tatty in places and has a genuinely diverse community. Take the high street, where the line-up includes down-at-heel greasy spoons, a homely Sardinian trattoria, Rio's naturist spa, the Owl Bookshop and Phoenicia Food Hall, for Mediterranean foods of all kinds.

Like Camden, it does have a great music scene, from Monday jazz at the Oxford to big-league bands at the HMV Forum. But there's also something of a restaurant scene explosion happening up Kentish Town Road and Highgate Road: Pizza East and Chicken Shop (both from the Soho House group), rice balls at Arancini Factory, and the tiny but sensational Italian Anima e Cuore .

There are plenty of polished gastropubs (Oxford, Vine, Abbey), but also some unreconstructed boozers with football on the telly, frequented by men with dogs on string. Tapping the Admiral is a local favourite, but the grand dame of the neighbourhood is the Pineapple. A local institution since 1868, it's a vision of Victorian splendour. You can feel the history in the weathered wood of the joyously unmodernised main bar, and there are outdoor tables in case the weather's good. That other old-timer, legendary pub-cum-music venue the Bull & Gate, has come over all cocktail with the addition of the upstairs Boulogne Bar (joining the excellent Ladies & Gentlemen – housed in a former public toilet – and Knowhere Special, mere seconds away).

Off the main drag, there's some big-scale beauty in the buildings, with crescents of attractive Victorian terraces and the Grade II-listed St Pancras Public Baths on Prince of Wales Road, now called the Kentish Town Sports Centre. Also here is the Zabludowicz Collection, a great contemporary art gallery and one of the leading lights on the under-sized north London arts scene. Meanwhile, side streets lined with diminutive, pastel-painted terraced houses have a sweetly seaside feel – and not so sweet price tags.

Green spaces include Cantelowes Gardens, with its skatepark and children's play area, and the spacious City Farm, founded in 1972. For those craving more greenery, Hampstead Heath is a 15-minute walk away.

Belsize Park NW3

Derived from the French *bel assis*, the name Belsize Park means 'well situated'. Halfway up the hill to Hampstead from Camden Town, it was a Victorian development of notorious 18th-century pleasure gardens that once surrounded Belsize House (now demolished). Much of the estate had been owned by Eton College since the Middle Ages. Grand white-stuccoed terraces and red-brick mansions, most now converted into expensive one- or two-bed flats, were designed to compete with Kensington. The area is far more staid and salubrious than nearby Camden Town, but more bohemian than Hampstead.

On the area's high street, at the top end of Haverstock Hill, there are banks, a Budgens, chain restaurants, organic grocer Pomona, Daunt Books and the cosy Everyman Cinema. This part of London has no shortage of delis, including the Belsize Village Deli, butcher/deli/wine shop the Hampstead Butcher & Providore, and the Polish Beetroot Deli. England's Lane, at the lower end of Haverstock Hill, is more quirky and rarefied, with a slew of fine local pubs and popular brunch spots, notably the Belsize Park sister of Hampstead's popular Ginger & White café. Most delightful of all is Belsize Village, a pedestrianised oasis off Belsize Lane, with a good vet, excellent pharmacy and a(nother) deli, among other attractions.

Despite its proximity to Camden Town, Belsize Park is more geared towards a quiet drink and a meal than riotous nights out, with stately gastropubs such as the Hill catering for a well-off clientele. On Haverstock Hill, the Sir Richard Steele is a pleasingly old-fashioned drinking den with a cosily cluttered interior and a regular quiz night.

Hampstead NW3

First fashionable for its spa waters in the 18th century, Hampstead has long been London's most gorgeous hilltop hideaway. It resisted the Victorian expansion of the city by conserving Hampstead Heath, a wonderful high tract of open countryside, and by preserving its own rural character.

Now, many of the houses here cost as much as a farm. Though these may only be within reach of professional footballers and investment bankers, the area's artistic, literary and bohemian reputation is safe in the hands of a critical mass of genteel paupers.

A relatively large area, Hampstead has several different districts. South End Green is the most affordable, close to Hampstead Heath station, and given a rougher edge by its proximity to the Royal Free Hospital, Gospel Oak and Kentish Town. Fitzjohn's, on the other side of Rosslyn Hill, has avenues of fine, red-brick Victorian villas and lots of private schools. Christchurch, east of Heath Street, is particularly delightful; close to the Heath, it's a warren of steep, winding lanes with raised pavements, old houses and fabulous views. Burgh House is the headquarters of the influential residents' association, the Heath & Hampstead Society.

Hampstead tube emerges in Hampstead Village, where the High Street and Heath

TRANSPORT

Tube lines Central, Circle, Hammersmith & City, Jubilee, Metropolitan, Northern, Overground, Piccadilly, Victoria
Rail services into City Thameslink, Euston, King's Cross, St Pancras; Eurostar from St Pancras International
Main bus routes dozens of buses run through Camden and into central London – for a full list, visit www.tfl.gov.uk/buses

St Pancras Renaissance Hotel

Street provide most of the area's shops and nightlife, including the luxurious Everyman Cinema. There's plenty of fashion, with a decent assortment of mid-range brands. Kids can be indulged at traditional toyshop Happy Returns. Further east, in (otherwise barren) Gospel Oak, is Kristin Baybars' fascinating shop, full of exquisite miniaturist scenes and doll's house kits.

Hampstead's choice of eateries is on the increase. Jin Kichi (Japanese) and the Coffee Cup Café are long-time favourites. Off Haverstock Hill to the east, you'll find unpretentious Zara (Turkish) and family-friendly Mimmo la Bufala. On the High Street is a north London institution: Parisian street vendor La Crêperie de Hampstead has been serving crêpes and galettes to increasingly long queues of hungry punters since 1980.

Historic pubs dot the tangled backstreets and leafy lanes of Hampstead. The oldest is the wonderfully atmospheric 16th-century Spaniard's Inn; equally snug is the warren of wood-panelled rooms at the Holly Bush. The Wells tavern offers classy gastro fare, while at the Horseshoe you can match lunch with one of its own Camden Town Brewery beers. The Freemasons Arms is an ideal spot to spend lazy summer afternoons, with its expansive garden situated next to the southern entrance to the Heath.

The Heath is, of course, one of the area's biggest assets; at its northern end lies the elegant neoclassical Kenwood House. It also has three open-air swimming ponds: one for men, one for women and the third mixed. Local swimmers have won their battle to keep them open. There's a surfeit of schools in the area, many of them private, so congestion is hellish during the school run, the streets clogged with SUVs.

West Hampstead and South Hampstead NW6

Down the hill from Hampstead and separated by the roaring Finchley Road, West Hampstead is very much a district in its own right, with excellent train links into and out of London provided by the Overground, Underground and Thameslink. A number of businesses are moving to the area to take advantage of its convenient location while avoiding central London rents, but West Hampstead manages to retain an overriding residential feel.

Since West End Lane became a vibrant hub for eating and socialising, the area has emerged as a firm favourite with young professionals with more than a little income to spare. Arts-and-crafts enthusiasts are well-catered for at Art 4 Fun, where kids and adults can paint a range of ceramics in a relaxed café setting; the independent West End Lane Books, now in its third decade, continues to thrive at the heart of the community.

Today's West Hampstead is the dynamic love child of rough-and-ready Kilburn and grandiose Hampstead, sitting at the confluence of these two distinctive areas. Gentrification is on the up, however; the impressive West Hampstead Square development, located directly opposite West Hampstead tube station, will comprise 198 new homes, shops, restaurants, a food market and new landscaped open space.

In West Hampstead, West End Lane keeps everyone well fed. Among the pleasant neighbourhood cafés and restaurants (many of them also great for takeaways), there's Lebanese Cedar, Middle Eastern Lena's, gastropub the Alice House, and Modern British café/brasserie the Wet Fish. There are also occasional food markets outside the Thameslink station, and steaks aplenty at the Hampstead Butcher. A little further afield, on Fortune Green Road, is Nautilus, a proper chippy (eat-in or takeaway).

Down Broadhurst Gardens, once a no-go area beside the Jubilee line tracks, are a number of cafés and specialist shops: Wired Co for coffee, Cocoa Bijoux for chocolates and fascinating Pro Arte for stringed instruments, just opposite the ENO's rehearsal studios.

West Hampstead nightlife is concentrated around West End Lane. Bars – including perennial favourite the Gallery – predominate over traditional pubs, although the spacious Black Lion is a busy local, especially on a Sunday for its roast and evening quiz.

Few Londoners know of the existence of South Hampstead as an area, unless they're familiar with the London Overground station (which takes you one stop to Euston in 12 minutes). Property in South Hampstead consists mainly of stately red-brick mansion blocks or large detached villas such as those around Priory Road and Compayne Gardens. Several houses here remain gloriously spacious family homes, but many were converted into flats in the 1970s.

Primrose Hill NW1

This area just north of Regent's Park is popular with artists, musicians and actors. Relatively quiet, safe and desirable, Primrose

Koko, Camden

Hill attracts well-off Londoners to settle in its neatly painted four-storey Victorian terraced houses. The eponymous mound, essentially an extension of Regent's Park, is filled with dog-walkers and tourists enjoying the picturesque view of the London skyline.

Much of Primrose Hill is within a 15-minute walk of Chalk Farm tube station. Regent's Park Road and Gloucester Avenue are the local focal points, containing a pretty sprinkling of boutiques, cafés and constantly busy gastropubs. The high street remains unspoilt by chain stores and there's relatively little traffic. Consequently, Primrose Hill's house prices are nearly twice those of nearby Camden Town. The grand villas with views over Regent's Park fetch more than £10 million; a large terraced house in the centre of Primrose Hill currently costs approximately £5 million; and even two-bedroom conversion flats go for around £1 million.

There's a genuine village atmosphere, with independent shops ranging from hardware stores to designer boutiques thriving along the main streets. Gloucester Avenue is sprinkled with gems: Shikasuki for well-preserved vintage clothing and accessories; delicate jewellery at Sweet Pea; the Primrose Bakery, which has tables for eating in; and superior deli Melrose & Morgan.

Pubs here swing towards gastro – top are the Queens and the Lansdowne. For other dining options, Lemonia continues to serve a buzzing crowd with its excellent Greek-Cypriot cuisine; nearby Odette's, meanwhile, is the showcase restaurant for TV chef Bryn Williams. Vegetarians, vegans and even meat-eaters love the tasty raw delights at Manna, which claims to be the oldest vegetarian restaurant in the UK.

One potential cloud on the Hill horizon is the path of the future HS2 train line through

the area. Some fear the knock-on effect could change the area forever (and hurt those buoyant house prices).

Swiss Cottage NW3

Roads from St John's Wood and Chalk Farm converge at Swiss Cottage, named after the 19th-century chalet-style inn at its centre. Wedged between West Hampstead and Belsize Park, the area has some attractive houses, particularly to the west of Finchley Road, but is also home to more affordable flats above the many shops.

For shopping, Finchley Road has a convenient range of household names, plus the O2 Centre: home to Waterstones, Oliver Bonas, BoConcept Danish design, plenty of chain eateries (Nando's, Rossopomodoro, Byron, Yo Sushi) and a Vue cinema. Although the O2 Centre dominates Finchley Road, there are a couple of smaller places worth seeking

out: quirky pet grooming parlour Yuppy Puppy, Loft Coffee, Gail's bakery, Middle Eastern grill Mahdi, tiny Japanese grocer Natural Natural, Café Also (Mediterranean dishes with bookshop attached) and the cosy Arches wine bar. For something smarter, Bradleys serves Modern British cuisine with a southern French influence.

At Swiss Cottage Market, on Eton Avenue, you'll find a smattering of food stalls on Wednesday and Friday mornings – most notably the Merito Coffee stall, where the flat white is worth the queue – and general stalls (jewellery, clothing) on Saturdays.

For culture, Hampstead Theatre (by Swiss Cottage tube), celebrates new writing and attracts top talent, often prior to a West End transfer. Further north, past Finchley Road & Frognal station, Camden Arts Centre hosts regular exhibitions, events and courses for all ages, while the Freud Museum, in his former home, provides a fascinating insight into the man and his couch.

The Cottage apart, the most notable landmark is Swiss Cottage Library, designed by Sir Basil Spence. Its companion piece, the Swiss Cottage Leisure Centre, has been demolished, replaced by a state-of-the-art version with pool, spa, climbing wall and café.

Highgate and Dartmouth Park N6

Spilling out from the borough of Camden into Haringey, Highgate is known for its cemeteries – the wild and wonderful West Cemetery and the more ordered, municipal East Cemetery, wherein lies Karl Marx. The neighbourhood as a whole is far from dead, though, with a buoyant property market and one of the capital's most active community groups, the Highgate Society. The area isn't quite as expensive to live in as Hampstead, but it's not far behind. Highgate also shares many of Hampstead's advantages, such as its elevation and, of course, the lovely Heath.

See the whole of London in model form at New London Architecture, Store Street.

Dartmouth Park, east of the Heath and just south of the cemeteries, isn't a park at all. It's a residential area on the slopes up to Highgate, characterised by late 19th-century terraced and semi-detached houses good enough for Ed Miliband. Dartmouth Park's residents converge in the row of pleasant café terraces on Swain's Lane after a constitutional swim in Hampstead Ponds or a walk on nearby Parliament Hill, with its protected view over London. Once called Traitor's Hill, it's now affectionately known as Kite Hill, for obvious reasons.

Highgate Village is the prime place to reside in this neck of the woods – and talking of woods, Highgate Wood and Queen's Wood (both across borough boundaries in Haringey, but close) are lovely examples of protected ancient woodland, both originally part of the Forest of Middlesex. Other parks include the very pretty Waterlow Park and equally beautiful Kenwood House, both given to the nation by philanthropic landowners in more public-spirited times. The Village's gated roads housing wealthy families are virtually

free of the background hum of traffic. Such semi-rural serenity comes at a price, as does living anywhere very close to the Village, with its pretty shops and famous pub, the Flask.

Around Pond Square, most houses are Victorian or Georgian, while some even older properties, built around the time of Charles II, can be glimpsed on the Grove. Five-bedroom, 18th-century piles will set you back almost £3 million in this select enclave. High-end estates, such as the Holly Lodge Estate, are also popular, while Berthold Lubetkin's Highpoint flats, intended for workers in the 1930s, now house the chattering classes.

Upmarket boozers filled with cliquey locals are the norm. The Wrestlers and Angel Inn are pleasant spots for a pint, while the Bull has turned into a brewpub, with a wonderful array of beers and US-style grub. Along Archway Road, the late-licensed Boogaloo marks a total change of pace with its superb jukebox, eclectic DJ nights and occasional celebrity clientele.

The area's favourite cafés are most often set inside its parks. The café at Lauderdale House inside Waterlow Park has a suntrap terrace and gorgeous views across to Hampstead Heath; the Brew House at Kenwood House sits in a secluded sunken garden within the grounds; and the Pavilion Café in Highgate Wood (in Haringey) is on the edge of the central glade where cricketers play at the weekends in crisp whites. High Tea of Highgate, on the High Street, is a good alternative to the park cafés.

For culture, Upstairs at the Gatehouse in Highgate Village offers enjoyably ambitious productions in a small space, while Jackson's Lane on Archway Road has a wide variety of performances and classes on the calendar.

For shopping, there are good family butchers on Dartmouth Park's Swains Lane and in Highgate Village, plus a Saturday farmers' market in the grounds of William Ellis School (entrance at the bottom of Parliament Hill). Residents head to nearby Kentish Town, Muswell Hill or Crouch End for a more thorough weekly shop.

Eating

Alice House 283-285 West End Lane, NW6 1RD (7431 8818, www.thealicehouse.co.uk).
Anima e Cuore 129 Kentish Town Road, NW1 8PB (7267 2410).
Arancini Factory 115A Kentish Town Road, NW1 8PB (3648 7941, www.arancinibrothers.com).

Booking Office St Pancras Renaissance, Euston Road, NW1 2AR (7841 3566, www.booking officerestaurant.com).

Bradleys 25 Winchester Road, NW3 3NR (7722 3457, www.bradleysnw3.co.uk).

Brew House Kenwood House, Hampstead Lane, NW3 7JR (8341 5384, www.companyofcooks.com).

La Brocca 273 West End Lane, NW6 1QS (7433 1989, www.labrocca.co.uk).

Café Also 1255 Finchley Road, NW11 0AD (8455 6890, www.cafealso.com).

Camino & Bar Pepito 3 Varnishers Yard, Regent Quarter, N1 9FD (7841 7331, www.camino.uk.com).

Caravan Granary Building, Granary Square, N1C 4AA (7101 7661, www.caravankingscross.co.uk).

Cedar 202 West End Lane, NW6 1SG (3602 0862, www.thecedarrestaurant.co.uk).

Chicken Shop 79 Highgate Road, NW5 1TL (3310 2020, www.chickenshop.com).

Chin Chin Laboratorists 49-50 Camden Lock Place, NW1 8AF (07885 604284, www.chinchinlabs.com).

Cigala 54 Lamb's Conduit Street, WC1N 3LW (7405 1717, www.cigala.co.uk).

Coffee Cup Café 74 Hampstead High Street, NW3 1QX (7435 7565, www.villabiancagroup.co.uk).

La Crêperie de Hampstead 77 Hampstead High Street, NW3 1RE (7445 6767).

Fryer's Delight 19 Theobald's Road, WC1X 8SL (7405 4114).

Gilbert Scott St Pancras Renaissance, Euston Road, NW1 2AR (7278 3888, www.thegilbertscott.co.uk).

Ginger & White 4A-5A Perrin's Court, NW3 1QS (7431 9098, www.gingerandwhite.com).

Grain Store 1-3 Stable Street, Granary Square, N1C 4AB (7324 4466, www.grainstore.com).

Haché 24 Inverness Street, NW1 7HJ (7485 9100, www.hacheburgers.com).

High Tea 50 Highgate High Street, N6 5HX (8348 3162, www.highteaofhighgate.com).

Hook 63-65 Parkway, NW1 7PP (7482 0475, www.hookrestaurants.com).

Ippudo Central Saint Giles, St Giles High Street, WC2H 8AG (7240 4469, www.ippudo.co.uk).

Jin Kichi 73 Heath Street, NW3 6UG (7794 6158, www.jinkichi.com).

Kanada-Ya 64 St Giles High Street, WC2H 8LE (7240 0232, www.kanada-ya.com).

Kerb Lewis Cubitt Square, Stable Street, N1C 4AA (www.kerbfood.com).

Lemonia 89 Regent's Park Road, NW1 8UY (7586 7454, www.lemonia.co.uk).

Lena's 267 West End Lane, NW6 1QS (7443 5666, www.lenascafe.com).

Loft Coffee Company 4 Canfield Gardens, NW6 3BS (7372 2008).

Mahdi 2 Canfield Gardens, NW6 3BS (7625 4344).

Manna 4 Erskine Road, NW3 3AJ (7722 8028, www.mannav.com).

Mimmo la Bufala 45A South End Road, NW3 2QB (7435 7814, www.mimmolabufala.co.uk).

Nautilus 27-29 Fortune Green Road, NW6 1DU (7435 2532).

North Sea Fish Restaurant 7-8 Leigh Street, WC1H 9EW (7387 5892, www.northseafish restaurant.co.uk).

Odette's 130 Regent's Park Road, NW1 8XL (7586 8569, www.odettesprimrosehill.com).

Pavilion Café Muswell Hill Road, N10 3JN (8444 4777).

Pizza East 79 Highgate Road, NW5 1TL (3310 2000, www.pizzaeast.com).

La Porchetta 33 Boswell Street, WC1N 3BP (7242 2434, www.laporchetta.net).

Porky's 18 Chalk Farm Road, NW1 8AG (7428 0998, www.porkys.co.uk).

Prufrock 23-25 Leather Lane, EC1N 7TE (7242 0467, www.prufrockcoffee.com).

Q Grill 29-33 Chalk Farm Road, NW1 8AJ (7267 2678, www.q-grill.co.uk).

Queen's Head & Artichoke 30-32 Albany Street, NW1 4EA (7916 6206, www.the artichoke.net).

Retsina 48-50 Belsize Lane, NW3 5AR (7431 5855, www.retsina-london.com).

Singapore Garden 83 Fairfax Road, NW6 4DY (7624 8233, www.singaporegarden.co.uk).

Ted 47-51 Caledonian Road, N1 9BU (3763 2080, www.tedrestaurants.co.uk).

Wet Fish Café 242 West End Lane, NW6 1LG (7443 9222, www.thewetfishcafe.co.uk).

Yumchaa 1 Granary Square, N1C 4AA (7209 9641, www.yumchaa.com).

Zara 11 South End Road, NW3 2PT (7794 5498, www.zararestaurant.co.uk).

HIGHS & LOWS

Eurostar on your doorstep

Hampstead Heath

Live music

Celebrity overkill

Tourist hell

Drinking

Abbey Tavern 124 Kentish Town Road, NW1 9QB (7267 9449, www.abbey-tavern.com).
Angel Inn 37 Highgate High Street, N6 5JT (8341 5913, www.theangelhighgate.co.uk).
Arches 7 Fairhazel Gardens, NW6 3QE (7624 1867).
Boogaloo 312 Archway Road, N6 5AT (8340 2928, www.theboogaloo.co.uk).
Bradley's Spanish Bar 42-44 Hanway Street, W1T 1UT (7636 0359).
Bull 13 North Hill, N6 4AB (8341 0510, www.thebullhighgate.co.uk).
Bull & Gate 389 Kentish Town Road, NW5 2TJ (7347 0905, www.bullandgatenw5.co.uk).
Flask 77 Highgate West Hill, N6 6BU (8348 7346, www.theflaskhighgate.com).
Freemasons Arms 32 Downshire Hill, NW3 1NT (7433 6811, www.freemasonsarms.co.uk).
Hawley Arms 2 Castlehaven Road, NW1 8QU (7428 5979, www.thehawleyarms.co.uk).
Hill 94 Haverstock Hill, NW3 2BD (7267 0033, www.thehilllondon.com).
Holly Bush 22 Holly Mount, NW3 6SG (7435 2892, www.hollybushhampstead.co.uk).
Horseshoe 28 Heath Street, NW3 6TE (7431 7206, www.thehorseshoehampstead).
Knowhere Special 296 Kentish Town Road, NW5 2TG (www.knowherespecial.com).
Ladies & Gentlemen 2 Highgate Road, NW5 1NR (www.ladiesandgents.co).
Lamb 94 Lamb's Conduit Street, WC1N 3LZ (7405 0713, www.youngs.co.uk).
Lansdowne 90 Gloucester Avenue, NW1 8HX (7483 0409, www.thelansdownepub.co.uk).
Lock Tavern 35 Chalk Farm Road, NW1 8AJ (7482 7163, www.lock-tavern.com).
Museum Tavern 49 Great Russell Street, WC1B 3BA (7242 8987, www.taylor-walker.co.uk).
Oxford 256 Kentish Town Road, NW5 2AA (7485 3521, www.metropolitanpubcompany.com).
Pineapple 51 Leverton Street, NW5 2NX (7284 4631).
Queens 49 Regent's Park Road, NW1 8XD (7586 0408, www.thequeensprimrosehill.co.uk).
Sir Richard Steele 97 Haverstock Hill, NW3 4RL (7483 1261, www.faucetinn.com/sirrichardsteele).
Tapping the Admiral 77 Castle Road, NW1 8SU (7267 6118, www.tappingtheadmiral.co.uk).
Vine 86 Highgate Road, NW5 1PB (7209 0038, www.metropolitanpubcompany.com).
Wells 30 Well Walk, NW3 1BX (7794 3785, www.thewellshampstead.co.uk).
Wrestlers 98 North Road, N6 4AA (8340 4297, www.thewrestlershighgate.com).
Ye Old Mitre 1 Ely Place, EC1N 6SJ (7405 4751, www.yeoldemitreholborn.co.uk).

Shopping

Aesop 50 Lamb's Conduit Street, WC1N 3LH (7404 4555, www.aesop.com).
Albion Wine Shippers 56 Lamb's Conduit Street, WC1N 3LW (7242 0873, www.albionwine shippers.co.uk).
Beetroot Deli 92 Fleet Road, NW3 2QX (7424 8544, www.beetrootdeli.co.uk).
Belsize Village Deli 39 Belsize Lane, NW3 5AS (7794 4258).
Bikefix 48 Lamb's Conduit Street, WC1N 3LH (7405 1218, http://bikefix.co.uk).
Black Truffle 52 Warren Street, W1T 5NJ (7388 4547, www.blacktruffleshoes.com).
Blade Rubber Stamps 12 Bury Place, WC1A 2JL (7831 4123, www.bladerubberstamps.co.uk).
Bookmarks 1 Bloomsbury Street, WC1B 3QE (7637 1848, www.bookmarksbookshop.co.uk).
Contemporary Ceramics Centre 63 Great Russell Street, WC1B 3BF (7242 9644, www.cpaceramics.com).
Daunt Books (www.dauntbooks.co.uk); 193 Haverstock Hill, NW3 4QL (7794 4006); 51 South End Road, NW3 2QB (7794 8206).
Drink Shop Do 9 Caledonian Road, N1 9DX (7278 4335, www.drinkshopdo.com).
Folk 49 Lamb's Conduit Street, WC1N 3NG (7404 6458, www.folkclothing.com).
Gay's the Word 66 Marchmont Street, WC1N 1AB (7278 7654, www.gaystheword.co.uk).

Camden Lock

Hampstead Butcher & Providore 56 Rosslyn Hill, NW3 1ND (7794 9210, (www.hampsteadbutcher. com); 244 West End Lane, NW6 1LG (7794 0096).

Happy Returns 36 Rosslyn Hill, NW3 1NH (7435 2431).

Heal's 196 Tottenham Court Road, W1T 7LQ (7636 1666, www.heals.co.uk).

James Smith & Son 53 New Oxford Street, WC1A 1BL (7836 4731, www.james-smith.co.uk).

Judd Books 82 Marchmont Street, WC1N 1AG (7387 5333, www.juddbooks.com).

KC Continental Stores 26 Caledonian Road, N1 9DU (7837 0201).

Kristin Baybars 7 Mansfield Road, NW3 2JD (7267 0934).

London Review Bookshop 14 Bury Place, WC1A 2JL (7269 9030, www.londonreviewbookshop.co.uk).

Louis' Pâtisserie 32 Heath Street, NW3 6DU (7435 9908).

Melrose & Morgan 42 Gloucester Avenue, NW1 8JD (7722 0011, www.melroseandmorgan.com).

Mystical Fairies 12 Flask Walk, NW3 1HE (7431 1888, www.mysticalfairies.co.uk).

Natural Natural 1 Goldhurst Terrace, NW6 3HX (7287 1499, www.natural-natural.co.uk).

O2 Centre Finchley Road, NW3 6LU (7794 7716, www.o2centre.co.uk).

Oliver Spencer 62 Lamb's Conduit Street, WC1N 3LW (7269 6444, www.oliverspencer.co.uk).

Owl Bookshop 209 Kentish Town Road, NW5 2JU (7485 7793).

People's Supermarket 72-78 Lamb's Conduit Street, WC1N 3LP (7430 1827, www.thepeoples supermarket.org).

Persephone Books 59 Lamb's Conduit Street, WC1N 3NB (7242 9292, www.persephone books.co.uk).

Phoenicia Food Hall 186-192 Kentish Town Road, NW5 2AE (7267 1267, www.phoenicia foodhall.co.uk).

Pomona 179 Haverstock Hill, NW3 4QS (7916 2676, www.pomonafoods.co.uk).

Primrose Bakery 69 Gloucester Avenue, NW1 8LD (7483 4222, www.primrose-bakery.co.uk).

Royal Mile Whiskies 3 Bloomsbury Street, WC1B 3QE (7436 4763, www.royalmilewhiskies.com).

School of Life 70 Marchmont Street, WC1N 1AB (7833 1010, www.theschooloflife.com).

Shikasuki 67 Gloucester Avenue, NW1 8LD (7722 4442, www.shikasuki.com).

Skoob Unit 66, The Brunswick Centre, WC1N 1AE (7278 8760, www.skoob.com).

Sweet Pea 77 Gloucester Avenue, NW1 8LD (7449 9292, www.sweetpeajewellery.com).

Swiss Cottage Market Eton Avenue, NW3 3EU (www.lfm.org.uk).

Universal Works 37 Lamb's Conduit Street, WC1N 3NG (3632 2115, www.universalworks.co.uk).

VX 73 Caledonian Road, N1 9BT (7833 2315, www.vegancross.com).

Yuppy Puppy 198 Finchley Road, NW3 6BX (7794 2066, www.theyuppypuppy.co.uk).

Things to do

Cinemas & theatres

Bloomsbury Theatre 15 Gordon Street, WC1H 0AH (3108 1000, www.thebloomsbury.com).
Camden People's Theatre 58-60 Hampstead Road, NW1 2PY (7419 4841, www.cptheatre.co.uk).
Curzon Bloomsbury Brunswick Square, WC1N 1AW (0330 500 1331, www.curzoncinemas.com).
Drill Hall 16 Chenies Street, WC1E 7EX (7307 5061, www.rada.ac.uk). Lesbian- and gay-focused performance art and activities.
Etcetera Theatre 265 Camden High Street, NW1 7BU (7482 4857, www.etceteratheatre. com). Mini theatre above the Oxford Arms pub.
Everyman Cinema (0871 906 9060, www. everymancinema.com); 203 Haverstock Hill, NW3 4QG; 5 Holly Bush Vale, NW3 6TX.
Hampstead Theatre Eton Avenue, NW3 3EU (7722 9301, www.hampsteadtheatre.com).
Horse Hospital Colonnade, WC1N 1JD (7833 3644, www.thehorsehospital.com). Offbeat arts venue.
Kings Place 90 York Way, N1 9AG (7520 1490, www.kingsplace.co.uk). Purpose-built cultural venue, with a concert hall and two galleries.
New Diorama Theatre 15-16 Triton Street, NW1 3BF (7383 9034, www.newdiorama.com). New 80-seat performance space presenting drama, music and comedy.
Odeon (0871 224 4007, www.odeon.co.uk); 14 Parkway, NW1 7AA; 96 Finchley Road, NW3 5EL.
Place 17 Duke's Road, WC1H 9PY (7121 1100, www.theplace.org.uk). Leading contemporary dance centre.
Shaw Theatre 100-110 Euston Road, NW1 2AJ (7666 9037, www.shaw-theatre.com).
Theatro Technis 26 Crowndale Road, NW1 1TT (7387 6617, www.theatrotechnis.com). Fringe theatre established in 1957.
Upstairs at the Gatehouse Corner of Hampstead Lane & North Road, N6 4BD (8340 3488, www.upstairsatthegatehouse.com).
Vanburgh Theatre RADA, 62-64 Gower Street, WC1E 6ED (7636 7076, www.rada.ac.uk).
Vue Finchley Road O2 Centre, 255 Finchley Road, NW3 6LU (0871 224 0240, www.myvue.com).

Galleries & museums

Blain Southern 4 Hanover Square, W1S 1BP (7493 4492, www.blainsouthern.com)
British Museum Great Russell Street, WC1B 3DG (7323 8299, www.thebritishmuseum.ac.uk).
Camden Arts Centre Arkwright Road, NW3 6DG (7472 5500, www.camdenartscentre.org). Galleries, studios, a café and landscaped gardens.

Cartoon Museum Old Dairy, 35 Little Russell Street, WC1A 2HH (7580 8155, www.cartoon museum.org).
Fenton House Windmill Hill, NW3 6SP (7435 3471, www.nationaltrust.org.uk). Collection of antique musical instruments, sunken gardens and an orchard.
Freud Museum 20 Maresfield Gardens, NW3 5SX (7435 2002, www.freud.org.uk). Former home of Sigmund and daughter Anna.

Take folk-dancing classes at Cecil Sharp House.

House of Illustration 2 Granary Square, N1C 4BH (3696 2020, www.houseofillustration.org.uk).
Keats House Keats Grove, NW3 2RR (7332 3868, www.keatshouse.cityoflondon.gov.uk). The Romantic poet's last British home.
Kenwood House Hampstead Lane, NW3 7JR (0370 333 1181, www.english-heritage.org.uk). Impressive neoclassical house on Hampstead Heath.
New London Architecture The Building Centre, 26 Store Street, WC1E 7BT (7636 4044, www.newlondonarchitecture.org).
Sir John Soane's Museum 13 Lincoln's Inn Fields, WC2A 3BP (7405 2107, www.soane.org). Former home of 18th-century architect, showcasing his collection of art and artefacts.
Zabludowicz Collection 176 Prince of Wales Road, NW5 3PT (7428 8940, www.zabludowicz collection.com). Contemporary art in an impressive, restored Methodist chapel.

Other attractions

Bloomsbury Festival www.bloomsbury festival.org.uk.
British Library 96 Euston Road, NW1 2DB (0330 333 1144, www.bl.uk). One of the greatest libraries in the world. Access to the Reading Rooms requires a reader pass.
Kentish Town City Farm 1 Cressfield Close, NW5 4BN (7916 5421, www.ktcityfarm.org.uk).
Pirate's Castle Oval Road, NW1 7EA (7267 6605, www.thepiratecastle.org). Canalside activity centre for young people.

Gigs, clubs & comedy

Barfly 49 Chalk Farm Road, NW1 8AN (7688 8994, www.thebarflylondon.com). Music venue.
Camden Head 100 Camden High Street, NW1 0LU (7485 4019, www.camdenhead.com). Comedy upstairs.
Cecil Sharp House 2 Regent's Park Road, NW1 7AY (7485 2206, www.cecilsharphouse.org).

Dingwalls 11 Middle Yard, NW1 8AB (7428 5929, www.dingwalls.com).

Dome 2A Dartmouth Park Hill, NW5 1HL (7272 8153, www.dometufnellpark.co.uk).

Dublin Castle 94 Parkway, NW1 7AN (07949 575149, www.thedublincastle.com). Music venue and pub.

Egg London 200 York Way, N7 9AX (7871 7111, www.egglondon.net).

Electric Ballroom 184 Camden High Street, NW1 8QP (7485 9006, www.electricballroom. co.uk). Music venue and club.

Forge 3-7 Delancey Street, NW1 7NL (7383 7808, www.forgevenue.org).

Forum 9-17 Highgate Road, NW5 1JY (7428 4099, www.theforumlondon.com). Music venue.

Green Note 106 Parkway, NW1 7AN (7485 9899, www.greennote.co.uk).

Invisible Dot 2 Northdown Street, N1 9BG (7424 8918, www.theinvisibledot.com).

Jazz Café 5 Parkway, NW1 7PG (7485 6834, www.thejazzcafelondon.com). Music venue.

Koko 1A Camden High Street, NW1 7JE (7388 3222, www.koko.uk.com). Music venue and club.

Lock Tavern 35 Chalk Farm Road, NW1 8AJ (7482 7163, www.lock-tavern.com).

Monkey Business Comedy Club (07932 338203, www.monkeybusinesscomedyclub.co.uk). Held at the Oxford (Thur) and Tolli (Sat).

Oxford 256 Kentish Town Road, NW5 2AA (7485 3521, www.metropolitanpubcompany.com). Jazz.

Roundhouse Chalk Farm Road, NW1 8EH (0300 678 9222, www.roundhouse.org.uk). Pioneering arts venue.

Scala 275 Pentonville Road, N1 9NL (7833 2022, www.scala.co.uk). Music venue and club.

Stillery 18 Kentish Town Road, NW1 9NX (7284 2131, www.thestillery.co.uk).

Underworld 174 Camden High Street, NW1 0NE (7482 1932, www.theunderworldcamden.co.uk).

Water Rats 328 Gray's Inn Road, WC1X 8BZ (www.thewaterrats.com). Music venue.

Green spaces

Camley Street Nature Park 12 Camley Street, N1C 4PW (7833 2311, www.wildlondon.org.uk). Meadow, woodland and ponds by the canal.

Cantelowes Gardens NW1 9AA (7974 8765, www.camden.gov.uk). Playground, sports pitches, skatepark and BMX.

Coram's Fields 93 Guilford Street, WC1N 1DN (7837 6138, www.coramsfields.org).

Grays Inn Walks South Square, WC1R 5ET (7458 7800, www.graysinn.org.uk). Historic private gardens open to the public (noon-2.30pm Mon-Fri).

Hampstead Heath (7332 3322, www.hampstead heath.net). Grassland, woodland, swimming ponds and Kenwood House.

Kilburn Grange NW6 2JL (7974 8961, www. camden.gov.uk). Sports pitches, rose garden, adventure playground and waterpark.

Lincoln's Inn Fields WC2A 3TL. London's largest square, dating back to the 1630s.

St Pancras Gardens Pancras Lane, NW1 1UL (7419 6679, www.posp.co.uk). Churchyard of St Pancras Old Church, one of the oldest sites of Christian worship in Europe. Includes Soane's monument to his wife.

Tavistock Square Gardens WC1H 9LD (7974 1693, www.camden.gov.uk). Includes statue of Gandhi and a tree commemorating the victims of Hiroshima.

Waterlow Park N6 5HG (www.waterlowpark.org. uk). Landscaped park on hillside with great views.

Gyms & leisure centres

Armoury 25 Pond Street, NW3 2PN (7431 2263, www.jubileehalltrust.org). Private.

Central YMCA 112 Great Russell Street, WC1B 3NQ (7343 1844, www.ymca.co.uk). Private.

Kentish Town Sports Centre Grafton Road, NW5 3DU (7974 7000, www.better.org.uk).

Mallinson Sports Centre Bishopswood Road, N6 4NY (8342 7272, www.highgateschool.org.uk). Private.

Oasis Sports Centre 32 Endell Street, WC2H 9AG (7831 1804, www.better.org.uk).

Pancras Square Leisure 5 Pancras Square, N1C 4AG (7974 5555, www.better.org.uk). Pool, gym, jacuzzi and sauna.

Swiss Cottage Leisure Centre Adelaide Road, NW3 3NF (7974 2012, www.better.org.uk).

Talacre Community Sports Centre Dalby Street, NW5 3AF (7974 8765, www.better.org.uk).

Triyoga 57 Jamestown Road, NW1 7DB (7483 3344, www.triyoga.co.uk).

Outdoor pursuits

Hampstead Heath Swimming Ponds
Hampstead Heath, NW5 1QR (7332 3773, www. cityoflondon.gov.uk/hampstead).

Parliament Hill Lido Parliament Hill Fields, Gordon House Road, NW5 2LT (7485 3873, www. cityoflondon.gov.uk/openspaces).

Schools

Primary

There are 39 state primary schools in Camden, 20 of which are church schools. There are also 22 independent primaries, including one French school, one international school and two Montessori schools. See www.camden. gov.uk, www.ofsted.gov.uk and www.education. gov.uk/edubase for more information.

Secondary

Acland Burghley School 93 Burghley Road, NW5 1UJ (7485 8515, www.aclandburghley.camden.sch.uk).

Camden School for Girls Sandall Road, NW5 2DB (7485 3414, www.camdengirls.camden. sch.uk). Girls only.

Collège Français Bilingue de Londres 87 Holmes Road, NW5 3AX (7993 7400, www.cfbl. org.uk). Bilingual; private.

Great Ormond Street Hospital for Children School Great Ormond Street, WC1N 3JH (7813 8269, www.gosh.camden.sch.uk).

Hampstead School Westbere Road, NW2 3RT (7794 8133, www.hampsteadschool.org.uk).

Haverstock School 24 Haverstock Hill, NW3 2BQ (7267 0975, www.haverstock.camden.sch.uk).

Maria Fidelis Convent School 34 Phoenix Road, NW1 1TA (7387 3856, www.mariafidelis.camden. sch.uk). Roman Catholic; girls only.

Parliament Hill School Highgate Road, NW5 1RL (7485 7077, www.parliamenthill.camden.sch.uk). Girls only; mixed sixth form.

Regent High School Chalton Street, NW1 1RX (7387 0126, www.regenthighschool.org.uk).

La Sainte Union Catholic Secondary School Highgate Road, NW5 1RP (7428 4600, www. lasainteunion.org.uk). Roman Catholic; girls only.

South Hampstead High School 3 Maresfield Gardens, NW3 5SS (7435 2899, www.shhs.gdst. net). Girls only; private.

UCL Academy Adelaide Road, NW3 3AQ (7449 3080, www.uclacademy.com).

University College School Frognal, NW3 6XH (7435 2215, www.ucs.org.uk). Boys only; mixed sixth form; private.

William Ellis School Highgate Road, NW5 1RN (7267 9346, www.williamellis.camden.sch.uk). Boys only; mixed sixth form.

Property

Local estate agents

Alexanders www.alexanders-uk.com
Apple Green Lettings www.applegreen
lettings.co.uk
Black Katz www.blackkatz.com
Burghleys Estate Agents www.burghleys.com
Camden Bus Estate Agents www.camden
bus.co.uk
Christo & Co www.christo.co.uk
Cool Cribs http://coolcribs.co.uk
Day Morris Associates www.daymorris.com
Dennis & Hayes www.dennisandhayes.co.uk
Duke & Herzog www.dukeandherzog.com
Frank Harris & Co www.frankharris.co.uk
Jeremy Bass www.jeremybass.co.uk
London Residential www.londonresidential.
uk.com

Marsh & Parsons www.marshandparsons.co.uk
Matthew James www.matthewjames.co.uk
McHugh & Co www.mchughandco.com
Olivers www.oliverstown.com
Ringley www.ringley.co.uk

Local knowledge

www.camdennewjournal.com
www.gasholder.london
www.hamhigh.co.uk
www.heathandhampsteadsociety.org.uk
www.highgatesociety.com
www.kentishtowner.co.uk
www.kentishtowninvestigations.
wordpress.com
www.kingscrossenvironment.com
www.lovecamden.org
www.westhampsteadlife.com

Camden

USEFUL INFO

Borough size
2,179 hectares

Population
237,400

Ethnic mix
White 69.9%
Asian or Asian British 14.2%
Black or Black British 7.3%
Chinese or other 4.8%
Mixed 3.8%

London borough of Camden
Camden Town Hall, Judd Street, WC1H
9JE (7974 4444, www.camden.gov.uk)

Council run by
Labour

MPs
Hampstead & Kilburn, Tulip Siddiq
(Labour); Holborn & St Pancras,
Keir Starmer (Labour)

Main recycling centre
Regis Road Recycling Centre, Regis
Road, NW5 3EW (3620 4026,
www.wiseuptowaste.org)

Council tax
£891.32 to £2,673.62

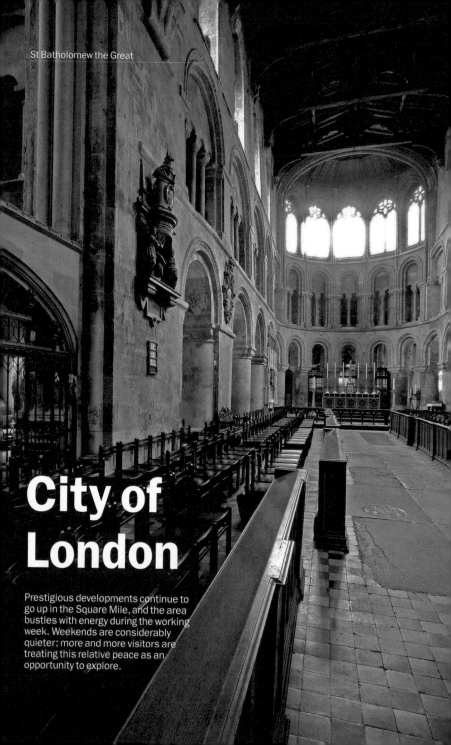

City of London

Prestigious developments continue to go up in the Square Mile, and the area bustles with energy during the working week. Weekends are considerably quieter; more and more visitors are treating this relative peace as an opportunity to explore.

Neighbourhoods

The City EC2, EC3, EC4

One of the joys of the City is the population ebb and flow that ensures it never stays the same. By day, it's mobbed by some 350,000 office workers, plus a veritable army of City of London police officers, cycle couriers, tourists and white-van drivers. By night, and at weekends, the streets are less busy although nowhere near as deserted as they were 15 years ago, thanks to the increase in the number of bars, restaurants and shops. This is especially apparent at the One New Change complex – which offers a great view of the dome of St Paul's and beyond from its rooftop viewing area – and around redeveloped Paternoster Square, where the knock-on effect of the crowds surging over the Millennium Bridge from Tate Modern gives the place a definite buzz at weekends.

The boundaries of the City are roughly delineated by the old Roman city walls, but the few thousand full-time residents of the district are actually squeezed into a much smaller area. Most of the elegant townhouses built after the Great Fire of London in 1666 were destroyed by German bombing in World War II, transformed into offices, or knocked down and replaced with office blocks by generations of town planners. Residents have been left to make the best of the small pockets of housing tucked away between the major monuments, tower blocks and Wren churches.

With the focus very much on office space, amenities such as parks and children's play areas are in short supply, though the City is home to more than 150 small 'city gardens' (see www.cityoflondon.gov.uk) and there's always the river to gaze at. What's more, the architecture is the most fascinating in London, with the showily modern ('the Gherkin' or the Lloyd's of London building) sitting alongside the beautifully ancient (St Bartholomew the Great is London's oldest parish church); statues and other public artworks are also plentiful. Construction is a constant – major, skyline-altering projects in the last few years include the Leadenhall Building ('the Cheesegrater') and 20 Fenchurch Street ('the Walkie-Talkie').

Among the most desirable residences are the handful of Georgian townhouses that escaped the Blitz, found in clusters around Fenchurch Street, Fleet Street and Liverpool Street station. Most are broken up into luxury apartments, attracting young high-flyers who enjoy the proximity of the bars and restaurants in Islington and Tower Hamlets. Gardens and parking spaces are almost unheard of, but most residents are happy to trade the luxury of space for the convenience of living so centrally.

This is one of the easiest places in London in which to flag down a black cab and with plentiful buses, and train and tube stations every few hundred yards, it's transport heaven. The glitzy new Blackfriars tube and rail station now extends over Blackfriars Bridge, with entrances on both sides of the river. The Crossrail project is having a big impact on the areas around Liverpool Street and Moorgate; by its completion in late 2018, the City will be even better connected.

London's oldest (and richest) local authority, the City has its peculiarities: its own police force; numerous archaic traditions; and it owns land well beyond its borders (Epping Forest and Hampstead Heath, for example). Unlike anywhere else in the UK, local elections are non party political, and businesses as well as individuals are allowed to vote. Crime of the kind that affects homeowners is well below the London average. However, post-work binge drinking is one black mark on this otherwise enviable record.

Inevitably, the City is not a cheap place to eat, and expense-account dining is everywhere. An antidote can be found at the Café Below, where breakfasts and brasserie

Around Smithfield Market are several late-night-cum-early-morning or 24-hour cafés. Try Ferrari's.

dishes are served in the courtyard and crypt of St Mary-le-Bow Church. Other affordable venues include Hummus Bros, Patty & Bun, and City Câphé, a small Vietnamese café serving great bánh mi. Chain restaurants – Pizza Express, Wagamama and so on – are everywhere. More interesting venues include Vivat Bacchus, where a serious wine list is balanced by an easygoing attitude and South African-influenced food, and our favourite City haunt – trad fish restaurant Sweetings (open for lunch on weekdays only). A new food hub has been created at Broadgate Circle, with offerings ranging from a branch of the

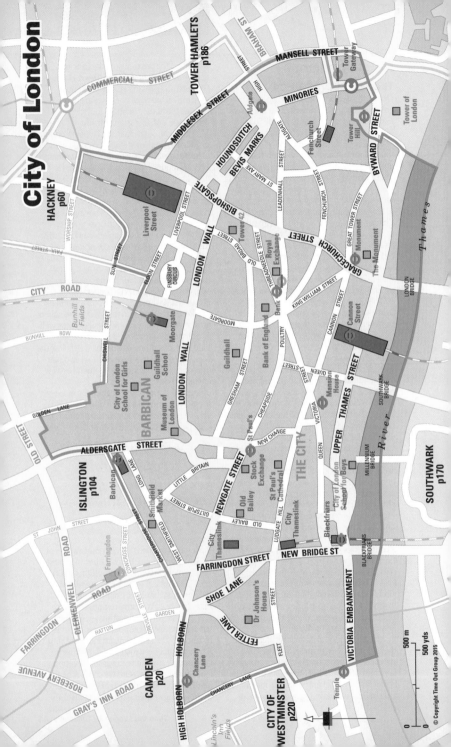

Franco Manca chain with its well-priced sourdough pizza to Yauatcha City's dim sum and premium mains.

Bar and pub chains have a very strong presence here, but there are some wonderfully historic boozers and wine bars, and glam cocktail bars way up in the sky such as Sushisamba and City Social Bar; these two also have eateries attached. The area around Liverpool Street heaves with City workers on Thursday and Friday nights, all with annihilation on their minds. A safer bet might be adjacent Spitalfields in Tower Hamlets, though the bar at the smart South Place Hotel is worth trying.

Retailing in the City has undergone a huge shake-up in recent years: the biggest transformation was the arrival of the One New Change centre in 2010. But, as elsewhere in the Square Mile, although the architecture (courtesy of Jean Nouvel) may be interesting, the shops are identikit. Fashion chains predominate at One New Change, while the swanky Royal Exchange complex has a slew of luxury brands.

The area around St Paul's and Paternoster Square has also become lively at weekends. The smartest options here are bar-restaurants Paternoster Chop House (British) and the Restaurant at St Paul's (also British, and housed within the cathedral). Jamie Oliver and Gordon Ramsay have gone head to head at One New Change with Barbecoa and Bread Street Kitchen, respectively.

Cheapside has yet more clothing chains and a big Tesco, but some originality is added to the mix with Daunt Books; for a little more charm, wander down the Dickensian Bow Lane. Also scenic is historic Leadenhall Market, to the east, which is packed with shops and stalls. The occasional one-off gem remains – visit F Flittner barbers (est 1904) on Moorgate for a glimpse of how things used to be.

It's worth remembering that, due to the tidal nature of the daytime population, many pubs, restaurants and shops close over the weekend.

Smithfield and Barbican EC1, EC2

In recent years, renovation of the area around Smithfield Market has provided plenty of loft apartments in converted warehouses and office buildings. The plan to demolish a set of Victorian buildings on the west side of Smithfield Market (running along Farringdon Road) and replace them with shops and offices has been the subject of much (ongoing) debate. Many of the buildings are by Horace Jones, the architect who designed the rest of the market, but they have been allowed to lie derelict for years.

The atmosphere in this area most resembles next-door Clerkenwell (in the borough of Islington); there are still local shops and small businesses, as well as bars and destination restaurants. Aside from the handsome meat market, the main landmark is historic St Bartholomew's Hospital. The pretty streets between St Barts and Aldersgate contain some very covetable houses – the area oozes character.

Smithfield is a fruitful location for restaurants, and further rich pickings can be had on St John Street. Thanks to Fabric (the destination club that draws enormous weekend queues), the bars on Charterhouse Street pull in a vibrant crowd – wedge-shaped Charterhouse, for example, and the multifaceted Smiths of Smithfield, are both popular pre-club pit-stops. The Fox & Anchor pub offers good British food and a more relaxed atmosphere.

The Barbican Estate, easily the City's most famous residential address, houses about half the City of London's population and is highly sought after. The advantages

TRANSPORT

Tube lines Central, Circle, District, DLR, Metropolitan, Northern, Waterloo & City
Rail services Blackfriars, Cannon Street, City Thameslink, Fenchurch Street, Liverpool Street and Moorgate stations
Main bus routes Dozens of buses run through the City of London during the day; for a full list, visit www.tfl.gov.uk/buses. Night buses N8, N11, N15, N21, N26, N35, N47, N55, N63, N76, N133; 24-hour buses 23, 25, 43, 149, 214, 242, 243, 271, 344
River boat services Blackfriars Pier

are obvious: it's very central, with fantastic transport links and an arts complex on your doorstep, yet quiet and peaceful at weekends. A midcentury modern masterpiece, the Barbican terraces and towers were designed by architects Chamberlain, Powell & Bon, and built between 1964 and 1975 (the Barbican arts centre wasn't finished until 1982). The whole estate covers around 40 acres and has just over 2,000 apartments (of well over 100 different types, ranging from studio flats to penthouses).

It also contains the City of London School for Girls, the Museum of London (though a move to Smithfield Market is being mooted) and the Guildhall School of Music & Drama (the last also has new facilities across the road in the Heron, which also holds 284 luxury flats). By 2016, the Barbican will also house the London Film School. Just to the north, on Fann Street, the Golden Lane Estate is becoming increasingly popular for fans of the same era; the houses and flats were designed by the same architects, and are also Grade II listed.

The honeypot effect of the Barbican can be seen in the new developments clustered around it: not only the Heron on Moor Lane, but also Roman House (an office block converted to smart apartments) on Wood Street.

The Barbican complex offers several dining options, none of them compelling. The most interesting choices close by are the Jugged Hare, a smart gastropub, and Bad Egg, a diner by Neil Rankin on the ground floor of the large City Point office building.

HIGHS & LOWS

No more commuting – you're already here

Bars and clubs

History – this is the original London

Few burglaries

Antisocial drinking during the week

Lack of independent shops

Very quiet at weekends

The atmosphere changes to the west of St Paul's, with fewer high-rise trophy buildings. Ludgate Hill, Fleet Street and the winding lanes and alleyways running off them are packed tight with old buildings (some of them containing tucked-away flats as well as the more obvious offices). The newspaper industry may have disappeared, but the legal world remains, keeping places such as venerable wine bar El Vino going. There are plenty of historic pubs in the area, but the most striking is the art-nouveau-meets-Arts-and-Crafts Blackfriar. Towards Temple, the well-funded gardens of the Inns of Court offer some respite from the traffic.

Eating

Bad Egg City Point, 1 Ropemaker Street, EC2Y 9AW (3006 6222, www.badegg.london).
Barbecoa 20 New Change Passage, EC4M 9AG (3005 8555, www.barbecoa.com).
Bread Street Kitchen 10 Bread Street, EC4M 9AJ (3030 4050, www.breadstreetkitchen.com).
Café Below St Mary-le-Bow Church, Cheapside, EC2V 6AU (7329 0789, www.cafebelow.co.uk).
City Câphé 17 Ironmonger Lane, EC2V 8EY (www.citycaphe.com).
Ferrari's 8 West Smithfield, EC1A 9JR (7236 7545).
Hummus Bros 128 Cheapside, EC2V 6BT (7726 8011, www.hbros.co.uk).
Jugged Hare 49 Chiswell Street, EC1Y 4SA (7614 0134, www.thejuggedhare.com).
Paternoster Chop House Warwick Court, Paternoster Square, EC4M 7DX (7029 9400, www.paternosterchophouse.co.uk).
Patty & Bun 22-23 Liverpool Street, EC2M 7PD (7621 1331, www.pattyandbun.co.uk).
Restaurant at St Paul's St Paul's Cathedral, St Paul's Churchyard, EC4M 8AD (7248 2469, www.restaurantatstpauls.co.uk).
Sweetings 39 Queen Victoria Street, EC4N 4SA (7248 3062, www.sweetingsrestaurant.com).
Vivat Bacchus 47 Farringdon Street, EC4A 4LL (7353 2648, www.vivatbacchus.co.uk).
Yauatcha City Broadgate Circle, EC2M 2QS (3817 9888, www.yauatcha.com).

Drinking

Blackfriar 174 Queen Victoria Street, EC4V 4EG (7236 5474, www.nicholsonspubs.co.uk).
Charterhouse 38 Charterhouse Street, EC1M 6JH (7608 0858, www.charterhousebar.co.uk).
City Social Bar 24th floor, Tower 42, 25 Old Broad Street, EC2N 1HQ (7877 7703, www.citysocial london.com).

Blackfriars Bridge

Fabric 77A Charterhouse Street, EC1M 3HN (7336 8898, www.fabriclondon.com). Nightclub.
Fox & Anchor 115 Charterhouse Street, EC1M 6AA (7250 1300, www.foxandanchor.com).
Smiths of Smithfield 67-77 Charterhouse Street, EC1M 6HJ (7251 7950, www.smithsofsmithfield. co.uk).
South Place Hotel 3 South Place, EC2M 2AF (3503 0000, www.southplacehotel.com).
Sushisamba 38th & 39th floors, Heron Tower, 110 Bishopsgate, EC2N 4AY (3640 7330, www. sushisamba.com).
El Vino (www.elvino.co.uk); 47 Fleet Street, EC4Y 1BJ (7353 6786); 30 New Bridge Street, EC4V 6BJ (7236 4534); 125 London Wall, EC2Y 5AP (7600 6377).

Shopping

Daunt Books 61 Cheapside, EC2V 6AX (7248 1117, www.dauntbooks.co.uk).
F Flittner 86 Moorgate, EC2M 6SE (7606 4750, www.fflittner.com).
House of Fraser 68 King William Street, EC4N 7HR (0844 800 3718, www.houseoffraser.co.uk).
Leadenhall Market Whittington Avenue, off Gracechurch Street, EC3V 1LR (7929 1073, www.leadenhallmarket.co.uk).
One New Change EC4M 9AF (7002 8900, www.onenewchange.com).
Royal Exchange Cornhill & Threadneedle Street, EC3V 3LR (www.theroyalexchange.com).

Things to do

Cinemas & theatres

Barbican Centre Silk Street, EC2Y 8DS (7638 8891, www.barbican.org.uk). Major arts centre with theatres, an art gallery and three cinemas. Also the home of the London Symphony Orchestra and the BBC Symphony Orchestra.
Guildhall School of Music & Drama Silk Street, Barbican, EC2Y 8DT (7628 2571, www.gsmd. ac.uk). Recitals open to the public; free.

Galleries & museums

Bank of England Museum Entrance on Bartholomew Lane, EC2R 8AH (7601 5545, www.bankofengland.co.uk/museum).
Barbican Art Gallery Level 3, Barbican Centre, Silk Street, EC2Y 8DS (7638 8891, www.barbican. org.uk). Contemporary art and photography.
Dr Johnson's House 17 Gough Square, EC4A 3DE (7353 3745, www.drjohnsonshouse.org). Wonderfully atmospheric museum celebrating the life and works of Samuel Johnson.
Guildhall Art Gallery Guildhall Yard, off Gresham Street, EC2V 5AE (7332 3700, www.guildhallartgallery.cityoflondon.gov.uk). Works by Constable, Reynolds and Rossetti.
Museum of London London Wall, EC2Y 5HN (7001 9844, www.museumoflondon.org.uk).
Museum of Methodism & John Wesley's House Wesley's Chapel, 49 City Road, EC1Y 1AU (7253 2262, www.wesleyschapel.org.uk).

Tower Bridge Exhibition Tower Bridge, SE1 2UP (7403 3761, www.towerbridge.org.uk). The history of the bridge. Stunning views from the high-level (glass) walkways.

Tower of London Tower Hill, EC3N 4AB (0844 482 7777, www.hrp.org.uk). The English Crown Jewels, ravens, Beefeaters, tourists and nearly 1,000 years of history. (Actually in Tower Hamlets.)

Other attractions

College of Arms Queen Victoria Street, EC4V 4BT (7248 2762, www.college-of-arms.gov.uk). Heraldic and genealogical history.

Guildhall Gresham Street, EC2P 2EJ (7606 3030, www.guildhall.cityoflondon.gov.uk). Home of the Corporation of London.

Monument Monument Street, EC3R 8AH (7626 2717, www.themonument.info). Built in 1677 to commemorate the Great Fire of London. Spectacular views from the top.

Old Bailey Central Criminal Court, corner of Newgate Street & Old Bailey, EC4M 7EH (7248 3277, www.justice.gov.uk). The public galleries allow viewing of trials.

St Bartholomew the Great West Smithfield, EC1A 9DS (7606 5171, www.greatstbarts.com). The City's finest medieval church.

St Paul's Cathedral Ludgate Hill, EC4M 8AD (7246 8357, www.stpauls.co.uk).

Sky Garden 20 Fenchurch Street, EC3M 3BY (3772 0020, www.skygarden.london). Viewing complex in the soaring 'Walkie-Talkie' building.

Green spaces

Bunhill Fields Burial Ground 38 City Road, EC1Y 1AU (www.cityoflondon.gov.uk). Burial place of William Blake, John Bunyan, Daniel Defoe and Susannah Wesley.

Inner Temple Gardens Middle Temple Lane, EC4Y 9AT (www.innertemple.org.uk). Peaceful courtyards and gardens amid the historic barristers' chambers, open to the public weekday afternoons. Middle Temple Gardens (www.middletemplehall.org.uk), adjacent, serve as more of an events venue these days.

Postman's Park EC1A (www.cityoflondon.gov.uk). Entrances via St Martin's Le-Grand and Aldersgate Street and King Edward Street. Pretty and unusual; home to George Frederick Watt's Memorial to Heroic Self Sacrifice.

Gyms & leisure centres

Barbican YMCA 2 Fann Street, EC2Y 8BR (7628 0697, www.cityymca.org). Private.

City (London) Fitness & Wellbeing Centre 4 Cousin Lane, EC4R 3XJ (3773 2628, www.nuffieldhealth.com). Private.

Citypoint Club Citypoint, 1 Ropemaker Street, EC2Y 9AW (7920 6200, www.thecitypointclub.co.uk). Private.

Golden Lane Leisure Centre Fann Street, EC1Y 0SH (7250 1464, www.fusion-lifestyle.com).

LA Fitness (www.lafitness.co.uk); 20 Little Britain, EC1A 7DH (7600 0900); 48 London Wall, EC2M 5QB (7628 9876); St Botolph Building, 141 Houndsditch, EC3A 7DH (7337 3400). Private.

Slim Jim's Health Club 1 Finsbury Avenue, EC2M 2PF (7247 9982, www.slim-jims.co.uk). Private.

Outdoor pursuits

Broadgate Ice Rink Broadgate Circle, EC2M 2QS (0845 653 1424, www.broadgate.co.uk/ice). Seasonal ice skating.

Schools

Primary

There is only one state primary school within the City of London (the Sir John Cass's Foundation Primary School) and two independents (St Paul's Cathedral School and the Charterhouse Square School). See www.cityoflondon.gov.uk, www.education.gov.uk/edubase and www.ofsted.gov.uk for more information.

Secondary

There are no state secondary schools, but the borough has an arrangement with Tower Hamlets to provide places. Local children also get priority admission to the City of London Academy in Southwark.

City of London School for Boys Queen Victoria Street, EC4V 3AL (7489 0291, www.clsb.org.uk). Boys only; private.

City of London School for Girls St Giles' Terrace, EC2Y 8BB (7847 5500, www.clsg.org.uk). Girls only; private.

Property

Local estate agents

Chancery Estates www.chanceryestates.co.uk
Chase Evans www.chaseevans.co.uk
Frank Harris & Company www.frankharris.co.uk
Hamilton Brooks www.hamiltonbrooks.co.uk
Lawlor Property www.lawlorproperty.co.uk
Lawrence Ward www.lawrenceward.co.uk
Scott City www.scottcity.co.uk
Thomas Michael www.thomasmichael.co.uk

Local knowledge

www.barbicanlifeonline.com
www.barbicanliving.co.uk

Barbican

USEFUL INFO

Borough size
290 hectares

Population
8,200

Ethnic mix
White 82.3%
Asian or Asian British 8.4%
Black or Black British 3.7%
Chinese or other 3.5%
Mixed 2.0%

City of London Corporation
Guildhall, Gresham Street, EC2P 2EJ
(7606 3030, www.cityoflondon.gov.uk)

MPs
Cities of London & Westminster, Mark
Field (Conservative)

Main recycling centre
The City does not have a recycling
centre. See www.cityoflondon.gov.uk
for alternatives

Council tax
£628.96 to £1,886.88

Greenwich

Greenwich is known for its world-class heritage sites and as the birthplace of time (well, the Prime Meridian). Steeped in maritime history, today it's also home to one of London's largest entertainment complexes, on the Greenwich Peninsula. Further east, though, the borough is monotonously residential.

AVERAGE PROPERTY PRICE

Detached	Terraced
£644,566	£340,124
Semi-detached	Flat
£414,886	£318,353

AVERAGE RENTAL PRICE PER WEEK

Room	1 bed
£96	£222
Studio	2 bed
£178	£288
	3 bed
	£334

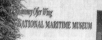

National Maritime Museum, Greenwich

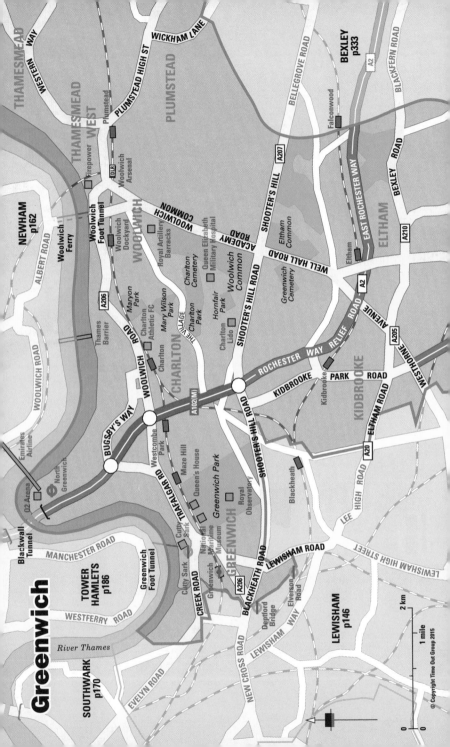

Neighbourhoods

Greenwich SE10

Is it possible to think of a more beautiful place to live than Greenwich? The perfectly preserved historic streets of Royal Hill, Crooms Hill and all those in between are charm itself, stretching uphill beside the park until they hit Blackheath. There are serious Georgian townhouses with bow windows and plenty of stories to tell, and more diminutive cottages with no less character. On Royal Hill, there's the dream shopping parade of fishmonger (the Fishmonger), butcher (Drings), cheesemonger (the Cheeseboard), greengrocer (the Creaky Shed) and florist (Karen Wolven), as well as the Hill Mediterranean restaurant, the tiny Royal Teas café, Meantime Brewery's Greenwich Union pub and old-timer Richard I; on Crooms Hill, the Greenwich Theatre is an off-West End venue that attracts some top thespian talent and a loyal local following.

The serenity doesn't last, though. From the station along to Deptford Bridge, Greenwich High Road (the wrong end of town) has been invaded by apartment blocks and hotels; the centre of town is besieged by traffic and chain restaurants; Wren's Old Royal Naval College is overrun with students (it's now home to the University of Greenwich); and the riverfront and markets are filled with tourists.

Greenwich's markets are spread across different sites, including a central covered market (currently in the process of an upgrade, with the addition of a new roof). There are simple fruit 'n' veg stalls on Wednesdays; antiques and collectibles on Tuesdays; Thursdays and Fridays; and contemporary crafts and design at the weekend, always with a strong street-food presence too. Permanent fixtures in the surrounding units include Greenwich Printmakers, Goddards pie shop and Mr Humbug sweets.

Elsewhere, amid the studenty clothes shops and chain eating, are several interesting shops and cafés: Halcyon Books, Casbah Records, the Music & Video Exchange, seasonal restaurant Inside, Jamie's Italian, Rhodes Bakery, Peyton & Byrne, and the cosy, family-run Peter de Wit's Café. There are plenty of good pubs in the area (seriously – far too many to list here); those by the river include the Trafalgar Tavern (where Gladstone and his Cabinet would come for whitebait) and, a little further along, the Cutty Sark, serving since 1795. Riverside dining includes the capital's best-located chains (Nando's, Byron), with their riverside roof terraces, just off Cutty Sark Gardens.

Greenwich Park is yet another treasure, a rolling landscape that climbs up the hillside to the Royal Observatory and some excellent views. This is also the best vantage point from which to appreciate the orderly beauty of the Queen's House, National Maritime Museum and Old Royal Naval College (not for nothing is this a UNESCO World Heritage Site), not to mention the majestic sweep of the Thames and the badlands of deepest east London beyond.

If you can't afford to live the Royal Hill dream, there are plenty of more modest streets stretching eastwards from the Old Royal Naval College, between Trafalgar Road and the river, as well as a string of new apartments beginning to fill the riverside right round to the Greenwich Peninsula.

Greenwich Peninsula SE10

Greenwich Peninsula is finally becoming a place to be. The O2 (or 'Millennium Dome', as anyone over 40 still insists on calling it; or 'North Greenwich Arena', as pretty much no one does) still dominates this near-island in the Thames, but there are now plenty more reasons to go, or even stay: the spirited Now Gallery, serious eating at Stevie Parle's Craft and the Greenwich Kitchen, off-beat theatre at the Jetty (soon to have a permanent site), the Emirates Air Line cable car (useless as a piece of transport infrastructure; brilliant for

Charlton Toy Library in historic Charlton House is a brilliant resource for parents. Hire a toy for a couple of weeks, then return it when your little one gets bored.

cheap thrills), and Europe's largest golf driving range. Down by the Blackwall Tunnel approach road, there's megaclub Studio 338, a multiplex cinema, dim sum at the huge Saikei Chinese restaurant in the Holiday Inn, and London's original craft brewery, Meantime, now with added dining in the Tasting Rooms.

And there's more to the O2 itself than just stadium bands, blockbuster sports tournaments and what feels like the world's longest food court. There's Brooklyn Bowl, Gran Turismo racing pods at Nissan Innovation Experience, Sky Studios' free behind-the-scenes experience, and Up at the O2, which allows you to climb over the top of the dome itself.

Although the centre of the peninsula is essentially a car park servicing the O2, the riverside edges feature a peaceful ecology park, designated cycling and jogging tracks, an imaginative children's playground and the Millennium Village apartment blocks, designed with a friendly neighbourhood feel. Lots more of the same is planned over the next 25 years, on an even huger scale.

Charlton SE7 and Kidbrooke SE3

One look at Woolwich Road, and it's a wonder that anyone ever ventures further east than Greenwich Peninsula. Traffic creaks wearily on towards Woolwich with little excitement save a brief entanglement with the ever-congested Blackwall Tunnel approach road. Travel in the same direction by train, however, and you pass through Maze Hill, Westcombe Park and Charlton, where the attractiveness of this strip of south-east London becomes more apparent. The whole hillside (marketed as 'Charlton Slopes') is filled with family-friendly period streets – not as head-turning as those in nearby Greenwich and Blackheath, perhaps, but a tempting alternative. There are also plenty of schools and the lovely Maryon Wilson Park, with its own children's zoo.

The historic hub is Charlton Village – not an estate agents' marketing ploy, it was once a bona fide village and the main road is actually called Charlton Village. You can still spot historic elements such as the drinking fountain, St Luke's parish church and Blackheath Rugby Club – the world's oldest. The star turn, though, is Charlton House, which dates back to 1612 and is considered one of the finest surviving Jacobean mansions. It's now a prime wedding venue, but also houses a fantastic toy library and a great café, the Mulberry Tea Rooms.

Unfortunately for lovers of artisanal bakeries, fancy restaurants or arty boutiques, there aren't any (although the Village Green Grocers does appear to have entered into the 'village' spirit). The most exciting shops here are probably the very niche Charlton Reptiles & Aquatics, and Bowes shoe repairs, which looks like it's been there since they laid the railway. That's if anywhere's actually open. You'll find a bit more commercial life over in Westcombe Park and Blackheath Standard (including the Royal Standard pub).

Charlton Park, where the terrain flattens out on the other (southern) side of Charlton Road, is a great neighbourhood resource; a big, open patch of playgrounds, sports pitches and kickabout space surrounded by tree-lined streets. Its park café (Old Cottage Coffee Shop) is worth a mention – it's done out inside like a Victorian parlour with standard lamps and stacks of second-hand books. Then there's the much-loved Charlton Lido, located on the far side of the park by Shooters Hill Road.

Given that it shares a demographic and property portfolio similar to many classically gentrified neighbourhoods, Charlton's ordinariness comes as either a surprise or a relief, depending on your point of view. This could be down to it being that bit more awkward to get to.

Across Shooters Hill Road is the once no-go area of Kidbrooke, now the subject of a £750-million redevelopment programme. This has included the demolition of the infamous Ferrier Estate – one of the largest in London – and the building of, you guessed it, Kidbrooke Village, with commuter-friendly apartments and townhouses, plus a supermarket, gym, pool and newly created Cator Park.

Woolwich and Plumstead SE18, Thamesmead SE28

Past the Thames Barrier, the Royal Borough of Greenwich starts to get considerably shabbier. The South Circular ploughs through

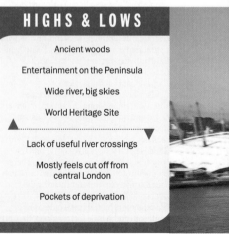

HIGHS & LOWS

Ancient woods

Entertainment on the Peninsula

Wide river, big skies

World Heritage Site

▲ ⋯⋯⋯⋯⋯⋯⋯⋯⋯ ▼

Lack of useful river crossings

Mostly feels cut off from central London

Pockets of deprivation

Woolwich, joined to the north bank not by anything as practical as a bridge but by the Woolwich Ferry – free and fun, but not that useful if the weather's bad or you're in a hurry. The A2 and A20 thunder through Eltham, so that much of this stretch of south-east London feels like a monotonous swathe of housing carved up by roads, interspersed with wide expanses of ancient woodland and common.

Concerted effort (and quite a lot of money) has been put into regenerating Woolwich town centre, and the results are beginning to show. On exiting Woolwich Arsenal station (now linked up to the DLR as well as being on a rail line into Charing Cross, creating new commuting possibilities), General Gordon Square provides a firm statement of intent. There's bold landscaping and water features, dominated by the Big Screen, drawing crowds to watch everything from major sporting events to live opera broadcasts. Around it are the Grade II-listed Equitable House (where the Woolwich Building Society began life – now home to the Woolwich Equitable pub) and 2014 Carbuncle Cup-winner Woolwich Central, a glazed apartment block with striped metal cladding housing a giant Tesco.

The new riverside park of Royal Arsenal Gardens has created a pleasant green space. Beresford Square has also received some love, but remains home to the daily market. Shopping along Powis Street is still fairly unexciting, though the arrival of a few chains shows a growing confidence in the area. Wellington Street, meanwhile, has acquired

the eye-catching Woolwich Centre, which provides council services, a modern and expanded library, a café, and an exhibition and meeting space. Unsurprisingly, new riverside apartment blocks (including the large Royal Arsenal Riverside development) are taking advantage of Woolwich's assets.

Regeneration may be afoot, but Woolwich is still all about history – specifically military history. This was the site of the country's main arsenal and ammunitions manufacturing for more than two centuries, finally closing in 1967. You can learn more at the Firepower experience at the Royal Artillery Museum. It's also still home to the Royal Artillery Barracks and was where a certain north London football team was born in 1886.

Even Thamesmead, whose 1960s and '70s urban planning formed the backdrop to *A Clockwork Orange* and Jonathan Harvey's coming-of-age love story *Beautiful Thing*, is undergoing regeneration. Greenwich and Bexley councils (which Thamesmead straddles) are working with the Peabody housing association on a ten-year, £200-million regeneration project to build 700 new homes.

Nearby Plumstead houses London's largest Nepalese community, and consequently hotly recommended momo restaurants such as tiny De Namaste. Over in Eltham, London becomes faceless residential suburbia, but history still pops up with surprises. Eltham Palace is a stunning art deco house attached to a Tudor hall, run by English Heritage; Well Hall Pleasaunce is a Tudor barn, now occupied by the Heritage Restaurant & Bar.

Emirates Air Line

Eating

Craft Peninsula Square, SE10 0SQ (8465 5910, www.craft-london.co.uk).
De Namaste 158 Plumstead Road, SE18 7DY (8333 2232).
Goddards 22 King William Walk, SE10 9HU (8305 9612, www.goddardsatgreenwich.co.uk).
Greenwich Kitchen Peninsula Square, SE10 0SQ (8305 9757, www.greenwichkitchen.com).
Hill 89 Royal Hill, SE10 8SE (8691 3926, www.thehillgreenwich.com).
Inside 19 Greenwich South Street, SE10 8NW (8265 5060, www.insiderestaurant.co.uk).
Jamie's Italian 17-19 Nelson Road, SE10 9JB (3667 7087, www.jamieoliver.com).
Mulberry Tea Rooms Charlton House, Charlton Road, SE7 8RE (www.charltonhouse.org).
Old Cottage Coffee Shop Charlton Park, SE7.
Peter de Wit's Café 21 Greenwich Church Street, SE10 9BJ (8305 0048, www.peterdewits cafe.co.uk).
Peyton & Byrne 20-22 Greenwich Church Street, SE10 9BJ (3422 1455, www.peytonandbyrne.co.uk).
Rhodes Bakery 37 King William Walk, SE10 9HU (8858 8995, www.paulrhodesbakery.co.uk).
Royal Teas 76 Royal Hill, SE10 8RT (8691 7240, www.royalteascafe.co.uk).
Saikei Holiday Inn Express, 85 Bugsby's Way, SE10 0GD (8269 1638, www.saikei-restaurant.com).
Tasting Rooms Lawrence Trading Estate, Blackwall Lane, SE10 0AR (8293 1111, www.meantimebrewing.com).

Drinking

Cutty Sark 4-6 Ballast Quay, SE10 9PD (8858 3146, www.cuttysarkse10.co.uk).
Greenwich Union 56 Royal Hill, SE10 8RT (8692 6258, www.greenwichunion.com).
Richard I 52-54 Royal Hill, SE10 8RT (8692 2996, www.richardthefirst.co.uk).
Trafalgar Tavern Park Row, SE10 9NW (8858 2909, www.trafalgartavern.co.uk).
Woolwich Equitable Equitable House, General Gordon Square, Vincent Road, SE18 6AB (8309 8126, www.woolwichequitable.com).

Shopping

Casbah Records at the Beehive 320-322 Creek Road, SE10 9SW (8858 1964, www.casbah records.co.uk).
Cheeseboard 26 Royal Hill, SE10 8RT (8305 0401, www.cheese-board.co.uk).
Creaky Shed 20 Royal Hill, SE10 8RT (8269 0333, www.thecreakyshed.co.uk).

Drings 22 Royal Hill, SE10 8RT (8858 4032, www.drings.co.uk).
Fishmonger Rear of 26 Royal Hill, SE10 8RT (07880 541485, www.thefishmongerltd.com).
Greenwich Market SE10 9HZ (8269 5096, www.greenwichmarketlondon.com).
Greenwich Printmakers 1A Greenwich Market, SE10 9HZ (8858 1569, www.greenwich-printmakers.co.uk).
Halcyon Books 1 Greenwich South Street, SE10 8NW (8305 2675, www.halcyonbooks.co.uk).
Karen Woolven 18 Royal Hill, SE10 8RT (8858 1112, www.kwfloraldesign.co.uk).
Mr Humbug 12 Greenwich Market, SE10 9HZ (7790 4345, www.mrhumbug.com).
Music & Video Exchange 23 Greenwich Church Street, SE10 9BJ (8858 8898, www.mgeshops.com).

Things to do

Cinemas & theatres
Big Screen General Gordon Square, SE18 6HD (www.royalgreenwich.gov.uk). Live broadcasts.
Greenwich Picture House 180 Greenwich High Road, SE10 8NN (0871 902 5732, www.picturehouses.co.uk).
Greenwich Theatre Crooms Hill, SE10 8ES (8858 7755, www.greenwichtheatre.org.uk).
Odeon Greenwich Bugsby's Way, SE10 0QJ (0871 224 4007, www.odeon.co.uk).

Galleries & museums
Charlton Athletic Museum North Stand, Charlton Athletic FC, The Valley, Floyd Road, SE7 8BL (8333 4000, www.thecharltonathletic museum.co.uk).
Cutty Sark King William Walk, SE10 9HT (8312 6608, www.rmg.co.uk).
Fan Museum 12 Crooms Hill, SE10 8ER (8305 1441, www.thefanmuseum.org.uk). More than 3,500 fans from around the world.
Firepower, Royal Artillery Museum Royal Arsenal, SE18 6ST (8312 7103, www.firepower.org.uk). Artillery through the ages.
National Maritime Museum Romney Road, SE10 9NF (8858 4422, information 8312 6565, tours 8312 6608, www.rmg.co.uk). Explore more than 500 years of maritime history.
Now Gallery The Gateway Pavilions, Peninsula Square, SE10 0SQ (3770 2212, www.nowgallery.co.uk).
Old Royal Naval College King William Walk, SE10 9HU (8269 4747, tours 8269 4799, www.greenwichfoundation.org.uk). Built by Sir Christopher Wren at the turn of the 17th century. At the heart of the Maritime Greenwich World Heritage Site.

Greenwich Market

TRANSPORT

Tube DLR, Jubilee
Rail services into Cannon Street, Charing Cross, London Bridge, Victoria
Main bus routes into central London night buses N1, N21; 24-hour buses 53, 188
River Woolwich Ferry (cars and foot passengers); Greenwich Pier, North Greenwich Pier and Woolwich Arsenal Pier
Cable car Emirates Air Line

Royal Observatory & Planetarium Blackheath Avenue, SE10 8XJ (8858 4422, www.rmg.co.uk). Also by Wren. Home of Greenwich Mean Time and the Prime Meridian line.

Thames Barrier 1 Unity Way, SE18 5NJ (8305 4188, www.gov.uk/the-thames-barrier). Learn about London's flood defence system.

Other attractions

Charlton House Charlton Road, SE7 8RE (8856 3951, www.charlton-house.org). Grand Jacobean manor house. Now home to Charlton Toy Library (www.charltontoylibrary.co.uk).

Eltham Palace & Gardens Court Yard, SE9 5QE (8294 2548, www.english-heritage.org.uk). Medieval royal palace and art deco home.

Emirates Air Line Edmund Halley Way, SE10 0FR (www.emiratesairline.co.uk). Cable car to Royal Docks. Oyster cards accepted.

Greenwich & Docklands International Festival (GDIF) (8305 1818, www.festival.org). Highly acclaimed festival held each year in June.

Greenwich Festivals (8921 8390, www. greenwichfestivals.co.uk). Info on local shindigs.

Greenwich Tourist Information Centre Pepys House, 2 Cutty Sark Gardens, SE10 9LW (0870 608 2000, www.visitgreenwich.org.uk).

Maryon Wilson Animal Park Flamsteed Road, SE7 8HT (07842 073583, www. maryonwilsonanimalpark.org.uk).

Queen's House Romney Road, SE10 9NF (8858 4422, www.rmg.co.uk). Home to the National Maritime Museum's art collection – and a ghost.

Ranger's House (Wernher Collection) Chesterfield Walk, SE10 8QX (8294 2548, www.english-heritage.org.uk). Medieval and Renaissance art, housed in an 18th-century villa.

St Alfege's Greenwich Church Street, SE10 9BJ (8244 4323, www.st-alfege.org).

Sky Studios The O2, Peninsula Square, SE10 0DX (http://rewards.sky.com/home/sky-at-the-o2). Go behind the scenes, see the Iron Throne, read the news – it's all possible here.

Up at the O2 Peninsula Square, SE10 0DX (8463 2680, www.theo2.co.uk/do-more-at-the-o2/up-at-the-o2). Climb the roof for a new perspective.

Gigs, clubs & comedy

Greenwich Comedy Festival Various venues (www.greenwichcomedyfestival.co.uk).

O2 Peninsula Square, SE10 0DX (0844 856 0202, www.theo2.co.uk). Includes the O2 Arena music venue, IndigO2, an 11-screen Cineworld cinema, and various restaurants and attractions.

Studio 338 338 Boord Street, SE10 0PF (8293 6669, www.studio338.co.uk).

Up the Creek 302 Creek Road, SE10 9SW (8858 4581, www.up-the-creek.com).

Green spaces

For more details, see www.royalgreenwich.gov.uk.
Avery Hill Bexley Road, SE9. Winter garden, rose garden, sports facilities and play area.
Bostall Heath & Woods Bostall Hill, SE2. Large expanse of grass and woodland.
Charlton Park Charlton Park Road, SE7. Sports pitches and cafés. Home to Jacobean Charlton House.
Green Chain Walk Linking green spaces from Thamesmead to Crystal Palace, a 10,359-hectare network across around 300 parks and open spaces.
Greenwich Park Shooters Hill Road, SE10. Oldest of London's Royal Parks.
Hornfair Park Shooters Hill Road, SE18. Formal gardens, BMX track, sports pitches and lido.
Maryon Wilson Park Maryon Road, SE7. Landscaped park with animal centre.
Oxleas Wood Shooters Hill, SE9. Vast area of ancient woodland.
Plumstead Common Plumstead Common Road, SE18. Nature conservation area.
Royal Arsenal Gardens Warren Lane, SE18. This man-made riverside park includes a conservation meadow. Skateboard park.

Gyms & leisure centres

Better Gym 4-6 Green Place, SE10 0PE (8305 0673, www.better.org.uk). Private.
Coldharbour Leisure Centre Chapel Farm Road, SE9 3LX (8851 8692, www.better.org.uk).

Craft, Greenwich Peninsula

Crown Woods College 145 Bexley Road, SE9 2QN (www.better.org.uk). After school and during holidays only.
David Lloyd Kidbrooke Park Road, at Weigall Road, SE12 8HG (0345 129 6796, www.david lloyd.co.uk). Private.
Eltham Centre 2 Archery Road, SE9 1HA (8921 4344, www.better.org.uk).
FitSpace Gym Woolwich 1 Macbean Street, SE18 6LW (0344 409 8145, www.fitspacegyms. co.uk). Private.
Greenwich Centre 12 Lambarde Square, SE10 9GB (3795 0600, www.better.org.uk). Two pools.
PhysioActive Old Bank House, Mottingham Road, SE9 4QZ (8857 6000, www.physioactive. com). Private.
Thamesmere Leisure Centre Thamesmere Drive, SE28 8RE (8311 1119, www.better.org.uk).
Thomas Tallis School 154 Kidbrooke Park Road, SE3 9PY (www.better.org.uk). After school and during holidays only.
Warehouse, Sports & Performing Arts Centre Speranza Street, SE18 1NX (8855 8289, www.better.org.uk).
Waterfront Leisure Centre Woolwich High Street, SE18 6DL (8317 5010, www.better.org.uk). Pool.

Outdoor pursuits

Blackheath Sports Club The Rectory Field, Charlton Road, SE3 8SR (8858 1578, www. blackheathsportsclub.co.uk). Cricket, tennis and squash. Also home to Blackheath Rugby Club (http://blackheathrugby.co.uk).
Charlton Lido & Lifestyle Club Hornfair Park, Shooters Hill Road, SE18 4LX (8856 7389, www. gll.org). 50m heated outdoor pool. Gym, open-air cycle studio and tennis courts.
Goals Soccer Centre Baldon Sports Ground, Sidcup Road & Eltham Palace Road, SE9 5LU (8912 0600, www.goalsfootball.co.uk).
Royal Blackheath Golf Club Court Road, SE9 5AF (8850 1795, www.royalblackheath.com). Established in 1608.
Shooters Hill Golf Club Lowood, Eaglesfield Road, SE18 3DA (8854 6368, www.shgc.uk.com). Year-round 18-hole course.
Southmere Boating Centre Binsey Walk, SE2 9TU (8310 2452, www.southmereboating. co.uk). Kayaking, sailing and powerboating.
Sutcliffe Park Athletics Track Eltham Road, SE9 5LW (8294 0701, www.gll.org). International-standard track and events stadium.

Spectator sports

Charlton Athletic FC The Valley, Floyd Road, SE7 8BL (8333 4000, www.cafc.co.uk).

Schools

Primary

Greenwich has 65 state primary schools, 17 of which are church schools. There are also eight independent schools, including a Steiner school and a theatre academy. See www.greenwich.gov.uk, www.education.gov.uk/edubase and www.ofsted.gov.uk for more information.

Secondary

Colfe's School Horn Park Lane, SE12 8AW (8852 2283, www.colfes.com). Private.

Corelli College Corelli Road, SE3 8EP (8516 7977, www.corellicollege.org.uk).

Eltham Hill School & Post-16 Eltham Hill, SE9 5EE (8859 2843, www.elthamhill.greenwich.sch.uk). Girls only; mixed sixth form.

Harris Academy Greenwich Queenscroft Road, SE9 5EQ (8859 0133, www.harris greenwich.org.uk).

John Roan School Maze Hill, SE3 7UD (8516 7555, www.thejohnroan.greenwich.sch.uk).

Plumstead Manor School Old Mill Road, SE18 1QF (3260 3333, www.plumsteadmanor.com). Girls only; mixed sixth form.

St Paul's Academy Finchale Road, SE2 9PX (8311 3868, www.stpaulsacademy.org.uk).

St Thomas More Catholic Comprehensive School Footscray Road, SE9 2SU (8850 6700, www.stmcomprehensive.org). Roman Catholic.

St Ursula's Convent School 70 Crooms Hill, SE10 8HN (8858 4613, www.stursulas.com). Roman Catholic; girls only.

Shooters Hill Post-16 Campus Red Lion Lane, SE18 4LD (8319 9700, www.shootershill.ac.uk). Sixth form only.

Woolwich Ferry

Stationers' Crown Woods Academy 145 Bexley Road, SE9 2PT (8850 7678, www.crown woods.org.uk).
Thomas Tallis School Kidbrooke Park Road, SE3 9PX (8856 0115, www.thomastallisschool. com).
Woolwich Polytechnic School Hutchins Road, SE28 8AT (8310 7000, www.woolwich poly.greenwich.sch.uk). Boys only.

Property

Local estate agents
Alan Ives Estates www.rightmove.co.uk
Beaumont Gibbs www.beaumontgibbs.com
Cockburn www.cockburn-online.co.uk
Conran Estates www.conranestates.co.uk
Felicity J Lord www.fjlord.co.uk/greenwich
Harrison Ingram www.harrisoningram.co.uk

JLL www.jll.co.uk
John Payne www.johnpayne.com
Maritime Properties www.maritime-properties.co.uk
Oliver Bond www.rightmove.co.uk
Pick Me Properties www.pickme properties.co.uk
Redwood Estates www.redwood estates.co.uk

Local knowledge

http://853blog.com
www.allthingsgreenwich.co.uk
www.charltonchampion.co.uk
www.greenwichsociety.org.uk
www.newsshopper.co.uk
www.royalgreenwich.gov.uk
www.thegreenwichphantom.co.uk

USEFUL INFO

Borough size
4,733 hectares

Population
270,200

Ethnic mix
White 73.9%
Black or Black British 10.9%
Asian or Asian British 8.2%
Chinese or other 3.5%
Mixed 3.4%

London borough of Greenwich
The Woolwich Centre, 35 Wellington Street, SE18 6HQ (8854 8888, www.royalgreenwich.gov.uk)

Council run by
Labour

MPs
Eltham, Clive Efford (Labour); Greenwich & Woolwich, Matthew Pennycook (Labour); Erith & Thamesmead, Teresa Pearce (Labour)

Main recycling centre
Nathan Way Waste Transfer Station, Nathan Way, SE28 0AF (8312 1177)

Council tax
£853.27 to £2,559.82

Hackney

One of the capital's most exciting boroughs, Hackney suffers its share of inner-city problems (unemployment, crime and urban decay). But it's a district that's been on its way up over the past decade, with large pockets that are now well and truly gentrified. It has a cutting-edge creative scene, fantastic Vietnamese and Turkish food, animated bars and clubs, and countless devoted locals who wouldn't dream of living anywhere else.

AVERAGE PROPERTY PRICE

Detached £757,645	**Terraced** £721,494
Semi-detached £934,577	**Flat** £503,288

AVERAGE RENTAL PRICE PER WEEK

Room £124	**2 bed** £385
Studio £231	**3 bed** £500
1 bed £300	**4+ bed** £650

Dalston Roof Park

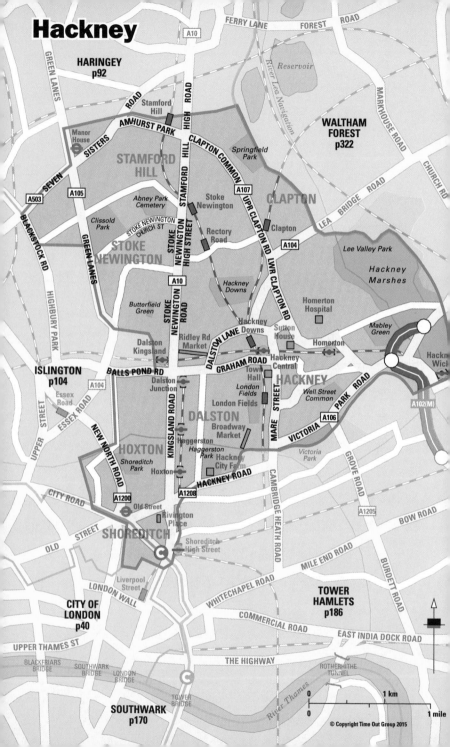

Neighbourhoods

Shoreditch and Hoxton E2

It's been years since living in this bit of east London was at the cutting edge of cool. These days, Shoreditch is virtually synonymous with gentrification, and the artists and creatives have been replaced by Silicon Roundabout start-ups, tech entrepreneurs and City boys. But the expensive warehouse conversions and 'loft apartments' still look out over swathes of council flats and betting shops, especially to the north of the 'Shoreditch Triangle' between Curtain Road, Shoreditch High Street and Old Street.

The flat-white economy drives Shoreditch by day, as laptop-tappers seeking Wi-Fi and caffeine flood the area's huge number of coffee shops (go to Allpress for the quality, Shoreditch Grind for the vibes). Shopping is another big draw: streetwear from the wildly successful Boxpark pop-up mall on Bethnal Green Road, or designer fare and pricey homewares on Shoreditch High Street and Redchurch Street (APC, House of Hackney, Labour and Wait, Hostem). There are two great record shops too: Sister Ray at the Ace Hotel, and Flashback on Bethnal Green Road.

High-quality groceries and fancy deli items are on offer at the excellent Grocery on Kingsland Road. For high-quality cuisine, there's the Boundary restaurant in Terence Conran's hotel of the same name (also home to old-school-style caff and bakery the Albion). Lyle's serves modish British food in white, airy surroundings, and Hoi Polloi, in the Ace Hotel, has British food in a wood-panelled space with a mid-century vibe. If you're looking for something less slick, head a few doors north for the row of Vietnamese canteens (Sông Quê and Mien Tay are local favourites), or traditional pie and mash shop F Cooke on Hoxton Street.

Tucked behind all this, between Redchurch Street and Columbia Road (technically in Tower Hamlets, spiritually in Shoreditch) is the Boundary Estate, an early example of a social housing scheme, built in 1900. The handsome (Grade II-listed) brick tenements radiating out from the central mound of Arnold Circus are now highly desirable to private buyers, though there are still high proportions of private renters and local authority tenants. Tucked away in the corner, hidden inside an old school, you'll

also find daytime-only Rochelle Canteen, serving exquisite seasonal lunches.

Shoreditch nightlife is changing fast, but despite some scandalous venue closures, it's still possible to have a good night out here. XOYO hosts world-class DJs and live acts every week, and the Book Club and the Queen of Hoxton are always good for offbeat fun. The Macbeth pub has sweaty R&B nights and messy live shows; the Old Blue Last is a great place to catch rising bands; Red Gallery hosts art, clubs and gigs; and the Bridge Café serves beer and coffee till late in its boudoir-like upstairs lounge. All are worth a visit before a controversial series of new glass tower blocks, the proposed Bishopsgate Goodsyard development, turns the area into an outcrop of the City. Come back, Nathan Barley – all is forgiven!

The streets around Old Street (Rivington Street, Leonard Street, Curtain Road) are still crammed with restaurants, bars and design shops, with apartments and, more often, offices and studios above.

Many of the cafés, bars and restaurants are siblings of cafés, bars and restaurants you'll find in other popular central London neighbourhoods, but a few come with character and add gravitas to the area: there's high-end contemporary cuisine at Clove Club in Shoreditch Town Hall, Iberian fine dining at Eyre Brothers and small British plates at Fifteen, founded by Jamie Oliver.

SCP was a pioneer when it opened on Curtain Road in 1985, selling furniture and homewares by design stars and upcoming talent. Its magnetic field quickly attracted like-minded aesthetes into the area and, consequently, during the annual London Design Festival in September, Shoreditch and Hoxton are hopping.

Dalston and Haggerston E8

It's hard to think of another London neighbourhood that's changed as much as Dalston in the past few years – somewhere along the line, the area became synonymous with hipsterdom and youthful creativity. It's not an unjustified reputation but, needless to say, it's not the whole story.

The change is most obvious at night: ten years ago, the wide high street of Kingsland Road, which morphs into Stoke Newington Road as it heads north, was saved from nocturnal desolation by 24-hour Turkish shops and Turkish ocakbaşı restaurants. The shops and restaurants are still there,

Clissold House Café

but now they've been joined by a buzzing mix of bars and clubs.

Metrosexual Dalston Superstore kicked off the action. Now, weekend nights see the pavement crammed with revellers waiting to get into the Alibi, the Nest and Vogue Fabrics, or standing outside bars such as Birthdays. People come from all over, especially since Dalston Junction, on the East London branch of the Overground, opened a little way down from Dalston Kingsland station, on the Overground line from Stratford to Richmond.

Despite the rate of change in this protean neighbourhood – a pound shop gone here,

an African fabric shop disappeared there – there's still plenty of old Dalston left. The area's commercial heart remains Ridley Road market, one of the best places in London to buy African and Caribbean (and European) ingredients.

A vibrant cultural life is centred around two poles: the Dalston Culture House art space, home to the Vortex jazz bar, on the open space of Gillett Square; and the converted paint and print factory complex on Ashwin Street – near to the flash new Dalston Square apartment complex – that now houses the Arcola Theatre, left-field music venue Café Oto and, in the summer

months, the trendy Dalston Roof Park. Just off Gillett Square is the Servant Jazz Quarters, a classic cocktail bar with live jazz in the basement. Then there's Dalston's stalwart cultural survivor: the long-established Rio cinema, a gorgeous art deco movie-house – its blue sign a beacon from afar – with mainstream and independent screenings. Off the main drag is live music venue the Shacklewell Arms, a Caribbean boozer in a former life, the colourful dancefloor a nod to its previous incarnation.

Turkish ocakbaşı restaurants are still holding their own, particularly on Stoke Newington Road. Alongside Mangal II and the original Mangal in Arcola Street, standouts include 19 Numara Bos Cirrik and Tava. These sit-down restaurants have been joined by a string of casual Turkish café-bars, among them the Evin Café Bar and Red Art Café. On Kingsland Road, there's non-Turkish bistro-style eating at urban-rustic A Little of What You Fancy, and – possibly Dalston's most serious restaurant – chef Stevie Parle's venture, modern Italian Rotorino.

Among the neighbourhood pubs, the Railway Tavern, near Dalston Kingsland station on a road heading towards Mildmay, has a convivial atmosphere and craft beers, while the Haggerston on Kingsland Road is a popular late-night haunt. There are myriad new-style cafés too but, on a summer day, where better to enjoy a beverage than the outdoor café in the peaceful retreat that is the Dalston Eastern Curve urban garden?

The southern stretch of Stoke Newington Road is now home to several interesting independent shops, such as vintage store Pelicans & Parrots, which has one branch for clothes and another for homewares (with a rum bar hidden below). There's also a huge branch of vintage emporium Beyond Retro and Kristina Records vinyl shop.

Away from the hustle of the high street, Dalston is surprisingly quiet and residential, particularly south of Balls Pond Road, where roads are lined with gracious early Victorian homes. To the south-west is De Beauvoir, a leafy area with grand Dutch-gabled houses. North of Balls Pond Road, heading towards Stoke Newington, houses are solid Victorian and Edwardian.

The opening of Haggerston station in 2010 (on the East London branch of the London Overground) pumped new life into this area immediately south of Dalston. Housing here is a combination of lovely old streets and squares such as Albion Square (one of this part of the world's most desirable addresses), smart new-build flats and older council blocks.

Downham Road is home to loud and lively US-style barbecue and craft beer joint Duke's Brew & Cue, and there's action under the railway arches with the board-game café Draughts. Otherwise, the canalside – popular for summer strolls – is the focus of both modern housing development and eating and drinking. Ribbons of high-spec new-builds line Regent's Canal and its offshoot Kingsland Basin. At the far end of Kingsland Basin (also accessible from Hertford Road) is laid-back and airy Japanese café Toconoco, with a children's play area and healthy noodle and rice-ball dishes. Back on the canal's main drag, the Proud Archivist serves modern British food all day in an airy space with a gallery, and Arepa & Co introduces Londoners to Venezuelan dishes.

Stoke Newington N16

Heading north from Dalston, the vibe changes. The high street here (first called Stoke Newington Road, then Stoke Newington High Street) is more workaday, and trendy incursions are fewer, though increasing.

Stoke Newington Church Street, considered the area's heart by many, is a striking contrast: a bijou strip of boutiques, second-hand bookshops, cafés, restaurants, estate agents and, despite fierce local protest, a branch of Nando's.

Stoke Newington was once a country village, and traces remain in the much-loved green space of Clissold Park. The Victorian age turned Stoke Newington into a working-class suburb. The 1970s and '80s saw it colonised by 'alternative' Londoners, including members of the Angry Brigade. The alternative reputation is pretty dated now, and Church Street teeters on the edge of established-posh with branches of Jojo Maman Bébé and Wholefoods Market, and an upmarket butcher, Meat N16. The popularity of the area with families is reflected in shops such as Olive Loves Alfie and Route 73 Kids (named for Stokie's favourite bus route). Ooh Lou Lou Cakery is a cute cake shop. However, the street is saved from chichi overkill by a strong streak of vintage, with shops including Ribbons & Taylor and Collectif.

Church Street is crammed with cafés – filled with parents and children at weekends – including the Green Room Café & Florist; the Spence bakery does great artisan bread and has a small café too. The street does less well with proper restaurants, although it is home to the original branch of South Indian mini-chain Rasa and sister restaurant Rasa Travancore (which also serves meat and fish dishes), and pizzeria and trattoria Il Bacio.

Back on the High Street, evergreen landmarks include the Ottoman-style Aziziye Mosque (known locally as the Blue Mosque), with its own Turkish general store and restaurant; the immense, green-tiled, Victorian Rochester Castle pub, a pre-gentrification stalwart that has the claim to fame of being the first Wetherspoons; and the long-established Stoke Newington Bookshop. These veterans are joined by numerous Turkish barbers and general stores, and utilitarian homewares shops.

Eating on the High Street used to be all about the Turkish restaurants, and these still abound (Testi is one of the best). Another well-established eaterie of note is smart Thai restaurant YumYum, in a large Georgian house set back from the road, just north of the junction with Church Street. However, the number of trendy, freelance-friendly cafés and bars, typically with exposed-brick walls and a rough-and-ready look, is increasing.

These include coffee spot the Lazy Social; Etcetera, which serves breakfasts, drinks and tapas; and the Haberdashery, for brunch, lunch and modern British dinners. Other newcomers are Original Sin, little sister of Shoreditch's Happiness Forgets and a purveyor of equally superb cocktails, and tapas restaurant Black Pig in White Pearls.

There's a variety of fine pubs in the area: the best are on Church Street and around, variously appealing to Guinness drinkers (Auld Shillelagh), the child-laden (Prince) and the child-avoiding (Rose & Crown). The huge White Hart on the High Street has a large beer garden that's gorgeously green in summer. And tucked away in the backstreets, the Shakespeare has bare floors, good beers and loyal regulars.

Stoke Newington's disparate residents are united by their love of Clissold Park, a vast tree-lined expanse with tennis courts, an enclosure for deer, duck ponds and a kids' paddling pool. An upgrade brought a new playground, two new ponds, a skatepark, improved landscaping and a smart new café in the park's 18th-century manor, Clissold House. Another popular spot for a promenade is the atmospheric and overgrown Abney

Swim outdoors in heated London Fields Lido.

Park Cemetery, final resting place of many Victorians, including the founder of the Salvation Army.

Social housing aside, much of Stoke Newington's housing stock is made up of Victorian and Edwardian terraces. The streets around Church Street, in particular, are known for their sweet, small (and now pricey) Victorian homes. The days of finding cheap property in any part of Stoke Newington are long gone, despite the fact that transport links aren't the greatest. Reaching the City or the West End involves a 40-minute bus journey or a 15-minute train ride from Stoke Newington or Rectory Road station. Alternatively, buses pass along the High Street every few minutes, day and night – and can drop you off at Dalston Kingsland or Dalston Junction stations, for links to the West End or the City – and you can cycle to Islington in ten minutes and the City in 20. The nearest tube stations are Finsbury Park and Manor House on the border with Haringey.

Stamford Hill N16

Few districts are as strongly associated with one community as Stamford Hill. The streets north of Stoke Newington (from around the junction with Manor Road to the north of Amhurst Park) are home to most of London's 30,000 Hasidic Jews. The Hasidim follow a strict form of Judaism, adhering to specific codes of dress and behaviour. On Saturdays, large, distinctively dressed families walking to synagogue are a familiar sight. This is a culturally fascinating area, though there's little mixing between the Hasidic community and the rest of the local population.

Most of the shops and services are clustered around the intersection of Stamford Hill and Clapton Common. Kosher food shops and bakeries join a typical London high-street melange of launderettes, dodgy-looking outlets selling mobile phone accessories and fast-food joints.

On Stamford Hill, the area's main traffic-clogged thoroughfare, the road is hemmed in by ugly council blocks, but the surrounding terraces are bright and inviting, with numerous Hasidic schools, synagogues and community centres. Some of the best housing is around Manor Road and Lordship Park; the adjacent reservoir has the popular Castle Climbing Centre and the West Reservoir Water Sports Centre. But the little-known jewel in Stamford Hill's crown is Springfield Park, to the east of Clapton Common. The park slopes down to the River Lea with glorious views from the top over the river to the Walthamstow Marshes. There are wooded areas, a park café, a riverside path and a bridge over to the wilds of the Marshes.

Seven Sisters tube station is a short hop north of the area, and Stamford Hill rail station is just west of the main junction, on Amhurst Park.

Hackney E8/E9

The original working-class London suburb, Hackney was founded in Roman times near a ford across the River Lea. Once a rural idyll, it grew into a busy industrial centre in the Victorian era before sliding into decline after World War II. Over the next few decades, Hackney became the heartland of social disintegration in the capital; stark housing estates mushroomed, unemployment soared and Hackney Council picked up the European record for most demolitions by a local authority.

These days, large pockets of gentrification are drawing wealthy professionals to the area,

Regent's Canal

TRANSPORT

Tube Northern, Overground, Piccadilly
Rail services into Liverpool Street
Main bus routes into central London 8, 21, 26, 29, 30, 35, 38, 48, 55, 56, 73, 76, 106, 141, 153, 205, 253, 259, 388, 394, 476; night buses N8, N19, N26, N29, N35, N38, N41, N55, N73, N76, N253, N279; 24-hour buses 43, 149, 214, 242, 243, 271, 341

but Hackney still has many pockets of poverty and high crime. Hackney's Mare Street was one of the hotspots for the 2011 riots. But if you were hoping to beat the house-price inflation that has blighted Stoke Newington, Victoria Park and De Beauvoir, you've already missed the boat.

The main artery of Hackney is Mare Street, which runs south past the stately art deco Hackney Town Hall to Bethnal Green and Whitechapel. The area is known locally as Hackney Central, after the nearby train station, and has recently become a nightlife spot with the opening of gig space/restaurant Oslo, next to the station. The modernist Technology & Learning Centre (housing a library and the Hackney Museum) and the impressively restored Hackney Empire theatre (one of the best community theatres in London) are still going, and the dynamic Hackney Picturehouse cinema, in the old Ocean music venue, has brought a new vitality to this stretch of Mare Street.

Artistic endeavour in Hackney is focused on London Fields, a popular green space just west of Mare Street that is rammed with hipsters in the summer (as are Dalston and, to the east, Hackney Wick). Driven from Old Street by soaring rents, painters and sculptors colonised the warehouses and factories around London Fields, creating their own mini-Hoxton, complete with cutting-edge art spaces such as the Hothouse 'creative cluster' on Richmond Road and Netil House on Westgate Street. Another big draw of the area is the London Fields Lido, which reopened in 2006 after 20 years of neglect, and which has become a key community asset. A huge number of new-wave independent shops and cafés can be found on über-trendy Broadway Market, Wilton Way (just north of London Fields) and in the railway arches next to London Fields rail station, which now harbour one of the city's best bakeries – E5 Bakehouse – as well as the artisan London Fields Brewery. There's a very different kind of shopping in an incongruous post-industrial setting around Chatham Place, just off Morning Lane: a small hub of designer outlet stores; Burberry, Aquascutum and Pringle of Scotland each have a store here.

Out of hours, freelancers hang out in the Pub on the Park on the edge of London Fields or in the pubs and cafés on Broadway Market. The Saturday market is one of the liveliest in London, attracting many of the gourmet food stalls that set up at Spitalfields. Wealthier

market regulars might live in the grand Victorian townhouses to the west of London Fields, or the warehouse apartments that line the Regent's Canal (which provides a handy back route to Islington and Victoria Park).

In the far south-east of Hackney, Well Street Common nudges up against Victoria Park, just over the borough border in Tower Hamlets. Houses here are grand and expensive, and residents take full advantage of the park, pubs, cafés and restaurants along villagey, family-friendly Lauriston Road.

Solid local restaurants in the area include the family-friendly Frizzante at Hackney City Farm, a branch of Franco Manca pizza parlour on Broadway Market, old-fashioned pie and mash shop F Cooke (with branches on Hoxton Street and Broadway Market), East European eaterie Little Georgia and industrial-chic Italian restaurant Lardo on Richmond Road. Good Turkish choices in Hackney Central include Anatolia Ocakbaşı and Tad Bistro, while Tre Viet and Green Papaya are Vietnamese favourites. Reliable watering holes, meanwhile, include the Dove, a Belgian beer specialist, and the Cat & Mutton gastropub on Broadway Market; the Prince George on Parkholme Road, with Victorian decor, real ales and loyal regulars; and the Spurstowe Arms on Greenwood Road.

Broadway Market is an essential port of call for foodies. The street's popular Saturday market – where Hackneyites stock up on fancy olive oil and freshly made gourmet lunches – joins the excellent independent shops on the street, including long-running French deli L'Eau à la Bouche and the Pavilion bakery, opened by the Victoria Park café in 2015. There are some great boutiques on the street too – don't miss shoe and accessory outlet Black Truffle, and Hub shop, for stylish mens- and womenswear.

Hackney Central is on the London Overground line, and the borough has decent bus and train services.

Hackney Wick and Homerton E9

It is only very recently that Hackney Wick and Homerton, on the east side of the borough, recovered from the collapse of their Victorian industries. Both areas offer a mix of council estates, new-build flats and factory warehouses, the latter now inhabited by an international breed of creatives (including big names such as the Chapman Brothers, Gavin Turk and Bridget Riley), who can often be found in the canalside Crate Bar & Pizzeria.

Homerton also has Victorian and Edwardian terraces, and the focal point of Homerton Hospital, while Hackney Wick feels quite isolated and very much in its own post-industrial world, caught between the A12 and the River Lea (though the savvy know the Overground will get them in and out in a trice).

There's culture in Hackney Wick in the form of arts centre the Stour Space, which hosts exhibitions and has performance and studio spaces, and the Yard Theatre. Annual arts festival Hackney Wicked (www.hackneywickedfestival.co.uk) is emblematic of the area's brave new era. For many, however, it's all about the parties, with weekend warehouse raves going on until the small hours. There's a chance for recovery at Counter Café on Roach Road (perfect for breakfast, especially the house-roast coffee), while its neighbour Muff Customs does a nice line in breakfast burritos and custom motorbikes. For a reminder of the area's history, H Forman & Son on Stour Road is London's oldest salmon smoker and they have a massive pink – and, yes, salmon-shaped – factory. Near the station, the Hackney Pearl has mismatched furniture, a vibrant atmosphere and quality food.

With Stratford just across the Lea, residents have seen big changes from the Olympic regeneration programme – and while some of this has been positive (new housing developments, cleaned-up streets, a new Olympic swimming pool), the inevitable increase in prices isn't good news for all residents.

Clapton E5

Squeezed between Hackney Central and Walthamstow Marshes, Clapton has long been seen as the less attractive younger sibling to Hackney proper; but this image has been rapidly changing over the past few years, with gentrification much in evidence, especially at the southern end of Lower Clapton Road. Indeed, Clapton's 'Murder Mile' epithet – earned from various shootings at notorious nightclubs that once graced the neighourhood – does now appear to be a distant memory. The Clapton of today is more about sourdough pizza joints (Sodo, Yard Sale), trendy cafés (119 Lower Clapton) and craft beer shops (Clapton Craft) than guns and crime.

Well-established bars and pubs include music bar Biddle Bros, and the Elderfield and the Crooked Billet, two supremely likeable boozers – the latter with a large beer garden.

Hackney Downs corner boozer the Pembury Tavern is equally egalitarian, and known for its real ales, pizzas and bar billiards table, while the Windsor Castle and Clapton Hart

Take advantage of all the brilliant sports facilities just the other side of the River Lea.

are both reconstituted gastropubs that attract a pleasingly mixed crowd. For upmarket cuisine, head to Scandinavian-inspired charcuterie bar Verden, at the top of Clarence Road, or to Shane's on Chatsworth. Maeve's Kitchen (stews) and Dom's Place (Turkish wraps) provide cheaper, more homely alternatives.

While prices have risen dramatically here, as in most of the surrounding area, the borough's current appeal for many is its relaxed mix of old and new. Though most of the old pubs, like the ones above, have been regenerated (for better or for worse – though mainly for better), many of the jerk-chicken and small local businesses remain, and there's a tangible desire to preserve the current equilibrium. The area's community-focused spirit is exemplified by the popular Palm 2 grocery store next to prettified Clapton Pond (the area's 'village green'); run by Turkish owner Abdul Saluk – something of a local celebrity – the cornershop upped its game with the arrival of Tesco next door, and now offers a popular coffee bar and a great range of locally made food, such as gözleme pancakes and E5 Bakehouse bread.

Chatsworth Road Market – selling gourmet food, vintage bric-a-brac and crafts on Sundays – was reinstated in 2010, following its demise in the 1980s, and is now doing for Clapton what the reintroduction of Broadway Market did for London Fields. Rents are rising as a result, with worries for the many small shops and cafés based here (such as the excellent Triangle, Botany, Hop toy shop and L'Epicerie 56).

The green open spaces of Springfield Park (its southern reaches are accessible from Upper Clapton), Hackney Downs, Hackney Marshes and Walthamstow Marshes (across the River Lea in the borough of Waltham Forest) are another huge appeal of the area – particularly for young families – while the canal towpath is a popular stretch for joggers, cyclists and dog-walkers. There are also narrowboat berths for hire here. The wide spaces of Hackney Marshes are home to a famous series of football pitches. Hackney Downs has tennis and basketball courts, and further afield – across the River Lea – are the Lee Valley Ice Centre and Lee Valley Riding Centre.

The massive Lea Bridge roundabout splits Clapton in two. Lower Clapton has the best of the shops and amenities, while Upper Clapton has the area's train station (on the line to Liverpool Street). Frequent day and night buses connect Clapton with the City and surrounding districts. Housing stock is dominated by council estates, Victorian terraces and new-builds. There are a few historic gems – most notably, the gorgeous Georgian terraces around Sutton House (on the edge of Homerton) and in leafy Clapton Square.

Eating

119 Lower Clapton 119 Lower Clapton Road, E5 0NP (8533 9763).
A Little of What You Fancy 464 Kingsland Road, E8 4AE (7275 0060, www.alittleofwhat youfancy.info).
Albion 2-4 Boundary Street, E2 7DD (7729 1051, http://albioncaff.co.uk).
Allpress 58 Redchurch Street, E2 7DP (7749 1780, www.allpressespresso.com).
Anatolia Ocakbaşı 253 Mare Street, E8 3NS (8986 2223, www.anatolya.co.uk).
Arepa & Co 58A De Beauvoir Crescent, N1 5SB (7923 3507, www.arepaandco.com).
Black Pig in White Pearls 61 Stoke Newington High Street, N16 8EL (7249 1772, www.blackpig withwhitepearls.co.uk).
Boundary Restaurant 2-4 Boundary Street, E2 7DD (7729 1051, www.theboundary.co.uk).
Cat & Mutton 76 Broadway Market, E8 4QJ (7249 6555, www.catandmutton.com).
Clissold House Café Clissold Park, Stoke Newington Church Street, N16 9HJ (7221 4804, www.clissoldpark.com).
Counter Café 7 Roach Road, E3 2PA (07834 275920, www.counterproductive.co.uk).
Crate Bar & Pizzeria The White Building, Unit 7, Queen's Yard, E9 5EN (8533 3331, www.cratebrewery.com).
Dalston Eastern Curve Garden Café 13 Dalston Lane, E8 3DF (www.dalstongarden.org).
Dom's Place 199 Lower Clapton Road, E5 8EG (8985 5454, www.doms-place.com).
Etcetera 86 Stoke Newington High Street, N16 7PA (7684 4763, www.facebook.com/baretcetera).

Evin Café 115 Kingsland High Street, E8 2PB (7254 5634, www.evincafe.co.uk).
F Cooke 9 Broadway Market, E8 4PH (7254 6458); 150 Hoxton Street, N1 6SH (7729 7718).
Franco Manca 52 Broadway Market, E8 4QJ (7254 7249, www.francomanca.co.uk).
Frizzante Hackney City Farm, 1A Goldsmith's Row, E2 8QA (7739 2266, www.frizzanteltd.co.uk).
Green Papaya 191 Mare Street, E8 3QT; 97 Kingsland Road, E2 8AG (www.green-papaya.com).
Green Room Café 113 Stoke Newington Church Street, N16 0UD (7923 1877, www.flowersn16.co.uk).
Haberdashery 170 Stoke Newington High Street, N16 7JL (3643 7123, www.the-haberdashery.com).
Hackney Pearl 11 Prince Edward Road, E9 5LX (8510 3605, www.thehackneypearl.com).
Lardo 197-201 Richmond Road, E8 3NJ (8985 2683, www.lardo.co.uk).
Lazy Social 101 Stoke Newington High Street, N16 0PH (7254 7684).
Little Georgia 87 Goldsmith's Row, E2 8QR (7739 8154, www.littlegeorgia.co.uk).
Maeve's Kitchen 181 Lower Clapton Road, E5 8EQ (8533 1057, www.maeveskitchen.com).
Mangal 10 Arcola Street, E8 2DJ (7275 8981, www.mangal1.com).
Mangal II 4 Stoke Newington Road, N16 8BH (7254 7888, www.mangal2.com).
Mien Tay 122 Kingsland Road, E2 8DP (7729 3074, www.mientay.co.uk).
19 Numara Bos Cirrik I 34 Stoke Newington Road, N16 7XJ (7249 0400, www.cirrik1.co.uk).
Proud Archivist 2-10 Hertford Road, N1 5SH (3598 2626, www.theproudarchivist.co.uk).
Rasa 55 Stoke Newington Church Street, N16 0AR (7249 0344, www.rasarestaurants.com).
Rasa Travancore 56 Stoke Newington Church Street, N16 0NB (7249 1340, www.rasarestaurants.com).
Red Art Café 113 Kingsland High Street, E8 2PB (7254 3256).
Rochelle Canteen Rochelle School, Arnold Circus, E2 7ES (7729 5677, www.arnoldand henderson.com).
Rotorino 434 Kingsland Road, E8 4AA (7249 9081, www.rotorino.com).
Shane's on Chatsworth 62 Chatsworth Road, E5 0LS (8985 3755, www.shaneson chatsworth.com).
Shoreditch Grind 213 Old Street, EC1V 9NR (7490 7490, www.shoreditchgrind.com).
Sodo 126 Upper Clapton Road, E5 9JY (8806 5626, www.sodopizza.co.uk).
Sông Quê Café 134 Kingsland Road, E2 8DY (7613 3222, www.songque.co.uk).

Spence Bakery 161 Stoke Newington Church Street, N16 0UH (7249 4927, www.thespence.co.uk).

Tad 261 Mare Street, E8 3NS (8986 2612, www.tadrestaurant.co.uk).

Tava 17 Stoke Newington Road, N16 8BH (7249 3666, www.tavarestaurant.co.uk).

Testi 38 Stoke Newington High Street, N16 7PL (7249 7151, www.testirestaurant.co.uk).

Toconoco Unit A, 28 Hertford Road, N1 5QT (7249 8394, www.toconoco.com).

Tre Viet 245-249 Mare Street, E8 3NS (8533 7390, www.treviet.co.uk).

Verden 181 Clarence Road, E5 8EE (8986 4723, www.verdene5.com).

Yard Sale Pizza 105 Lower Clapton Road, E5 0NP (3602 9090, www.yardsalepizza.com).

YumYum 187 Stoke Newington High Street, N16 0LH (7254 6751, www.yumyum.co.uk).

Drinking

Auld Shillelagh 105 Stoke Newington Church Street, N16 0UD (7249 5951, www.theauld shillelagh.co.uk).

Biddle Bros 88 Lower Clapton Road, E5 0QR (www.facebook.com/biddlebros).

Birthdays 33-35 Stoke Newington Road, N16 8BJ (7923 1680, www.birthdaysdalston.com).

Bridge 15 Kingsland Road, E2 8AE (07833 393272, www.facebook.com/thebridge15).

Cat & Mutton 76 Broadway Market, E8 4QJ (7249 6555, www.catandmutton.com).

Clapton Hart 231 Lower Clapton Road, E5 8EG (8985 8124, www.claptonhart.com).

Crooked Billet 84 Upper Clapton Road, E5 9JP (3058 1166, www.e5crookedbillet.co.uk).

Dalston Superstore 117 Kingsland High Street, E8 2PB (7254 2273, www.dalston superstore.com).

Dove 24-28 Broadway Market, E8 4QJ (7275 7617, www.dovepubs.com).

Draughts 337 Acton Mews, E8 4EA (www.draughtslondon.com).

Duke's Brew & Cue 33 Downham Road, N1 5AA (3006 0795, www.dukesbrewandque.com).

Elderfield 57 Elderfield Road, E5 0LF (8986 1591, www.facebook.com/theelderfield).

Haggerston 438 Kingsland Road, E8 4AA (7923 3206, www.thehaggerstonpub.com).

Prince George 40 Parkholme Road, E8 3AG (7254 6060, www.remarkablerestaurants.co.uk).

Pub on the Park 19 Martello Street, E8 3PE (7923 3398, www.pubonthepark.com).

Railway Tavern 2 St Jude Street, N16 8JT.

Rochester Castle 145 Stoke Newington High Street, N16 0NY (7249 6016, www.jdwetherspoon. co.uk).

Rose & Crown 199 Stoke Newington Church Street, N16 9ES (7923 3337, www.roseand crownn16.co.uk).

Servant Jazz Quarters 10A Bradbury Street, N16 8JN (7684 8411, www.servantjazzquarters.com).

Shakespeare 57 Allen Road, N16 8RY (7254 4190, www.remarkablerestaurants.com).

Spurstowe Arms 68 Greenwood Road, E8 1AB (7923 3115, www.thespurstowearms.com).

White Hart 69 Stoke Newington High Street, N16 8EL (7254 6626, www.whitehartstoke newington.com).

Windsor Castle 135 Lower Clapton Road, E5 8EQ (8985 6096, www.thewindsorcastleclapton.com).

Shopping

APC 5 Redchurch Street, E2 7DJ (7729 7727, www.apc.fr).

Aquascutum 8 Chatham Place, E9 6LT (3096 1863, www.aquascutum.co.uk).

Aziziye Mosque General Store 117 Stoke Newington Road, N16 8BU (7254 0046).

Beyond Retro 92-100 Stoke Newington Road, N16 7XB (7923 2277, www.beyondretro.com).

Black Truffle 4 Broadway Market, E8 4QJ (7923 9450, www.blacktruffleshoes.com).

Botany 5 Chatsworth Road, E5 0LH (07583 934366, www.botanyshop.co.uk).

Boxpark 2 Bethnal Green Road, E1 6GY (7033 2899, www.boxpark.co.uk).

Broadway Market Broadway Market, E8 (www.broadwaymarket.co.uk).

Burberry 29-31 Chatham Place, E9 6LP (8328 4287, http://uk.burberry.com).

Chatsworth Market Chatsworth Road, E5 (www.chatsworthroade5.co.uk).

Clapton Craft 97 Lower Clapton Road, E5 0NP (3643 2669, www.claptoncraft.co.uk).

Collectif 31 Stoke Newington Church Street, N16 0NX (7241 5023, www.collectif.co.uk).

E5 Bakehouse Arch 395, Mentmore Terrace, E8 3PH (8525 2890, www.e5bakehouse.com).

L'Eau à La Bouche 35-37 Broadway Market, E8 4PH (7923 0600, www.labouche.co.uk).

L'Épicerie 56 56 Chatsworth Road, E5 0LS (7503 8172, www.lepicerie56.com).

Flashback Records 131 Bethnal Green Road, E2 7DG (3780 1900, www.flashback.co.uk).

Grocery 54-56 Kingsland Road, E2 8DP (7729 6855, www.thegroceryshop.co.uk).

H Forman & Son Stour Road, Fish Island, E3 2NT (8525 2399, www.formans.co.uk).

Hop 68 Chatsworth Road, E5 0LS (8525 1347, www.hoptoyshop.co.uk).

Hostem 41-43 Redchurch Street, E2 7DJ (7739 9733, www.hostem.co.uk).

Crate Brewery, Hackney Wick

House of Hackney 131-132 Shoreditch High Street, E1 6JE (7739 3901, www.house ofhackney.com).

Hub 2A Ada Street, E8 4QU (7923 9354, www. hubshop.co.uk).

JoJo Maman Bébé 58 Stoke Newington Church Street, N16 0NB (7254 2292, www.jojomaman bebe.co.uk).

Kristina Records 44 Stoke Newington Road, N16 7XJ (7254 2130, www.kristinarecords.com).

Labour and Wait 85 Redchurch Street, E2 7DJ (7729 6253, www.labourandwait.co.uk).

London Fields Cycles 281 Mare Street, E8 1PJ (8525 0077, www.londonfieldscycles.co.uk).

Meat N16 104 Stoke Newington Church Street, N16 0LA (7254 0724, www.meatlondon.co.uk).

North One Garden Centre 25A Englefield Road, N1 4EU (7923 3553, www.n1gc.co.uk).

Olive Loves Alfie 84 Stoke Newington Church Street, N16 0AP (7241 4212, www.oliveloves alfie.co.uk).

Ooh Lou Lou Cakery 121 Stoke Newington Church Street, N16 0TD (07968 699110, www. oohloulou.com).

Palm 2 152-156 Lower Clapton Road, E5 0QJ (07434 958073, www.palm2.co.uk).

Pavilion Bakery 18 Broadway Market, E8 4QJ (www.pavilion-bakery.com).

Pelicans & Parrots 40 Stoke Newington Road, N16 7XJ (7249 9177, www.pelicansandparrots.com).

Pringle of Scotland 90 Morning Lane, E9 6NA (8985 9735, www.pringlescotland.com).

Ribbons & Taylor 157 Stoke Newington Church Street, N16 0UH (7254 4735).

Ridley Road Market Ridley Road, E8 2LH (www.ridleyroad.co.uk).

Route 73 Kids 92 Stoke Newington Church Street, N16 0AP (7923 7873, www.route73 kids.co.uk).

Sister Ray at Ace Hotel 100 Shoreditch High Street, E1 6JQ (7729 3142, www.sisterray.co.uk).

Stoke Newington Bookshop 159 Stoke Newington High Street, N16 0NY (7249 2808, www.stokenewingtonbookshop.co.uk).

Stoke Newington Farmers' Market St Paul's Church, Stoke Newington High Street, N16 7UY (7502 7588, www.growingcommunities.org).

Triangle 92A Chatsworth Road, E5 0LS (www. trianglestore.co.uk).

Whole Foods Market 32-40 Stoke Newington Church Street, N16 0LU (7254 2332, www. wholefoodsmarket.com).

Things to do

Cinemas & theatres

Arcola Theatre 24 Ashwin Street, E8 3DL (7503 1646, www.arcolatheatre.com). Enterprising fringe theatre.

Hackney Empire 291 Mare Street, E8 1EJ (8985 2424, www.hackneyempire.co.uk). Restored Edwardian music hall; shows run from stand-up comedy to Shakespeare.

Hackney Picturehouse 270 Mare Street, E8 1HE (0871 902 5734, www.picturehouses. co.uk).

Rio Cinema 107 Kingsland High Street, E8 2PB (7241 9410, www.riocinema.org.uk).

Yard Theatre Unit 2A, Queen's Yard, E9 5EN (07548 156266, www.theyardtheatre.co.uk).

Galleries & museums

Geffrye Museum 136 Kingsland Road, E2 8EA (7739 9893, www.geffrye-museum.org.uk). Domestic interiors from the 1600s to the present, housed in Georgian almshouses. There are regular changing exhibitions too – the annual Christmas one is a must-see.

Hackney Museum 1 Reading Lane, E8 1GQ (8356 3500, www.hackney.gov.uk).

Red Gallery 1-3 Rivington Street, EC2A 3DT (7613 3620, www.redgallerylondon.com).

Rivington Place Rivington Place, EC2A 3BA (7749 1240, www.rivingtonplace.org). Public gallery and library dedicated to visual arts and photography.

Stour Space 7 Roach Road, E3 2PA (8985 7827, www.stourspace.co.uk). Arts centre with exhibitions and performance spaces.

Sutton House 2-4 Homerton High Street, E9 6JQ (8986 2264, www.nationaltrust.org.uk). This atmospheric red-brick Tudor mansion is the oldest home in east London.

Victoria Miro Gallery 16 Wharf Road, N1 7RW (7336 8109, www.victoria-miro.com).

Gigs, clubs & comedy

Alibi 91 Kingsland High Street, E8 2PB (7249 2733, www.thealibilondon.co.uk).

Book Club 100-106 Leonard Street, EC2A 4XS (7684 8618, www.wearetbc.com).

Café Oto 18-22 Ashwin Street, E8 3DL (7923 1231, www.cafeoto.co.uk).

Dalston Roof Park The Print House, 18-22 Ashwin Street, E8 3DL (7275 0825, www. facebook.com/dalstonroofpark). Summer only opening times.

Dalston Superstore 117 Kingsland High Street, E8 2PB (7254 2273, www.dalstonsuperstore.com).

Macbeth 70 Hoxton Street, N1 6LP (7749 0600, www.themacbeth.co.uk).

Nest 36 Stoke Newington Road, N16 7XJ (7275 9336, www.ilovethenest.com).

Old Blue Last 38 Great Eastern Street, EC2A 3ES (7739 7033, www.theoldbluelast.com).

Oslo 1A Amhurst Road, E8 1LL (3553 4831, www. oslohackney.com).

Queen of Hoxton 1-5 Curtain Road, EC2A 3JX (7422 0958, www.queenofhoxton.com).

Shacklewell Arms 71 Shacklewell Lane, E8 2EB (7249 0810, www.shacklewellarms.com).

Vogue Fabrics 66 Stoke Newington Road, N16 7XB (7682 0408, www.voguefabrics dalston.com).

Vortex Jazz Club 11 Gillett Square, N16 8AZ (7254 4097, www.vortexjazz.co.uk).

XOYO 32-37 Cowper Street, EC2A 4AP (www.xoyo.co.uk).

Hackney City Farm; London Fields Lido; London Fields

HIGHS & LOWS

Bike culture

Bars and clubs

Independent shops

Turkish ocakbaşı restaurants

Overground rail

▲ ⋯⋯⋯⋯⋯⋯⋯⋯ ▼

Overdevelopment of Shoreditch

Still lots of inner-city problems

Canal path packed at weekends

Green spaces

See www.hackney.gov.uk.

Abney Park Cemetery Stoke Newington High Street, N16 0LH.

Clissold Park Stoke Newington Church Street & Green Lanes, N16 9HJ. Aviary, butterfly dome, animals, pond dipping, fountains, paddling pool and playgrounds, and a café in a Grade II*-listed mansion, Clissold House.

De Beauvoir Square N1 4LG. Noted rose gardens.

Hackney City Farm 1A Goldsmith's Row, E2 8QA (7729 6381, http://hackneycityfarm.co.uk).

Hackney Downs Downs Park Road, E5 8NP. Basketball, floodlit sports pitches, athletics track.

Hackney Marshes Homerton Road, E9 5PF.

London Fields E8 3EU.

Springfield Park E5 9EF.

Gyms & leisure centres

Britannia Leisure Centre 40 Hyde Road, N1 5JU (7729 4485, www.better.org.uk). Swimming pool.

Castle Climbing Centre Green Lanes, N4 2HA (8211 7000, www.castle-climbing.co.uk).

Clissold Leisure Centre 63 Clissold Road, N16 9EX (7254 5574, www.better.org.uk). Swimming pool.

King's Hall Leisure Centre 39 Lower Clapton Road, E5 0NU (8985 2158, www.better.org.uk). Swimming pool.

Queensbridge Sports & Community Centre 30 Holly Street, E8 3XW (7923 7773, www.better.org.uk).

Space 31 Falkirk Street, N1 6HF (7613 9525, www.hackneysportscentre.com). Private.

Outdoor pursuits

Hackney Marshes Homerton Road, E9 5PF (8986 7955, www.better.org.uk). A record-breaking 82 football, rugby and cricket pitches.

Lea Rowing Club The Boathouse, Spring Hill, E5 9BL (8806 8282, www.learc.org.uk).

London Fields Lido London Fields West Side, E8 3EU (7254 9038, www.better.org.uk). Dating from 1936, this art deco lido reopened in autumn 2006 after lying derelict for 20 years.

West Reservoir Water Sports Centre Green Lanes, N4 2HA (8442 8116, www.better.org.uk).

Schools

Primary

There are 53 state primary schools in Hackney, 11 of which are church schools and two of which are Jewish schools. There are also 21 independent primaries, including eight Jewish schools and two Muslim schools. See www.learningtrust.co.uk, www.education.gov.uk/edubase and www.ofsted.gov.uk for more information.

Secondary

Bridge Academy Laburnum Street, E2 8BA (7749 5240, www.bridgeacademy.hackney.sch.uk).

BSix Brooke House Sixth Form College Kenninghall Road, E5 8BP (8525 7150, www.bsix.ac.uk).

Cardinal Pole Catholic School 205 Morning Lane, E9 5RB (8985 5150, www.cardinalpole.co.uk). Roman Catholic.

Clapton Girls' Academy Laura Place, Lower Clapton Road, E5 0RB (8985 6641, www.clapton.hackney.sch.uk). Girls only.

Haggerston School Weymouth Terrace, E2 8LS (7739 7324, www.haggerston.hackney.sch.uk).

Mossbourne Community Academy Downs Park Road, E5 8JY (8525 5200, www.mossbourne.hackney.sch.uk).

Our Lady's Convent High School 6-16 Amhurst Park, N16 5AF (8800 2158, www.ourladys.hackney.sch.uk). Roman Catholic; girls only; mixed sixth form.

Petchey Academy Shacklewell Lane, E8 2EY (7275 1500, www.petcheyacademy.org.uk).

Skinners' Academy Woodberry Grove, N4 1SY (8800 7411, www.skinnersacademy.org.uk).

Stoke Newington School Clissold Road, N16 9EX (7241 9600, www.sns.hackney.sch.uk).

Urswick School Paragon Road, E9 6NR (8985 2430, www.theurswickschool.co.uk). Church of England.

Property

Local estate agents

Base Property Specialist www.baseps.co.uk

Bennett Walden of Hackney www.bwofhackney.co.uk

Blake Stanley www.blakestanley.co.uk

City & Urban www.cityandurbaninternational.com

Courtneys www.courtneys-estates.com

Davey Stone www.daveystone.com

Keatons www.keatons.com

PG Estates www.pgestates.com

Philips Estates www.phillipsestates.co.uk

Shaw & Co www.shawco.com

Sovereign House www.sovereign-house.com

Local knowledge

www.chatsworthroade5.co.uk
www.hackneycitizen.co.uk
www.hackneygazette.co.uk
www.hackney.gov.uk/w-hackneytoday.htm
www.n16mag.com

Hackney Empire

USEFUL INFO

Borough size
1,905 hectares

Population
265,400

Ethnic mix
White 62.7%
Black/Black British 18.2%
Asian/Asian British 11.0%
Mixed 4.2%
Chinese or other 4.0%

London Borough of Hackney
Town Hall, Mare Street, E8 1EA (8356
3000, www.hackney.gov.uk)

Council run by
Labour

MPs
Hackney North & Stoke Newington,
Diane Abbott (Labour); Hackney South
& Shoreditch, Meg Hillier (Labour)

Main recycling centre
Hornsey Street Waste & Recycling Centre,
40 Hornsey Street, N7 8HU (8884 5645,
www.londonwaste.co.uk)

Council tax
£862.30 to £2,586.90

Hammersmith
& Fulham

Close proximity to central London doesn't stop the Fulham half of the borough from sometimes feeling like a county town, with its refined streets, cosy pubs, private schools and upper-class sports. Likewise, being in Zone 2 doesn't stop Shepherd's Bush and Hammersmith from being entertainment and shopping sensations.

AVERAGE PROPERTY PRICE

Detached £1,823,729	**Terraced** £1,211,107
Semi-detached £1,506,014	**Flat** £617,694

AVERAGE RENTAL PRICE PER WEEK

Room £161	**2 bed** £395
Studio £231	**3 bed** £550
1 bed £310	**4+ bed** £810

Hammersmith & Fulham

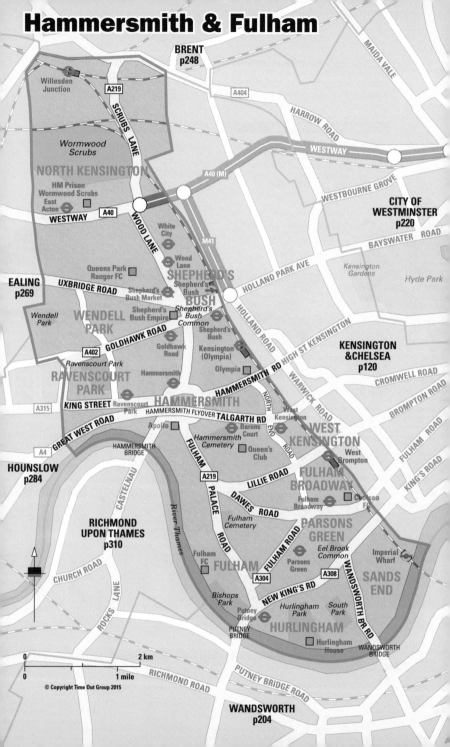

BRENT
p248

Willesden
Junction

A219

SCRUBS LANE

A404

MAIDA VALE

HARROW ROAD

WESTWAY

Wormwood
Scrubs

NORTH KENSINGTON

A40 (M)

WESTBOURNE GROVE

CITY OF
WESTMINSTER
p220

HM Prison
Wormwood Scrubs
East
Acton

A40

WESTWAY

WOOD LANE

White
City

M41

Wood
Lane

BAYSWATER ROAD

Kensington
Gardens

Hyde Park

EALING
p269

UXBRIDGE ROAD

Queens Park
Ranger FC

SHEPHERD'S
BUSH

Shepherd's
Bush

HOLLAND PARK AVE

Wendell
Park

WENDELL
PARK

Shepherd's
Bush Market

Shepherd's
Bush Empire

Shepherd's
Bush
Common

Shepherd's
Bush

HOLLAND ROAD

KENSINGTON
& CHELSEA
p120

A402

GOLDHAWK ROAD

Goldhawk
Road

Kensington
(Olympia)

HIGH ST KENSINGTON

CROMWELL ROAD

RAVENSCOURT
PARK

Ravenscourt Park

Hammersmith

Olympia

HAMMERSMITH RD

WARWICK ROAD

BROMPTON ROAD

A315

KING STREET

Ravenscourt
Park

HAMMERSMITH

NORTH END

West
Kensington

WEST
KENSINGTON

FULHAM ROAD

KING'S ROAD

GREAT WEST ROAD

HAMMERSMITH FLYOVER

TALGARTH RD

West
Brompton

A4

HAMMERSMITH
BRIDGE

Apollo

Hammersmith
Cemetery

Barons
Court

Queen's
Club

FULHAM

END ROAD

HOUNSLOW
p284

CASTELNAU

A219

LILLIE ROAD

FULHAM
BROADWAY

RICHMOND
UPON THAMES
p310

River Thames

PALACE

DAWES ROAD

Fulham
Cemetery

Fulham
Broadway

Chelsea
FC

CHURCH ROAD

ROCKS LANE

ROAD

FULHAM ROAD

PARSONS
GREEN

Fulham FC

FULHAM

Parsons
Green

Eel Brook
Common

Imperial
Wharf

SANDS
END

A304

NEW KING'S RD

A308

WANDSWORTH BR RD

Bishops
Park

Hurlingham
Park

South
Park

Putney
Bridge

HURLINGHAM

0   2 km

PUTNEY
BRIDGE

Hurlingham
House

WANDSWORTH
BRIDGE

0   1 mile

© Copyright Time Out Group 2015

RICHMOND ROAD

PUTNEY BRIDGE ROAD

WANDSWORTH
p204

Neighbourhoods

Shepherd's Bush W12 and Olympia W14

Everything changed at Shepherd's Bush with the arrival of Westfield London in 2008, and the mega mall isn't finished yet – a flagship four-floor John Lewis store is set to be built at the White City end of the complex by 2017, along with 1,300 new homes. Bush residents may have been sceptical about the dropping of a luxury mega mall on their doorstep, but weatherproof Westfield's arrival has been pretty positive, bringing together more than 250 shops, a 17-screen cinema and chain eats galore (Five Guys, Pho, Busaba and the like). It also brought a raft of infrastructure improvements to the area, including two new stations: Wood Lane on the Hammersmith & City line and Shepherd's Bush station on the London Overground rail line.

Other aspects of the Bush have slowly improved too. The eternally grotty Green received a modern makeover in 2013 with a decent playground and artist Elliott Brook's impressive *Goaloids* rotating, football-themed sculpture, though the park's position marooned in a sea of nose-to-tail traffic on the A217 means it'll never rival Kensington Gardens. Round the outside, things are slowly changing too, as pound shops become coffee shops, and kebab shops become, well, more coffee shops. The most spectacular addition is the £30 million, 317-room four-star Dorsett Shepherd's Bush hotel, which occupies the vast Grade II-listed building that started life in the 1920s as the Pavilion Cinema. Maybe the Bush is on its way to becoming 'Shey-Boo' after all.

Fortunately, grunge cred is restored a few doors along at the O2 Shepherd's Bush Empire, with gigs by Hawkwind and Death Cab for Cutie filling the calendar. Pre-gig drinking and dining options have improved considerably of late, with venues such as the Defector's Weld, with its smart pub, 'snug' cocktail bar and unobtrusive DJ sounds; the newly revamped Sindercombe Social serving Ruby Jean's eclectic burgers (pickled onion Monster Munch, emmental and thousand island topping, anyone?); and Aberdeenshire export BrewDog, featuring a bare-brick interior and 40 craft beers on tap. For a smarter soirée, the peking duck at the Dorsett's Shikumen is a triumph.

Culture continues round the corner at the Bush Theatre, now housed in the old library

on Uxbridge Road but still punching well above its weight. A little further along, past renowned Middle Eastern supermarket Al-Abbas and authentic Greek taverna Vine Leaves, is the wonderfully ornate Bush Hall (an intimate space for gigs), which has spread out to include the Music House for Children and artfully distressed Bush Hall Dining Rooms. Beyond here, Uxbridge Road is an unprepossessing ribbon of cheap call centres and carpet retailers, but keep the faith and you'll reach the handsomely refurbished Princess Victoria pub, which brings gastro flair to this far-flung part of W12. Running between Uxbridge and Goldhawk roads, Shepherd's Bush Market offers a wonderful counterbalance to Westfield's WAGs, flogging an intriguing mix of just about everything you can think of, from fruit and veg and fabrics to reggae music and wedding gowns, though its long-term future is uncertain.

Most of the property near the Green is made up of flats, with a couple of ugly tower blocks dominating the green itself. Heading

The Lyric Hammersmith – a newly-refurbished theatre punching well above its weight.

towards Olympia, there's a change as Shepherd's Bush becomes 'Blythe Village' – at least in the eyes of the local estate agents – and family houses dominate along attractive roads such as Bolingbroke Road and Sterndale Road. All village life is here, too, including Saturday farmers' market Brook Green Market & Kitchen on Bolingbroke Road, and several decent eating options: Italian at Pentolino, gastro treats at the

TRANSPORT

Tube lines Central, Circle, District, Hammersmith & City, Overground, Piccadilly

Main bus routes into central London 7, 9, 10, 11, 22, 74, 211, 414; night buses N7, N9, N10, N11, N22, N74, N97, N207; 24-hour buses 14, 27, 94, 148

River boat services Chelsea Harbour Pier

HIGHS & LOWS

The massive Westfield London –
shoppers' paradise

Maggie's West London at
Charing Cross Hospital – top-class
cancer support

Football at Chelsea, Fulham and QPR

Posh sports! Anyone for croquet?

Historic riverside pubs

Gigs galore

King Street remains grotty and
unappealing

The massive Westfield London –
shopping refusenik purgatory

Low on green space

Eternal traffic

Shepherd's Bush Market

Havelock Tavern, posh pizzas at the Bird in Hand, and steak and chips (and little else) at Popeseye. Nearby Olympia Exhibition Centre, on the border with Kensington & Chelsea, hosts a variety of trade shows, including in its newly revamped Olympia 2 hall, but local resentment towards the traffic it creates is only set to increase as its calendar grows to accommodate events from the now defunct Earl's Court, such as the Ideal Home Show.

Hammersmith W6

The heart of Hammersmith is a congested and noisy mess, thanks to the thundering A4, rickety Hammersmith flyover and the often gridlocked gyratory around Hammersmith Broadway, where the tube and bus station are situated. Talk continues to rage about converting the flyover to a flyunder, and reconnecting the area with the river. For now, though, the barrier remains, with the south side overlooked by the looming edifice of the Grade II-listed art deco Eventim Apollo. Between here and the river, the area is dominated by a couple of large council estates before emerging at the Thames itself, awash with vast development under the moniker of Fulham Reach. Butting up against the city's oldest suspension bridge, Hammersmith Bridge, multitasking arts venue Riverside Studios, which opened in 1975, is undergoing a major revamp and is due to reopen in late 2017, complete with three studios, a cinema and a riverside walkway that will open up a path from Barnes Bridge to Craven Cottage. The other side of Hammersmith Bridge, towards Chiswick, is a more sedate scene, with grand riverside houses and atmospheric pubs lining the Thames Path, including the Old Ship, with its happy marriage of Thames views and outside space, and the 17th-century Dove.

Shopping is centred on busy King Street, which leads west to Chiswick. It's a pretty down-at-heel thoroughfare, providing the usual raft of Primark, mobile phone outlets and charity shops, plus an unappealing shopping centre, Kings Mall. Further on lies Lowiczanka Polish Cultural Centre, home to a theatre, restaurant and the largest Polish library outside Poland. Opposite is Hugh Grant's alma mater, Latymer Upper, a leading independent school that stretches all the way down to the river. Next door, Pallingswick House is currently being converted into the new home of Toby Young's much talked-about West London Free School, the first

of its kind when it opened for 'classical liberal' education in 2011. Unfortunately, no conversion seems in the pipeline for the hideous Hammersmith Town Hall extension, with an equally gloomy Cineworld cinema next door. Luckily, though, you're spoilt for post-film eats here, with a global mix of excellent local eateries – trusty old-timers such as Saigon, Saigon (Vietnamese), Shilpa (Indian) and Anarkali (Indian), plus new arrivals such as L'Amorosa, opened in 2014 by former Zafferano head chef Andy Needham, and new upmarket fish-and-chip place WP Fish & Chips.

Noisy chain pubs used to dominate the area around the tube station, but things are improving slowly if rather predictably, with chains such as Byron and Tiger Bills Thai creating a more sober (if rather soulless) vibe. Better options, perhaps, are the wonderfully inventive vegetarian food at the long-running Gate, sustainable fish and chips at Kerbisher & Malt, or deli treats at Brook's Counter & Table. If you're after a sip of something stronger, the Hampshire Hog 'pub and pantry' is the pick of the hostelries on King Street. Culture comes to the fore here, too, with the revamped Lyric Theatre dominating the attractive open space of Lyric Square – when the sun's shining, the fountains and café chairs create an almost continental vibe.

Traffic-clogged Shepherd's Bush Road is a decidedly unappealing stretch of tarmac, its sole redeeming feature – the Hammersmith Palais, built in 1919 as a dance hall and once a legendary gig venue – now transformed into a bright, airy student halls of residence. Next door, student standbys Wagamama and Belushi's keep the new kids on the block entertained. Across the road, high walls keep the riffraff from peering in on the playing fields of top London day school St Paul's Girls' School.

With SPGS, Latymer Upper and Godolphin & Latymer all within a hockey stick of each other, the area is rich with top independent schools. As a result, large family homes attract premium prices in the streets either side of Brook Green, a thin wedge of grass with a handful of tennis courts. There are still plenty of conversion flats, though – this is one of the largest private rented sectors in London – and modern luxury apartment blocks are mushrooming around focal Hammersmith Broadway.

Hammersmith isn't the finished article yet, but the landscape is changing rapidly in this previously maligned part of W6. But for a taste of just how good Hammersmith could be if it does ever finally reconnect with the river, save up and head down to the legendary River Café, where Ruth Rogers is still cooking up a storm after more than 25 years. Take a seat on the terrace overlooking the river and Shepherd's Bush Road will seem a million miles away.

Brackenbury Village and Ravenscourt Park W6

This area – bounded by King Street to the south and Hammersmith Grove to the east – is an island of middle-class calm in a sea of urban through-traffic. It feels quite distinct from surrounding Hammersmith and Shepherd's Bush. At its green heart is appealing Ravenscourt Park, a much-needed open space in a very built-up part of the capital. Come Guy Fawkes Night, it offers the best fireworks display in west London, and the brilliant Carter's Steam Fair is an annual visitor. The park is extensive, with good facilities – there are tennis courts galore, a bowling green, several playgrounds, a summer paddling pool, astroturf pitches and a decent café run by Fait Maison – and besieged by Brackenbury families at the weekends. At the southern end of the park is the W6 Garden Centre, nestling underneath the arches of the District line above – tucked in among the ornamentals is a new café serving Sally Clarke quiches and the like.

Minimal traffic and some of west London's best state schools (John Betts Primary, West London Free School) make the area enormously popular with young families, as do the rows of pretty terraced cottages that dominate the area (although prices are pushing many prospective villagers further west to Acton in search of familial space). Wingate Road is probably the area's most desirable address, with its pastel-coloured houses going for £2 million and above. Such assets, combined with clever estate agent marketing (the 'Village' is a recent addition to Brackenbury), also draw media types eager for a quick commute to White City. Another asset is a number of decent drinking holes in the 'village', including long-running local gastro hero the Anglesea Arms, the more pubby but equally popular Andover Arms, the second branch of Fulham's Butcher's Hook (replacing the Thatched House), and gourmet pizza pub the Oak W12, all within a ten-minute pram push of each other. For finer dining, the Brackenbury restaurant reopened in early 2014 in the hands of Ossie Gray (son of the late Rose Gray of River Café fame) and chefs Humphrey Fletcher and Andy Morris, who come with impressive CVs. Just opposite are Brackenburys Deli, a centre of latte life, and that most important element of a true 'village' moniker, a wonderful family butcher in the shape of John Stenton. Well, all those SITCOMs (single income, two children, oppressive mortgage) have to source their noisettes d'agneau from somewhere.

Brackenbury isn't the only village in town any more, though, with those clever marketeers at it again to the north of Ravenscourt Park – this time with the newly created 'Askew Village'. Anyone who's been down Askew Road in the last 20 years may choke at the thought of gentrification, but this rat-run road between Uxbridge Road and Goldhawk Road now has village cred in spades, with the Ginger Pig gourmet butcher, the brilliant Laveli Bakery, fine wine and cheese at Askewine, mid-century modern kit at Max Inc, and solid gastro grub at the Eagle, a pub with a show-stealing beer garden. And if you fancy a bit of old-school Askew, classic eateries Adam's Café (North African) and Sufi (Persian) face each other across the street.

Housing stock is still slightly more affordable this side of Goldhawk Road, and young families are swarming into Askew side roads such as Bassein Park Road and Wendell Road for a slice of village life. The latter is home to the prestigious Leiths School of Food & Wine, the ideal place to brush up your skills for the W6 dinner-party circuit.

West Kensington and Barons Court W14

Straddling the affluent border between Hammersmith & Fulham and Kensington & Chelsea, West Kensington boasts some desirable neighbourhoods, although they're hemmed in somewhat by the major traffic arteries of North End Road, Talgarth Road and Lillie Road, and the area becomes a real rat run during term time. Rents here are higher than in most boroughs, but the area is popular for a reason: if you can ignore the traffic, Barons Court has a villagey vibe around the tube station and a stand-out, award-winning organic local butcher, HG Walter, which had a smart revamp in 2014. It supplies many of London's top restaurants, so expect premium prices for its premium cuts. Next door is another handsome enterprise, C'est Ici, a decent Gallic spot for croissants, cakes and coffee. The District line is just moments away, providing direct access to central London and the City (another reason its capacious houses are a popular buy).

Whatever your poison, nearby North End Road is prime bar-hopping territory. Music venue Black Velvet has become a top choice for soul, funk and disco lovers. The Albion public house is a beloved (and reputedly haunted) watering hole, while the Curtains Up gastropub in Barons Court serves British food and ales, bustling banter, and some decent pub theatre in the 60-seater basement.

Along with Kensington Olympia, the Queen's Club in Barons Court puts the area on the London map (and brings crowds of visitors when there's an event on). Opened in 1886, Queen's claims to be the first multi-purpose sports complex in the world. It's the home of the eponymous pre-Wimbledon tennis tournament and boasts 27 outdoor lawn tennis courts. The area also has one of Britain's oldest drama schools, Lamda (opened in 1861 as the London Academy of Music), alma mater of Benedict Cumberbatch, Rory Kinnear, Martin Shaw and David Suchet. Its president, actor Timothy West, is currently spearheading an £18.4 million redevelopment of its Talgarth Road campus.

West Kensington has some decent housing stock. Victorian terrace houses in the Gunter Estate conservation area, north of Talgarth Road, were developed by brothers James and Robert Gunter, whose family built large areas of South Kensington and Chelsea. There are also several mansion-flat blocks, with the most impressive in the Fitzgeorge & Fitzjames conservation area. Schools-wise, Fulham Prep on Greyhound Road is a popular independent prep school, while Fulham Boys School is a flagship free school which opened to 'boys of all faiths and no faith' in late 2014.

Beyond the salubrious confines of Queen's Club, green space is at something of a premium in the area, but Normand Park and the adjoining Fulham Pools provide space to run, play and swim just off the Lillie Road.

Fulham SW6

Few areas encapsulate the changes experienced by Londoners in recent decades quite as manifestly as Fulham. Once a mainly working class neighbourhood populated by those employed in the messy industries close to the river, Fulham was gradually gentrified from the 1960s, a process that has since accelerated into super-gentrification, with the ultra-wealthy moving in to displace the upper middle class. There's now little of

Hammersmith riverside

the industrial heritage remaining, bar a gorgeous listed kiln on New King's Road, once the location of John Dwight's famous Fulham Pottery works.

West of Putney Bridge sits Fulham Palace in Bishops Park, formerly the manor house of the Bishop of London and now a museum. Bordering the river, it also features tennis courts and the popular Drawing Room Café, and holds a popular annual fireworks display.

The park leads to the sedate home ground of Fulham FC, London's oldest professional football club. The streets immediately north are known as the 'alphabet streets' and are generally grander than Fulham's usual stock of Victorian terraces, with large gardens that

The Clothworkers' Centre, an outpost of the V&A, houses the museum's amazing collection of costumes through the ages.

are much sought after. The alphabet streets meet at the major east–west thoroughfare of Fulham Palace Road, something of a traffic blackspot but also the location of Drink of Fulham, a beer shop specialising in boutique ales. Heavy traffic is a bugbear of locals, partly caused by the area's relatively poor public transport links, being served only by Putney Bridge tube station on the District line and a handful of buses. It can give the area a strangely suburban feel for somewhere so central, and also means the streets are filled with 4x4s during school-run hours.

The main shopping thoroughfares are Fulham High Street and the New King's Road, where you can find a range of exclusive boutiques, antiques shops, gyms, upmarket bars and restaurants. Particularly pleasant browsing can be had at Circa Vintage for clothes and jewellery.

More affordable shopping can be had at the North End Road street market. Recommended restaurants include a trio of excellent Italians – Sapori Sardi, La Pizzica and Pappa Ciccia – and the Lebanese café Mes Amis, while decent pubs include the Eight Bells by Putney Bridge station and the Crabtree in the far west of the area. There's also a decent fish and chips place, Fishers, on Fulham High Street.

Parsons Green and Fulham Broadway SW6

Fulham Broadway has gradually transformed from being Chelsea's shabby cousin at the wrong end of the Fulham Road, to a destination in its own right. That's partly down to the shopping centre built on top of Fulham Broadway tube, which includes various chain shops and restaurants, as well as a nine-screen cinema and gym. Like the rest of the area, it gets incredibly busy on the days when Chelsea FC are at home – their Stamford Bridge stadium is 100 yards up the road and causes major congestion and changes to bus routes on match days. Fans and locals have plenty of pubs and restaurants to choose from, with highlights being the Michelin-starred Harwood Arms, the splendid, secretive country-style boozer Fox & Pheasant, the Butcher's Hook, Malt House and an outpost of Bodean's rib joint.

Head south, either via Eel Brook Common, a fat comma of grass containing a playground and sports pitches, or the shops of Fulham Road, and you'll reach the well-scrubbed enclave of Parsons Green. There's more of a sleepy Cotswolds village feel here, with fine houses surrounding the stately green triangle, overlooked by the huge White Horse pub (sometimes referred to as the 'sloaney pony'), an excellent ale pub as well as a decent restaurant. Across the green is the Duke on the Green, less grand but pleasing enough, and the trendy Aragon House; Fulham Road is home to decent gastropub the Brown Cow. The streets are filled with delis and restaurants, including top Italian Nuovi Sapori; Koji, a bustling Japanese place; and cut-above kebab shop (Jamie Oliver is apparently a fan) Kebab Kid. And, of course, a farmers' market on Sundays. There's plenty of fine shopping round here, too, including tailor Marc Wallace, Deuxième for women's clothes, as well as independent bookshop Nomad and funky stationery shop Tinc.

Lying south of the New King's Road, this area is a tale of two estates. One is the exclusive Peterborough Estate, built in the 19th century for local workers. Conversions, extensions and increasing gentrification due to the Chelsea overspill have combined to make these elaborately detailed red-brick houses highly sought after (especially the original 500 'Lion' houses, so-named because of their miniature rooftop stone lions). Nearby is the Sullivan Estate – an area known for 'hoodie' street-gang kids and petty crime. The clash can be an uncomfortable one.

Catering to the richest residents is the exclusive Hurlingham Club, located at 18th-century Hurlingham House. Best described as a country mansion (site of many a glittering party), it sits in 42 acres of riverside grounds, with facilities for tennis, croquet, cricket, bowls, golf, squash and swimming. But before you get ideas above your station – the waiting list for membership is full. An alternative is South Park, a wide expanse of green, with tennis courts, a couple of cricket pitches, a fun playground and a pizza van.

Sand's End and Imperial Wharf SW6

For decades, this has been a relatively forgotten corner of south-west London, stymied from development by industrial infrastructure – gas cylinders, the Lots Road power station – and poor public transport connections. Change first came in the shape of Chelsea Harbour, which sits pretty much on the border of Imperial Wharf and Sand's End and offers a rather anodyne – and unwelcoming – example of early luxury development in the shape of expensive hotels and apartments, a health centre and the odd restaurant, such as the Design Café in the Design Centre. It used to be a coal yard, but little of that has been allowed to survive.

This outpost of luxury living was for a long time somewhat isolated, but now the rest of the area is starting to catch up. That's been driven by the arrival of Imperial Wharf station on the London Overground train line, meaning it's now less than ten minutes to Clapham Junction. This was accompanied by the Imperial Wharf development, a modern take on Chelsea Harbour – the same ethos, but with a more inclusive approach, desperate to draw people to the area. To that end, there is (among the usual hotels and apartments) a range of restaurants such as Blue Elephant (Thai) and Yamal Alsham (Middle Eastern), as well as pubs (Young's Waterside Bar & Kitchen), shops (jewellery store Tateossian), a dance studio and events such as a jazz festival.

One imagines the Lots Road power station development will be along similar lines. This two-chimneyed brick cathedral once had four chimneys and was known as the 'Chelsea monster' when it powered the Underground, but has been rechristened Chelsea Riverside and will eventually feature the usual array of shops, homes, hotels and restaurants in ten separate buildings, including two larger towers.

Around these mammoth complexes, less institutional treats linger in streets largely made up of classic London terraces. Lots Road is a good modern take on the traditional pub near the power station, while further west, the Sands End and the Hurlingham Pub & Kitchen offer a similar service, as does the Rose to the north, between the King's Road and the gasworks. The gasworks has been colonised by Core One, a group of nine antiques dealers, artisan workshops and furniture warehouses. More furniture shopping can be done along Wandsworth Bridge Road, where you can also find cafés, delis, hair stylists and the very popular Randalls Butchers.

Entertainment comes in the form of the 606 Club, a jazz venue on Lots Road, while children adore the Gambado indoor play centre – with hundreds of activities including dodgems, laser play and climbing walls – and Clip 'n Climb, a feast of vertical challenges in colours only a child could love. The Imperial Wharf development has also bequeathed a small park, Imperial Park, with a sensory garden, children's playground and boating pond.

Eating

Adam's Café 77 Askew Road, W12 9AH (8743 0572, www.adamscafe.co.uk).

L'Amorosa 278 King Street, W6 9NH (8563 0300, www.lamorosa.com).

Anarkali 303-305 King Street, W6 9NH (8748 1760, www.anarkalifinedining.com).

Anglesea Arms 35 Wingate Road, W6 0UR (8749 1291, www.angleseaarmspub.co.uk).

Bird in Hand 88 Masbro Road, W14 0LR (7371 2721, www.thebirdinhandlondon.com).

Blah Blah Blah 78 Goldhawk Road, W12 8HA (8746 1337).

Blue Elephant Imperial Wharf, Townmead Road, SW6 2UB (7751 3111, www.blue elephant.com).

Bodean's 4 Broadway Chambers, SW6 1EP (7610 0440, www.bodeansbbq.com).

Brackenbury 129-131 Brackenbury Road, W6 0BQ (8741 4928, www.brackenbury restaurant.co.uk).

Brown Cow 676 Fulham Road, SW6 5SA (7384 9559, www.thebrowncowpub.co.uk).

Byron 10 Hammersmith Grove, W6 0ND (8741 9677, www.byronhamburgers.com).

C'est Ici 47 Palliser Road, W14 9EB (7381 4837).

Curtains Up 28A Comeragh Road, W14 9HR (7386 7543, www.geronimo-inns.co.uk/london-the-curtains-up).

Design Café Design Centre, Chelsea Harbour, SW10 0XE (7351 5362, www.dcch.co.uk/Design-Cafe).

Drawing Room Café Fulham Palace, Bishops Park, SW6 6EA (7736 3233, www.fulhampalace.org).

Eagle 215 Askew Road, W12 9AZ (8746 0046, www.geronimo-inns.co.uk/london-the-eagle).

Fait Maison www.fait-maison.co.uk; 245 Goldhawk Road, W12 8EU (8222 8755); Tea House, Ravenscourt Park, W6 0UL (8563 9291).

Fishers 19 Fulham High Street, SW6 3JH (7371 5555, www.fishersfishandchips.co.uk).

Gate 51 Queen Caroline Street, W6 9QL (8748 6932, www.thegaterestaurants.com).

Harwood Arms Corner of Walham Grove & Farm Lane, SW6 1QP (7386 1847, www.harwoodarms.com).

Havelock Tavern 57 Masbro Road, W14 0LS (7603 5374, www.havelocktavern.com).

Karma Restaurant 44 Blythe Road, W14 0HA (7602 0333, www.karma-westkensington.co.uk).

Kebab Kid 90 New King's Road, SW6 4LU (7737 0427).

Kerbisher & Malt 164 Shepherd's Bush Road, W6 7PB (3556 0228, www.kerbisher.co.uk).

Koji 58 New King's Road, SW6 4LS (7731 2520, www.koji.restaurant).

Lowiczanka 1st floor, Polish Cultural Centre, 238-246 King Street, W6 0RF (8741 3225, www.posk.org).

Mes Amis 1 Rainville Road, W6 9HA (7385 5155).

Oak 243 Goldhawk Road, W12 8EU (8741 7700, www.theoakw12.com).

Pappa Ciccia 105-107 Munster Road, SW6 5RQ (7384 1884, www.pappaciccia.com).

Pentolino 71 Blythe Road, W14 0HP (3010 0091, www.pentolinarestaurant.co.uk).

La Pizzica 744-746 Fulham Road, SW6 5SJ (7731 3762, www.lapizzicalondon.co.uk).

Popeseye Steak House 108 Blythe Road, W14 0HD (7610 4578, www.popeseye.com).

River Café Thames Wharf, Rainville Road, W6 9HA (7386 4200, www.rivercafe.co.uk).

Saigon Saigon 313-317 King Street, W6 9NH (8748 6887, www.saigon-saigon.co.uk).

Sapori Sardi 786 Fulham Road, SW6 5SL (7731 0755, www.saporisardi.co.uk).

Shikumen Dorsett Hotel, 58 Shepherd's Bush Green, W12 8QE (8749 9978, www.shikumen.co.uk).

Shipla 206 King Street, W6 0RA (8741 3127, www.shilparestaurant.co.uk).

Sufi 70 Askew Road, W12 9BJ (8834 4888, www.sufirestaurant.com).

Tiger Bills Thai 135 King Street, W6 9JG (8741 1315, www.tigerbills.co.uk).

Vine Leaves Taverna 71 Uxbridge Road, W12 8NR (8749 0325, www.vineleavestaverna.co.uk).

WP Fish & Chips 262 King Street, W6 0SP (8846 9860, www.fishxchips.co.uk).

Yamal Alsham 5 Imperial Wharf, The Boulevard, SW6 2UB (3010 1100, www.yamalalsham.co.uk).

Drinking

Albion 121 Hammersmith Road, W14 0QL (7603 2826, www.thealbionpub.com).

Andover Arms 57 Aldensley Road, W6 0DL (8748 2155, www.theandoverarms.com).

Aragon House 247 New King's Road, SW6 4XG (7731 7313, www.aragonhouse.net).

Black Velvet London 3 North End Cresscent, W14 8TG (7602 6834, www.blackvelvetlondon.co.uk).

BrewDog 15-19 Goldhawk Road, W12 8QQ (8749 8094, www.brewdog.com).

Butcher's Hook 115 Dalling Road, W6 0ET (8741 6283, www.thebutchershook.co.uk).

Crabtree Rainville Road, W6 9HA (7385 3929, www.thecrabtreew6.co.uk).

Defector's Weld 170 Uxbridge Road, W12 8AA (8749 0008, www.defectors-weld.com).

Drink of Fulham 349 Fulham Palace Road, SW6 6TB (7610 6795, www.drinkoffulham.com).

Dove 19 Upper Mall, W6 9TA (8748 9474, www.dovehammersmith.co.uk).

Duke on the Green 253 New King's Road, SW6 4XG (7736 2777, www.dukeonthegreen.co.uk).

Eight Bells 89 Fulham High Street, SW6 3JS (7736 6307).

Fox & Pheasant 1 Billing Road, SW10 9UJ (7352 2943, www.foxandpheasant-chelsea.co.uk).

Hampshire Hog 227 King Street, W6 9JT (8748 3391, www.thehampshirehog.com).

Hurlingham Pub & Kitchen 360 Wandsworth Bridge Road, SW6 2TZ (7610 9816, www.thehurlingham.co.uk).

Lots Road 114 Lots Road, SW10 0RJ (7352 6645, www.foodandfuel.co.uk).

Malt House 17 Vanston Place, SW6 1AY (7084 6888, www.malthousefulham.co.uk).

Old Ship 25 Upper Mall, W6 9TD (8748 2593, www.oldshipw6.co.uk).

Princess Victoria Pub 217 Uxbridge Road, W12 9DH (8749 5886, www.princessvictoria.co.uk).

Rose 1 Harwood Terrace, SW6 2AF (7731 1832, www.therosefulham.co.uk).

Sands End 135-137 Stephendale Road, SW6 2PR (7731 7823, www.thesandsend.co.uk).

Sindercombe Social 2 Goldhawk Road, W12 8QD (8746 1288, www.thesindercombesocial.co.uk).

White Horse 1-3 Parsons Green, SW6 4UL (7736 2115, www.whitehorsesw6.com).

Young's Waterside Bar & Kitchen Riverside Tower, The Boulevard, Imperial Road, SW6 2SU (7371 0802, www.watersidelondon.com).

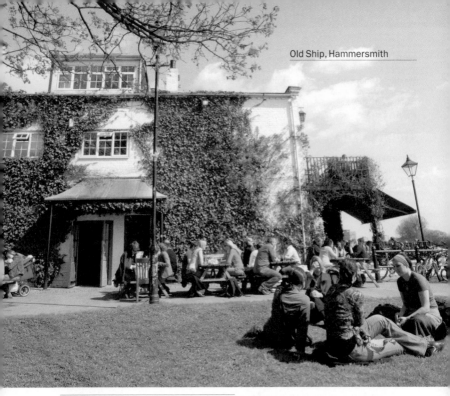

Old Ship, Hammersmith

Shopping

Al-Abbas 258-262 Uxbridge Road, W12 7JA (8740 1932).

Askewine 84 Askew Road, W12 9BJ (8746 1585, www.askewine.com).

Brackenburys Deli 22 Aldensley Road, W6 0DH (8748 7388, www.brackenburys.co.uk).

Broadway Shopping Centre The Broadway, W6 9YE (8563 0131, www.hammersmith broadway.co.uk).

Brook Green Market & Kitchen Bolingbroke Road, W14 0AA (www.brookgreenmarket.co.uk).

Brook's Counter & Table 140 Shepherd's Bush Road, W6 7PB (7602 0664, www.counter andtable.com).

Circa Vintage Clothes 64 Fulham High Street, SW6 3LQ (7736 5038, www.circavintage.com).

Core One The Gasworks, 2 Michael Road, SW6 2AN (7731 7171, www.coreoneantiques.com).

Deuxième 299 New King's Road, SW6 4RE (7736 3696, www.deuxieme.co.uk).

Fulham Broadway Centre Fulham Road, SW6 1BW (7385 6965, www.fulhambroadway.co.uk).

Ginger Pig 137-139 Askew Road, W12 9AU (8740 4297, www.thegingerpig.co.uk).

HG Walter 51 Palliser Road, W14 9EB (7385 6466, www.hgwalter.com).

John Stenton 55 Aldensley Road, W6 0DH (8748 6121, www.johnstenton.com).

Kings Mall Shopping Centre King Street, W6 0PZ (8741 2121, www.kings-mall.co.uk).

Laveli Bakery 5 Churchfield Road, W3 6BH (8993 6490, www.lavelibakery.com).

Marc Wallace 261 New King's Road, SW6 4RB (7736 6795, www.marcwallace.com).

Max Inc 106 Askew Road, W12 9BL (07973 121879, www.maxinc.co.uk).

Nomad Books 781 Fulham Road, SW6 5HA (7736 4000, www.nomadbooks.co.uk).

North End Road Street Market North End Road (8753 3916, www.lbhf.gov.uk).

Nuovi Sapori 295 New King's Road, SW6 4RE (7736 3363).

Randalls Butchers 113 Wandsworth Bridge Road, SW6 2TE (7736 3426).

Shepherd's Bush Market off Goldhawk Road, W12 (www.shepherdsbushmarket.co.uk).

Tateossian 6 The Boulevard, Imperial Wharf, SW6 2UB (7731 6424, www.tateossian.com).

Tinc 705 Fulham Road, SW6 5UL (7731 4044, www.tinc.uk.com).

W6 Garden Centre 17 Ravenscourt Avenue, W6 0SL (8563 7112, www.w6gardencentre.co.uk).
Westfield London Ariel Way, W12 7SL (http://uk.westfield.com/london).
Wholefoods 63-97 Kensington High Street, W8 5SE (7368 4500, www.wholefoodsmarket.com).

Things to do

Cinemas & theatres
Bush Theatre 7 Uxbridge Road, W12 8LJ (8743 3584, www.bushtheatre.co.uk).
Cineworld Hammersmith 207 King Street, W6 9JT (0871 200 2000, www.cineworld.co.uk).
Lyric Hammersmith Lyric Square, King Street, W6 0QL (8741 6850, www.lyric.co.uk). Excellent local theatre.
Riverside Studios Crisp Road, W6 9RL (8237 1000, www.riversidestudios.co.uk). Performance arts plus repertory cinema. Reopening in 2017.
Vue 0871 224 0240, www.myvue.com; Fulham Broadway Centre, Fulham Road, SW6 1BW; West 12 Centre, Shepherd's Bush Green, W12 8PP.

Galleries & museums
Fulham Palace Bishop's Avenue, SW6 6EA (7736 3233, www.fulhampalace.org). Museum, gallery, gardens – and a fine café.
Kelmscott House 26 Upper Mall, W6 9TA (8741 3735, www.williammorrissociety.org). William Morris's 1878-96 home is a private house, but the basement and coach house are open to the public on Thursday and Saturday afternoons.
V&A's Clothworkers' Centre Blythe House, 23 Blythe Road, W14 0QX (7942 2000, www.vam.ac.uk). Costume archives, open by appointment.

Gigs, clubs & comedy
606 Club 90 Lots Road, SW10 0QD (7352 5953, www.606club.co.uk).
Black Velvet London 3 North End Crescent, W14 8TG (7602 6834, www.blackvelvetlondon.co.uk).
Bush Hall 310 Uxbridge Road, W12 7LJ (8222 6955, www.bushhallmusic.co.uk). Chamber concerts and low-key rock shows.
Eventim Apollo Queen Caroline Street, W6 9QH (8563 3800, www.eventimapollo.com). Powerhouse music venue with a 5,000 capacity.
O2 Shepherd's Bush Empire Shepherd's Bush Green, W12 8TT (0844 477 2000, www.o2shepherdsbushempire.co.uk). Great mid-sized music venue.

Green spaces
For more details, see www.lbhf.gov.uk.
Bishops Park Bishop's Avenue, SW6. Play and sports facilities, gardens, meadows and a lake.

Hurlingham Park Hurlingham Road, SW6. Play area, sports pitches, tennis courts, bowling green.
Ravenscourt Park Ravenscourt Avenue, W6. Garden centre and café, play areas, sports courts and pitches. One of the borough's foremost parks.
Wormwood Scrubs Open Space Scrubs Lane, W12. Nature reserve, model aircraft runway, sports pitches and the Linford Christie Outdoor Sports Centre.

Gyms & leisure centres
Charing Cross Sports Club Aspenlea Road, W6 8LH (8741 3654, www.ccsclub.co.uk). Private.
Clip 'n Climb 19 Michael Road, SW6 2ER (7736 2271, www.clipnclimbchelsea.co.uk).
David Lloyd Unit 24, Fulham Broadway Retail Centre, Fulham Road, SW6 1BW (0345 129 6792, www.davidlloyd.co.uk). Private.
Fitness First www.fitnessfirst.co.uk; West 12 Centre, Shepherd's Bush Green, W12 8PP (8743 4444); 26-28 Hammersmith Grove, W6 7HA (8742 6140). Private.
Fulham Pools Normand Park, Lillie Road, SW6 7ST (7471 0450, www.lbhf.gov.uk).
Gambado 7 Station Court, Townmead Road, SW6 2PY (www.gambado.com).
Hammersmith Fitness & Squash Centre 1 Chalk Hill Road, W6 8DW (8741 8028, www.better.org.uk).
Lillie Road Fitness Centre Lillie Road, SW6 7PH (7381 2183, www.better.org.uk).
Phoenix Fitness Centre & Janet Adegoke Swimming Pool Bloemfontein Road, W12 7DB (8735 4900, www.better.org.uk).
Thirtysevendegrees 10 Beaconsfield Terrace Road, W14 0PP (7610 4090, www.thirtysevendegrees.co.uk). Private.
Virgin Active www.virginactive.co.uk; Normand Park, Lillie Road, SW6 7ST (7471 0450); 181 Hammersmith Road, W6 8BS (8741 0487); 188A Fulham Road, SW10 9PN (7352 9452). Private.

Outdoor pursuits
Linford Christie Outdoor Sports Centre Artillery Way, off Du Cane Road, W12 0DF (07908 788739, www.lbhf.gov.uk).
Queen's Club Palliser Road, W14 9EQ (7386 3400, www.queensclub.co.uk). Upmarket tennis club.

Spectator sports
Chelsea FC Stamford Bridge, Fulham Road, SW6 1HS (0871 984 1905, www.chelseafc.com).
Fulham FC Craven Cottage, Stevenage Road, SW6 6HH (0843 208 1234, www.fulhamfc.com).
Queen's Park Rangers FC Loftus Road Stadium, South Africa Road, W12 7PA (0844 477 7007, www.qpr.co.uk).

Queen's Club Palliser Road, W14 9EQ (7386 3400, www.queensclub.co.uk). Pre-Wimbledon tennis championship.

Schools

Primary
There are 35 state primary schools in Hammersmith & Fulham, including 12 church schools. There are also 12 independent primaries, including one Muslim school, one French school, one theatre school and one Montessori school. See www.lbhf.gov.uk, www.education.gov.uk/edubase and www.ofsted.gov.uk for more information.

Secondary
Burlington Danes Academy Wood Lane, W12 0HR (8735 4950, www.burlingtondanes.org).
Fulham Boys School Gibbs Green Estate, W14 9LY (7381 7100, www.fulhamboysschool.org).
Fulham College Boys' School Kingwood Road, SW6 6SN (7381 3606, www.fulhamcollegeboys.net). Boys only.
Fulham Cross Girls' School Munster Road, SW6 6BP (7381 0861, www.fulhamcross.net). Girls only.
Godolphin & Latymer School Iffley Road, W6 0PG (8741 1936, www.godolphinandlatymer.com). Private; girls only.
Hammersmith Academy Cathnor Road, W12 9JD (8222 6000, www.hammersmithacademy.org).
Hurlingham & Chelsea School Peterborough Road, SW6 3ED (7731 2581, www.hurlingham andchelsea.org.uk).
Lady Margaret School Parsons Green, SW6 4UN (7736 7138, www.ladymargaret.lbhf.sch.uk). Church of England; girls only.
Latymer Upper School King Street, W6 9LR (8629 2024, www.latymer-upper.org). Private.
London Oratory School Seagrave Road, SW6 1RX (7385 0102, www.london-oratory.org). Roman Catholic; boys only; mixed sixth form.
Phoenix High School The Curve, W12 0RQ (8749 1141, www.phoenixhighschool.org).
Sacred Heart High School 212 Hammersmith Road, W6 7DG (8748 7600, www.sacredhearthighschool hammersmith.org.uk). Roman Catholic; girls only.
St Paul's Girls Brook Green, W6 7BS (7603 2288, spgs.org). Private; girls only
West London Free School Bridge Avenue, W6 0LB (8600 0670, www.westlondonfreeschool.co.uk).

Property

Local estate agents
Chard www.chard.co.uk
Douglas & Gordon www.douglasandgordon.com
Featherstone Leigh www.featherstoneleigh.co.uk

Finlay Brewer www.finlaybrewer.co.uk
Goss & Co www.gossandco.com
Haus Properties www.hausproperties.co.uk
Horton & Garton www.hortonandgarton.co.uk
Kerr & Co www.kerrandco.com
Lawsons & Daughters www.lawsonsand daughters.com
Marsh & Parsons www.marshandparsons.co.uk
Peter Woods www.peterwoods.co.uk

Local knowledge

www.fulhamsociety.org
www.fulhamsw6.com
www.hammersmithtoday.co.uk
www.shepherdsbushw12.com
www.w14london.ning.com

USEFUL INFO

Borough size
1,640 hectares

Population
181,700

Ethnic mix
White 76.0%
Black or Black British 9.0%
Asian or Asian British 8.2%
Mixed 3.7%
Chinese or other 3.2%

London Borough of Hammersmith & Fulham
Town Hall, King Street, W6 9JU (8748 3020, www.lbhf.gov.uk).

Council run by
Labour

MPs
Chelsea & Fulham, Greg Hands (Conservative); Hammersmith, Andy Slaughter (Labour)

Main recycling centre
Western Riverside Waste Authority, Western Riverside Transfer Station, Smugglers Way, SW18 1JS (8871 2788, www.wrwa.gov.uk)

Council tax
£681.88 to £2,045.62

Haringey

Leafy suburban splendour meets grim deprivation in what is one of the capital's most multicultural boroughs. But regeneration is afoot, making troubled neigbourhoods such as Tottenham interesting places to be.

AVERAGE PROPERTY PRICE

Detached £1,470,743	**Terraced** £509,318
Semi-detached £680,178	**Flat** £419,618

AVERAGE RENTAL PRICE PER WEEK

Room £126	**1 bed** £300
Studio £230	**2 bed** £385
	3 bed £504

DOZE @ WRH..
..QUALITY VANDALISM..
...SINCE 1985

Parkland Walk, from Finsbury Park to Highgate

Neighbourhoods

Finsbury Park and Stroud Green N4

Affectionately known as 'Little Algiers', Finsbury Park is home to London's largest Algerian population, as well as plenty of students, surly youths with low-slung trousers, boozy Arsenal fans and families priced out of Crouch End. It's also starting to develop new cultural hubs such as Furtherfield Gallery, a digital art and community space in the green splendour of the 112-acre, Grade II-listed park itself, and artsy playhouse Park Theatre on Clifton Terrace.

Finsbury Park, an area that straddles the Haringey/Islington border, is not the most beautiful of environs. Road junctions and railway bridges characterise its well-connected centre but Victorian and Edwardian buildings mix in with the council blocks creating some pockets of nicety. The terraced houses of Woodstock, Perth and Ennis roads sell for upwards of £425,000.

Shoppers aren't spoilt for choice here, with traditional boozers flanking late-opening Turkish and Caribbean grocers, Italian delis, and Latin American and Thai restaurants (Finsbury Park is nothing if not multicultural). There's a scattering of bookstores and antique shops, such as the eccentric Eighty-Seven. Or you can bunny-hop to the world's only specialist Sylvanian Families shop for all your miniature figurine needs. For classic steel-framed bikes, you can't beat Sargent & Co.

However, there are some great eateries squeezed between the 24-hour off-licences and fried-chicken shops, mainly on Mountgrove Road (heading towards Clissold Park) or Stroud Green Road (leading up to Crouch Hill). For lunch, Fink's Salt & Sweet is the deli of choice, or head to Jai Krishna for delicious, good-value, vegetarian Indian food. Dotori is a local favourite, with its heady mix of Japanese and Korean cuisine, as is Osteria Tufo for tasty Italian fare.

Hidden away in the backstreets behind the park is the huge Faltering Fullback pub, known for its homely atmosphere and vertical garden, which will make you feel like an Ewok out on the razz. The World's End is laid-back, with Sunday acoustic sessions, while the Silver Bullet, outside the station, is one of the few late-closing options.

A local landmark is the Castle Climbing Centre, a Victorian pumphouse for the New River converted into an impressive bouldering course that turns the heads of non-local drivers as they pass it on Green Lanes. But if you really want to party, get your mind into the gutter at Rowans Tenpin Bowl – cheap booze, arcade games, bowling, and you can order in pizza from next door. It's like being 12 years old again, but with beer.

Another landmark is the North London Central Mosque. Previously called Finsbury Park Mosque (which it continues to be known as locally), the mosque was rebranded as a way of dissociating itself with extremist preacher Abu Hamzah and foiled shoe-bomber Richard Reid.

While the north end of the borough is dyed-in-the-wool Spurs, Finsbury Park is spitting distance from the Emirates Stadium, which gives rise to possibly the neighbourhood's most prominent landmark, right by Finsbury Park station – the massive Arsenal Store.

Crouch End N8

As Haringey spreads west from Tottenham and Wood Green to Muswell Hill, leafy N8 sits in between. Geographically down the hill from Highgate, it appeals to media types and actors who don't have the income and/or the 4x4 mindset of its wealthier neighbouring enclaves. However, the price of a first-floor flat in Crouch End has overtaken what you'd have paid for the whole house 15 years ago.

That said, you'll still find places to get your keys cut and your laundry done on the Broadway – Crouch End's shopping and social hub, a mix of high-street names, friendly boutiques and upmarket butchers' shops. Main thoroughfares get you south-ish to Finsbury Park and Archway tube stations in 10 to 15 minutes, and head north towards Muswell Hill, Turnpike Lane and Alexandra Palace, also 10 minutes away by bus. That's right, there's no tube station, but Hornsey rail station has quick links to Finsbury Park and Highbury & Islington, with Old Street and Moorgate on the same line, in less than 25 minutes. Plus Crouch Hill station is on the Overground.

Crouch End is proud of its village feel – and not just to compensate for that lack of Underground station. Even its recent openings, such as the excellent Art House N8 (voted *Time Out* readers' favourite local cinema in its first year) and the Earl Haig Hall bar and venue, have eased themselves into the area's casual local vibe, furnished with second-hand chairs and tables and run by young, well-informed staff. Add to these the local drama groups, gig nights and annual arts festivals, plus the nearby excellent Park Theatre, and Crouch End is a self-contained cultural haven with little thought of Zone 1 for its weekend pleasure.

The drinking and dining scene also reflects the mix of well-heeled residents and first-London-job renters. Although casual café-bar restaurants are the norm and as popular with couples in the evening as they are with parents and their pre-schoolers in the day, there are a handful of more ambitious gaffs, most notably Bar Esteban (Spanish) and Bistro Aix (French). There are a couple of large old boozers, the prettiest being the Kings Head and the Queens, though the most characterful is the Harringay Arms, an unreconstructed bar much loved by older locals and younger trendies wanting to escape the mainstream night-out crowd.

The Broadway is focused around the landmark clock tower (built in 1895 as a monument to a councillor who promoted the establishment of local green spaces). With the newly refurbished Park Road Pools & Fitness complex (indoor pools, a summer

Alexandra Palace Park offers tree-climbing sessions, with ropes and safety equipment.

lido and gym on hand), as well as gyms such as Virgin Active, plus a local cricket club and the parks, there are plenty of ways for residents to work off evenings spent in the above-mentioned restaurants.

The long tree-lined avenues just off the Broadway are the most sought after, along with the massive Victorian and Edwardian homes along the top of the hill heading towards Finsbury Park and the streets rising up Shepherd's Hill towards Highgate tube. Where Tottenham Lane heads towards Turnpike Lane, things become less gentrified, with the appearance of the area's estates, though even at this extreme of Crouch End there are charming streets around Priory Park, and you'd do well to find a bargain to buy anywhere south of Hornsey High Street.

Crouch End's café menus are geared towards children in search of 'babyccinos' as much as adults wanting free Wi-Fi and a matcha latte, and anyone who's had to

negotiate hurrying pushchairs on the narrow pavements will testify that this is a family-oriented part of London. Shops such as Soup Dragon (toys and clothes) and Pickled Pepper Books (a café and children's bookshop) reflect the child focus, and primary education is generally strong in N8. For secondary education, the pushier parents start to look for homes in Muswell Hill as Year 7 approaches, in the hope of getting into Fortismere School, but the increasingly positive performance of pupils at Crouch End's large secondary school Highgate Wood has seen its catchment area shrink rapidly in recent years.

Muswell Hill N10

Haringey may be the tenth most-deprived district in England but you wouldn't know it in Muswell Hill. Sitting atop a steep hill leading up from Crouch End, this is the borough's own Hampstead. It's one of the few places that really lives up to the 'village London' tag. Once home to one of London's greatest bands, the Kinks, it's now filled with affluent jobs-in-media types.

Among the area's leafy avenues and stately semi-detached residences lies Alexandra Palace – the home of TV. Opened in 1873, it had to be rebuilt after burning to the ground just 16 days later. Reopened two years down the line, it went on to become the site of the first BBC television broadcast, in 1936, before suffering another catastrophic fire in 1980. Nowadays, there are 196 acres of grounds, an ice-rink at the building's north end and a bar with expansive views of north London. Events are what it does best: it has a tradition of mass-capacity gigs that includes a legendary 1967 Pink Floyd performance. Alexandra Palace train station provides a fast link to central London.

There are a large number of tempting boutiques – Whistles, Mint Velvet, White Stuff, and a few indie fashion stores beckon along Muswell Hill Broadway and Fortis Green Road. The Broadway also boasts high-end shoe shop Kate Kuba, ensuring that the well-heeled stay that way.

W Martyn on the Broadway is typical of the true charm of Muswell Hill: a proper old-fashioned family business, with shelves piled high with preserves, dried fruits, coffees and sweet treats. Locals are keen supporters of independent traders, including Art for Art's Sake (art supplies) and Crocodile Antiques (quirky homewares). There's also Les Aldrich's redoubtable classical music shop, the excellent Muswell Hill Bookshop and the knowledgeable Children's Bookshop (both on Fortis Green Road), which has regular visits from big-name authors. And the self-explanatory Cheeses of Muswell Hill.

Although there are lots of places to eat out, it's a bit chain-dominated, with branches of child-friendly Giraffe, Pizza Express and ASK, as well as Carluccio's and Maison Blanc, but it also has famed fish-and-chips shop Toff's (est 1968).

For one-off deli and diner experiences, there's Feast, Fasta (both on Fortis Green Road) and plenty of other options that don't happen to start with an F. Or give Chriskitch on Tetherdown a go. Its counter groans with incredible bakes and vast bowlfuls of salad. When the sun's out, the tables out front are the perfect place to soak up the N10 atmosphere.

The best pubs are a stroll away. The Clissold Arms has fireside tables, an impressive wine list and outside tables for dining. Heading down towards Crouch End, there's Victoria Stakes, which is grand and airy, with the added bonus of a sobering climb back up Muswell Hill afterwards. For home consumption, N10-ers head to Prohibition Wines, where owners Paul and Louise host regular tastings.

Wood Green and Bounds Green N22

Very much the borough's nerve centre, Wood Green contains Haringey's main courthouse (the beautiful Georgian townhouse-style Wood Green Crown Court), Haringey Council's major administrative headquarters, and numerous bus routes. Once upon a time, higher rail fares compared with the rest of the borough made it home to Haringey's moneyed residents, but the fact that its current main purpose is as the borough's retail heart has been a great social leveller.

There are two multi-screen cinemas, a shopping centre and a high street crammed with major chain stores. The ugly Mall Shopping City dominates Wood Green: its more than 80 retailers include branches of Argos, TK Maxx and Boots alongside high-street fashion (Topman, New Look,

HIGHS & LOWS

Ally Pally

Craft breweries

Crouch End eating

Football

Lee Valley

Multicultural shopping

Great views

▲ .... ▼

Finsbury Park station tunnels

Lack of nightlife

Late-night drunks on the N29 night bus

Poverty

Tottenham gang culture

Tottenham Hale gyratory

Crouch End

Next) and one of the cinemas, as well as a clutch of eateries, from standard chains to a US-style diner, Turkish restaurant and cafés. Outside the mall, on the High Road, are branches of Primark and Lidl, while just off the main drag, the Big Green Bookshop is a great local independent. Apart from the numerous chains, the better eating options are out of central Wood Green: to the west towards Alexandra Palace, modern European bar-brasserie Mosaica at the Chocolate Factory; and to the north, Fatisa pizzeria.

The streets regularly throng with a crowd that varies from well-heeled Muswell Hillites kitting out the kids to sportswear-clad B-boys. Indeed, diversity is the watchword here: it's estimated that over 200 languages are spoken in Haringey, with Caribbean, African, Asian, Chinese, Albanian, Greek, Irish and Turkish Cypriot ethnic groups all represented in the area. Property is a good deal more affordable than in the borough's swankier neighbourhoods – you might pick up a one-bed flat for around £250,000.

As the middle-classes increasingly colonise the quieter and more residential Bounds Green, a classic late-Victorian railway suburb of decent-sized semis with gardens, the Greek grocery shops and takeaways there are being joined by more individual options. Running east from Bowes Park rail station, Myddleton Road has the fine café the Step and well-thought-of Greek restaurant Vrisaki, as well as a Greek Orthodox icon seller, a tailor and the former *Mary Celeste* clothes shop George Moore, currently being revamped. Here too is a regular but not yet frequent market (www.myddletonroadmarket.co.uk), mostly comprising street-food stalls plus some plants and crafts. In the other direction from the tube, the Ranelagh is the pick of the pubs: good food, good beer and a good mix of punters.

Harringay N4, N8

Harringay (confusingly, spelled differently from the borough of Haringey in which it sits) might have its low points – the constant traffic jam along Green Lanes and its scuffy appearance for starters – but it has its highs too. With a mixed community that reflects Turkish, Kurdish, Italian, Greek and Polish nationalities, Green Lanes has an astonishingly cosmopolitan mix and its terraced sprawl is good for first-time buyers and renting.

The stretch of Green Lanes in Harringay is known for its Turkish and Middle Eastern food shops – try Turkish Food Market and Yasar Halim. Nearby, the unpromising-looking Andreas Michli & Son stocks brilliant Greek, Cypriot and Turkish specialities.

Only the oldest London cabbies will recall Harringay dog stadium – that area, close to Harringay Green Lanes Overground station, is now a retail park with a vast Sainsburys, Next, Homebase and other high street names.

However, for something more inspiring than the usual arterial-road scenery, Harringay does have a few gems worth seeking out. Harringay Market is a weekend community affair with stalls for doing your weekly shop and for grabbing a bite to eat (previously on Mattison Road, it's now on Portland Gardens). The vast Finsbury Park also has two long borders with Harringay's streets, and these days scrubs up rather well, with a new outdoor gym near Endymion Road gate, and the Furtherfield art gallery at the park's McKenzie Pavilion. On Green Lanes, the stately Salisbury Hotel pub offers a strong list of real ales, live jazz, a weekly quiz night and tasty roasts by the fireside.

A series of terraced Victorian streets runs horizontally between the two major

north–south roads (Green Lanes and Wightman Road) and is known to locals as 'the Ladder'. Many of the period houses have been split into two or more flats, with Falkland Road and Fairfax Road enjoying a little more variety than many of the other roads on the Ladder, thanks to the small Fairland Park. On Pemberton Road and Mattison Road, the old red brick buildings and playgrounds of South Harringay School and the bridges over the New River Canal break up the uniform terraced views. If you're lucky, at the right time of year you might even see swans nesting.

Wood Green's busy shops are a ten-minute walk away and there are good bus links to Camden. But the area's main transport links are Harringay Stadium station on the Overground network, Harringay station on the line into Moorgate and King's Cross, and Manor House tube station, which is on the Piccadilly Line. It's worth noting that Manor House is on the Zone 2/3 border, handy for saving a few quid on your weekly commute.

Tottenham N17

Tottenham has one of the highest unemployment rates in London, and Northumberland Park is officially one of the most deprived areas in the country. There are recognised problems with gang culture and illegal landlords exploiting immigrant families. But there is also an energy and a will to change that's making Tottenham an exciting place to be right now.

Following on from the riots of 2011 – the neighbourhood's most recent low – the town of Tottenham has seen drastic improvement and has come to be recognised as a hidden gem to live in for its easy and accessible routes to key parts of central London.

The preponderance of densely packed terraced housing (the best surviving examples are largely on the west side of the High Road, particularly in Church Road and Cemetery Road) has led to a surfeit of low-income residents, but money has been pumped into regeneration. New homes have been built, which has brought in more first-time buyers and young professionals. There are plans for a total of more than 10,000 new homes and 5,000 new jobs.

Recently completed Hale Village – a £400 million development opposite Tottenham Hale station built by Lee Valley Estates and the Newlon Housing Trust – includes more than 500 affordable homes, as well as private housing, a hotel, shopping and eating facilities,

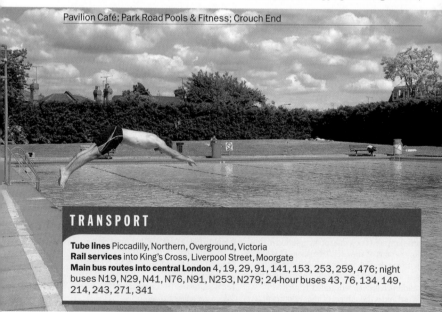

Pavilion Café; Park Road Pools & Fitness; Crouch End

TRANSPORT

Tube lines Piccadilly, Northern, Overground, Victoria
Rail services into King's Cross, Liverpool Street, Moorgate
Main bus routes into central London 4, 19, 29, 91, 141, 153, 253, 259, 476; night buses N19, N29, N41, N76, N91, N253, N279; 24-hour buses 43, 76, 134, 149, 214, 243, 271, 341

and an 'eco' park. There's also new student accommodation Unite next to the station.

The relentlessly straight High Road powers through the middle of Tottenham; it's what was once the Roman Ermine Street, starting as Kingsland Road back down in Hoxton and keeping on going right out of London. Today's glut of Spurs merchandise shops, phone shops, tawdry takeaways and uninviting pubs are dispiriting, but green shoots are visible, especially around Tottenham Green, where the baroque beauty of the old town hall has been brought back to life. In the old fire station, urban interventionists Create London are planning to open Chicken Town in September 2015, a healthy alternative to the ubiquitous fried chicken shops, and designed to provide local jobs and training while encouraging teenagers to eat better. Further north, on Stoneleigh Road, is CAMRA award-winning pub the Beehive, and out along West Green, steak and shisha joint the Banc.

The Seven Sisters area, or South Tottenham, is beginning to feel fairly gentrified (and, needless to say, some people are already calling it 'SoTo'). A strong Colombian and Peruvian community remains, often to be found in Pueblito Paisa Café feeding on the sublime empanadas.

And those light industrial estates don't just house metal merchants and sign companies any more – there's been an artisanal invasion: Wildes Cheese (you can buy direct from the dairy or find them at Alexandra Palace Farmers' Market); Redemption Brewery; Beavertown Brewery Tap Room; and Craving Coffee café and bar.

Improvements are also steadily underway for the mess that is Tottenham Hale Gyratory, turning the one-way car race into a two-way system, and expanding the bus station. The retail park has useful high-street stores including B&Q, JD Sports and Argos.

The thing that puts Tottenham on the map and makes the name recognisable to people around the world is, of course, the football club, a particular point of pride for locals. Spurs' trusty White Hart Lane stadium will be replaced by a much larger space-age stadium next door, due for completion in time for the start of the 2017/18 season. This comes with flats and shops, as well as 20,000 extra seats for fans. The rundown area around the stadium has been rebranded 'High Road West' and is the subject of redevelopment by Haringey Council.

Among the modern developments, the area retains its fair share of history: the 16th-century Bruce Castle manor house occupies the site of a castle once owned by Robert the Bruce (it now includes a small museum).

If Tottenham's gritty urbanity gets too much, face east. The estates and gyratory systems are bang up against the Lee Valley, East London's no-longer-hidden asset. This means open expanses of reservoir (look out for the Ferry Boat pub), Tottenham and Walthamstow marshes, Lee Valley Park, Markfield Park (with its beam engine museum) and riverside walks.

And don't forget: those straight roads and handy rail stations can whisk you up to Stansted Airport or down to Liverpool Street station in no time.

Eating

Banc 261 Green Road, N15 3BH (8888 8898, www.thebanc.co.uk).
Bar Esteban 29 Park Road, N8 8TE (8340 3090, www.baresteban.com).
Bistro Aix 54 Topsfield Parade, Tottenham Lane, N8 8PT (8340 6346, www.bistroaix.co.uk).
Chicken Town Tottenham Green, N15 (chicken-town.co.uk).
Chriskitch 7A Tetherdown, N10 1DN (8411 0051, www.chriskitch.com).
Craving Coffee The Mill Co Project, Gaunson House, Markfield Road, N15 4QQ (8808 3178, www.cravingcoffee.co.uk).
Dotori 3A Stroud Green Road, N4 2DQ (7263 3562).
Fasta Fortis Green Road, N10 3HN (8444 3003, www.fasta.co.uk).
Fatisa Pizzeria 292 High Road, Wood Green, N22 8JZ (8888 9008, www.fatisa.co.uk).
Feast 46 Fortis Green Road, N10 3HN (8444 4957, www.feastonthehill.co.uk).
Fink's Salt & Sweet 70 Mountgrove Road, N5 2LT (7684 7189, www.finks.co.uk).
Jai Krishna 161 Stroud Green Road, N4 3PZ (7272 1680).
Mosaica at the Factory Unit C005, The Chocolate Factory, Clarendon Road, N22 6XJ (8889 2400, www.mosaicarestaurant.com).
Osteria Tufo 67 Fonthill Road, N4 3HZ (7272 2911, www.osteriatufo.co.uk).
Pueblito Paisa Café 231 High Road, Seven Sisters, N15 5BT.
Step 101 Myddleton Road, N22 8NE (3302 2412, www.thestep.co.uk).
Toff's 38 Muswell Hill Broadway, N10 3RT (8883 8656, www.toffsfish.co.uk).
Vrisaki 73 Myddleton Road, N22 8LZ (8889 8760).

Drinking

Beavertown Brewery Tap Room Unit 17-18, Lockwood Industrial Park, Mill Mead Road, N17 9QP (8525 9884, www.beavertownbrewery.co.uk).
Beehive Stoneleigh Road, N17 9BQ (8808 3567, beehiven17.com).
Clissold Arms 105 Fortis Green, N2 9HR (8444 4244, www.clissoldarms.co.uk).
Earl Haig Hall 18 Elder Avenue, N8 9TH (8347 0545, www.earlhaighall.com).
Faltering Fullback 19 Perth Road, N4 3HB (7272 5834, www.thefullback.co.uk).
Ferry Boat Ferry Lane, N17 9NG (8808 4980, www.theferryboatlondon.co.uk).
Harringay Arms 153 Crouch Hill, N8 9QH (8292 3624, www.theharringayarms.com).
King's Head 2 Crouch End Hill, N8 8AA (8340 1028, www.thekingsheadcrouchend.co.uk).
Queens 26 Broadway Parade, N8 9DE (8340 2031, www.thequeenscrouchend.co.uk).
Ranelagh 82 Bounds Green Road, N11 2EU (8361 4382, www.theranelaghn11.co.uk).
Salisbury Hotel 1 Grand Parade, Green Lanes, N4 1JX (8800 9617).
Victoria Stakes 1 Muswell Hill, N10 3TH (8815 1793, www.victoriastakes.com).
World's End 21-23 Stroud Green Road, N4 3EF (7281 8679, www.capitalpubcompany.com).

Shopping

Alexandra Palace Farmers' Market Hornsey Gate Entrance, Alexandra Palace Way, N22 7AY (8365 2121, www.alexandrapalace.com, www.weareccfm.com).
Andreas Michli & Son 405-411 St Ann's Road, N15 3JL (8802 0188).
Arsenal Store Unit 6/9, Station Place, N4 2DH (7272 1000, www.arsenal.com).
Art for Art's Sake 203 Muswell Hill Broadway, N10 1DE (8442 0512).
Big Green Bookshop Unit 1, Brampton Park Road, N22 6BG (8881 6767, www.biggreenbookshop.com).
Cheeses of Muswell Hill 13 Fortis Green Road, N10 3HP (8444 9141).
Children's Bookshop 29 Fortis Green Road, N10 3HP (8444 5500, www.childrensbookshoplondon.com).
Crocodile Antiques 120 Muswell Hill Broadway, N10 3RU (8444 0273, www.crocodileantiques.com).
Eighty-Seven 87 Blackstock Road, N4 2DR (07751 906739).
Feast Deli 56 Fortis Green Road, N10 3HN (8444 0836, www.feastdeli.co.uk).
Harringay Market 11 Portland Gardens N4 1HU (07412 757335, www.marketmate.co.uk/markets/Harringay-Market).

Kate Kuba 71 Muswell Hill Broadway, N10 3HA (8444 1227, www.katekuba.co.uk).
Les Aldrich 98 Fortis Green Road, N10 3HN (8883 5631, www.lesaldrichmusic.co.uk).
Mall Shopping City 159 High Road, Wood Green, N22 6YQ (8888 6667, www.themall.co.uk).
Mint Velvet 172 Muswell Hill Broadway, N10 3SA (8883 8043, www.mintvelvet.co.uk).
Muswell Hill Bookshop 72 Fortis Green Road, N10 3HN (8444 7588, www.muswellhillbookshop.com).
Myddleton Road Market Bowes Park, N22 (www.myddletonroadmarket.co.uk).
North London Hospice 44 Fortis Green Road, N10 3HN (8444 8131, www.northlondonhospice.org).
Pickled Pepper Books 10 Middle Lane, N8 8PL (8632 0823).
Prohibition Wines 34 Fortis Green Road, N10 3HN (8444 4804, www.prohibitionwines.com).
Sargent & Co 75 Mountgrove Road, N5 2LT (7359 7642, www.sargentandco.com).
Soup Dragon 27 Topsfield Parade, Tottenham Lane, N8 8PT (8348 6931, www.soup-dragon.co.uk).
Spurs Megastore 1-3 Park Lane, N17 0JT (8365 5042, www.tottenhamhotspur.com).
Sylvanian Families 68 Mountgrove Road, N5 2LT (7226 1329, www.sylvanianstorekeepers.com).
Treehouse 7 Park Road, N8 8TE (8341 4326).
Turkish Food Market 385-387 Green Lanes, N4 1EU (8340 4547).
Whistles 175 Muswell Hill Broadway, N10 3RS (8883 1143, www.whistles.com).
White Stuff 188 Muswell Hill Broadway, N10 3SA (8842 0974, www.whitestuff.com).
Wildes Cheese (07758 755248, wildescheese.co.uk).
W Martyn 135 Muswell Hill Broadway, N10 3RS (8883 5642, www.wmartyn.co.uk).
Yasar Halim 493 Green Lanes, N4 1AL (8348 1074).

Things to do

Cinemas & theatres

Art House 159A Tottenham Lane, N8 9BT (8245 3099, www.arthousecrouchend.co.uk).
Cineworld Wood Green Wood Green Shopping City, The Mall, off Noel Park Road, N22 6LU (0871 200 2000, www.cineworld.co.uk).
Jacksons Lane 269A Archway Road, N6 5AA (8341 4421, www.jacksonslane.org.uk). Arts centre in a converted Edwardian church, offering activities and workshops.
Odeon Muswell Hill Fortis Green Road, N10 3HP (0871 224 4007, www.odeon.co.uk).
Park Theatre Clifton Terrace, N4 3JP (7780 6876, www.parktheatre.co.uk).
Vue Wood Green Hollywood Green, 180 High Road, Wood Green, N22 6EJ (0871 224 0240, www.myvue.com).

Galleries & museums

Bruce Castle Museum Lordship Lane, N17 6RT (8808 8772, www.haringey.gov.uk). Local history.
Furtherfield Gallery The McKenzie Pavilion, Finsbury Park, Endymion Road, N4 2NQ (8802 2827, www.furtherfield.org).
Markfield Beam Engine & Museum Markfield Park, Markfield Road, N15 4RB (01707 873628, www.mbeam.org).

Other attractions

Alexandra Palace Ice Rink Alexandra Palace Way, N22 7AY (8365 2121, www.alexandrapalace.com).
Castle Climbing Centre Green Lanes, N4 2HA (8211 7000, www.castle-climbing.co.uk).
Earl Haig Hall 18 Elder Avenue, N8 9TH (8347 0545, www.earlhaighall.com). Pub that also hosts various classes and events.
Rowans Tenpin Bowl 10 Stroud Green Road, N4 2DF (8800 1950, www.rowans.co.uk).
Segway Rally Alexandra Palace Way, N22 7AY (8365 2121, www.alexandrapalace.com).

Gigs, clubs & comedy

Alexandra Palace Alexandra Palace Way, N22 7AY (8365 2121, www.alexandrapalace.com).
Downstairs at the King's Head 2 Crouch End Hill, N8 8AA (8340 1028, www.downstairsatthe kingshead.com).
Silver Bullet 5 Station Place, N4 2DH (7619 3639, www.thesilverbullet.co.uk).

Green spaces

For more details, see www.haringey.gov.uk.
Alexandra Park Alexandra Palace Way, N22. Boating lake, pitch and putt, skatepark, café, garden centre and amazing views.
Bruce Castle Park Lordship Lane, N17. In the grounds of a Grade I-listed 16th-century manor house. Sports facilities, paddling pool.
Chestnuts Park St Ann's Road, N15. Basketball, tennis, playground, café and wildflower meadow.
Coldfall Wood Creighton Avenue, N10. Ancient woodland. Nature trail.
Finsbury Park Endymion Road, Seven Sisters Road and Green Lanes, N4. Grade II-listed. Sports facilities, skatepark, boating lake, café, playground.
Highgate Wood N10. Lies between Haringey, East Finchley and Highgate Village. Ancient woodland with a café and sports ground.
Lordship Recreation Ground Lordship Lane, N17. Adventure playground, BMX rack, sports pitches, lake, paddling pool, playground and skatepark. Eco-Hub and Shell Theatre.
Markfield Park Crowland Road, N15 4RB. Waterside park with play areas, beam engine museum and café.

Parkland Walk Local Nature Reserve Stretches from N4 to N10 following a disused railway line.
Priory Park Middle Lane, N8. Sport facilities, café, paddling pool and playground. Conservation area and heritage trail.
Queen's Wood Muswell Hill Road, N10. Nature reserve with ancient woodland. Café.
Railway Fields Green Lanes, opposite Haringey Green Lanes station, N4 1ES. Nature reserve.
Tottenham Marshes Watermead Way, N17 0XD (0845 677 0600, www.visitleevalley.org.uk). Wildlife area with canalside walking and cycle paths.

Gyms & leisure centres

Bodyworks Gym Unit 5, Fountayne House, Fountayne Road, N15 4QJ (8808 6580, www.bodyworksgym.co.uk). Private.
Broadwater Farm Community Centre Adams Road, N17 6HE (8801 4115, www.fusion-lifestyle.com).
easyGym The Mall, Wood Green Shopping Centre, 98-100 High Street, N22 6YG (www.easygym.co.uk). Private.
Factory Gym & Dance Centre 407-409 Hornsey Road, N19 4DX (7272 1122, www.factorylondon.com). Private.
Finsbury Park Sports Facility Hornsey Gate, Endymion Road, N4 0XX (8802 9139, www.finsburyparksportspartnership.org.uk).
Gym London Lebus Street, N17 9FD (0844 384 3282, www.thegymgroup.com). Private.
Laboratory Spa & Health Club The Avenue, N10 2QE (8482 3000, www.labspa.co.uk). Private.
North London YMCA 184 Tottenham Lane, N8 8SG (8340 6088, www.ymcahornsey.org.uk). Private.
Park Road Pools & Fitness Park Road, N8 8JN (8341 3567, www.haringey.gov.uk).
Selby Centre Selby Road, N17 8JL (8885 5499, www.selbytrust.co.uk). Private.
Tottenham Green Pools & Fitness 1 Philip Lane, N15 4JA (8885 7300, www.fusion-lifestyle.com).
White Hart Lane Community Sports Centre (New River Sport & Fitness) White Hart Lane, N22 5QW (8881 2323, www.haringey.gov.uk).
Zone Gym Cypress House, 2 Coburg Road, N22 6UJ (8881 8222, www.zonegym.co.uk). Private.

Outdoor pursuits

Crouch End Cricket Club Shepherd's Cot Playing Fields, Park Road, N8 8JJ (07834 169188, www.crouchendcricket.com).
Highgate Golf Course Denewood Road, N6 4AH (8340 1906, www.highgategc.co.uk).
Muswell Hill Golf Club Rhodes Avenue, N22 7UT (8888 1764, www.muswellhillgolfclub.co.uk).
Stoke Newington West Reservoir Centre Green Lanes, N4 2HA (8442 8116, www.better.org.uk).

Spectator sports

Tottenham Hotspur FC Bill Nicholson Way, 748 High Road, Tottenham, N17 0AP (0344 499 5000, ticket office 0344 844 0102, www. tottenhamhotspur.com).

Schools

Primary

There are 54 state primary schools in Haringey, 17 of which are church schools. There are also ten independent primaries, including one Muslim school, one Montessori school and one Steiner school. See www.haringey.gov.uk, www.education. gov.uk/edubase and www.ofsted.gov.uk for more information.

Secondary

Alexandra Park School Bidwell Gardens, N11 2AZ (8826 4880, www.apsch.org.uk).
Channing School for Girls The Bank, N6 5HF (8340 2328, www.channing.co.uk). Girls only; private.
Fortismere School (8365 4400, www.fortismere. haringey.sch.uk); North Wing, Creighton Avenue, N10 1NS; South Wing, Tetherdown, N10 1NE.
Gladesmore Community School Crowland Road, N15 6EB (8800 0884, www.gladesmore.com).
Greig City Academy High Street, Hornsey, N8 7NU (8609 0100, www.greigcityacademy.co.uk). Church of England.
Heartlands High School Station Road, N22 7ST (8826 1230, www.heartlands.haringey.sch.uk).
Highgate School North Road, N6 4AY (8340 1524, www.highgateschool.org.uk). Private.
Highgate Wood School Montenotte Road, N8 8RN (8342 7970, www.hws-haringey.sch.uk).
Hornsey School for Girls Inderwick Road, N8 9JF (8348 6191, www.hsg.haringey.sch.uk). Girls only.
Northumberland Park Community School Trulock Road, N17 0PG (8801 0091, www. northumberlandpark.haringey.sch.uk).
Park View West Green Road, N15 3QR (8888 1722, www.parkview.haringey.sch.uk).
St Thomas More Catholic School Glendale Avenue, N22 5HN (8888 7122, www.stthomas moreschool.org.uk). Roman Catholic.
Woodside High School White Hart Lane, N22 5QJ (8889 6761, www.woodsidehighschool.co.uk).

Property

Local estate agents

Anthony Pepe http://anthonypepe.com
Barbara Gibson Properties www.bgibson.co.uk
Black Katz www.blackkatz.com

CJ Delemere www.cjdelemere.com
Davies & Davies www.daviesdavies.co.uk
Hobarts http://hobarts.co.uk
Liberty www.libertyestateagents.com
Tatlers www.tatlers.co.uk
Thomas & Co http://thomasproperty.net
Wilkinson Byrne www.wilkinsonbyrne.co.uk
WJ Meade www.wjmeade.co.uk

Local knowledge

www.crouchendradio.co.uk
www.hamhighbroadway.co.uk
www.haringeyindependent.co.uk
www.harringayonline.com
www.thecrouchendproject.co.uk
www.tottenhamjournal.co.uk
www.tottenham-today.co.uk

USEFUL INFO

Borough size
2,960 hectares

Population
271,000

Ethnic mix
White 66.3%
Black or Black British 15.9%
Asian or Asian British 9.6%
Mixed 4.4%
Chinese or other 3.8%

London Borough of Haringey
Civic Centre, High Road, Wood Green, N22 8LE (8489 0000, www.haringey.gov.uk)

Council run by
Labour

MPs
Hornsey & Wood Green, Catherine West (Labour); Tottenham, David Lammy (Labour)

Main recycling centres
Park View Road Reuse & Recycling Centre, Park View Road, N17 9AY; Western Road Reuse & Recycling Centre, Western Road, N22 6UG

Council tax
£986.23 to £2,958.65

Islington

People living in Islington enjoy the best of both worlds. The borough's inner-city location means proximity to the capital's financial district, but it's also a desirable place for families seeking a taste of small-town life.

AVERAGE PROPERTY PRICE		AVERAGE RENTAL PRICE PER WEEK	
Detached £1,653,411	**Terraced** £1,040,043	**Studio** £227	**2 bed** £440
Semi-detached £1,092,497	**Flat** £575,676	**1 bed** £325	**3 bed** £575
			4+ bed £700

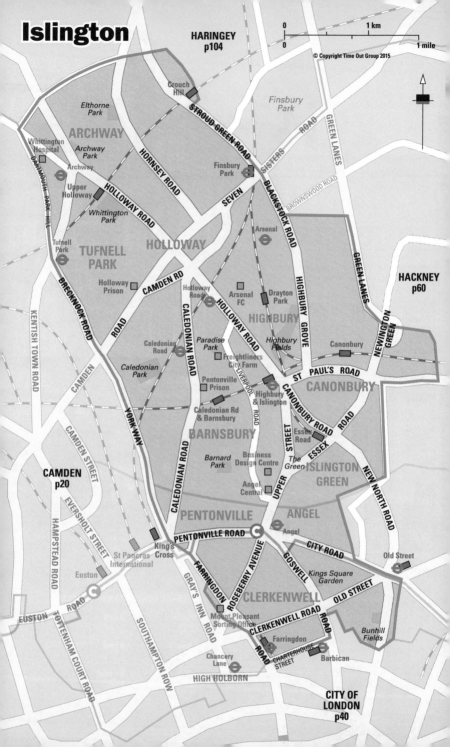

Islington

0   1 km
0   1 mile

© Copyright Time Out Group 2015

Crouch Hill

Elthorne Park

STROUD GREEN ROAD

Finsbury Park

ARCHWAY

Whittington Hospital

Archway Park

Archway

Upper Holloway

HORNSEY ROAD

HOLLOWAY ROAD

Finsbury Park

SEVEN SISTERS ROAD

BLACKSTOCK ROAD

GREEN LANES

BROWNSWOOD ROAD

Whittington Park

DARTMOUTH PARK HILL

Tufnell Park

TUFNELL PARK

HOLLOWAY

Arsenal

BRECKNOCK ROAD

Holloway Prison

CAMDEN RD

Holloway Road

Arsenal FC

Drayton Park

HIGHBURY

HIGHBURY GROVE

GREEN LANES

NEWINGTON GREEN

KENTISH TOWN ROAD

ROAD

CALEDONIAN ROAD

HOLLOWAY ROAD

Caledonian Road

Paradise Park

Highbury Fields

Canonbury

CAMDEN

Caledonian Park

Freightliners City Farm

LIVERPOOL ROAD

Highbury & Islington

St PAUL'S ROAD

CANONBURY

CANONBURY ROAD

ESSEX ROAD

YORK WAY

Pentonville Prison

Caledonian Rd & Barnsbury

BARNSBURY

Barnard Park

Business Design Centre

Essex Road

The Green

UPPER STREET

ISLINGTON GREEN

NEW NORTH ROAD

CAMDEN STREET

HAMPSTEAD ROAD

EVERSHOLT STREET

Angel Central

PENTONVILLE

ANGEL

Euston

St Pancras International

King's Cross

PENTONVILLE ROAD

Angel

CITY ROAD

Old Street

ROSEBERY AVENUE

GOSWELL ROAD

Kings Square Garden

OLD STREET

EUSTON ROAD

TOTTENHAM COURT ROAD

SOUTHAMPTON ROW

FARRINGDON ROAD

GRAY'S INN ROAD

Mount Pleasant Sorting Office

CLERKENWELL

CLERKENWELL ROAD

Farringdon

CHARTERHOUSE STREET

Barbican

Bunhill Fields

Chancery Lane

HIGH HOLBORN

Neighbourhoods

Angel and Pentonville N1

With a deceptively pretty name for a crowded bustle of streets, Angel spans the interchange of Upper Street, Pentonville Road and St John Street. On one side is the unobtrusive – but consistently busy – Angel tube station. On the other is a not-unpleasant but fairly dreary collection of banks, pubs, supermarkets and Angel Central (formerly the N1 Centre). This is a small shopping centre with well-known high-street names and one of the area's two cinemas; the other, the Everyman Screen on the Green, further along Upper Street, shows more independent films and is a real looker when lit up at night. Other classy entertainment options further along Upper Street are the King's Head pub-theatre and much-loved music venue the Union Chapel.

The work and shopping crowds don't particularly make for a peaceful walk down the Angel end of Upper Street. It's equally hard to negotiate at night – the area has become entrenched as a night-out destination, with all that entails (chain pubs and soulless bars; rowdy passers-by and a pavement decorated in shattered glass and vomit).

There are, however, some stand-out bars and pubs scattered around the Angel area – organic specialist the Duke of Cambridge has teamed up with veg-box provider Riverford to present a uniquely ethical menu; the Drapers Arms is an elegant gastropub with a seasonal menu. When it comes to bars, 69 Colebrooke Row is the place to go for top-notch cocktails, although its tiny size and huge popularity mean the place fills up quickly. The Four Sisters and the Library are also worthy contenders.

There's plenty of choice when it comes to cafés and restaurants too. Close to Angel station, a clutch of Mexican food bars have sprung up, including burrito whizzes Chilango. In the vicinity, Sasa Sushi, the Afghan Kitchen, quiet Thai restaurant Isarn and classy Turkish venue Pasha provide a quick snapshot of the area's culinary diversity. The Islington branch of Ottolenghi has a café tucked behind an enticing window display of takeaway goodies.

Upper Street has a number of designer homewares and fashion outlets, including trendy clothes store Diverse and midcentury modern furniture shop TwentyTwentyOne. Cross Street, which links Upper Street and Essex Road, has Coexistence (lighting), Farrow & Ball, Aesop (beauty products), Scandi women's boutique Wild Swans and Dinny Hall (jewellery).

Running parallel to Upper Street, Islington High Street (which turns into Essex Road) is a more relaxed version of its neighbour. Off this is pedestrianised Camden Passage. An attractive strip, once lined with antiques shops, it's now home to independent shops and a few nice cafés; the CoffeeWorks Project is a good pick, as is Kipferl for Austrian coffee and food. Contemporary fashion outlet Workshop and the African Waistcoat Company are worth a look, as is gourmet chocolatier, Paul A Young. The higgledy-piggledy Pierrepont Arcade still sells antiques, and there are periodic antiques, book and vintage clothes markets here.

Just behind Angel Central, Chapel Market is a crowded cacophony of stalls, cheap food spots, and shops ranging from tatty to useful; it's also home to the Islington

The regular DWS designer warehouse sample sales off Seven Sisters Road have kept the sartorially savvy well dressed for decades.

Farmers' Market on Sundays. Alpino is an inexpensive and unpretentious Italian snack bar that serves generous portions of pasta alongside full English breakfasts. There's also a selection of pubs open late at the far end of the street, including the Joker of Penton Street.

Leading away from Angel in the King's Cross direction, Pentonville Road is a dull stretch. The hard edges are softened by a Georgian terrace and the Crafts Council headquarters at the Angel end, but essentially it's a traffic-laden thoroughfare with purpose-built student accommodation and a few tower blocks towards King's Cross.

Islington Green and Canonbury N1

Islington Green is a residential area just behind Angel. In parts it's beautiful and leafy, in others it's hard-bitten and neglected – in short, a prime example of the borough's dual personality.

Essex Road forms the boundary between Islington Green to the east and Canonbury to the west. It has a decent mix of useful everyday stores and some excellent food shops – wholefoods chain Planet Organic, Steve Hatt fishmongers and James Elliot butchers – interspersed with quirky gems such as Get Stuffed taxidermists, ramshackle vintage store Past Caring and the Polish Pottery Shop. Eating options include Italian restaurant the Food Lab and delightful haberdashery Ray-Stitch, which doubles as a small café.

Canonbury itself is noticeably quiet and moneyed. In the roads around smart Canonbury Square, terraced houses sell for millions (particularly the Georgian ones). Eating options include the open-plan pub and kitchen the Snooty Fox – complete with leather sofas and 1960s-style jukebox, renovated Victorian pub the Cellars and relaxed Nordic-chic venue 3Course (simple Scandinavian food and great open sandwiches).

Highbury N5

Highbury has developed into a trendy high-end shopping, eating and living zone – though still dominated by Highbury Fields, Islington's largest green space.

Just near Highbury Fields, gathered closely together in a cluster of foodie goodness, are tiny cheesemonger/deli La Fromagerie, Meek & Wild Fishmongers, and restaurants and cafés such as Dear Pizza and Turkish eaterie İznik. Further up Blackstock Road, Cremeria Vienna doles out Italian ice-cream.

Though Arsenal Stadium is gone – redeveloped into Highbury Square and surrounding flats – the Arsenal Museum at the club's Emirates Stadium stands as testament to the area's football loyalties.

At the eastern end of Highbury is Newington Green, a more mixed area than ever-smarter Highbury, and home to the cornucopia that is Newington Green Fruit & Vegetables. There are lots of cheap and cheerful eating options here: tapas at boho Trangallán, the vegetarian/vegan Acoustic Café, contemporary Indian Cinnamon Lounge and the kid-friendly That Place on the Corner; Paradise Fish Bar gets a good rep for fish and chips. Dissenting Academy is a refurbished pub with entertainment most nights.

Barnsbury N1

A residential refuge tucked to the north-west of Angel, Barnsbury is served by Liverpool Road, running parallel to Upper Street and

Everyman Screen on the Green, Upper Street

the glass-fronted Business Design Centre, all the way up to Holloway Road. Packed with Edwardian terraces, it's generally much quieter than Upper Street – lacking the buzz as well as the sleaze – but can be noisy due to the regular presence of police cars using it as a short cut to trouble in Angel and beyond. The roads connecting the two parallel thoroughfares make for some of Islington's choicest residences – fairly quiet, with easy access to amenities. Almeida Street is particularly appealing, home to both a classy theatre and a smart French restaurant of the same name.

Caledonian Road is scruffier, with strong working-class associations, but has good travel options, including both Piccadilly line and rail stations, making it a popular spot for lower-end renters and buyers. Many properties on the 'Cally Road' itself are above the likes of bookies and kebab shops; elsewhere, expect to find mostly ex-local authority conversions. At its southern end, however, Caledonian Road has experienced a knock-on effect from the huge regeneration of King's Cross. The other principal residents of note are those serving at Her Majesty's pleasure in Pentonville prison.

Archway N19 and Holloway N7

Nobody goes to Holloway for the sake of their Instagram feed but, despite the fact that its high street is essentially a dual carriageway, the place has some charm. A huge Odeon cinema and London Metropolitan University lend the place some character (notably in the case of the Daniel Libeskind Graduate Centre), and the various Zone 2 staples are all present and correct (pound shops, fried-chicken outlets, caffs and an Argos). It's gritty without being scary, and shopping in the Nags Head Market for veg and kitchen utensils on a Saturday morning will give you a taste of the eclectic nature of the area.

Many of Holloway's drinking holes are too busy catering to the Emirates Stadium's hordes to be noteworthy, but cosy local the Swimmer at the Grafton Arms is a very comfortable place to while away the hours, and (towards Highbury) the Horatia and the Lamb are both welcoming and well stocked.

You've not had a night out in Holloway, however, without ending up in the Big Red, a lively rock bar with pool tables, low lighting and a late licence. Holloway Road pie emporium Piebury Corner started out as a couple of entrepreneurs selling gourmet pies from their front garden to passing football

Morito, Exmouth Market

fans on match days – a tradition it continues to honour in its stall at the corner of Gillespie and Avenell roads.

Gentrification is creeping in at the Islington end – witness cafés such as EZ & Moss, Le Péché Mignon and Vagabond N7, all of which serve great coffee and food.

Though well-served for the more practical things in life thanks to an enormous Morrisons and a Waitrose, Holloway is not a great day out for window-shoppers. The odd bargain has been known to out itself from the piles of tat sold on weekend mornings at the Grafton School Market, and junk shop Ooh-La-La is a great place to rummage for vintage furniture and random surprises, but for gifts, clothing or homewares, your best bet is N7's own department store, Selbys.

Scruffy Archway is seeing various improvements. Though unlovely around its Northern line station and throbbing traffic hub – not to mention the rather ugly Archway Tower – the area is being slowly dragged from the mire. Proximity to both classy, suburban Highgate and buzzy, urban Islington makes it an increasingly alluring proposition for buyers and renters; council discussion regarding major redevelopment of the area seems endless.

Gastropubs the Landseer and St John's Tavern are decent places to dine, while the Spoke provides good breakfasts and burgers.

Tufnell Park N19

Tufnell Park is the well-heeled corner of Holloway. It used to be the sort of place that attracted actors, print journalists and writers, but its desirability and prices means newcomers are more likely to be City workers, lawyers or TV stars.

Part of its attraction is the acreage of handsome Victorian houses – the larger ones long converted into flats. And although the borough of Islington has few sizeable green spaces, Tufnell Park is walking distance from Hampstead Heath and Highgate Cemetery.

At Tufnell Park Northern line station, where several roads meet, there has been an explosion of chichi shops and top-notch local restaurants, with the effect extending along Fortess Road, Junction Road and Brecknock Road. Shops include fishmonger Jonathan Norris, butcher Meat N5, and interiors and homewares shop Future and Found. Restaurants run from Shoe Shop, where Australian chef Paul Merrony cooks up a storm, to tapas venue Del Par, the Ethiopian

Lalibela, family friendly café Bear + Wolf, and exotic ice-cream parlour Ruby Violet.

The area's pubs – the Junction Tavern and Lord Palmerston – have a gastro edge, but there's still a good number of music venues left from Tufnell Park's more bohemian days, including Aces & Eights, Boston Music Room and the Dome.

Clerkenwell and Farringdon EC1

South from Angel towards the City lies the mystery province of Finsbury, near Rosebery Avenue, an area designation that's been all but abandoned. It occasionally crops up on maps and in the names of public buildings,

In need of an exotic ingredient for an Ottolenghi recipe? Excellent Turkish shop Korkmaz Food Centre will sort you out.

causing confusion with Finsbury Park some way to the north. Some locals refer to it as Clerkenwell, a few as Mount Pleasant – after the large Royal Mail sorting office, itself named after an old rubbish dump – while most stick to the safer Islington.

Regardless, it's a lively, attractive area – kept young thanks to City University and its various sites around Northampton Square, and kept classy thanks to world-renowned dance theatre Sadler's Wells. There's a wide range of housing stock: the modernist Spa Green estate, warehouse conversions, new-build apartments, the 19th-century model dwellings of the Peabody estate, and Georgian and Victorian terraces.

In Exmouth Market, the area also has one of Islington's gems: a thriving pedestrianised strip that boasts great bars, restaurants, shops and food stalls. The embarrassment of riches includes modish global food at Caravan, Japanese option Nécco, seafood at Bonnie Gull, table-football bar Café Kick and destination diner Moro. The last offers Spanish-North African crossover dishes and has spawned Morito tapas and meze bar next door. For great coffee (and bagels) head to Brill. Nearby gastropubs include London's original gastropub, the Eagle (opened in 1991). Also worth a look are the Easton, the Exmouth Arms and the

Wilmington. Just round the corner is the historic Quality Chop House (now an excellent Modern European restaurant).

Shopping highlights include Family Tree with its idiosyncratic gifts and clothes, modern jeweller EC One, Bagman & Robin vending characterful, colourful bags of all sizes and Sweet with its bread and pâtisserie.

To the south lies Clerkenwell proper, bordered by the rather blank Farringdon Road to the west and Smithfield meat market to the south. The area was once home to craftsmen, especially watchmakers, and there's still a fantastically old-school bookbinder, but it's now London's design district with showrooms for high-end furniture-makers such as Cappellini, Domus, Knoll and Vitra, and an annual design festival for professionals (www.clerkenwelldesignweek.com).

There are several galleries tucked away down Great Sutton Street – they've followed the architects who pioneered Clerkenwell's gentrification in the 1990s. Zaha Hadid, who has her practice in a former school building near Exmouth Market, has also opened a gallery here. You can find the architecture crowd drinking and networking at the Slaughtered Lamb, or getting their punctures mended at bike shop-cum-café Look Mum No Hands!

The area north of Old Street is a bit of a hinterland between the bustling areas of Clerkenwell and Shoreditch, and the buttoned-up City. The large number of tech companies in the vicinity of Old Street roundabout has given rise to the nickname Silicon Roundabout, though even they are in danger of being priced out of the neighbourhood. The roundabout itself lacks aesthetic merit, but Moorfields Eye Hospital on City Road and Hawksmoor's St Luke's Church on Old Street are gems.

Clerkenwell Green is an attractive focal point; good-natured pub crowds spill out on to the expansive pavements during the summer. Round the corner in a narrow side street is the Jerusalem Tavern, run by organic brewery St Peter's. St John's Square outside the Zetter Townhouse and Zetter hotel has become a relaxed public space, with tables from the Modern Pantry restaurant spilling outdoors on warm days. Craft Central on the square is where to browse and buy craft and design.

St John Street is another restaurant hotspot – pioneered by chef Fergus Henderson with his British venue St John. Given the influence

of architects in this part of London, it's no surprise that he trained as one too. Joining him along the road these days are Portal (high-end Portuguese), Vinoteca (new-wave foodie wine bar), Foxlow (ribs) and Kurz & Lang (wurst).

Farringdon station is part of the Crossrail network, and the already vastly improved Thameslink/tube station serves thousands of commuters, as do a clutch of sandwich bars and convenience stores around the transport hub.

The big warehouse spaces around Smithfield meat market have allowed a strong nightlife scene to flourish. This means a non-stop flow of people at weekends – hence the likes of late-night diner Tinseltown, one of the few places in London to serve through to the wee small hours. Clubbers also benefit from the early-opening pubs and cafés catering for market traders.

Eating

3Course 412 Essex Road, N1 3PJ (7998 8651, www.3course.co.uk).
Acoustic Café 60 Newington Green, N16 9PX (7288 1235).
Afghan Kitchen 35 Islington Green, N1 8DU (7359 8019).
Almeida 30 Almeida Street, N1 1AD (7354 4777, www.almeida-restaurant.co.uk).
Alpino 97 Chapel Market, N1 9EY (7837 8330).
Bear + Wolf Café 153 Fortess Road, NW5 2HR (3601 1900, www.bearandwolfcafe.com).
Bonnie Gull Seafood Bar 50-57 Exmouth Market, EC1R 4QL (3122 0047, www.bonniegull seafoodbar.com).
Brill 27 Exmouth Market, EC1R 4QL (7833 9757).
Caravan 11-13 Exmouth Market, EC1R 4QQ (7833 8115, www.caravanonexmouth.co.uk).
Chilango 27 Upper Street, N1 0PN (7704 2123, chilango.co.uk).
Cinnamon Lounge 20 Newington Green, N16 9PU (7241 2222, www.cinnamon-lounge.biz).
CoffeeWorks Project 96-98 Islington High Street, N1 8EG (7424 5020, www.coffeeworks project.com).
Cremeria Vienna 145 Blackstock Road, N4 2JS (07427 617229).
Dear Pizza 35 Highbury Park, N5 2AA (7354 9309).
Eagle 159 Farringdon Road, EC1R 3AL (7837 1353, www.theeaglefarringdon.co.uk).
Easton 22 Easton Street, off Rosebery Avenue, WC1X 0DS (7278 7608, www.theeastonpub.co.uk).

EZ & Moss 183 Holloway Road, N7 8LX (7619 9523).

Food Lab 56 Essex Road, N1 8LR (7226 1001, www.foodlablondon.com).

Foxlow 69-73 St John Street, EC1M 4AN (7014 8070, www.foxlow.co.uk).

Isarn 119 Upper Street, N1 1QP (7424 5153, www.isarn.co.uk).

Íznik 19 Highbury Park, N5 1QJ (7704 8099, www.iznik.co.uk).

Kipferl 20 Camden Passage, N1 8ED (7704 1555, www.kipferl.co.uk).

Kurz & Lang 1 St John Street, EC1M 4AA (7992 2923, www.kurzandlang.com).

Lalibela 137 Fortess Road, NW5 2HR (7284 0600, www.lalibelarestaurant.co.uk).

Modern Pantry 47-48 St John's Square, EC1V 4JJ (7553 9210, www.themodernpantry.co.uk).

Morito 32 Exmouth Market, EC1R 4QE (7278 7007, www.morito.co.uk).

Moro 34-36 Exmouth Market, EC1R 4QE (7833 8336, www.moro.co.uk).

Nécco 52-54 Exmouth Market, EC1R 4QE (7713 8575, www.necco.co.uk).

Ottolenghi 287 Upper Street, N1 2TZ (7288 1454, www.ottolenghi.co.uk).

Paradise Fish Bar 141 Newington Green Road, N1 4RA (7354 3669).

Pasha 301 Upper Street, N1 2TU (7226 1454, www.pashaislington.co.uk).

Le Péché Mignon 6 Ronalds Road, N5 1HX (7607 1826, www.lepechemignon.co.uk).

Piebury Corner 209-211 Highbury Corner, N7 8DL (7700 5441, www.pieburycorner.com).

Quality Chop House 88-94 Farringdon Road, EC1R 3EA (7278 1458, www.thequalitychop house.com).

Ruby Violet 118 Fortess Road, NW5 2HL (7609 0444, www.rubyviolet.co.uk).

St John 26 St John Street, EC1M 4AY (7251 0848, www.stjohnrestaurant.com).

Sasa Sushi 422 St John Street, EC1V 4NJ (7837 1155, www.sasasushi.co.uk).

Shoe Shop 122A Fortess Road, NW5 2HL (7267 8444, www.shoeshoplondon.com).

Spoke 710 Holloway Road, N19 3NH (7263 4445, www.thespokelondon.com).

That Place on the Corner 1-3 Green Lanes, N16 9BS (7704 0079, www.thatplaceonthecorner.co.uk).

Tinseltown 44-46 St John Street, EC1M 4DF (7689 2424, www.tinseltown.co.uk).

Trangallán 61 Newington Green, N16 9PX (7359 4988, www.trangallan.com).

Vagabond N7 105 Holloway Road, N7 8LT (www.vagabond.london).

Vinoteca 7 St John Street, EC1M 4AA (7253 8786, www.vinoteca.co.uk).

Drinking

69 Colebrooke Row 69 Colebrook Row, N1 8AA (07540 528593, www.69colebrookerow.com).

Aces & Eights 156-158 Fortess Road, NW5 2HP (7485 4033, www.acesandeightssaloonbar.com).

Big Red 385 Holloway Road, N7 0RY (7609 6662).

Café Kick 43 Exmouth Market, EC1R 4QL (7837 8077, www.cafekick.co.uk).

Cellars 125 Newington Green Road, N1 4RA (7684 2447, www.thecellarsnewingtongreen.com).

Dissenting Academy 92 Mildmay Park, N1 4PR (7249 6430).

Drapers Arms 44 Barnsbury Street, N1 1ER (7619 0348, www.thedrapersarms.com).

Duke of Cambridge 30 St Peter's Street, N1 8JT (7359 3066, www.dukeorganic.co.uk).

Four Sisters 25 Canonbury Lane, N1 2AS (7226 0955, www.thefoursistersbar.co.uk).

Horatia 98-100 Holloway Road, N7 8JE (7682 4857, www.thehoratia.co.uk).

Jerusalem Tavern 55 Britton Street, EC1M 5UQ (7490 4281, www.stpetersbrewery.co.uk).

Joker of Penton Street 58 Penton Street, N1 9PZ (7837 3891, www.joker.pub).

Junction Tavern 101 Fortess Road, NW5 1AG (7485 9400, www.junctiontavern.co.uk).

Lamb 54 Holloway Road, N7 8JL (7619 9187, www.thelambn7.co.uk).

Landseer 37 Landseer Road, N19 4JU (7263 4658).

Library 235 Upper Street, N1 1RU (7704 6977).

Lord Palmerston 33 Dartmouth Park Hill, NW5 1HU (7584 1578).

St John's Tavern 91 Junction Road, N19 5QU (7272 1587, www.stjohnstavern.com).

Slaughtered Lamb 34-35 Great Sutton Street, EC1V 0DX (7253 1516, www.theslaughtered lambpub.com).

Snooty Fox 75 Grosvenor Avenue, N5 2NN (7354 9532, www.snootyfoxlondon.co.uk).

Swimmer at the Grafton Arms 13 Eburne Road, N7 6AR (7281 4632).

Wilmington 69 Rosebery Avenue, EC1R 4RL (7837 1384, www.metropolitanpubcompany.com).

Zetter Townhouse 49-50 St John's Square, EC1V 4JJ (7324 4444, www.thezettertownhouse.com).

Shopping

Aesop 56 Cross Street, N1 2BA (7148 0349, www.aesop.com/uk).

African Waistcoat Company 33 Islington Green, N1 8DU (7704 9698, www.africanwaistcoat company.com).

Angel Central 21 Parkfield Street, N1 0PS (7359 2674, www.angelcentral.co.uk).

Bagman & Robin 47 Exmouth Market, EC1R 4QL (7833 8780, www.bagmanandrobin.com).

Chapel Market N1 9EX (www.islington.gov.uk).

Coexistence 288 Upper Street, N1 2TZ (7354 8817, www.coexistence.co.uk).

Craft Central 33-35 St John's Square, EC1M 4DS (7251 0276, www.craftcentral.org.uk).

Designer Warehouse Sales 5/6 Islington Studios, Thane Villas, N7 7NU (7697 9888, www.designerwarehousesales.com). At time of writing, an autumn 2015 relaunch was planned.

Dinny Hall 292 Upper Street, N1 2TU (7704 1543, www.dinnyhall.com).

Diverse 294 Upper Street, N1 2TU (7359 8877, www.diverseclothing.com).

EC One 41 Exmouth Market, EC1R 4QL (7713 6185, www.econe.co.uk).

Euphorium Bakery (www.euphoriumbakery. com); 79 Upper Street, N1 0NU (7288 8788); 202 Upper Street, N1 1RQ (7704 6905); 26A Chapel Market, N1 9EN (7837 7010).

Family Tree 53 Exmouth Market, EC1R 4QL (7278 1084, www.familytreeshop.co.uk).

Farrow & Ball 38 Cross Street, N1 2BG (7226 2627, www.farrow-ball.com).

La Fromagerie 30 Highbury Park, N5 2AA (7359 7440, www.lafromagerie.co.uk).

Future & Found 225A Brecknock Road, N19 5AA (7267 4772, www.futureandfound.com).

Get Stuffed 105 Essex Road, N1 2SL (7226 1364, www.thegetstuffed.co.uk).

Grafton School Market Bowman's Place, off Holloway Road, N7 (01992 717198, www. makinginroads.org).

Islington Farmers' Market Chapel Market, between Penton Street and Baron Street, N1 9PZ (7833 0338, www.lfm.org.uk).

James Elliot 96 Essex Road, N1 8LU (7226 3658, www.jameselliottbutchers.co.uk).

Knoll 91 Goswell Road, EC1V 7EX (7236 6655, www.knoll-int.com).

Korkmaz Food Centre 363-365 Holloway Road, N7 0RN (7700 1608).

Look Mum No Hands! 49 Old Street, EC1V 9HX (7490 3928, www.lookmumnohands.com).

Meat 147 Fortess Road, NW5 2HR (7267 2591, www.meatlondon.co.uk).

Meek & Wild Fishmongers 13 Highbury Park, N5 1QJ (7226 3331).

Newington Green Fruit & Vegetables 109 Newington Green Road, N1 4QY (7354 0990).

Ooh-La-La 147 Holloway Road, N7 8LX (7609 0455).

Past Caring 54 Essex Road, N1 8LR.

Paul A Young Fine Chocolates 33 Camden Passage, N1 8EA (7424 5750, www.paula young.co.uk).

Pierrepont Arcade Market Camden Passage, N1 8EG (www.camdenpassageislington.co.uk).

Polish Pottery Shop 65 Essex Road, N1 2SF (7704 2800, www.polishpotteryshop.co.uk).

Ray-Stitch 99 Essex Road, N1 2SJ (7704 1060).

Selbys 384-400 Holloway Road, N7 6PR (7607 2466, www.james-selby.co.uk).

Steve Hatt 88-90 Essex Road, N1 8LU (7226 3963).

Sweet 64A Exmouth Market, EC1R 4QP (7713 6777, www.sweetdesserts.co.uk).

TwentyTwentyOne 274-275 Upper Street, N1 2UA (7288 1996, www.twentytwentyone.com).

Vitra 30 Clerkenwell Road, EC1M 5PG (7608 6200, www.vitra.com).

Wild Swans 54 Cross Street, N1 2BA (7354 8681, www.wild-swans.com).

Workshop 19 Camden Passage, N1 8EA (7226 3141, www.camdenpassageislington.co.uk).

HIGHS & LOWS

Artisanal food shops

Great restaurants

Close to the City

Cycle routes

The A1 and Archway roundabout

Lack of large green spaces

Rowdy pubs in Angel

Drapers Arms, Angel

Things to do

Cinemas & theatres

Almeida Theatre Almeida Street, N1 1TA (7359 4404, www.almeida.co.uk). Award-winning theatre.

Everyman Screen on the Green 83 Upper Street, N1 0NP (0871 906 9060, www.everyman cinema.com).

King's Head 115 Upper Street, N1 1QN (7478 0160, www.kingsheadtheatre.org). A pioneer of the pub-theatre scene.

Little Angel Theatre 14 Dagmar Passage, off Cross Street, N1 2DN (7226 1787, www. littleangeltheatre.com). This acclaimed puppet theatre celebrated its 50th birthday in 2011.

Odeon Holloway 419-427 Holloway Road, N7 6LJ (0871 224 4007, www.odeon.co.uk).

Pleasance London Carpenters Mews, North Road, N7 9EF (7609 1800, www.pleasance.co.uk). Sister venue to the Edinburgh Pleasance.

Rosemary Branch 2 Shepperton Road, N1 3DT (7704 6665, www.rosemarybranch.co.uk). Friendly, eccentrically decorated freehouse with a 60-seat theatre upstairs.

Sadler's Wells Rosebery Avenue, EC1R 4TN (0844 412 4300, www.sadlerswells.com). One of the world's premier dance venues.

Vue Islington Angel Central shopping centre, 36 Parkfield Street, N1 0PS (0871 224 0240, www.myvue.com).

Galleries & museums

Arsenal Museum Northern Triangle Building, 75 Drayton Park, N5 1BU (7619 5003, www. arsenal.com).

Cubitt 8 Angel Mews, N1 9HH (7278 8226, www.cubittartists.org.uk). Artist-run gallery and studio space.

Estorick Collection of Modern Italian Art 39A Canonbury Square, N1 2AN (7704 9522, www.estorickcollection.com). Work by Italian painters such as Balla, Boccioni and Carra.

London Canal Museum 12-13 New Wharf Road, N1 9RT (7713 0836, www.canalmuseum.org.uk). Housed in a former 19th-century ice warehouse built for the ice-cream maker Carlo Gatti.

Museum of the Order of St John St John's Gate, St John's Lane, EC1M 4DA (7324 4005,

TRANSPORT

Tube lines Circle, Hammersmith & City, Metropolitan, Northern, Overground, Piccadilly, Victoria

Rail services into King's Cross, Moorgate, plus Thameslink stations

Main bus routes into central London 4, 17, 19, 29, 30, 38, 55, 56, 73, 76, 91, 141, 153, 205, 274; night buses N19, N29, N38, N41, N55, N73, N253; 24-hour buses 43, 214, 243, 271, 341, 390

www.museumstjohn.org.uk). Recently revamped museum charting the evolution of the medieval Order of Hospitaller Knights to its modern incarnation as the renowned ambulance service.
Parasol Unit 14 Wharf Road, N1 7RW (7490 7373, www.parasol-unit.org). Contemporary art venue.
Zaha Hadid Design Gallery 101 Goswell Road, EC1V 7EZ (7253 5147, www.zaha-hadid-design. com). Showcase for work by the architect of the Olympic Aquatics Centre.

Other attractions

Business Design Centre 52 Upper Street, N1 0QH (7288 6272, www.businessdesigncentre. co.uk). Exhibition space for conferences and trade fairs; also some major art and design shows.
Candid Arts Trust 3-5 Torrens Street, EC1V 1NQ (7837 4237, www.candidarts.com). Two Victorian warehouses behind Angel tube, with exhibition and rehearsal space, artists' studios, a film-screening room and an excellent café.
Crafts Council 44A Pentonville Road, N1 9BY (7806 2500, www.craftscouncil.org.uk). Reference library open Wed and Thur.

Camden Passage Market; Ruby Violet

Freightliners Farm Sheringham Road, N7 8PF (7609 0467, www.freightlinersfarm.org.uk).
Marx Memorial Library 37A Clerkenwell Green, EC1R 0DU (7253 1485, www.marx-memorial-library.org).

Gigs, clubs & comedy

Boston Music Room 178 Junction Road, N19 5QQ (7272 8153, www.bostonmusicroom.co.uk).
Dome 2A Dartmouth Park Hill, NW5 1HL (7272 8153, www.dometufnellpark.co.uk).
Garage 20-22 Highbury Corner, N5 1RD (7619 6721, www.thegaragehighbury.com).
Hen & Chickens 109 St Paul's Road, N1 2NA (7704 2001, www.henandchickens.com). Well-established comedy joint.
Lexington 96-98 Pentonville Road, N1 9JB (7837 5371, www.thelexington.co.uk).
LSO St Luke's 161 Old Street, EC1V 9NG (7638 8891, www.lso.co.uk/lsostlukes). Restored Hawksmoor church used for rehearsals by the London Symphony Orchestra, and for gigs.
O2 Academy Angel Central, 16 Parkfield Street, N1 0PS (7288 4400, www.o2academyislington. co.uk). Slightly soulless venue; London's lack of mid-size spaces means this has become a default haunt for international cult acts.
Union Chapel Compton Terrace, off Upper Street, N1 2UN (7226 1686, www.unionchapel.org.uk).

Green spaces

For more details, see www.islington.gov.uk.
Barnard Park Copenhagen Street, N1. Playground and waterplay and sports facilities.
Bunhill Fields City Road, EC1 (www.cityoflondon. gov.uk). Famous residents in this cemetery include William and Catherine Blake, John Bunyan and Daniel Defoe.
Culpeper Gardens Tolpuddle Street, N1. Community garden with ponds, ornamental beds and vegetable plots.
Elthorne Park Hazellville Road, N19. Floodlit sports pitches, playground and walled peace garden.
Gillespie Park 191 Drayton Park, N5. Ponds, meadows and woodland; good for birdwatching. Ecology Centre open to visitors.
Highbury Fields Highbury Crescent, N5. Large grassy area popular for barbeques and community events. Playground, waterplay, sandpit, sports facilites, café, orchard and wildlife area.
Paradise Park MacKenzie Road, N7. Playground, sports pitch, green gym, pétanque, chess tables, birdwatching, various meadows, and a peace garden. Includes a Children's Centre.
Rosemary Gardens Southgate Road, N1. Playground, waterplay and floodlit sports courts.

Spa Fields Skinner Street, EC1. Lavender garden, cornfield meadow, playground and tarmac pitches.

Thornhill Bridge Community Gardens Caledonian Road, N1. Canalside gardens with playground and community artworks.

Tufnell Park Playing Fields Campdale Road, N19. Includes a playground and two tennis courts, as well as full-sized pitches.

Whittington Park Holloway Road, N7. Sports facilities, waterplay, woodland, wildlife area, pond and ecology garden.

Gyms & leisure centres

Archway Leisure Centre McDonald Road, N19 5DD (7281 4105, www.gll.org).

Cally Pool 229 Caledonian Road, N1 0NH (7278 4676, www.gll.org).

CitySport City University London, Franklin Building, 124 Goswell Road, EC1V 7DP (7040 5656, www.citysport.org.uk).

Dowe Dynamics Gym 1-2 Central Hall Buildings, Archway Close, N19 3UB (7281 2267, www. dowedynamics.com). Private.

Factory 407 Hornsey Road, N19 4DX (7272 1122, www.factorylondon.com). Private.

Finsbury Leisure Centre Norman Street, EC1V 3PU (7253 1303, www.gll.org).

Fitness First (www.fitnessfirst.co.uk); 60 Featherstone Street, EC1Y 8NQ (0840 571 2913); Unit A, East Stand, Highbury Stadium Square, Avenall Road, N5 1FE (0844 412 9958). Private.

Highbury Pool & Gym Highbury Crescent, N5 1RR (7704 2312, www.gll.org).

Ironmonger Row Baths 1-11 Ironmonger Row, EC1V 3AA (3642 5520, www.gll.org).

Islington Boxing Club 20 Hazellville Road, N19 3LP (07920 280230, www.islingtonboxingclub.org).

Maximum Fitness 144 Fortess Road, NW5 2HP (7482 3941, www.maxfit.co.uk). Private.

Ozone Health & Fitness Club 1 King's Cross Road, WC1X 9HX (7698 4039, www. ozonehealthandfitness.co.uk). Private.

Sobell Leisure Centre & Ice Rink Hornsey Road, N7 7NY (7609 2166, www.gll.org).

Virgin Active (www.virginactive.co.uk); 333 Goswell Road, EC1V 7DG (7014 9700); 33 Bunhill Row, EC1Y 8LP (7448 5454); 27 Essex Road, N1 2SD (7288 8200). Private.

Outdoor pursuits

Islington Tennis Centre Market Road, N7 9PL (3793 6880, www.gll.org).

Spectator sports

Arsenal FC Emirates Stadium, Hornsey Road, N7 7AJ (switchboard 7619 5003, stadium tours 7619 5000, www.arsenal.com).

Schools

Primary

There are 45 state primary schools in Islington, 15 of which are church schools. There are also seven independent primaries, including one Montessori school and one Steiner school. See www.islington. gov.uk, www.education.gov.uk/edubase and www.ofsted.gov.uk for more information.

Secondary

Central Foundation Boys' School Cowper Street, EC2A 4SH (7253 3741, www.central foundationboys.co.uk). Boys only.

City of London Academy Islington Prebend Street, N1 8PQ (7226 8611, www.cityacademy islington.org.uk).

Elizabeth Garrett Anderson School Donegal Street, N1 9QG (7837 0739, www.egaschool.co.uk). Girls only.

Highbury Fields School Highbury Hill, N5 1AR (7288 1888, www.highburyfields.islington.sch.uk). Girls only.

Highbury Grove School 8 Highbury Grove, N5 2EQ (7288 8900, www.highburygrove.islington.sch.uk).

Holloway School Hilldrop Road, N7 0JG (7607 5885, www.holloway.islington.sch.uk).

Islington Arts & Media School Turle Road, N4 3LS (7281 5511, www.iamschool.co.uk).

Italia Conti Academy of Theatre Arts 23 Goswell Road, EC1M 7AJ (7608 0044, www. italiaconti.com). Private theatre school.

Mount Carmel Catholic College for Girls Holland Walk, Duncombe Road, N19 3EU (7281 3536, www.mountcarmel.islington.sch.uk). Roman Catholic; girls only.

St Aloysius' College 30 Hornsey Lane, N6 5LY (7561 7800, www.sta.islington.sch.uk). Roman Catholic; boys only.

St Mary Magdalene Academy Liverpool Road, N7 8PG (7697 0123, www.smmacademy.org).

Property

Local estate agents

Hotblack Desiato www.hotblackdesiato.co.uk
Jeffrey Nicholas www.jeffreynicholas.co.uk
JTM Homes www.jtmhomes.co.uk
My Pad London www.mylondonpad.co.uk
Myspace www.myspaceuk.com

Local knowledge

www.islingtongazette.co.uk
www.islingtonnow.co.uk
www.islingtontribune.com
www.mytufnellpark.com

Highbury Fields

USEFUL INFO

Borough size
1,486 hectares

Population
224,600

Ethnic mix
White 72.7%
Black or Black British 10.1%
Asian or Asian British 9.4%
Chinese or other 3.9%
Mixed 3.9%

London Borough of Islington
222 Upper Street, N1 1XR (7527 2000,
www.islington.gov.uk)

Council run by
Labour

MPs
Islington North, Jeremy Corbyn (Labour);
Islington South & Finsbury, Emily
Thornberry (Labour)

Main recycling centre
Household Reuse & Recycling Centre,
40 Hornsey Street, N7 8HU (8884 5645,
www.islington.gov.uk)

Council tax
£850.67 to £2,552.02

Kensington & Chelsea

The name has become synonymous with 'posh' thanks to its palatial properties, world-class museums, sumptuous shopping, glitzy hotel restaurants, Sloane Rangers and, more recently, Russian oligarchs. It also boasts the capital's most expensive address.

AVERAGE PROPERTY PRICE

Detached	Terraced
£4,973,592	£2,956,360

Semi-detached	Flat
£3,529,814	£1,092,706

AVERAGE RENTAL PRICE PER WEEK

Studio	2 bed
£284	£624

1 bed	3 bed
£450	£1,000

	4+ bed
	£1,150

Kensington

Neighbourhoods

Kensington W8

Kensington High Street, once the site of offbeat shopping (legendary Biba, funky indoor Kensington Market, fashion-forward Hyper Hyper) and independent shops, has long been lined with chain stores: a big M&S, lots of mid-range fashion outlets and the flagship branch of Whole Foods. For a glimpse of a more traditional Kensington, walk up Kensington Church Street, where the pricier boutiques and antiques parlours seem more suited to the grand stucco-fronted houses that line the backstreets. Alternatively, head south into Pembroke Square and mooch around the century-old Rassells garden centre, which has pretty much overgrown the entire garden square. Just around the corner, and well hidden from passing traffic, is the bucolic Scarsdale Tavern, with tables outside for summer drinks. Also nearby is Michelin-starred Kitchen W8.

There are a few characterful places tucked away in the streets between High Street Ken and Notting Hill: Dirty Bones (hip hot dogs), Yashin (sushi), Geales (posh fish and chips), and kitsch Alpine re-enactment Bodo's Schloss (cheese in all its forms). And let's not forget old-timers such as Kensington Place and Clarke's. Drinks-wise, the Elephant & Castle and Churchill Arms are both extremely popular watering holes; the latter serves great-value Thai in a plant-filled annexe.

The old Derry & Tom's department store building (once home to the aforementioned Biba), by the tube station, hides Kensington Roof Gardens – not a new addition to the hipster rooftop-everything trend, but an ornate 1930s creation that was once the largest roof garden in Europe, famous for its resident flamingos. Here, you can dine at Babylon or party at the Club (the wild weekend daytime 'drunch' parties attract a sloaney/model crowd).

The other end of Kensington High Street is marked by the former Commonwealth Institute. This behemoth, which introduced many a young child to the Empire's furthest outposts, abuts Holland Park. The Grade II*-listed building, having lain dormant for many years, is being redeveloped to become the home of the Design Museum (relocated from near Tower Bridge) by 2017, though it's now somewhat hidden away behind the luxury flats being built alongside to help fund the whole project.

Outdoor types, especially in-line skaters and cyclists, gravitate towards Kensington Gardens (which merges with Hyde Park). The cultural crowd heads for the Serpentine Gallery, a former 1930s tearoom that hosts feted international artists, and its new Sackler Gallery, which was designed by Zaha Hadid. Its temporary summer pavilions are always an architectural event, as well as providing an alternative park café.

Families head for the brilliant (but at times oppressively busy) Diana, Princess of Wales Memorial Playground, with its pirate ship and urban beach, while a stroll around the Round Pond makes for a traditional Sunday afternoon jaunt. It's easy to forget all about the dense traffic of Kensington Road as you admire the swans, geese and model yachts out on the water.

Holland Park W11

Holland Park, a relatively tranquil area full of extravagant Georgian and Victorian terraces, is another of the borough's exclusive and expensive residential neighbourhoods with properties regularly valued at more than £10 million. A number of countries also maintain embassies in the neighbourhood. The smart shops and restaurants along traffic-filled Holland Park Avenue, which cuts through the area on its way from Notting Hill Gate to Shepherd's Bush, include some respected names: Lidgate's butchers, which has been around for 160 years; baker Maison Blanc; independent bookseller Daunt Books; and authentic Italian restaurant the Edera, known for its truffles and intimate vibe. Clarendon Cross is another delightful local shopping spot: browse in well-loved boutique the Cross; stock up on fine kitchenware at Summerill & Bishop; or have lunch and a pedicure at the London outpost of Babington House's Cowshed spa, which doubles as a café. Also here is the famous Julie's Restaurant & Champagne Bar, a celebrity magnet since 1969 and a rock 'n' roll retreat for everyone from the Rolling Stones to Stella McCartney. It was undergoing a revamp in 2015 and was due to reopen in September.

Holland Park itself is an impressively planned and surprisingly untouristy public space where peacocks roam freely. There's a wonderfully tranquil Japanese garden complete with a waterfall and a bridge across the carp-filled pond, a far less peaceful adventure playground, an art gallery, a famous orangery, a summer open-air opera

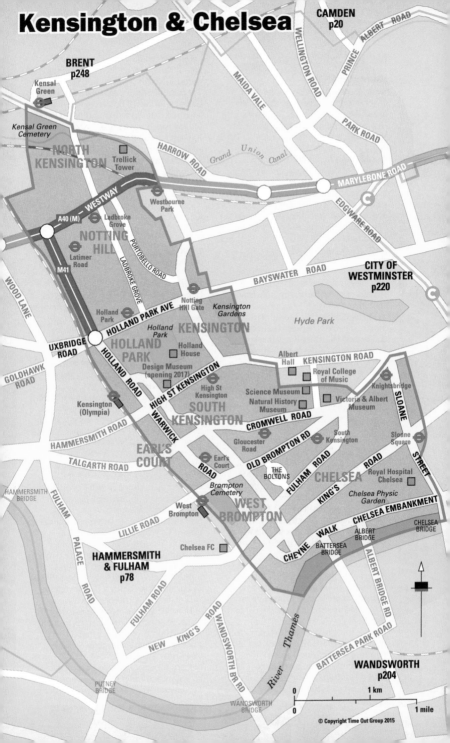

season and one of the city's most handsomely situated youth hostels. The Belvedere restaurant, a popular spot for Sunday lunch, is set in the exquisite former ballroom of Holland House. Located just a short stroll away, Leighton House Museum was once the residence of the Victorian artist Frederic, Lord Leighton. Visit for the lavish marble and tiled interior and collection of paintings.

If Holland Park is relatively sedate, that all changes at the western end of Holland Park Avenue when it encounters Shepherd's Bush.

South Kensington SW7

South Kensington is best known for its Museum Mile, one of the most visited parts of London and home to the triumvirate of the Natural History, Science and V&A museums. Where once the trek from tube to entrance was fairly grim, and even the underground passage was preferable to dodging traffic above ground, the considered landscaping of Exhibition Road – now kerb-free and shared equally between cars and pedestrians as part of an urban-planning experiment – has brought life on to the streets. Museums spill out from their confines with street activities and there are plenty of pavement cafés too. The route – which leads up to Hyde Park, the Albert Hall and the Albert Monument, past several other venerable institutions – now has the sense of occasion it deserves.

For such an unavoidably touristy part of town, there are now a lot of genuinely good places to eat in the area, especially along Harrington Road and Old Brompton Road, as well as chains such as Gails, Comptoir Libanais and Fernandez & Wells near the station. Options include Iddu (Sicilian), Tendido Cero and Cambio de Tercio (smart tapas), and Yashin Ocean House (Japanese). There's also Ognisko at the Polish Hearth Club on Exhibition Road, and eastern European stalwart Daquise, which has been serving Polish fare for more than 60 years. And for the super-sweet toothed, there's Maître Choux's pimped-up eclairs and cupcake queen Hummingbird's creations.

This distinctly elegant part of the capital has a strong French accent thanks to the nearby Lycée Français and Institut Français. There's architectural splendour at nearly every turn in this neighbourhood, from the florid Italianate Brompton Oratory Catholic church to the iconic Royal Albert Hall (technically, just outside the borough – but this whole neighbourhood is sometimes referred to as 'Albertopolis' due to its Victorian heritage).

Besides tourists, French expats and diplomats, South Kensington is home to a sizeable student population (the Royal College of Art, Royal College of Music, Imperial College and numerous language schools are all here) and lots of embassies. There's also a

Notting Hill's Coronet cinema also puts on fringe theatre under the auspices of the Print Room.

self-styled design quarter around Brompton Road/Fulham Road, with the Conran Shop as its mothership, supported by Skandium, Divertimenti and Smallbone of Devizes.

Earl's Court SW5 and West Brompton SW10

It's a safe bet that almost every Londoner has taken a journey through the capital that involved passing through Earl's Court, with its District and Piccadilly line interchange. Above ground, Earl's Court connects with South Kensington via the very busy Cromwell Road (A4). Further local amenities can be found dotted around Gloucester Road, but the area otherwise remains a sprawl of side streets, hotels, private garden squares, youth hostels and bedsits; the last often have sadly crumbling interiors behind their imposing stuccoed façades.

There's a transient spirit to the district (traditionally, it has attracted antipodeans over for a few years of adventure), which does at least make for an appealing cultural mix; Hogarth Road, for example, has some interesting Filipino grocers and cafés. The site previously covered by the Earl's Court Exhibition Centre, and 77 acres around it, will be redeveloped into a new neighbourhood of mid-rise buildings, parkland, public spaces, offices and 7,500 new homes, though it's not expected to be fully realised until 2030.

In contrast to Earl's Court, neighbouring West Brompton is a classy residential area, incorporating plenty of high-value property, including the facing crescents of the Boltons. The district's most memorable landmark is Brompton Cemetery, on Fulham Road; the many famous graves include that of the suffragette pioneer Emmeline Pankhurst.

From here, it's a short walk to Stamford Bridge, home of Chelsea FC – just over the border in Hammersmith & Fulham.

Chelsea SW3

Chelsea today holds a reputation as one of London's most affluent neighbourhoods, home to the Sloane Ranger, and their brasher modern equivalent as seen on reality show *Made in Chelsea*. Boasting a parade of high-end fashion boutiques and top-quality eateries, this area has long since evolved from its 1960s swinging London roots and punk-rock revolution heyday.

Take a stroll from Chelsea's main tube station, Sloane Square, through to World's End along the King's Road (originally Charles II's private route from St James's Palace) and treat yourself at one of the many cafés and quirky gelaterias along the way. Standouts are L'Eto and Amorino – serving some of the best Italian ice-cream around, in a huge variety of flavours. Fashion retail outlets are out in force, ranging from the eclectic Zadig & Voltaire and Sandro to high-street chains such as Banana Republic. Most tastes are catered for, though nothing is likely to come cheap. Budding stylists enjoy Deuxième on New King's Road for one-off vintage pieces, and Vivienne Westwood's original World's End shop (opened with Malcolm McLaren in 1970 as Let It Rock), easily recognisable by its backwards-running clock.

Tucked off the King's Road away from the traditional hustle and bustle are a selection of high-end gastropubs: the long-enduring Pig's Ear and wonderfully refurbished Cross Keys, which once had JMW Turner, Dylan Thomas and Bob Marley as regulars. An *MiC* favourite is the Phene by Cheyne Walk (recently saved in a campaign headed by Hugh Grant), while the Goat on Fulham Road channels a relaxed lounge setting with a mood-lit upstairs bar and a great selection of cocktails.

The upmarket dining experience continues to grow with the recently opened Ivy Chelsea Garden (part of the famous Ivy group), showcasing British fare in a beautiful outdoor

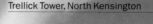

Trellick Tower, North Kensington

HIGHS & LOWS

Kensington Gardens, especially the Diana Memorial Playground

Chelsea Pensioners in their scarlet uniforms

Notting Hill Carnival if you're in the party mood

Some of the best museums in the world

Designer shopping

Very central

Disappointed tourists looking for the 'real' Notting Hill

Those pretty squares in Notting Hill are private

Notting Hill Carnival if you're not in the party mood

High prices – and not just the homes

Clubs with no-jeans dress codes

garden setting complete with terrace and orangery. Alternatively, brush shoulders with celebrities in Gordon Ramsay's restaurant on Royal Hospital Road or Bluebird on King's Road. The more budget-inclined turn to old-school faves the Stockpot, Chelsea Kitchen and Mona Lisa further up near World's End.

Dominating Sloane Square is Peter Jones, still the spiritual home of the upper middle classes. John Betjeman once said that, when the end of the world came, he wanted to be in the haberdashery department 'because nothing unpleasant could ever happen there.'

The Royal Court Theatre, next to Sloane Square tube station, has been providing a platform for up-and-coming writers since it sent shockwaves around the world with its première of John Osborne's *Look Back in Anger* in 1956. Get there early on Mondays to secure £10 tickets. The Saatchi Gallery has also made its home at this end of the King's Road, taking over the neoclassical Duke of York's headquarters building.

Late-night clubbers should dress to impress – trainers and slacks are a no-go in these parts. Guy Pelly (chum to the royals) runs Mexican basement club Tonteria on Sloane Square; Raffles, Embargo and JUJU on King's Road are hotspots for classy, sophisticated partiers – playing a mixture of electro, house and pop music – while Boujis, often cited as one of Prince Harry's preferred clubs, lies just next door to South Kensington tube station. Those more inclined to live performances can visit the 606 Jazz Club, hidden away in a basement entrance on Lots Road – music is varied, so pick your night accordingly.

Much of Chelsea's exclusivity is down to its labelling as a global ultra-prime residential area. The period streets behind King's Road are indeed charming, but unless you are loaded (or your parents are), living here may be difficult. Even the moorings along blue-plaque-edged Chelsea Embankment are considerably classier than those on the Regent's Canal. There are, however, several council estates dotted around the area: Wiltshire Close, and the 1970s World's End estate, a series of interconnected tower blocks that make fans of municipal housing weak at the knees. Rental options vary, but nothing comes cheap unless you are willing to live a little outside: prices fall dramatically closer towards Earl's Court and Fulham Broadway, but you'll still be well within distance to enjoy the lifestyle Chelsea offers.

Knightsbridge SW1

While much of Knightsbridge technically falls under the aegis of the City of Westminster, it seamlessly continues on from designer-label central Sloane Street (Prada, Chanel, Jimmy Choo) as a ritzy, label-saturated enclave. The main drag is dominated by two temples to conspicuous consumption: the over-the-top Harrods (local residents treat its food halls as their corner shop, and you'll always find something novel), and the more restrained, fashion-conscious Harvey Nicks. It also has one of London's most expensive addresses, One Hyde Park, located next to the Mandarin Oriental hotel, its 80 or so flats starting at around the £20-million mark. There isn't much affordable housing in SW7, although some people manage to rent tiddly bedsits in the area's tucked-away streets.

The restaurant scene in Knightsbridge is similar: high quality, high prices. The Capital serves haute cuisine in the exclusive environs of its namesake hotel; the Mandarin Oriental has Dinner by Heston Blumenthal and the less expensive Bar Boulud. There's also first-rate French restaurant Racine, Japanese bar-restaurant Zuma, sleekly appointed Indian and Pakistani restaurant Amaya, and Chinese destination Mr Chow, one of London's oldest Chinese restaurants. Ramsay-affiliated Pétrus and the Berkeley hotel's Koffman's consistently impress for haute cuisine; at the other end of the scale entirely is O Fado, a homely basement restaurant that's London's oldest Portuguese eaterie. Meanwhile, fabulously decorated Russian restaurant Mari Vanna has provided the local oligarchs with a home from home.

Notting Hill W11

When you first arrive in Notting Hill, don't be surprised if you're overcome with a wash of disappointment. Traffic-clogged Notting Hill Gate isn't the most attractive high street out there but, like all living, breathing things in the world, it has its charms and interesting features, which makes exploring worthwhile.

No, we're not talking about a daredevil hop over a residential garden wall à la Hugh Grant and Julia Roberts: that's asking for trouble – via a call to the police from the £1,500 fee-paying, key-holding residents. We're talking about the little gems that hide among the chain stores, fast-food joints and traffic lights.

Before leaving the congested pavement of Bayswater Road, your first stop should be the Gate Cinema, which offers an experience that harks back to a bygone era, with plush velvet seats, a schedule of National Theatre showings and selected contemporary films that'll make your weekly trip to the flicks a little more special. Your next should be the recently refurbished Coronet, a former theatre that has been reclaimed as a hybrid cinema and drama studio that was featured in – you guessed it – *Notting Hill*.

And what's a movie without dinner? The immediate area around Notting Hill Gate has many new, hip eateries that'll make visiting here worth the trip. From Italian small plates at Polpo Notting Hill to creative Greek food at Mazi, British small plates (there seems to be a theme) at the Shed to full-on Indian cuisine at Chakra, there are plenty of flavours to explore before venturing off into the heart of Notting Hill: Portobello Road Market.

Yes, it's clichéd. Yes, you can barely move for tourists at the weekend. But the market is the hub of activity round here. Featuring a funky mix of vintage clothes shops, hip boutiques, specialist stores and record shops (Honest Jon's is famed across London), there's plenty to see on this legendary strip.

Food is also becoming big business in the area: burger franchise Honest Burger has laid down its roots along with Pizza East, Hummingbird, Gail's Bakery and a whole host of other popular names. You'll also find the hallowed Electric, which is yet another arts cinema but this time accompanied by a noteworthy restaurant – the Electric Diner. Always buzzing with local trendies, it proves that west London hasn't been forsaken for the east by all.

For those looking for a rather quieter day out, plenty of boutique shops, pubs and restaurants can be found dotted around. On Ledbury Road, you'll not only find the Michelin-starred restaurant the Ledbury, but also the original (and tiny) Ottolenghi, Beach Blanket Babylon and the always-busy Walmer Castle pub. The junction of Ledbury Road and Westbourne Grove is boutique central – beautiful clothes and accessories for beautiful people, and beautiful items for beautiful homes.

Head over to Westbourne Park Road and you'll come across the American diner Lucky 7, and pretty authentic Mexican food at Crazy Homies. And if you're just after a nice pint with the possibility of some decent fodder, then the Prince Bonaparte on Chepstow Road and the Commander on Hereford Road are calling your name.

But you can't really mention Notting Hill without the district's most famous celebration. The area is best known for hosting Europe's largest street party, the Notting Hill Carnival, a raucous celebration of the neighbourhood's Afro-Caribbean heritage. The Carnival emerged as a positive stand against the race riots of the 1960s. Four decades later, it draws around a million revellers to these streets and neighbouring North Kensington every August bank holiday weekend.

North Kensington W10

On the northern side of the Westway, North Kensington has the edgiest feel of any neighbourhood in the borough. Ladbroke Grove, so gentrified at the Holland Park end, is here lined with late-night shops and fast-food joints, and overlooked by local-authority housing. There are also some handsome houses, long since converted into flats and grimy from decades of traffic fumes, but still very much in demand. Café Oporto and Lisboa Pâtisserie signal a mini Portuguese enclave, and Bay Sixty6 turns the thundering Westway to its advantage by using it to shelter an indoor skatepark.

The district was built around the St Charles and Princess Louise hospitals, giant Victorian edifices that have been softened slightly with revamps. Buildings in the area certainly contrast with each other: take Barlby Road, for instance, which has snug-looking terraced houses as well as the imposing 1911 Pall Mall Depository, which now contains office units and a café. North Kensington is also the spiritual home to the 'Notting Hill Set', a powerful clique of Conservatives that includes David Cameron and George Osborne.

At the area's northernmost boundary, you'll find the green oasis of Kensal Green Cemetery, the first of London's grand Victorian burial grounds and final resting place of Trollope, Thackeray and Isambard Kingdom Brunel. Also here are the striking canalside studios of Kensal Town; designer Tom Dixon's HQ, home to his Dock Kitchen; and the borough-run Canalside Activity Centre, which focuses on youth recreation.

Finally, mention should be made of what is surely North Kensington's most famous building: architect Ernö Goldfinger's 31-storey Trellick Tower, originally designed as cheap social housing in 1972. It has shrugged off a troubled reputation to become one of the most sought-after addresses in the area – now Grade II* listed, it is a modernist icon.

Eating

Amorino 67A King's Road, SW3 4NT (7730 3591, www.amorino.com).

Babylon Kensington Roof Gardens, Derry Street, W8 5SA (7368 3993, www.virginlimitededition.com).

Bar Boulud Mandarin Oriental Hyde Park, 66 Knightsbridge, SW1X 7LA (7201 3899, www.barboulud.com/london).

Belvedere off Abbotsbury Road, in Holland Park, W8 6LU (7602 1238, www.belvedererestaurant.co.uk).

Bluebird 350 King's Road, SW3 5UU (7559 1000, www.bluebird-restaurant.co.uk).

Bodo's Schloss 2A Kensington High Street, W8 4PT (7937 5506).

Cambio de Tercio 163 Old Brompton Road, SW5 0LJ (7244 8970, www.cambiodetercio.co.uk).

Capital 22-24 Basil Street, SW3 1AT (7591 1200, www.capitalhotel.co.uk).

Chakra 157-159 Notting Hill Gate, W11 3LF (7229 2115, www.chakralondon.com).

Chelsea Kitchen 451 Fulham Road, SW10 9UZ (3055 0088, www.thechelseakitchen.co.uk).

Clarke's 122-124 Kensington Church Street, W8 4BH (7221 9225, www.sallyclarke.com).

Comptoir Libanais 1-5 Exhibition Road, SW7 2HE (7225 5006, www.comptoirlibanais.com).

Crazy Homies 125 Westbourne Park Road, W2 5QL (7727 6771, www.crazyhomies.com).

Daquise 20 Thurloe Street, SW7 2LT (7589 6117, www.daquise.co.uk).

Dinner by Heston Blumenthal Mandarin Oriental Hyde Park, 66 Knightsbridge, SW1X 7LA (7201 3833, www.dinnerbyheston.com).

Dirty Bones 20 Kensington Church Street, W8 4EP (7920 6434, www.dirty-bones.com).

Dock Kitchen Portobello Docks, 342-344 Ladbroke Grove, Kensal Road, W10 5BU (8962 1610, www.dockkitchen.co.uk).

Edera 148 Holland Park Avenue, W11 4UE (7221 6090, www.edera.co.uk).

Electric Diner 191 Portobello Road, W11 2ED (7908 9696, www.electricdiner.com).

L'Eto 149 King's Road, SW3 5TX (7351 7656, www.letocaffe.co.uk).

Geales (www.geales.com); 1 Cale Street, SW3 3QT (7965 0555); 2 Farmer Street, W8 7SN (7727 7528).

Gordon Ramsay 68 Royal Hospital Road, SW3 4HP (7352 4441, www.gordonramsay.com).

Honest Burger 189 Portobello Road, W11 2ED (7229 4978, www.honestburgers.co.uk).

Iddu 47 Harrington Road, SW7 3ND (7589 1991, www.iddulondon.com).

Julie's Restaurant & Champagne Bar 135 Portland Road, W11 4LW (7229 8331, www.juliesrestaurant.com).

Kensington Place 201 Kensington Church Street, W8 7LX (7727 3184, www.kensingtonplace-restaurant.co.uk).

Kitchen W8 11-13 Abingdon Road, W8 6AH (7937 0120, www.kitchenw8.com).

Koffman's The Berkeley, Wilton Place, SW1X 7RL (7107 8844, www.the-berkeley.co.uk).

Ledbury 127 Ledbury Road, W11 2AQ (7792 9090, www.theledbury.com).

Lisboa Pâtisserie 57 Golborne Road, W10 5NR (8968 5242).

Royal Court Bar and Kitchen

TRANSPORT

Tube lines Bakerloo, Central, Circle, District, Hammersmith & City, Piccadilly, Overground
Rail services into Clapham Junction, Victoria
Main bus services into central London 9, 11, 19, 22, 74, 137; night buses N7, N9, N11, N18, N19, N22, N52, N74, N97, N137, N207; 24-hour buses 7, 10, 14, 18, 23, 27, 94, 148, 390
River boat services Cadogan Pier (under Albert Bridge) and Chelsea Harbour Pier

Lucky 7 Diner 127 Westbourne Park Road, W2 5QL (7727 6771, www.lucky7london.co.uk).
Mari Vanna Wellington Court, 116 Knightsbridge, SW1X 7PJ (7225 3122, www.marivanna.ru/london).
Mazi 12-14 Hillgate Street, W8 7SR (7229 3794, www.mazi.co.uk).
Mr Chow 151 Knightsbridge, SW1X 7PA (7589 7347, www.mrchow.com).
Mona Lisa 417 King's Road, SW10 0LR (7376 5447).
Ognisko 55 Prince's Gate, Exhibition Road, SW7 2PN (7589 0101, www.ogniskorestaurant.co.uk).
Ottolenghi 63 Ledbury Road, W11 2AD (7727 1121, www.ottolenghi.co.uk).
Pétrus 1 Kinnerton Street, SW1X 8EA (7592 1609, www.gordonramsay.com).

The venerable Royal Geographical Society houses an incredible collection of globes.

Pizza East 310 Portobello Road, W10 5TA (8969 4500, www.pizzaeastportobello.com).
Polpo 126-128 Notting Hill Gate, W11 3QG (7229 3283, www.polpo.co.uk).
Shed 122 Palace Gardens Terrace, W8 4RT (7229 4024, www.theshed-restaurant.com).
Stockpot 273 King's Road, SW3 5EN (7823 3175, www.stockpotchelsea.co.uk).
Tendido Cero 174 Old Brompton Road, SW5 0BA (7370 3685, www.cambiodetercio.co.uk).
Yashin 1A Argyll Road, W8 7DB (7938 1536, www.yashinsushi.com).
Zuma 5 Raphael Street, SW7 1DL (7584 1010, www.zumarestaurant.com).

Drinking

Beach Blanket Babylon 45 Ledbury Road, W11 2AA (7229 2907, www.beachblanket.co.uk).
Churchill Arms 119 Kensington Church Street, W8 7LN (7727 4242, www.churchill armskensington.co.uk).
Commander 47 Hereford Road, W2 5AH (7229 1503, www.thecommanderbar.com).
Cross Keys 1 Lawrence Street, SW3 5NB (7351 0686, www.thecrosskeyschelsea.co.uk).
Elephant & Castle 40 Holland Street, W8 4LT (7937 6382, www.nicholsonspubs.co.uk).
Goat 333 Fulham Road, SW10 9QL (7352 1384, www.goatchelsea.com).
Phene 9 Phene Street, SW3 5NY (7352 9898, www.thephene.com).
Pig's Ear 35 Old Church Street, SW3 5BS (7352 2908, www.thepigsear.info).

Prince Bonaparte 80 Chepstow Road, W2 5BE (7313 9491, www.theprincebonapartew2.co.uk).
Scarsdale Tavern 23A Edwardes Square, W8 6HE (7937 1811, www.scarsdaletavern.co.uk).
Walmer Castle 59 Ledbury Road, W11 2AJ (7229 4620, www.walmercastlenottinghill.co.uk).

Shopping

Banana Republic Duke of York Square, 23 King's Road, SW3 4LY (7730 4704. www. bananarepublic.co.uk).
Conran Shop Michelin House, 81 Fulham Road, SW3 6RD (7589 7401, www.conranshop.co.uk).
Cowshed Clarendon Cross 119 Portland Road, W11 4LN (7078 1944, www.cowshed clarendoncross.com).
Cross 141 Portland Road, W11 4LR (7727 6760, www.thecrossshop.co.uk).
Daunt Books 112-114 Holland Park Avenue, W11 4UA (7727 7022, www.dauntbooks.co.uk).
Deuxième 299 New King's Road, SW6 4RE (7736 3696. www.deuxieme.co.uk).
Divertimenti 227-229 Brompton Road, SW3 2EP (7581 8065, www.divertimenti.co.uk).
Gail's 45 Thurloe Street, SW7 2LQ (7584 7499, www.gailsbread.co.uk).
Harrods 87-135 Brompton Road, SW1X 7XL (7730 1234, www.harrods.com).
Harvey Nichols 109-125 Knightsbridge, SW1X 7RJ (7235 5000, www.harveynichols.com).
Honest Jon's 278 Portobello Road, W10 5TE (8969 9822, www.honestjons.com).
Hummingbird Bakery (7851 1795, www. hummingbirdbakery.com; 47 Old Brompton Street, SW7 3JP; 133 Portobello Road, W11 2DY.
Lidgate's 110 Holland Park Avenue, W11 4UA (7727 8243, www.lidgates.com).
Maison Blanc 102 Holland Park Avenue, W11 4UA (7221 2494, www.maisonblanc.co.uk).
Peter Jones Sloane Square, SW1W 8EL (7730 3434, www.peterjones.co.uk).
Portobello Road Market (7727 7684, www. portobelloroad.co.uk, www.rbkc.gov.uk).
Rassells 80 Earl's Court Road, W8 6EQ (7937 0481, www.rassells.com).
Sandro 190 King's Road, SW3 5XP (7352 8382, www.sandro-paris.com).
Skandium 245-249 Brompton Road, SW3 2EP (7584 2066, www.skandium.com).
Smallbone of Devizes 220 Brompton Road, SW3 2BB (7581 9989, www.smallbone.co.uk).
Summerill & Bishop 100 Portland Road, W11 4LQ (7229 1337, www.summerillandbishop.com).
Whole Foods Market The Barkers Building, 63-97 Kensington High Street, W8 5SE (7368 4500, www.wholefoodsmarket.com).

World's End (Vivienne Westwood) 430 King's Road, SW10 0LJ (7352 6551, www.worldsendshop. co.uk, www.viviennewestwoodonline.co.uk).
Zadig & Voltaire 194 King's Road, SW3 5XP (7351 2231, www.zadig-et-voltaire.com).

Things to do

Cinemas & theatres
Ciné Lumière Institut Français, 17 Queensbury Place, SW7 2DT (7871 3515, www.institut-francais.org.uk). Mostly screens films in French, with English subtitles.
Cineworld (0871 200 2000, www.cineworld.co.uk); 279 King's Road, SW3 5EW; 142 Fulham Road, SW10 9QR.
Coronet 103 Notting Hill Gate, W11 3LB (7727 6705, www.the-print-room.org). Much-loved cinema undergoing refurbishment at time of writing; also home to Print Room theatre company. Main auditorium scheduled to reopen later in 2015.
Curzon Chelsea 206 King's Road, SW3 5XP (0330 500 1331, www.curzoncinemas.com).
Electric Cinema 191 Portobello Road, W11 2ED (7908 9696, www.electriccinema.co.uk).
Gate Cinema 87 Notting Hill Gate, W11 3JZ (0871 902 5731, www.picturehouses.co.uk).
Gate Theatre 11 Pembridge Road, W11 3HQ (7229 0706, www.gatetheatre.co.uk).
Odeon Kensington 263 Kensington High Street, W8 6NA (0871 224 4007, www.odeon.co.uk).
Royal Court Theatre Sloane Square, SW1W 8AS (7565 5000, www.royalcourttheatre.com).
Science Museum IMAX Exhibition Road, SW7 2DD (0870 870 4868, www.sciencemuseum.org.uk).

Galleries & museums
Carlyle's House 24 Cheyne Row, SW3 5HL (7352 7087, www.nationaltrust.org.uk). The home of writer Thomas Carlyle offers an intriguing snapshot of Victorian life.
Leighton House Museum 12 Holland Park Road, W14 8LZ (7602 3316, www.rbkc.gov.uk/leightonhousemuseum).
National Army Museum Royal Hospital Road, SW3 4HT (7730 0717, www.national-army-museum.ac.uk). Exhibits run from 15th-century Agincourt to contemporary peacekeeping.
Natural History Museum Cromwell Road, SW7 5BD (information 7942 5011, switchboard 7942 5000, www.nhm.ac.uk).
Saatchi Gallery Duke of York's HQ, King's Road, SW3 4LY (www.saatchi-gallery.com).
Science Museum Exhibition Road, SW7 2DD (0870 870 4868, www.sciencemuseum.org.uk).
Victoria & Albert Museum Cromwell Road, SW7 2RL (7942 2000, www.vam.ac.uk).

Other attractions
Brompton Oratory Thurloe Place, Brompton Road, SW7 2RP (7808 0900, www.brompton oratory.com). England's second-largest Catholic church (after Westminster Cathedral).
Chelsea Physic Garden 66 Royal Hospital Road, SW3 4HS (7352 5646, www.chelseaphysic garden.co.uk).
Ecology Centre Holland Park, Ilchester Place, W8 6LU (7938 8186, www.rbkc.gov.uk).
Goethe-Institut 50 Princes Gate, Exhibition Road, SW7 2PH (7596 4000, www.goethe.de/london). German cultural institute.
Institut Français 17 Queensberry Place, SW7 2DT (7871 3515, www.institut-francais.org.uk). French cultural institute; includes Ciné Lumière.
Kensington Palace W8 4PX (0844 482 7777, bookings 0844 482 7799, www.hrp.org.uk). Reopened spring 2012 after major renovation, with restored gardens, new courtyard terrace and café.
Notting Hill Carnival (www.thenottinghill carnival.com). Late Aug bank holiday.
Royal Hospital Chelsea Royal Hospital Road, SW3 4SR (7881 5200, www.chelsea-pensioners.co.uk).

Gigs, clubs & comedy
606 Club 90 Lots Road, SW10 0QD (7352 5953, www.606club.co.uk).
Boujis 43 Thurloe Street, SW7 2LQ (7584 2000, www.boujis.com).
Cadogan Hall 5 Sloane Terrace, SW1X 9DQ (7730 4500, www.cadoganhall.com). Fine classical concert hall, home to the Royal Philharmonic.
Club Kensington Roof Gardens, Derry Street, off Kensington High Street, W8 5SA (7368 3971, www.virginlimitededition.com). Private members' club.
Embargo República 533 King's Road, SW10 0TZ (7351 5038, www.embargorepublica.com).
Juju 316-318 King's Road, SW3 5UH (7351 5998, www.jujulondon.com).
Notting Hill Arts Club 21 Notting Hill Gate, W11 3JQ (7460 4459, www.nottinghillartsclub.com). Specialist music and arts venue.
Raffles 287 King's Road, SW3 5EW (7351 4964, www.rafffleschelsea.com).
Royal Albert Hall Kensington Gore, SW7 2AP (7589 8212, www.royalalberthall.com). World-famous concert hall known for classical performances, including the Proms; also hosts pop and rock concerts.
Royal College of Music Prince Consort Road, SW7 2BS (7591 4300, www.rcm.ac.uk).
Tabernacle 35 Powis Square, off Portobello Road, W11 2AY (7221 9700, www.tabernaclew11.com).
Tonteria 7-12 Sloane Square, SW1W 8EG (7881 5991, www.tonteria.co.uk).

Green spaces

For more details, see www.rbkc.gov.uk.

Emslie Horniman's Pleasance Bosworth Road, W10. Playground, floodlit sports pitches, contemporary art and Voysey Garden.

Holland Park Ilchester Place, W8. Playground, sports facilities, Kyoto Japanese garden, woodland, open-air opera and remains of Holland House. Base of the borough's ecology service.

Kensington Memorial Park St Mark's Road, W10. Playground, waterplay and sports.

Little Wormwood Scrubs Dalgarno Gardens, W10. Grassland, woodland and adventure playground. Designated a Site of Nature Conservation Importance.

Gyms & leisure centres

Aquilla Health Club 11 Thurloe Place, SW7 2RS (7225 0225, www.aquillahealthclub.com). Private.

Bay Sixty6 10 Acklam Road, W10 5QZ (8969 4669, www.nikesbbaysixty6.com/park). Indoor skatepark.

BodyWorksWest 11 Lambton Place, W11 2SH (7229 2291, www.bodyworkswest.co.uk). Private.

Chelsea Sports Centre Chelsea Manor Street, SW3 5PL (7352 6985, www.better.org.uk).

David Lloyd Point West 116 Cromwell Road, SW7 4XR (0345 129 6709, www.davidlloyd leisure.co.uk). Private.

Fitness First Petersham House, 29-37 Harrington Road, SW7 3HD (0844 571 2933, www.fitness first.co.uk). Private.

Harbour Club Watermeadow Lane, SW6 2RW (7371 7700, www.harbourclub.co.uk). Private.

Kensington Leisure Centre Silchester Road, W10 6EX (3793 8210, www.better.org.uk).

LAX South Kensington 63-81 Pelham Street, SW7 2NJ (7838 0500, www.lafitness.co.uk). Private.

Soho Gyms Earl's Court 254 Earl's Court Road, SW5 9AD (7370 1402, www.sohogyms. com). Private.

Virgin Active (www.virginactive.co.uk); 3rd floor, 17A Old Court Place, W8 4PL (0845 270 9128); 188A Fulham Road, SW10 9PN (0845 270 4085); 119-131 Lancaster Road, W11 1QT (0845 270 2102). Private.

Westway Sports & Fitness Club 3-5 Thorpe Close, W10 5XL (8960 2221, www.westway.org). Private.

Outdoor pursuits

Canalside Centre Canal Close, W10 5AY (8968 4500, www.rbkc.gov.uk).

Westway Sports & Fitness Centre 1 Crowthorne Road, W10 6RP (8969 0992, www.westway.org).

Schools

Primary

There are 26 state primary schools, 15 of which are church schools. There are 25 independent primaries, including one Spanish school and one French school. See www.rbkc.gov.uk, www.education.gov.uk/edubase and www.ofsted.gov.uk for more information.

Secondary

Cardinal Vaughan Memorial School 89 Addison Road, W14 8BZ (7603 8478, www.cvms.co.uk). Roman Catholic; boys only; mixed sixth form.

Chelsea Academy Lots Road, SW10 0AB (7376 3019, www.chelsea-academy.org). Church of England.

Francis Holland School 39 Graham Terrace, SW1W 8JF (7730 2971, www.fhs-sw1.org.uk). Girls only; private.

Holland Park School Campden Hill Road, W8 7AF (7908 1000, www.hollandparkschool.co.uk).

Queen's Gate 133 Queen's Gate, SW7 5LE (7589 3587, www.queensgate.org.uk). Girls only; private.

St Thomas More Language College Cadogan Street, SW3 2QS (7589 9734, www.stmlc.co.uk). Roman Catholic.

Sion Manning RC Girls' School 75 St Charles Square, W10 6EL (8969 7111, www.sion-manning. com). Roman Catholic; girls only.

Property

Local estate agents

Anthony Sharp www.anthony-sharp.com

Bruten & Company www.brutens.com

Campden Estates www.campdenestates.co.uk

Carter Jonas www.carterjonas.co.uk

Chard www.chard.co.uk

Chelsea International www. chelseainternational.co.uk

Draker Lettings www.draker.co.uk

Farrar www.farrar.co.uk

Home House Estates www.homehouse estates.co.uk

Jeremy Jacob www.jeremyjacob.co.uk

Marsh & Parsons www.marshandparsons.co.uk

Maskells www.maskells.co.uk

Westways www.westways.co.uk

Local knowledge

www.getwestlondon.co.uk
www.heritage.com/chelsea_standard
www.kctimes.co.uk
www.kcwtoday.co.uk
www.nottinghillpost.com
www.peopleofportobello.com
www.thehill.co.uk

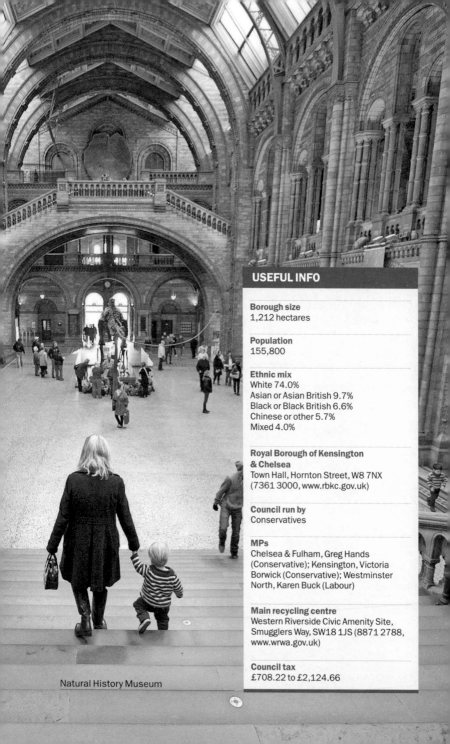

Natural History Museum

USEFUL INFO

Borough size
1,212 hectares

Population
155,800

Ethnic mix
White 74.0%
Asian or Asian British 9.7%
Black or Black British 6.6%
Chinese or other 5.7%
Mixed 4.0%

Royal Borough of Kensington & Chelsea
Town Hall, Hornton Street, W8 7NX
(7361 3000, www.rbkc.gov.uk)

Council run by
Conservatives

MPs
Chelsea & Fulham, Greg Hands
(Conservative); Kensington, Victoria
Borwick (Conservative); Westminster
North, Karen Buck (Labour)

Main recycling centre
Western Riverside Civic Amenity Site,
Smugglers Way, SW18 1JS (8871 2788,
www.wrwa.gov.uk)

Council tax
£708.22 to £2,124.66

Lambeth

A multicultural microcosm of everything London has to offer, Lambeth mixes nightlife with high culture, street food with family-friendly gastropubs, and attractive period housing with deprived estates.

Pop Brixton

AVERAGE PROPERTY PRICE

Detached £973,684	**Terraced** £669,481	
Semi-detached £764,973	**Flat** £490,355	

AVERAGE RENTAL PRICE PER WEEK

Room £121	**2 bed** £345
Studio £192	**3 bed** £464
1 bed £283	**4+ bed** £624

Neighbourhoods

South Bank, Waterloo and Lambeth North SE1

If ever you're stuck for something to do of a weekend, the South Bank is the place to head. There's always something going on in or, more likely, around these big cultural venues – there's the BFI IMAX, BFI Southbank, Hayward Gallery, London Aquarium, London Eye, National Theatre, Royal Festival Hall and the purple, upside down cow-shaped summertime comedy tent Udderbelly. The public spaces and riverside location lend themselves to markets, music, play fountains, roof gardens and skateboarding. And in the case of the Southbank Centre complex, 50 per cent of everything that goes on is free.

The concrete walkways are now filled with good places to eat, drink and shop. The Southbank Centre Shop itself trades on the complex's 1950s heritage, while RFH's Skylon restaurant offers classic river views. Not to be outdone, the National Theatre has added some rather good bars (the Understudy) and restaurants (the Green Room), and opened up its own concrete terraces.

And there's more happening in the streets behind. The Cut, home to the Old and Young Vic theatres, is where to go for pre-theatre dinner or post-theatre supper. Popular venues include Tas with its meze dishes, the Anchor & Hope gastropub and – at the far end, near Southwark station – the Scandinavian Baltic, and Mar i Terra with its tapas.

A frisson of cool has been added by the Vaults, an alternative arts establishment in the arches under Waterloo station where anything might happen: burlesque balls, immersive theatre experiences or a zombie Blitz. The fact that you have to play hunt-the-venue down graffiti-covered backstreets adds to the allure.

Easier to spot, but just a stone's throw away, is Lower Marsh Market, where stalls and street-food vendors line this quiet but characterful street. Somehow, it's still a nook of independents catering to specific needs: Ian Allan Book & Model Shop; Radio Days vintage emporium; I Knit London; Travelling Through travel bookshop; Top Wind flute shop; and JB's Records. Smarter shops are starting to appear, though. There's also Scootercaffè, Café del Marsh and a growing number of galleries including Orso Major and Gallery 223.

The stretch of river between Westminster and Lambeth bridges has the classic views of the Houses of Parliament on the opposite bank. It's also home to the Archbishop of Canterbury in Lambeth Palace, parts of which date to the 13th century. The Archbishop is lucky enough to have the Garden Museum for a neighbour.

Opposite Lambeth North tube station is Morley College, a fantastic resource for adult-education courses and evening classes. This stretch between Waterloo and Elephant & Castle may feel like a glorified bus route, but it hides a few pretty pockets such as West Square. The area is dominated, though, by the Imperial War Museum, a majestic building surrounded by public gardens.

Vauxhall SE11/SW8

Changes are afoot in Vauxhall, as London's relentless redevelopment machine rolls over another relatively neglected area. To be fair, Vauxhall has been on the radar for a while now – MI6 (the Secret Intelligence Service) moved here in the 1990s, ostentatiously housed in an extraordinarily ugly pile, while St George's Wharf is an early example of London's irresponsible attitude to riverside development – this hideous complex has twice been nominated for the Carbuncle Cup, an award for Britain's worst building.

Vauxhall's problem has long been the gigantic roundabout that occupies what should be its centre. The area was once the site of the Georgian Vauxhall Pleasure Gardens, but all that remains of those days is a small park, recently renamed after the old attraction. Vauxhall's riverside location then saw it become a place for industry – Marmite and Royal Doulton were based here, as was Vauxhall Motors. Now, the few remaining industrial sites are being transformed as part of the massive Nine Elms project, spearheaded by the new US Embassy, due to open just over the borough boundary in Wandsworth in 2017. Mixed-use developments – One Nine Elms, Vauxhall Cross, Vauxhall Square – have been approved, while the big one is the venture that will eventually see homes, offices and retail added to New Covent Garden Market. The ugly roundabout remains but people are now prepared to overlook it.

The place already has a buzz thanks to the new Damien Hirst gallery on Newport Street. A huge space converted from five warehouses, it features free contemporary shows, work from Hirst's own vast collection, a restaurant and shop. Other treats include the bucolic Vauxhall City Farm, while the wonderful Brunswick House is home to architectural

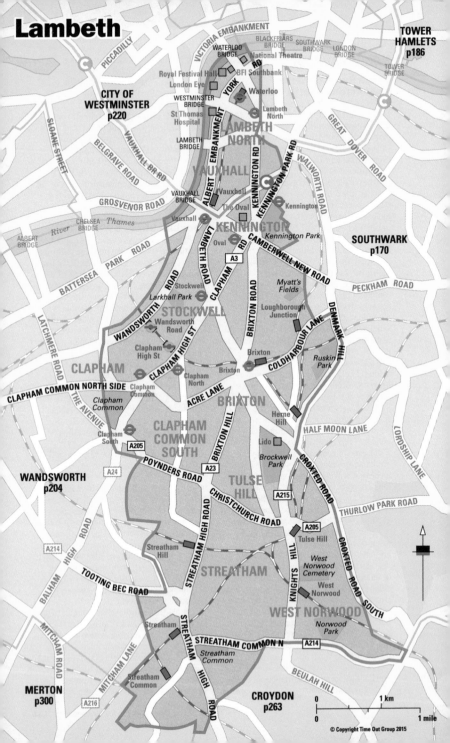

Lambeth

TOWER
HAMLETS
p186

CITY OF
WESTMINSTER
p220

SOUTHWARK
p170

WANDSWORTH
p204

MERTON
p300

CROYDON
p263

VICTORIA EMBANKMENT
BLACKFRIARS BRIDGE
SOUTHWARK BRIDGE
LONDON BRIDGE
TOWER BRIDGE
PICCADILLY
WATERLOO BRIDGE
National Theatre
RD
BFI Southbank
Royal Festival Hall
London Eye
Waterloo
YORK
WESTMINSTER BRIDGE
St Thomas Hospital
Lambeth North
LAMBETH NORTH
LAMBETH BRIDGE
ALBERT EMBANKMENT
VAUXHALL
VAUXHALL BR RD
BELGRAVE ROAD
GROSVENOR ROAD
VAUXHALL BRIDGE
Vauxhall
The Oval
KENNINGTON RD
KENNINGTON PARK RD
WALWORTH ROAD
GREAT DOVER ROAD
Kennington
Vauxhall
KENNINGTON
CHELSEA BRIDGE
Thames
River
ALBERT BRIDGE
LAMBETH ROAD
Oval
RD
Kennington Park
A3
CAMBERWELL NEW ROAD
PECKHAM ROAD
SLOANE STREET
BATTERSEA PARK ROAD
PARK ROAD
Myatt's Fields
ROAD
Stockwell
Loughborough Junction
STOCKWELL
BRIXTON ROAD
DENMARK HILL
LATCHMERE ROAD
WANDSWORTH
Larkhall Park
Wandsworth Road
Wandsworth Road
Brixton
COLDHARBOUR LANE
Ruskin Park
CLAPHAM HIGH ST
Clapham High St
Brixton
Clapham North
Brixton
LORDSHIP LANE
CLAPHAM
THE AVENUE
CLAPHAM COMMON NORTH SIDE
Clapham Common
ACRE LANE
BRIXTON
HALF MOON LANE
CLAPHAM COMMON SOUTH
Clapham South
BRIXTON HILL
Herne Hill
A205
A24
Clapham Common
Lido
Brockwell Park
CROXTED ROAD
POYNDERS ROAD
A23
TULSE HILL
THURLOW PARK ROAD
A214
BALHAM HIGH ROAD
CHRISTCHURCH ROAD
A215
CROXTED ROAD SOUTH
TOOTING BEC ROAD
STREATHAM HIGH ROAD
Streatham Hill
A205
Tulse Hill
KNIGHTS HILL
West Norwood Cemetery
West Norwood
STREATHAM
WEST NORWOOD
Norwood Park
MITCHAM LANE
Streatham
STREATHAM HIGH ROAD
STREATHAM COMMON N
A214
Streatham Common
MITCHAM ROAD
Streatham Common
BEULAH HILL
A216

0   1 km
0   1 mile

© Copyright Time Out Group 2015

salvage company LASSCO (who usually have great bits of furniture to look at) as well as the excellent Brunswick House restaurant. Other restaurants include veggie Bonnington Centre Café (founded by squatters), Dirty Burger and the Counter Brasserie. Foodies are further served by a summer street-food market and the superb Italo Deli on Bonnington Square. Decent local pubs include the ace Vauxhall Griffin and the Black Dog.

Despite having potential scene-stealers such as Damien Hirst and MI6 as neighbours, Vauxhall is still probably best known as one of London's gay centres. Much of that is to do with the legendary Royal Vauxhall Tavern, which hosts a variety of club nights and burlesque shows, and has acted as a magnet for other gay venues including the Hoist (leather bar), Fire (popular with the party crowd), Eagle London (cruisey) and a branch of Chariots (the gay-sauna chain). Some clubs open all day Sunday; how they will get on with Vauxhall's incoming residents remains to be seen.

Kennington and Oval SE11

Just half a mile south of the river, Kennington is primarily residential, but with plenty of bars, restaurants and shops. It is well served by the Northern line, and by the end of 2015 there will be a brand-new cycle superhighway running from Oval to Pimlico. The area is full of contrasts, with grand Georgian houses and attractive squares, as well as ex-council blocks and some smart modern developments. It's also within reach of the parliamentary division bell, which allows eight minutes for MPs to leg it back to Westminster if an important vote is about to happen – which is why so many MPs live here.

Kennington Park caters for a wide range of sports with a concrete skate bowl, tennis courts and an AstroTurf pitch for football or hockey; the secluded Cleaver Square, nearby, is ideal for spending summer afternoons playing boules. For many, however, Kennington is all about cricket, with the Kia Oval ground sending the neighbourhood into a beer-fuelled hysteria that can often be heard for miles around.

For food, there's French fish restaurant Lobster Pot and the elegant Kennington Tandoori, as well as top brunch spot the Oval Lounge. The area also boasts a number of good pubs, including the Brown Derby, the Prince of Wales and the Fentiman Arms, where the cider garden is well worth a visit in the summer months – not to mention

South London Pacific, a courageously camp Hawaiian bar and nightclub, open to 3am.

For entertainment, the Ovalhouse and the White Bear pub-theatre, or comedy nights at the Tommyfield, are perfect for spotting new talent. But the Kennington pub quiz is the place to be on a Sunday night.

Stockwell SW9

Just beside Brixton, and on the way to Clapham, Stockwell is overshadowed by both its better-known neighbours. Its claims to fame are one of the country's best skateparks, a Grade II*-listed bus garage, higher than average crime rates, and the largest Portuguese community outside the Iberian peninsula.

A lesser-known fact is that Stockwell was once home to Vincent van Gogh, whose former house at 87 Hackford Road has a blue plaque. There's also the local air-raid-shelter-turned-war-memorial complete with colourful murals, and 19th-century St Michael's Church with stained-glass windows by John Trinick.

Property-wise, Stockwell is a mix of Victorian terraces jostling for space with council and ex-council blocks. There's charming Larkhall Park, but this is not the most visually attractive place. The 1970s Angell Town Estate (once so rife with gang culture that taxi drivers refused to go there) has been rebuilt with strong environmental credentials and a softer aesthetic. What was Isabel Street has been resurrected as Van Gogh Walk, a community space with planting inspired by the artist's paintings.

Bakeries, bars, cafés and Portuguese restaurants cluster around South Lambeth Road and Stockwell Road. There's Funchal Bakery, O Cantinho de Portugal, Bar Estrela, Grelha d'Ouro and – over on Wandsworth Road – A Toca. Round the corner in the Porto Restaurant on Landor Road is the HQ of FC Porto's official London supporters' club.

Other popular eateries in the area include Rustico, offering proper Italian cooking in an unpromising parade of shops, taverna Mar Azul, and La Fonda de Maria – serving Colombian and Peruvian specialities.

Local boozers vary from meat markets to more genteel establishments. Among the best are the Canton Arms, sibling of Waterloo's Anchor & Hope, and the Cavendish Arms.

Brixton SW2/SW9

Emerge from Brixton tube and you're hit by the cacophony of Brixton Road: ticket touts trading that night's big-name band at Brixton

South Bank

Academy, shouting above the noise of buskers and street preachers, as a conga line of buses draws up for commuters to fight over, and police sirens race by on their way to sort out yet another fracas. Boring, Brixton ain't.

This very Caribbean corner of Zone 2, once scarred by drugs, gangs and rioting (OK, none of these have disappeared entirely) has also been colonised by middle-class professionals staking a claim on its wealth of Victorian housing, and hipsters creating a vibrant food scene. The traditional street market still fills Electric Avenue most days, and the railway arches along Atlantic Road and Station Road remain a busy mix of phone shops, grocers and cafés – at least until Network Rail's proposed redevelopment turfs them out.

As for that food scene, you find it in the covered markets of Brixton Village and Market Row, where small independent traders have taken over long-empty units to create a catering sensation. Some, such as Franco Manca and Honest Burgers, have grown into mini chains; others are much-loved locals – Mama Lan (dumplings), KaoSarn (Thai), Cornercopia (local produce and pop-ups), Fish, Wings & Tings (jerk), Elephant (Pakistani thalis), Federation Coffee and Carioca (fejoda). There are bars, cheese shops and artisanal bakeries, but it's not all food. People also come here for African fabrics, hardware, vinyl, wig shops and more. With music playing and most of the dining done outside the units, it's like one big street party

(under cover, with blankets provided). You can eat from any continent – there's even Osakan *okonomiyaki* at Okan if you want really niche. As well as the dominant Caribbean culture, there's a strong Colombian presence; the empanadas at El Rancho de Lalo are great.

Vying to be the new Brixton Village is Pop Brixton, a container park by the railway station that is all about giving space to local startups. There's Zoe's Ghana Kitchen, Baba G (Indian fusion) and Donostia Social Club (pintxos), as well as vintage clothes, cheap workspaces, gigs, events and a garden.

Indeed, there's been lots of (much needed) investment in Brixton, both in terms of public money and personal commitment. Landscaping of Windrush Square has provided a versatile public piazza for markets and events (and demos), and a home for the Black Cultural Archives. At the same time, there's been underinvestment in local-authority housing, with many tenants protesting about feeling pushed out of their homes in favour of big-money developers. Architecturally loved estates – such as Cressingham Gardens on the edge of Brockwell Park – have been left fighting for survival.

The local music scene still thrives thanks to venues such as the aforementioned Brixton Academy, which hosts international stars and souped-up club nights, and longstanding indie favourite the Windmill pub. There's also jazz at the Effra Hall Tavern, and experimental and international music upstairs at the Ritzy cinema. These, along with numerous clubs such as Electric Brixton, the Prince of Wales, Jamm and Dogstar – and the 24-hour Victoria line weekend tube – ensure that the high street is often as busy at 6am as it is at 6pm.

Though the focus of attention is currently on the central markets, Brixton Road and Coldharbour Lane, there's also a lot happening – though perhaps at a lower volume – on the many routes out of the neighbourhood. Up Acre Lane, towards Clapham, there's Boqueria tapas and the Grand Union, with one of London's best beer gardens. Meanwhile, Naughty Piglets wine bar serving Lyonnaise tapas, Effra Social and the raucous Hootananny are giving Brixton Water Lane, towards Herne Hill, its own lease of life.

Clapham and Clapham North SW4

Nobody knew it at the time, but Clapham was something of a trailblazer back in the 1980s. This was the first part of south London to get a serious dose of gentrification, and while this was initially concentrated at the top of the High Street near the common, its tendrils have since snaked to all the surrounding streets and to Clapham North. That means the area has arguably London's best concentration of bars and restaurants outside the West End, plus some of its most annoying pullovers-round-shoulders, rugger-bugger residents. Generally speaking, the further you go from the Common, the cheaper the housing – but it is relative. This

is one of London's most expensive postcodes, notwithstanding the odd council estate.

One landmark is the Clapham Picturehouse, a well programmed and very comfortable arthousey cinema on Venn Street, where there's also an excellent Saturday food market. The High Street from here to Clapham North is crammed with chain restaurants – everything from Bodean's to Nando's – but if you want something a little different, there are several superb venues. Many are centred around Clapham Old Town, the network of streets west of the High Street facing the common, where you will find the acclaimed Dairy (its spin-off the Manor is nearby), excellent French venue Trinity, Modern British at 22 North Street and some terrific ice-cream at Nardulli's.

Elsewhere is the cheap and delightful Mama Lan for dumplings, the brilliant Brickwood Coffee & Bread and, at Clapham North, Tsunami for sushi. Old-timers such as the Pepper Tree, a cheapish Thai canteen on the main drag, are worth a look as high standards force the best from every kitchen. Even the local public toilet has been turned into an upmarket restaurant, WC Wine & Charcuterie, now operating from the subterranean Victorian lavs by Clapham Common tube.

Much the same is true of the pubs – yes, the bars on the High Street are awful, especially at weekends or when there's a rugby match on the big screens – but dotted around are several gems, including the Landor (which also has a theatre), the Rose & Crown, the Craft Beer

Company, Bread & Roses and the Belle Vue; most backstreets harbour their own newly gastrofied boozer.

Clapham stinks of money, and one result is that the area has terrific facilities. Of course there's the huge expanse of the Common itself (which has a decent café called Fields) but there's also a recently refurbished leisure centre and swimming pool on Clapham Manor Street and the swanky Clapham One on the High Street, which houses a café, library and performance space. There are also serious shops, from the delightful Clapham Books, installed in new premises on the Pavement, to Moen the butcher and the hugely popular bakery-café Breads Etcetera. Scattered around those are several gift shops, antiques places, jewellery designers and general purveyors of high-quality bric-a-brac – Places & Spaces or Woodlark – ensuring the town is constantly busy. These days, even the celebs are in on the act: actor Neil Pearson has a rare book shop that does brisk business in the Old Town for moneyed locals happy to spend £2,500 on a first-edition Nabokov. Only in Clapham.

Clapham South and Clapham Park SW2/SW4

Stretching from the south side of Clapham Common across to Brixton Hill, Clapham Park is a typical London suburb. Stuck between Streatham, Clapham, Brixton and Balham, you'll find a bit of everything here – good pubs, neighbourhood restaurants, unexpected parks such as Agnes Riley Gardens, sprawling housing estates – all spread around street after street of terraced houses: some exceptionally grand, others about as unpretentious as Zone 2 ever manages. It's the sort of place where it's easy to get lost, but also where something interesting or unusual may be around the next corner.

The bit most people have heard about is Abbeville Road, which is one of those London streets that thinks it's a village and can be as delightful as it is smug. This is banker-bonus territory, so a house will set you back a few million, but the restaurants are correspondingly great, whether it's French (clock-themed bistro Le Bonne Heure), Modern European (the Abbeville Kitchen), Modern British (Bistro Union), Mexican (Comensal) or trendy but reasonably priced fish and chips (Kerbisher & Malt). There's also a clutch of places around Clapham South tube such as the Georgian, which doubles as a boozer. Otherwise you have to head all the way over

to Brixton Hill, through the estates of Clapham Park, where you'll find Lisboa Grill and – in Brixton Prison – a restaurant staffed by inmates called the Clink.

Decent pubs include the Rookery, just across the road from the Windmill, which itself is a grand coaching inn on Clapham Common – on a summer day, its beer garden has a magnetic effect on locals. Abbeville Road has the Abbeville but the best drinking place in the area is undoubtedly the other Windmill towards Brixton, a pub and music venue with a terrifically eclectic bookings policy.

For shops, you really need to stick to Abbeville Road, where there are several gift and antique shops including Grand Passion and delis such as Macfarlanes, plus a branch of Ginger Pig butchers and numerous estate agents. There are nice small parks – Windmill Gardens has a great community feel, for instance, as well as a remarkably surviving windmill from 1816 that is open for occasional tours. But the area's anchor is obviously Clapham Common, a massive expanse of green that has enough space for everybody: footballers, joggers, kite-flyers, rich mums doing buggy-aerobics, anglers, sunbathers and daytime drinkers. All of London can be found here, weather permitting.

Streatham SW16

Streatham High Road, all 1.8 miles of it, has been classed as the UK's worst high street and its most polluted; in fact, it's more accurate to call it the most quintessentially 'London' high street. Starting at the southern end, where things are still quite pleasant, there's Streatham Common (a welcome green space worth exploring, up to the Rookery gardens and café), the spankingly rebuilt ice rink (with pool attached), and Hideaway jazz club. The buses that clog the main stretch of the High Road largely terminate here at Streatham rail station. (Not to be confused with Streatham Common station, hidden down behind Barrow Road, or Streatham Hill station, about a mile north towards Brixton.) And apart from the biggest Tesco most of us have ever seen, this locale is characterised by small shops and cafés serving a multitude of nationalities.

The area's sizeable Somali community is visible around the cluster of cafés at the top of Gleneagle Road. By contrast, the next junction, at Streatham Green, is all about the big Manor Arms pub (with secluded beer garden) and the farmers' market (weekly on Saturdays).

The central section of Streatham High Road hasn't done much for the area's reputation. It's the bit that everyone sees when they are stuck in traffic waiting to head off west to Tooting and its famous Bec or ploughing on south along the A23 to Croydon. Among the pawn shops, betting shops, hair-braiding salons, supermarkets and chain restaurants, however, there are a few places worth looking out for: Whole Meal Café is a vegetarian-vegan venue, around since 1978; Beyrouths is a meze and grill joint, good for big groups and small children; Brooks & Gao and Boyce da Roca are popular cafés; the White Lion and the Horse & Groom are the pubs of choice, the former something of a live music hub.

Along here, the Brazilian and Portuguese communities are served by specialist grocers, cafés and a capoeira school. The Eastern European community is looked after by several Polish delis, a Romanian mini market and cake shop called Dracula.

At Streatham Hill station, and around the bottom of Leigham Court Road, there's a subtle change for the better. Here, you'll find a couple of award-winning Italian delis: Thompson, its windows crammed with *arancini*, *caprese* (Italian brownies), *ciambella* (doughnuts) and other freshly made treats; and Fish Tale, with its fresh-fish counter and jars of flavoured balsamic vinegars. There's also old-school chippy Kennedy's (hear the crunch of the batter) and a branch of Balfe's Bikes. Hood is probably the nearest Streatham has to a destination restaurant, but it won't be alone for long.

The residential streets are just as varied as the High Road. Those towards Tooting Bec and around Streatham Common station are more uniform, but those that scramble over the hill towards West Norwood offer all sorts of unexpected surprises. There are intimate mews, all kinds of housing (Arts and Crafts, Edwardian, Victorian), and big mansion blocks including the art deco Pullman Court on Streatham Hill itself. Period details abound, in a lived-in-and-loved way rather than in a show-off style.

West Norwood and Tulse Hill SE27

This very urban slice of south London abuts genteel West Dulwich on one side and flows up and over the hill into Streatham on the other.

At one end, under-appreciated Tulse Hill sits huddled around the train station and the South Circular's one-way system, its Victorian terraces and light-industrial units housing glass-blowers and other local artisans. But the recent sprucing-up of the Tulse Hill Hotel – now a grand gastropub with boutique rooms – may shunt the neighbourhood on to the south London map.

At the other end, slightly raised above the dust of Norwood Road and still exhibiting signs of its grander Victorian past, is West Norwood. It is dominated by Grade II*-listed St Luke's Church and the 40-acre South Metropolitan Cemetery (one of London's 'magnificent seven'), established in the 19th century and celebrated for its Gothic Revival architecture. More retiring but equally lovely

Streatham Common is considerably less crowded than Clapham Common. Seek out the pretty Rookery garden.

is the Old Library on Knight's Hill, designed by Sidney Smith of Tate Britain fame.

The long straight stretch of Norwood Road linking the two is where you'll find the workaday shops along with an impressively multicultural selection of cafés. In just a couple of hundred metres, you can encounter Afro-Caribbean, Iberian, Italian and Portuguese examples, plus a Polish grocery displaying a Brazilian flag. Especially worth stopping at are the much-loved deli Beamish & McGlue, the authentically retro Electric Café and the growing, hyper-local mini-chain Blackbird Bakery.

The classic middle-class catnip is up in the Knight's Hill triangle around the church and station (roughly 20 minutes into Victoria and served by plenty of buses). You can get gluten-free cakes at Cul de Sac, interior-design services at Revamp Interiors and gastropubbery at the Great North Wood, which is named after the sylvan swathes that covered the ridge from Forest Hill to Norwood. For beer and chat, try the relaxed Hope pub; for smoothies, babygrows and stretch-mark oil, head for Otter Trading; the Book & Record Bar has soul nights and vinyl; the Portico Gallery does evening classes, exhibitions and a great deal more besides. Cap all this with some good schools – and a shiny new leisure centre – and you can see why families are flocking here.

But this is also a down-to-earth, can-do sort of place. There are enough business and industrial spaces for local people to work near home, which keeps the high street full of life at any time of day. Artisan activity and community spirit is strong, as demonstrated by the monthly West Norwood Feast (local arts and crafts, food fair, furniture, live music, vintage clothes), the popularity of the South London Theatre, the work of L'Arche disability support centre (www.larchelondon.org.uk) and an active Trussell Trust food bank. In 2017, the local library is joining forces with Picturehouse Cinemas to breathe new multifunctional life into Nettlefold Hall.

Finally, those taking advantage of the relatively affordable house prices in the area – and the substantial supply of decent-sized family homes and conversion flats – benefit from some great local stores and facilities: the well-stocked and extremely helpful London Decorators Merchants paint shop, auction house Roseberys, a garden centre and several self-storage warehouses.

Eating

22 North Street 22 North Street, SW4 0HB (3583 3702, www.22northstreet.co.uk).
Abbeville Kitchen 47 Abbeville Road, SW4 9JX (8772 1110, www.abbevillekitchen.com).
Anchor & Hope 36 The Cut, SE1 8LP (7928 9898, www.anchorandhopepub.co.uk).
A Toca 343 Wandsworth Road, SW8 2JH (7627 2919, www.atoca-lambeth.co.uk).
Baba G Pop Brixton, Brixton Station Road, SW9 8PB (07725 230995, www.bhangraburger.com).
Baltic 74 Blackfriars Road, SE1 8HA (7928 1111, www.balticrestaurant.co.uk).
Bar Estrela 111 South Lambeth Road, SW8 1UZ (7793 1051).
Beyrouths 20-21 High Parade, Streatham High Road, SW16 1EX (7998 1853, www.beyrouths.com).
Bistro Union 40 Abbeville Road, SW4 9NG (7042 6400, www.bistrounion.co.uk).

Le Bonne Heure 31 Abbeville Road, SW4 9LA (3417 3056, www.labonneheure.co.uk).
Bonnington Centre Café 11 Vauxhall Grove, SW8 1TD (7820 7466, www.bonnington cafe.co.uk).
Boyce da Roca Leigham Hall Parade, Streatham High Road, SW16 1DR (8769 0099).
Brickwood Coffee & Bread 16 Clapham Common South Side, SW4 7AB (7819 9614, www.brickwoodlondon.com).
Brooks & Gao 28 Streatham High Road, SW16 1DB (www.netberg.com/brooksandgao).
Brunswick House 30 Wandsworth Road, SW8 2LG (7720 2926, www.brunswickhouse.co).
Café del Marsh 44 Lower Marsh, SE1 7RG (07976 226905).
Carioca Market Row, 25-27 Coldharbour Lane, SW9 8LB (7095 9052).
Clink Her Majesty's Prison Brixton, Jebb Avenue, SW2 5XF (8678 9007, www.theclinkcharity.org).
Comensal 32 Abbeville Road, SW4 9NG (8673 7272, www.comensal.co.uk).
Cornercopia 65 Brixton Village Market, Coldharbour Lane, SW9 8PS (07919 542233, www.brixtoncornercopia.co.uk).
Counter Brasserie Arch 50, 7-11 South Lambeth Place, SW8 1SP (3693 9600, www.counterrestaurants.com).
Cul de Sac 2 Knight's Hill, SE27 0HY (07939 573806).
Dairy 15 The Pavement, SW4 0HY (7622 4165, www.the-dairy.co.uk).
Dirty Burger Arch 54, 6 South Lambeth Road, SW8 1SS (7074 1444, www.eatdirtyburger.com).
Donostia Social Club Pop Brixton, Brixton Station Road, SW9 8PB (07961 844464, www.donostiasocialclub.co.uk).
Electric Café 258 Norwood Road, SE27 9AJ (8670 3114).
Elephant 55 Brixton Village Market, Coldharbour Lane, SW9 8PS (07590 389684, www.elephantcafeonline.blogspot.co.uk).
Federation Coffee Unit 77-78, Brixton Village Market, Coldharbour Lane, SW9 8PS (http://federationcoffee.com).

TRANSPORT

Tube lines Bakerloo, Jubilee, Northern, Overground, Victoria, Waterloo & City
Rail services into Charing Cross, City Thameslink, London Bridge, Victoria, Waterloo
Main bus routes into central London 1, 2, 3, 4, 26, 35, 42, 45, 59, 68, 76, 77, 87, 133, 137, 168, 171, 172, 436, 521, RV1, X68; night buses N1, N2, N3, N35, N44, N68, N76, N133, N137, N155, N171, N343, N381; 24-hour buses 12, 88, 139, 159, 176, 188, 243, 341, 344
River boat services Festival Pier, South Bank and St George Wharf Pier, Vauxhall

Fields 2 Rookery Road, SW4 9DD (www.fieldscafe.com).

Fish, Wings & Tings 3 Granville Arcade, Coldharbour Lane, SW9 8PR (no phone).

La Fonda de Maria 273A Clapham Road, SW9 9BQ (3730 0659).

Franco Manca Unit 4, Market Row, SW9 8LD (7738 3021, www.francomanca.co.uk).

Funchal Bakery 141-143 Stockwell Road, SW9 9TN (7733 3134).

Georgian 27 Balham Hill, SW12 9DX (8675 4975, www.georgianrestaurant.co.uk).

Great North Wood 3 Knight's Hill, SE27 0HS (8766 0351, www.thegreatnorthwood.co.uk).

Green Room 101 Upper Ground, SE1 9PP (7452 3630, www.greenroom.london).

Grelha d'Ouro 151-153 South Lambeth Road, SW8 1XN (7735 9764).

Hood 67 Streatham Hill, SW2 4TX (3601 3320, www.hoodrestaurants.com).

Honest Burgers 12 Brixton Village Market, Coldharbour Lane, SW9 8PR (7733 7963, www.honestburgers.co.uk).

KaoSarn 2 & 96 Brixton Village Market, Coldharbour Lane, SW9 8PR (7095 8922).

Kennedy's 5 Leigham Court Road, SW16 2ND (8769 1003).

Kennington Tandoori 313 Kennington Road, SE11 4QE (7735 9247, www.kenningtontandoori.com).

Kerbisher & Malt 50 Abbeville Road, SW4 9NF (3417 4350, www.kerbisher.co.uk).

Lisbon Grill 256A Brixton Hill, SW2 1HF (8671 0600, www.lisbon-grill.co.uk).

Lobster Pot 3 Kennington Lane, SE11 4RG (7582 5556, www.lobsterpotrestaurant.co.uk).

Madeira Pâtisserie 46A-C Albert Embankment, SE1 7TL (7820 1117, www.madeiralondon.co.uk).

Mama Lan (www.mamalan.co.uk); Unit 18, Brixton Village Market, Coldharbour Lane, SW9 8PR; 8 The Pavement, SW4 0HY.

Manor 148 Clapham Manor Street, SW4 6BX (7720 4662, www.themanorclapham.co.uk).

Mar Azul 124 Clapham Road, SW9 0LA (7820 0464, www.marazulseafoodrestaurantlondon.co.uk).

Mar i Terra 14 Gambia Street, SE1 0XH (7928 7628, www.mariterra.co.uk).

Nardulli's 29 The Pavement, SW4 0JE (7720 5331, www.nardulli.co.uk).

Naughty Piglets 28 Brixton Water Lane, SW2 1PE (7274 7796, www.naughtypiglets.co.uk).

O Cantinho de Portugal 137 Stockwell Road, SW9 9TN (7924 0218, www.cantinho-de-portugal.co.uk).

Okan 39 Brixton Village Market, Coldharbour Lane, SW9 8PR (www.okanbrixtonvillage.com).

Otter Trading 21 Knight's Hill, SE27 0HS (8670 6923).

Oval Lounge 24 Clapham Road, The Oval, SW9 0JG (7735 8882, www.theovallounge.co.uk).

Pepper Tree 19 Clapham Common South Side, SW4 7AB (7622 1758, www.thepeppertree.co.uk).

Porto Restaurant 82 Landor Road, SW9 9PE (3601 3181, www.portorestaurant.co.uk).

El Rancho De Lalo 94-95 Brixton Village Market, SW9 8PS (7737 2648).

Rustico 271 Clapham Road, SW9 9BQ (7738 4563, www.rusticolondon.com).

Scootercaffè 132 Lower Marsh, SE1 7AE (7620 1421).

Skylon Southbank Centre, Belvedere Road, SE1 8XX (7654 7800, www.skylon-restaurant.co.uk).

Tas 33 The Cut, SE1 8LF (7928 2111, www.tasrestaurants.co.uk).

Trinity 4 The Polygon, SW4 0JG (7622 1199, www.trinityrestaurant.co.uk).

Tsunami 5-7 Voltaire Road, SW4 6DQ (7978 1610, www.tsunamirestaurant.co.uk).

Tulse Hill Hotel 150 Norwood Road, SE24 9AY (8671 7499, www.tulsehillhotel.com).

WC Wine & Charcuterie Clapham Common South Side, SW4 7AA (7622 5502, www.wcclapham.co.uk).

Whole Meal Café 1 Shrubbery Road, SW16 2AS (8769 2423, www.wholemealcafe.com).

Zoe's Ghana Kitchen Pop Brixton, Brixton Station Road, SW9 8PB (07931 602889, www.zoesghanakitchen.co.uk).

Brixton Village Market: Elephant (left) and Federation Coffee

Drinking

Abbeville 67-69 Abbeville Road, SW4 9JW (8675 2201, www.theabbeville.co.uk).
Belle Vue 1 Clapham Common South Side, SW4 7AA (7498 9473, www.bellevue-clapham.com).
Black Dog 112 Vauxhall Walk, SE11 5ER (7735 4440, www.theblackdogvauxhall.com).
Brown Derby 336 Kennington Park Road, SE11 4TP (7735 5122, www.thebrownderbypub. wordpress.com).
Canton Arms 117 South Lambeth Road, SW8 1XP (7582 8710, www.cantonarms.com).
Cavendish Arms 128 Hartington Road, SW8 2HJ (7498 7464, www.thecavendisharmsstockwell.co.uk).
Craft Beer Company 128 Clapham Manor Street, SW4 6ED (7498 9633, www.thecraftbeerco.com).
Eagle London 349 Kennington Lane, SE11 5QY (7793 0903, www.eaglelondon.com).
Effra Social 89 Effra Road, SW2 1DF (7737 6800, www.effrasocial.com).
Electric Brixton 1 Town Hall Parade, Brixton Hill, SW2 1RJ (7274 2290, www.electricbrixton.com).
Fentiman Arms 64 Fentiman Road, SW8 1LA (7793 9796, www.geronimo-inns.co.uk).
Fire 39 Parry Street, SW8 1RT (3242 0040, www.firelondon.net).
Grand Union 123 Acre Lane, SW2 5UA (7274 8794, www.grandunionbars.com).

Hootananny 95 Effra Road, SW2 1DF (7737 7273, www.hootanannybrixton.co.uk).
Hope 49 High Street, West Norwood, SE27 9JS (8670 2035, www.rampubcompany.co.uk).
Horse & Groom 60 Streatham High Road, SW16 1DA (8769 8895, www.horseandgroom-pub.co.uk).
Kennington 60 Camberwell New Road, SE5 0RS (7735 9990, www.thekennington.com).
Manor Arms Mitcham Lane, SW16 6LQ (3195 6888, www.themanorarms.com).
Prince of Wales 48 Cleaver Square, SE11 4EA (7735 9916, www.shepherdneame.co.uk).
Rookery 69 Clapham Common South Side, SW4 9DA (8673 9162, www.therookeryclapham.co.uk).
Rose & Crown 2 The Polygon, SW4 0JG (7720 8265).
Royal Vauxhall Tavern 372 Kennington Lane, SE11 5HY (7820 1222, www.vauxhalltavern.com).
South London Pacific 340 Kennington Road, SE11 4LD (7450 0796, www.southlondonpacific.com).
Tommyfield 185 Kennington Lane, SE11 4EZ (7735 1061, www.thetommyfield.com).
Understudy National Theatre, South Bank, SE1 9PX (7452 3000, www.nationaltheatre.org.uk).
Vauxhall Griffin 8 Wyvil Road, SW8 2TH (7622 0222, www.vauxhallgriffin.com).
White Lion 243 Streatham High Road, SW16 1BB (8677 3341, www.whitelion.org.uk).
Windmill Clapham Common South Side, SW4 9DE (8673 4578, www.windmillclapham.co.uk).

Shopping

Balfe's Bikes 87 Streatham Hill, SW2 4UB (8671 1984, www.balfesbikes.co.uk).
Beamish & McGlue 461 Norwood Road, SE27 9DQ (8761 8099, www.beamishandmcglue.com).
Book & Record Bar 20 Norwood High Street, SE27 9NR (8670 9568, www.thebookandrecordbar.co.uk).
Breads Etcetera 127 Clapham High Street, SW4 7SS (7720 3601).
Brixton Market Electric Avenue, Pope's Road, Brixton Station Road & Atlantic Road, SW9 (www.brixtonmarket.net).
Clapham Books 26 The Pavement, S4 0JA (7627 2797, www.claphambooks.com).
Dracula 32 Streatham High Road, SW16 1DB (3417 7840, www.dracula-shop.co.uk).
Fish Tale 9 Leigham Court Road, SW16 2ND (8664 7464, www.fishtale.co.uk).
Ginger Pig 55 Abbeville Road, SW4 9JW (8673 2251, www.thegingerpig.co.uk).
Grand Passion 42 Abbeville Road, SW4 9NG (8675 3499, www.grandpassion.co.uk).
Ian Allan Book & Model Shop 45-46 Lower Marsh, SE1 7RG (7401 2100, www.ianallanpublishing.com).
I Knit 106 Lower Marsh, SW6 1TE (7261 1338, www.iknit.org.uk).
Italo Deli 13 Bonnington Square, SW8 1TE (7450 3773, www.italodeli.co.uk).
JB's Records 108 Lower Marsh, SE1 7AB (7261 1968).
LASSCO Brunswick House, 30 Wandsworth Road, SW8 2LG (7394 2100, www.lassco.co.uk).
London Decorators Merchants 547-549 Norwood Road, SE27 9DL (8655 9595, www.ldmdirect.co.uk).
Macfarlanes 48 Abbeville Road, SW4 9NF (8673 5373, www.macfarlanesdeli.co.uk).
M Moen & Sons 24 The Pavement, SW4 0JA (7622 1624, www.moen.co.uk).
Places & Spaces 30 Old Town, SW4 0LB (7498 0998, www.placesandspaces.com).
Radio Days 87 Lower Marsh, SE1 7AB (7928 0800, www.radiodaysvintage.co.uk).
Revamp Interiors 33 Bellevue Road, SW17 7EF (8767 7222, www.revampinteriors.co.uk).
Roseberys 70-76 Knight's Hill, SE27 0JD (8761 2522, www.roseberys.co.uk). Auction house.
Southbank Centre Shop Festival Terrace, SE1 8XX (7921 0771, http://shop.southbankcentre.co.uk).
Streatham Farmers' Market Streatham Green, SW16 5SD (www.weareccfm.com).
Thompson 2 Streatham High Road, SW16 1DB (8677 1197).
Top Wind 2 Lower Marsh, SE1 7RJ (7401 8787, www.topwind.com).

Travelling Through 131 Lower Marsh, SE1 7AE (www.travellingthrough.co.uk).
Venn Street Market Venn Street, SW4 0AT (7622 8259, www.vennstreetmarket.co.uk).
West Norwood Feast Various venues (www.westnorwoodfeast.com).
Woodlark 32 Old Town, SW4 0LB (7720 3312, www.woodlarkclapham.co.uk).

Things to do

Cinemas & theatres

Above the Stag Theatre Arch 17, Miles Street, SW8 1RZ (www.abovethestag.com).
BFI London IMAX 1 Charlie Chaplin Walk, SE1 8XR (0330 333 7878, www.bfi.org.uk). The UK's biggest cinema screen with plenty of 3D spectaculars.

Learn a new skill at Morley College (www.morleycollege.ac.uk).

BFI Southbank Belvedere Road, SE1 8XT (7928 3232, www.bfi.org.uk). London's best cinema, with an unrivalled programme of retrospective seasons and previews.
Bread & Roses 68 Clapham Manor Street, SW4 6DZ (7498 1779, www.breadandrosespub.com). Pub with comedy, music and theatre.
Clapham Picturehouse 76 Venn Street, SW4 0AT (0871 902 5727, www.picturehouses.co.uk).
Landor 70 Landor Road, SW9 9PH (7737 7276, www.landortheatre.co.uk). Pub theatre.
LOST 208 Wandsworth Road, SW8 2JU (7622 9208, www.losttheatre.co.uk).
National Theatre South Bank, SE1 9PX (7452 3000, www.nationaltheatre.org.uk). Theatre complex with four auditoria: the Olivier, Lyttleton, Dorfman and a temporary space that was added in 2013.
Odeon Streatham 47-49 Streatham High Road, SW16 1PW (0871 224 4007, www.odeon.co.uk).
Old Vic The Cut, SE1 8NB (0844 871 7628, www.oldvictheatre.com).
Omnibus 1 Clapham Common Northside, SW4 0QW (7498 4699, www.omnibus-clapham.org). Multi-arts centre.
Ovalhouse 52-54 Kennington Oval, SE11 5SW (admin 7582 0080, box office 7582 7680, www.ovalhouse.com). Theatre and gallery with strong community and young persons' programmes.
Ritzy Brixton Oval, Coldharbour Lane, SW2 1JG (0871 902 5739, www.picturehouses.co.uk). Much-loved local cinema, with café and jazz bar.

South London Theatre The Old Fire Station, 2A Norwood High Street, SE27 9NS (box office 8670 3474, www.southlondontheatre.co.uk).

White Bear Theatre 138 Kennington Park Road, SE11 4DJ (7793 9193, www.whitebeartheatre. co.uk). Pub theatre.

Vaults Leake Street, SE1 7NN (7401 9603, www. the-vaults.org). Kitchen, gallery and theatre.

Young Vic 66 The Cut, SE1 8LZ (7922 2922, www.youngvic.org).

Galleries & museums

Black Cultural Archives 1 Windrush Square, SW2 1EF (3757 8500, www.bcaheritage.org.uk).

Florence Nightingale Museum St Thomas' Hospital, 2 Lambeth Palace Road, SE1 7EW (7620 0374, www.florence-nightingale.co.uk). The life and work of 'the lady with the lamp'.

Gallery 223 137-139 Lower Marsh, SE1 7AE (www.gallery223.co.uk).

Garden Museum Lambeth Palace Road, SE1 7LB (7401 8865, www.gardenmuseum.org.uk). The world's first horticultural museum.

Hayward Gallery Belvedere Road, SE1 8XX (7960 4200, www.southbankcentre.co.uk/venues/hayward-gallery). One of London's top galleries, presenting a mix of contemporary and older work.

Museum of the Royal Pharmaceutical Society 1 Lambeth High Street, SE1 7JN (7572 2210, www. rpharms.com). The history of pharmaceuticals.

Newport Street Gallery Newport Street, SE11 6AJ (www.newportstreetgallery.com). Hirst's personal collection in a new gallery scheduled to launch in October 2015.

Orso Major Art 19 Lower Marsh, SE1 7RJ (3289 5553, www.orsomajor.com).

Portico Gallery Knight's Hall, 23A Knight's Hill, SE27 0HS (8761 7612, www.porticogallery.org.uk).

Other attractions

Brixton Windmill Blenheim Gardens, SW2 5EU (7926 6056, www.brixtonwindmill.org). Restored windmill used as an educational attraction.

Lambeth Palace Lambeth Palace Road, SE1 7JU (7898 1200, www.archbishopofcanterbury.org). Official residence of the Archbishop of Canterbury.

London Aquarium County Hall, Westminster Bridge Road, SE1 7PB (0871 663 1678, www. visitsealife.com/london). One of Europe's largest aquatic exhibitions; giant tanks and touch pools.

London Eye Riverside Building, County Hall, Westminster Bridge Road, SE1 7PB (0871 781 3000, www.londoneye.com).

Vauxhall City Farm 165 Tyers Street, SE11 5HS (7582 4204, www.vauxhallcityfarm.org). Community farm and gardens, with beekeepers and riding lessons.

Gigs, clubs & comedy

Dogstar 389 Coldharbour Lane, SW9 8LQ (7733 7515, www.dogstarbrixton.com).

Effra Hall Tavern 38 Kellett Road, SW2 1EB (7274 4180). Jazz pub.

Hideaway 2 Empire Mews, SW16 2BF (8835 7070, www.hideawaylive.co.uk).

Hoist Railway Arches 47B & 47C, South Lambeth Road, SW8 1SR (7735 9972, www.thehoist.co.uk).

Jamm 261 Brixton Road, SW9 6LH (07517 465613, www.brixtonjamm.org).

O2 Academy Brixton 211 Stockwell Road, SW9 9SL (7771 3000, www.o2academybrixton.co.uk). Major concert venue.

Prince of Wales 467-469 Brixton Road, SW9 8HH (7095 1978, www.pow-london.com).

Southbank Centre Belvedere Road, SE1 8XX (7960 4200, www.southbankcentre.co.uk). Three concert halls – the majestic Royal Festival Hall, smaller Queen Elizabeth Hall and diminutive Purcell Room – cover classical and contemporary music and dance.

Udderbelly Jubilee Gardens, off Belvedere Road, SE1 8XX (0844 545 8282, www.underbelly.co.uk). Comedy and music; summer only.

Windmill Brixton 22 Blenheim Gardens, SW2 5BZ (8671 0700, http://windmillbrixton.co.uk).

Green spaces

For more details, see www.lambeth.gov.uk.

Archbishop's Park Carlisle Lane, SE1 (www. archbishopspark.org). With gardening club.

Brockwell Park Dulwich Road, SE24 (www. brockwellpark.com). Playground and BMX track.

Clapham Common Windmill Drive, SW4 (www. claphamcommon.org). Skate park, fishing and a great pub café.

Kennington Park Kennington Park Road, SE11 (www.kenningtonpark.org). Gardens, sports pitches and café.

Max Roach Park Brixton Road, SW9. Adventure playground.

Myatt's Fields Park Calais Street, SE5 (www. myattsfieldspark.info). Sports pitches, gardens and waterplay.

Ruskin Park Denmark Hill, SE5 (www. friendsruskinpark.org.uk). Sports pitches, community garden and bandstand.

Vauxhall Pleasure Gardens Tyers Street, SE11.

Streatham Common Streatham High Road, SW16. Includes the Rookery formal garden.

Gyms & leisure centres

Brixton Recreation Centre 27 Brixton Station Road, SW9 8QQ (7095 5100, www.better.org.uk). Busy programme of classes includes fencing and wheelchair basketball.

Clapham Leisure Centre 141 Clapham Manor Street, SW4 6DB (7627 7900, www.better.org.uk). State-of-the-art gym and 25m pool.

Ferndale Community Sports Centre Nursery Road, SW9 8PB (0845 130 8998, www.better.org.uk).

Fitness First Blue Star House, 234-244 Stockwell Road, SW9 9SP (0844 571 2828, www.fitnessfirst. co.uk). Private.

Flaxman Sports Centre Carew Street, SE5 9DF (7926 1054, www.better.org.uk).

Paris Gym 73 Goding Street, SE11 5AW (7735 8989, www.parisgym.com). Men only; private.

Soho Gym 95-97 Clapham High Street, SW4 7TB (7720 0321, www.sohogyms.com). Private.

South Bank Club 124-130 Wandsworth Road, SW8 2LD (7622 6866, www.southbankclub.co.uk). Private.

Streatham Ice & Leisure Centre 390 Streatham High Road, SW16 6HX (8677 5758, www.better. org.uk).

Virgin Active (www.virginactive.co.uk); 4-20 North Street, SW4 0HG (7819 2555); 20 Ockley Road, SW16 1UB (8769 8686). Private.

West Norwood Health & Leisure Centre 25 Devane Way, SE27 0DF (8761 1159, www. better.org.uk). Classes; 25m pool.

Outdoor pursuits

Brockwell Lido Brockwell Park, Dulwich Road, SE24 0PA (7274 3088, www.fusion-lifestyle.com). Indoor gym attached.

Ebony Horse Club 51 Millbrook Road, SW9 7JD (7738 3478, www.ebonyhorseclub.org). Small community riding centre.

Spectator sports

Kia Oval Surrey County Cricket Club, SE11 5SS (0844 375 1845, www.kiaoval.com).

Schools

Primary

There are 59 state primary schools in Lambeth, including 21 church schools and one Muslim school. There are also nine independent primaries, including two Muslim schools. See www.lambeth. gov.uk, www.education.gov.uk/edubase and www.ofsted.gov.uk for more information.

Secondary

Archbishop Tenison's School 55 Kennington Oval, SE11 5SR (7735 3771, www.tenisons.com). Church of England; boys only.

Bishop Thomas Grant School Belltrees Grove, SW16 2HY (8769 3294, www.btg.ac). Roman Catholic.

Dunraven School 94-98 Leigham Court Road, SW16 2QB (8677 2431, www.dunraven.org.uk).

Elmgreen School Elmcourt Road, SE27 9BZ (8766 5020, www.the-elmgreen-school.org.uk).

Evelyn Grace Academy 255 Shakespeare Road, SE24 0QN (7737 9520, www.evelyngrace academy.org).

Lambeth Academy Elms Road, SW4 9ET (7819 4700, www.lambeth-academy.org).

Lilian Baylis Technology School 323 Kennington Lane, SE11 5QY (7091 9500, www.lilianbaylis.com).

London Nautical School 61 Stamford Street, SE1 9NA (7928 6801, www.lns.org.uk). Boys only.

Norwood School Crown Dale, SE19 3NY (8670 9382, www.thenorwoodschool.org).

Platanos College Clapham Road, SW9 0AL (7733 6156, www.platanoscollege.com).

La Retraite RC School Atkins Road, SW12 0AB (8673 5644, www.laretraite.lambeth.sch.uk). Roman Catholic; girls only.

St Gabriel's College Langton Road, SW9 6UL (7793 3901, www.saintgabrielscollege.org).

St Martin-in-the-Fields CE School 155 Tulse Hill, SW2 3UP (8674 5594, www.stmartins. academy). Church of England; girls only.

Property

Local estate agents

Aspire www.aspire.co.uk

Beresford Residential www. beresfordresidential.com

Brooks www.brooksestateagents.com

Daniel Cobb www.danielcobb.co.uk

Field & Sons www.fieldandsons.co.uk

George Lynch www.georgelynch.co.uk

Harmens www.harmens.co.uk

Jacksons www.jacksonsestateagents.com

Keating Estates www.keatingestates.com

Lloyd & Co www.lloydandcoproperties.com

Martin Barry www.martinbarrypartnership.co.uk

Murray Estates www.murray-estates.co.uk

Xander Matthew www.xandermatthew.com

Local knowledge

www.brixtonblog.com
www.brixtonbuzz.com
www.heartstreatham.co.uk
www.incredibleediblelambeth.org
www.loveclapham.com
www.lovevaux.com
www.shopinstreatham.com
www.shoutstreatham.com
www.streathamguardian.co.uk
www.streathamsociety.org.uk
www.totallyclapham.co.uk
www.vauxhallcivicsociety.org.uk
www.waterlooquarter.org

Cleaver Square

USEFUL INFO

Borough size
2,681 hectares

Population
322,000

Ethnic mix
White 67.5%
Black or Black British 17.4%
Asian or Asian British 7.6%
Mixed 4.2%
Chinese or other 3.3%

London borough of Lambeth
Town Hall, Brixton Hill, SW2 1RW
(7926 1000, www.lambeth.gov.uk)

Council run by
Labour

MPs
Dulwich & West Norwood, Helen
Hayes (Labour); Streatham, Chuka
Umunna (Labour); Vauxhall, Kate
Hoey (Labour)

Main recycling centre
Vale Street Recycling Centre, Vale
Street, SE27 9PH (7926 9000,
www.lambeth.gov.uk)

Council tax
£825.80 to £2,477.40

Lewisham

With beautiful wooded hills looking out over gritty urban wastes, Lewisham is the original *jolie laide* borough. Regeneration schemes – to improve housing, schools, parks and sports facilities – and well-networked transport links mean its popularity is on an upward trajectory.

AVERAGE PROPERTY PRICE

Detached	Terraced
£785,812	£410,586
Semi-detached	Flat
£507,784	£320,714

AVERAGE RENTAL PRICE PER WEEK

Room	1 bed
£109	£216
Studio	2 bed
£173	£276
	3 bed
	£345

Brockley Market

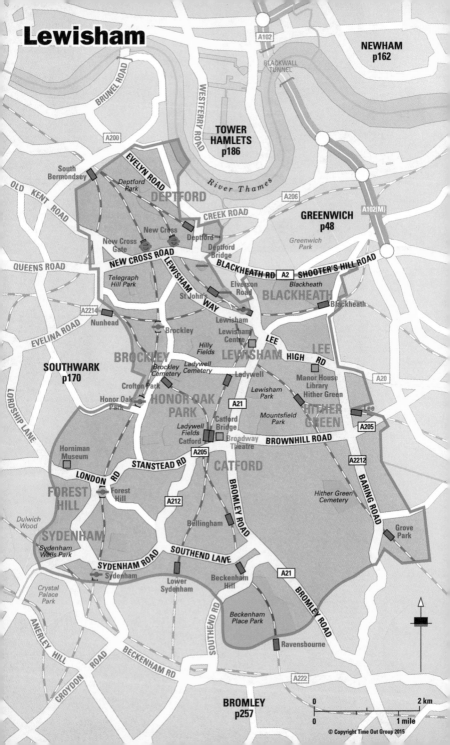

Lewisham

Neighbourhoods

New Cross and Telegraph Hill SE14

New Cross is a teeming blend of Goldsmiths art students, hoodies and young creative professionals living around the smoggy A2 and its great knots of infrastructure. This edgy, bohemian atmosphere sets up the perfect growing conditions for gentrification, and a preponderance of affluent, semi-famous, creative types are settling and breeding in the big houses around Telegraph Hill Park.

In days gone by, the independent New Cross spirit rose up in a proud moment in Lewisham's history: in 1977, the biggest street battle against fascists since the Battle of Cable Street in 1936 took place here, on Clifton Rise. The area's appealingly nonconformist nature, these days evident in local traders' vociferous rejection of the supermarket chains, is manifested in some delightful one-off shops, cafés, bars and pubs.

Up the steeply climbing wide roads, away from the gentle chaos of the main drag, Telegraph Hill is a largely unspoilt residential area with some impressive, bay-fronted Edwardian houses. The park of the same name offers inspiring views over the city and has great play facilities (including a fabulous slide) and Hill Station, a community-run café.

New Cross's music pubs throb with bands and leftish debate. Indie-leaning Amersham Arms is popular, and has launched the career of many a Mercury Prize winner. Further down towards Peckham, there's the Montague Arms – once a barmy English pub with zebra heads and maritime knick-knacks, it has been resurrected as London's only steampunk bar. With many of the original features still intact, it's an eccentric blend of the kitsch and anarchic, and also serves big helpings of unpretentious British food.

In New Cross, students tuck into fiery dishes at tiny Thailand, or Turkish barbecue at Meze Mangal. Highlights among the many new offerings in the area are New Cross House, a pub that does a good line in pizzas, and the London Particular, spearheading gentrification with its café-cum-restaurant (and batches of braised fennel and celeriac fritters). Jointly owned aviation-themed LP Bar next door sells coffee during the day and craft beers by night. The latest contender is Birdie Num Nums, a hipster hangout where the jeans are as skinny as the lattes.

There's little in the way of shopping here, but look out for fabulous costumier Prangsta, and independent grocer the Allotment, where as much of the produce as possible is local or from Kent.

Deptford and St John's SE8

Those who always rejoiced in the maritime charm of atmospheric, riverside Deptford now have to acknowledge its officially trendy status. Thankfully, some of the cobbled cut-throughs and ancient terraces are protected by preservation orders, but the old wharves and muddy river flats are disappearing under residential developments at Convoys Wharf and Greenwich Reach.

Deptford is still a joy to explore. By way of an introduction, take a stroll down picturesque Tanners Hill before crossing New Cross Road and weaving your way along Deptford High Street. A mix of pound shops and pie-and-mash caffs, with a lively multicultural market – stalls sell everything

Join urban hippies at Hilly Fields' mini Stonehenge for the summer and winter solstices.

from fruit and vegetables to second-hand clothes and household junk – this is a very old-school retail experience. For a proper old-fashioned flea market, visit Deptford on Wednesday or Saturday.

The Deptford Project is a £47 million regeneration scheme that, when finished in late 2015, will hold over 100 new homes, arch-space workshops, shops, restaurants and a new market square – all situated next to Deptford railway station.

Veer down beautiful Albury Street, built in the early 18th century and all the more elegant for its proximity to the chaotic High Street. Between here and Church Street stands the Queen Anne church of St Paul's, where there's a plaque to Myididdee, a Tahitian who sailed with Captain Bligh and died in Deptford in 1793. Follow Church Street riverward to find St Nicholas's Church, where Christopher Marlowe is rumoured to have been buried following his violent end in a Deptford pub, or go east to Creekside, Deptford's artists' quarter. This slightly spooky area, with its mudflats and rotting hulls of old boats, is lit up by sudden flashes of artistic licence. The skull and crossbones carvings on the gateposts of St Nicholas' Church inspired the original pirate flag. It's also home to Cockpit Arts – a charity that supports designer-makers – as well as the studios and workshops of the neighbourhood's many creative souls.

Laban, the contemporary dance centre, is housed in an iridescent, coloured-Perspex building that – when you look at it from the Ha'penny Hatch Bridge – looks like it's been marooned on the muddy creek. New apartment buildings are springing up around it. If you really want to get stuck in to this area's (natural) history, pull on your gumboots and get down to the Creekside Centre, which runs some satisfyingly muddy Sunday walks.

Away from the river, St John's sits between Deptford and Lewisham town centres. Developed in the mid 19th century as New Deptford, it's a handsome conservation pocket, with lots of spacious Victorian and Edwardian houses clustered around its own station and church.

Deptford's budget eating places include AJ Goddard's and Manze's pie and mash shops. The Big Red Pizza Bus is a nostalgic treat, a Routemaster-turned-restaurant, where the crunchy-based pizzas are matched with local Greenwich Meantime beer. Peckish drinkers at the Job Centre (guess what it used to be) can take advantage of successive 'kitchen hijacks' with their beer; for more global flavours, there's Panda Panda (Vietnamese) and Chaconia (Trinidadian).

Real ales, good Sunday lunches and unpretentious charm can be found at the Dog & Bell. The Birds Nest is a punk, sticky-floored sort of boozer with an eclectic line-up and good-value meals, while the Bunker Club is the only disco in town – with Goldsmiths College nearby, it has a packed, student-facing vibe.

Blackheath SE3

With the lovely old All Saints church surrounded by green pastures, and all the attributes of a thriving market town, Blackheath, part of London's first conservation area, is the pride of the borough. Granted, the incessant traffic that thunders through the greensward (the A2 bisects it) taints the bucolic atmosphere, but this wealthy enclave's position beside the main route from London to Dover has earned it a place in history. Wat Tyler amassed an army of peasants on Blackheath, before marching to protest against the poll tax in 1381, and Henry VIII first clapped eyes on Anne of Cleves here, to well documented mutual disappointment, in 1540.

Hungry hikers tramping inland from their Thames walk via Greenwich are rewarded by numerous cafés and restaurants populating the two high streets of what locals fondly call 'Blackheath Village'. There are family-friendly stalwarts (Giraffe, Pizza Express, with Strada nearby), well-regarded local independents (Chapters, Buenos Aires, Everest Inn) and brasher newcomers such as the Argentinian steakhouse CAU.

There are lots of cafés, and they make a killing on a Sunday, when runners and walkers come to Blackheath to brunch, lunch and cream-tea the calories back. A branch of Gail's has opened, joining Boulangerie Jade, Hand Made Food, Tzigano's, the Village Deli and Black Vanilla. Like many well-heeled outer London districts, Blackheath has a tempting branch of upmarket ready-meal pusher Cook cleverly situated near the station.

There are plentiful drinking options. Most locals cite the Princess of Wales as the liveliest, most attractive pub. The Hare & Billet is another old favourite. Beer lovers also enjoy Zero Degrees (great wood-fired pizzas too), while Le Bouchon is the sort of serious-minded French wine bar (also serving fromage and charcuterie from the farmers' market by the station) that could only survive somewhere like Blackheath.

Smart chains are beginning to dominate the shop fronts: Whistles, Jigsaw, Fatface and JoJo Maman Bébé give an idea of the demographic here. A further hint comes in the form of branches of Fired Earth, Farrow & Ball and old-timer Neal's Yard Remedies. Independents include Blackbird (fair-trade womenswear), Raffles (men's clothes and a sideline in vintage toys) and Hortus (a gorgeously appointed garden shop and landscape-design company).

On the western edge of the village, where roads lead to Lee, Hither Green or Lewisham, Blackheath Concert Halls and the Conservatoire cater for the area's cultural and arts educational needs, with comedy, concerts, classes, a music school and a nursery. But one of the loveliest places in Blackheath Village is still the Age Exchange Reminiscence Arts centre, newly refurbished to accommodate the local library and an exhibition space. It's an exercise in nostalgia, with a café, garden and an army of lively OAP volunteers on hand with amazing tales of yesteryear.

Lewisham SE13

Approaching the fleshpots of Lewisham Town from the coffee-scented gentility of Blackheath, Hither Green or Ladywell gives the impression of descending into chaos. That shouldn't last too long – the all-new Lewisham Gateway, which is the cover-all term for the renaissance of the town centre (including a huge Barrett development called Renaissance) is unfolding at speed. The hoardings around these, variously called Thurston Point, Portrait and Confluence Place, depict idealistic projections of airy waterside plazas and apartment blocks, plus a Premier Inn. Lewisham will be unrecognisable. Meanwhile, the already notorious roundabout, where roads to Greenwich, Lee, Catford or New Cross clog with buses and intimidate nervous drivers, has become a sort of triangulabout, where tempers fray every day.

Another subject in the big gentrification conversation is the proposed Bakerloo line extension, which promises Lewisham and Catford (and even Bromley) the revitalising effect of the Underground in exchange for the eight-an-hour trains that currently trundle up to London Bridge and Charing Cross from these parts. The locals are torn between the obvious house-price benefits of being on the tube, and the inevitable transport chaos that would ensue while it takes shape.

A multicoloured monument to health and fitness, the Glass Mill Leisure Centre opened in 2013. Its patchwork of glass panes, reminiscent of the children's book character Elmer the Elephant, flash on and off, triggered by noises within, much to the irritation of the people living in the neighbouring flats.

The wholesome air that the Glass Mill bestows is soon dispelled across the road in the shopping centre, which squats unappealingly alongside a popular street market. The Lewisham Centre has far too many pound shops in among the youth-friendly chains (H&M, Tiger, TK Maxx, Primark, Next, Body Shop). It smells delicious, though, thanks to the proliferation of food concessions.

Food shopping options outside the mall are varied. The market has multiple fruit and veg stalls, while Lewis Grove, which runs alongside the marketplace, provides delicatessens and attractive eateries: celebrated Italian deli Gennaro's (now calling itself, mundanely, the Italian Food Centre);

a lovely Polish deli; Turkish restaurant Levante; and Totó & Peppe, a pizzeria and pasta restaurant.

If you don't like fried chicken, Lewisham's eating choices are otherwise pretty limited. The Darjeeling Indian restaurant has won a few 'best local curry' gongs, and the basic-but-efficient Sri Lankan, Everest Curry King, on Loampit Vale is consistently good. Or there's much-loved Maggie's (an Irish diner for meat and two veg) and a proper cor-blimey chippy called Something Fishy which closes at 5.30pm.

The dearth of good eating places is probably why the hungry hipsters of Lewisham fell on Street Feast (www.street feastlondon.com) with such glad cries when it descended on the derelict Lewisham Model Market (196 Lewisham High Street); expect more Dalston glamour in future summers too.

We haven't found a decent pub in the centre of Lewisham – you have to go to Ladywell, Blackheath or New Cross – but the local youth enjoy the Fox & Firkin for its cheap beer and open-mic nights.

Ladywell SE4/SE13

Between Catford and Lewisham lies the apotheosis of urban villages, Ladywell. Since its council endowment with flagstones, planters and benches, it's looking handsome. What's more, it ticks more best-kept-village boxes than many rural communities: post office, excellent deli, greengrocer, bakery (the Larder), one of the best independent hardware shops, a sandwich shop, a newsagent, two thoughtfully stocked gift and card shops (Slater & King, Zenubian) and two cafés, Oscar's and Le Délice (fantastic French pâtisserie).

Ladywell is also blessed with the sort of pubs you could waste far too much time in. The Ravensbourne Arms is a pleasant space with great beer and a consistently good menu. The Ladywell Tavern and attached gallery, under its new ownership, is blossoming.

The village even nestles among rolling pastures (of sorts): Ladywell Fields flanks the recently saved Lewisham Hospital; patients in wheelchairs often come out to take the air. A little tributary of the river Ravensbourne has been diverted to provide pond-dipping and paddling opportunities for children. A branch of the Jimmy Mizen Foundation, a charming little café called Ten Thousand Hands, opened here in 2014, and has become a pleasant lunching spot for hospital staff.

On the other side of Ladywell Village rears Hillyfields, an undulating choice for local runners, who refuel afterwards at Pistachios in the Park with cappuccinos and cakes, and earnestly discuss their PBs. This is a very wholesome community.

Standing on Hillyfields' highest point is Prendergast, one of the best schools in the area, a girls' comprehensive with a mixed sixth form. Prendergast sixth formers, young mums with toddlers and personal trainers make full use of the mini 'Stonehenge' on Hillyfields, a great picnicking spot.

The empty space where Ladywell Leisure Centre once stood is to be the venue for one of the country's first 'pop-up villages', which will provide temporary housing for 24 families. The colourful, Lego-like blocks will have ground-floor units for business and community use. The villagey vibe continues.

Brockley, Crofton Park and Honor Oak SE4

The popular neighbourhood of Brockley has plenty to recommend it – which is probably why many people who move here stay for decades. There are big houses and conversion flats along the wide roads that run towards Hilly Fields and Lewisham Way, modest terraces to the west of Brockley Road and down through Crofton Park to Honor Oak, plenty of schools, fast rail links (including the Overground) into town, attractive cafés, an award-winning chippie (Brockley's Rock) and one of south London's busiest and best food markets in the carpark of Lewisham College.

It's a relatively laid-back area, populated by creative and family-oriented types. Find them sipping flat whites at child-friendly cafés such as Browns of Brockley, Broca, Arlo & Mo and Brockley Mess; consuming something stronger or more filling at cosy pub Jam Circus; or dining at the Gantry or the Orchard. It's even considered cool enough now for a branch of hip hairdresser Blue Tit and brewer Late Knights' London Beer Dispensary, while the pockets of light industrial units up by Brockley Cross hide small producers such as the Brockley Brewery and Blackwoods Cheese Company.

Also here is the well-respected Brockley Jack pub-theatre, and the grand old Rivoli Ballroom, swathed in plush red velvet and dripping with gilt. It started life as the Crofton Park Picture Palace in 1913 before conversion in the 1950s, but its ballroom dances, jive nights and other knees-ups remain a huge draw.

Neighbouring Honor Oak often gets overlooked – not quite Brockley, not quite East Dulwich, not quite Forest Hill. But the suburban station's promotion to the Overground is proving a draw for young professionals. At rush hour, Honor Oak Park is a bit of a traffic rat-run, but it's also home to pretty outlets such as Jumping Bean gift shop, a growing number of cafés (My Jamii also works with young people who've struggled in mainstream education) and Mamma Dough pizzeria. Round the corner on Brockley Rise is the area's celebrated Indian restaurant, Babur Brasserie.

The place gets its name from the majestic Oak of Honor at the top of One Tree Hill – in fact, a whole wood's worth of trees with fantastic views and a historic beacon, lit on occasions such as the Diamond Jubilee.

Lee and Hither Green SE12/SE13

The Lewisham end of Lee High Road starts chaotically: a jumble of shabby shopfronts and far too many chicken shops, with the odd little curiosity, such as a vinyl record shop or Unique Cakes 4 U, a celebration cakes emporium displaying confections of alarming fluorescence. The Harlequin fancy-dress store continues the party atmosphere.

The road starts to smarten up as Lewisham gives way to Lee; pause to admire handsome

HIGHS & LOWS

Family-friendly cafés, especially in Brockley and Hither Green

Good connections into town

Creative types. Pubs host local TV comedians trying out new material

The views from One Tree Hill and Horniman Gardens

Traffic galore on the A2, A21, South Circular, and other major thoroughfares

Redevelopment at Lewisham roundabout causing chaos

Little happening south of Catford

Allodi Accordians, the centre for all of London's accordion needs since 1978. A newcomer to Lee High Road's diverse curiosities is Ruby & Norm, which rather portentously bills itself as 'Southeast London's most inspirational culture store'. It is, in fact, a large, shabby junk/vintage/second-hand emporium, with coffee machines and cake stands and a programme of acupuncture, baby massage, yoga and so on.

Brockley Market – the best in the borough.

It all becomes a little less shabby chic and more solidly middle class in Lee, where a preponderance of lovingly conserved terraces and quite grand detached houses have long been the quiet attraction. Lee will never be hip in that joyously, slightly grubby way of more central Lewisham communities; it feels too wealthy for that. Businesses cater for the well heeled: there are architects' studios and interior design businesses, and the smart, airy coffee shop and gallery With Jam and Bread, run by Jennie Milsom, author of *Café Life London*. The woman knows her beans, which are currently sourced from south London roaster Volcano. In the evenings, there's Harvey's Bistro, praised for its fish dishes, and the jolly Ristorante Carola on Lee Road. Ageing rockers love the Old Tiger's Head for beer and locally fledged pop stars.

The blot on Lee's landscape is generally agreed to be the somewhat flyblown and mostly boarded up Leegate shopping centre. It's due for demolition, and in its stead will rise… more mixed-use retail/restaurant/housing developments with a 'new anchor foodstore' (that's Asda) and plenty of 'green boulevards' involving much tree planting on wider pavements. Everyone in Lee except Sainsbury's seems OK with this, so long as the Asda remains 'largely hidden'.

Once you've turned your back on Leegate and walked in a southerly direction through the pretty Manor House Gardens (there's a heronry on the lake, an 18th-century ice house in the grounds and a branch of Pistachios in the Park for coffee and ice-cream), you'll pass more dinky – though expensive – terraces on your way to Hither Green. This is a quietly right-on district of Lewisham that keeps Catford at park's length (it's the other side of Mountsfield Park, but Hither Green residents don't like to think about it).

Hither Green is a credit to FUSS (Friends and Users of Staplehurst Shops), who keep the street flowerboxes filled and arrange Christmas and summer fairs and festivals. Its star turns are You Don't Bring Me Flowers (the winsome flower shop, café, community hub and purveyer of Catford honey and locally made jam and chutney), the Hither Green Deli and the gastro-oriented Station Hotel. On Hither Green Lane, the Café of Good Hope was established to honour the memory of 16-year-old Jimmy Mizen, who was murdered not far from here in 2008. It's a lovely space and the coffee and brunches are well presented and generous. On Saturdays in spring and summer, it's home to a Vietnamese supper club. Just next door, a little children's boutique and toy store called Cissie Wears was opened in response to the area's popularity with young families.

When they can get a babysitter, the parents make a date with Haven't Stopped Dancing Yet (www.haventstoppeddancingyet.co.uk), a 1970s mum-and-dad-dancing disco experience that takes place regularly in St Swithun's Church Hall. The church also sustains a community choir, quiz nights and other well-attended events.

Catford SE6

Once considered beyond the pale, Catford is having its moment in the sun, thanks to numerous freelance journalists having invested in the cheapest (and often biggest) family houses in south-east London, then writing pieces about how trendy it is. Their evidence? The whispers about the Bakerloo line, as well as Barrett Homes' shiny new Catford Green development between Catford and Catford Bridge stations, and the Catford Constitutional Club ('CatCon' to its friends). This is housed in what was the old Conservative club on Catford Broadway, all original chandeliers and wattle-and-daub ceilings. Despite starting out looking like a squat, it has been a resounding success, specialising in local ale and cider, and turning out high-quality pub grub from a brand-new kitchen. The Tuesday quiz night is extremely popular and the antique lavatories are a joy.

Catford Broadway – all spruced up and looking lively with a Costa, independent cafés and a great little street market – is a pleasant place to be these days, with the art deco Broadway still Catford's pride and joy. Of course, Catford is a poor area, with more than its fair share of pound, pawn and charity shops, but there are diamonds in the rough. Everyone loves the wonderful Chinese foodstore (FLK) by the station, where you can buy extraordinary ingredients and be told in great detail what to make with them. Great little Vietnamese, Turkish and African foodstores offer an alternative to Tesco.

The Waterlink Way, alongside the Ravensbourne River, is a pedalling pleasure.

The main green space, Mountsfield Park, is shared with Hither Green; this is where Lewisham People's Day takes place every July. Major improvements mean the playground is now all handsome wood, and there's a large community orchard and vegetable garden laid out, ready for rosy-cheeked Catfordians to get busy with the apple presses in autumn.

For younger residents, a night out in Catford is a blowout in Nando's followed by pudding over the road in Kaspa's, an ice-cream shop and café that looks like a night club. Older, more discerning diners still favour Pizzeria Italiana, happy in its hiding place underneath the brutalist Eros House, Sapporo Ichiban on the Broadway or the rather classy Turkish Mekân at the beginning of Bromley Road.

Forest Hill SE23

'Creative', 'community', 'friendly', 'foodie', 'family', 'arty'... these words crop up repeatedly when Forest Hill residents are asked to sum up their home.

Creative could apply to the legion of actors, designers, comedians, filmmakers, jewellery makers, and glass artists who live and socialise in the area, but is specifically found at galleries-cum-cafés such as Canvas & Cream and Montage, and the artists' studios of Havelock Walk.

Foodie could mean any of the increasing number of cafés – St David Coffee House, the Archie Parker, Aga's Little Deli – or shops such as the Butchery and retro sweet shop Sugar Mountain, or the Saturday famers' market at Horniman Gardens.

Friendliness you'll find in spades at neighbourhood pubs such as the Sylvan Post (housed in a former post office, with the strongrooms now private booths) or at the ED Comedy nights at the Hob pub.

Community spirit is everywhere, but galvanised at DoopoDoopo (home to film clubs, food nights, DJ nights and workshops, as well as providing a retail outlet specifically for local designers and makers) and craft heaven Stag & Bow. Being largely ranged around a busy junction on the South Circular hasn't done Forest Hill any favours, but local businesses have pulled together to introduce cohesion to the disparate high streets, supporting events such as Forest Hill Fashion Week and regular local festivals, or planting an informal edible high street.

Families benefit from one of London's most eccentric and child-friendly museums, the Horniman (its gardens have some of the best views in London), and a new swimming pool and leisure centre.

Property-wise, you can find everything in these hilly streets: flats in a converted church, art deco mansion blocks, Victorian terraces, 1970s townhouses, roomy conversion flats, or 1930s semis clinging to steep slopes. Particularly popular is the area around Church Rise, just behind the station, and the houses along Perry Vale (where the house names spell out that of their architect, local turn-of-last-century builder Ted Christmas).

It's an eclectic area full of surprises. Explore and you never know what you'll find – an old Wren spire, a nature reserve around a forgotten fragment of a disused canal, or a German Lutheran church.

Sydenham SE26

Sydenham folk, used to being dismissed as a bit suburban, have firmly joined the rest of the capital. Rail and Overground networks swiftly connect them to central and east London, and they no longer have to trek up to Forest Hill or Crystal Palace for a drink or a decent coffee. Low-key cafés have begun to congregate along Kirkdale: bijou bar/restaurant/café 161, Fig & Pistachio and IBS French Bakery joining longstanding fixture Blue Mountain Café. There's an inevitable rebranding as 'Kirkdale Village', and a council-led facelift is in the offing.

Upper Sydenham, leading down from Sydenham Hill, benefits from having pretty Sydenham Wells Park as its focus, named after the area's 17th-century medicinal springs, now sporting a great water-jet playground.

Lawrie Park is the desirable address (its vista was once painted by Camille Pissarro). Some early houses remain along the broad tree-lined avenues, joined by, among others,

New Cross House

TRANSPORT

Tube lines DLR, Overground
Rail services into Cannon Street,
Charing Cross, London Bridge, Victoria
Main bus routes into central London
21, 47, 171, 172, 185, 188; night
buses N21, N36, N47, N89, N171,
N343; 24-hour buses 53, 176,
188, 453

some 1920s mock Tudor homes built by celebrated local architect Ted Christmas and groups of classic 1970s townhouses. Just off the high street, the area's worst-kept secret is the Thorpes (Earlsthorpe, Kingsthorpe…), an Edwardian conservation area abutting Mayow Park.

Community spirit is high. Kirkdale Books has for decades been a hub of events. More recently, Sydenham has gained a monthly Saturday artisans' market in Venner Square and Queensthrope Square, joining an annual arts fair, a Christmas fair, and the odd pop-up.

The busy high street is fairly standard; once past gastro-ish pub the Dolphin and the Lovely Gallery, Sydenham Road leads on with increasing grimness to Bell Green, which makes up in usefulness (a mega Sainsbury's, the Bridge Leisure Centre) what it lacks in aesthetic appeal. The addition of some shiny new apartment blocks, however, suggests someone has a better future planned for this area – and the sudden turn into leafy suburbia on crossing into Lower Sydenham makes this less implausible than it sounds.

Eating

161 161 Kirkdale, SE26 4QJ (3602 7980).
AJ Goddard 203 Deptford High Street, SE8 3NT (8692 3601).
Archie Parker 55A Dartmouth Road, SE23 3HN (8699 4818, www.thearchieparker.com).
Arlo & Moe 340 Brockley Road, SE4 2BT (07749 667207).
Babur Brasserie 119 Brockley Rise, SE23 1JP (8291 2400, www.babur.info).
Big Red Pizza Bus 30 Deptford Church Street, SE8 4RZ (3490 8346, www.bigredpizza.co.uk).
Birdie Num Nums 11 Lewisham Way, SE14 6PP (8692 7223, www.birdienumnums.co.uk).
Black Vanilla 32 Tranquil Vale, SE3 0AX (8852 0020, www.black-vanilla.com).
Blue Mountain Café 260 Kirkdale, SE26 4NP (8659 6016, www.bluemo.co.uk).
Broca 4 Coulgate Street, SE4 2RW (8691 0833, www.brocafoods.com).
Brockley Mess 55 Brockley Road, SE4 2QZ (07530 423749, www.thebrockleymess.com).
Brockley's Rock 317 Brockley Road, SE4 2QZ (8694 1441, www.brockleysrock.co.uk).
Browns of Brockley 5 Coulgate Street, SE4 2RW (8692 0722).
Buenos Aires 17 Royal Parade, SE3 0TL (8318 5333, www.buenosairescafe.co.uk).
Café of Good Hope 216 Hither Green Lane, SE13 6RT (8852 7888, www.cafeofgoodhope.co.uk).

Café Oscar's 48 Ladywell Road, SE13 7UX (8314 5581, www.cafe-oscars.com).
Canvas & Cream 18 London Road, SE23 3HF (8699 9589, www.canvasandcream.com).
CAU 10-12 Royal Parade, SE3 0TL (8318 4200, www.caurestaurants.com).
Chaconia 26 Deptford High Street, SE8 4AF (8692 8815, www.chaconia.net).
Chapters 43-45 Montpelier Vale, SE3 0TJ (8333 2666, www.chaptersblackheath.com).
Darjeeling 134 Lee High Road, SE13 5PR (8473 8222, www.darjeeling-lewisham.co.uk).
Le Délice 38 Ladywell Road, SE13 7UZ (8690 3238, www.facebook.com/ledeliceladywell).
Everest Curry King 24 Loampit Hill, SE13 7SW (8691 2233).
Everest Inn 41 Montpelier Vale, SE3 0TJ (8852 7872, www.everestinnblackheath.co.uk).
Fig & Pistachio 101 Kirkdale, SE26 4QJ (8291 0025, www.figandpistachio.co.uk).
Gantry 188 Brockley Road, SE4 2RL (8469 0043, www.thegantry.co.uk).
Harvey's Bistro 121 Lee Road, SE3 9DS (8318 2116, www.harveyslondon.co.uk).
Hill Station Telegraph Hill Centre, Kitto Road, SE14 5TY (7635 2955, www.hillstation.org.uk).
Kaspa's 97 Rushey Green, SE6 4AF (8461 2817, www.kaspas.co.uk).
Levante 11 Lewis Grove, SE13 6BG (8355 3522, www.levanterestaurant.co.uk).
London Particular 399 New Cross Road, SE14 6LA (8692 6149, www.thelondonparticular.co.uk).
Maggie's 322 Lewisham Road, SE13 7PA (8244 0339, www.maggiesrestaurant.co.uk).
Mamma Dough 76-78 Honor Oak Park, SE23 1DY (8699 5196, www.mammadough.co.uk).
Manze's 204 Deptford High Street, SE8 3PR (8692 2375, www.manzepieandmash.com).
Mekân 11-13 Bromley Road, SE6 2TS (7998 1598, www.mekanrestaurant.co.uk).
Meze Mangal 245 Lewisham Way, SE4 1XF (8694 8099, www.mezemangal.co.uk).
Montage 33 Dartmouth Road, SE23 3HN (7207 9890).
My Jamii Café 3 Honor Oak Park, SE23 1DX (www.myjamiicafe.com).
Orchard 5 Harefield Road, SE4 1LW (8692 4756, www.thebrockleyorchard.com).
Panda Panda 8 Deptford Broadway, SE8 4PA (8616 6922, www.panda-panda.co.uk).
Pistachios in the Park Hilly Fields (8694 3674, www.pistachiosinthepark.org.uk); Manor House Gardens (8852 5381).
La Pizzeria Italiana 3 Eros House, Brownhill Road, SE6 2EF (8461 4606, www.lapizzaitalia.com).
Ristorante Carola 151-157 Lee Road, SE3 9DJ (8617 3544, www.ristorantecarola.co.uk).

St David Coffee House 5 David's Road, SE23
3EP (8291 6646, www.stdavidcoffeehouse.co.uk).
Sapporo Ichiban 13 Catford Broadway, SE6 4SP
(8690 8487).
Something Fishy 119 Lewisham High Street,
SE13 6AT (8852 7075).
Ten Thousand Hands Ladywell Fields, SE13.
Thailand 15 Lewisham Way, SE14 6PP (8691
4040, www.thethailandonline.com).
Totó & Peppe 13 Lewis Grove, SE13 6BG
(8852 5787).
With Jam & Bread 386 Lee High Road, SE12
8RW (8318 4040, www.withjamandbread.com).

Drinking

Amersham Arms 388 New Cross Road, SE14
6TY (8469 1499, www.theamershamarms.com).
Birds Nest 32 Deptford Church Street, SE8 4RZ
(8692 1928, www.thebirdsnestpub.com).
Le Bouchon 72 Tranquil Vale, SE3 0BN
(www.lebouchonwinebar.co.uk).
Catford Constitutional Club Catford Broadway,
SE6 4SP (8613 7188, www.catfordconstitutional
club.com).
Dog & Bell 116 Prince Street, SE8 3JD (8692
5664).
Dolphin 121 Sydenham Road, SE26 5HB (8778
8101, www.thedolphinsydenham.com).
Fox & Firkin 316 Lewisham High Street, SE13
6JZ (8690 0969, www.foxfirkin.com).
Hare & Billet 1A Hare and Billet Road, SE3 0QJ
(8852 2352, www.hareandbillet.com).
Hobgoblin 272 New Cross Road, SE14 6AA
(8692 3193).
Jam Circus 330-332 Brockley Road, SE4 2BT
(8692 3320, www.jamcircus.com).
Job Centre 120-122 Deptford High Street, SE8
4NS (8692 6859, http://jobcentredeptford.com).
Ladywell Tavern 80 Ladywell Road, SE13 7HS
(8690 7184, www.ladywelltavern.com).
London Beer Dispensary 389 Brockley Road,
SE4 2PH (8694 6962, www.lateknightsbrewery.
co.uk).
LP Bar 401 New Cross Road, SE14 6LA (8691
8822, www.thelpbar.co.uk).
Montague Arms 289 Queen's Road, SE14 2PA
(7639 4923, www.montaguearms.com).
New Cross House 316 New Cross Road, SE14
6AF (8691 8875, www.thenewcrosshouse.com).
Old Tiger's Head 351 Lee High Road, SE12 8RU
(8244 2014).
Princess of Wales 1A Montpelier Row, SE3 0RL
(8852 5784, www.princessofwalespub.co.uk).
Ravensbourne Arms 323 Lewisham High
Street, SE13 6NR (8613 7070, www.ravensbourne
arms.com).

Station Hotel 14 Staplehurst Road, SE13 5NB
(8463 0367, www.stationhotelhithergreen.co.uk).
Sylvan Post 24-28 Dartmouth Road, SE23 3XZ
(8291 5712, http://sylvanpost.com).
Zero Degrees 29-31 Montpelier Vale, SE3 0TJ
(8852 5619, www.zerodegrees.co.uk).

Shopping

Aga's Little Deli 49 Dartmouth Road, SE23
3HN (07889 760915).
Allodi Accordions 143-145 Lee High Road,
SE13 5PF (8244 3771, www.accordions.co.uk).
Allotment 318 New Cross Road, SE14 6AF
(3583 5953, www.theallotment.uk.com).
Black Vanilla 32 Tranquil Vale, SE3 0AX
(8852 0020, www.black-vanilla.com).
Blackbird 28 Blackheath Village, SE3 9SY
(8852 5550).
Blue Tit 258 Brockley Road, SE4 2SF (8305
8060, www.bluetitlondon.com).
Boulangerie Jade 44 Tranquil Vale, SE3 0BD
(8318 1916, www.boulangeriejade.com).
Brockley Brewery 31 Harcourt Road, SE4 2AJ
(07814 584338, http://brockleybrewery.co.uk).
Brockley Market Lewisham College car park,
Lewisham Way, SE4 1UT (07900 905708, www.
brockleymarket.com).

Lewisham Model Market
– the regular summer
pop-up putting Lewisham
on the hipster map.

Butchery 49 London Road, SE23 3TY (8291 4219).
Cissy Wears 212A Hither Green Lane, SE13 6RT
(8852 8687, www.cissywears.com).
Cockpit Arts 18-22 Creekside, SE8 3DZ (8692
4463, www.cockpitarts.com).
Cook 18 Tranquil Vale, SE3 0AX (8852 8082,
www.cookfood.net).
DoopoDoopo 15 Dartmouth Road, SE23 3HN
(3632 5041, http://doopodoopo.co.uk).
FLK 3 Station Buildings, Catford Road, SE6 4QZ
(8690 8938, www.flkchinesegroceries.co.uk).
Gail's 3 Blackheath Village, SE3 9LA (8852 3127,
www.gailsbread.co.uk).
Hand Made Food 40 Tranquil Vale, SE3 0BD
(8297 9966, www.handmadefood.com).
Harlequin Party Shop 254 Lee High Road, SE13
5PL (8852 0193, www.harlequinparty.co.uk).
Hither Green Deli 13 Staplehurst Road, SE13
5ND (8297 1754).
Hortus 26 Blackheath Village, SE3 9SY (8297
9439, www.hortus-london.com).

Gennaro 23 Lewis Grove, SE13 6BG (8852 1370, www.facebook.com/italianfoodlondon).
IBS French Bakery 138 Kirkdale, SE26 4QJ (07588 535570).
Jumping Bean 45 Honor Oak Park, SE23 1EA (8314 4747, www.facebook.com/jumpingbeanshop).
Kirkdale Bookshop & Gallery 272 Kirkdale, SE26 4RS (8778 4701, www.kirkdalebookshop.com).
Larder 71 Ladywell Road, SE13 7JA (8314 5797, www.thelarderdeli.com).
Lewisham Centre Molesworth Street, SE13 7HB (8852 0094, www.lewishamshopping.co.uk).
Prangsta 304 New Cross Road, SE14 6AF (8694 9869, www.prangsta.co.uk).
Raffles 49 Montpelier Vale, SE3 0TJ (8852 0018).
Ruby & Norm 266-268 Lee High Road, SE13 5PL (www.facebook.com/rubynorm).
Slater & King 46 Ladywell Road, SE13 7UZ (07545 973085, www.slaterandking.co.uk).
Stag & Bow 8 Dartmouth Road, SE23 3XU (8291 4992, http://stagandbow.com).
Sugar Mountain 57a Dartmouth Road, SE23 3HN (www.sugarmountaindartmouthroad.co.uk).
Tziganos 15-17 Montpelier Vale, SE3 0TA (8852 9226, www.tziganos.com).
Unique Cakes 4 U 37 Lee High Road, SE13 5NS (8318 2233, www.uniquecakes4u.com).
Village Deli 1-3 Tranquil Vale, SE3 0BU (8852 2015).
You Don't Bring Me Flowers 15 Staplehurst Road, SE13 5ND (8297 2333, www.youdontbringmeflowers.co.uk).

Zenubian 218 Algernon Road, SE13 7AN (07535 090865, www.zenubian.com).

Things to do

Cinemas & theatres

Albany Douglas Way, SE8 4AG (8692 4446, www.thealbany.org.uk). Community arts centre.
Broadway Theatre Catford Road, SE6 4RU (8690 0002, www.broadwaytheatre.org.uk).
Deptford Film Club Various venues (www.deptfordfilmclub.org).
Laban Theatre Laban Building, Creekside, SE8 3DZ (8463 0100, www.trinitylaban.ac.uk). Independent conservatoire for contemporary dance.
New Cross & Deptford Free Film Festival Various venues (www.freefilmfestivals.org).

Galleries & museums

Horniman Museum & Gardens 100 London Road, SE23 3PQ (8699 1872, www.horniman.ac.uk). Natural-history and anthropological displays, café, aquarium and animal enclosure.
Lewisham Arthouse 140 Lewisham Way, SE14 6PD (8691 9113, www.lewishamarthouse.co.uk). Gallery in an impressive Edwardian hall.
Lovely Gallery 140 Sydenham Road, SE26 5JZ (3686 1328, www.thelovelygallery.com).
Montage 33 Dartmouth Road, SE23 3HN (7207 9890).

Horniman Museum

Other attractions

Age Exchange Reminiscence Arts
11 Blackheath Village, SE3 9LA (8318 9105,
www.age-exchange.org.uk). Local history
shared by the people who remember it.
Creekside Discovery Centre 14 Creekside,
SE8 4SA (8692 9922, www.creeksidecentre.org.uk).
Environmental education centre with monthly
low-tide walks.

Gigs, clubs & comedy

Amersham Arms 388 New Cross Road, SE14
6TY (8469 1499, www.theamershamarms.com).
Blackheath Halls 23 Lee Road, SE3 9RQ (8463
0100, www.trinitylaban.ac.uk). Concerts (classical
and contemporary), community events and more.
Brockley Jack Studio Theatre 410 Brockley
Road, SE4 2DH (8291 6354, www.brockleyjack.
co.uk). Stages theatre, music and comedy.
Also home to a film club (www.brockleyjack
filmclub.co.uk).
Conservatoire 19-21 Lee Road, SE3 9RQ (8852
0234, www.conservatoire.org.uk). Independent
arts centre.
ED Comedy at the Hob 7 Devonshire Road,
SE23 3HE (8855 0496, http://thehobforesthill.
co.uk/ed-comedy).
Rivoli Ballroom 350 Brockley Road, SE4 2BY
(8692 5130, www.therivoli.co.uk). Stylish old
ballroom used for tea dances and classes.
The Venue 2A Clifton Rise, SE14 6JP (8692
4077, www.thevenuelondon.com).

Green spaces

Further details at www.lewisham.gov.uk.
Beckenham Place Park BR3 5BP. The borough's
largest green space includes ancient woodland,
a municipal golf course and the routes of both
the Green Chain Walk and the Capital Ring.
Blackheath Shooters Hill Road, SE3. Huge
historic heath.
Cornmill Gardens & River Mill Park Loampit
Vale, SE13.
Forster Memorial Park Whitefoot Lane, SE6
2NZ. Skate park and BMX track.
Hilly Fields Adelaide Avenue, SE4 1LE. Running
club, café and mini stone circle.
Ladywell Fields SE13. Adventure playground,
skate park, tennis courts, river walk, waterpumps.
Manor House Gardens Taunton Road, SE13
5SU. Walled flower garden, lake, fountain and
historic ice-house.
Mountsfield Park Stainton Road, SE6 1AN.
Tennis courts and sports pitches.
One Tree Hill Honor Oak Park, SE23 3LE.
Historic woods with a great view.
Pepys Park Millard Road, SE8 3GB. Riverside
park with landscaped play areas.
Sydenham Wells Park Wells Park Road, SE26
6LA. Gardens, playground and waterplay.
Telegraph Hill Park Kitto Road, SE14 5TW.
Great slide.
Waterlink Way Signposted river walk from
Sydenham to the Thames along the rivers Pool
and Ravensbourne.

Gyms & leisure centres

Bridge Leisure Centre Kangley Bridge Road,
SE26 5AQ (8778 7158, www.fusion-lifestyle.com).
Colfe's Leisure Centre Horn Park Lane, SE12
8AW (8297 9110, www.colfes.com/leisurecentre).
Private. Outside school hours only.
Downham Health & Leisure Centre 7-9
Moorside Road, BR1 5EP (8461 9200, www.1life.
co.uk). Includes a GP, dentist, library and
community hall.
Forest Hill Pools Dartmouth Road, SE23 3HZ
(8291 8730, www.fusion-lifestyle.com).
Forest Hill School Sports Centre Bampton
Road, SE23 2XN (8699 9343, www.fusion-lifestyle.
com). Out of school hours only.
Glass Mill Leisure Centre 41 Loampit Vale, SE13
7FT (0303 303 0111, www.fusion-lifestyle.com).
Ladywell Arena Silvermere Road, SE6 4QX (8314
1986, www.fusion-lifestyle.com).
MFA Bowl 11-29 Belmont Hill, SE13 5AU (0843 290
8911, www.mfabowl.com).
Wavelengths Leisure Centre Giffin Street, SE8
4RJ (8694 9400, www.fusion-lifestyle.com).

Outdoor pursuits

Beckenham Golf Course Beckenham Place Park,
Beckenham Hill Road, BR3 5BP (8650 2292, www.
glendale-golf.com). An 18-hole public golf course.
Catford Soccer Jubilee Ground, Canadian Avenue,
SE6 4SW (8690 1111, www.catfordsoccer.co.uk).

Spectator sports

Millwall Football Club The Den, Zampa Road,
SE16 3LN (7232 1222, www.millwallfc.co.uk).

Schools

Primary

There are 69 state primary schools in Lewisham,
including 20 church schools. There are also eight
independents. See www.lewisham.gov.uk/education
and learning, www.education.gov.uk/edubase and
www.ofsted.gov.uk for more information.

Secondary

Addey & Stanhope School 472 New Cross Road,
SE14 6TJ (8305 6100, www.as.lewisham.sch.uk).
Bonus Pastor Catholic College Winlaton Road,
BR1 5PZ (8695 2100, www.bonuspastor.co.uk).
Roman Catholic.
Christ the King College www.ctksfc.ac.uk
Aquinas Sprules Road, SE4 2NL (7358 2400);
Belmont Grove, SE13 5GE (8297 9433). Sixth
form only.
Conisborough College Conisborough
Crescent, SE6 2SE (8461 9600, www.
conisboroughcollege.co.uk).

Deptford Green School Edward Street, SE14 6AN
(8691 3236, www.deptfordgreen.lewisham.sch.uk).
Forest Hill School Dacres Road, SE23 2XN (8699
9343, www.foresthillschool.co.uk). Boys only;
mixed sixth form.
Haberdashers' Aske's Hatcham College 135
Pepys Road, SE14 5SF (7652 9500, www.haaf.org.uk).
Haberdashers' Aske's Knights Academy
Launcelot Road, BR1 5EB (7652 9500,
www.haaf.org.uk).
Prendergast Ladywell School Manwood
Road, SE4 1SA (8690 1114, www.prendergast-
ladywell.com).
Prendergast School Hilly Adelaide Avenue, SE4
1LE (8690 3710, www.prendergast-school.com).
Girls only; mixed sixth form.
St Dunstan's College Stanstead Road, SE6 4TY
(8516 7200, www.stdunstans.org.uk). Private.
St Matthew Academy St Joseph's Vale, SE3 0XX
(8853 6250, www.stmatthewacademy.co.uk).
Sedgehill School Sedgehill Road, SE6 3QW
(8698 8911, www.sedgehill-lewisham.co.uk).
Sydenham School Dartmouth Road, SE26 4RD
(8699 6731, www.sydenham.lewisham.sch.uk).
Girls only.
Trinity School Taunton Road, SE12 8PD (8852
3191, www.trinitylewisham.org).

Property

Local estate agents

Acorn Estate Agents www.acorn.ltd.uk
Benjamin Matthews www.benjamin-
matthews.co.uk
Bryan Keegan www.bryanandkeegan.co.uk
Cannon Kallar www.cannonkallar.co.uk
Mark Beaumont www.markbeaumont.com
Pedder www.pedderproperty.com
Peter James Estates www.peterjames
estates.co.uk
Property World www.propertyworlduk.net
Rocodells www.rocodells.co.uk
Sebastian Roche www.sebastianroche.com
Sexton & Co www.saxtonest.co.uk

Local knowledge

www.brockleycentral.blogspot.com
www.foresthillsociety.com
www.mercury-today.co.uk
www.ourhithergreen.com
www.se23.com
http://see3.co.uk
www.southeastcentral.co.uk
http://sydenham.org.uk
www.sydenhamsociety.com
http://totally-locally.co.uk

Blackheath

USEFUL INFO

Borough size
3,515 hectares

Population
294,000

Ethnic mix
White 66.2%
Black or Black British 19.0%
Asian or Asian British 6.7%
Mixed 4.2%
Chinese or other 3.8%

London borough of Lewisham
Lewisham Town Hall, Catford Road, SE6
4RU (8314 6000, www.lewisham.gov.uk)

Council run by
Labour

MPs
Lewisham East, Heidi Alexander (Labour);
Lewisham Deptford, Vicky Foxcroft
(Labour); Lewisham West & Penge,
Jim Dowd (Labour)

Main recycling centre
Reuse & Recycling Centre Civic Amenities
Site, Landmann Way, SE14 5RS (8314
7171, www.lewisham.gov.uk)

Council tax
£903.57 to £2,710.70

Newham

The 2012 Olympics were a game changer for this neck of east London, bringing world-class sports facilities, a landscaped public park and one of Europe's biggest shopping centres, as well as creating useful new transport connections, rediscovering the River Lea and, of course, prompting property prices to rocket.

AVERAGE PROPERTY PRICE

Detached £367,835	**Terraced** £283,580
Semi-detached £320,011	**Flat** £341,251

AVERAGE RENTAL PRICE PER WEEK

Room £104	**1 bed** £207
Studio £175	**2 bed** £276
	3 bed £322

Roof East, Stratford

Neighbourhoods

Stratford E15/E20 and Forest Gate E7

Long before the 2012 Olympic jamboree, Stratford had been Newham's heart. Amid all the oppressively same-same concrete, there was always a little culture – focused at the doughty Theatre Royal, the Picturehouse cinema next door, the Stratford Circus arts centre and the Discover children's story centre – as well as shedloads of transport. There was even a kind of shopping mall: the permanently down-at-heel Stratford Centre, with its pound-a-bowl fruit sellers and chain stores.

Shopping is now all about Westfield Stratford City, which opened as Europe's largest urban shopping centre in 2011. Directly opposite the Stratford Centre and easily accessible from the station, it is anchored by John Lewis and Marks & Spencer and contains pretty much every high-end chain and enough entertainment (bowling alley, casino, multi-screen cinema) to keep you indoors all day. It's also home to a legion of the glossier restaurant chains (Busaba Eathai, Jamie's Italian, the Real Greek, Wahaca); there's also a Comptoir Libanais (Mediterranean), Franco Manca (pizza) and Rosa's (Vietnamese). You'll find a great range of beer at Tap East – it's run by the people behind the Rake in Borough Market – and Balans Soho Society offers cocktails, but our favourite pub in the area is on the far side of the Stratford Centre: the King Edward VII, known locally as the King of Prussia (a World War I joke), is a rare example in Stratford of a proper pub with decent beer and food.

Other alternatives for a tipple outside the retail behemoth include the bar at the Theatre Royal, which has regular free entertainment, and the Railway Tavern with its late licence (until midnight). If you're on Gerry Raffles Square, you can eat at Pizza Express, while in season (from May) check out the terrific Roof East (www.roofeast.com), which provides eats, drinks, screenings and other events on the roof of the Stratford Centre car park.

What of the Queen Elizabeth Olympic Park, which hosted the 2012 Games? It's as impressive as you'd have a right to expect for a cool £8.77 billion. Closest to Westfield, the curly-whirly red scaffolding of Anish Kapoor's lofty ArcelorMittal Orbit peers down on Zaha Hadid's excellent London Aquatics Centre – both open to the public. To get into the Olympic Stadium itself,

you'll need to attend a major sports event or buy a West Ham United season ticket when the club takes up residence there from the start of the 2016/17 season. There are numerous public artworks dotted around the park, some terrific playgrounds (Tumbling Bay is amazing) and lovely landscaping around the meandering streams. In the north, the VeloPark (centred on the superb velodrome, but with BMX and other cycling trails attached) caters for London's current cycling obsession. There are a couple of decent cafés here too: in the north, the Unity Kitchen Café and, on the Greenway along the park's westerly flank, Moka East in the View Tube. Hipsters pedal right across the park and over the River Lea to Hackney Wick for coffee at the Counter Café or pizzas at Crate Brewery.

Of undoubted benefit are Stratford's excellent transport links: the DLR; the Central and Jubilee tube lines; London Overground; the main line from Liverpool Street and Essex; and the high-speed Javelin train down to Kent. Crossrail will have a stop here too from 2018. Stansted Airport is less than an hour by coach, and then there's London City Airport in the Royal Docks. Stratford is definitely easy to leave – Canary Wharf is five minutes away, the City ten, the West End no more than 20 – it may not, however, remain easy to stay.

The social aspects of the area's 'Olympic legacy' are contested. The Athletes' Village has been reinvented as East Village and is turning into a relaxed community with its own film festival and fairs. But the changed definition of 'affordable' has left much of the park's promised housing beyond the reach of local residents, although the new Chobham Academy school and the health centre (formerly the Olympic polyclinic) are welcome. House-hunters have already pushed on to the more suburban climes of Forest Gate and Manor Park with their leafy Victorian streets. A community hub is building up around Forest Gate station and Woodgrange Road, with cafés such as Coffee7, a Saturday market and the craft showcase Number 8 Forest Gate Emporium. Meanwhile, the Woodgrange Estate conservation area around the station is particularly sought after. The neighbourhood also benefits from great curry houses, fantastic open spaces (Wanstead Flats spill over from the adjacent borough of Redbridge) and one of London's best-stocked craft beer pubs (the Wanstead Tap).

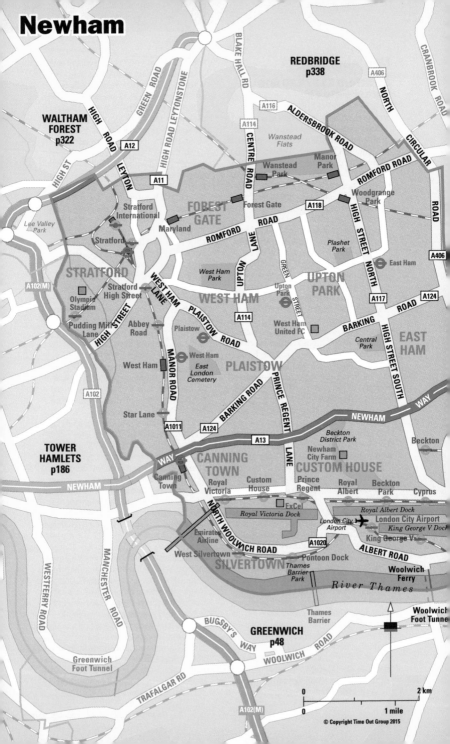

Plaistow E13/E15, Upton Park E6/E13, and East and West Ham E6/E7/E15

There is a hard-to-shake feeling that the further south you travel in the borough, and the closer you get to the old docks, the worse everything becomes. This isn't the most prosperous area, and classic inner-city problems such as crime, overcrowding, pollution and unemployment abound. But that doesn't mean locals don't know how to have a good time. As you enter High Street North in East Ham, you really get an impression of a strong and mutually supportive community.

Newham was formed in 1965 by the merging of the former Essex county boroughs of East Ham and West Ham into Greater London. Both neighbourhoods have an ethnically diverse but integrated population: cockney meets the Indian subcontinent but also Africa, the Caribbean and eastern Europe.

In this highly multicultural area, Green Street is the place with the most pronounced South Asian flavour. With Indian and Pakistani clothes shops and restaurants, it is almost that community's local equivalent to Oxford Street. You can see this at boutiques such as Damini's, sari shop Henna Mehndi and the smart new East Shopping Centre, a mall of Asian brands. By contrast, Queen's Market by Upton Park tube provides the sort of trading banter you'd expect from a barrowload of East Enders, and round the corner on Barking Road you'll find longstanding independent Newham Bookshop organising literary events.

As well as being known for shopping, Green Street is also known for food. For ice-cream, head to Afters, a black and pink, 1950s-themed ice-cream parlour that keeps children of all ages happy. There is also a smattering of curry houses, among them vegetarian venues such as Amitas and Vijay's Chawalla. If you're hankering after a taste of the old East End, however, try Queen's Fish Bar on Green Street or the historic (and CAMRA-listed) Black Lion in nearby Plaistow.

In the north-east of the borough, leafy side streets continue off High Street North into East Ham; the streets named for poets around Plashet Park and the area known as the Burges Estate (which extends towards the Barking Relief Road) are quiet and anonymous. Central Park, an oasis of greenery that ties together many of the quieter Victorian residential streets in the heart of East Ham, is another popular locale. Further west, the area bordering West Ham Park, particularly Ham Park Road, has some excellent housing stock. West Ham Park itself is one of the borough's many fine open spaces, with cricket nets, football pitches and tennis courts.

The Hams even have some respectable architecture in the form of the attractive old Town Hall, East Ham's Underground station, the ornate Boleyn Cinema and Victorian-style houses. Perhaps the borough's most important landmark, though, is the Boleyn Ground, also known as Upton Park and home to the pride of the East End: West Ham United. As of the 2016/17 season, however, they will be playing their football at the former Olympic Stadium; the Boleyn Ground has been sold to Galliard Homes, which is planning more than 800 units on the site, including some 15-storey apartment blocks. How many will be affordable, for shared ownership or social housing, is still under negotiation.

As you head further west, into Plaistow, housing becomes less attractive and places of interest dwindle. But even here, you've got the Greenway, a four-mile walking and cycling artery that follows the path of the Northern Outfall Sewer (above it, not through it), linking Hackney and Beckton, as well as the green and pleasant Lee Valley Park, with Three Mills Island (containing film studios and a cluster of historical mill buildings) at the confluence of the local rivers. As development and regeneration continues along the Lee Valley, this broken part of London is gradually being stitched back together.

TRANSPORT

Tube lines Central, District, DLR, Hammersmith & City, Jubilee, Overground
Rail services into Liverpool Street, St Pancras
Main bus routes into central London 115; night buses N8, N15; 24-hour bus 25
River services Woolwich Ferry
Airports London City
Cable car Emirates Air Line crosses the Thames from ExCeL London at the Royal Docks to the O2 arena south of the river

Canning Town, Custom House and the Royal Docks E16

The view from the Woolwich ferry as it berths at North Woolwich Pier sums up this bit of London: the remnants of the docks; unloved and unassimilated modern architecture; and, precariously intermingled, some surprising green spaces. For many years, the parks provided the only real highlights in an area dominated by ugliness: the sprawling estates, the vast hangar of ExCeL London (the events and exhibition centre), the huge scar of the Beckton Sewage Treatment Works and the impressively bleak expanses of the Royal Docks themselves (the King George V, the Royal Albert and the Royal Victoria).

But transformation is under way. Crossrail will open a station at Custom House in 2018 and the brownfield sites around the Royal Docks have been designated an Enterprise Zone, into which will pour £1 billion of investment. The aim is to create a hub for Asian business on 35 acres of land by the Royal Albert Dock.

Sandwiched between the Royal Victoria Dock and the Thames, Silvertown Quays is already under redevelopment, with a new bridge planned to connect the area to Custom House. Formerly a Victorian workers' township, named after the boss of a 19th-century rubber firm, Silvertown used to be a favourite zone for connoisseurs of post-industrial decay; it is still sometimes assailed by the sickly smells of an animal-rendering plant and the Tate & Lyle sugar refinery. But the urbanists' landmarks – the Grade II-listed Silo D and the gently decaying Millennium Mills, soon to undergo £12 million-worth of government-funded renovation – are destined to take their place among new business premises and flats.

Newham Council had already made substantial improvements at the west end of Royal Victoria Dock, including the opening of the Crystal, with its high-quality interactive displays on ecological and urban-planning themes. It's an easy dockside walk from ExCeL London, where a cluster of restaurants and bars service the conference trade, and it sits alongside the embarkation point for the Emirates Air Line cable car, swinging tourists and curious Londoners across the river to the O2 arena. The dock contains the WakeUp Docklands watersports centre, which has wakeboarding opportunities and bars, as well as the historic steam coaster SS *Robin*, open for occasional tours while renovations

are completed. To the east on the Royal Albert Dock is the London Regatta Centre, which trains rowers and dragon-boat racers. Apart from the Crystal's fine café, the area's best restaurant is also on the Royal Albert: Yi-Ban serves good Cantonese food and has views across to London City Airport.

South of Silvertown is Thames Barrier Park, with a café, sculpted gardens and a children's play area, while just the other side of the airport, Beckton District Park stretches beyond the A13; next door is a city farm. Perhaps the most surprising green space, though, is Bow Creek Ecology Park. Just south-west of Canning Town station, this former ironworks and coal wharf is now a sweet little nature reserve that occupies the peninsula made by a particularly serpentine bend of the Lea. It forms a cluster of attractions either side of Leamouth, including the East India Dock Basin wildlife sanctuary and the lighthouse and art installations of Trinity Buoy Wharf.

Parks aside, Canning Town is basically a transport hub – a key interchange on the easterly sections of the DLR – amid a maze of residential streets that are starting to attract the buy-to-let crowd and middle-class, first-time buyers. Rathbone Market, just the other side of the A13 from the station, is a focal point for regeneration by the council.

But North Woolwich and Custom House form a windblown desert of dockland with oases of 'luxury flats' and modern hotels. On the positive side, there's the main campus of the University of East London (UEL), whose SportsDock training centre is open to the public. Two spurs of the DLR run to this corner of Newham, one of which leads directly to the bijou London City Airport.

Eating

Afters 166-168 Green Street, E7 8JT (8257 7056, www.aftersoriginal.co.uk).

Amitas 124-126 Green Street, E7 8JQ (8472 1839, www.amitasvegetarian.com).

Coffee7 10 Sebert Road, E7 0NQ (8534 7774, www.coffee7.co.uk).

Counter Café 7 Roach Road, E3 2PA (07834 275920, www.counterproductive.co.uk).

Moka East The View Tube, The Greenway, Marshgate Lane, E15 2PJ (07506 870837).

Queen's Fish Bar 406 Green Street, E13 9JJ (8471 2457).

Roof East Floors 7&8, Stratford Centre multi-storey car park, Great Eastern Way, E15 1XE (7515 7153, www.roofeast.com).

Discover

Unity Kitchen Café Timber Lodge, 1A Honour Lea Avenue, Queen Elizabeth Olympic Park, E20 1DY (7241 9076, www.unitykitchen.co.uk).
Vijay's Chawalla 268-270 Green Street, E7 8LF (8470 3535, www.vijayschawalla.co.uk).
Yi-Ban London Regatta Centre, 101 Dockside Road, E16 2QT (7473 6699, www.yi-ban.com).

Drinking

Black Lion 59-61 High Street, Plaistow, E13 0AD (8472 2351, www.blacklionplaistow.co.uk).
Crate Brewery The White Building, Unit 7, Queen's Yard, E9 5EN (07834 275687, www.cratebrewery.com).
King Edward VII 47 Broadway, E15 4BQ (8534 2313, www.kingeddie.co.uk).
Railway Tavern Hotel 131 Angel Lane, E15 1DB (8534 3123, www.railwaytavernhotel.co.uk).

Shopping

Damini's 277A Green Street, E7 8LJ (8503 4200, www.daminis.com).
East Shopping Centre 232-236 Green Street, E7 8LE (8969 1333, www.eastshoppingcentre.com).
Henna Mehndi 316-318 Green Street, E13 9AP (8471 7916, www.hennamehndi.co.uk).

Newham Bookshop 745-747 Barking Road, E13 9ER (8552 9993, www.newhambooks.co.uk).
Number 8 Forest Gate Emporium 8 Sebert Road, E7 0NQ (8534 3424).
Queen's Market Green Street, E13 9BA (8472 4730, www.friendsofqueensmarket.org.uk).
Rathbone Market Barking Road, E16 1EH (0845 262 0138, www.rathbonemarket.com). After redevelopment, it will move to Market Square.
Stratford Centre 54A Broadway, E15 5NG (8536 5350, www.stratfordshopping.co.uk).
Westfield Stratford City Stratford Avenue, E20 1EJ (8221 7300, http://uk.westfield.com).

Things to do

Cinemas & theatres

Boleyn Cinema 7-11 Barking Road, E6 1PW (8471 4884, www.boleyncinemas.com). Indian films.
Brick Lane Music Hall 443 North Woolwich Road, E16 2DA (7511 6655, www.bricklanemusic hall.co.uk).
Stratford Circus Arts Centre Theatre Square, E15 1BX (0844 357 2625, www.stratford-circus.com).
Stratford East Picturehouse Stratford Centre, Salway Road, E15 1BX (8555 3366, bookings 0871 902 5740, www.picturehouses.co.uk).

Theatre Royal Stratford East Gerry Raffles Square, E15 1BN (8534 0310, www.stratfordeast.com).
Vue Westfield Stratford City, E20 1ET (0871 224 0240, www.myvue.com). One of the largest all-digital cinemas in Europe, with 17 screens.
Wanstead Tap 352 Winchelsea Road, E7 0AQ (www.thewansteadtap.com). Gigs, cinema, events.

Other attractions

All Star Lanes 2nd Floor, Westfield Stratford City, E20 1ET (3167 2434, www.allstarlanes.co.uk). Bowling alley.
ArcelorMittal Orbit 3 Thornton Street, Queen Elizabeth Olympic Park, E20 2AD (0333 800 8099, www.arcelormittalorbit.com). Artist Anish Kapoor's tangled steel viewing platform.
Crystal 1 Siemens Brothers Way, Royal Victoria Dock, E16 1GB (7055 6400, www.thecrystal.org).
Discover 383-387 High Street, Stratford, E15 4QZ (8536 5555, www.discover.org.uk). The UK's first story centre for children.
Emirates Air Line Emirates Royal Docks station, 27 Western Gateway, E16 4FA (www.emirates airline.co.uk). Cable car.
ExCeL London 1 Western Gateway, Royal Victoria Dock, E16 1XL (7069 5000, www.excel-london.co.uk).
House Mill Three Mills Island, E3 3DU (8980 4626, www.housemill.org.uk). Grade I-listed tidal mill.
Newham City Farm King George Avenue, E16 3HR (0300 124 0123, www.activenewham.org.uk/newham-city-farm). Main entrance Stansfeld Road.
SS *Robin* Millennium Mills Pier, 2D/2E Royal Victoria Dock, E16 1UQ (7998 1343, www.ssrobin.org). The world's oldest complete steam coaster.

Green spaces

For more details, see www.newham.gov.uk.
Arc in the Park Hermit Road Recreation Ground, Bethell Avenue, E16 4JT (07827 236940, www.community-links.org). Adventure playground.
Beckton District Park North Park, Tollgate Road, E16 3SW; South Park, Stansfeld Road, E6 5LT. Fishing, sports pitches and woodland.
Bow Creek Ecology Park Bidder Street, E16 9ST (0845 677 0600, www.visitleevalley.org.uk). Nature reserve on former ironworks, shipyard and coal wharf.
City of London Cemetery Aldersbrook Road, E12 5DQ (8530 2151, www.cityoflondon.gov.uk).
Greenway Five-mile footpath and cycleway from Beckton to Victoria Park, via the Queen Elizabeth Olympic Park.
Queen Elizabeth Olympic Park E20 (0800 0722 110, www.queenelizabetholympicpark.co.uk). The former Olympic Park, now 227ha of landscaped space, waterways and cafés, with sport and other events all year round.

Thames Barrier Park North Woolwich Road, E16 2HP (7476 3741, www.london.gov.uk). Riverside landscaped gardens, café and playground overlooking the Thames Barrier.
Wanstead Flats (www.wansteadflats.org.uk). Most southerly part of Epping Forest, spilling across the borough border from Redbridge.
West Ham Park Upton Lane, E7 9PU (www.cityoflondon.gov.uk). Sports pitches, paddling pool and ornamental gardens.

Gyms & leisure centres

Atherton Leisure Centre 189 Romford Road, E15 4JF (8536 5500, www.gll.org). Reopening spring 2016.
Balaam Leisure Centre Balaam Street, E13 8AQ (7476 5274, www.gll.org).
East Ham Leisure Centre 324 Barking Road, E6 2RT (8317 5000, www.gll.org).
Lee Valley Hockey & Tennis Centre Eton Manor, Leadmill Lane, Queen Elizabeth Olympic Park, E20 3AD (0845 677 0604, www.visitleevalley.org.uk). Includes disability programmes.
Lee Valley VeloPark Abercrombie Road, Queen Elizabeth Olympic Park, E20 3AB (0845 677 0603, www.visitleevalley.org.uk). Track cycling, BMXing and road and mountain biking.
London Aquatics Centre Queen Elizabeth Olympic Park, E20 2ZQ (8536 3150, www.londonaquaticscentre.org). Tom Daley's training pool is also open to the public.
Newham Leisure Centre 281 Prince Regent Lane, E13 8SD (7511 4477, www.gll.org).
Peacock Gymnasium Peacock House, Caxton Street North, E16 1JL (7511 3799, www.peacockgym.com). Private.

Outdoor pursuits

Docklands Equestrian Centre 2 Clapsgate Lane, E6 6JF (7473 4951, www.docklandsequestrian centre.com). Riding lessons for all ages.
London Regatta Centre 1012 Dockside Road, E16 2QT (7511 2211, www.london-regatta-centre.org.uk).
Outdoors in the City Canning Town Recreation Ground, Freemasons Road, E16 3PY (07951 050152, www.outdoorsinthecity.co.uk).
WakeUp Docklands G21B, Waterfront Studios, 1 Dock Road, E16 1AG (07983 149600, www.wake updocklands.com). Wake- and paddleboarding.

Spectator sports

Copper Box Arena Queen Elizabeth Olympic Park, E20 2ST (8221 4900, www.better.org.uk/leisure/copper-box-arena).
Lee Valley VeloPark Abercrombie Road, Queen Elizabeth Olympic Park, E20 3AB (0845 677 0603, www.visitleevalley.org.uk).

London Aquatics Centre Queen Elizabeth Olympic Park, E20 2ZQ (8536 3150).
Olympic Stadium Loop Road, Queen Elizabeth Olympic Park, E20 2ST (0845 267 2012, queenelizabetholympicpark.co.uk).
West Ham United FC Boleyn Ground, Green Street, E13 9AZ (8548 2748, www.whufc.com). Until summer 2016, then at the former Olympic Stadium.

Schools

Primary

There are 62 state primary schools in Newham, including ten church schools. There are also six independent primaries, including three Muslim schools. See www.newham.gov.uk, www.education.gov.uk/edubase and www.ofsted.gov.uk for information.

Secondary

Brampton Manor Academy Roman Road, E6 3SQ (7540 0500, www.bramptonmanor.newham.sch.uk).
Cumberland School Oban Close, E13 8SJ (7474 0231, www.cumberland.org.uk).
Eastlea Community School Pretoria Road, E16 4NP (7540 0400, www.eastlea.newham.sch.uk).
Forest Gate Community School Forest Lane, E7 9BB (8534 8666, www.forestgate.newham.sch.uk).
Kingsford Community School Kingsford Way, E6 5JG (7476 4700, www.kingsfordschool.com).
Langdon Academy Sussex Road, E6 2PS (8471 2411, www.langdon.newham.sch.uk).
Lister Community School St Mary's Road, E13 9AE (8471 3311, www.lister.newham.sch.uk).
Little Ilford School Browning Road, E12 6ET (8478 8024, www.littleilford.newham.sch.uk).
Newham College London High Street South, E6 6ER (8257 4000, www.newham.ac.uk).
NewVic Plaistow Prince Regent Lane, E13 8SG (7473 4110, www.newvic.ac.uk).
Plashet School Plashet Grove, E6 1DG (8471 2418, www.plashet.newham.sch.uk). Girls only.
Rokeby School Barking Road, E16 4DD (7540 5620, www.rokeby.newham.sch.uk). Boys only.
Royal Docks Community School Prince Regent Lane, E16 3HS (7540 2700, www.royaldocks. newham.sch.uk).
St Angela's Ursuline School St George's Road, E7 8HU (8472 6022, www.stangelas-ursuline.co.uk). Roman Catholic; girls only; mixed sixth form.
St Bonaventure's Boleyn Road, E7 9QD (8472 3844, www.stbons.org). Roman Catholic; boys only; mixed sixth form.
Sarah Bonnell School Deanery Road, E15 4LP (8534 6791, www.sarahbonnellonline.co.uk). Girls only.
Stratford School Academy Grosvenor Road, E7 8JA (8471 2415, www.stratford.newham.sch.uk).

Property

Local estate agents

Aston Fox www.astonfox.co.uk
Canary Properties www.canaryproperties.co.uk
Charles Hamilton Estates www.charles hamiltonestates.co.uk
Charles Living & Son www.charlesliving.com
David Daniels www.daviddaniels.co.uk
Filtons www.filtons.com
Get Living London www.getlivinglondon.com
Marvel Estates www.marvelestates.com
McDowalls www.mcdowalls.com
Samuel King www.samuelking.co.uk
Spencers Property www.spencersproperty.co.uk

Local knowledge

www.newham.com
www.newham.gov.uk
www.newhamrecorder.co.uk

USEFUL INFO

Borough size
3,620 hectares

Population
332,700

Ethnic mix
White 44.7%
Asian or Asian British 30.3%
Black or Black British 16.5%
Chinese or other 4.5%
Mixed 4.1%

London Borough of Newham
1000 Dockside Road, E16 2QU (8430 2000, www.newham.gov.uk)

Council run by
Labour

MPs
East Ham, Stephen Timms (Labour);
West Ham, Lyn Brown (Labour)

Main recycling centre
Jenkins Lane Reuse & Recycling Centre, Jenkins Lane, IG11 0AD (8591 3834, www.newham.gov.uk)

Council tax
£827.09 to £2,481.26

Southwark

Gentrification and widespread regeneration have turned Southwark into a borough of layers: popular cultural attractions and riverside walks to the north; green spaces and smart food shops in the south; and regenerating housing estates and vibrant high streets across the middle. As reconstruction continues, this is a borough on the move – upwards.

AVERAGE PROPERTY PRICE	
Detached £1,188,265	**Terraced** £611,505
Semi-detached £769,587	**Flat** £530,376

AVERAGE RENTAL PRICE PER WEEK	
Studio £220	**3 bed** £425
1 bed £288	**4+ bed** £529
2 bed £345	

Bussey Building, Peckham

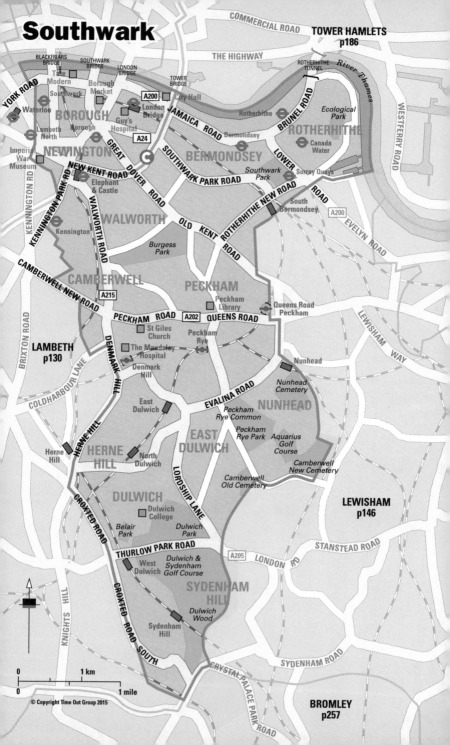

Neighbourhoods

Bankside and Borough SE1

Bankside has historically been a place of entertainment and fun, hedonism and artistic delight. Though industrial right up to the 1980s (as was much of London's riverside – hard to believe now), Bankside is once again a vibrant cultural quarter. Aside from the big guns – Tate Modern and Shakespeare's Globe – there are Bankside Gallery, Jerwood Space, Menier Chocolate Factory, Union Theatre and the Rose Playhouse.

Despite being lodged between some of the capital's main tourist sites, this is still a very residentially minded quarter. Coin Street Community Builders have been guardians of the five hectares to the east of Waterloo Bridge since the mid '80s, defending it from large-scale office proposals and championing family and affordable housing. The result has been some innovative house-building, relaxed retail spaces such as Gabriel's Wharf, and much of the Oxo Tower being given over to affordable housing and retail studio space for designer/makers.

Southwark tube station has brought the Jubilee line to Bankside, as well as some sculptural office blocks and new apartments. Developments along Union Street, Southwark Street and around the junction of the Cut and Blackfriars Road are fed by Scandinavian stalwart Baltic, tucked-away Mar i Terra, and architect-owned Table, though the Blue Fin building behind Tate Modern houses a useful range of wholesome chains such as Japanese takeaway Tsuru.

Borough Market has gone from being London's foodie hub to a tourist hotspot, packed most days with sellers touting hot food and artisanal produce. However, we'd still recommend a drink at the tiny Rake (serving around 130 beers at any one time) or traditional Market Porter, a meal at Roast (modern British) or Tapas Brindisa, or doughnuts from Bread Ahead; or simply indulge your cheese fantasies at Neal's Yard.

The Shard, London's tallest building, piercing the sky 87 storeys above London Bridge station, can be glimpsed up every side street. Chinese restaurant Hutong, on the 33rd floor, is just one of the places to eat and drink.

'The Borough' proper, south of the market, is an interesting place to explore. Dickensian connections are rife – most notably Marshalsea Road, near the site of the (long-gone) debtors' prison. Craft and design showcase Contemporary Applied Arts brings things back into the 21st century.

Elephant & Castle and Walworth SE17

Elephant & Castle is currently a work in progress. A century ago, it was considered the Piccadilly of south London for its shops and general bustle; now, the plots around the multi-lane double roundabout form one giant building site as estates come down and shiny new towers go up – part of a massive £1.5 billion regeneration of south London's traffic gateway. By 2025, more than 3,000 new homes should have been built, a proportion of them affordable housing.

As one community is unceremoniously broken up and shipped out, others are taking hold. Transient sites and condemned spaces spawn community gardens, makeshift galleries such as Hotel Elephant and temporary container parks (the Artworks) holding street-food stalls and start-ups.

With two major universities at its heart – London College of Communication and Southbank University – Elephant & Castle is a very studenty area, with increasing numbers of purpose-built residences. Factor in nightclubs such as the Coronet, Ministry of Sound and Corscia Studios; a street market; a cheap and cheerful bowling alley (Palace Superbowl); and that it's walking distance from central London, and you can see how the attractions might outweigh the incessant traffic.

South London's Colombian community also converges on the area, particularly on Sundays, when the numerous South American cafés (Chatica, Bodeguita and so on) that populate the unloved shopping centre and the railway arches beneath come alive with lunching families and Latin dance classes. Mamuska!, also inside the shopping centre, provides Polish beer and a taste of (eastern European) home. Dragon Castle, at the top of Walworth Road, attracts the dim sum connoisseur; neighbouring Longdan Express oriental supermarket caters for homesick Asian students and those who know their noodles.

Walworth Road, stretching away towards Burgess Park and Camberwell, is a lively and somewhat anarchic mix of nondescript shops, among which can be found health shop G Baldwin & Co (established 1844), the Cumming Museum (currently being restored following a devastating fire) and East Street

Market – one of London's oldest, biggest and busiest traditional street markets.

The Old Kent Road has never really moved on from its place as the cheapest spot on the Monopoly board, but it's important enough to actually be on the board in the first place. This area may be a bit rough and ready, but it has potential written all over it. Not only is it incredibly close to central London, but repeated mutterings about extending the Bakerloo line out to Hayes via New Cross must ring up build signs in developers' eyes. To be fair, even the Old Kent Road has its moments, with a few handsome Victorian streets surviving behind the main road, and a multicultural mix of cafés. Catch it while you can – it's only a matter of time before the towers of Elephant & Castle creep down here.

Bermondsey SE1

Bermondsey Street, stretching off behind London Bridge station, is a popular place for creative professionals, and one of London's main dining destinations. Many small-scale businesses have found studio space in the area, alongside larger organisations such as the Fashion & Textile Museum, London Glassblowing and the White Cube gallery. In response, Bermondsey Street is now lined with great cafés and restaurants, among them Casse-Croûte (French), José (Spanish), and Zucca (Italian), as well as pretty boutiques such as Bermondsey 167.

A less-worn track along pretty Snowfields, behind King's College and Guy's Hospital, brings you to cosy pubs such as the Rose, jeweller Alex Monroe and a beautiful Guinness Trust Victorian housing estate. At the other end of the street, down at Bermondsey Square, despite the gentrification, the famous Antiques Market still takes place every Friday (6am-2pm). A farmers' market redresses the balance on Saturdays.

Deeper into Bermondsey, development has been progressing apace with attractive new-build apartments along Tower Bridge Road, and around the quieter Spa Road area. At weekends, foodies flock to the shops and stalls of Maltby Street Market, based along Ropewalk, under the railway arches of Druid Street and around Spa Terminus. Permanent fixtures include 40 Maltby Street (artisanal wines and small-plates restaurant), Tozino tapas bar, St John Bakery, the London Honey Company, Mons cheesemongers and Kernel Brewery. It's also a good opportunity to browse architectural salvage specialist LASSCO. Away from the fray, relaxed local restaurant the Grange covers every weather base with an open fire and courtyard garden.

Shad Thames was one of the original warehouse developments in the 1980s – and is still sought after (at ten times the price). Also still going strong after decades of service are Le Pont de La Tour and the Butler's Wharf Chop House, where those deep of pocket can dine in the shadow of Tower Bridge. And the money is spreading east. Swathes of new apartment blocks have also been built in the strip between Jamaica Road and the river. A top tip for design fans (aside from the Design Museum, which will be moving to Kensington by 2017) is Vitrapoint, where you can often pick up ex-display furniture for vastly reduced prices. Tower Bridge Road boasts the original M Manze, serving pie, mash and liquor since 1902; at the other end of the scale, Story Restaurant serves stellar British dishes from bright young chef Tom Sellers. Looking for a quiet riverside pint far away from the Tower Bridge crowds? The Angel has been pulling them for centuries.

Rotherhithe and Surrey Quays SE16

To many, Surrey Quays is essentially an uninspiring shopping centre and retail park (Decathlon, Hollywood Bowl, Tesco), transport hub (bus station, Overground, and Canada Water tube) and thoroughfare (the busy Lower Road and nearby Rotherhithe Tunnel), but step further into Southwark's watery peninsula and Surrey Quays is a peaceful place. Eerily so.

Most of the docks were filled in during the 1980s, creating an area that's primarily residential but empty of humans much of the time. It's retained a tremendous sense of space thanks to Greenland Dock (home to the Surrey Docks Watersports Centre) and the width and stillness of the Thames. There are, of course, plenty of modern waterside apartments (of varying degrees of architectural merit) and more than 200 moorings in the South Dock Marina – including a World War II US Army tug and the Wibbly Wobbly pub boat. On a weekday, one of the few places you're likely to see another living soul is along the Thames Path, which darts in and out between private blocks but is popular with walkers, cyclists and joggers. It also passes through the delightful Surrey Docks Farm, which has the Piccalilli Café and farm shop as well as pettable livestock.

The heart of the peninsula has been given over to the Stave Hill Ecology Park, where it's worth climbing to the top of Stave Hill, not just for the view, but for the relief map showing the docks as they were in 1896.

As almost everything here is either water, housing or ecology park, places to eat and drink are limited. Local favourites include the Yellow House (grills and pizza) and Le Cigale on Lower Road, local pubs the Ship & the Whale and the Blacksmith's Arms, and Vietnamese eaterie Café East (in the unlikely location of the corner of the Odeon car park).

The Young Vic offers discounts and free tickets for Southwark residents.

For commuters, a river shuttle runs from the Hilton Hotel across to Canary Wharf.

The small cluster of historic buildings around Rotherhithe station, now branded as 'Rotherhithe Village' and surrounded by some early warehouse conversions, is a charming spot and a world apart from the congested Rotherhithe Tunnel that shoots beneath to Limehouse.

The Brunel Museum is keeper of the area's history, housed in the pumping house for Brunel's 1843 tunnel – the world's first thoroughfare to run under a navigable river. Opposite is the Mayflower pub, named after the pilgrims' boat, which was moored here before her voyage to America. Down the side of the pub, Church Steps give public access to the foreshore at low tide.

Camberwell SE5

Aside from being the subject of a *Withnail and I* quote about a carrot-shaped joint, Camberwell hasn't attracted much fame in recent decades. But things are changing.

Camberwell's Zone 2 status (situated between popular neighbours Peckham, Brixton and Dulwich) and affordable, run-down period housing stock means moustachioed hipsters and nesting thirtysomethings are invading in droves. Walk along the tree-lined streets surrounding the pretty community park of Myatt's Fields and you can barely hear the birdsong above the noise of belt sanders at work on Victorian floorboards. Slowly but surely, the pawnbrokers and

betting shops of Camberwell Church Street are becoming artisanal bakeries and bicycle cafés. If the decades-long deliberation over where to extend the Bakerloo line favours Camberwell, the double-edged sword of gentrification will undoubtedly fall heavily on the area's close-knit community.

Exactly where Camberwell starts and stops is a pretty grey area. But whatever its boundaries, you're certainly not limited to greasy spoons for breakfast (if you want one of those, head to Johnnies on Coldharbour Lane). Choose from Fowlds just south of Burgess Park (a café in a Victorian workshop, as lovely as it is tiny) to No.67 on Peckham Road (airy café/restaurant inside the South London Gallery) or Love Walk at the foot of Denmark Hill (good coffee).

A shopping paradise, Camberwell ain't – especially with the area being sliced up by the crossroads at Camberwell Green. The bustling and huge Cowling & Wilcox art-supplies store is a marker of the types the area continues to attract thanks to the well-regarded art school. With its local festivals and farmers' market, Camberwell has the feeling of an area on the up.

Camberwell Church Street, heading towards Peckham, is crowded with an increasingly good selection of bars and restaurants: Silk Road (award-winning Szechuan food), Stormbird (craft beer), Van Hing (Vietnamese), FM Mangal (kebabs), and Angels & Gypsies (tapas) and its sister bar the Communion.

Among the mix of terraces, mansion blocks, local-authority estates and a converted Victorian hospice is the anomaly that is Camberwell Grove – a stunning avenue of Georgian townhouses that shows how well-to-do this area once was.

Even the bleak area north of Camberwell Green is showing green shoots. The multi-million pound makeover of Burgess Park has been a huge success, turning a no-go zone into one filled with life, colour, cyclists, joggers and historical nods to the time when it was a canal, and attracting plenty of mixed new residential development around its perimeter (though the much maligned Aylesbury Estate still hangs in there).

The unassuming Pasha Hotel on Camberwell Road hides a Turkish spa and hammam, as well as the joyously odd Kyrgyz Kazakh House restaurant: a room festooned with floor cushions, belly dancers, musicians and an actual stream that you have to cross by a bridge. For non-belly-dancing pubs, the

Camberwell Arms does a great Sunday lunch, the Crooked Well does good gastro, the Sun of Camberwell is chilled and charming with a decent beer garden, and the Tiger is a party pub with a late licence that's tempted many a south Londoner to stop off on their way home from a night out in town.

The area's big landmarks up Denmark Hill are King's College Hospital (and its 'as seen on TV' A&E department) and the Salvation Army HQ. Ruskin Park, next door, provides the area's green lung, good views and another peaceful residential enclave.

Heading down Coldharbour Lane, Loughborough Junction, just over the borough border into Lambeth, clings to Camberwell's regenerating coat-tails, despite being overshadowed by the notorious Loughborough Estate. 'Creative' estate agents short of desirable SW9 flats are reinventing the streets around Loughborough Junction as 'Brixton East', and Lambeth Council has plans for a facelift. Current finds include Whirled Cinema (tiny cinema in the railway arches), Harbour Cycles, the House in the Junction (perpetrators of fun local urban interventions) and a community garden. The Thameslink station is handy too.

Peckham SE15

Peckham, which has been 'on the up' for about a decade, has suddenly been fast-tracked. Gourmet burgers, vinyl shops, pop-up bars, art parties and its own hyperlocal newspaper, the *Peckham Peculiar*, have appeared. Even the 7/11 has rebranded itself as the 'Village Grocer' and stocked up on craft beer.

Rye Lane is the main drag, and still has its multicultural buzz thanks to a mix of Nigerian grocers, halal butchers, market stalls, pound shops, Afro-Caribbean hair shops, evangelical churches and an extremely affordable cinema.

Duck down an unpromising passageway and you'll find the rambling Bussey Building – a former cricket-bat factory, now hipster HQ – home to the CLF Art Café club nights, Rye Wax vinyl, community yoga classes, pay-what-you-can work spaces, artists' studios, street art and more. In the summer, from the rooftop bar and cinema, you can wave across the railway tracks to fellow drinkers in Frank's, which sits on the top floor of a multi-storey car park.

Plans are afoot to develop or at least clean up the area around Peckham Rye station (which has great connections into Victoria and London Bridge and out to Kent, plus Clapham and east London thanks to the Overground), but it's already quite lively under the railway arches on Blenheim Grove with the Peckham Refreshment Rooms, the Brick Brewery (the local craft-ale producer), Bar Story and others. Down towards the Rye, Blue Tit hair salon and breakfast-to-dinner restaurant Pedler are raising the tone, while over on Consort Road you'll find pan-Balkan meze at Peckham Bazaar. In the opposite direction, on Peckham High Road, Persian food specialist Persepolis has become something of an institution.

The smart area is Bellenden Road, a huddle of independent shops and restaurants surrounded by leafy residential streets that

HIGHS & LOWS

World-class theatres and galleries

Good schools

Well-stocked food markets

▲ ······················· ▼

No tube in many parts

Elephant & Castle is one big building site

Sweeping gentrification is pushing many residents out

Southwark Street

include Victorian terraces (filling up with young families) and some larger period piles, as well as interesting nooks and crannies such as plant-filled Choumert Square. It's middle-class heaven, with coffee shops, the Review bookshop, gigs at the Peckham Liberal Club, a bike shop, fair-trade clothes shop Bias, Melange for handmade-chocolate, award-winning butcher Flock & Herd, and artisanal groceries at the General Store. There are some

Peckham's Bussey Building is a community hub for clubbing, theatre, workshops, yoga, pop-ups and more.

superb restaurants, such as Artusi (modern Italian), Ganapati (south Indian) and the Begging Bowl (Thai street food), not forgetting an ace pub quiz, great pizzas and guest ales nearby at the shabby-chic Gowlett.

Some of the love is spreading one stop up the rail line to the period houses, new-build apartments and regenerating estates around Queens Road Peckham station. Here, Penge brewer Late Knights has set up Beer Rebellion (ten keg beers, four ciders and four cask ales), Blackbird Bakery has moved into the railway arches and a local group is hoping to establish a 'High Line' walkway to Peckham Rye.

Traditionally, Peckham's proximity to Camberwell College of Arts has brought plenty of artists and creatives into the area. And it shows. There's street art everywhere, as well as exhibition spaces such as the high-profile South London Gallery (its No.67 café/ restaurant is good too), the south-east outpost of the international Hannah Barry Gallery, community space Peckham Platform and tiny local showcase the Sunday Painter.

East Dulwich SE22

For somewhere that's not even on the tube, East Dulwich sure is popular. Its ample supply of three-bed Victorian terraces get snapped up and quickly filled with babies, loft conversions and kitchen extensions. Whether that's down to the good schools, green spaces (Dulwich Park, Peckham Rye, Goose Green and nearby Dulwich Woods), plentiful bus routes into town, indie shops, great food, brand-new Picturehouse cinema or the camaraderie that comes precisely

from not being on the Underground network, no one's quite sure.

A high percentage of self-employed/ homeworkers (entrepreneurs, actors, media-types) and maternity-leave mums ensures that, on weekdays, the many cafés are filled with loners with laptops and ladies (and babies) who lunch. At weekends, Northcross Road market provides a lively focus, and in the evenings, when the twentysomethings get back from their office jobs, the numerous pubs, bars and restaurants keep Lordship Lane up late.

Innovative bistro Toasted, Boulangerie Jade, the French House (Alsace tartine) and a branch of pizzeria Franco Manca have joined gastropub the Palmerston, restaurant Franklins (big on all things local and seasonal), unpretentious pub the EDT (East Dulwich Tavern) and several decent curry houses and Turkish grills along Lordship Lane. No babysitter? William Rose butcher, Moxon's fishmonger, Pretty Traditional greengrocer, Burro e Salvia handmade pasta, healthfood-oriented grocer SMBS, Brick House Bread, several serious wine and/or beer shops and the Cheese Block will make sure you still eat and drink very well indeed.

Locals are fiercely protective of their independent shops and boutiques – the likes of Mrs Robinson, Ed, the Fresh Flower Company and Rye Books – and every six months there's an outcry as another rumour of a big chain surfaces on the extremely active online forum. Roullier White, an emporium of quality English produce and perfumes that you'd be hard pressed to find anywhere else, even pulls in Japanese tourists.

While the action is focused on Lordship Lane, the further away you get up the hill, the larger the houses, the better the views and the wealthier the inhabitants. Across Forest Hill Road, beside Peckham Rye, a set of 1930s streets provides popular family homes and a splendid art deco apartment block, Mundania Court.

Nunhead SE15

The heart of the historic village of Nunhead, which traces its roots back to 1680 and the Old Nun's Head pub at its centre, is the cluster of shops around Nunhead Green. Several – Ayres the Bakers, Soper's fishmonger and Smith's butcher's, all much-loved family-run businesses – have been here for generations. Newer arrivals along this strip point to the direction Peckham's quieter, overlooked sibling is heading: Papa Bear, stocking mid-century modern furniture; the Beer Shop craft-beer pub, Bambuni deli and coffee shop; pretty AG Flowers; Rat Race Cycles; Charlie Foxtrot Vintage; and more eclectic outlets including Mummy J textiles and stringed-instrument maker John Procter.

The green itself is looking better than ever after a community-led makeover, and a community centre is under construction. Surrounding Victorian streets are cheaper here than many neighbourhoods, or you can pick up a bargain on the 1970s Tappesfield Estate near the station.

Nunhead is an area of two halves, separated by the rambling Victorian cemetery, one of the finest examples of its kind and filled with listed monuments. Up the hill, away from the station and shops, things get even quieter and more residential. But not so residential that they don't have room for one of London's best pubs, the Ivy House. Threatened with closure and being turned into flats, it was collectively bought by thirsty locals (371 shareholders) and is currently being run as London's first cooperatively owned pub, complete with folk nights, local bands and a great selection of beers and ciders from the numerous local microbreweries. Because that's the sort of neighbourhood this is.

It's also the sort of neighbourhood that has allotments with an active bee-keeping community, an annual free film festival (shared with Peckham), annual art trail and food festival (www.nunheadarttrail.co.uk), toddler-centric café with play corner (the Dish & the Spoon), youth-run radio station (Reprezent FM) and a friendly nine-hole golf course (Aquarius).

Peckham Rye, an open expanse of green, both divides Nunhead and East Dulwich, and brings them together. Features include formal gardens, an adventure playground, a café and a skate park, while grassy areas are marked out for football, rugby and Aussie rules.

Herne Hill SE24

Well-heeled Herne Hill is a quiet sort of place, despite the constant traffic jam at its centre. Pedestrianisation of the area in front of the station has created an attractive focus for a charming collection of shops: wool shop, sweet shop, butcher, greengrocer, junk shop, Blackbird Bakery and Herne Hill Books. On Sundays, it's filled with food and craft stalls. Even the station itself (trains to Victoria, Thameslink destinations or on to Kent and Surrey) is nice enough to have its own community piano.

The forgotten strip of shops along Dulwich Road is blinking into life with the Society for the Protection of Unwanted Objects (a junk shop by any other name), ethical clothes shop Lowie, and brewpub the Florence, before heading Brixton-wards via the series of popular residential streets known collectively as 'the poets'. Elsewhere, there's top-quality neighbourhood restaurant Number 22; Olley's is a perennial favourite for fish and chips; and pretty Tales on Moon Lane draws families from far and wide with its well-chosen children's books and pretty window displays.

The area is dominated by Brockwell Park, an attractive space with a great playground, BMX track, miniature railway, walled garden, and community greenhouse. The park hosts the incongruous annual Lambeth Country Show and is home to Brockwell Lido, spruced up a few years ago with an indoor gym and a popular café.

Along Stradella and Winterbourne roads, things start to get very upmarket indeed (five or six bedrooms; some properties just advertised as 'POA'), although some interesting low-rise estates along Half Moon Lane and the Judith Kerr German school provide down-to earth respite. One of the most exciting features of the area, tucked away behind the houses of Burbage Road, is the historic Herne Hill Velodrome, used as a venue in the 1948 Olympics, which still hosts races, club training and kids' classes.

TRANSPORT

Tube lines Bakerloo, Jubilee, Northern, Overground
Rail services into Blackfriars, Charing Cross, London Bridge, Victoria
Main bus routes into central London 1, 17, 21, 35, 40, 42, 45, 47, 48, 63, 68, 100, 133, 141, 148, 171, 172, 521, RV1; night buses N1, N21, N35, N47, N63, N68, N133, N155, N171, N343, N381; 24-hour buses 12, 36, 37, 43, 53, 148, 149, 176, 188, 453
River boat services Bankside Pier, London Bridge Pier, Rotherhithe Pier and Surrey Quays Pier

Dulwich Village, West Dulwich and Sydenham Hill SE21

Dulwich Village is one of those places that really shouldn't be in London: white wooden signposts, neat gravel driveways, independent wine merchant Dulwich Vintner, Romeo Jones deli, a florist, men in tweed, loads of greenery and not a cashpoint in sight (so vulgar). Some shops, such as Village Books and Green's Village Toy Shop, have been there forever; others, such as Jane Newbury, have freshened things up with contemporary home accessories and pretty prints.

Swap touristy Borough Market for in-the-know Maltby Street.

Gail's bakery is a popular post-school or post-dogwalking treat, but sadly pubgoers will have to wait until 2016 for the reopening of the village's focal point, the Crown & Greyhound, currently undergoing extensive restoration to provide a boutique hotel.

Dulwich is major public-school territory – JAGS, Alleyn's, Dulwich College and their various feeder prep schools – and much of the area is carpeted with playing fields. The main visitor attraction is Dulwich Picture Gallery, designed by Sir John Soane and opened in 1817. The world's first purpose-built public art gallery, it ensures it's still relevant by curating street-art projects and using its permanent collection of Old Masters to inspire playful exhibitions.

Though most of the village itself is out of range of any buyers without a few million to spare, the 'North Dulwich Triangle', opposite North Dulwich station, has sturdy Edwardian terraces, many converted into flats. The quiet culs-de-sac of the 1920s Sunray Estate conservation area, built under the 'Homes Fit for Heroes' campaign, offer a taste of garden-city living.

Hop across the South Circular, and through the capital's only functioning tollgate (on College Road), and you're met with Dulwich Wood and the Dulwich Estate, stretching from London Road to Gipsy Hill. Well-kept residential estates such as Peckarman's Wood and Great Brownings are midcentury modern dream homes with a sylvan setting.

West Dulwich, half in Lambeth, feels like deep, suburban south London, but it's only 13 minutes from Victoria by train or a short bus ride from Brixton. The area has a good supply of big period houses and some popular shops and restaurants – Dulwich Books, Dulwich Trader, the Rosendale gastropub, Da Porcini (Italian), traditional outfitters Thomas School & Sport and Alleyn Park Garden Centre – mainly clustered around the junction of Croxted Road and Park Hall Road.

Eating

40 Maltby Street SE1 3PA (7237 9247, www.40maltbystreet.com).

Angels & Gypsies 29-33 Camberwell Church Street, SE5 8TR (7703 5984, www.angelsand gypsies.com).

Artusi 161 Bellenden Road, SE15 4DH (3302 8200, www.artusi.co.uk).

Baltic 74 Blackfriars Road, SE1 8HA (7928 1111, www.balticrestaurant.co.uk).

Bambuni 143 Evelina Road, SE15 3HB (7732 4150, www.bambuni.co.uk).

Begging Bowl 168 Bellenden Road, SE15 4BW (7635 2627, www.thebeggingbowl.co.uk).

La Bodeguita Unit 222, Elephant & Castle Shopping Centre, SE1 6TE (7701 9166, www.labodeguita.co.uk).

Boulangerie Jade 145 Lordship Lane, SE22 8HX (8613 6161, www.boulangeriejade.com).

Butlers Wharf Chop House 36E Shad Thames, SE1 2YE (7403 3403, www.chophouse-restaurant.co.uk).

Café East 100 Redriff Road, Surrey Quays Leisure Park, SE16 7LH (7252 1212, www.cafeeastpho.co.uk).

Casse-Croûte 109 Bermondsey Street, SE1 3XB (7407 2140, www.cassecroute.co.uk).

Chatica 2 Elephant Street, SE17 1LB (7277 4485, www.lachatica.com).

La Cigale 172 Lower Road, SE16 2UN (7237 0444).

Crooked Well 16 Grove Lane, SE5 8SY (7252 7798, www.thecrookedwell.com).

Da Porcini 7 Croxted Road, SE21 8SZ (8670 4444, www.daporcini.co.uk).

Dish & the Spoon 61 Cheltenham Road, SE15 3AF.

Dragon Castle 100 Walworth Road, SE17 1JL (7277 3388, www.dragon-castle.com).

FM Mangal 54 Camberwell Church Street, SE5 8QZ (7701 6677, www.thecrookedwell.com).

Fowlds 3 Addington Square, SE5 7JZ (3417 4500, www.fowldscafe.com).

Franco Manca 21 Lordship Lane, SE22 8EW (8299 4017, www.francomanca.co.uk).

Franklins 157 Lordship Lane, SE22 8HX (8299 9598, www.franklinsrestaurant.com).

French House 52 Lordship Lane, SE22 8HJ (3441 2090, www.thefrenchhouse.co).

Gail's 91 Dulwich Village, SE21 7BJ (8693 1787, www.gailsbread.co.uk).

Ganapati 38 Holly Grove, SE15 5DF (7277 2928, www.ganapatirestaurant.com).

Grange 103 Grange Road, SE1 3BW (7231 6563, www.grangepub.co.uk).

Hutong Level 33, The Shard, 31 St Thomas Street, SE1 9RY (3011 1257, www.hutong.co.uk).

Johnnies 104-106 Coldharbour Lane, SE5 9PZ.

José 104 Bermondsey Street, SE1 3UB (7403 4902, www.josetapasbar.com).

Kyrgyz Kazakh House Pasha Hotel, 158 Camberwell Road, SE5 0EE (7277 2228).

Lido Café Brockwell Lido, Dulwich Road, SE24 0PA (7737 8183, www.thelidocafe.co.uk).

Love Walk 81 Denmark Hill, SE5 8RS (7703 9898, www.lovewalkcafe.co.uk).

Mamuska! Unit 233, Elephant & Castle Shopping Centre, SE1 6TE (3602 1898, www.mamuska.net).

Mar i Terra 14 Gambia Street, SE1 0XH (7928 7628, www.mariterra.co.uk).

M Manze 87 Tower Bridge Road, SE1 4TW (7407 2985, www.manze.co.uk).

No.67 South London Gallery, 67 Peckham Road, SE5 8UH (7252 7649, www.number67.co.uk).

Number 22 22 Half Moon Lane, SE24 9HU (7095 9922, www.number-22.com).

Olley's 65-69 Norwood Road, SE24 9AA (8671 8259, www.olleys.info).

Palmerston 91 Lordship Lane, SE22 8EP (8693 1629, www.thepalmerston.co.uk).

Peckham Bazaar 119 Consort Road, SE15 3RU (7732 2525, www.peckhambazaar.com).

Peckham Refreshment Rooms 12-16 Blenheim Grove, SE15 4QL (7639 1106, www.peckham refreshment.com).

Pedler 58 Peckham Rye, SE15 4JR (3030 5015, www.pedlerpeckhamrye.com).

Le Pont de la Tour 36D Shad Thames, SE1 2YE (7403 8403, www.lepontdelatour.co.uk).

Roast Floral Hall, Borough Market, Stoney Street, SE1 1TL (0845 034 7300, www.roast-restaurant.com).

Rosendale 65 Rosendale Road, SE21 8EZ (8761 9008, www.therosendale.co.uk).

Silk Road 49 Camberwell Church Street, SE5 8TR (7703 4832).

Stormbird 25 Camberwell Church Street, SE5 8TR (7708 4460, www.thestormbirdpub.co.uk).

Story Restaurant 199 Tooley Street, SE1 2JX (7183 2117, www.restaurantstory.co.uk).

Peckham Rye Park café; Burgess Park BMX

Table 83 Southwark Street, SE1 0HX (7401 2760, www.thetablecafe.com).

Tapas Brindisa 18-20 Southwark Street, SE1 1TJ (7357 8880, www.brindisatapas kitchens.com).

Toasted 36-38 Lordship Lane, SE22 8HJ (8693 9021, www.toastdulwich.co.uk).

Tozino LASSCO Ropewalk, Maltby Street, SE1 3PA (www.bartozino.com).

Tsuru Bankside 4 Canvey Street, SE1 9AN (7928 2228, www.tsuru-sushi.co.uk).

Van Hing 42 Camberwell Church Street, SE5 8QZ (7703 9707).

Yellow House 126 Lower Road, SE16 2UE (7231 8777, www.theyellowhouse.eu).

Zucca 184 Bermondsey Street, SE1 3TQ (7378 6809, www.zuccalondon.com).

Drinking

Angel 101 Bermondsey Wall East, SE16 4NB (7394 3214).

Bar Story 213 Blenheim Grove, SE15 4QL (7635 6643, www.barstory.co.uk).

Beer Rebellion 129 Queen's Road, SE15 2ND (www.lateknightsbrewery.co.uk).

Beer Shop 40 Nunhead Green, SE15 3QF (7732 5555, www.thebeershoplondon.co.uk).

Blacksmith's Arms 257 Rotherhithe Street, SE16 5EJ (7064 4355, www.blacksmithsarms rotherhithe.co.uk).

Brick Brewery Arch 209, Blenheim Grove, SE15 4QL (07747 787636, www.brickbrewery.co.uk).

Communion Bar 29-33 Camberwell Church Street, SE5 8TR (7703 5984, www.communion bar.com).

Crown & Greyhound 73 Dulwich Village, SE21 7BJ (8299 4976, www.thecrownandgreyhound.co.uk).

East Dulwich Tavern 1 Lordship Lane, SE22 8EW (8693 1316, www.eastdulwichtavern.com).

Florence 131-133 Dulwich Road, SE24 0NG (7326 4987, www.florencehernehill.com).

Frank's 10th floor, Peckham Multi-Storey Car Park, 95A Rye Lane, SE15 4ST (www.franks cafe.co.uk).

Gowlett 62 Gowlett Road, SE15 4HY (7635 7048, www.thegowlett.com).

Ivy House 40 Stuart Road, SE15 3BE (7277 8233, www.ivyhousenunhead.com).

Market Porter 9 Stoney Street, SE1 9AA (7407 2495, www.markettaverns.com).

Mayflower 117 Rotherhithe Street, SE16 4NF (7237 4088, www.mayflowerpub.co.uk).
Old Nun's Head 15 Nunhead Green, SE15 3QQ (7639 4007, www.theoldnunshead.co.uk).
Rake 14A Winchester Walk, SE1 9AG (7407 0557, www.utobeer.co.uk).
Rose 123 Snowsfields, SE1 3ST (7403 0168, www.therosepublichouse.co.uk).
Ship & Whale 2 Gulliver Street, SE16 7LT (7237 7072, www.shipandwhale.co.uk).
Sun of Camberwell 61-63 Coldharbour Lane, SE5 9NS (7737 5861, www.suncamberwell.com).
Tiger 18 Camberwell Green, SE5 7AA (7703 5246, www.thetigerpub.com).
Wibbly Wobbly Greenland Dock, Rope Street, SE16 7SZ (7232 2320).

Shopping

AG Flowers 139 Evelina Road, SE15 3HB (7277 6523, www.a-gflowers.co.uk).
Alex Monroe 37 Snowsfields, SE1 3SU (7378 6061, www.alexmonroe.com).
Alleyn Park Garden Centre 77 Park Hall Road, SE21 8ES (8670 7788, www.alleynpark.co.uk).
Ayres the Bakers 131-133 Evelina Road, SE15 3HB (7639 0648).
Blue Tit 26 Peckham Rye, SE15 4JR (7064 5073, www.bluetitlondon.com).
Bread Ahead 3 Cathedral Street, SE1 9DE (7407 7853, www.breadahead.com).
Bermondsey 167 167 Bermondsey Street, SE1 3UW (7407 3137, www.bermondsey167.com).
Bermondsey Square Antiques Market Bermondsey Square, SE1 3FD (7492 4868, www.bermondseysquare.com).
Bias 143 Bellenden Road, SE15 4DH (7732 3747, www.biasboutique.com).
Blackbird Bakery 208 Railton Road, SE24 0JT (7095 8800, www.blackbirdbakerylondon.co.uk); Queen's Road, SE15 2ND (7732 7711).
Borough Market 8 Southwark Street, SE1 1TL (7407 1002, www.boroughmarket.org.uk).
Brick House Bread 1 Zenoria Street, SE22 8HP (www.brickhousebread.com).
Burro e Salvia 151 Lordship Lane, SE22 8HX (8693 0331, www.burroesalvia.co.uk).
Camberwell Farmers' Market Camberwell Green, SE5 7PR.
Charlie Foxtrot Vintage 108 Evelina Road, SE15 3HL (www.facebook.com/charliefoxtrotvintage).
Cheese Block 69 Lordship Lane, SE22 8EP (8299 3636).
Contemporary Applied Arts 89 Southwark Street, SE1 0HX (7620 0086, www.caa.org.uk).
Cowling & Wilcox 8-12 Orpheus Street, SE5 8RR (7703 1342, www.cowlingandwilcox.com).

Decathlon Canada Water Retail Park, Surrey Quays Road, SE16 2XU (7394 2000, www.decathlon.co.uk).
Dulwich Books 6 Croxted Road, SE21 8SW (8670 1920, www.dulwichbooks.co.uk).
Dulwich Trader 9-11 Croxted Road, SE21 8SZ (8761 3457, www.rigbyandmac.com).
Dulwich Vintner 85-87 Dulwich Village, SE21 7BJ (8299 1051, www.dulwichvintners.co.uk).
East Street Market East Street, SE17 1EL (Street Trading Office 7525 6000, www.southwark.gov.uk).
Ed 41 Northcross Road, SE22 9ET (8299 6938, www.rigbyandmac.com).
FC Soper 141 Evelina Road, SE15 3HB (7639 9729, www.fcsoper.com).
Flock & Herd 155 Bellenden Road, SE15 4DH (7635 7733, www.flockandherd.com).
Fresh Flower Company 39 Northcross Road, SE22 9ET (8693 6088, www.freshflower.co.uk).
G Baldwin & Co 171 Walworth Road, SE17 1RW (7703 5550, www.baldwins.co.uk).
General Store 174 Bellenden Road, SE15 4BW (7642 2129, www.generalsto.re).
Green's Village Toy Shop 31 Dulwich Village, SE21 7BN (8693 5938).
Harbour Cycles 200 Coldharbour Lane, SE5 9QH (7274 5008, www.harbourcycles.co.uk).
HA Smith & Sons 111-113 Evelina Road, SE15 3HB (7639 2941).
Herne Hill Books 289 Railton Road, SE24 0LY (7998 1673, www.hernehillbooks.com).
Jane Newbery 33 Dulwich Village, SE21 7BN (8693 2634, www.janenewbery.co.uk).
John Procter 40 Nunhead Green, SE15 3QF (07779 040789, www.johnprocter.com).
Kernel Brewery Arch 11, Dockley Road Industrial Estate, Dockley Road, SE16 3SF (7231 4516, www.thekernelbrewery.com).
LASSCO 41 Maltby Street, SE1 3PA (7394 8061, www.lassco.co.uk).
London Glassblowing 62-66 Bermondsey Street, SE1 3UD (7403 2800, www.londonglassblowing.co.uk).
London Honey Company Arch 7, Spa South, off Spa Road, SE16 3FJ (www.thelondonhoneycompany.co.uk).
Longdan Express 128-132 Walworth Road, SE17 1JL (7701 2566, www.longdan.co.uk).
Lowie 115 Dulwich Road, SE24 0NG (7733 0040, http://ilovelowie.com).
Maltby Street Market Ropewalk, SE1 2HQ (www.spa-terminus.co.uk, www.maltby.st).
Melange Chocolate 184 Bellenden Road, SE15 4BW (07722 650711, www.themelange.com).
Mons Unit 2, Voyager Business Park, SE16 4RP (7064 6912, www.mons-cheese.co.uk).

Moxon's 149 Lordship Lane, SE22 8HX (8299 1559, www.moxonsfreshfish.com).

Mrs Robinson 128-130 Lordship Lane, SE22 8HD (8693 0693, www.mrsrobinsonshop.co.uk).

Mummy J 34 Nunhead Green, SE15 3QF (07956 341256).

Neal's Yard Dairy 6 Park Street, SE1 9AB (7367 0799, www.nealsyarddairy.co.uk).

Papa Bear 32 Nunhead Green, SE15 3QF (07957 313994, www.papabearlondon.com).

Persepolis 28-30 Peckham High Street, SE15 5DT (7639 8007, www.foratasteofpersia.co.uk).

Pretty Traditional 47 North Cross Road, SE22 9ET (8693 7169).

Rat Race Cycles 118 Evelina Road, SE15 3HL (7732 1933, www.ratracecycles.com).

Review 131 Bellenden Road, SE15 4QY (7639 7400, www.reviewbookshop.co.uk).

Romeo Jones 80 Dulwich Village, SE21 7AJ (8299 1900, www.romeojones.co.uk).

Roullier White 125 Lordship Lane, SE22 8HU (8693 5150, www.roullierwhite.com).

Rye Books 45 Upland Road, SE22 9EF (3581 1850, www.ryebooks.co.uk).

Rye Wax CLF Art Café basement, Bussey Building, 133 Rye Lane, SE15 4ST (7732 3176, www.ryewax.com).

St John Bakery 72 Druid Street, SE1 2DU (7237 5999, www.stjohngroup.uk.com).

SMBS Foods 75 Lordship Lane, SE22 8EP (8693 7792).

Society for the Protection of Unwanted Objects 125 Dulwich Road, SE24 0NG (07817 538872).

Tales on Moon Lane 25 Half Moon Lane, SE24 9JU (7274 5759, www.talesonmoonlane.co.uk).

Thomas Schoolwear 8 Croxted Road, SE21 8SW (8766 7400, www.thomasschoolwear.co.uk).

Village Books 1D Calton Avenue, SE21 7DE (8693 2808, www.village-books.co.uk).

Vitrapoint Ground Floor, Luna House, 37 Bermondsey Wall West, SE16 4RN (7064 9681, www.vitrapointuk.com).

William Rose Butchers 126 Lordship Lane, SE22 8HD (8693 9191, www.williamrose butchers.com).

Things to do

Cinemas & theatres

East Dulwich Picturehouse 116A Lordship Lane, SE22 8HD (0871 902 5749, www.picture houses.co.uk).

Menier Chocolate Factory 53 Southwark Street, SE1 1RU (7378 1713, www.menierchocolate factory.com). Gallery, restaurant, theatre and rehearsal space.

Odeon Cinema Surrey Quays Surrey Quays Leisure Park, Redriff Road, SE16 7LL (0871 224 4007, www.odeon.co.uk).

Old Vic 103 The Cut, SE1 8NB (7928 2651, www.oldvictheatre.com).

Peckham Plex 95A Rye Lane, SE15 4ST (0844 567 2742, www.peckhamplex.com).

Rose Playhouse 56 Park Street, SE1 9AR (7261 9565, www.rosetheatre.org.uk).

Shakespeare's Globe 21 New Globe Walk, Bankside, SE1 9DT (7902 1400, www.shakespearesglobe.com).

Siobhan Davies Dance 85 St George's Road, SE1 6ER (7091 9650, www.siobhandavies.com).

Southwark Playhouse 77-85 Newington Causeway, SE1 6BD (7407 0234, southwark playhouse.co.uk).

Unicorn Theatre 147 Tooley Street, SE1 2HZ (7645 0560, www.unicorntheatre.com). A purpose-built theatre for children.

Whirled Cinema 259-260 Hardess Street, SE24 0HN (7737 6153, www.whirledcinema.com).

Young Vic 66 The Cut, SE1 8LZ (7922 2922, www.youngvic.org).

Galleries & museums

Bankside Gallery 48 Hopton Street, SE1 9JH (7928 7521, www.banksidegallery.com).

Brunel Museum Railway Avenue, SE16 4LF (7231 3840, www.brunel-museum.org.uk).

Clink Prison Museum 1 Clink Street, SE1 9DG (7403 0900, www.clink.co.uk). Prison exhibition with re-creation of original cells.

Cuming Museum (7525 2332, www.southwark. gov.uk/cumingmuseum). Local history museum, in temporary accommodation; see website for details.

Design Museum 28 Shad Thames, SE1 2YD (7403 6933, www.designmuseum.org). Moving to Kensington in 2017.

Dilston Grove Southwark Park, SE16 2UA (7237 1230, www.cgplondon.org). Café/gallery.

Dulwich Picture Gallery Gallery Road, SE21 7AD (8693 5254, www.dulwichpicturegallery.org.uk).

Fashion & Textile Museum 83 Bermondsey Street, SE1 3XF (7407 8664, www.ftmlondon.org).

Gallery@oxo Oxo Tower Wharf, Bargehouse Street, SE1 9PH (7021 1686, www.oxotower.co.uk).

Hannah Barry Gallery 4 Holly Grove, SE15 5DF (7732 5453, www.hannahbarry.com).

Imperial War Museum Lambeth Road, SE1 6HZ (7416 5000, www.iwm.org.uk).

Jerwood Space 171 Union Street, SE1 0LN (7654 0171, www.jerwoodspace.co.uk).

Old Operating Theatre Museum & Herb Garret 9A St Thomas Street, SE1 9RY (7188 2679, www. thegarret.org.uk). A 16th-century herb loft and 17th-century operating theatre.

Peckham Platform 89 Peckham High Street, SE15 5RS (7358 9645, www.peckham platform.com).
South London Gallery 65-67 Peckham Road, SE5 8UH (7703 6120, www.southlondongallery.org).
Sunday Painter 1st Floor, 12-16 Blenheim Grove, SE15 4QL (07811 138350, www. the sundaypainter.co.uk).
Tate Modern Bankside, SE1 9TG (7887 8888, www.tate.org.uk).
White Cube 144-152 Bermondsey Street, SE1 3TQ (7930 5373, www.whitecube.com).

Other attractions

Dulwich Festival (www.dulwichfestival.co.uk). Music, theatre, poetry and art; held in May.
Golden Hinde II Pickfords Wharf, Clink Street, SE1 9DG (7403 0123, www.goldenhinde.com).
HMS Belfast The Queen's Walk, SE1 2JH (7940 6300, www.iwm.org.uk).
Hollywood Bowl The Mast Leisure Park, 3A Teredo Street, SE16 7LW (0844 826 1470, www. hollywoodbowl.co.uk).
London Dungeon Riverside Building, County Hall, Westminster Bridge Road, SE1 7PB (0871 423 2240, www.thedungeons.com).
Palace Superbowl First Floor, Elephant & Castle Shopping Centre, SE1 6TE (7277 0001, www.palacesuperbowl.com).
Shard 32 London Bridge Street, SE1 9SG (0844 499 7111, www.the-shard.com).
Southwark Cathedral London Bridge, SE1 9DA (7367 6700, www.southwark.anglican.org).
Surrey Docks Farm Rotherhithe Street, SE16 5ET (7231 1010, www.surreydocksfarm.org.uk).

Gigs, clubs & comedy

CLF Art Café Bussey Building, 133 Rye Lane, SE15 4ST (7732 5275, www.clfartcafe.org).
Coronet Theatre 28 New Kent Road, SE1 6TJ (7701 1500, www.coronettheatre.co.uk).
Corsica Studios 4-5 Elephant Road, SE17 1LB (7703 4760, www.corsicastudios.com).
Ministry of Sound 103 Gaunt Street, SE1 6DP (0870 060 0010, www.ministryofsound.com).
Peckham Liberal Club 24 Elm Grove, SE15 5DE (7639 1093, www.peckhamliberalclub.org).

Green spaces

Belair Park Gallery Road, SE21 7AB (7525 2000, www.southwark.gov.uk). Tennis courts (operating on a first-come, first-served basis), a skateboard park, an adventure playground and a duck pond.
Brockwell Park Dulwich Road, SE24 0PA (www.lambeth.gov.uk/places/brockwell-park).
Burgess Park Albany Road, SE5 7QH (7525 2000, www.southwark.gov.uk).

Dulwich Park College Road, SE21 7BQ (7525 2000, www.southwark.gov.uk). Boating lake, duck pond and recumbent bicycles for hire.
Nunhead Cemetery Linden Grove, SE15 3LP (7525 2000, www.southwark.gov.uk). Victorian Grade II*-listed cemetery with monthly guided walks among its historic monuments.
Peckham Rye Park & Common Peckham Rye, SE15 3UA (7525 2000, www.southwark.gov.uk). Skate park, formal gardens, football and rugby pitches, adventure playground and children's playgrounds.
Southwark Park Gomm Road, SE16 2EH (7525 2000, www.southwark.gov.uk).
Stave Hill Ecological Park Salter Road, SE16 6AX (7525 2000, www.southwark.gov.uk).

Gyms & leisure centres

Club at County Hall County Hall, Westminster Bridge Road, SE1 7PB (7902 8023, www. marriottleisure.co.uk).
Dojo Physical Arts 10-11 Milroy Walk, SE1 9LW (7928 3000, www.physical-arts.com).
JAGS Sports Club Red Post Hill, SE24 9JN (8613 6500, www.jagssportsclub.co.uk).
Peckham Pulse Healthy Living Centre 10 Melon Road, SE15 5QN (7708 6200, www.fusion-lifestyle.com).
Seven Islands Leisure Centre 100 Lower Road, SE16 2TU (7237 3296, www.fusion-lifestyle.com).
Yogarise Bussey Building, 133 Rye Lane, SE15 4ST (7732 2122, www.yogarisepeckham.com). Offers community yoga classes.

Outdoor pursuits

Aquarius Golf Club 41 Marmora Road, SE22 0RY (8693 1626, www.aquariusgolfclub.co.uk).
Brockwell Lido Brockwell Park, Dulwich Road, SE24 0PA (7274 3088, www.fusion-lifestyle.com).
Burgess Park BMX Burgess Park, Albany Road, SE5 7QH (7525 2000, www.southwark. gov.uk).
Dulwich & Sydenham Hill Golf Club Grange Lane, College Road, SE21 7LH (8693 3961, www.dulwichgolf.co.uk).
Dulwich Riding School Dulwich Common, SE21 7EX (8693 2944, www.dulwichridingschool.co.uk).
Herne Hill Velodrome 104 Burbage Road, SE24 9HE (7737 4647, www.hernehillvelodrome.com).
Surrey Docks Watersports Centre Rope Street, SE16 7SX (0844 893 3888, www.fusion-lifestyle.com).

Spectator sports

Dulwich Hamlet Football Club Edgar Kail Way, SE22 8BD (7274 8707, www.dulwich hamletfc.co.uk).

Schools

Primary

There are 68 state primary schools in the borough of Southwark, 20 of which are church schools. There are also six independent primaries. See www.southwark.gov.uk, www.education.gov.uk/edubase and www.ofsted.gov.uk for more information.

Secondary

Alleyn's School Townley Road, SE22 8SU (8557 1500, www.alleyns.org.uk). Private.

ARK All Saints Academy 140 Wyndham Road, SE5 0UB (7450 5959, www.arkallsaintsacademy.org).

ARK Globe Academy Harper Road, SE1 6AG (7407 6877, www.arkglobeacademy.org).

Bacon's College Timber Pond Road, SE16 6AT (7237 1928, www.baconscollege.co.uk).

Charter School Red Post Hill, SE24 9JH (7346 6600, www.charter.southwark.sch.uk).

City of London Academy Southwark 240 Lynton Road, SE1 5LA (7394 5100, www.cityacademy.co.uk).

Dulwich College Dulwich Common, SE21 7LD (8693 3601, www.dulwich.org.uk). Boys only; private.

Harris Academy Bermondsey 55 Southwark Park Road, SE16 3TZ (7237 9316, www.harrisbermondsey.org.uk). Girls only.

Harris Academy Peckham 112 Peckham Road, SE15 5DZ (7703 4417, www.harrispeckham.org.uk).

Harris Girls' Academy East Dulwich Homestall Road, SE22 0NR (7732 2276, www.harrisdulwich girls.org.uk). Girls only.

James Allen's Girls' School (JAGS) 144 East Dulwich Grove, SE22 8TE (8693 1181, www.jags.org.uk). Girls only; private.

Kingsdale Foundation School Alleyn Park, SE21 8SQ (8670 7575, www.kingsdalefoundation school.org.uk).

Notre Dame Roman Catholic Girls' School 118 St George's Road, SE1 6EX (7261 1121, www.notre dame.southwark.sch.uk). Roman Catholic; girls only.

Sacred Heart Catholic School Camberwell New Road, SE5 0RP (7274 6844, www.sacredheart.southwark.sch.uk). Roman Catholic.

St Michael's Catholic College Llewellyn Street, SE16 4UN (7237 6432, www.stmichaelscollege.org.uk). Roman Catholic.

St Saviour's & St Olave's School New Kent Road, SE1 4AN (7407 1843, www.ssso.southwark.sch.uk). Church of England; girls only.

St Thomas the Apostle College Hollydale Road, SE15 2EB (7639 0106, www.stac.uk.com). Roman Catholic; boys only.

Walworth Academy Shorncliffe Road, SE1 5UJ (7450 9570, www.walworthacademy.org).

Property

Local estate agents

Andrew Scott Robertson www.as-r.co.uk
Burnet Ware www.burnetware.com
Gareth James www.garethjames.com
Harvey & Wheeler www.harveywheeler.com
Pedder www.pedderproperty.com
Pickwick Estates www.pickwickestates.com
Roy Brooks www.roybrooks.co.uk
Wooster & Stock www.woosterstock.co.uk

Local knowledge

www.belowtheriver.co.uk
www.eastdulwichforum.co.uk
www.hernehillforum.org.uk
www.london-se1.co.uk
www.lovenunhead.co.uk
www.peckhampeculiar

USEFUL INFO

Borough size
2,886 hectares

Population
306,700

Ethnic mix
White 65.9%
Black or Black British 17.4%
Asian or Asian British 8.3%
Chinese or other 4.5%
Mixed 3.8%

Southwark Council
160 Tooley Street, SE1 2QH (7525 5000, www.southwark.gov.uk)

Council run by
Labour

MPs
Camberwell & Peckham, Harriet Harman (Labour); Dulwich & West Norwood, Helen Hayes (Labour); Bermondsey & Old Southwark, Neil Coyle (Labour)

Main recycling centre
43 Devon Street, SE15 1AL (7525 2000)

Council tax
£804.76 to £2,414.28

Tower Hamlets

Tower Hamlets is a living record of London's history: successive waves of immigrants forming strong communities, the mini-Manhattan regeneration of Docklands and the chic overhaul of Spitalfields are all part of the story of this eclectic borough.

Rough Trade East, Brick Lane.

AVERAGE PROPERTY PRICE

Detached	Terraced
£609,152	£513,541
Semi-detached	Flat
£478,823	£471,819

AVERAGE RENTAL PRICE PER WEEK

Room	1 bed
£137	£300
Studio	2 bed
£274	£370
	3 bed
	£480

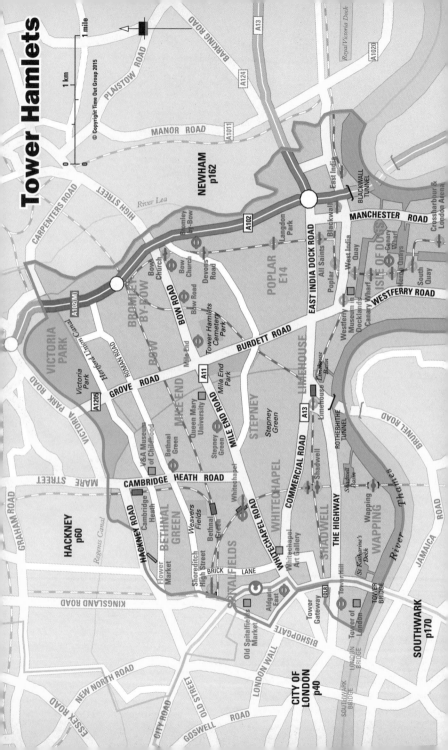

Neighbourhoods

Spitalfields and Brick Lane E1

Spitalfields has long been a first place of
refuge for communities new to London.
Over the years, it has housed groups such
as French Huguenots evading persecution
by Catholics, and Ashkenazi Jews escaping
Russian pogroms. Today, the neighbourhood's
most prominent immigrant community is
Bangladeshi, based on and around Brick
Lane. Central to life here is the Brick Lane
Mosque (opened 1976), which started life as
a French Protestant church (1743) and then
became a Methodist chapel (1819) and the
Spitalfields Great Synagogue (1889) before
becoming a mosque.

You know an area has lost its edge,
however, when groups of clipboard-wielding
schoolchildren filling out local history work-
sheets can be seen trailing the streets. The
seedier side of Spitalfields has become a
distant memory as the City has crept closer:
office blocks loom above the sanitised old
market, and the prostitutes on Commercial
Street have been replaced by Nando's, Pizza
Express and a few less formulaic restaurants
(Hawksmoor, St John Bread & Wine, Poppies
fish and chips, and Copita del Mercado).

There's always something going on inside
the covered market (antiques, art fairs, crafts,
vintage), and always crowds, while the
permanent shops and restaurants tend to
look more towards City workers than East
End locals. Among the more interesting are
Canteen with its Brit grub, the Peloton & Co
cycle café, retro grocer A Gold and corner
deli Verde & Company.

There is, though, plenty of the old
Spitalfields left beyond the inescapable
Jack the Ripper walking tours. Thanks to the
assiduous work of the Spitalfields Historic
Buildings Trust (founded in 1977 when the
City first started bulging eastwards), rows
of exquisite Georgian houses still stand on
Hanbury, Princelet and Fournier streets in
the shadow of Hawksmoor's masterpiece,
Christ Church. Keep an eye out for local
residents Gilbert & George too, frequently
to be seen strolling the streets in tandem,
living artwork that they are.

One block east of Commercial Street,
Brick Lane was once synonymous with curry.
Nowadays, 'street art' walking tours almost
outnumber the hawkers outside the Bengali
restaurants at the south end of the Lane, and
the north end has been colonised by cafés

(including the infamous Cereal Killer), vintage
shops and galleries. There are still some good
shops down Cheshire Street (Beyond Retro,
Comfort Station, Duke of Uke). Bagels are
also big, doled out all day and night by two
rival bakeries a few doors apart: Brick Lane
Beigel Bake and Beigel Shop.

Sunday is market day on both Brick Lane
and Petticoat Lane (west of Commercial
Street), and there's some gold to be found
among the tat – check out Brick Lane's Sunday
(Up)Market. The former Truman Brewery
complex now houses one of London's best
record shops, Rough Trade East, as well as two
popular watering holes: Café 1001 and the Big
Chill Bar. Plus there's always the superb Pride
of Spitalfields and the Commercial Tavern:
two top pubs respectively serving the old East
Enders and the new. Things may be changing
faster than ever here, but there'll always be
time to stop for a pint.

*The best range of
markets in London,
from fashion to fruit
and veg to junk.*

Whitechapel and Stepney E1

In the shadow of the swanky new towers at
Aldgate, the historic centre of the old East
End somehow contrives to remain rough and
ready. There's a dense, diverse and sometimes
fractious population here: old cockney voices
are still heard, and there are many students
and commuters, but the most characteristic
face of Whitechapel is Asian. The area's
Muslim community, centred on the East
London Mosque and the Whitechapel
Market, is close-knit and deeply rooted,
and must be one of the main reasons that
this bit of town is still holding out against
the ongoing tarting-up of the East End.

For those who like their London a bit
more chichi, Whitechapel can be an acquired
taste. There's only one surefire way to lure
in reluctant outsiders: the food. The curry
cognoscenti dodge the Brick Lane hawkers
and head to Tayyabs, Needoo Grill or Lahore
for real-deal Pakistani grills (and queues
serious enough to attest to the quality).
Down past the tube, there are two hip new
arrivals: an atmospheric Dirty Burger, and
the Foxcroft & Ginger café (top-notch for
brunch). Drinking in Whitechapel is harder

Wilton's Music Hall, Wapping

than eating: plenty of old East End boozers have turned into chicken shops or bookies, but the George Tavern in Stepney is a much-loved exception, and scruffily bohemian pub Indo serves great pizzas and good beer.

For fascinating and eclectic local history, all you have to do here is walk the streets, but there are a few bona fide attractions too. The excellent Whitechapel Gallery has doubled its size and increased its scope for ambitious exhibitions. Stepney has the Genesis, one of London's best independent cinemas, and the Troxy: a palatial art deco ex-cinema that puts on terrific gigs and club events, plus mixed martial arts bouts and elaborate weddings. The Royal London Hospital Museum, in an old crypt, tells the stories of Jack the Ripper and the Elephant Man. For cheerier outings, there's Stepney City Farm next to Stepney Green (one of the few decently sized parks in the area).

The completion of Crossrail in 2018 could finally see the clean-up of Whitechapel, and there are already major development plans brewing. For now, it's the extraordinary jumble of people and buildings and traffic that makes Whitechapel and Stepney special. For better or worse, there's always something going on here.

Bethnal Green E2

Situated between buzzing Shoreditch and Hackney's Mare Street, and in prime position on the Central line, Bethnal Green ticks all the boxes for those looking east. Like much of east London, there's not a great deal of uniformity in terms of housing after the bombardment of World War II, so the result is a network of streets that each appear to have their own character. Much of the area is in Zone 1, and it's only a few stops away from the middle of London.

The main drag is along Bethnal Green Road, which joins up with Shoreditch High Street. Here you'll find a good-sized Tesco,

fast food joints, pubs and greasy spoons – namely the family-run E Pellicci, with queues out the door on Saturday mornings. The Star of Bethnal Green, just across the road, is also a pub-quiz favourite for locals. Nearby is Weavers Fields, a decent-sized green space complete with children's play area and two football pitches. Residents enjoy the annual Bonfire Night fireworks display here.

Cambridge Heath Road, which meets Bethnal Green Road at the tube station, has been on the art gallery circuit for years – influential gallery owner Maureen Paley set up in nearby Herald Street in 1999; now it's also becoming a sought-after food and drink

Columbia Road Flower Market

TRANSPORT

Tube lines Central, District, DLR, Hammersmith & City, Metropolitan, Overground
Rail services into Fenchurch Street, Liverpool Street
Main bus routes into central London 15, 48, 55, 100, 205, 388; night buses
N8, N15, N26, N55, N108; 24-hour buses 8, 25, 26, 108, 277
River boat services Canary Wharf Pier, Masthouse Terrace Pier and St Katharine
Docks Pier

destination. The Town Hall Hotel is home to Jason Atherton's Typing Room, which shares the space with Matt Whiley's Peg + Patriot cocktail bar; Whiley also runs the acclaimed Talented Mr Fox cocktails, consultancy and events business.

Early 2014 saw the railway arches just across from the station open up to house a parade of bars and eateries including Mother Kelly's NY-style tap room and bottle shop, and Mission wine bar. Meanwhile, out along Old Ford Road is vegetarian/vegan institution the Gallery Café, which keeps its carbon footprint small by using locally sourced produce, including Allpress coffee and E5 bread.

Locals also have the choice of two adequate budget gyms (Muscle Works and Soho Gyms), as well as York Hall – the famous boxing venue. It seems the rising house prices in nearby areas such as Shoreditch have brought a vibrant crowd to Bethnal Green, much to its advantage.

Creative types have pitched up on the border of Hackney along Vyner Street, which has its own microcosm of galleries and trendy cafés in and among a number of modern apartment buildings. In the next street, there's slick sit-down dining at Bistrotheque (with in-house bar Manchichi).

Pressed up against Shoreditch, Columbia Road is best known for its Sunday flower market – a multicoloured frenzy for locals and tourists, with the Royal Oak pub serving the heartiest of roasts, Lily Vanilli creating quirky baking, and Jones Dairy Café dishing out tea and bagels. It's a charming shopping street with charming shops (perfumer Angela Flanders, carefully curated furniture at Two Columbia Road, illustrator Rob Ryan's Ryantown, and kids' clothes at Bob & Blossom), though some are open only at weekends. The quaint terraced houses around neighbouring Jesus Green are the most highly desired in the area, so expect prices to match, but there are also some architecturally noteworthy tower blocks in which you'll get a bargain and great views.

Mile End E1/E3

The City may only be a mile away, but its glittering skyscrapers on the horizon appear to be in a different world. Mile End still feels down-at-heel, with few of the pockets of cool found in neighbouring Bethnal Green. The legacy of wartime bomb damage and slum clearances means property here is a hotchpotch of 18th-century terraces and expansive housing estates – lyrical inspiration for both Pulp and Dizzee Rascal. In an attempt to shake this image, a number of chic apartment blocks have popped up in recent years along Palmers Road on the west bank of the Regent's Canal. For the most part, social housing and rentals make up the area's stock, but for those who do choose to buy here, prices remain lower than in many other parts of Tower Hamlets.

One particular apartment block on the bank houses Ink, a pleasantly out-of-place Nordic restaurant serving modernist plates. Opposite is the Palm Tree, a splendid East End boozer offering a number of guest ales and live music, which attracts a mix of jolly punters, old and young. In summer you can grab a pint, sit on the grass and take in the hustle and bustle of the floating canal market. The Greedy Cow, an exotic burger joint on Grove Road, is also popular.

Parts of this neighbourhood may lack glamour, but it offers excellent transport connections (with the Hammersmith & City, District and Central tube lines, as well as numerous bus routes) and Mile End Park – a series of green areas adjacent to the canal. The park crosses busy Mile End Road by means of an ingenious bridge carpeted with grass and trees, beneath which is a handy hub of restaurants, coffee shops and a Budgens. Residents also make good use of the pleasant canal path, the Mile End Climbing Wall, and the leisure centre, complete with swimming pool and five-a-side pitches.

Opposite the park, Queen Mary University gives the area a vibrant, studenty feel, with majestic older buildings sitting alongside the award-winning modern architecture of the university campus.

Victoria Park E3/E9

Despite being a ten-minute walk from the nearest tube (Bethnal Green or Mile End), the extra distance is worth it. This lush parkland is a welcome oasis in the heart of the East End.

Victoria Park, straddling Tower Hamlets and Hackney, is London's third-largest cultivated green space after Hyde Park and Regent's Park. Providing sports facilities, play areas, boat hire and even a deer enclosure, the park is perhaps most famous across London for its open-air concerts and festivals. On the west side of the park, overlooking the lake, the Pavilion Café is a magnet for families and groups of friends enjoying a Farmhouse Full English, among other delights.

The park is split in two by Grove Road. Follow the road north and you'll find Lauriston Road, with a cluster of independent delis, butchers, gastropubs and bistros. Vietnamese restaurant Namo is a popular eaterie, and the Royal Inn on the Park is a busy watering hole in the summer with a decent-sized beer garden. The popularity of this hub has grown so much that now, on warm days and weekends, it's rammed with families and visitors, sampling the artisanal ice-creams and dipping into the homeware shops. It's no wonder that this leafy neighbourhood, with streets lined with

H Foreman & Son on Fish Island, by the Lee Navigation, is Britain's oldest salmon curer.

attractive Victorian townhouses, is a property hotspot for young families.

The Regent's Canal borders the west of the park, and the Hertford Union Canal flows along the south, both serving as perfect (if crowded) pathways for cyclists, walkers and joggers. Along each, you'll find an array of newly built flats and houses. Head east to Cadogan Terrace and there are some beautiful four-storey houses overlooking the green. Unfortunately, council clearances in the 1960s robbed these dwellings of some of their neighbours and those that remain back on to another 1960s addition – the A12 flyover, beyond which the canal connects to the River Lee Navigation.

Where the waterways meet, Fish Island has had something of an Olympic revival since the games were held on the opposite bank of the River Lea. It's now frequented by artists and young professionals, many spilling over from neighbouring Hackney Wick. Its post-industrial warehouses and swanky new apartments are complemented by Forman's restaurant and salmon smokery, as well as excellent canalside hangout the Counter Café (based within Stour Space creative studios).

Bow and Bromley-by-Bow E3, and Poplar E14

Poplar is essentially a thoroughfare for the Blackwall Tunnel and the A13. The area, which once housed local dockers, is today mostly residential, with a handful of fast-food joints and budget convenience stores. There's a mix of Georgian terraced houses, modern

social housing and celebrated brutalist architecture such as Ernö Goldfinger's Balfron Tower – an icon of 1960s local authority ambition and sibling to west London's better-known Trellick Tower – and Robin Hood Gardens by Alison and Peter Smithson, another local authority housing project, completed in 1972. At time of writing, Balfron Tower was involved in a controversial gentrification scheme, while Robin Hood Gardens was scheduled for eventual demolition as part of a major redevelopment.

There is little to shout about Poplar's main high street, but Chrisp Street Market, the site of Britain's first pedestrian shopping centre, is a hub for locals with a thriving market and various festivals.

Bow has undergone substantial regeneration in preparation for the Olympics and afterwards. This is visible in the abundance of new housing developments, and the sprucing up of council homes. A residential highlight is Bow Quarter. Set within the former Bryant & May match factory (which held the famous match girls' strike of 1888), it is a complex of luxury, warehouse-style apartments, complete with gym and pool, aimed at the young professional.

More traditional architecture is found in and around sought-after Tredegar Square, with its towering, well-kept Georgian houses. The Morgan Arms nearby provides excellent gastro grub. Further towards Victoria Park is Roman Road and its friendly street market. This, and the traditional pie-and-mash offering from G Kelly (a pillar of the community since 1937), captures Bow's cockney charm. More recently, the area has benefited from the Nunnery Gallery, providing a space for artists to showcase their work on the ground floor of a former convent, as well as the Chisenhale building, offering studios and a dance space.

There are dozens of small shops along Roman Road. Not just pawnbrokers and discount shoe stores, but boutiques such as independent designer Barüch, and Anchor + Hope, which has locally-made homewares as well as clothes. For affordable vintage furniture, try 353 Vintage, while retro sales are held at the Bow Bells pub on Bow Road. Also on Roman Road, Fiesta Café does a generous English breakfast, and there's La Table des Saveurs for brunch or pastries, or Zealand Café for a caffeine hit.

To the east of Bow sits Bromley-by-Bow. Its urban sprawl isn't too aesthetically pleasing: industrial units, supermarkets, highways and council estates. However, just across Bow Creek (and the border with Newham) are the charming cobbles and historic buildings of Three Mills Island, close to the ecologically rich Three Mills Green – a vast green space with a truly exciting adventure playground.

Wapping and Shadwell E1, and Limehouse E14

The glass-fronted apartments of Wapping and Limehouse sit at odds with much of the world around them. Affluent incomers buying off-plan flats may be surprised to see what exists outside the picture frame: rows of estates and a brutal main road drawing traffic into the Rotherhithe Tunnel.

At least one half of Wapping has retained a cobbled-street village feel: the waterside area, with its charming old pubs, is one of the finer examples of restoration in East London. Several restaurants also pepper the High Street, such as Il Bordello, pulling in loyal customers since 1998. The recent addition of Wapping Market adds a hustle and bustle on Sundays to the otherwise quiet neighbourhood, serving a range of locally sourced meats, veg, cheese, artisanal goods and fresh street food. Another space that has seen a revival is the illustrious Wilton's Music Hall, steeped in history, which attracts music and theatre audiences from across London.

The other half of the district is earmarked for regeneration: the prison-like enclosure of the former News International office complex has been purchased by a company looking to develop 1,800 new homes. The development will also preserve a Grade II-listed warehouse that will eventually house restaurants, cafés and offices. King Edward VII Memorial Park provides a calm green space beside the river, but plans for a 'super sewer' to run through the area will see the park affected by site set-up and construction work from 2016 for nearly four years.

After its failure as a shopping centre, Tobacco Dock has been reinvented as an exhibition and festival space, sparing one of the finer 19th-century dockside warehouses.

Nearby Shadwell is an incongruous mix of dated social housing and smart new apartment buildings around the DLR station and Watney Street Market that appear to be attracting the young professionals. Victualler on Garnet Street and Bottega on Wapping Wall bring fine wine and Italian dining respectively. In addition, Shadwell Basin is an excellent watersports and adventure centre.

Further east, Limehouse Basin marina has a similar feel, with a mix of expensive new architecture and Victorian buildings. The Narrow, Gordon Ramsay's popular gastropub, is here, and a walk along the scenic riverside path will take you past the historic Grapes pub, described by Dickens in *Our Mutual Friend* and now co-owned by local resident Sir Ian McKellen.

Back westwards towards the City lies Tower Bridge and the Tower of London. Next door, in St Katharine's Dock – aside from 19th-century Ivory House with its distinctive clock tower – the sense of history all but disappears. This modern yacht-filled marina is overlooked by pricey penthouses, coffee chains, pubs and restaurants.

Docklands and Isle of Dogs E14

Very few cities ever have the chance to regenerate an area the size of Docklands without suffering a war or major catastrophe; very few people gave such a project a chance of working in London. And yet, three decades on, Canary Wharf is a successful, bustling part of the city – a hub for business, a destination for shopping and an increasingly popular place to live. For much of the 19th century, these were the busiest docks in the world, employing up to 50,000 people. The project that Margaret Thatcher's government started in 1981 is now a workplace for twice that number.

The Wharf is featured in just about every film about London. Want a shot that sums up London as a business centre? Go to Canary Wharf. Want a cool-looking transport system? Look no further than the cathedral-like, Norman Foster-designed Underground station here, or his brand new Crossrail station, complete with roof garden. There is, however, an undeniable sterility to the place – a feeling of not really being in London – particularly when the wind blows down the skyscraper-lined streets. And those skyscrapers no longer dominate the city like they once did: Canary Wharf once had the UK's three tallest buildings, but most have been outstripped by the City's Heron Tower and Leadenhall Building, and London Bridge's the Shard.

Local residents have plentiful amenities – gyms, a vast underground shopping mall packed with high-street names and a Waitrose, waterside bars, a cinema, a good museum, some fun public art – and weekends are no longer the lonely experience they were in the 1990s. But it does all feel very corporate: there is a lack of good independent eateries and cool boutiques, and a complete absence of corner shops. But then Canary Wharf never pretended to be edgy – take it as it is, and there's plenty to enjoy.

Billingsgate Fish Market, relocated from Blackfriars, is a pocket of real 'cor blimey London' with its own traditions and by-laws. Catering mainly to wholesale customers, there are nevertheless great stalls here for the individual, selling seafood, snacks, accessories and cooking utensils.

Smart chains dominate the dining opportunities, and benefit from two of Canary Wharf's chief characteristics: views and water. Plateau (French), on the fourth floor of Canada Place, Goodman (steak), and the Dock Seafood Restaurant (what it says) exploit the former; Royal China (Chinese), Le Secret des Rôtisseurs (rotisserie chicken) and Gaucho (Argentinian steaks) make the most of their waterside location. The pubs, by contrast, are far from gastro (with the exception of the Gun on Coldharbour) and the estates are grim.

If the ripples of prosperity were expected to be felt all the way down the Isle of Dogs, they've taken a long time to arrive. New housing developments are being built, but only the privileged few are able to afford a piece of the waterfront. Although there are more shops, more places to go out and better transport links, this area remains in the shadow of its high-rise neighbours. But 'the Island' has a wonderful green space at its heart in Mudchute Park – a fabulous resource for both residents and visitors, and home to Mudchute City Farm.

Eating

Bistrotheque 23-27 Wadeson Street, E2 9DR (8983 7900, www.bistrotheque.com).

Il Bordello 81 Wapping High Street, E1W 2YN (7481 9950, www.ilbordello.com).

Bottega 70 Wapping Wall, E1W 3SS (7481 0095, www.bottegawapping.com).

Canteen 2 Crispin Place, off Brushfield Street, E1 6DW (0845 686 1122, www.canteen.co.uk).

Cereal Killer Café 139 Brick Lane, E1 6SB (3601 9100, www.cerealkillercafe.co.uk).

Copita del Mercado 60 Wentworth Street, E1 7AL (7426 0281, www.copitadelmercado.com).

Counter Café Stour Space, 7 Roach Road, E3 2PA (07834 275920, www.counterproductive.co.uk).

Dirty Burger 27A Mile End Road, E1 4TP (3727 6165, www.eatdirtyburger.com).

Dock Seafood Restaurant 2 Mastmaker Road, E14 9AW (7515 4334, www.thedockseafood restaurant.com).

E Pellicci 332 Bethnal Green Road, E2 0AG (7739 4873).

Fiesta Café 548 Roman Road, E3 5ES (8880 6931).

Forman's Restaurant & Bar Stour Road, Fish Island, E3 2NT (8525 2365, www.formans.co.uk).

Foxcroft & Ginger 68 Mile End Road, E1 4TT (3602 3371, www.foxcroftandginger.co.uk).

Gallery Café St Margaret's House Settlement, 21 Old Ford Road, E2 9PL (8980 2092, www. stmargaretshouse.org.uk).

Gaucho Grill 29 Westferry Circus, E14 8RR (7987 9494, www.gauchorestaurants.co.uk).

G Kelly 414 Bethnal Green Road, E2 0DJ (7739 3603, http://gkelly.london).

Goodman 3 South Quay, E14 9RU (7531 0300, www.goodmanrestaurants.com).

Greedy Cow 2 Grove Road, E3 5AX (8983 3304, http://greedycow.com).

Gun 27 Coldharbour, E14 9NS (7515 5222, www.thegundocklands.com).

Hawksmoor 157A Commercial Street, E1 6BJ (7426 4850, www.thehawksmoor.com).

Ink 44 Palmers Road, E2 0TA (8983 6634, http://inkrestaurant.co.uk).

Jones Dairy Café 23 Ezra Street, E2 7RH (7739 5372, www.jonesdairy.co.uk).

Lahore Kebab House 2-10 Umberton Street, E1 1PY (7481 9737, www.lahore-kebabhouse.com).

Lily Vanilli 6 The Courtyard, Ezra Street, E2 7RH (www.lilyvanilli.com/the-bakery).

Mission Arch 250, Paradise Row, E2 9LE (7613 0478, www.missione2.com).

Morgan Arms 43 Morgan Street, E3 5AA (8980 6389, www.morganarmsbow.com).

Namo 176 Victoria Park Road, E9 7HD (8533 0639, http://namo.co.uk).

Narrow 44 Narrow Street, E14 8DP (7592 7950, www.gordonramsay.com).

Needoo Grill 85-87 New Road, E1 1HH (7247 0648, www.needoogrill.co.uk).

Pavilion Café Victoria Park, Crown Gate West, E9 7DE (8980 0030).

Plateau 4th Floor, Canada Place, E14 5ER (7715 7100, www.plateau-restaurant.co.uk).

Poppies 6-8 Hanbury Street, E1 6QR (7247 0892, www.poppiesfishandchips.co.uk).

Royal China 30 Westferry Circus, E14 8RR (7719 0888, www.rcguk.co.uk).

St John Bread & Wine 94-96 Commercial Street, E1 6LZ (7251 0848, www.stjohngroup.uk.com).

Spitalfields Market

HIGHS & LOWS

Traces of the old East End

Canary Wharf's public spaces

Chic and cheap eats

Vintage shopping

Cultural mix

▲ ····································· ▼

Pockets of bleakness and real poverty

Blackwall Tunnel approach road

The sterilisation of Spitalfields

Curry hawkers on Brick Lane

Le Secret des Rôtisseurs 37 Westferry Circus, E15 8RR (7719 0950, www.eatlesecret.co.uk).
La Table de Saveurs 494-496 Roman Road, E3 5LU (8983 0386).
Tayyab's 83-89 Fieldgate Street, E1 1JU (7247 6400, www.tayyabs.co.uk).
Typing Room Town Hall Hotel, Patriot Square, E2 9NF (7871 0461, www.typingroom.com).
Zealand Road Coffee Shop 391 Roman Road, E3 5QS (07940 235493).

Drinking

Big Chill Bar Dray Walk, Old Truman Brewery, 91 Brick Lane, E1 6QL (7392 9180, www.wearebigchill.com).
Bow Bells 116 Bow Road, E3 3AA (0871 951 1000).
Cafe 1001 Old Truman Brewery, 91 Brick Lane, E1 6QL (7247 6166, www.cafe1001.co.uk).
Commercial Tavern 142-144 Commercial Street, E1 6NU (7247 1888).
Grapes 76 Narrow Street, E14 8BP (7987 4396, www.thegrapes.co.uk).
Manchichi 23-27 Wadeson Street, E2 9DR (8983 7900, www.bistrotheque.com).
Mother Kelly's 251 Paradise Row, E2 9EL (7012 1244, www.motherkellys.co.uk).
Palm Tree 127 Grove Road, E3 5BH (8980 2918).
Peg + Patriot Town Hall Hotel, Patriot Square, E2 9NF (8709 4528, www.typingroom.com).
Pride of Spitalfields 3 Heneage Street, E1 5LJ (7247 8933).
Royal Inn on the Park 111 Lauriston Road, E9 7JH (8985 3321, www.royalinnonthepark.com).
Royal Oak 73 Columbia Road, E2 7RG (7729 2220, www.royaloaklondon.com).
Star of Bethnal Green 359 Bethnal Green Road, E2 6LG (7458 4480, www.starofbethnal green.co.uk).

Shopping

353 Vintage 353 Roman Road, E3 5QR (07955 755992, www.353vintage.co.uk).
A Gold 42 Brushfield Street, E1 6AG (7247 2487, www.agoldshop.com).
Anchor + Hope 363 Roman Road, E3 5QR (www.anchorandhopelondon.co.uk).
Angela Flanders 96 Columbia Road, E2 7QB (7739 7555, www.angelaflanders-perfumer.com).
Barüch 451 Roman Road, E3 5LX (7998 9280, www.baruchboutique.com).
Beigel Shop 155 Brick Lane, E1 6SB (7729 0826).
Beyond Retro 110-112 Cheshire Street, E2 6EJ (7613 3636, www.beyondretro.com).
Billingsgate Market Trafalgar Way, E14 5ST (7987 1118, www.cityoflondon.gov.uk).

Bob & Blossom 140 Columbia Road, E2 7RG (7739 4737, www.bobandblossom.com).
Brick Lane Beigel Bake 159 Brick Lane, E1 6SB (7729 0616).
Brick Lane Market Brick Lane (north of railway bridge), Cygnet Street and Sclater Street, E1; Bacon Street, Cheshire Street, E2 (7364 1717, www.visitbricklane.org).
Chrisp Street Market Market Square, E14 6EQ (0845 262 0846, www.towerhamletsarts.org.uk).
Columbia Road Flower Market Columbia Road, between Gosset Street and Royal Oak pub, E2 (www.columbiaroad.info).
Comfort Station 22 Cheshire Street, E2 6EH (7033 9099, www.comfortstation.co.uk).
Duke of Uke 88 Cheshire Street, E2 6EH (3583 9728, www.dukeofuke.co.uk).
Old Spitalfields Market Commercial Street, between Lamb Street and Brushfield Street, E1 (7247 8556, www.oldspitalfieldsmarket.com).
Peloton + Co 4 Market Street, E1 6DT (7183 5282, www.pelotonco.cc).
Petticoat Lane Market Middlesex, Goulston, New Goulston, Toynbee, Wentworth, Old Castle, Cobb, Leyden and Strype streets, E1 (7364 1717, www.towerhamlets.gov.uk).
Roman Road Market Roman Road, between Parnell Road and St Stephen's Road, E3 (7364 1717, www.romanroadlondon.com).
Rough Trade East Dray Walk, Old Truman Brewery, 91 Brick Lane, E1 6QL (7392 7788, www.roughtrade.com).
Ryantown 126 Columbia Road, E2 7RG (7613 1510, http://robryanstudio.com/ryantown/).
Sunday (Up)Market Old Truman Brewery, entrances on Elys Yard, Brick Lane, Hanbury Street, E1 6QL (7770 6028, www.sundayupmarket.co.uk).
Two Columbia Road 2 Columbia Road, E2 7NN (7729 9933, www.twocolumbiaroad.co.uk).
Verde & Company 40 Brushfield Street, E1 6AG (7247 1924, www.verdeandco.co.uk).
Victualler 69 Garnet Street, E1W 3QS (7481 9694, www.victualler.co.uk).
Wapping Market Shadwell Pierhead, Wapping Wall, E1W 3SG (8691 4918, www.wappingmarket.com).
Whitechapel Road Market Whitechapel Road, between Vallance Road and Cambridge Heath Road, E1 1DT (www.towerhamlets.gov.uk).

Things to do

Cinemas & theatres
Cineworld West India Quay Hertsmere Road, E14 4AL (0871 200 2000, www.cineworld.co.uk).
Electric Shoreditch 64-66 Redchurch Street, E2 7DP (3350 3490, www.electriccinema.co.uk).

Whitechapel Road Market

Mile End Genesis Cinema 93-95 Mile End Road, E1 4UJ (7780 2000, www.genesis-cinema.co.uk).
Rich Mix 35-47 Bethnal Green Road, E1 6LA (7613 7498, www.richmix.org.uk).
The Space 269 Westferry Road, E14 3RS (7515 7799, space.org.uk).
Wilton's Music Hall Graces Alley, E1 8JB (7702 2789, www.wiltons.org.uk).

Galleries & museums

Chisenhale Gallery 64-84 Chisenhale Road, E3 5QZ (8981 4518, www.chisenhale.org.uk).
Museum of Diversity and Immigration 19 Princelet Street, E1 6QH (7247 5352, www.19princeletstreet.org.uk).
Museum of London Docklands No.1 Warehouse, West India Quay, Hertsmere Road, E14 4AL (7001 9844, www.museumoflondon.org.uk). Huge museum covering everything from slavery and London Bridge to the Blitz and Docklands' development.
Nunnery 183 Bow Road, E3 2SJ (8709 7774, www.bowarts.org/nunnery). Bow Arts Trust gallery, splendidly located in a former Carmelite nunnery.
Ragged School Museum 46-50 Copperfield Road, E3 4RR (8980 6405, www.raggedschool museum.org.uk). A look at Dr Barnardo's Victorian education of the East End's urchins.

Royal London Hospital Museum & Archives St Phillip's Church, Newark Street, E1 2AA (7377 7608, www.medicalmuseums.org).
V&A Museum of Childhood Cambridge Heath Road, E2 9PA (8983 5200, www.museumof childhood.org.uk). The V&A's East End offshoot.
Whitechapel Art Gallery 77-82 Whitechapel High Street, E1 7QX (7522 7888, www.whitechapel.org). Leading contemporary gallery.

Other attractions

Centre of the Cell Blizard Institute, 4 Newark Street, E1 2AT (7882 2562, www.centreofthecell. org). A science education 'pod', suspended so you can watch medical researchers at work in their labs.
Dennis Severs' House 18 Folgate Street, E1 6BX (7247 4013, www.dennissevershouse.co.uk). Curious but fascinating period reconstruction: a 'still-life drama' in a splendid Huguenot house.
East London Mosque & London Muslim Centre 46-92 Whitechapel Road, E1 1JX (7650 3000, www.eastlondonmosque.org.uk).
Idea Stores (7364 4332, arena.yourlondonlibrary. net/web/tower-hamlets). Library and more.
Mudchute Park and Farm Pier Street, E14 3HP (7515 5901, www.mudchute.org).
Spitalfields City Farm Buxton Street, E1 5AR (7247 8762, www.spitalfieldscityfarm.org).

Typing Room, Bethnal Green

Stepney City Farm Stepney Way, E1 3DG (7790 8204, www.stepneycityfarm.org).
Trinity Buoy Wharf/Container City 64 Orchard Place, E14 0JW (7515 7153, www.trinitybuoywharf. com). Art space and artists' studios.
Whitechapel Bell Foundry 32-34 Whitechapel Road, E1 1DY (7247 2599, www.whitechapel bellfoundry.co.uk).

Gigs, clubs & comedy

93 Feet East Old Truman Brewery, 150 Brick Lane, E1 6QL (7770 6006, www.93feeteast.co.uk).
Bethnal Green Working Men's Club 42-44 Pollard Row, E2 6NB (7739 7170, www.workers playtime.net).
Canary Wharf Comedy Club East Wintergarden, 43 Bank Street, E14 5AB.
George Tavern 373 Commercial Road, E1 0LA (7790 7335, www.thegeorgetavern.co.uk).
Troxy 490 Commercial Road, E1 0HX (7790 9000, www.troxy.co.uk).

Green spaces

For more details, see www.towerhamlets.gov.uk.
Allen Gardens Buxton Street, E1. Play areas, pitches and a small city farm
Bow Creek Ecology Park Bidder Street, E16 9ST (0845 677 0600, www.visitleevalley.org.uk).

Nature reserve on former ironworks, shipyard and coal wharf.
Cemetery Park Southern Grove, E3 (8983 1277). One of London's 'Magnificent Seven' historic cemeteries, now a nature reserve and park, with the Soanes Centre, offering science workshops, and Ackroyd Drive Greenlink to Mile End Park.
Island Gardens Saunders Ness Road, E14. Waterfront park across the Thames from Greenwich.
Jubilee Park Canary Wharf, E14 5NY. Landscaped public space.
King Edward VII Memorial Park Glamis Road, E1. Riverside park, sports facilities and play area.
Mile End Park E3 (7364 0902). Stretches along the Regent's Canal from St Paul's Way to Roman Road. Includes an ecology park/pavilion, arts park/ pavilion, go-karting, skatepark and a climbing wall.
Millwall Park Stebondale Street, E14. Sports facilities and play areas.
Three Mills Green Three Mill Lane, E3 3DU (0845 677 0600, www.visitleevalley.org.uk). A green and one of the best adventure playgrounds in London.
Victoria Park Grove Road, E3 5TB (7634 2494). Boating lakes, fishing, flower gardens and a paddling pool; sports facilities, bowling green and skatepark. Outdoor gigs and festivals.
Weavers Fields Mape Street, E2 6HW. Football pitches, children's play area and community café.

Tayyabs, Whitechapel

Gyms & leisure centres

Canary Riverside Health Club West Ferry Circus, E14 8RR (0845 270 4084, www.virgin active.co.uk). Private.

Chisenhale Dance Space 64-84 Chisenhale Road, E3 5QZ (8981 6617, www.chisenhale dancespace.co.uk).

Island Sports Trust George Green's Secondary School, 100 Manchester Road, E14 3DW (7001 9441, www.islandsportstrust.co.uk).

John Orwell Sports Centre Tench Street, E1W 2QD (7488 9421, www.better.org.uk).

Mile End Climbing Wall Haverfield Road, E3 5BE (8980 0289, www.mileendwall.org.uk).

Mile End Park Leisure Centre 190 Burdett Road, E3 4HL (8709 4420, www.gll.org).

Mile End Park Stadium Rhodeswell Road, E14 7TW (8709 4420, www.gll.org).

St George's Leisure Centre 221 The Highway, E1W 3BP (7709 9714, www.gll.org). Swimming pool and gym.

Soho Gyms 221 Grove Road, E3 5SN (8981 7964).

Tiller Centre Tiller Road, E14 8PX (7987 5211, www.better.org.uk).

Whitechapel Sports Centre 55 Durwood Street, E1 5BA (7247 7538, www.gll.org).

York Hall Leisure Centre Old Ford Road, E2 9PL (8980 2243, www.gll.org). Also includes Spa London (8709 5845, www.spa-london.org).

Outdoor pursuits

Docklands Sailing & Watersports Centre 235A Westferry Road, Millwall Dock, E14 3QS (7537 2626, www.dswc.org).

Revolution Karting Arches 422-424, Mile End Park, 418-419 Burdett Road, E3 4AA (7538 5195, www.gokartinglondon.co.uk).

Shadwell Basin Outdoor Activity Centre 3-4 Shadwell Pierhead, Glamis Road, E1W 3TD (7481 4210, www.shadwell-basin.org.uk).

Schools

Primary

There are 65 state primary schools in Tower Hamlets, 16 of which are church schools. There are also three independent primaries: one Muslim school and two Montessori schools. See www.tower hamlets.gov.uk, www.education.gov.uk/edubase and www.ofsted.gov.uk for more information.

Secondary

Bethnal Green Academy Gosset Street, E2 6NW (7920 7900, www.bgtc.org.uk).

Bishop Challoner Catholic Federation of Schools 352 Commercial Road, E1 0LB (7791 9500, www.bishop-learningvillage.towerhamlets.sch. uk). Roman Catholic; separate schools for boys and girls; mixed sixth form.

Bow School 24 Twelvetrees Crescent, E3 3QW (8980 0118, www.bow-school.org.uk). Boys only; mixed sixth form.

Central Foundation Girls' School 25-33 Bow Road, E3 2AE (8981 1131, www.central. towerhamlets.sch.uk). Girls only.

George Green's School 100 Manchester Road, E14 3DW (7987 6032, www.georgegreens.com).

Langdon Park School Byron Street, E14 0RZ (7987 4811, www.langdonparkschool.co.uk).

Morpeth School Portman Place, E2 0PX (8981 0921, www.morpethschool.org.uk).

Mulberry School for Girls Richard Street, E1 2JP (7790 6327, www.mulberry.towerhamlets.sch.uk). Girls only.

Oaklands School Old Bethnal Green Road, E2 6PR (7613 1014, www.oaklands.tower hamlets.sch.uk).

Raines Foundation School Approach Road, E2 9LY (8981 1231, www.rainesfoundation.org.uk).

St Paul's Way Trust School 125 St Paul's Way, E3 4FT (7987 1883, www.spwt.net).

Sir John Cass Foundation & Redcoat Church of England Secondary School Stepney Way, E1 0RH (7790 6712, www.sjcr.net). Church of England.

Stepney Green Maths, Computing & Science College Ben Jonson Road, E1 4SD (7790 6361, www. stepneygreen.towerhamlets.sch.uk). Boys only.

Swanlea School 31 Brady Street, E1 5DJ (7375 3267, www.swanlea.towerhamlets.sch.uk).

Property

Local estate agents

Alexander David Property www.alexander davidproperty.co.uk

Atkinson McLeod www.atkinsonmcleod.com

Capital Square www.capital-square.co.uk

Claremont Estates www.claremontestates.co.uk

Daveys of Spitalfields www.daveys.co

Ellis & Co www.ellisandco.co.uk

Elms Estate Agents www.elmsestates.co.uk

Estates & Lets www.estatesandlets.com

Franklyn James www.franklynjames.co.uk

Future Pad www.futurepadlondon.com

Lloyds Residential www.lloydsres.com

Peach Properties www.peachproperties.com

Tarn & Tarn www.tarn-tarn.co.uk

Local knowledge

www.eastlondonadvertiser.co.uk
www.madeinshoreditch.co.uk
www.shoreditchradio.co.uk
www.spitalfieldslife.com

Canary Wharf

USEFUL INFO

Borough size
1,978 hectares

Population
287,200

Ethnic mix
White 57.1%
Asian/Asian British 30.6%
Black/Black British 6.3%
Chinese or other 3.1%
Mixed 2.8%

London Borough of Tower Hamlets
Town Hall, Mulberry Place, 5 Clove
Crescent, E14 2BG (7364 5000,
www.towerhamlets.gov.uk)

Council run by
Labour

MPs
Bethnal Green & Bow, Rushanara Ali
(Labour); Poplar & Limehouse, Jim
Fitzpatrick (Labour)

Main recycling centre
Tower Hamlets Reuse & Recycling Centre,
Yabsley Street, E14 9RG (7364 5004,
www.towerhamlets.co.uk)

Council tax
£787.02 to £2,361.04

Wandsworth

While glitzy apartment complexes dominate the riverfront, and well-to-do professionals congregate around the commons, the borough's traditionally shabbier high streets are pulling in a cooler crowd.

AVERAGE PROPERTY PRICE

Detached £1,636,225	**Terraced** £798,809
Semi-detached £972,857	**Flat** £483,329

AVERAGE RENTAL PRICE PER WEEK

Room £117	**1 bed** £305
Studio £219	**2 bed** £368
	3 bed £483

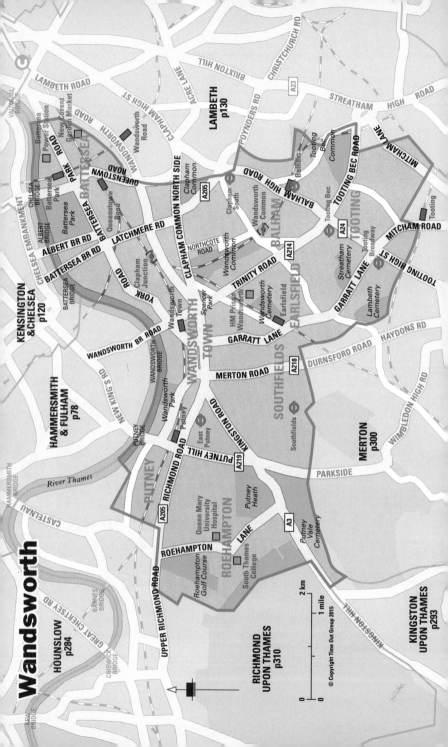

Neighbourhoods

Battersea SW11

Synonymous with its bridge, dogs' home and power station (currently undergoing an enormously ambitious redevelopment), Battersea's prime riverside is now lined with luxury apartments – and there's more to come, including the new US embassy at Nine Elms. This whole area is going to be a building site for years.

On the plus side, all this endeavour has forced an improvement in transport links, plus a proposed Northern line spur to Battersea and Nine Elms. Oh, and there's a heliport, should you require one, between Battersea and Wandsworth bridges.

Prettier by far is Battersea Park with its adventure playground, children's zoo, fountains and peace pagoda. And in the evening, there are the romantic lights of Albert Bridge – the one used in all the films. Beautiful mansion blocks line the park along Prince of Wales Drive, with council blocks clustered around Queenstown Road station behind.

West of Battersea Bridge, chichi Battersea Square (off Vicarage Crescent) is lined with cafés and restaurants. There's also excellent neighbourhood brasserie Galapagos on Battersea High Street, which has more of a villagey vibe, and crazy pizza party joint Bunga Bunga on Battersea Bridge Road, with bright young hedge-funders and Sloaney types letting their hair down thanks to prosecco and Elvis impersonators.

There's a hub of activity around the junction of Latchmere and Battersea Park roads. Although a little traffic-infested from cars heading to and from the bridges, it's brought to life by the excellent Latchmere pub theatre: come for the show, stay for the beer. The area's supporting cast includes cocktail bar the Lost Angel (sharing premises with the Gaslight Grill steakhouse), the Fox & Hounds gastropub, and a fair number of posh boutiques and upmarket interiors shops – because we're not far from Chelsea, after all. Milliner Edwina Ibbotson will sort you out with a titfer for Ascot and there's a great Sunday afternoon car boot sale at Battersea Park School.

Property around the triangle formed by Queenstown and Silverthorne roads, known as the Parktown Estate conservation area (or 'the Diamond' to locals) is much in demand, with townhouses and Victorian terraced cottages that sell for upwards of half a million. Queenstown Road is also a good place to head for eats – perhaps the Argentine grill Santa Maria del Sur.

Clapham Junction SW11

This area, named for its famous railway station, is actually in Battersea rather than Clapham proper. It's the busiest rail junction in Europe, incidentally, a boon to south Londoners who want to get pretty much anywhere. The neighbourhood around the interchange is buzzing. There are plenty of shops along St John's Hill and Lavender Hill, a Jongleurs comedy club, and performing-arts powerhouse Battersea Arts Centre – it was devastated by fire in early 2015 but continues to put on work.

North of the station, around Grant Road, the Winstanley Estate is often in the local news for all the wrong reasons. In contrast, the Shaftesbury Park Estate, south-east of Clapham Junction, is a conservation zone of about 1,200 homes. These are mostly two-storey cottages plus a few larger houses, all with Gothic Revival flourishes, built by the Artisans', Labourers' & General Dwellings Company in 1873-77. Many are owned by the Peabody Trust.

Northcote Road is one of south London's best shopping streets. Familiar names appealing to the not-so-down-at-heel include Cath Kidston, Question Air, Space NK… you get the picture. There are also lots of independent food and drink shops serving the considerable dinner-party demographic: Dove for meat, Hamish Johnston for cheese, Hive for honey, Philglas & Swiggot for wine. The area doesn't lack for kids' clothes stores, either, in the shape of JoJo Maman Bébé and Quackers, while One Small Step One Giant Leap has kids' shoes.

French cake shop Aux Merveilleux de Fred is evidence of the huge influx of French families over the past three or four years, presumably priced out of South Kensington; you can't walk down Northcote Road without hearing French spoken. And let's not forget the lively street market, although it's more about cupcakes than cockneys. The best restaurant is Lola Rojo, which serves innovative tapas.

Battersea Rise – leading up the hill towards Clapham Common – is lined with bars and restaurants. Some of these establishments can get a bit loud and loutish when denizens have had a few too many, but there's always the easygoing Northcote pub or beer

Tube District , Northern, Overground
Rail services into Victoria, Waterloo
Main bus routes into central London 19, 22, 35, 44, 74, 77, 87, 137, 414; night buses N19, N22, N35, N44, N74, N87, N133, N137, N155; 24-hour buses 14, 344
River boat services Putney Pier, Wandsworth River Quarter Pier
Heliport Bridges Court, London SW11 3BE (www.londonheliport.co.uk)

Battersea Power Station

specialist the Draft House for a marginally more sedate crowd. Smartest of all is Soif, which has superb wines.

The most sought-after housing is here, too, 'between the commons' as the estate agents say. There are big properties, competitive schools and green space galore; wealthy thirtysomethings who have made a mint in law or finance come here to raise families.

Down on the Balham edge of Wandsworth Common, the area becomes the epitome of metro-suburbia around Bellevue Road. Wave at a TV actor as they stroll the chic streets in search of trinkets at Tickled Pink or a Michelin-starred meal at Chez Bruce.

This leafy borough oozes quaint tea-shop charm paired with sleek business chic. Wandsworth is blessed with five times the amount of green space that Hyde Park has, making it the ideal spot for busy City workers needing a cold beer overlooking the common after a day's trading. The Hope is especially good, its views setting the scene for a perfect early summer evening at the pub.

So, if Clapham Junction and environs is all really part of Battersea, where's Clapham proper? Over the borough boundary in Lambeth.

Wandsworth Town SW18

Wandsworth caters for all. It accommodates those who want to show off their skills at a live-music night at the Ship pub; those interested in perusing work at the Oil & Water Contemporary Art Gallery; parents who want the best education for their children; and kids who want to feel safe when venturing out on their own for the first time, perhaps to the local Southside Shopping Centre.

This once bedraggled, 1970s mall stands proudly in the heart of Wandsworth; less chocolate-brown these days, now more chrome-clad, classy and almost futuristic. Although this was considered the 'dodgy end' of Wandsworth not so long ago, it now boasts a branch of Planet Organic, where you can buy gluten-free buckwheat fusilli.

Sky-high premiums are, of course, paid for river views in Wandsworth's ever-developing Thames-side quarter. Mega-developments include Battersea Reach, which dominates the riverfront at the south end of Wandsworth Bridge, and Point Pleasant right next to Wandsworth Park. Little Victorian terraces and the antique Cat's Back pub add charm, but mostly Wandsworth Riverside is like a whole new town, daunting in its shininess.

Despite the waterside construction eruption, the huge Southside Shopping Centre and the major arterial roads, there's still a villagey patch of old Wandsworth, beside Wandsworth Town station. Known as the Tonsleys after the names of several roads, it has retained its Victorian character with picturesque neighbourhood shops and cafés along largely traffic-free Old York Road. Needless to say, even a two-bed Victorian cottage in this enclave won't leave you much change from a million.

Past the madness that is the A3 one-way system, there's a cluster of decent restaurants on St John's Hill, the road that heads over to Clapham Junction. The mix includes relaxed café-restaurant Ben's Canteen; the tranquil Birdhouse Café; high-end chippy Fish Club; Thai-flavoured Kaosarn; Edwardian-themed cocktail bar and restaurant Powder Keg Diplomacy; and bijou café-deli Urban Gourmet.

Wandsworth's main landmark remains Young's Ram Brewery, founded in 1512 but sadly decommissioned in 2006. It's soon to become known as the Ram Quarter once the space has been renovated into 661 studio, two- and three-bed apartments. Its brewing legacy lives on in local pubs: the historic Alma on Old York Road has a cellar full of Young's kegs and is great for a swift half with friends, a family occasion or a raucous comedy night.

The neighbourhood's sense of community is second to none, but it certainly comes at a price: up to £1 million for a three-bedroom period home.

Putney SW15

Riverside locations, green space and a wholesome reputation make Putney a middle-class favourite. Putney Embankment is all pubs-by-the-Thames and rowing clubs rather than residential developments, though the upmarket apartment blocks of Putney Wharf have appeared on the Wandsworth side of Putney Bridge.

What's not to like? Planes, trains and automobiles. Namely, the incessant noise of the Heathrow flight path, oversubscribed rush-hour carriages trundling into Waterloo, the lack of tube stations in the westerly reaches, and the clogged South Circular (A205) and Roehampton Lane (A306). Other turn-offs are the stupidly high house prices – for some really quite boring terraced three-beds – and a sense of being lost in the suburbs.

Putney High Street is busy and lined with chains, though the Exchange Shopping Centre is a pleasant, well-appointed mall with a smarter selection of shops such as Jojo Maman Bébé, Neuhaus and Waitrose. Need cheap art for your new home? Try Will's Art Warehouse on Lower Richmond Road, 'the Oddbins of the art world'.

The area has history, though. In 1647, St Mary's Church – by the bridge – hosted the New Model Army's Putney Debates, a significant step on the road to modern parliamentary democracy; and the open spaces of Putney Heath were once a popular location for duelling.

Upper Richmond Road is where you'll find a selection of the area's best restaurants: Ma Goa showcasing Portuguese-influenced Goan specialities; family-run French bistro L'Auberge; well-established Japanese venue Chosan; and the magnificent new French restaurant Gazette. Further towards Barnes is a branch of steak specialist Popeseye.

The High Street tends towards chain restaurants such as Wagamama and Byron, but also has family-oriented Eddie Catz, Spanish outpost La Mancha, and Enoteca Turi, a classy Italian with a superb wine list. Il Mascalzone, meanwhile, serves up tasty pizza from a wood-fired oven and authentic Italian charm. Off the High Street, Royal China is reliable for dim sum and daily specials, and local favourite Emile's offers French and modern British fare.

Towards the river, on Lower Richmond Road, you'll find the flagship branch of the Thai Square chain, housed in a striking modern building next to Putney Bridge. For artisanal coffee, try nearby Grind.

The Boat Race is the biggest thing to happen to Putney each year (early spring), though the Great River Race (autumn) is much more fun to watch. The riverside path offers pleasant walks towards Barnes and beyond. Away from the Thames, Putney Heath, together with neighbouring Wimbledon

Northcote Road, Clapham Junction

Common, accounts for half of all London's heathland. There's also Wandsworth Park, where you can follow the Putney Sculpture Trail or practise your swing at Putt in the Park.

Putney's pubs include the handsome Duke's Head by the river, while the nearby Half Moon has a live music pedigree that belies the area's lack of street cred – Elvis Costello used to have a residency here, and a recent relaunch introduced popular comedy night Gits & Shiggles. The Prince of Wales on Upper Richmond Road does a cracking roast, while other decent pubs include the Coat & Badge, the unpretentious Whistle & Flute, and fantastic ale pub the Bricklayer's Arms on Waterman Street. Putney Station is a bright, modern wine bar with good food. If late-night drinking and dancing floats your boat, there's always the Fez Club on Upper Richmond Road or the Toy Shop on Putney High Street, where the creative scamps behind the bar serve cocktails in a robot's torso.

Popular residential developments include the Sir Giles Gilbert Scott building, a handsome Grade II-listed red brick construction in Whitelands Park, just off Sutherland Grove from West Hill. Also in the park, new-build Hannay House is part of the council's shared ownership scheme for key workers.

Roehampton SW15

Wandsworth's most westerly outpost is Roehampton, which in parts is more like down-at-heel Surrey suburbia than London. Just east of Richmond Park, Alton Estate is one of the largest council estates in the country, a vast swathe of low- and high-rise, modernist concrete architecture. West Alton, inspired by French architect Le Corbusier, is now Grade II-listed. Elsewhere are smatterings of council housing and some attractive tree-lined roads.

There are students galore here, studying at Roehampton University, South Thames College and Queen Mary's Hospital, the main structure of which was built in 1712 and later enlarged by Sir Edwin Lutyens. Grade I-listed Roehampton House and other parcels of former hospital land are being turned into smart housing schemes, designed to be in keeping with the grand buildings hereabouts.

The Putney Heath district is the poshest neighbourhood, with huge, elaborate Edwardian houses more in keeping with the stockbroker belt. Off the north-west edge of the heath, Roehampton Village is also a desirable quarter, with families living in

picturesque terraced properties, near a high street that has a good mix of independent shops, a pub and a parish church. Famous names buried or cremated at Putney Vale Cemetery, on the other side of the A3, include archaeologist Howard Carter (who discovered Tutankhamun's tomb), Formula One champion racing driver James Hunt, actor Jon Pertwee (the third Doctor Who) and English folk-rock legend Sandy Denny.

Earlsfield and Southfields SW18

Just a few years ago, it was considered to be the poor relation of neighbours Battersea and Putney, but now Earlsfield is the hidden wonder of Wandsworth.

A property gem, it's an area on the rise with a recently redeveloped train station and hundreds of new apartments and townhouses underway. Earlsfield's traditional Victorian and Edwardian terraces and maisonettes are

Balham's Banana Cabaret is a great place to catch big-name comedians, as well as those on the way up.

popular with families looking for affordable, spacious homes with a garden in the Big Smoke. Its brilliant primary schools – such as the Beatrix Potter School on Magdalen Road – are also a big draw. Earlsfield station makes central London easily commutable, with trains taking just 12 minutes to Waterloo and 15 minutes to Victoria.

Garratt Lane is the heart of Earlsfield and offers fantastic cafés, gastropubs, organic delis and other independent businesses. Here's where you'll find most of the good eateries: great pub grub at the Jolly Gardeners; Mel's Vintage Beats & Breakfast decorated with old album sleeves; and the modern European Sylvan Oak. Meanwhile, if you want to see your food barbecued before your eyes, try sensational Korean restaurant Cah-Chi. In the same vein, at Brazilian venue Nabrasa, skewers of grilled meat are brought to your table in a seemingly endless procession.

Pubs are plentiful. The Earlsfield gastropub started life as the ticket office of the adjacent station; the Wandle, named after the River Wandle flowing parallel to Garratt Lane, is said to serve Earlsfield's finest steaks and hosts live music too. For cocktails, try the Graffiti Cocktail Bar with more than a hundred on the menu.

Earlsfield is close to fantastic parks and green spaces that attract many cyclists, dog walkers and runners; Garratt Green, Garratt Park and King George's Park all have acres of play areas, sports pitches and tennis courts. Kids never get the chance to be bored as there's plenty for them to do. Prime examples include It's a Kid's Thing, an award-winning play and sports facility for under-nines, and Mini Potters for pottery painting.

Southfields, on the other side of the Wandle, has grander houses; there are plenty of handsome Victorian terraces and semis with large, mature gardens. The neatly appointed properties in 'the Grid' – south-east of the station – are the most sought after; similar houses around Wimbledon Park Road are also popular. The agreeable cafés and shops on Replingham Road give it the peaceful air of a Home Counties town. Although Southfields has a tube, it's on the slow District line so it's quicker to use Earlsfield's Overground station.

Balham SW12

Balham is Clapham South's rock-chick little sister, hiding its six-bedroom Victorian terraces like a coy teenager trying to fit in with the cool kids. It's slowly outpricing its original stock of residents, but the incoming City money is keen to keep up shabby-chic appearances. Leave the franchises behind, and grab a panini and a rich roast coffee at Bertie & Boo. Waitrose looms, though, reminding residents that they're not quite as rock'n'roll as Tooting.

Balham can offer a great night out. Catch a show at the Bedford: comedy, music, theatre. This characteristically English pub attracts some seriously high-profile comedians. After a giggle, move on to the Balham Bowls Club, or the BBC as it's known by local residents. The club is like a time machine: from the chewing-gum-splatted streets of Balham, you step into a 1960s working men's club, though the selection of craft beers and ales will pull you back into the 21st century.

A short walk from the green spaces of Clapham and Tooting Bec, Balham is ideally placed for young families and professionals. There's also plenty of Victorian housing stock, including pretty residential streets by Tooting Bec Common, while young professionals untroubled by plans for procreation invest in serviced flats in Du Cane Court, a distinctive 1937 art deco apartment block on Balham High Road.

If the numerous cafés and bars are all too much, and the parks too bucolic, the Northern line provides an easy transport link into the centre. Or hop on the Overground and explore the rest of south London.

Tooting SW17

This lively, diverse area is fast becoming the hub of south-west London, and it's easy to see why. Walk along Upper Tooting Road, from Tooting Broadway station to Tooting Bec, and you'll feel like you've walked across the world. A vast array of restaurants provide exotic tastes and smells; these include East African Asian, Gujarati, South Indian, Pakistani and Sri Lankan – an authentic flavour of multicultural London.

If you're a curry-lover then clearly you're in the right place. Some of the city's best South Asian food is found in Tooting, with Upper Tooting Road being the curry corridor. At Onam Kerala, staff pride themselves on using the same spices and other ingredients used in Keralan kitchens; Dosa n Chutny combines the intense and aromatic flavours of south Indian and Sri Lankan cuisine; Apollo Banana Leaf on the High Street also serves good, cheap and fiery Sri Lankan dishes. Throw in excellent Asian food stores and it's a true food village; check out Deepak on Greaves Place and Shiv Darshan on Upper Tooting Road, which is great for *farsan* (savoury snacks).

Searching for something a little less spicy? How about restaurant-cum-bakery Graveney & Meadow, burger joint Honest Burger or Aussie café Mud? There's also a branch of Soho House's Chicken Shop.

For drinking and socialising, there's the well-named Little Bar for cocktails and craft beers; the standard-sized Antelope on Mitcham Road; former tramshed the Tooting Tram & Social; and the huge Castle on Tooting High Street, with a vast beer garden featuring huts with their own seating and heating.

Tooting High Street and Mitcham Road have high-street chains, but the area also boasts two fantastic indoor markets – Broadway Market is one of the largest in London, with more than 90 stalls selling everything from fresh fruit and vegetables to flowers, saris and fashion accessories.

When it comes to house hunting, Tooting's large period homes and excellent schools attract plenty of young families, but it's more competitively priced than neighbours

Battersea Park

Clapham and Balham; being in the London Borough of Wandsworth, it also has one of the lowest council tax rates in the capital. However, don't expect a bargain – plenty of property speculators have focused on Tooting and numerous tiny, expensive flats are being squeezed into defunct commercial buildings.

Tooting Bec is the posher bit, while Tooting Broadway has quiet Edwardian and Victorian streets; both tube stops are popular with smug commuters who can always get a seat on the Northern line going into town. House-hunters favour Furzedown, near Tooting Bec – especially those trying to get into the catchment area for Graveney School – and the more affordable Edwardian terraces of Tooting Broadway. The residential roads around the two local commons, Wandsworth and Tooting Bec, are very smart, with plenty of properties over a million pounds.

Aside from the curries, houses, schools and transport, the area's other selling point is its large green spaces and sports facilities. Tooting Bec Common offers 89 hectares of open parkland, wildlife areas and woods. It's also home to Tooting Bec Lido – England's largest freshwater swimming pool.

Eating

Apollo Banana Leaf 190 Tooting High Street, SW17 0SF (8696 1423).

L'Auberge 22 Upper Richmond Road, SW15 2RX (8874 3593, www.ardillys.com).

Ben's Canteen 140 St John's Hill, SW11 1SL (7228 3260, www.benscanteen.com).

Bertie & Boo 162 Balham High Road, SW12 9BW (8772 1562, www.bertieandboo.com).

Birdhouse 123 St John's Hill, SW11 1SZ (7228 6663, www.birdhou.se).

Bunga Bunga 37 Battersea Bridge Road, SW11 3BA (7095 0360, www.bungabunga-london.com).

Cah-Chi 394 Garratt Lane, SW18 4HP (8946 8811, www.cahchi.com).

Chez Bruce 2 Bellevue Road, SW17 7EG (8672 0114, www.chezbruce.co.uk).

Chicken Shop 141 Tooting High Street, SW17 0SY (8767 5200, www.chickenshop.com).

Dosa n Chutny 68 Tooting High Street, SW17 0RN (8767 9200, www.dosanchutny.com).

Earlsfield 511 Garratt Lane, SW18 4SW (8871 4221, www.theearlsfield.com).

Emile's 96-98 Felsham Road, SW15 1DQ (8789 3323, www.emilesrestaurant.co.uk).

Enoteca Turi 28 Putney High Street, SW15 1SQ (8785 4449, www.enotecaturi.com).

Fish Club 189 St John's Hill, SW11 1TH (7978 7115, www.thefishclub.com).

Galapagos 169 Battersea High Street, SW11 3JS (8488 4989).

Gaslight Grill 339 Battersea Park Road, SW11 4LS (7622 2112, www.gaslightgrill.co.uk).

Gazette 147 Upper Richmond Road, SW15 2TX (8789 6996, www.gazettebrasserie.co.uk/putney).

Graveney & Meadow 40 Mitcham Road, SW17 9NA (8672 9016, www.graveneyand meadow.com).

Grind 79 Lower Richmond Road, SW15 1ET (8789 5101, www.grindcoffee.com).

Honest Burgers 72 Tooting High Street, SW17 0RN (3601 5700, www.honestburgers.co.uk).

Kaosarn 110 St John's Hill, SW11 1SJ (7223 7888).

Lola Rojo 78 Northcote Road, SW11 6QL (7350 2262, www.lolarojo.net).

If you can sing in tune, join the friendly South West London Choral Society (www.swlcs. org.uk), established in 1886.

Ma Goa 242-244 Upper Richmond Road, SW15 6TG (8780 1767, www.ma-goa.com).

Marco Polo Riverside Quarter, Eastfields Avenue, SW18 1LP (8874 6800, www.marcopolo.uk.net).

Il Mascalzone 41 Putney High Street, SW15 1SP (8785 4793, www.ilmascalzone.com).

Mel's Vintage Beats & Breakfast 573 Garratt Lane, SW18 4ST (8944 5718, www.foodandfuel.co.uk).

Mud 141 Mitcham Road, SW17 9PE (8767 7893, www.mudtooting.co.uk).

Nabrasa 505 Garratt Lane, SW18 4SW (8871 3875, www.nabrasa.co.uk).

Onam 219 Tooting High Street, SW17 0SZ (8767 7655, www.onamrestaurant.co.uk).

Popeseye 277 Upper Richmond Road, SW15 6SP (8788 7733, www.popeseye.com).

Powder Keg Diplomacy 147 St John's Hill, SW11 1TQ (7450 6457, www.powderkegdiplomacy.co.uk).

Santa Maria del Sur 129 Queenstown Road, SW8 3RH (7622 2088, www.santamariadelsur.com).

Soif 27 Battersea Rise, SW11 1HG (7223 1112, www.soif.co).

Sylvan Oak 558-560 Garratt Lane, SW17 0NY (8944 7944, www.sylvanoakearlsfield.co.uk).

Thai Square 2-4 Lower Richmond Road, SW15 1LB (8780 1211, www.thaisq.com).

Urban Gourmet 201 St John's Hill, SW11 1TH (3441 1200, www.urban-gourmet.co.uk).

Drinking

Alma 499 Old York Road, SW18 1TF (8870 2537, www.almawandsworth.com).
Antelope 76 Mitcham Road, SW17 9NG (8672 3888, www.theantelopepub.com).
Balham Bowls Club 7-9 Ramsden Road, SW12 8QX (8673 4700, www.balhambowlsclub.com).
Bedford 77 Bedford Hill, SW12 9HD (8682 8940, www.thebedford.co.uk).
Bricklayer's Arms 32 Waterman Street, SW15 1DD (8782 0222, www.bricklayers-arms.co.uk).
Castle 38 Tooting High Street, SW17 0RG (8672 7018, www.castletooting.com).
Cat's Back 86-88 Point Pleasant, SW18 1NN (8617 3448, www.thecatsback.com).
Coat & Badge 8 Lacy Road, SW15 1NL (8788 4900, www.geronimo-inns.co.uk).
Devonshire 39 Balham High Road, SW12 9AN (8673 1363, www.dukeofdevonshirebalham.com).
Draft House 94 Northcote Road, SW11 6QW (7924 1814, www.drafthouse.co.uk).
Duke's Head 8 Lower Richmond Road, SW15 1JN (8788 2552, www.dukesheadputney.co.uk).
Fez Club 200B Upper Richmond Road, SW15 2SH (8780 0123, www.putneyfez.com).
Fox & Hounds 66-68 Latchmere Road, SW11 2JU (7924 5483, www.thefoxandhoundspub.co.uk).
Graffiti Cocktail Bar 561 Garratt Lane, SW18 4SR (8944 9009, www.graffitibar.co.uk).
Half Moon 93 Lower Richmond Road, SW15 1EU (8790 9383, www.geronimo-inns.co.uk).
Hope 1 Bellevue Road, SW17 7EG (8672 8717, www.thehopepub.co.uk).
Jolly Gardeners 214 Garratt Lane, SW18 4EA (8870 8417, www.thejollygardeners.co.uk).
Latchmere 503 Battersea Park Road, SW11 3BW (7223 3549, www.thelatchmere.co.uk).
Little Bar 145 Mitcham Road, SW17 9PE (8672 7317).
Lost Angel 339 Battersea Park Road, SW11 4LS (7622 2112, www.lostangel.co.uk).
Northcote 2 Northcote Road, SW11 1NT (7223 5378, www.geronimo-inns.co.uk).
Prince of Wales 138 Upper Richmond Road, SW15 2SP (8788 1552, www.foodandfuel.co.uk).
Putney Station 94-98 Upper Richmond Road, SW15 2SP (8780 0242, www.brinkleys.com).
Ship 41 Jews Row, SW18 1TB (8870 9667, www.theship.co.uk).
Tooting Tram & Social 46-48 Mitcham Road, SW17 9NA (8767 0278, www.tootingtramandsocial.co.uk).
Toy Shop 32 Putney High Street, SW15 1SQ (8704 1188, www.thetoyshopbar.com).
Wandle 332 Garratt Lane, SW18 4EJ (8874 4209, www.metropolitanpubcompany.com).

Whistle & Flute 46-48 Putney High Street, SW15 1SQ (8780 5437, www.fullers.co.uk).

Shopping

Aux Merveilleux de Fred 55 Northcote Road, SW11 1NP (7223 0771, www.auxmerveilleux.com).
Balham Farmers' Market Chestnut Grove Primary School, junction of Chestnut Grove & Hearnville Road, SW12 8JZ (7833 0338, www.lfm.org.uk/markets/balham). Saturday.
Battersea Car Boot Sale Harris Academy, Battersea Park Road, SW11 5AP (07941 383588, www.batterseaboot.com). Sunday.
Broadway Market 21-23 Tooting High Street, SW17 0SN (8672 4760, www.tootingmarket.com).
Deepak Food 953-959 Garratt Lane, SW17 0LR (8767 7819).
Designer Alterations 14 Ingate Place, SW8 3NS (7498 4360, www.designandalter.com).
Dove & Son Ltd 71 Northcote Road, SW11 6PJ (7223 5191, www.dovethebutchers.co.uk).
Edwina Ibbotson 45 Queenstown Road, SW8 3RG (7498 5390, www.edwinaibbotson.co.uk).
Hamish Johnston 48 Northcote Road, SW11 1PA (7738 0741, www.hamishjohnston.com).
Hatty Bloom (8767 6753, www.hattybloom.com); Tickled Pink, 2 Bellevue Parade, SW17 7RQ; Sugarbag Blue, 567 Garratt Lane, SW18 4SR.
Hive Honey Shop 93 Northcote Road, SW11 6PL (7924 6233, www.thehivehoneyshop.co.uk).
JoJo Maman Bébé (www.jojomamanbebe.co.uk); 39 Bedford Hill, SW12 9EY (8675 1906); 72 Northcote Road, SW11 6QL (7223 8510); Unit 30, The Exchange, SW15 1TW (8780 5165).
Northcote Music 155C Northcote Road, SW11 6QB (7228 0074, www.northcotemusic.co.uk).
Northcote Road Antiques Market 155A Northcote Road, SW11 6QB (7228 6850, www.spectrumsoft.net/nam.htm).
Oil & Water 340 Old York Road, SW18 1SS (8704 4327, www.oilandwater.co.uk).
One Small Step One Giant Leap (www.onesmallsteponegiantleap.com); 49 Northcote Road, SW11 1NJ (7223 9314); Unit D2, The Exchange, SW15 1TW (8789 2046).
Philglas & Swiggot 21 Northcote Road, SW11 1NG (7924 4494, www.philglas-swiggot.com).
Planet Organic 52 Garratt Lane, SW18 4FT (8877 8330, www.planetorganic.com).
Putney Exchange Shopping Centre Putney High Street, SW15 1TW (8780 1056, www.putneyexchange.co.uk).
Quackers 155D Northcote Road, SW11 6QB (7978 4235).
Question Air 143-145 Northcote Road, SW11 6PX (7924 6948, www.question-air.com).

Shiv Darshan 169 Upper Tooting Road, SW17 7TJ (8682 5173).
Southside Shopping Centre Wandsworth High Street, SW18 4TF (8870 2141, www.southsidewandsworth.com).
Will's Art Warehouse 180 Lower Richmond Road, SW15 1LY (8246 4840, www.wills-art.com).

Things to do

Cinemas & theatres

Battersea Arts Centre (BAC) Lavender Hill, SW11 5TN (7223 2233, www.bac.org.uk). Forward-thinking theatre specialising in new writers and companies.
Cineworld Wandsworth Southside Shopping Centre, Wandsworth High Street, SW18 4TF (0871 200 2000, www.cineworld.co.uk).
Odeon Putney 26 Putney High Street, SW15 1SN (0871 224 4007, www.odeon.co.uk).
Putney Arts Theatre Ravenna Road, SW15 6AW (8788 6943, www.putneyartstheatre.org.uk).
Tara Arts Theatre 356 Garratt Lane, SW18 4ES (8333 4457, www.tara-arts.com). Cross-cultural (British-Asian) enterprise producing quality community theatre. New theatre currently being built upon the grounds of the old.
Theatre 503 The Latchmere, 503 Battersea Park Road, SW11 3BW (7978 7040, www.theatre503.com).

Galleries & museums

Hua Unit 7B, Albion Riverside Building, 8 Hester Road, SW11 4AX (7738 1215, www.hua-gallery.com). Specialises in contemporary Chinese art.

Pump House Gallery Battersea Park, SW11 4NJ (8871 7572, www.pumphousegallery.org.uk). Tiny art gallery in a 19th-century building.

Other attractions

Battersea Dogs & Cats Home 4 Battersea Park Road, SW8 4AA (0843 509 4444, www.battersea.org.uk). Visitors are welcome at this world-famous animal sanctuary, home to around 180 dogs and 100 cats at any once time.

Look out for the sign at the start of Albert Bridge commanding marching soldiers to break step.

Battersea Park Children's Zoo Chelsea Bridge Gate, Queenstown Road, SW11 4NJ (7924 5826, www.batterseaparkzoo.co.uk).
Eddie Catz 68-70 Putney High Street, SW15 1SF (3475 5268, www.eddiecatz.com).
It's a Kids Thing 279 Magdalen Road, SW18 3NZ (8739 0909, www.itsakidsthing.co.uk).
Mini Potters 430 Garratt Lane, SW18 4HN (8944 7466, www.minipotters.co.uk).

Gigs, clubs & comedy

Bedford 77 Bedford Hill, SW12 9HD (8682 8940, www.thebedford.com).
Half Moon 93 Lower Richmond Road, SW15 1EU (8780 9383, www.geronimo-inns.co.uk). One of London's longest-running music venues.

Green spaces

For more information see www.wandsworth.gov.uk
Battersea Park SW11 4NJ. Sports pitches and tennis courts, adventure playground, children's zoo, lake, ornamental gardens and café.
Clapham Common Windmill Drive, SW4 9DE. Huge open space with playgrounds, sports pitches and skatepark. Popular festivals.
King George's Park SW18 4GB. Sports pitches, tennis courts, bowling green and Wandle trail.
Leaders Gardens Putney Embankment, SW15 1LW. Small riverside park with tennis courts.
Tooting Common SW16 1RU. Athletics track, fishing, horse riding, sports pitches, activity centre, wildlife areas and lido.
Wandsworth Common SW12 8PB. Ecological and ornamental areas, sports pitches, tennis and bowling, fishing lake and children's playground.
Wandsworth Park Putney Bridge Road, SW18 1PP. Riverside park with pitch-and-putt.

Gyms & leisure centres

Balham Leisure Centre Elmfield Road, SW17 8AN (8772 9577, www.placesforpeopleleisure.org).
Furzedown Recreation Centre Ramsdale Road, SW17 9BP (8767 6542, www.wandsworth.gov.uk). Floodlit pitches and tennis courts.
Latchmere Leisure Centre Burns Road, SW11 2DY (7207 8004, www.placesforpeopleleisure.org).
Nuffield Health (www.nuffieldhealth.com); Wandsworth Fitness & Wellbeing Centre King George's Park, Burr Road, SW18 4SQ (8874 1155); Battersea Fitness & Wellbeing Centre Sheepcote Lane, Burns Road, SW11 5BT (7228 4400). Private.

Physical Culture Studios Studios 21-22, The Arches, Winthorpe Road, SW15 2LW (8780 2172, www.physicalculture.co.uk). Private.
Putney Leisure Centre Dryburgh Road, SW15 1BL (8785 0388, www.placesforpeopleleisure.org).
Roehampton Sport & Fitness Centre Laverstoke Gardens, off Danesbury Avenue, SW15 4JB (8785 0535, www.placesforpeopleleisure.org).
Sivananda Yoga Vedanta Centre, 51 Felsham Road, SW15 1AZ (8780 0160, www.sivananda. co.uk). Long-established yoga centre.
Tooting Leisure Centre Greaves Place, SW17 0NE (8333 7555, www.placesforpeopleleisure.org).
Wandle Recreation Centre Mapleton Road, SW18 4DN (8871 1149, www.placesforpeople leisure.org).
Yorky's 24-28 York Road, SW11 3QA (7228 6266). Private.

Outdoor pursuits

Central London Golf Centre Burntwood Lane, SW17 0AT (8871 2468, www. clgc.co.uk). Nine holes.
Go Ape Battersea Park, SW11 4NJ (0333 331 7419, www.goape.co.uk). Treetop walks and zipwires.
London Rowing Club Putney Embankment, SW15 1LB (8788 1400, www.londonrc.org.uk). Courses and recreational rowing.
Thames Rowing Club Putney Embankment, SW15 1LB (8788 0798, www.thamesrc.co.uk).
Tooting Bec Lido Tooting Bec Road, SW16 1RU (8871 7198, www.placesforpeopleleisure.org). Home of the South London Swimming Club (www.slsc.org.uk).

Tooting Bec Lido

HIGHS & LOWS

Good schools

Low council tax

Parks, heaths, commons and becs

Tooting's curry corridor

▲ ⋯⋯⋯⋯⋯⋯⋯⋯⋯⋯⋯ ▼

Nowhere to park

Pricey

Riverside colonised by luxury developments

Too many 4x4s

Schools

Primary

There are 55 state primary schools in the borough, including 17 church schools and one Muslim school. There are also 22 independent primaries, including one French school, one Montessori school and one Steiner school. See www.wandsworth.gov.uk, www.education.gov.uk/edubase and www.ofsted.gov.uk for more information.

Secondary

Ark Putney Academy Pullman Gardens, SW15 3DG (8788 3421, www.arkputneyacademy.org).

Ashcroft Technology Academy 100 West Hill, SW15 2UT (8877 0357, www.atacademy.org.uk).

Bolingbroke Academy Wakehurst Road, SW11 6BF (7924 8200, www.arkbolingbrokeacademy.org).

Burntwood School Burntwood Lane, SW17 0AQ (8946 6201, www.burntwoodschool.com). Girls only; mixed sixth form.

Chestnut Grove Academy 45 Chestnut Grove, SW12 8JZ (8673 8737, www.chestnutgrove.wandsworth.sch.uk).

Emanuel School Battersea Rise, SW11 1HS (8870 4171, www.emanuel.org.uk). Private.

Ernest Bevin College Beechcroft Road, SW17 7DF (8672 8582, www.ernestbevin.org.uk).

Graveney School Welham Road, SW17 9BU (8682 7000, www.graveney.org).

Harris Academy Battersea 401 Battersea Park Road, SW11 5AP (7622 0026, www.batterseaparkschool.org).

Putney High School 35 Putney Hill, SW15 6BH (8788 4886, www.putneyhigh.gdst.net). Girls only; private.
St Cecilia's Sutherland Grove, SW18 5JR (8780 1244, www.saintcecilias.wandsworth. sch.uk). Church of England.
St John Bosco College Princes Way, SW19 6QE (8246 6000, www.sjbc.wandsworth.sch.uk). Roman Catholic.
Southfields Academy 333 Merton Road, SW18 5JU (8875 2600, www.southfieldsacademy.com).

Property

Local estate agents
Andrews www.andrewsonline.co.uk
Cochrane & Wilson www.cochraneandwilson.com

Craigie & Co www.craigie-co.co.uk
First Union www.first-union.co.uk
Jacksons Estate Agents www.jacksonsestateagents.com
John Thorogood www.john-thorogood.co.uk
Time2move www.time2move.com

Local knowledge

www.lavenderhill.co.uk
http://putneysw15.com
www.southlondonpress.co.uk
http://tooting-news.dailyprss.co.uk
www.tootinglife.com
www.wandsworthguardian.co.uk
www.wandsworthsw18.com

Balham Bowls Club

USEFUL INFO

Borough size
3,426 hectares

Population
318,000

Ethnic mix
White 77.0%
Asian or Asian British 8.5%
Black or Black British 8.1%
Mixed 3.3%
Chinese or other 3.2%

Wandsworth Borough Council
The Town Hall, Wandsworth High Street, SW18 2PU (8871 6000, www.wandsworth.gov.uk)

Council run by
Conservatives

MPs
Battersea, Jane Ellison (Conservative); Putney, Justine Greening (Conservative); Tooting, Sadiq Khan (Labour)

Main recycling centres
Western Riverside Civic Amenity Site, Smugglers Way, SW18 1JS (8871 2788, www.wrwa.gov.uk); Cringle Dock Civic Amenity Site, Cringle Street, SW8 5BX (7622 1046)

Council tax
£451.77 to £1,409.10

City of Westminster

This borough encompasses the stuccoed streets of Pimlico, the tourist magnet that is Covent Garden, the heavily guarded environs of Whitehall and the gay bars of Soho. Variety in spades, in other words.

AVERAGE PROPERTY PRICE

Detached £2,125,140	**Terraced** £2,083,820
Semi-detached £2,182,672	**Flat** £931,247

AVERAGE RENTAL PRICE PER WEEK

Studio £300	**2 bed** £625
1 bed £450	**3 bed** £896

Liberty

Neighbourhoods

Covent Garden WC2

Although it figures high on every tourist's agenda, Covent Garden is more than just an entertainment centre. True, the area is synonymous with the Royal Opera House, offers daily alfresco entertainment on its central piazza, is surrounded by theatres and has one of the capital's most popular museums: the London Transport Museum. True, too, that it is always thronged with shoppers and merrymakers. Yet there's a big residential community as well, and many independent businesses.

The colonnaded old fruit and veg market is still the hugely popular shopping centrepiece, perennially lively or unbearably crowded and commercial, depending on your point of view. (It's crazy now to think that when the business and the traders moved to new premises in Nine Elms in 1974, the plan was to bulldoze the old place and drive a ring road through it.) Off the central piazza, Floral Street has more interesting boutiques (Paul Smith was a pioneer of the area) and Long Acre has high-street brands, while Southampton Street has the hiking and camping shops. For travel books and maps, seek out Stanfords; Cybercandy has imported sweets from around the world.

Sadly, the very grand-sounding Strand is actually quite dull save for the beautiful art deco Savoy hotel and theatre. Where it meets Waterloo Bridge, though, is Somerset House, which has plenty to offer Londoners: an ice rink in the winter, outdoor films and concerts in the summer, year-round exhibitions and Skye Gyngell's restaurant Spring. At the other end of Strand is Trafalgar Square, officially London's central point as marked just outside Charing Cross station.

North across Long Acre (venturing into the borough of Camden) is Neal Street, largely filled with trainer shops, and secluded Neal's Yard, associated with some of the area's earliest tenants: Neal's Yard Dairy, Neal's Yard Remedies and Monmouth Coffee. Some of the capital's most attractive commercial streets are here, radiating from Seven Dials, a road junction marked by a pillar bearing six sundials, itself acting as the seventh. Between the numerous slick urbanwear boutiques, you'll find saucy sex shop Coco de Mer, perspex jewellery queen Tatty Devine, London perfumer Miller Harris, the bargain CD and DVD shop Fopp, and

sci-fi and fantasy favourite Forbidden Planet on Shaftesbury Avenue. The area also has an entire beauty hall's worth of those mid-range brands: Bare Minerals, Benefit, Caudalie, Kiehl's, Shu Uemura…

Covent Garden has plenty of places to eat to suit all budgets, with many offering pre- and post-theatre deals for those attending the many local theatres. The big hitters are Balthazar and the Delaunay, while Opera Tavern has a cult following. Cheaper places include Battersea Pie, Mishkin's Jewish diner and Sesame. There are also plenty of pubs, another legacy of the market days; beer-drinkers tend to favour the Harp and the Lamb & Flag.

Surprisingly for such a central location, Covent Garden still has a strong residential element. Yes, there's the odd multi-million-pound apartment for sale, and many 'houses' are now used for offices, but the denizens of such places share amenities with long-term residents and those living in local Peabody Trust housing, such as Davey's Court on Bedfordbury. More desirable residential areas can be found at Ching Court, off Shelton Street, and the flats opposite Phoenix Garden, a delightful wildlife nook tucked away behind St Giles-in-the-Fields church. Towards Kingsway, big Victorian buildings such as decommissioned primary schools have been converted into flats – quiet Macklin Street and Newton Street have a number of these.

Soho W1

Everyone's complaining about the death of Soho, that the West End's centre of sleaze has lost its sex appeal. Westminster Council's drive to combat drugs and street prostitution has cleaned the place up in a way that's been welcomed by most, but soaring rents have driven out a lot of the more, ahem, 'interesting' establishments and colourful characters, while opening the door to sanitised new housing and hundreds of decent places to eat.

Tamer it may be, but Soho is still somewhere to go to have a good time. Behind Shaftesbury Avenue's theatres, there's a serious restaurant scene happening. There are too many great venues to mention – and hot new spots opening every week (see www.timeout.com for the latest names) – but the top-notch dim sum at Yauatcha and the Modern European cooking at 10 Greek Street stand out, while Polpo is partially to blame for the small-plates, no-bookings trend. There's

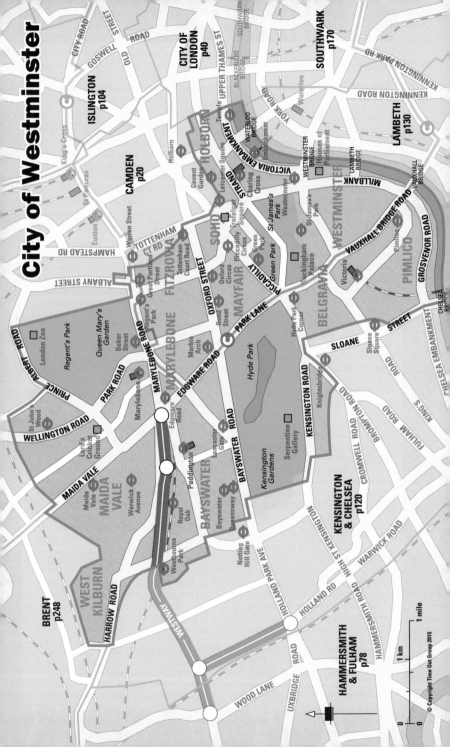

also plenty of interesting eating on a much cheaper scale: Bo Drake (Korean barbecue), Bone Daddies (noodles), Herman ze German (wurst) and Pitt Cue (pulled pork). Soho's famous coffee houses of the 1950s and '60s have been replaced by a new generation, including Flat White and Milk Bar.

Carnaby Street is still the main shopping street, though it's dominated by trainer shops. More interesting is the 'Newburgh Quarter' behind it, home to studiously hip boutiques such as Flying Horse and Fred Perry, and grooming parlour Pankhurst. Kingly Court, on the other side of Carnaby Street, is also having a moment, with several decent places to eat. And don't dismiss Liberty; beyond its signature prints, there are incredibly well-sourced selections of everything from perfume to chocolate.

Old Soho lives on at various venues: legendary pubs the French House and the Coach & Horses; delightful pâtisserie Maison Bertaux; Italian delis I Camisa and Lina's; 24-hour Bar Italia; and jazz club Ronnie Scott's. The much-reduced sex industry is now centred around the backstreets off Brewer Street, such as Tisbury Court.

London's gay community in particular still feels Soho's pull, drawn to the bars and clubs around Old Compton Street: the Admiral Duncan, Freedom Bar, G-A-Y, Shadow Lounge and the Yard. A strong music scene survives around Berwick Street and Broadwick Street thanks to Reckless Records, Sister Ray and Sounds of the Universe. On annual Record Store Day, stages are set up and the streets are heaving.

The daytime population is very media-centric; there's a multitude of film production houses in the area – and this is very much part of Soho's character. Above the shops and restaurants is a still staunchly residential stratum, which is defended by the Soho Society, housed by Soho Housing (www.sohoha.org.uk), and educated by the tiny Soho Parish Primary School.

The area between Leicester Square and Shaftesbury Avenue is the domain of the LCCA (London Chinatown Chinese Association), centred on Gerrard Street; you can't miss its ersatz oriental street trimmings. The Chinese community first opened restaurants and shops here in the 1950s, and Chinatown's way of life, like much of Soho, was established in the halcyon days of cheap rents and slummy streets; today, these streets are valuable real estate.

The choice of places to eat can be rather overwhelming, and the service famously curt; some favourites include Baozi Inn, Café TPT and Joy King Lau. There are also plenty of Chinese supermarkets, where you can source authentic ingredients.

The huge Crossrail development at Tottenham Court Road has had a massive impact on the area. On Charing Cross Road, legendary venue the Astoria has been lost and the specialist music shops of Denmark Street are under threat. Going from strength to strength, though, is Foyles, the independent bookshop and resident of the street since 1906, now in even bigger and better premises.

Mayfair W1

Bordered by the five-star hotels of Park Lane, the flagship stores of Oxford Street and Regent Street, and the smart institutions of Piccadilly, Mayfair is generally thought of as the epitome of posh. It's where the titled feel at home. You'll find them on weeknights at private members' clubs such as 5 Hertford Street and Annabel's, or dining in the many pricey-but-dull restaurants; at weekends, they go to the country. But as far as living here goes, the slightly shabby English upper crust is being pushed out by new money bling. Houses and flats are now home to embassies and hedge fund companies, and Georgian façades hide the sort of accommodation that has its own cinema, gym and panic room.

But just because you can't live here doesn't mean that you can't enjoy it. Grand squares and hidden alleyways make Mayfair a fun place to explore. The original Mayfair is Shepherd Market, site of the 18th-century May Fair; find it by ducking down under a building off Curzon Street. The pedestrianised streets and pavement restaurants here have a smaller scale and slower pace than everything around. It's populated with curiosities such as L'Autre (a Polish-Mexican bistro which also claims to be Mayfair's oldest wine lodge), the London Coin Galleries and Turmeaus ('fine cigar merchant and blenders of splendid tobacco', established 1817).

At the other extreme of the glitzometer is Bond Street (New and Old), lined with designer labels (Burberry, Chanel, Prada), jewellers (Asprey, Tiffany & Co) and galleries (the Fine Art Society, Halcyon Gallery). This street is all about the money, but we can still dream. In the meantime, auction house Sotheby's is a good place to catch public exhibitions prior to a sale.

A few streets over – on Albermarle and Dover streets – there's a fresher crowd: Victoria Beckham, Jimmy Choo (men's fashion), McQ (Alexander McQueen) and the six-storey Dover Street Market, an emporium devised by Comme des Garçons designer Rei Kawakubo, with exclusive lines from other cutting-edge names.

Elsewhere, Mount Street has become a hub for the new generation of London designers: Christopher Kane, Roksanda Ilincic, Jenny Packham, Nicholas Kirkwood and Solange Azagury-Partridge. Between them, they provide fashions for men, women and children, bridal gowns, shoes and jewellery. Legendary seafood restaurant Scott's keeps the flag flying for eats, while just behind the shops is shady haven Mount Street Gardens.

Mid-range brands can be found on and around South Moulton Street, including brilliantly edited fashion at Browns and a Paul Smith sale shop down an alley behind the Handel House Museum. A totally different kind of shopping experience can be had at Grays Antique Market – around 200 dealers offer a spectacular range of wares.

The huge number of smart hotels in the area means a huge number of super-smart hotel bars. Superb cocktails are to be had at the Connaught's Coburg Bar and Connaught Bar, and also at the Beaumont's American Bar. Also worth seeking out are the Keeper's House, tucked away off the corner of the Royal Academy's courtyard, and the Windmill pub, where pies are a speciality.

Marylebone W1

A couple of decades ago, Marylebone was a reasonably affordable part of Westminster. Today, rents and prices match those of its expensive neighbours.

The rebranding of the pretty High Street into desirable 'Marylebone Village' has been a roaring success. Despite having Oxford Street just to the south, it could belong to an affluent provincial town. Some of its best-known independent shops are La Fromagerie (with its legendary climate-controlled cheese room), rare-breed butcher Ginger Pig, pretty chocolatier Rococo, Daunt Books, and ribbons and trimmings emporium VV Rouleaux. There's also a number of middle- to upmarket clothing stores and some contemporary jewellery shops such as Cox & Power or Kabiri. On a more neighbourhood level, there's still a farmers' market that sets up in the car park behind Waitrose.

Another lovely place to browse is Chiltern Street, with specialists such as Cire Trudon candles, Cadenhead's Whisky Shop & Tasting Rooms, and a high concentration of bridal shops. It's also the location of the Chiltern Firehouse, one of the capital's hottest and hardest-to-book restaurants.

More easily accessible venues include trattoria Briciole, Dinings with its innovative Japanese cuisine, and New Zealand trailblazer the Providores & Tapa Room. Plus there's plenty of very fine dining spread between Marylebone High Street, Marble Arch and Baker Street: Galvin Bistrot de Luxe, the Orrery (which also has a rooftop terrace) and the inspirational Italian Locanda Locatelli, to name just a few.

Lisson Grove, which heads north-west from here, was once all slums; much of the housing stock is ex-council. While the large Lisson Green Estate overlooking the canal can be intimidating, the streets between Lisson Grove and Edgware Road are more enticing. Still on the Grove (but at the other end of the market), the gated Belvedere development has two-bed flats for £500,000, and there's a small supply of bijou Georgian houses. Otherwise, you might want to look into buying one of the houseboats on the canal. Bell Street is one of the more interesting roads hereabouts,

Shaftesbury Avenue

home to the Lisson Gallery, plus a couple of second-hand bookshops. The other standout is Church Street, which has a weekend street market but is otherwise almost completely given over to antiques shops; Alfie's Antique Market has loads.

New building in the as-yet-unprettified quarter of Baker Street is throwing more housing into the Marylebone mix. Much of it is expensive – but you would be living next to the formal flower beds, waterfowl-strewn lakes and playing fields of Regent's Park, and close to London Zoo.

Busy Edgware Road creates a definitive edge to the neighbourhood as traffic ploughs on northwards up towards Kilburn and, eventually, the M1 motorway. Its attraction is the banks of Middle Eastern restaurants on either side, including Abu Zaad, Maroush and Ranoush Juice.

Fitzrovia W1

Unlike its neighbours, Marylebone and Bloomsbury (where crescents, squares and lofty terraces were created by wealthy, empire-building landowners), Fitzrovia was developed on a smaller scale by minor landowners. This left the streets feeling less well organised, but the area has a low-key, arty, crafty and businesslike vibe – though

the huge Fitzroy Place development on the site of the old Middlesex Hospital has brought a new slickness to the neighbourhood. There are a few fashion wholesale businesses, an increasing number of 'new media' offices, the famous BT Tower, and loads of cafés, pubs and restaurants.

The neighbourhood's name comes from 18th-century Fitzroy Square (just into the borough of Camden), designed by Robert Adam. It's handsome but not too grand – it doesn't lose its residential feel. It has a history of artistic and literary residents; community operas are sometimes performed in the square (www.fitzroysquareopera.co.uk).

Charlotte Street, over towards Tottenham Court Road, is the dining district; there's often a hot new place with queues outside. Lasting successes include Roka (Japanese), while nearby is Jason Atherton's glamorous dining room Berners Tavern, which is housed in the new Edition Hotel.

Another good patch is up Great Titchfield Street and Eastcastle Street – a short hop from the frenzy of Oxford Circus but with a community atmosphere thanks to those who work there. There's all-day dining (and drinking) at Riding House Café, vegetarian self-service at Ethos and some serious coffee-drinking at Kaffeine.

There are plenty of relaxed pubs dotted around the area (the Cock, the King & Queen, and the Newman Arms) and a number of great bars: Oskar's (attached to splendid restaurant Dabbous), the Remedy and underground den Lucky Pig. But the one every Londoner is destined to end up in once in their lifetime, usually when they're already drunk, is Bradley's Spanish Bar, a shabby place down scuzzy Hanway Street, famed for its vinyl jukebox.

Westminster and St James's SW1

The wider borough may be called the City of Westminster but this inner circle, around Westminster Abbey, takes the Westminster name for itself.

This is a po-faced land of civil servants; the ministries that line Whitehall, as well as Downing Street with its heavily guarded security gate, are strictly off limits. But it does have one of London's best Indian restaurants, Cinnamon Club, housed in a Grade II-listed Victorian library – a favourite with MPs. Away from the Houses of Parliament, around Horseferry Road for example, streets take on a quieter, more residential feel and there are even some Peabody estates to house low-paid key workers.

St James's Park is essentially the Queen's front garden – leafier and more pleasant than Green Park, with the bonus of pelicans on the lake. Between the Mall and Piccadilly is the genteel neighbourhood of St James's, which is characterised by gentlemen's clubs and some of London's oldest shops: Berry Bros & Rudd wine merchants, Fortnum & Mason, DR Harris shaving products and Lock & Co hatters.

In Regency times, Piccadilly was the very height of fashion as men started to take great pride in their appearance. The covered arcades – Burlington, Piccadilly and the Royal – still offer elegant browsing, policed by uniformed beadles.

Victoria, Pimlico and Belgravia SW1

Like many areas in Zone 1, Victoria is defined by its transport termini. The streets around them are crowded, dominated by backpackers, commuters, package tourists, passport applicants, theatregoers and various other scuttlers on their way somewhere else. Currently, it's also affected by a giant building site around the station.

Victoria Street, the main street linking Parliament Square to Victoria station, is full of chain stores, with only the stripy Roman Catholic cathedral offering interest, both to Catholics and those looking to enjoy the fabulous views from the campanile.

Pimlico started off very smartly, with Thomas Cubitt building white stucco dwellings and garden squares for Lord Grosvenor in 1825. When land was sold off and charitable housing body the Peabody Trust built estates for the poor, the smart money lost interest. After World War II, large public-housing estates were built on the area's bombsites and fine houses were converted into flats, so all pretence to exclusivity was lost for decades.

The London Library in St James's Square is a less aloof alternative to the British Library.

Still, Pimlico is central, and pockets of Zone 1 smartness give the whole district panache. In fact, property of any calibre is expensive here. Pimlico's extensive local authority housing stock includes the Lillington Gardens Estate, off Tachbrook Street. This high-density, low-rise, red-brick affair was built in the 1970s and now has Grade II-listed status. Hide Tower, on Regency Street, was built in the late 1950s and is run by a tenant management organisation. Its flats have fantastic views over London and attract high prices.

Down by the river is Dolphin Square, a self-contained village of pieds-à-terre for important (and wealthy) people. The fortress-like, red-brick 1930s block is home to a health club, smart restaurant and a little art deco parade of shops.

Both Pimlico and Victoria folk enjoy the reflected glory afforded by their proximity to Belgravia. Belgravia, however, remains aloof. Like Mayfair, it gets its blue blood from the aristocratic Grosvenor family, who still own much of it. Current residents of its stucco palaces tend to be Russian oligarchs and embassies. Off Eaton Square (one of the capital's most prestigious addresses), Elizabeth Street has several charming shops including Les Senteurs (rare perfumes), Peggy Porschen (cakes), Philip Treacy (millinery) and Mungo & Maud (chic dog boutique).

Bayswater W2

Westminster's most multifaceted district, Bayswater is a pleasing mix of once-grand mansions, hotels and architecturally significant pleasure palaces, plus some great places to eat and drink. Bayswater's big council estate, Hallfield, which was designed by architect Sir Denys Lasdun of National Theatre fame, gives its residents spectacular views over west London from top-floor flats that are very much in demand on the private market.

Queensway is Bayswater's backbone and is one big, noisy conservation area. There's the splendid Edwardian-era Whiteleys shopping centre, a great building filled with the usual shops. The rest of the street is full of Middle Eastern cafés and restaurants.

To the south lie Kensington Gardens and the excellent playground dedicated to the memory of the late Princess of Wales. The built-up areas of Paddington and Bayswater both gain from their proximity to these royal green acres, which merge to the east with Hyde Park.

At the northern end of Queensway lies the beautiful Porchester Centre, one of the few surviving examples of the Victorian Turkish baths that once proliferated in Britain. West of Queensway, on Moscow Road, the Greek Orthodox Cathedral of St Sophia, with its impressive Byzantine icons and golden mosaics, adds to the area's cosmopolitan charm.

North of Bayswater lies Westbourne Green, a high-priority area for Westminster Council's regeneration plans. Its challenging position by Harrow Road and the Westway does the place few favours, but impressive openings, such as the Westminster Academy secondary school and Stowe Community Centre, are bringing new hope to an area dominated by high-rise council homes.

Paddington W2

Always something of the poor relation to neighbours Bayswater and Marylebone, Paddington's revival has been centred round what was previously seen as its chief drawback – the brownfield meeting point of canal, rail and road at its centre. Paddington station's renovation was completed in 2011, emphasising the elegant roof designed by Isambard Kingdom Brunel. In 2018, an architecturally striking Crossrail station will drive further footfall to an already busy quarter of the city.

The main focus of the area's redevelopment has been at Paddington Basin, a once-dilapidated dead-end arm of the Regent's Canal, now called Paddington Waterside. This is a massive ultra-modern, mixed-use development of shiny towers that combines flats and offices with numerous shops and restaurants, such as the excellent Chinese venue Pearl Liang. Paddington Waterside is an immense project, covering an area the size of Soho, and when completed it will serve 30,000 office workers. Accessibility has been vastly improved – nearly a mile of new towpath has been laid, as have five pedestrian bridges, most notably Thomas Heatherwick's Rolling Bridge; it curls up to allow water traffic to pass, and repeats the feat every Friday at noon. A more conspicuous landmark will arrive in 2016: 1 Merchant Square, with 42 storeys of apartments, boutique hotels and a rooftop bar. It looks a bit like a cucumber and will be the tallest building in Westminster.

Around the station, a shabby authenticity remains along with the occasional gem, such as the Frontline Club, a bar and restaurant with a focus on international journalism, and the Victoria, a classic London backstreet pub. The streets and squares get increasingly chichi as you head south towards Hyde Park, with the area known as Connaught Village crammed with fine shops and expensive bars and restaurants. Paddington in general is filled with hotels, including several on Westbourne Terrace, once known as the finest street in London.

Past the thundering Westway, Paddington Green conservation area, centred round St Mary's Church, provides some tranquility, and the streets then become better groomed the closer you get to the mansion blocks of Maida Vale.

Maida Vale W9

When Robert Browning coined the term 'Little Venice', he was describing the point where the Paddington arm of the Grand Union Canal meets the Regent's Canal. South Maida Vale's most poetic citizen is remembered forever at friendly Browning's Pool, where narrowboats adorned with pelargonium house cafés and galleries; the Puppet Theatre Barge is here too.

Continuing west on the canal path leads the unwary to the equally charming Westbourne Green and its tower blocks, while a stroll east along the towpath will bring you to Regent's

Park. The area around Little Venice and Clifton Gardens is an affluent part of town. The white stucco houses are tall; the shops are geared to the luxury market.

More affordable accommodation is available north-west towards Paddington Recreation Ground, at Maida Vale's northerly extreme. Not only is this a popular spot for families to get some air but there are some great facilities for sportsmen and women, as well as weekly clubs, holiday clubs and tennis coaching.

At Elgin Avenue, which bisects the district west to east, Kilburn craic starts to impinge on Maida Vale's sanity; but the residential roads that lead off it are lined by solid Victorian terraces with wrought-iron balconies and by handsome blocks of well-proportioned mansion flats. The atttactive apartments of Westside Court and pretty Delaware Road are much sought after. It's a quiet, cosy part of the world, with few shops and businesses. The refurbished Elgin bar now attracts a younger crowd serving good food – morning, noon and night – while Roma's Café on Elgin Avenue is still one of the best places in the area for tea and cake.

Maida Vale's shops mainly cater to affluence. Some of the best are Raoul's Deli, Sheepdrove Organic Farm Family Butcher, the Baker & Spice bakery-café and superior wine merchant the Winery – plus the venerable Clifton Nurseries. Likewise, the restaurants attract a similar clientele.

The Waterway and sister establishment the Summerhouse allow you to eat on a level with, and partially floating on, the canal. Don't miss the fabulous Bridge House; across the water, the beautiful Prince Alfred has great food and drink. Near Warwick Avenue tube, the Warrington on Randolph Avenue is a splendid affair, with leather sofas and fine British cooking.

You'll find the locals in the Warwick Castle on Warwick Place. After a pint or two, pop next door to Kateh, a Persian restaurant where you can get a whole array of tempting dishes, or to Gogi on Edgware Road for Korean food cooked at your table.

St John's Wood NW8

Smart, desirable and pricey, St John's Wood is a northerly outpost of Westminster that's just too quirky to be labelled a mere suburb. Although its stucco villas, spacious 19th-century housing and well-maintained, purpose-built apartments – the last dating

from careful 1950s redevelopment – all reek of provincial prosperity, St John's Wood has global appeal.

The biggest attraction is the famous Abbey Road recording studios and, of course, that zebra crossing (watch out for tourists holding up traffic by trying to recreate the Beatles album cover), though Lord's Cricket Ground, which keeps the area busy all summer, ranks a pretty close second.

The High Street is now mainly lined with chain shops, estate agents and restaurants. The usual upmarket fashion outlets and high-class food stores are here, including quality butcher Kent & Sons and family-run deli Panzer's – a veritable institution crammed with international fare.

Eateries along St John's Wood High Street feed well-heeled shoppers who ogle pastries at Maison Blanc or tuck into Jewish dishes at Harry Morgan's. There's also a fine, old pub called the Ordnance on Ordnance Hill.

At the end of the High Street, St John's Wood Church Gardens is a nice space for a quiet read or a picnic, and also has a good play area. In the adventure playground on St John's Wood Terrace, parents can leave their kids under supervision for a couple of pounds.

The neighbourhood has always been wealthy, and its proximity to gracious Regent's Park keeps the house prices high. More affordable property can be found in the apartment blocks along busy St John's Wood Road, but these are more often available as short-term lets.

Eating

There are hundreds of great shops, bars and restaurants in central London. For in-depth reviews and all the latest openings see www.timeout.com.

10 Greek Street 10 Greek Street, W1D 4DH (7734 4677, www.10greekstreet.com).
Abu Zaad 128 Edgware Road, W2 2DZ (7224 8382, www.abuzaad.co.uk).
L'Autre 5B Shepherd Street, W1J 7HP (7499 4680).
Baker & Spice 20 Clifton Road, W9 1SU (7289 2499, www.bakerandspice.uk.com).
Balthazar 4-6 Russell Street, WC2B 5HZ (3301 1155, www.balthazarlondon.com).
Baozi Inn 26 Newport Court, WC2H 7JS (7287 6877, www.baoziinnlondon.com).
Bar Italia 22 Frith Street, W1D 4RF (7437 4520, www.baritaliasoho.co.uk).

Battersea Pie Lower Ground Floor, 28 The Market, WC2E 8RA (7240 9566, www.batterseapiestation.co.uk).

Berners Tavern 10 Berners Street, W1T 3LF (7908 7979, www.bernerstavern.com).

Bo Drake 6 Greek Street, W1 4DE (www.bodrake.co.uk).

Bone Daddies 31 Peter Street, W1F 0AR (7287 8581, www.bonedaddies.com).

Briciole 20 Homer Street, W1H 4NA (7723 0040, http://briciole.co.uk).

Café TPT 21 Wardour Street, W1D 6PN (7734 7980).

Chiltern Firehouse 1 Chiltern Street, W1U 7PA (7073 7676, www.chilternfirehouse.com).

Cinnamon Club Old Westminster Library, 30-32 Great Smith Street, SW1P 3BU (7222 2555, www.cinnamonclub.com).

Delaunay 55 Aldwych, WC2B 4BB (7499 8558, www.thedelaunay.com).

Dinings 22 Harcourt Street, W1H 4HH (7723 0666, www.dinings.co.uk).

Ethos 48 Eastcastle Street, W1W 8DX (3581 1538, www.ethosfoods.com).

Flat White 17 Berwick Street, W1F 0PT (7734 0370, www.flatwhitesoho.co.uk).

Galvin Bistrot de Luxe 66 Baker Street, W1U 7DJ (7935 4007, www.galvinrestaurants.com).

Gogi 451 Edgware Road, W2 1TH (7724 3018, www.gogi-restaurant.com).

Harry Morgan's 29-31 St John's Wood High Street, NW8 7NH (7722 1869, www.harryms.co.uk).

Herman Ze German 33 Old Compton Street, W1D 5JU (7734 0431, www.herman-ze-german.co.uk).

Joy King Lau 3 Leicester Street, WC2H 7BL (7437 1132, www.joykinglau.com).

Kaffeine 66 Great Titchfield Street, W1W 7QJ (7580 6755, http://kaffeine.co.uk).

Kateh 5 Warwick Place, W9 2PX (7289 3393, www.katehrestaurant.co.uk).

Locanda Locatelli 8 Seymour Street, W1H 7JZ (7935 9088, www.locandalocatelli.com).

Maison Bertaux 28 Greek Street, W1D 5DQ (7437 6007, www.maisonbertaux.com).

Maison Blanc 37 St John's Wood High Street, NW8 7NG (7586 1982, www.maisonblanc.co.uk).

Maroush 21 Edgware Road, W2 2JE (7723 0773, www.maroush.com).

Milk Bar 3 Bateman Street, W1D 4AG (7287 4796).

Mishkin's 25 Catherine Street, WC2B 5JS (7240 2078, www.mishkins.co.uk).

Monmouth Coffee 27 Monmouth Street, WC2H 9EU (7232 3010, www.monmouthcoffee.co.uk).

Opera Tavern 23 Catherine Street, WC2B 5JS (7836 3680, www.operatavern.co.uk).

Orrery 55 Marylebone High Street, W1U 5RB (7616 8000, www.orrery-restaurant.co.uk).

Pearl Liang 8 Sheldon Square, W2 6EZ (7289 7000, www.pearlliang.co.uk).

Pitt Cue 1 Newburgh Street, W1F 7RB (7287 5578, www.pittcue.co.uk).

Polpo 41 Beak Street, W1F 9SB (7734 4479, www.polpo.co.uk).

Providores & Tapa Room 109 Marylebone High Street, W1U 4RX (7935 6175, www.theprovidores.co.uk).

Ranoush Juice Bar 43 Edgware Road, W2 2JR (7723 5929).

Raoul's 13 Clifton Road, W9 1SZ (7289 7313, www.raoulsgourmet.com).

Riding House Café 43-51 Great Titchfield Street, W1W 7PQ (8968 0202, www.ridinghousecafe.co.uk).

Roka 37 Charlotte Street, W1T 1RR (7580 6464, www.rokarestaurant.com).

Roma's Café 302 Elgin Avenue, W9 1JS (7289 0906).

Scott's 20 Mount Street, W1K 2HE (7495 7309, www.caprice-holdings.co.uk).

Sesame 23 Garrick Street, WC2E 9BN (7240 4879, www.sesamefood.co.uk).

Walk from Trafalgar Square to Lancaster Gate with greenery all the way: St James's Park, Green Park, Hyde Park.

Spring Somerset House, Lancaster Place, Strand, WC2R 1LA (3011 0115, http://springrestaurant.co.uk).

Summerhouse Blomfield Road, W9 2PA (7286 6752, www.thesummerhouse.co).

Yauatcha 15-17 Broadwick Street, W1F 0DL (7494 8888, www.yauatcha.com).

Drinking

Admiral Duncan 54 Old Compton Street, W1D 5PA (7437 5300).

American Bar The Beaumont, Brown Hart Gardens, W1K 6TF (7499 1001, www.thebeaumont.com).

Bradley's Spanish Bar 42-44 Hanway Street, W1T 1UT (7636 0359).

Bridge House 13 Westbourne Terrace Road, W2 6NG (7266 4326, www.thebridgehouselittlevenice.co.uk).

Coach & Horses 29 Greek Street, W1D 5DH (7437 5920, www.thecoachandhorses soho.co.uk).

Coburg Bar The Connaught, Carlos Place, W1K 2AL (7499 7070, www.theconnaught hotellondon.com).
Cock Tavern 27 Great Portland Street, W1W 8QE (7631 5002).
Comptons 51-53 Old Compton Street, W1D 6HN (3238 0163, www.faucetinn.com).
Connaught Bar The Connaught, Carlos Place, W1K 2AL (7499 7070, www.theconnaught hotellondon.com).
Elgin Bar 255 Elgin Avenue, W9 1NJ (7625 5511, www.theelgin.com).
French House 49 Dean Street, W1D 5BG (7437 2477, www.frenchhousesoho.com).
Frontline Club 13 Norfolk Place, W2 1QJ (7479 8950, www.frontlineclub.com).
Harp 47 Chandos Place, WC2N 4HS (7836 0291, www.harpcoventgarden.com).
Keeper's House Royal Academy of Arts, Burlington House, Piccadilly, W1J 0BD (7300 5881, www.keepershouse.org.uk).
King & Queen 1 Foley Street, W1W 6DL (7636 5619, www.thekingandqueenpub.com).
Lamb & Flag 33 Rose Street, WC2E 9EB (7497 9504).
Lucky Pig 5 Clipstone Street, W1W 6BB (7436 0035, www.theluckypig.co.uk).
Newman Arms 23 Rathbone Street, W1T 1NG (7636 1127, www.newmanarms.co.uk).
Ordnance Arms 29 Ordnance Hill, NW8 6PS (7722 0278).
Oskars Bar Dabbous, 39 Whitfield Street, WIT 2SF (7323 1544, www.dabbous.co.uk).
Prince Alfred & Formosa Dining Rooms 5A Formosa Street, W9 1EE (7286 3287, www.theprincealfred.com).
Remedy 124 Cleveland Street, W1T 6PQ (3489 3800, www.theremedylondon.com).

Victoria 10A Strathern Place, W2 2NH (7724 1191, www.fullers.co.uk).
Warrington 93 Warrington Crescent, W9 1EH (7286 8421, www.faucetinn.com).
Warwick Castle 6 Warwick Place, W9 2PX (7266 0921, www.metropolitanpubcompany.com).
Windmill 6-8 Mill Street, W1S 2AZ (7491 8050, www.windmillmayfair.co.uk).
Yard 57 Rupert Street, W1D 7PL (7437 2652, http://yardbar.co.uk).

Shopping

Alfie's Antique Market 13-25 Church Street, NW8 8DT (7723 6066, www.alfiesantiques.com).
Baker & Spice 20 Clifton Road, W9 1ST (7289 2499, www.bakerandspice.uk.com).
Berry Bros & Rudd 3 St James's Street, SW1A 1EG (0800 280 2440, www.bbr.com).
Browns (www.brownsfashion.com); 24-27 South Molton Street, W1K 5RD (7514 0016); Browns Labels for Less, 50 South Molton Street, W1K 5SB (7514 0052).
Burlington Arcade Piccadilly, W1J 0QJ (7630 1411, www.burlington-arcade.co.uk).
Cadenhead's Whisky Shop & Tasting Rooms 26 Chiltern Street, W1U 7QF (7935 6999, www.whiskytastingroom.com).
Christopher Kane 6-7 Mount Street, W1K 3BH (7493 3111, www.christopherkane.com).
Cire Trudon 36 Chiltern Street, W1U 7QJ (7486 7590, www.ciretrudon.com).
Clifton Nurseries 5A Clifton Villas, W9 2PH (7289 6851, www.clifton.co.uk).
Coco de Mer 23 Monmouth Street, WC2H 9DD (7836 8882, www.coco-de-mer.co.uk).
Cox & Power 35C Marylebone High Street, W1U 4QA (7935 3530, www.coxandpower.com).

Dolphin Square; Covent Garden Piazza

Cybercandy 3 Garrick Street, WC2E 9BF (0845 838 0958, www.cybercandy.co.uk).
Daunt Books 83-84 Marylebone High Street, W1U 4QW (7224 2295, www.dauntbooks.co.uk).
Dover Street Market 17-18 Dover Street, W1S 4LT (7518 0680, www.doverstreetmarket.com).
DR Harris 29 St James's Street, SW1A 1HB (7930 3915, www.drharris.co.uk).
Flying Horse Indigos Goods 8 Newburgh Street, W1F 7RJ (7287 1404, www.flying horseindigogoods.com).
Fopp 1 Earlham Street, WC2H 9LL (7845 9770, www.fopp.com).
Forbidden Planet 179 Shaftesbury Avenue, WC2H 8JR (7420 3666, www.forbiddenplanet.com).
Fortnum & Mason 181 Piccadilly, W1A 1ER (7734 8040, www.fortnumandmason.co.uk).
Foyles 107 Charing Cross Road, WC2H 0DT (7437 5660, www.foyles.co.uk).
La Fromagerie 2-6 Moxon Street, W1U 4EW (7935 0341, www.lafromagerie.co.uk).
Ginger Pig 8-10 Moxon Street, W1U 4EW (7935 7788, www.thegingerpig.co.uk).
Grays Antique Market 58 Davies Street & 1-7 Davies Mews, W1K 5AB (7629 7034, www.graysantiques.com).
I Camisa & Son 61 Old Compton Street, W1D 6HS (7437 7610, www.icamisa.co.uk).
Jenny Packham 3A Carlos Place, Mount Street, W1K 3AN (7493 6295, www.jennypackham.com).
Jimmy Choo 35A Dover Street, W1S 4NH (7495 8007, www.jimmychoo.com).
Kabiri 37 Marylebone High Street, W1U 4QE (7224 1808, www.kabiri.co.uk).
Kent & Sons 59 St John's Wood High Street, NW8 7NL (7722 2258, www.kents-butchers.co.uk).
Kingly Court Carnaby Street, opposite Broadwick Street, W1B 5PW (7333 8118, www.carnaby.co.uk).

Liberty Regent Street, W1B 5AH (7734 1234, www.liberty.co.uk).
Lina Stores 18 Brewer Street, W1F 0SH (7437 6482, www.linastores.co.uk).
Lock & Co 6 Saint James's Street, SW1A 1EF (7930 8874, www.lockhatters.co.uk).
London Coin Galleries 6 Shepherd Street, W1J 7JE (7493 0498, www.lcgcoins.com).
Marylebone Farmers' Market Cramer Street car park, behind Marylebone High Street, W1U 4EA (7833 0338, www.lfm.org.uk). 10am-2pm Sun.
McQ by Alexander McQueen 14 Dover Street, W1S 4LW (7318 2220, www.mcq.com/gb).
Miller Harris 14 Monmouth Street, WC2H 9HB (7836 9378, www.millerharris.com).
Mungo & Maud 79 Elizabeth Street, SW1W 9PJ (7022 1207, www.mungoandmaud.com).
Neal's Yard Dairy 17 Shorts Gardens, WC2H 9AT (7240 5700, www.nealsyarddairy.co.uk).
Neal's Yard Remedies (www.nealsyardremedies.com); 15 Neal's Yard, WC2H 9DP (7379 7222); 45 St John's Wood High Street, NW8 7NJ (7586 1647).
Nicholas Kirkwood 5 Mount Street, W1K 3NE (7290 1404, www.nicholaskirkwood.com).
Pankhurst 10 Newburgh Street, W1F 7RN (7287 9955, www.pankhurstlondon.com).
Panzer's 13-19 Circus Road, NW8 6PB (7722 8596, www.panzers.co.uk).
Paul Smith (www.paulsmith.co.uk); 40-44 Floral Street, WC2E 9TB (7379 7133); Paul Smith Sale Shop, 23 Avery Row, W1K 4AX (7493 1287).
Peggy Porschen 116 Ebury Street, SW1W 9QQ (7730 1316, www.peggyporschen.com).
Philip Treacy 69 Elizabeth Street, SW1W 9PJ (7730 3992, www.philiptreacy.co.uk).
Piccadilly Arcade SW1Y 6NH (7647 3000, www.piccadilly-arcade.com).

HIGHS & LOWS

As central as it gets

World-beating shopping

World-beating galleries

Royal Parks

▲ .... ▼

Too central for some

Huge inequality within the borough

Raoul's Deli 8-10 Clifton Road, W9 1SS (7289 6649, www.raoulsgourmet.com).

Reckless Records 30 Berwick Street, W1F 8RH (7437 4271, www.reckless.co.uk).

Rococo 45 Marylebone High Street, W1U 5HG (7935 7780, www.rococochocolates.com).

Roksanda 9 Mount Street, W1K 3NG (7613 6499, www.roksanda.com).

Royal Arcade 12 Abemarle Street & 28 Old Bond Street, W1S 4SD (no phone).

Les Senteurs 71 Elizabeth Street, SW1W 9PJ (7730 2322, www.lessenteurs.com).

Sheepdrove Organic Farm Family Butcher 5 Clifton Road, W9 1SZ (7266 3838, www. sheepdrove.com).

Sister Ray Berwick Street Market, 75 Berwick Street, W1F 8RP (7734 3297).

Solange Azagury-Partridge 5 Carlos Place, W1K 3AP (7792 0197, www.solange.co.uk).

Sounds of the Universe 7 Broadwick Street, W1F 0DA (7734 3430, www.soundsofthe universe.com).

Stanfords 12-14 Long Acre, WC2E 9LP (7836 1321, www.stanfords.co.uk).

Tatty Devine 44 Monmouth Street, WC2H 9EP (7836 2685, www.tattydevine.com).

Turmeaus 1 White Horse Street, Shepherd Market, W1J 7LB (7624 3351, www.cigarsltd.co.uk).

Victoria Beckham 36 Dover Street, W1S 4NH (7042 0700, www.victoriabeckham.com).

VV Rouleaux 102 Marylebone Lane, W1U 2QD (7224 5179, www.vvrouleaux.com).

Whiteleys 151 Queensway, W2 4YN (7229 8844, www.whiteleys.com).

Winery 4 Clifton Road, W9 1SS (7286 6475, www.thewineryuk.com).

Things to do

There are hundreds of venues and galleries in the City of Westminster – these are just a few. For the latest shows, visit www.timeout.com.

Cinemas & theatres

Adelphi Theatre Strand, WC2R 0NS (0844 412 4651, www.reallyuseful.com).

BBC Maida Vale Studios Delaware Road, W9 2LG (www.bbc.co.uk/showsandtours/venues/bbc_maida_vale_studios). Home to the BBC Radiophonic Workshop.

Coliseum St Martin's Lane, WC2N 4ES (7836 0111, www.eno.org). Home of the English National Opera.

Curzon (0330 500 1331, www.curzoncinemas.com); 38 Curzon Street, W1J 7TY; 99 Shaftesbury Avenue, W1D 5DY.

Dominion Theatre Tottenham Court Road, W1T 7AQ (7927 0900, www.dominiontheatre.org.uk).

Everyman (0871 906 9060, www.everyman cinema.com); 96-98 Baker Street, W1U 6TJ; 215 Sutherland Avenue, W9 1RU.

Leicester Square Theatre 6 Leicester Place, WC2H 7BX (7734 2222, www.leicestersquare theatre.com).

Lyceum Theatre Wellington Street, WC2E 7RQ (7420 8100, www.londontheatredirect.com).

Novello Theatre Aldwych, WC2B 4LD (0844 482 5170, www.delfontmackintosh.co.uk).

Open Air Theatre Regent's Park, NW1 4NR (0844 375 3460, box office 0844 826 4242, www. openairtheatre.org). Alfresco theatre, perfect for summery Shakespeare romps.

Piccadilly Comedy Club The Comedy Pub, 7 Oxendon Street, SW1Y 4EE (07568 352828, www.piccadillycomedy.co.uk).

Piccadilly Theatre 16 Denman Street, W1D 7DY (0844 871 7627, www.atgtickets.com).

Picturehouse Central 13 Coventry Street, W1D 7DH (0871 902 5747, www.picturehouses.com).

Prince Charles Cinema 7 Leicester Place, WC2H 7BP (7494 3654, www.princecharlescinema.com).

Prince of Wales Theatre Coventry Street, W1D 6AS (0844 482 5115, www.delfontmackintosh.co.uk).

Puppet Theatre Barge opposite 35 Blomfield Road, W9 2PF (7249 6876, www.puppetbarge.com).

Queen's Theatre Shaftesbury Avenue, W1D 6BA (0844 482 5160, www.delfontmackintosh.co.uk).

Regent Street Cinema 309 Regent Street, W1B 2UW (7911 5050, www.regentstreetcinema.com). The UK's first cinema, now restored.

Royal Opera House Bow Street, WC2E 9DD (7304 4000, www.royaloperahouse.org).

St James's Church 197 Piccadilly, W1J 9LL (7734 4511, www.sjp.org.uk). Lunchtime and evening concerts.

St Martin-in-the-Fields Trafalgar Square, WC2N 4JJ (7766 1100, www.stmartin-in-the-fields.org). 18th-century church, known for its classical concerts.

Shaftesbury Theatre 210 Shaftesbury Avenue, WC2H 8DP (7379 5399, www.shaftesbury theatre.com).

Soho Theatre 21 Dean Street, W1D 3NE (7478 0100, www.sohotheatre.com).

Theatre Royal Drury Lane Catherine Street, WC2B 5JF (0844 412 4660, www.londontheatre direct.com).

Wigmore Hall 36 Wigmore Street, W1U 2BP (7935 2141, www.wigmore-hall.org.uk). Top concert venue for chamber music and song.

Galleries & museums

Benjamin Franklin House 36 Craven Street, WC2N 5NF (7839 2006, www.benjamin franklinhouse.org).

Chiltern Firehouse

Tube, rail and bus Dozens of tube, rail and bus services run through the City of Westminster; for maps and service information, visit www.tfl.gov.uk
Commuter and leisure boat services Embankment Pier, Millbank Pier, Savoy Pier, Westminster Pier

ICA (Institute of Contemporary Arts) The Mall, SW1Y 5AH (7930 3647, www.ica.org.uk). Long-running alternative arts venue.

Lisson Gallery (7724 2739, www.lissongallery. com); 29 Bell Street, NW1 5BY; 52-54 Bell Street, NW1 5DA. Contemporary art.

London Transport Museum Covent Garden Piazza, WC2E 7BB (7379 6344, www.ltmuseum.co.uk).

National Gallery Trafalgar Square, WC2N 5DN (7747 2885, www.nationalgallery.org.uk).

National Portrait Gallery St Martin's Place, WC2H 0HE (7306 0055, www.npg.org.uk).

Royal Academy of Arts Burlington House, Piccadilly, W1J 0BD (7300 8000, www.royal academy.org.uk).

Serpentine Gallery Kensington Gardens, W2 3XA (7402 6075, www.serpentinegallery.org). Excellent art exhibitions and summer pavilion.

Somerset House Strand, WC2R 0RN (7845 4600, www.somersethouse.org.uk). Includes the Courtauld Gallery (www.courtauld.ac.uk).

Tate Britain Millbank, SW1P 4RG (7887 8888, www.tate.org.uk).

Timothy Taylor 15 Carlos Place, W1K 2EX (7409 3344, http://timothytaylorgallery.com).

Victoria Miro 14 St George Street, W1S 1FE (3205 8910, www.victoria-miro.com).

Wallace Collection Hertford House, Manchester Square, W1U 3BN (7563 9500, www.wallace collection.org). Fine private art collection.

White Cube 25-26 Masons Yard, SW1Y 6BU (7930 5373, www.whitecube.com).

Other attractions

Buckingham Palace & Royal Mews
Buckingham Palace Road, SW1W 1QH (7766 7300, www.royal.gov.uk).

Houses of Parliament Parliament Square, SW1A 0AA (Commons information 7219 4272, Lords information 7219 3107, tours 0870 906 3773, www.parliament.uk).

Royal Courts of Justice Strand, WC2A 2LL (7947 6000, www.justice.gov.uk). Members of the public are allowed to attend certain trials.

Westminster Abbey 20 Dean's Yard, SW1P 3PA (7222 5152, tours 7654 4834, www.westminster-abbey.org).

Westminster Cathedral Victoria Street, SW1P 1QW (7798 9055, www.westminster cathedral.org.uk).

Gigs, clubs & comedy

229 229 Great Portland Street, W1W 5PN (7631 8379, www.229thevenue.com).

Amused Moose Moonlighting Nightclub 17 Greek Street, W1D 4DR (7287 3727, www. amusedmoose.com).

Boat Show *Tattershall Castle* (boat), Victoria Embankment, SW1A 2HR (07932 658895, www.boatshowcomedy.co.uk).

Borderline Orange Yard, Manette Street, W1D 4JB (7734 5547, www.theborderlinelondon.com).

Comedy Store 1A Oxendon Street, SW1Y 4EE (0844 871 7699, http://thecomedystore.co.uk).

Freedom Bar 60-66 Wardour Street, W1F 0TA (7734 0071, www.freedombarsoho.com).

G-A-Y 30 Old Compton Street, W1D 4UR (7494 2756, www.g-a-y.co.uk).

Heaven The Arches, Villiers Street, WC2N 6NG (7930 2020, www.heavennightclub-london.com).

Pizza Express Jazz Club 10 Dean Street, W1D 3RW (0845 602 7017, www.pizzaexpresslive.co.uk).

Ronnie Scott's 47 Frith Street, W1D 4HT (7439 0747, www.ronniescotts.co.uk). Famous, long-running jazz venue.

Shadow Lounge 5 Brewer Street, W1F 0RF (7317 9270, www.theshadowlounge.co.uk).

Social 5 Little Portland Street, W1W 7JD (7636 4992, www.thesocial.com).

Storm Nightclub 28A Leicester Square, WC2H 7LE (07760 488119, www.99clubcomedy.com). Includes 99 Club for comedy.

Green spaces

Green Park www.royalparks.org.uk.

Grosvenor Square W1A 2LQ. Large Georgian square, dominated by the US Embassy for a few more years.

Hyde Park www.royalparks.org.uk.

St James's Park www.royalparks.org.uk.

Paddington Recreation Ground Randolph Avenue, W9 1PD (7641 3642, www.gll.org). Facilities for tennis, cricket, football and athletics, plus a gym.

Regent's Park www.royalparks.org.uk.

Gyms & leisure centres

Jubilee Sports Centre Caird Street, W10 4RR (8960 9629, www.gll.org).

Porchester Centre Queensway, W2 5HS (7792 2919, www.gll.org).

Queen Mother Sports Centre 223 Vauxhall Bridge Road, SW1V 1EL (7630 5522, www.gll.org).

Queens Ice Rink & Bowling 17 Queensway, W2 4QP (7229 0172, www.queensiceandbowl.co.uk).

Seymour Leisure Centre Seymour Place, W1H 5TJ (7723 8019, www.gll.org).

Outdoor pursuits

Serpentine Swimming Club (http:// serpentineswimmingclub.com). Hardcore open-air swimming enthusiasts in Hyde Park.

Westminster Boating Base 136 Grosvenor Road, SW1V 3JY (7821 7389, www.westminster boatingbase.co.uk).

Spectator sports

Lord's Cricket Ground St John's Wood Road, NW8 8QN (Marylebone Cricket Club 7616 8500, tickets 7432 1000, www.lords.org).

Schools

Primary

There are 38 state primary schools in the borough, 26 of which are church schools. There are also 16 independent primaries, including one American, one French, one international and one Jewish school. See www.westminster.gov.uk, www.education.gov.uk/edubase and www.ofsted.gov.uk for information.

Secondary

Grey Coat Hospital Girls' School St Andrew's Building, Grey Coat Place, SW1P 2DY (7969 1998, www.gch.org.uk). Church of England; girls only.
King Solomon Academy Penfold Street, NW1 6RX (7563 6900, www.kingsolomonacademy.org).
Paddington Academy 50 Marylands Road, W9 2DR (7479 3900, www.paddington-academy.org.uk).
Pimlico Academy Lupus Street, SW1V 3AT (7828 0881, www.pimlicoacademy.org).
Portland Place 56-58 Portland Place, W1B 1NJ (7307 8700, www.portland-place.co.uk). Private.
Queen's College 43-49 Harley Street, W1G 8BT (7291 7000, www.qcl.org.uk). Girls only; private.
Quintin Kynaston School Marlborough Hill, NW8 0NL (7722 8141, www.qkschool.org.uk).
St Augustine's CE School Oxford Road, NW6 5SN (7328 3434, www.staugustineshigh.org). Church of England.
St George's Catholic School Lanark Road, W9 1RB (7328 0904, www.stgeorgesrc.org). Roman Catholic.
St Marylebone CE School 64 Marylebone High Street, W1U 5BA (7935 4704, www.stmarylebone school.com). Church of England; girls only; mixed sixth form.
Sylvia Young Theatre School 1 Nutford Place, W1H 5YZ (7258 2330, www.sylviayoungtheatreschool.co.uk). Private.
Westminster Academy 255 Harrow Road, W2 5EZ (7121 0600, www.westminsteracademy.biz).
Westminster City Boys' School 55 Palace Street, SW1E 5HJ (7641 8760, www.wcsch.com). Boys only; private.
Westminster School Little Dean's Yard, SW1P 3PF (7963 1000, www.westminster.org.uk). Boys only; mixed sixth form; private.

Property

Local estate agents

Bensons www.bensonsestateagents.co.uk
Cool Cribs http://coolcribs.co.uk

Curtis Residential www.curtisresidential.co.uk
Douglas & Gordon www.douglasandgordon.com
Fox Gregory ww.foxgregory.co.uk
James Taylor Property www.jamestaylor property.com
Manors www.manors.co.uk
Marsh & Parsons www.marshandparsons.co.uk
Robert Irving & Burns www.rib.co.uk
Wallsway www.wallsway.co.uk
York Estates www.yorkestates.co.uk

Local knowledge

www.fitzroviajournal.com.
www.marylebonejournal.com
www.maryleboneonline.co.uk
www.mayfairtimes.co.uk
www.mountstreetmayfair.co.uk
www.news.fitzrovia.org.uk
www.savesoho.com
www.thesohosociety.org.uk

USEFUL INFO

Borough size
2,149 hectares

Population
235,000

Ethnic mix
White 69.5%
Asian or Asian British 12.8%
Black or Black British 7.2%
Chinese or other 6.6%
Mixed 4.0%

Westminster City Council
Westminster City Hall, 64 Victoria Street, SW1E 6QP (7641 6000, www.westminster.gov.uk).

Council run by
Conservatives

MPs
Cities of London & Westminster, Mark Field (Conservative); Westminster North, Karen Buck (Labour)

Main recycling centre
Smugglers Way, SW18 1JS (8871 2788)

Council tax
£448.50 to £1,345.48

Outer Boroughs

Barnet

For London living with an edge, look elsewhere – Barnet's attractions are distinctly
suburban. The borough takes in traffic-clogged Hendon, Jewish Golders Green,
East, Central and North Finchley, wealthy and leafy Totteridge and, at the northern
edge, self-sufficient High Barnet. Oodles of 1930s semis, golf courses, excellent
schools and plentiful parkland are on offer along the way.

AVERAGE PROPERTY PRICE

Detached	Terraced
£1,045,669	£435,623

Semi-detached	Flat
£580,095	£330,087

AVERAGE RENTAL PRICE PER WEEK

1 bed	3 bed
£239	£390

2 bed	
£299	

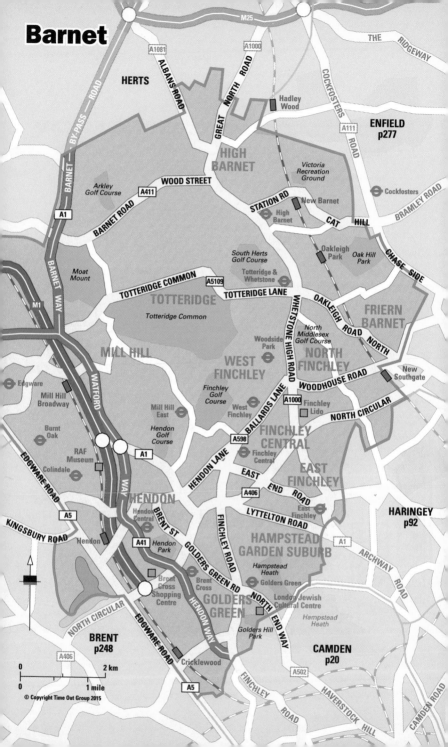

Barnet

HERTS

M25

A1081

A1000

THE RIDGEWAY

ALBANS ROAD

GREAT NORTH ROAD

BY-PASS ROAD

BARNET

Hadley Wood

COCKFOSTERS ROAD

ENFIELD
p277

A111

BRAMLEY ROAD

HIGH BARNET

Victoria Recreation Ground

Arkley Golf Course

WOOD STREET

A411

Cockfosters

BARNET ROAD

A1

STATION RD

High Barnet

New Barnet

CAT HILL

CHASE SIDE

BARNET WAY

M1

Moat Mount

South Herts Golf Course

Totteridge & Whetstone

A5109

TOTTERIDGE COMMON

TOTTERIDGE LANE

Oakleigh Park

Oak Hill Park

WHETSTONE HIGH ROAD

OAKLEIGH ROAD NORTH

FRIERN BARNET

TOTTERIDGE

Totteridge Common

MILL HILL

Woodside Park

North Middlesex Golf Course

NORTH FINCHLEY

New Southgate

WEST FINCHLEY

WOODHOUSE ROAD

NORTH CIRCULAR

Edgware

WATFORD

Finchley Golf Course

West Finchley

BALLARDS LANE

A1000

Finchley Lido

Mill Hill Broadway

Mill Hill East

A598

Hendon Golf Course

Burnt Oak

RAF Museum

A1

FINCHLEY CENTRAL

Finchley Central

Colindale

HENDON LANE

EAST END ROAD

EAST FINCHLEY

A406

East Finchley

HARINGEY
p92

EDGWARE ROAD

A5

WATFORD WAY

BRENT ST

HENDON

Hendon Central

A41

Hendon Park

LYTTELTON ROAD

A1

ARCHWAY ROAD

KINGSBURY ROAD

Hendon

GOLDERS GREEN RD

FINCHLEY ROAD

HAMPSTEAD GARDEN SUBURB

Hampstead Heath

Golders Green

Brent Cross Shopping Centre

Brent Cross

HENDON WAY

GOLDERS GREEN

London Jewish Cultural Centre

NORTH END WAY

Hampstead Heath

BRENT
p248

NORTH CIRCULAR

EDGWARE ROAD

Golders Hill Park

CAMDEN
p20

A406

0   2 km
0   1 mile

Cricklewood

A5

A502

FINCHLEY ROAD

HAVERSTOCK HILL

CAMDEN ROAD

© Copyright Time Out Group 2015

Neighbourhoods

Golders Green NW11

In a classic story of the suburbs, Golders Green was transformed by the introduction of the tube in 1907. The Golders Green Northern line station and a busy bus terminus lie at the neighbourhood's core, by a major junction that sees Golders Green Road crossing Finchley Road. Nearby is the majestic-looking Golders Green Hippodrome, now the El-Shaddai International Christian Centre. Signs at the station point the way to Golders Green Crematorium (opened 1902), where Sigmund Freud, George Bernard Shaw, Marc Bolan and Amy Winehouse were cremated.

The area has become synonymous with Jewish London, hence the presence of numerous kosher businesses, particularly along Golders Green Road and the stretch of Finchley Road by Temple Fortune. In order to observe the Jewish Shabbat, many of the district's businesses close from sunset on Friday to sunset on Saturday. The weekly reopening on Saturday night sees Golders Green buzzing with young people hanging out in the cafés, and local bakeries doing a roaring trade in salmon and cream cheese bagels.

Sunday, too, is a busy shopping day. Factory outlet Gold & Son, specialising in bargain suits and shoes, cheerfully advertises itself as 'the big red building on Golders Green Road'. Just up the road, genteel Temple Fortune is home to a number of small independents, including Brian's (kids' shoes), the Bookworm (kids' books) and Joseph's (more books).

Heading up the hill towards Hampstead, you'll find Golders Hill Park, a popular and nicely laid-out patch of greenery. A little further up the hill is the London Jewish Cultural Centre, attractively housed in Ivy House, where ballerina Anna Pavlova once lived.

With Golders Green home to a long-established Jewish community, it's no surprise that this is a great place to sample Jewish cuisine. Both Ashkenazi (Russian and east European) and Sephardi (Middle Eastern) dishes are generously represented. Since the sorry demise of both Solly's and Bloom's, bustling Sami's is the place to go for Israeli-style food, with generous portions of houmous, grilled meat and excellent salads. There's also supermarket Kosher Kingdom, Soyo café, classic Jewish deli Platters, fishmongers Sam Stoller & Son and JA Corney, and bustling bagel bakeries Carmelli and Daniels. Other kosher options include La Fiesta (Argentinian), Met Su Yan (Asian) and – relocated from Hendon – Isola Bella restaurant-café. Of course, it isn't all kosher food round here – for sushi, try Café Japan.

Hampstead Garden Suburb NW11

Bordered by arterial Falloden Way (A1) and Finchley Road, Hampstead Garden Suburb remains a relatively well-kept secret, although it's growing in popularity. Founded in 1907 by heiress Dame Henrietta Barnett, HGS was an idealistic piece of social engineering that aimed to provide housing for all social classes, from workers' cottages to grand residences for the toffs.

Gardens and green spaces played a central part in Dame Henrietta's vision; an average density of eight dwellings to an acre allowed for ample gardens. The attractive Arts and Crafts-style houses are much sought after – and, not surprisingly, command premium prices. The dream of the proletariat living next door to the elite died here long ago.

The buildings on the central square and at 140-142 Hampstead Way are frequently visited by fans of classic architecture and town planning but, despite the appealing exteriors, there is something stand-offish about the neighbourhood: the enclave was designed with religion and education at its centre and roads that deliberately kink to deter traffic; even the Lutyens churches bear stern notices forbidding ball games against their walls; and definitely no pubs.

There are no shops within Hampstead Garden Suburb either, but residents are well catered for by nearby Temple Fortune.

East Finchley N2 and Finchley Central N3

Of the several Finchleys, East Finchley is the only one inside the North Circular and offers the strongest sense of place, with an identity and community all of its own. It even has an art deco tube station topped with a striking figure of an archer.

Positioned cheek-by-jowl with Highgate and Muswell Hill, and with desirable Victorian and Edwardian housing stock, East Finchley appeals to a liberal, arty crowd, as evidenced by its lively annual arts festival. Although the homely high street – part of the Great North Road – is often congested, it is also narrow enough to allow for life on a human scale. Local businesses include such London high street rarities as a decent fishmonger (A Scott & Son), record shop (Alan's), greengrocer (Tony's Continental) and bookshop (Black Gull Books).

Adult learners are amply catered for by the Hampstead Garden Suburb Institute, while the jewel in the district's crown is the Phoenix Cinema. Opened in 1910 and one of the UK's oldest continuously operating picture houses, this deco gem is one of the capital's few remaining independent cinemas and is loyally supported by locals and big-name patrons, who now include Benedict Cumberbatch. Families, especially those with toddlers, make a beeline for Cherry Tree Wood and its playground, while the no less

The University of London Observatory at Mill Hill holds open evenings for the public, fortnightly on Fridays, October to March.

charming Coldfall Wood offers slightly more testing terrain and a wealth of flora and fauna to spot. The park hosts a community festival every summer.

The green fields of College Farm, formerly the showcase farm for Express Dairies, is a reminder of Finchley Central's rural past. Any pastoral feel, however, is long gone, with the area now seeing a high volume of traffic pass along its congested high street (Ballards Lane). Good transport links, both tube and buses, have attracted a mixed population, including a sizeable Jewish contingent, Japanese expats (catered for by Japanese food shop Atari-Ya) and a recent influx of young Poles. For a much-needed breath of fresh air, residents head to Victoria Park.

East Finchley has a limited but eclectic range of cuisines, from the rustic Italian fare of Bufi to the splendid Punjabi restaurant and takeaway, Majjo's. Finchley Central has the more sedate options of Rani, a Gujarati vegetarian restaurant, and the charming Vietnamese Vy Nam Café, while fine fish and chips and traditional seafood are on offer at Leon and Tony Manzi's perpetually popular fish restaurant, the Two Brothers. North Finchley has a branch of Khoai Café,

a good-quality Vietnamese restaurant. Those looking for reassuringly familiar chain eateries are well catered for on the North Circular, where Brent Cross Shopping Centre has branches of Carluccio's, Leon, Nando's, Pizza Express, Wagamama and Yo! Sushi.

And for a much-needed drink, East Finchley has the Bald Faced Stag gastropub, much improved after a 2014 refurb and now with excellent seasonal lunch and dinner menus. Over in Finchley Central, the Catcher in the Rye, with football on its TV screens, reasonably priced pub grub and quiz nights, is also popular.

Despite having its own tube station, West Finchley exists in Finchley Central's shadow. Primarily residential, it lacks a real shopping centre, but plus points include comparatively peaceful streets, views over the green belt and proximity to Finchley Golf Club.

North Finchley's most prominent landmark is the Artsdepot complex, which towers over Tally Ho Corner. It houses a well-appointed arts centre offering a good variety of reasonably priced entertainment, a bus depot and luxury apartments. For additional recreation, locals can head to nearby 1930s Finchley Lido (now housing a Vue cinema, fast-food outlets, a bowling alley and a swimming pool). The most desirable houses are tucked away in the peaceful streets around Woodside Park, the location of the nearest tube station.

Totteridge and Whetstone N20

Drive into Whetstone from the south and it seems distinctly unprepossessing: a B&Q sits opposite a large timber merchant, and Barnet House – the tall, grim tower block that contains Barnet Council's offices – looming in the background. However, turn left into Totteridge Lane, towards Totteridge Village, and you're soon travelling tree-lined lanes between substantial houses. Home to the seriously wealthy (including footballers and their WAGs), the mansions here are discreetly set back from the road and have fine green-belt views. However, despite the area's prosperity, Whetstone High Road shows little sign of conspicuous consumption – unless you count the branches of Waitrose and Marks & Spencer.

The prestigious South Herts Golf Club, its course designed by golf legend Harry Vardon, is among the area's hidden assets. Even further west, flanking Barnet Way,

Soyo, Golders Green

TRANSPORT

Tube line Northern
Rail services into King's Cross,
Moorgate
Main bus routes into central London
13, 16, 82, 113; night buses N13, N16;
24-hour buses 83, 134, 189

are Scratchwood and Moat Mount open spaces, constituting the largest area of woodland in Barnet.

Whetstone's bar-restaurant the Haven offers what passes for genuine glamour in this corner of Barnet – eat here or try a cocktail. Also in Whetstone, El Vaquero draws crowds for its Brazilian/Argentinian grilled meats (it has another branch in Mill Hill), while Italian joint Al Fresco is perpetually bustling.

One of Totteridge's best-known pubs, meanwhile, is the Orange Tree, which gets top marks for its picturesque location down tree-lined Totteridge Lane.

High Barnet EN5

Once a staging post on the main road to London, High Barnet still has a bit of an old-fashioned, out-of-town feel, which is much relished by the residents. 'Barnet Church' (actually St John the Baptist) is the dominating local landmark. It marks the start of the High Street, a narrow spot known appropriately as 'the squeeze'. The top of the church tower is meant to be the highest point between London and York; be that as it may, the tower certainly commands spectacular views. Historically, Barnet was famous for its fair, a major livestock-trading event. 'Barnet Fair', with the second word characteristically dropped, became cockney rhyming slang for 'hair'.

Even today, Barnet has a sense of community to match its parochialism,

with events such as Scout parades, church fêtes and cricket on the green. There's even a professional football team (Barnet FC, nicknamed the Bees), which commands a passionate following and regained its Football League status in 2015. Barnet Market, granted a charter by King John in 1199, plied a thriving trade in cattle; these days, traders operate on St Albans Road every Wednesday and Saturday, selling fish, meat, fresh fruit and veg, as well as flowers. High Barnet also has the Spires, a pleasant, low-level shopping centre constructed around small open-air squares, which offers the Body Shop, New Look, Waterstones and WH Smith. At the Monken Hadley end of the High Street, you'll find Bargain Buys (an Aladdin's cave of household goods), Wanders (chic footware) and the Present (fancily wrapped gifts).

Easy access to green spaces is much appreciated by residents, who walk their dogs, cycle and fly kites on the Common and Hadley Green (where the Battle of Barnet was fought in 1471, during the Wars of the Roses). There are also a number of traditional pubs: try Ye Olde Monken Holt or the White Lion. Ye Olde Mitre Inne offers a spruced-up trad pub vibe and the Sebright Arms is a firm local favourite. Eating options are fewer, but Chinese restaurant Emchai is a solid choice and the Village Greek, remarkably, is as homely as the name suggests.

On the downside, life here in the suburbs can be dull. Other than the flicks at the huge

1930s Odeon down the road, there is little cultural life on offer, and the fact that Barnet's yob element comes to the fore at night makes walking around after dark a depressing experience. Barnet is, however, seeing a steady influx of families from other parts of north London drawn by more affordable property prices and good schools.

Eating

Al Fresco 1327 High Road, Whetstone, N20 9HR (8445 8880, www.alfresco-restaurant.co.uk).
Bald Faced Stag 69 High Road, East Finchley, N2 8AB (8442 1201, www.thebaldfacedstagn2.co.uk).
Bufi 84 High Road, East Finchley, N2 9PN (8883 4720, www.bufirestaurants.com).
Café Japan 626 Finchley Road, NW11 7RR (8455 6854).
Emchai 78 High Street, Barnet, EN5 5SN (8364 9993).
La Fiesta 235 Golders Green Road, NW11 9ES (8458 0444, www.lafiestalondon.com).
Haven Bistro & Bar 1363-1365 High Road, Whetstone, N20 9LN (8445 7419, www.haven-bistro.co.uk).
Isola Bella 111A-113 Golders Green Road, NW11 8HR (8455 2228, www.isolabella.co.uk).
Khoai Café 362 Ballards Lane, N12 0EE (8445 2039, www.khoai.co.uk).
Majjo's 1 Fortis Green, N2 9JR (8883 4357, www.majjos.com).

Met Su Yan 134 Golders Green Road, NW11 8HP (8458 8088, www.metsuyan.co.uk).
Rani 7 Long Lane, N3 2PR (8349 4386, www.raniuk.com).
Sami's 118 Golders Green Road, NW11 8HB (8458 7003, www.samisrestaurant.co.uk).
Soyo 94 Golders Green Road, NW11 8HB (8458 8788).
Two Brothers Fish Restaurant 297-303 Regents Park Road, N3 1DP (8346 0469, www.twobrothers.co.uk).
El Vaquero 1105-1111 High Street, Whetstone, N20 0PT (8445 1882, www.elvaquero.co.uk).
Village Greek 24 Lytton Road, EN5 5BY (8449 1341, www.thevillagegreek.co.uk).
Vy Nam Café 371 Regents Park Road, N3 1DE (8371 4222, www.vynam.co.uk).

Drinking

Catcher in the Rye 317-319 Regents Park Road, N3 1DP (8343 4369, www.faucetinn.com).
Orange Tree 7 Totteridge Village, N20 8NX (8343 7031, www.theorangetreetotteridge.co.uk).
Sebright Arms 9 Alston Road, EN5 4ET (8449 6869, www.sebrightarmsbarnet.com).
White Lion 50 St Albans Road, EN5 4LA (8449 4560, www.white-lion-barnet.co.uk).
Ye Olde Mitre Inne 58 High Street, EN5 5SJ (8449 5701).
Ye Olde Monken Holt 193 High Street, EN5 5SU (8449 4280, www.yeoldemonkenholt-barnet.co.uk).

Royal Air Force Museum

Shopping

A Scott & Son 94 High Road, East Finchley,
N2 9EB (8444 7606, www.ascottandson.co.uk).
Alan's Records 218 High Road, East Finchley,
N2 9AY (8883 0234, www.alansrecords.com).
Atari-Ya (www.atariya.co.uk); 595 High
Road, North Finchley, N12 0DY (8446 6669);
15-16 Monkville Parade, NW11 0AL
(8458 7626).
Bargain Buys 4 High Street, Hadley Parade,
EN5 5SX (8440 7983).
Barnet Market Chipping Close, St Albans
Road, EN5 4LP (8440 0203, www.fobm.co.uk).
Black Gull Books 121 High Road, East Finchley,
N2 8AG (8444 4717).
Bookworm 1177 Finchley Road, NW11 0AA
(8201 9811, www.thebookworm.uk.com).
Brent Cross Shopping Centre NW4 3FP
(8202 8095, www.brentcross.co.uk).
Brian's 2 Halleswelle Parade, Finchley Road,
NW11 0DL (8455 7001).
Carmelli Bakery 126-128 Golders Green Road,
NW11 8HB (8455 2074, www.carmelli.co.uk).
Daniels 12-13 Halleswelle Parade, Finchley
Road, NW11 0DL (8455 5826, www.daniels
catering.co.uk).
Gold & Son Factory Outlet 110-114 Golders
Green Road, NW11 8HB (8905 5721, www.the
bigredbuilding.com).
JA Corney 16 Halleswelle Parade, Finchley
Road, NW11 0DL (8455 9588).

HIGHS & LOWS

Kosher cuisine, London's best bagels

Genuine village feel in some areas

Inspiration for cockney slang

Large chunks of green belt

Easy access to the M1

Lots of golf

Suburban and dull in some stretches

Traffic-laden roads

Only just in the A-Z

Lots of golf

Joseph's Bookstore 2 Ashbourne Parade,
1257 Finchley Road, NW11 0AD (8731 7575,
www.josephsbookstore.com).
Kosher Kingdom Russell Parade, NW11 9NN
(8455 1429, www.kosherkingdom.co.uk).
Platters 10 Halleswelle Parade, Finchley Road,
NW11 0DL (8455 7345).
Present 220-222 High Street, Barnet, EN5 5SZ
(8441 6400).
Sam Stoller & Son 28 Temple Fortune Parade,
Finchley Road, NW11 0QS (8458 1429).
Spires 111 High Street, EN5 5XY (8449 7505,
www.thespiresbarnet.co.uk). Shopping centre.
Tony's Continental 140 High Road, East Finchley
N2 9ED (8444 5545).
Wanders 180 High Street, Barnet, EN5 5SZ (8449
2520, www.wanders.co.uk).

Things to do

Cinemas & theatres

Artsdepot 5 Nether Street, Tally Ho Corner,
N12 0GA (8369 5454, www.artsdepot.co.uk).
Multidisciplinary arts venue, featuring comedy,
dance and theatre productions, plus lots of
activities for kids.
Bull Theatre 68 High Street, EN5 5SJ (8441 5010,
www.thebulltheatre.com).
Cineworld Staples Corner Retail Park, Geron Way,
NW2 6LW (0871 200 2000, www.cineworld.co.uk).
Odeon Barnet Great North Road, EN5 1AB (0333
006 7777, www.odeon.co.uk). No phone bookings.
Phoenix Cinema 52 High Road, N2 9PJ (8444
6789, www.phoenixcinema.co.uk).
Vue Great North Leisure Park, Chaplin Square,
N12 0GL (0871 224 0240, www.myvue.com).

Galleries & museums

Barnet Museum 31 Wood Street, EN5 4BE (8440
8066, www.barnetmuseum.co.uk). Local history
museum, holding everything from a fine costume
collection to archaeological remains.
Royal Air Force Museum Grahame Park Way,
NW9 5LL (8205 2266, www.rafmuseum.org.uk).
More than 100 aircraft (including a Lancaster and
a Spitfire) are displayed on the site of the original
London Aerodrome.

Other attractions

Barnet Walks (8440 6805, www.barnetwalks.
talktalk.net). Programme of guided history walks
in the borough running Feb-Dec.
JW3 341-351 Finchley Road, NW3 6ET (7433 8988,
www.jw3.org.uk). This combination of the London
Jewish Cultural Centre and the Jewish Community
Centre of London forms a hub offering a range of
courses, exhibitions, films, music and lectures.

University of London Observatory 553 Watford Way, NW7 2QS (3549 5807, www.ulo.ucl.ac.uk). Guided tours available if pre-booked.

Green spaces

For more details, see www.barnet.gov.uk.
Arrandene Open Space Wise Lane, NW7. Ancient hedgerows and abundant wildflowers.
Cherry Tree Wood Summerlee Avenue, N2. Sports facilities and play areas.
Coldfall Woods Creighton Avenue, N2, N10 (www.coldfallwoods.co.uk). Ancient woodland. Forms the boundary line between Barnet and Haringey.
Coppetts Wood Colney Hatch Lane, N10, N11, N12. Nature reserve.
Dollis Valley Green Walk Around ten miles in length, it links the green belt and Hampstead Heath, via the borough's green spaces. Follows Dollis Brook.
Edgewarebury Park Edgwarebury Lane, HA8. Sports pitches, playgrounds and café.
Friary Park Friary Road, N12. Landscaped grounds, a popular playground, a skateboard park and a child-friendly café.
Glebelands Summers Lane, N12. Nature reserve with trails and volunteer opportunities.
Golders Hill Park NW11. Adjoins Hampstead Heath, West Heath. Zoo, walled garden, water feature and duck ponds.
Hadley Green Great North Road, EN5. Trees, grassland and pond.
Hampstead Heath Extension Northerly Annexe, Hampstead Way, NW11. Created from farmland.
Moat Mount Open Space Barnet Way, EN5, Nature reserve. Outdoor activity centre.
Monken Hadley Common Camlet Way, EN5.
Oak Hill Park Parkside Gardens, EN4 (7261 0447). Sports facilities and play areas. Includes a nature reserve, Oak Hill Woods and Meadow, good for bat-spotting.
Rowley Green Rowley Lane, EN5 (01727 858901). Woods, grasslands and ponds. Includes a nature reserve.
Scratchwood Park Barnet Way, NW7. Nature reserve. Ancient woodland and muntjac deer. Model-plane airfield.
Totteridge Common N20.
Totteridge Fields Hendon Wood Lane, NW7. Nature reserve.
Victoria Park Ballards Lane, N3, N12. Grassland, playgrounds, sports facilities and gardens.

Gyms & leisure centres

Barnet Burnt Oak Leisure Centre Watling Avenue, HA8 0NP (8201 0982, www.better.org.uk).
Barnet Copthall Leisure Centre Champions Way, NW4 1PX (8457 9900, www.better.org.uk).

Church Farm Swimming Pool Church Hill Road, EN4 8XE (8368 7070, www.better.org.uk).
Compton Leisure Centre Summers Lane, N12 0RF (8361 8658, www.better.org.uk).
David Lloyd Finchley Leisure Way, High Road, Finchley, N12 0QZ (0345 129 6791, www.davidlloydleisure.co.uk). Private.
Finchley Lido Leisure Centre Chaplin House, Great North Leisure Park, Chaplin Square, N12 0GL (8343 9830, www.better.org.uk).
Hendon Leisure Centre Marble Drive, NW2 1XQ (8455 0818, www.better.org.uk).
Laboratory Spa & Health Club 1A Hall Lane, NW4 4TJ (8457 3300, www.labspa.co.uk). Private.
LA Fitness (www.lafitness.co.uk); East End Road, N3 2TA (8346 7253); 152-154 Golders Green Road, NW11 8HE (8731 7312). Private.
Oakleigh Park School of Swimming 100 Oakleigh Road North, N20 9EZ (8445 1911, www.swimoakleighpark.co.uk).
Virgin Active (www.virginactive.co.uk); 108-110 Cricklewood Lane, NW2 2DS (3582 4939); 260 Hendon Way, NW4 3NL (3582 4824); 264 Princess Park Manor, Royal Drive, N11 3BG (3582 4807). Private.

Outdoor pursuits

Arkley Golf Club Rowley Green Road, EN5 3HL (8449 0394, www.club-noticeboard.co.uk/arkley).
Finchley Golf Club Nether Court, Frith Lane, NW7 1PU (8346 5086, www.finchleygolfclub.com).
Hendon Golf Club Ashley Walk, Devonshire Road, NW7 1DG (8346 6023, www.hendongolfclub.co.uk).
Mill Hill Golf Club 100 Barnet Way, NW7 3AL (8959 2339, www.millhillgc.co.uk).
North Middlesex Golf Club The Manor House, Friern Barnet Lane, N20 0NL (8445 1604, www.northmiddlesexgc.co.uk).
Old Fold Manor Golf Club Old Fold Lane, EN5 4QN (8440 9185, www.oldfoldmanor.co.uk).
South Herts Golf Club Links Drive, N20 8QU (8445 2035, www.southhertsgolfclub.co.uk).

Spectator sports

Barnet FC The Hive, Camrose Avenue, HA8 6AG (8381 3800, www.barnetfc.com).

Schools

Primary

There are 76 state primaries in Barnet, including 23 church schools and nine Jewish schools. There are also 18 independent primary schools, including nine faith schools and one international school. See www.barnet.gov.uk, www.education.gov.uk/edubase and www.ofsted.gov.uk for more information.

Secondary

Ashmole Academy Cecil Road, N14 5RJ (8361
2703, www.ashmoleacademy.org).
Bishop Douglass School Hamilton Road, N2 0SQ
(8444 5211, www.bishopdouglass.barnet.sch.uk).
Roman Catholic.
Christ's College Finchley East End Road, N2 0SE
(8349 3581, www.christscollegefinchley.org.uk).
Boys only; mixed sixth form.
Compton School Summers Lane, N12 0QG (8368
1783, www.thecomptonschool.co.uk).
Copthall School Pursley Road, NW7 2EP (8959
1937, www.copthallschool.org.uk). Girls only.
East Barnet School 5 Chestnut Grove, EN4 8PU
(8344 2100, www.eastbarnet.barnet.sch.uk).
Finchley Catholic High School Woodside Lane,
N12 8TA (8445 0105, www.finchley.fluencycms.
co.uk). Roman Catholic; boys only; mixed sixth form.
Friern Barnet School Hemington Avenue, N11
3LS (8368 2777, www.friern.barnet.sch.uk).
Specialist arts college.
Hasmonean High School Holders Hill Road,
NW4 1NA (8203 1411, www.hasmonean.co.uk).
Jewish; boys only.
Hasmonean High School 2-4 Page Street, NW7 2EU
(8203 1411, www.hasmonean.co.uk). Jewish; girls only.
Hendon School Golders Rise, NW4 2HP (8202
9004, www.hendonschool.co.uk).
Henrietta Barnett School Central Square, NW11
7BN (8458 8999, www.hbschool.org.uk). Girls only.
Jewish Community Secondary School
Castlewood Road, EN4 9GE (8344 2220,
www.jcoss.org). Jewish.
London Academy Spur Road, HA8 8DE (8238
1100, www.londonacademy.org.uk).
Mill Hill County High School Worcester Crescent,
NW7 4LL (0844 477 2424, www.mhchs.org.uk).
Queen Elizabeth's Girls' School High Street,
Barnet, EN5 5RR (8449 2984, www.qegschool.org.
uk). Girls only.
Queen Elizabeth's School Queen's Road, EN5
4DQ (8441 4646, www.qebarnet.co.uk). Boys only.
St James' Catholic High School Great Strand,
NW9 5PE (8358 2800, www.st-james.barnet.sch.
uk). Roman Catholic.
St Mary's High School Downage, NW4 1AB
(8203 2827, www.st-maryshigh.barnet.sch.uk).
Church of England. Expected to close in 2016.
St Michael's Catholic Grammar School Nether
Street, N12 7NJ (8446 2256, www.st-michaels.
barnet.sch.uk). Roman Catholic; girls only.
Totteridge Academy Barnet Lane, N20 8AZ
(8445 9205, www.thetotteridgeacademy.co.uk).
Whitefield School Claremont Road, NW2 1TR
(8455 4114, www.whitefield.barnet.sch.uk).
Wren Academy Hilton Avenue, N12 9HB (8492
6000, www.wrenacademy.org). Church of England.

Property

Local estate agents

Adam Hayes www.adam-hayes.co.uk
Alpine www.alpinegroup.co.uk
Archers www.archersestateagents.co.uk
Douglas Martin www.douglasmartin.co.uk
Finchleys www.finchleys.com
Jeremy Leaf & Co www.jeremyleaf.co.uk

Local knowledge

www.barnetbugle.com
www.hgs.org.uk
www.the-archer.co.uk

USEFUL INFO

Borough size
8,675 hectares

Population
380,800

Ethnic mix
White 71.3%
Asian or Asian British 13.7%
Black or Black British 7.1%
Chinese or other 4.4%
Mixed 3.6%

London Borough of Barnet
Council Chambers Hendon Town Hall, The
Burroughs, NW4 4AX; *Customer-facing
departments* North London Business
Park, Oakleigh Road South, N11 1NP
(8359 2000, www.barnet.gov.uk);

Council run by
Conservatives

MPs
Chipping Barnet ,Theresa Villiers
(Conservative); Finchley & Golders
Green, Mike Freer (Conservative);
Hendon, Matthew Offord (Conservative)

Main recycling centre
Civic Amenity & Recycling Centre,
Summers Lane, N12 0RF (8362
0752, www.barnet.gov.uk)

Council tax
£931.38 to £2,794.14

Brent

Brent is the borough of temples, from gorgeous Hindu places of worship to the more traditional English style of communal experience at Wembley Stadium and the retail ecumenicalism of IKEA. It's also a cool place for a curry, has a surprising but welcome collection of green spaces, and there's even a site for watersports.

AVERAGE PROPERTY PRICE			AVERAGE RENTAL PRICE PER WEEK	
Detached £757,645	**Terraced** £482,470		**Room** £121	**1 bed** £253
Semi-detached £511,351	**Flat** £342,403		**Studio** £196	**2 bed** £315
				3 bed £388

Kensal Green Cemetery

Neighbourhoods

Kilburn and Brondesbury NW6

Kilburn is actually divided between three London boroughs (Brent, Camden and Westminster), with Kilburn High Road the boundary that divides them. The route dates back to pre-Roman times but today it's a traffic-laden path (the A5) lined with a number of local-run businesses mixed in with high street regulars such as Marks & Spencer and Primark, and a number of pound shops. Although an area that could do with some love, it's still popular for its daily market in Kilburn Square, the fairs and events at Grange Park, and the selection of restaurants and bars that line the street – not forgetting the politically inclined Tricycle Theatre.

Once known as 'Little Ireland', Kilburn's strong Irish identity is fading as many of the old residents are moving from the area, cashing in on rising house prices. A few classic Irish pubs are holding strong – some on Kilburn High Road, and the McGovern on Willesden Lane – but most have been converted to trendy bars. The consistently excellent Black Lion, with its gorgeously ornate Victorian decor, is a must-visit for discerning drinkers and handy for the Tricycle Theatre, while the unpretentious, late-opening Good Ship bar draws a lively crowd to its DJ/music and comedy nights. The hip and happening club Love and Liquor is a favourite place for those who want to party without West End prices.

The borough's budget bistros, Small & Beautiful and Little Bay in Kilburn, are popular with young professionals. On Kilburn High Road, other possibilities are Betsy Smith (global menu), Raw Brick (pizzeria and bar) and Woody Grill (Turkish, and handy for a late-night post-club meal).

Despite the influx of coffee chains and other indicators of affluence, Kilburn retains a slightly down-at-heel vibe. Housing stock ranges from large villas to handsome Victorian terraces. The good news is that prices remain consistently less painful than those in nearby West Hampstead and Maida Vale – though the stream of young and middle-aged professionals taking advantage means the cost will rise before long.

Residential Brondesbury stretches north and west of Kilburn, and includes Willesden Lane. It's another area with a varied ethnic mix, reflected in the many food shops selling Indian, Polish and Persian specialities, alongside a number of greasy spoons that offer no-nonsense fry-ups and butties.

Harlesden, Stonebridge and Church End NW10

Despite its often negative reputation, there's plenty to love about Harlesden. Around the famous clock tower is one of Brent's most vibrant shopping areas, with food stores catering for the local Caribbean, Asian and Brazilian communities, as well as discount shops and takeaways. Harlesden is buzzing: visit for some reggae on vinyl (from Hawkeye Records), all things African, and pound shops.

Brent grew and developed along with the arrival of the railways in the late 1880s, and this is very much reflected in Harlesden's predominantly late-Victorian properties. House sizes vary – north of the High Street, some are very large and quite a few have not yet been converted into flats. Prices reflect the area's longstanding notoriety and tend to be somewhat lower than you might expect.

Transport links (bus, tube and train) are good, though drivers have a hard time – Harlesden is a controlled-parking zone, and double-parking along the high street often causes gridlock at weekends. Locals can easily escape the hustle and bustle though. Grade II-listed Roundwood Park is a popular, gated green space, with a café, play area and some award-winning gardens. Harlesden's canalside Grand Junction Arms (just in Ealing) is great in summer.

West of Harlesden, Stonebridge has been transformed – at least from the outside – with high-rise blocks almost gone, replaced by new low-rises run by Brent Council and a housing association. Improvements include the colourful and contemporary £2.1 million family centre, Stonebridge Nursery.

Neighbouring Church End is also (slowly) getting a makeover and, with the new Central Middlesex Hospital in the middle of Park Royal, there's a note of optimism in a formerly bleak urban area. Church End sits between Harlesden, Willesden and Neasden, meeting Stonebridge on the other side of the railway tracks. Here, anonymous prefabs have been replaced with modern low-rise estates.

Kensal Rise and Kensal Green NW10

If Harlesden has an edgy reputation, Kensal Green is considered the chilled little sister with its arty, bohemian feel (Kensal Green Cemetery, just over the Kensington & Chelsea

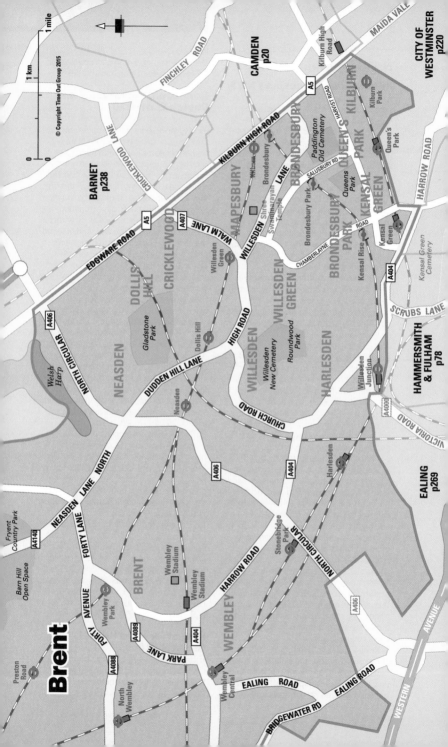

border, was a fashionable final resting place for Victorian writers and artists, as well as a number of modern day stars). Its cosy, compact terraces appeal to young professionals who can't afford Notting Hill. For the same price as a flat in Ladbroke Grove, you can buy a house – which is attracting a lot of families. In fact, estate agents often call this area 'Notting Hill borders', hence the dramatic increase in house prices in the past few years. At its southernmost tip, this part of Brent really is within spitting distance of Ladbroke Grove; housing stock ranges from swanky conversions and gated complexes to 1960s council estates, loft-style pads and terraces.

West of Kensal Green tube is a popular shopping area that also sports plenty of restaurants and takeaways. Transport links are decent, and the Kensal Rise end of Chamberlayne Road provides more local shopping options.

Kensal Rise itself has blossomed. House prices are on the up, though it's still cheaper than Queen's Park. As a result, it's a popular choice with young families. Property consists mainly of Victorian terraces and 1930s houses, both large and small, but it has witnessed a number of new low-rise developments; the north end of College Road is where most of the retail action happens. It has a middle-class vibe, with delis, alternative medicine treatment rooms and quirky boutiques.

As parts of the borough become increasingly fashionable, so too do its gastropubs. Paradise by Way of Kensal Green is an energetic gastropub of long standing, with lots of entertainment (music, comedy nights). Also of note is Harrow Road's William IV. Visit Behesht in Kensal Green for great Persian fare (grills, stews and salads), while in Queen's Park, the Salusbury satisfies those with gastropub leanings. There's also a branch of café/bakery Gail's here, and easygoing brasserie Jack's. The influx of families is catered for with child-friendly cafés such as Hugo's and Bel & Nev, and Sacro Cuore pizzas. But grown-ups are not forgotten – try Queen's Park cocktail bar the Shop.

On College Road in Kensal Rise, alternative health treatments can be had at Gracelands Yard. East on Chamberlayne Road is contemporary floristry courtesy of Scarlet & Violet, as well as Brooks butchers, Minkies

Deli, children's clothes shop Their Nibs, Supra clothes store, and a number of decent vintage furniture shops, including Niche and Howie & Belle. Salusbury Road has more shops, including women's boutique Iris, Queens Park Books, the contemporary Salusbury Wine Store and, on Sundays, a farmers' market at Salusbury Road Primary School.

Willesden and Willesden Green NW10, and Cricklewood NW2

Willesden High Road offers an array of restaurants, shops and takeaways. It is, however, a grimy thoroughfare, with slow-moving traffic.

Willesden has a large rental market as well as plenty of Victorian terraces that appeal to families and young professionals keen to get a foot on the property ladder. The area's Irish influence is less evident than it once was –

Make the most of the Lexi, the not-for-profit community cinema – see a show or volunteer.

nowadays, East European and Antipodean voices are more likely to be heard on the high street than Irish ones. Landmark Willesden Green Library has recently been 'upgraded' to luxury apartments, replaced by a new, smaller library offering a narrower range of facilities.

The Brent side of Cricklewood, meanwhile, shares many features with Kilburn; it's centred around the A5, grew up with the railways and was historically favoured by Irish immigrants. It has, however, a much more suburban feel, with wide roads and terraces. Transport links are good and it has its own bus station, but it's a walk to the nearest tube (Dollis Hill or Willesden Green).

Gladstone Park, which sits between Cricklewood, Willesden and Dollis Hill, is a big green space much used by families and dog walkers, with a café and a friendly feel. To the south of the park are a number of popular culs-de-sac with detached 1930s houses (these command a premium), while to the north are wide avenues of 1930s semis. This isn't the most fashionable part of town, but with its sizeable (and not entirely unreasonably priced) houses and suburban vibe, it's increasingly colonised by young families.

In Willesden, Sushi-Say remains a big draw – booking is essential. Vijay, Anjanaas and Kovalam comprise a pleasing cluster of South Indian specialists on Willesden Lane. For a classy coffee, pop into the café at the Tricycle Theatre. Kensal Rise caffeine needs are best fixed at family-friendly Gracelands, jerk cravings by Island on the Rise (a Caribbean restaurant on Station Terrace). In Willesden Green, bar-restaurant the Queensbury attracts a smart local crowd.

The salvage yards at Park Royal and Willesden Green are a bonus, and you can still buy Irish folk music from Mandy's Irish Shop. Also in Willesden is Edward's Bakery, in business since 1908.

Queen's Park NW6

Queen's Park has profited from the Notting Hill knock-on effect. The houses around the park command the best views and the highest prices, while the southern end of Salusbury Road provides plenty of upmarket shopping and dining options; adjacent Lonsdale Road has a strip of attractive eateries and small businesses.

Around the park, properties vary in size, with the largest sitting either side of the railway line to the north. The Avenue has some desirable, spacious 1930s houses with large gardens front and back. Prices are lower the further you stray from the park.

Queen's Park itself is gated (and managed by the City of London); dogs are not allowed to roam free, though children – and there are plenty of them in these parts – very much are. The café does brisk business, as does the pitch and putt course and the tennis courts. It gets very crowded in summer, when the playground is packed.

At the top of Salusbury Road is another station, Brondesbury Park (London Overground). This popular district offers appealing detached houses – many stone-clad and firmly gated – located around Mallorees School. Willesden Lane offers a slightly greyer version, with large Victorian piles, many of which have been turned into flats, and some new-builds and gated estates. The Mapesbury conservation area, meanwhile, is a world of its own, with 'urban villas' situated on wide avenues.

Dollis Hill and Neasden NW2/NW10

North of Dollis Hill underground station congregates a selection of small Edwardian terraces and a 1930s estate. The area has a sedate but cosmopolitan feel and is popular with British Asian, English and Irish families. There's a marked contrast with nearby Willesden's grimy urban vibe. Neasden is known for its IKEA but local shops are limited to a smattering near the station (most residents scoot off to Willesden, Neasden or Brent Cross for serious supplies); other amenities include imposing Gladstone Park.

Neasden, long the butt of *Private Eye* jokes, was named after its nose-shaped hill, which is today lined with streets of 1930s houses. More

Tricycle Theatre

HIGHS & LOWS

Big bands and high-profile football

Wembley's Indian restaurants

Relatively affordable housing, including newbuilds

Great transport links

Crowds for big gigs and football

Suburbs with faintly comical names such as Cricklewood or Neasden

Drab high streets

people are familiar with Neasden's traffic island than its slightly sad shopping centre. Outside the shopping area, this is a neighbourhood with a distinctly anonymous, suburban feel. For posh boutiques and fancy food, you'll need to look elsewhere, but with the nearby North Circular, plenty of buses and the Jubilee line at residents' disposal, access to neighbouring areas is easy.

The magnificent Shri Swaminarayan Mandir Hindu temple is also in Neasden, and open to visitors. Shayona, its community restaurant, offers pan-Indian vegetarian fare. Elsewhere, Oasis provides bargain Polish food in cheery surroundings. Chinese and Asian food superstore Wing Yip remains a Dollis Hill stalwart.

Wembley HA0/HA9

Wembley Stadium sits on the far side of the North Circular, but its magnificent arch can be seen for miles around. There's a steady stream of visitors to the stadium – and the neighbouring SSE Arena, Wembley – for concerts by big-name bands and for high-profile football matches.

The wider Wembley area has a strong community feel due largely to the extensive Gujarati and South Indian population. Consequently, it's not hard to find a good place for curry – try dosa specialist Sarashwathy Bavans, the vegetarian Sakonis, Gujarati-style thali café Asher's, or Lahore Village with its great falafels and barbecue rolls.

Decent-sized semi-detached houses, popular with families, can make the area feel like an American suburb, and a wealth of easy transport brings in commuters; it may be in Zone 4 but it's just a little over 20 minutes into central London. The newly opened London Designer Outlet, next to Wembley Stadium, is brand city: Adidas, Gap, Skechers, Villeroy & Boch and more. It's also a popular entertainments hub with a multi-screen cinema and restaurants.

Ealing Road – stunning by night when it's lit for the Diwali festival – offers a bustling mix of restaurants, travel agents advertising great deals to Mumbai, and shops selling gold jewellery, fabulous sari fabrics, Bollywood hits at Musik Zone, and huge piles of exotic fruit and veg at Fruit Asia and Fruity Fresh. The road is also home to the striking Shree Sanatan Hindu Mandir temple, Wembley Central Mosque and the glitzy Clay Oven banqueting suites, a popular venue for local wedding receptions.

Eating

Anjanaas 57-59 Willesden Lane, NW6 7RL (7624 1713, www.anjanaas.co.uk).
Asher's 224 Ealing Road, HA0 4QL (8795 2455).
Behesht 1082-1086 Harrow Road, NW10 5NL (8964 4477, www.behesht.co.uk).
Bel & Nev 15 Station Terrace, NW10 5RX (3720 8825).
Betsy Smith 77 Kilburn High Road, NW6 6HY (7624 5793, www.thebetsysmith.co.uk).
Gail's 75 Salusbury Road, NW6 6NH (7625 0068, www.gailsbread.co.uk).
Gracelands 118 College Road, NW10 5HD (8964 9161, www.gracelandscafe.com).
Hugo's 25 Lonsdale Road, NW6 6RA (7372 1232, www.hugosrestaurant.co.uk).
Island on the Rise 1 Keslake Mansions, Station Terrace, NW10 5RU (8969 0405).
Jack's 101 Salusbury Road, NW6 6NH (7624 8925, www.jacks-cafe.com).
Kovalam 12 Willesden Lane, NW6 7SR (7625 4761).
Lahore Village 131 Wembley Park Drive, HA9 8HQ (8902 6550).
Little Bay 228 Belsize Road, NW6 4BT (7372 4699, www.littlebay.co.uk).
Oasis 236 Neasden Lane, NW10 0AA (8450 5178).
Paradise by Way of Kensal Green 19 Kilburn Lane, W10 4AE (8969 0098, www.theparadise.co.uk).
Raw Brick 11 Kilburn Bridge, NW6 6HT (7624 2555).
Sacro Cuore 45 Chamberlayne Road, NW10 3NB (8960 8558, www.sacrocuore.co.uk).
Sakonis 127-129 Ealing Road, HA0 4BP (8903 1058, www.sakonis.co.uk).
Salusbury 50-52 Salusbury Road, NW6 6NN (7328 3286, www.thesalusbury.co.uk).
Sarashwathy Bavans 549 High Road, Wembley, HA0 2DJ (8902 1515, www.sarashwathy.com).
Shayona 54-62 Meadow Garth, NW10 8HD (8965 3365, www.shayonarestaurants.com).
Small & Beautiful 351 Kilburn High Road, NW6 7QB (7328 2637, www.small-and-beautiful.co.uk).
Sushi-Say 33B Walm Lane, NW2 5SH (8459 2971).
Vijay 49 Willesden Lane, NW6 7RF (7328 1087, www.vijayrestaurant.co.uk).
William IV 786 Harrow Road, NW10 5LX (8969 5955, www.williamivlondon.com).
Woody Grill 211-213 Kilburn High Road, NW6 7JG (7328 3160, www.woody-grill.com); 44 High Road Willesden, NW10 2QA (8451 2673).

Drinking

Black Lion 274 Kilburn High Road, NW6 2BY (7625 1635, www.blacklionguesthouse.com).
Good Ship 289 Kilburn High Road, NW6 7JR (07949 008253, www.thegoodship.co.uk).

Grand Junction Arms Acton Lane, NW10 7AD (8965 5670, www.gjapub.co.uk).
Love & Liquor 34 Kilburn High Road, NW6 5UA (7625 7500, www.loveandliquor.co.uk).
Queensbury 110 Walm Lane, NW2 4RS (8452 0171, www.thequeensbury.co.uk).
The Shop 75 Chamberlayne Road, NW10 3ND (8969 9399, www.theshopnw10.com).

Shopping

Brent Cross Shopping Centre Hendon, NW4 3FP (8202 8095, www.brentcross.co.uk). Not in the borough but a dominating presence nearby.
Brooks 91 Chamberlayne Road, NW10 3ND (8964 5678, www.brooksbutchers.com).
Edward's Bakery 269 High Road, Willesden Green, NW10 2RX (8459 3001, www.londonbakery.co.uk).
Fruit Asia 194-196 Ealing Road, HA0 4QD (8900 2850).
Fruity Fresh 111-113 Ealing Road, HA0 4BP (8902 9797, www.fruityfresh.com).
Hawkeye 2 Craven Park Road, NW10 4AB (8961 0866).
Howie & Belle 52 Chamberlayne Road, NW10 3JH (8964 4553, www.howieandbelle.com).
IKEA 2 Drury Way, North Circular Road, NW10 0TH (0845 355 1141, www.ikea.co.uk).
Iris 73 Salusbury Road, NW6 6NJ (7372 1777, www.irisfashion.co.uk).
London Designer Outlet Wembley Park Boulevard, HA9 0QL (8912 5210, www.london designeroutlet.com).
Minkies Deli 'Glasshouse', Chamberlayne Road, NW10 5RQ (8969 2182, www.minkiesdeli.co.uk).
Musik Zone 105A Ealing Road, HA0 4BP (8791 5266).
Niche The Mews Coachworks, 27 Mortimer Road, NW10 5QR (07931 666285, www.niche antiques.co.uk).
Park Royal Salvage Acton Lane, NW10 7AB (8961 3627).
Queens Park Books 87 Salusbury Road, NW6 6NH (7625 1008, www.queensparkbooks.co.uk).
Salusbury Winestore 54 Salusbury Road, NW6 6NN (7372 6664).
Scarlet & Violet 76 Chamberlayne Road, NW10 3JJ (8969 9446, www.scarletandviolet.com).
Supra 71 Chamberlayne Road, NW10 3ND (8968 6868, www.supralondon.com).
Their Nibs 79 Chamberlayne Road, NW10 3ND (8964 8444).
Willesden Green Architectural Salvage 189 High Road, NW10 2SD (8459 2947, www.willesdensalvage.com).
Wing Yip 395 Edgware Road, NW2 6LN (8450 0422, www.wingyip.com).

Things to do

Cinemas & theatres

Lexi 194B Chamberlayne Road, NW10 3JU (0871 704 2069, www.thelexicinema.co.uk). Social enterprise cinema.
Tricycle Theatre 269 Kilburn High Road, NW6 7JR (7328 1000, www.tricycle.co.uk). Theatre and cinema, plus café-bar and art gallery.

Galleries & museums

Brent Museum Willesden Green Cultural Centre, 95 High Road, NW10 2SF (8937 3600, www.brent. gov.uk/museum). Local history museum, closed since spring 2013 for redevelopment. Check website for scheduled reopening.

Other attractions

BAPS Shri Swaminarayan Mandir 105-119 Brentfield Road, NW10 8LD (8965 2651, www. londonmandir.baps.org). Temple dedicated to Bhagwan Swaminarayan and the Hindu faith.

Green spaces

Further details at http://brent.gov.uk.
Fryent Country Park Fryent Way, NW9. Designated local nature reserve running to more than 103 hectares.
Gladstone Park Dollis Hill Lane, NW2. Recreational area and sporting facilities.
Northwick Park The Fairway, HA0. Sports pitches and parkland.
Queen's Park Harvist Road, NW6. Ornamental gardens, playground, pitch and putt, paddling pool, café and sports facilites.
Roundwood Park Harlesden Road, NW10. Grade II-listed Victorian park with aviary, wildlife area, café and playground.
Welsh Harp Open Space & Reservoir Birchen Grove, NW9. Open water, marshes, trees and grassland, plus two bird hides. Site of Special Scientific Interest.

Gyms & leisure centres

Bridge Park Community Leisure Centre Harrow Road, NW10 0RG (8937 3730, www.brent. gov.uk).
Brondesbury Park Fitness & Wellbeing Centre 12 Sidmouth Road, NW2 5JY (0845 241 3799, www.nuffieldhealth.com).
Fitness First (www.fitnessfirst.co.uk); 492-498 High Road, HA9 7BH (0844 571 2972); 1st floor, 632-640 Kingsbury Road, NW9 9HN (0844 571 2889); 105-109 Salusbury Road, NW6 6RG (0844 571 2886).
Genesis Gym 333 Athlon Road, HA0 1EF (8566 8687, www.genesisgym.co.uk).

LivingWell Lakeside Way, HA9 0BU (8733 0610, www.livingwell.com).

Manor Health & Leisure 307 Cricklewood Broadway, NW2 6PG (8450 6464, www.themanorhealthandleisure.co.uk).

Vale Farm Sports Centre Watford Road, HA0 3HG (8908 6545, www.brent.gov.uk).

Willesden Sports Centre Donnington Road, NW10 3QX (8955 1120, www.brent.gov.uk).

Outdoor pursuits

Phoenix Outdoor Centre Welsh Harp Reservoir, Cool Oak Lane, NW9 7ND (07854 655968, www.phoenixcanoeclub.co.uk). Canoeing, windsurfing, orienteering and paddle parties.

Welsh Harp Sailing Club Welsh Harp Reservoir, Birchen Grove, NW9 8SA (www.welshharpsailing club.org). Sailing and windsurfing. The largest of several sailing clubs on the reservoir.

Spectator sports

SSE Arena, Wembley Arena Square, Engineers Way, HA9 0AA (8782 5566, www.ssearena.co.uk). Formerly known as Wembley Arena.

Wembley Stadium HA9 0WS (0844 980 8001, www.wembleystadium.com).

Schools

Primary

There are 51 state primary schools in Brent, 13 of which are church schools, three Jewish and one Muslim. There are also ten independent primaries, including two Muslim schools, one Montessori school, one Jewish school, one Hindu school and one Welsh school. See www.brent.gov.uk, www.education.gov.uk/edubase and www.ofsted.gov.uk for more information.

Paradise by Way of Kensal Green

TRANSPORT

Tube lines Bakerloo, Jubilee, Metropolitan, Overground, Piccadilly
Rail services into Clapham Junction, Euston, Marylebone
Main bus routes into central London 16, 18, 36, 52, 98; night buses N16, N18, N98; 24-hour buses 6, 189

Secondary

Alperton Community School Ealing Road, HA0 4PW (8902 2038, www.alperton.brent.sch.uk).

Al-Sadiq & Al-Zahra Schools 134 Salusbury Road, NW6 6PF (7372 7706, www.asazs.co.uk). Muslim.

ARK Academy Bridge Road. HA9 9JP (8385 4390, www.arkacademy.org).

ARK Elvin Academy Cecil Avenue, HA9 7DU (8902 6362, www.arkelvinacademy.org).

Brondesbury College 8 Brondesbury Park, NW6 7BT (8830 4522, www.brondesburycollege.co.uk). Boys only.

Capital City Academy Doyle Gardens, NW10 3ST (8838 8700, www.capitalcityacademy.org).

Claremont High School Academy Claremont Avenue, HA3 0UH (8204 4442, www.claremont-high.org.uk).

Convent of Jesus & Mary Language College Crownhill Road, NW10 4EP (8965 2986, www.cjmlc.co.uk). Roman Catholic; girls only.

Crest Boys' Academy Crest Road, NW2 7SN (8452 8700, www.thecrestboysacademies.org.uk). Boys only.

Crest Girls' Academy Crest Road, NW2 7SN (8452 4842, www.thecrestgirlsacademies.org.uk). Girls only.

JFS The Mall, HA3 9TE (8206 3100, www.jfs.brent.sch.uk). Jewish.

Kingsbury High School Princes Avenue, NW9 9JR (8206 3000, www.kingsburyhigh.org.uk).

Menorah High School 105 Brook Road, NW2 7BZ (8208 0500). Orthodox Jewish; girls only.

Newman Catholic College Harlesden Road, NW10 3RN (8965 3947, www.ncc.brent.sch.uk). Roman Catholic; boys only.

Preston Manor High School Carlton Avenue East, HA9 8NA (8385 4040, www.pmanor.brent.sch.uk).

Queen's Park Community School Aylestone Avenue, NW6 7BQ (8438 1700, www.qpcs.brent.sch.uk).

St Gregory's Catholic Science College Donnington Road, HA3 0NB (8907 8828, www.stgregorys.harrow.sch.uk). Roman Catholic.

School of the Islamic Republic of Iran 100 Carlton Vale, NW6 5HE (7372 8051). Muslim.

Swaminarayan School 260 Brentfield Road, NW10 8HE (8965 8381, www.swaminarayan.brent.sch.uk). Hindu.

Wembley High Technology College East Lane, HA0 3NT (8385 4800, www.whtc.co.uk).

Property

Local estate agents

Camerons Stiff & Co www.cameronsstiff.co.uk
Chelsea Square www.chelsea-square.co.uk
Daniels www.danielsestateagents.co.uk
Grey & Co www.greyandco.net
Hoopers www.hoopersestateagents.co.uk
Jorgensturner Estate Agents www.jorgensenturner.com
Mapesbury www.mapesburyproperty.co.uk
Margo's www.margos.co.uk
Mile Estates www.mileestates.co.uk
Portland Estate Agents www.portlandestateagents.co.uk

Local knowledge

www.getwestlondon.co.uk
www.harrowtimes.co.uk
www.kilburntimes.co.uk
www.park-life.org
www.wembleymatters.blogspot.com

USEFUL INFO

Borough size
4,323 hectares

Population
325,400

Ethnic mix
White 51.7%
Asian/Asian British 24.4%
Black/Black British 16.2%
Chinese or other 3.9%
Mixed 4.0%

London Borough of Brent
Brent Civic Centre. Engineers Way, Wembley HA9 0FT (8937 1234, www.brent.gov.uk)

Council run by
Labour

MPs
Brent Central, Dawn Butler (Labour); Brent North, Barry Gardiner (Labour); Hampstead & Kilburn, Tulip Siddiq (Labour)

Main recycling centre
Brent Reuse & Recycling Centre, Abbey Road, NW10 7TJ (8965 5497)

Council tax
£902.63 to £2,707.88

Bromley

Greater London's biggest borough – and its greenest – has outstanding schools as well as superb sports facilities and West End-lite shopping. No wonder families flock here.

AVERAGE PROPERTY PRICE

Detached	Terraced
£758,373	£339,050
Semi-detached	**Flat**
£425,745	£270,693

AVERAGE RENTAL PRICE PER WEEK

Room	1 bed
£112	£196
Studio	**2 bed**
£150	£265
	3 bed
	£322

Bromley High Street

Neighbourhoods

Penge SE20

Penge. There's always been something slightly risible about the name. *The Goon Show* used to send it up relentlessly. Well, it seems dear old Penge is having the last laugh. Folk realising that they can no longer afford to live in places like Clapham or East Dulwich are venturing Pengewards and finding themselves pleasantly surprised.

It's got a good selection of decent-sized and affordable Victorian and Edwardian family houses in broad streets left over from when this was a smart suburb, as well as everything on the property ladder up to that level, including some pretty railway cottages. (By 'affordable' read '47.5% below the London average'). It's got history and literary references (*Rumpole and the Penge Bungalow Murders*) and the attractive Royal Watermen's Almshouses, built in the early Victorian period for watermen and lightermen (now private homes). It has its own bus route, the 176, to Tottenham Court Road; three train stations (Kent House, Penge East and Penge West); and the Overground. And now it's got its own microbrewery (Late Knights), a pub theatre (above the popular Bridge House pub) and a circus school (My Aerial Home). Plus it's very handy for Crystal Palace Park and its sports centre, both run by Bromley Council.

The high street is still dominated by 'useful' shops (pound shops, grocers, hardware stores) but locals are very excited about their gorgeous little garden centre, Alexandra Nurseries, and its cake-laden café. There's also great loyalty to traditional butcher Murray Bros, Penge Food Centre (for herbs and spices), the Blue Belle and Blue Mountain cafés and, for more niche needs, Twang Guitars. The Goldsmiths Arms caters to the more modern pub-goer, but there's still plenty of old-fashioned boozers, though not as many as 150 years ago when Penge is said to have had 16 pubs on its High Street alone – one every 44 yards.

One stop further down the line from Penge West is Anerley, which may or may not be part of Penge, depending on whom you ask. Linking the two, Thicket Road, along the edge of Crystal Palace Park, is a unique place to live, with its views of the famous dinosaurs; other roads near the park are not to be sniffed at either. Not any more.

Beckenham BR3

Keep going through Penge and you'll hit Beckenham. While Penge clings to its London credentials, Beckenham looks longingly towards Kent.

Streets are leafy, especially those around Copers Cope Road, Kelsey Lane and Village Way, and the Park Langley conservation area. There's a good choice of properties of all sizes and price tags, including swathes of well-to-do 1920s and '30s suburban architecture. The wider residential areas and their houses (with drives and garages) have a reputation for being a bit *Footballers' Wives* as one local put it. A clue to the demographic is that Beckenham has one of south-east London's few branches of Waitrose.

Having a choice of railway stations, not to mention Overground and tram stops, makes Beckenham not just a convenient place to live, but also attractive to businesses keen to avoid central London rents.

For Bromley residents, Beckenham is also somewhere to go for a night out. This won't be a central London, Michelin-starred cuisine or cocktails in jam jars night out – or a West End show night out – but there are enough entertainments to make Beckenham something of a borough hub. There's a six-screen cinema and a range of decent places to eat, although largely of the old-school type, with tablecloths. These include La Rascasse (French), Sapore Vero (pizza), Zi' Teresa and Pierluigi's (Italian), and the smart Sea Salt (seafood), as well as a couple of Turkish mangal restaurants and Beckenham Curry Club in Elmers End. For pubs, try the Jolly Woodman or the 17th-century George Inn; for coffee, head for Fee & Brown. There are concerts and festivals on Beckenham Green, as well as regular farmers' markets. Other retail diversions include Beckenham Bookshop, the well-stocked Kitchen Range (kitchenalia plus cooking classes) and Villagers Sausages on the High Street.

TRANSPORT

Rail services into Charing Cross, London Bridge, Victoria
Trams to Beckenham Junction, Croydon, Elmers End, Wimbledon
Main bus routes into central London 176; night buses N3, N47
Airport Biggin Hill

Historically, the area was home to several manor houses, their estates now serving as municipal green spaces such as Kelsey Park or golf courses such as Langley Park. It's also a place of oddities such as the 'Chinese Garage' on Wickham Road, built in 1928 in the style of a pagoda.

Cricket fans unable to get into the Oval can often find tickets to lower-key matches at Kent County Cricket Ground on Worsley Bridge Road, while legendary cricketer WG Grace is buried in Beckenham Crematorium and Cemetery – as is Thomas Crapper of toilet fame.

It's all too easy to dismiss the southern suburbs but they have given birth to many cultural movers and shakers. Early in his career, local lad David Bowie ran the Beckenham Arts Lab club from the Three Tuns pub on the High Street, for instance, although it's now a branch of the Zizzi restaurant chain. But if it was good enough for the Thin White Duke…

Bromley BR1

Bromley has long been synonymous with good schools – state, grammar and independent – although its star performers, Newstead Wood and St Olave's Grammar, are within the borough in nearby Orpington rather than the town of Bromley itself.

For south Londoners of all boroughs, Bromley provides a less crowded alternative to Oxford Street, especially at the Intu Bromley shopping centre (formerly known as the Glades) and along the pedestrianised streets of the town centre. Teenagers congregate here on Saturdays to spend their allowances in Topshop and chain restaurants, while their younger siblings go wild on the flumes at the Pavilion leisure centre. The area's other mega shopping experience is Hayes Street Farm Boot Fair, a car boot sale in a huge field with hundreds of pitches and some serious bargain hunters; it runs fortnightly on Sundays from Easter to October, weather permitting.

The Old Town, by Bromley North station, is an enclave of Victorian terraces and semis, neighbourhood pubs and a few artisans' cottages. It's not foodie heaven, but there are a couple of decent places to eat, such as Aqua Mediterranean Bar & Grill on East Street, which is also popular for Sunday roasts. Further up Bromley Hill is the Indo-Nepalese Yak & Yeti, which also does takeaway food, while over in upmarket Sundridge Park is the Indian restaurant Cinnamon Culture.

Bromley has plenty of properties of all eras and sizes, and – as is common all over London – new-build schemes are adding to the mix. At time of writing, the £90 million St Mark's Square project was approaching completion; a redevelopment of part of the southern end of the town centre, it will create an 'urban lifestyle quarter' with new apartments, a hotel, a multiplex cinema and restaurants.

Eating

Aqua Mediterranean Bar & Grill 4-6 Market Parade, BR1 1QN (8460 2346, www.aquabar andgrill.co.uk).
Beckenham Curry Club 4 Goodwood Parade, Upper Elmers End Road, BR3 3QZ (8658 7608).
Blue Belle 182 Maple Road, SE20 8JB (8659 6505, www.bluebellecafe.co.uk).
Blue Mountain 201 Maple Road, SE20 8HU (8659 0564, www.bluemo.co.uk).
Cinnamon Culture 46 Plaistow Lane, BR1 3PA (8289 0322, www.cinnamonculture.com).
Fee & Brown 50 High Street, BR3 1AY (07944 038226, www.feeandbrown.com).
Pierluigi's 86-90 High Street, BR3 1ED (8663 3387, www.pierluigis.com).
La Rascasse 59-63 High Street, BR3 1AW (8650 2291, www.larascasse.com).
Sapore Vero 78 High Street, BR3 1ED (8658 0021, www.saporevero.com).
Sea Salt 2 Southend Road, BR3 1SD (8663 0994, www.seasaltbeckenham.com).
Yak & Yeti 16 Bromley Hill, BR1 4JX (8290 6386, www.yakandyeti.co.uk).
Zi' Teresa 141-143 Croydon Road, BR3 3RB (8658 9117, www.ziteresa.co.uk).
Zizzi 157 High Street, BR3 1AE (8658 2050, www.zizzi.co.uk).

Drinking

Bridge House 2 High Street, SE20 8RZ (8778 2100, www.bridgehousese20.co.uk).
George Inn 111 High Street, BR3 1AG (8663 3468, www.thegeorgeinnbeckenham.co.uk).
Goldsmiths Arms 3 Croydon Road, SE20 7TJ (8659 1242, www.goldsmithsarms.com).
Jolly Woodman 9 Chancery Lane, BR3 6NR (8663 1031).

Shopping

Alexandra Nurseries 56B Parish Lane, SE20 7LJ (8778 4145, www.alexandranurseries.co.uk).
Beckenham Bookshop 42 High Street, BR3 1AY (8650 9744, www.beckenhambooks.com).

Hayes Street Farm Boot Fair Hayes Lane, BR2 7LB (8462 1186, www.hayesstfarm.co.uk).
Intu Bromley High Street, BR1 1DN (8466 8899, www.intu.co.uk/bromley). Shopping centre.
Kitchen Range 220 High Street, BR3 1EN (8663 6323).
Murray Bros 146 High Street, SE20 7EU (8776 5535).
Penge Food Centre 197-199 High Street, SE20 7PF (8778 4090, www.pengefoodcentre.com).
Twang Guitars 94 High Street, SE20 7EZ (8676 0926, www.twangmusicacademy.com).
Villagers Sausages 91 High Street, BR3 1AG (8325 5475, www.englishsausages.com).

Things to do

Cinemas & theatres

Churchill Theatre High Street, BR1 1HA (0844 871 7620, www.atgtickets.com/bromley).
Empire Cinema 242 High Street, BR1 1PQ (0871 471 4714, www.empirecinemas.co.uk).
Odeon High Street, BR3 1DY (0871 224 4007, www.odeon.co.uk).

Galleries & museums

Ripley Arts Centre 24 Sundridge Avenue, BR1 2PX (8464 5816, www.bromleyarts.com).

Other attractions

Biggin Hill Airport 518 Churchill Road, Biggin Way, TN16 3BN (01959 578500, www.biggin hillairport.com).
Biggin Hill Heritage Hangar Hangar 528, Biggin Hill Airport, TN16 3BN (01959 576767, www.bigginhillheritagehangar.co.uk). Climb inside a Spitfire or go on a sortie.
Chislehurst Caves Caveside Close, Old Hill, BR7 5NL (8467 3264, www.chislehurst-caves.co.uk).
Crofton Roman Villa Crofton Road, BR6 8AF (01689 860939, www.cka.moon-demon.co.uk). Only Roman villa open to the public in Greater London.
Down House Luxted Road, BR6 7JT (01689 859119, www.english-heritage.org.uk). Charles Darwin's family home.

Green spaces

For more details, see www.bromley.gov.uk.
Bromley Common BR2, BR3. Woodland, golf course and lake.
Bromley Palace Park Stockwell Close, BR1 3DE. With an 18th-century Bishop's Palace, an icehouse, listed Pulham Rockeries, historic springs and a mock medieval folly.
Jubilee Country Park Thornet Wood Road, BR5 1BL. Local nature reserve with wildflower meadow, hedgerows and woodland.

Kelsey Park Manor Way, BR3 3LS. Extensive ornamental gardens with lakes and woodland.
Norman Park Hayes Lane, BR2 9EF. Children's play area and sports facilities.
Petts Wood Chislehurst, BR5 1NZ (01732 810378, www.nationaltrust.org.uk/petts-wood-and-hawkwood). National Trust woodland.
Scadbury Park Old Perry Street, BR7 6LS. Local nature reserve with trails, meadows, hedgerows and woodland.
Sparrow Wood & Crofton Heath Farrington Avenue, BR2 8BY. Open common and woodland.

Gyms & leisure centres

Biggin Hill Memorial Pool Church Road, TN16 3LB (01959 574468, www.mytimeactive.co.uk).
Bromley Indoor Bowls Centre Bodmin Close, BR5 4LX (01689 834341, www.bromleyibc.com).

Take a lamplit tour of Chislehurst Caves – more than 20 miles of historic limestone tunnels. Bands such as the Stones and Pink Floyd used to play there in the '60s and '70s.

Bromley Tennis Centre Avebury Road, BR6 9SA (01689 880407, www.bromleytenniscentre.co.uk).
Crystal Palace National Sports Centre Ledrington Road, SE19 2BB (8778 0131, www.better.org.uk). Olympic pool and diving centre, climbing wall, courts, pitches and beach volleyball.
Langley Park School for Girls Hawksbrook Lane, South Eden Park Road, BR3 3BE (8633 1906, www.lpgs.bromley.sch.uk/143/sports-centre). Various facilities; outside school hours only.
Pavilion Kentish Way, BR1 3EF (8313 9911, www.mytimeactive.co.uk). Leisure centre with swimming, fitness suite and classes.
Spa at Beckenham 24 Beckenham Road, BR3 4PF (020 8650 0233, www.mytimeactive.co.uk). Includes 25m pool, teaching pool and soft play.
Sundridge Park Lawn Tennis & Squash Rackets Club Lawn Close, off Garden Road, BR1 3NA (8464 9106, www.spltsrc.co.uk).
Walnuts Leisure Centre Lych Gate Road, BR6 0TJ (01689 870533, www.mytimeactive.co.uk). Pools, gym, sauna, steam room and soft play.
West Wickham Leisure Centre Station Road, BR4 0PY (8777 5686, www.mytimeactive.co.uk). Pool, fitness suite and pump room.

Outdoor pursuits

Beckenham Place Park Golf Course
Beckenham Hill Road, BR3 5BP (8650 2292,
www.glendalegolf.co.uk). Pay and play; 18 holes.
Bromley Golf Centre Magpie Hall Lane, BR2 8JF
(8462 7014, www.mytimeactive.co.uk). Nine-hole
course and driving range.
High Elms Golf Course High Elms Road, BR6
7JL (01689 858175, www.mytimeactive.co.uk).
Attractive 18-hole course near Downe.
Langley Park Golf Club Barnfield Wood Road,
BR3 6SZ (8658 6849, www.langleyparkgolf.co.uk).
Established 1910; 18 holes.

Spectator sports

Crystal Palace National Sports Centre
Ledrington Road, SE19 2BB (8778 0131, www.
better.org.uk). National track and field events,
as well as school sports days.
Kent County Cricket Ground Worsley Bridge
Road, BR3 1RL (01227 456886, www.kentcricket.
co.uk). Not Kent's main ground but it hosts very
occasional first-class games and some Twenty20.

Schools

Primary

There are 76 primary schools in the borough of
Bromley (including 16 Church of England and
Roman Catholic church schools). There are also
an additional 13 independent schools that take
primary-age children. See www.bromley.gov.uk,
www.education.gov.uk/edubase and www.ofsted.
gov.uk for more information.

Secondary

Babington House Elmstead Lane, BR7 5ES (8467
5537, www.babingtonhouse.com). Private.
Bishop Challoner School 228 Bromley Road,
BR2 0BS (8460 3546, www.bishopchallonerschool.
com). Private.
Bishop Justus Church of England School
Magpie Hall Lane, BR2 8HZ (8315 8130, www.
bishopjustus.bromley.sch.uk). Church of England.
Bromley High School Blackbrook Lane, BR1
2TW (8781 7000, www.bromleyhigh.gdst.net).
Girls only; private.

Alexandra Nurseries, Penge

HIGHS & LOWS

Easy route out to Kent and Sussex

Fantastic swimming pools

Great grammar schools

Green belt and Kent Downs

Self-contained for shopping

Boring for under-40 golf haters

Poor for arts, culture and eating out

Suburban mindset

The traffic in Bromley

Bullers Wood School St Nicholas Lane, Logs Hill, BR7 5LJ (8467 2280, www.bullerswood.bromley. sch.uk). Girls only; mixed sixth form.

Charles Darwin School Jail Lane, TN16 3AU (01959 574043, www.cdarwin.com).

Chislehurst School for Girls Beaverwood Road, BR7 6HE (8300 3156, www.chislehurstschoolfor girls.co.uk). Girls only.

Coopers School Hawkwood Lane, BR7 5PS (8467 3263, www.coopersschool.com).

Darrick Wood School Lovibonds Avenue, BR6 8ER (01689 850271, www.darrickwood. bromley.sch.uk).

Darul Uloom London Islamic School Foxbury Avenue, BR7 6SD (8295 0637, www.darululoom london.co.uk). Muslim; private.

Eltham College Grove Park Road, SE9 4QF (8857 1455, www.eltham-college.org.uk). Boys only; mixed sixth form; private.

USEFUL INFO

Borough size
15,013 hectares

Population
324,700

Ethnic mix
White 85.5%
Black/Black British 2.8%
Asian/Asian British 7.8%
Chinese or other 2.6%
Mixed 1.4%

London Borough of Bromley
Civic Centre, Stockwell Close, BR1 3UH (8464 3333, www.bromley.gov.uk)

Council run by Conservatives

MPs
Beckenham, Bob Stewart (Conservative); Bromley & Chislehurst, Bob Neill (Conservative); Lewisham West & Penge, Jim Dowd (Labour); Orpington, Jo Johnson (Conservative)

Main recycling centres
Waldo Road, Bromley, BR1 2QX; Churchfields Road, Beckenham, BR3 4QY (0300 303 8658, www.bromley.gov.uk)

Council tax
£883.43 to £2,650.28

Farringtons School Perry Street, BR7 6LR (8467 0256, www.farringtons.org.uk). Private.

Harris Academy Beckenham Beckenham Manor Way, BR3 3SJ (8650 8694, www.harrisbeckenham. org.uk). Formerly Kelsey Park Sports College.

Harris Academy Bromley Lennard Road, BR3 1QR (8778 5917, www.harrisbromley.org.uk). Formerly Cator Park School.

Hayes School West Common Road, BR2 7DB (8462 2767, www.hayes.bromley.sch.uk).

Kemnal Technology College Sevenoaks Way, DA14 5AA (8300 7112, www.ktc-tkat.org).

Langley Park School for Boys Hawksbrook Lane, South Eden Park Road, BR3 3BP (8639 4700, www.lpsb.org.uk). Boys only.

Langley Park School for Girls Hawksbrook Lane, South Eden Park Road, BR3 3BE (8663 4199, www.lpgs.bromley.sch.uk). Girls only.

Newstead Wood School Avebury Road, BR6 9SA (01689 853626, www.newsteadwood. bromley.sch.uk).

Priory School Tintagel Road, BR5 4LG (01689 819219, www.priory.bromley.sch.uk).

Ravensbourne School Hayes Lane, BR2 9EH (8460 0083, www.ravensbourne.bromley. sch.uk).

Ravens Wood School Oakley Road, BR2 8HP (01689 856050, www.ravenswood.bromley.sch.uk).

St Olave's Grammar School Goddington Lane, BR6 9SH (01689 820101, www.saintolaves.net).

Wickham Court School Layhams Road, BR4 9HW (8777 2942, www.wickhamcourt.org.uk). Private.

Property

Local estate agents

Alan de Maid www.alandemaid.co.uk
Browne Estates www.browne-estates.co.uk
Capital www.capitalestateagents.com
Curran & Pinner www.curranpinner.co.uk
David James www.djames.co.uk
Edward Ashdale www.edwardashdale.com
Humphriss & Ryde www.humphrissandryde. co.uk
JDM www.jdmonline.com
Langford Russell www.langfordrussell.co.uk
Proctors www.georgeproctor.co.uk
Vincent Chandler www.vincentchandler.co.uk

Local knowledge

www.biggin-hill-today.co.uk
www.bromleytimes.co.uk
www.bromley-today.co.uk
www.deserter.co.uk
www.pengetouristboard.co.uk

Croydon

London's most populous borough is a tough little thing compared to its unworldy neighbours Bromley and Sutton. From the unexpected Manhattan skyline of 'The Cronx' to the fantastic views, great restaurants and community events of Crystal Palace, this is a borough to be reckoned with.

AVERAGE PROPERTY PRICE

Detached £629,514	**Terraced** £289,657
Semi-detached £376,688	**Flat** £237,949

AVERAGE RENTAL PRICE PER WEEK

Studio £155	**3 bed** £299
1 bed £194	**4+ bed** £380
2 bed £253	

View from the top of Gipsy Hill

Neighbourhoods

Crystal Palace SE19

Crystal Palace occupies a privileged position in the topography of London – one of the highest points in the city, at 367 feet. The views, consequently, are amazing and the streets steep. The hub of the community is the central triangle formed by the one-way system of Church Road, Westow Hill and Westow Street, lined with bars, cafés and independent shops.

Vintage is big here and the area is best on a Sunday morning, when junk shops and stalls spill out on to the pavements of Church Road. For furniture, try Crystal Palace Antiques – spread over four treasure-packed floors – or Flaming Nora. Crazy Man Crazy, Et Pourquoi Pas?, Vintage Hart (housed in the White Hart pub) and Violet Betty's sell clothing, while at the eclectic Crystal Palace Vintage and at Haynes Lane Market you never know what might turn up. These are complemented by a growing number of slick new boutiques such as Forty Seven Hair (womenswear at the front, salon at the back) and menswear outlet Simon Carter.

In and around the central triangle, you'll also find the independent Bookseller Crow on the Hill, the Milkhouse Candle Co, the award-winning Good Taste (bottle shop, charcuterie and cheese) and the weekly Crystal Palace Food Market (10am-3pm Sat).

For restaurants, the neighbourhood punches well above its weight. There is Modern British cooking at the Exhibition Rooms; French-Algerian cuisine at Numidie; dependable bistro dishes at Joanna's; plus the modern buzz at Crystal Palace Market, which even has its own fishmonger and butcher. If you want a pint and a pub atmosphere with your nosh, try locals the Alma, the Sparrowhawk, Westow House or the White Hart, while there are also plenty of places for snacks and light meals: deli-café Comfort & Joy, the vegetarian Domali, Boyce da Roca (housed in a junk shop) and the decidedly French Café St Germain.

It's quite a contrast then to step from this hubbub into the hushed residential areas that lie immediately behind. There's a range of property, including converted workshops, modern housing, tucked-away mews and Victorian homes. As the area undulates towards the heights of Upper Norwood, there is green space too, such as the family-friendly Westow Park. Beulah Hill, looking

Church Road, Crystal Palace

out over to Croydon, has everything from historic Georgian villas to modest, modern family homes.

Meanwhile, careering down Gipsy Hill in the direction of Dulwich and central London, you'll find a mix of period streets and modern estates – some on the rough side – and a notable swathe of sharp-edged 1970s flats and townhouses. Community is strong around here: a network of community gardens called Patchwork Farm, campaigns to open a cinema, and the Palace Pint scheme (encouraging people to grow hops for a communal brew).

While Alexandra Palace on the other side of London has both an iconic television mast and a palace, the taller tower here stopped broadcasting analogue in 2012, and the palace burnt down in 1936. The old building, of cast iron and plate glass, occupied a prime site at the top of Crystal Palace Park, having been relocated from Hyde Park after the Great Exhibition of 1851. Designed by Joseph Paxton, it was an engineering sensation, and even today its ghost remains an icon of the area. Currently, the site is the subject of controversial rebuild plans.

Missing marvels aside, the rest of the park is a valuable local asset, although being caught between five boroughs, it hasn't always received the love it needs. The architecturally dynamic National Sports Centre at its heart is a great resource and includes an athletics stadium; Usain Bolt has raced here, while local schools get to use it for their sports days. It is repeatedly threatened by redevelopment plans, however. The maze, concert platform, mini farm, the Brown & Green café in Crystal Palace station at the park's southern edge and the famous dinosaur sculptures among the shrubbery make this far more than your average green space.

Croydon CR0

Croydon is so maligned that even its affectionate nickname – The Cronx – makes it sound like everybody is taking the piss. This is a town that once provoked Bromley boy David Bowie to call it his 'nemesis… everything I didn't want in my life' and has been the butt of jokes for decades. But changes are afoot.

After years in the doldrums, a £5 billion development scheme, spearheaded by a new Westfield shopping centre to replace the tired Whitgift, is underway, with the intention of transforming Croydon into a thriving

shopping hub. Several huge, unused tower blocks are being renovated as residential – or rebuilt entirely – as the town tries to take advantage of its transport links.

Croydon is brilliantly located – it takes around 20-30 minutes on the train to City Thameslink, London Bridge and Victoria stations – giving it great potential. It is surrounded by attractive suburbs – including Addiscombe, Coulsdon, Purley, Selsdon and Shirley – while golf courses, good schools and parks are abundant. As well as plenty of nice semis with big gardens, there are gems such as the Webb Estate, an Edwardian-era garden village for millionaires. The Waldrons, a Victorian crescent just outside the town centre, is another coveted area, while green spaces include Duppas Hill and Lloyd Park.

But the plan is to encourage people to live in central Croydon itself – and that is more of a tough sell, partly because a small motorway cuts the town in two. This was the result of 1960s planning that wanted to turn Croydon into London's Manhattan but left it looking more like Warsaw. It's here, however, that the major investment is taking place. Around 30 towers are in the offing, many along the lines of Saffron Square, a 43-storey pink eruption with housing, restaurants and shops around a public square. If Croydon is to become a success, it needs these to work and for the new Westfield shopping mall to act as a magnet, bringing in yet more interesting restaurants and retail.

As it stands, there are plenty of places to shop – as you might expect for a town with a huge high street and three shopping centres – but little that's non-branded. Surrey Street Market (Mon-Sat) is a great, old-school street market and there are furniture warehouses such as the landmark IKEA and John Lewis Home on the Purley Way. Restaurant recommendations include Bagatti's for

Italian, Albert's Table for Modern British and the theatrical Little Bay. Drinkers should try the Glamorgan on Cherry Orchard Lane, the jolly Oval Tavern or the Spread Eagle.

Also worth a look is Matthew's Yard, a new arts hub featuring a café, gallery and small theatre, while the old St George's Walk shopping centre has the excellent Rise art gallery. With Croydon's refurbishment bent on establishing the town as a 'Tech City', these sorts of quirky cultural corners should be on the up.

Croydon has two mainstream cultural spaces: the Clocktower is putting itself back together after heavy budget cuts but still has the Museum of Croydon and the reopened David Lean arthouse cinema; Fairfield Halls, described as the best concert hall in London by Simon Rattle, should be the focus of the area's cultural scene but needs investment – the council insists a renovation is forthcoming. They've been saying that for decades, but this time Croydon seems ripe for a new beginning.

Eating

Albert's Table 49C South End, CR0 1BF (8680 2010, www.albertstable.co.uk).
Bagatti's 56-58 South End, CR0 1DP (8686 9649, www.bagattis.com).
Boyce da Roca 28-30 Church Road, SE19 2ET (8771 2682).
Brown & Green Crystal Palace station, Station Road, SE19 2AZ (8659 0202, www.brownand greencafe.com).

HIGHS & LOWS

Family-friendly, top-flight football

Views from Crystal Palace

Purley Way IKEA

Trams

▲ ⋯⋯⋯⋯⋯⋯⋯⋯⋯⋯⋯⋯⋯ ▼

Croydon flyover

Walking up Gipsy Hill

Purley Way IKEA at the weekend

The butt of jokes

Café St Germain 16-17 Crystal Palace Parade, SE19 1UD (8670 3670, www.cafestgermain.com).
Comfort & Joy 79 Church Road, SE19 2TA (8771 1212).
Crystal Palace Market 3-7 Church Road, SE19 2TF (3475 7080, www.thecrystalpalace market.com).
Domali Café 8 Westow Street, SE19 3AH (8768 0096, www.domalicafe.co.uk).
Exhibition Rooms 69-71 Westow Hill, SE19 1TX (8761 1175, www.theexhibitionrooms.com).
Joanna's 56 Westow Hill, SE19 1RX (8670 4052, www.joannas.uk.com).
Little Bay 32 Selsdon Road, CR2 6PB (8649 9544, www.littlebaycroydon.co.uk).
Numidie 48 Westow Hill, SE19 1RX (8766 6166, www.numidie.co.uk).

Drinking

Alma 95 Church Road, SE19 2TA (8768 1885, www.thealmapub.com).
Glamorgan 81 Cherry Orchard Road, CR0 6BE (8688 6333, www.theglamorgan.co.uk).
Sparrowhawk 2 Westow Hill, SE19 1RX (8761 4831, www.thesparrowhawkpub.co.uk).
Spread Eagle 39-41 Katharine Street, CR0 1NX (8781 1134, www.spreadeaglecroydon.co.uk).
Westow House 79 Westow Hill, SE19 1TX (8670 0654, www.westowhouse.com).
White Hart 96 Church Rd, SE19 2EZ (8771 9389, www.thewhitehartse19.co.uk).

Shopping

Bookseller Crow on the Hill 50 Westow Street, SE19 3AF (8771 8831, www.booksellercrow.co.uk).
Crazy Man Crazy 18 Church Road, SE19 2ET (8653 6548, www.crazymancrazylondon.co.uk).
Crystal Palace Antiques Junction of Westow Hill & Jasper Road, SE19 1SH (8480 7042, www.crystalpalaceantiques.com).
Crystal Palace Food Market Haynes Lane, SE19 3AP (www.crystalpalacefoodmarket.co.uk).
Crystal Palace Vintage 35 Westow Street, SE19 3RW (8916 1626, www.crystalpalace vintage.com).
Et Pourquoi Pas? 45 Westow Street, SE19 3RW (07950 995360).
Flaming Nora 40 Church Road, SE19 2ET (7175 0111, www.flaming-nora.com).
Forty Seven Hair 47A Westow Street, SE19 3RW (8771 7170, www.fortysevenlondon.co.uk).
Good Taste 28 Westow Hill, SE19 1RX (8761 7455, www.goodtaste-fd.co.uk).
Haynes Lane Market Haynes Lane, off Westow Street, SE19 3AN (07968 168532). Fri-Sun only.

Milkhouse Candle Co 111 Church Road, SE19 2PR (8419 8306, www.milkhouse candles.co.uk).
Simon Carter 71 Westow Street, SE19 3RW (8768 1457, www.simoncarter.net).
Surrey Street Market Surrey Street, CR0 1RG.
Vintage Hart 96 Church Road, SE19 2EZ (07949 552926).
Violet Betty's 85 Church Road, SE19 2TA (8771 4998, www.violetbettys.com).
Whitgift Shopping Centre CR0 1LP (8688 8522, www.thewhitgiftcroydon.co.uk).

Things to do

Cinemas & theatres

David Lean Cinema Croydon Clocktower, Katharine Street, CR9 1ET (0333 666 3366, www.davidleancroydon.org.uk).
Fairfield Halls Park Lane, CR9 1DG (8688 9291, www.fairfield.co.uk). Arts, entertainment and conference centre.
Matthews Yard Studio 1 Matthews Yard, CR0 1FF (www.matthewsyard.com).
Vue Croydon Grant's 14 High Street, CR0 1GT (0871 224 0240, www.myvue.com).

Galleries & museums

Crystal Palace Museum Anerley Hill, SE19 2BA (8676 0700, www.crystalpalacemuseum.org.uk). Archive of the Palace.
Museum of Croydon Central Library, Croydon Clocktower, Katharine Street, CR9 1ET (8253 1022, www.museumofcroydon.com).
Rise Gallery 7-9 St George's Walk, CR0 1YH (8681 1279, www.rise-gallery.co.uk).

Other attractions

Croydon Airport Visitor Centre Airport House, Purley Way, CR0 0XZ (07779 681 035, www. croydonairport.org.uk). Once London's main airport (open 1st Sun of mth).
Shirley Windmill Postmill Close, CR0 5DY (8406 4676, www.shirleywindmill.org.uk). Regular open days May-Oct; group visits by arrangement.

Gigs, clubs & comedy

Oval Tavern 131 Oval Road, CR0 6BR (8686 6023, www.theovalcroydon.co.uk). Pub with live music and Saturday storytime session for families.

Green spaces

For more details, see www.croydon.gov.uk.
Biggin Woods Covington Way, SW16. Once part of the Great North Wood. Tennis courts.
Brickfields Meadow Dickensons Lane, Woodside Green, SE25. Dipping pond.

Crystal Palace Park SE19 2BS (www.bromley. gov.uk). Major sports centre, farm, maze, fishing lake, and dinosaurs lurking in the bushes.
Grangewood Park Grange Road, SE25. Woodland, gardens, tennis courts, plus playground.
Lloyd Park Coombe Road, CR0. Parkland, woodland, sports pitches and disc golf.
Norwood Grove Covington Way & Gibson's Hill, SW16. Mansion with ornamental gardens. Once part of Great Streatham Common.
Selsden Wood Nature Reserve Old Farleigh Road, Selsdon, CR2.
South Norwood Country Park Albert Road, SE25. Lake, viewing mound, meadows, playground, visitors' centre, and pitch and putt.
South Norwood Lake & Grounds Woodvale Avenue, SE25. Lake with sailing and fishing, sports pitches and woodland.
Wandle Park Vicarage Road, CR0. Skatepark.
Westow Park Church Road, SE19. Playground.

Gyms & leisure centres

New Addington Leisure Centre Central Parade, New Addington, CR0 0JB (01689 842553, www. fusion-lifestyle.com).
Purley Leisure Centre 50 High Street, Purley, CR8 2AA (8668 7251, www.fusion-lifestyle.com).
South Norwood Leisure Centre 164 Portland Road, SE25 4PT (8662 9464, www.fusion-lifestyle.com).
Thornton Heath Leisure Centre 100 The High Street, CR7 8LF (8689 5300, www.fusion-lifestyle.com).
Waddon Leisure Centre Purley Way, CR0 4RG (8760 0657, www.fusion-lifestyle.com).

Outdoor pursuits

Addington Golf Club 205 Shirley Church Road, CR0 5AB (8777 1055, www.addingtongolf.com).
Addington Palace Golf Club Addington Park, Gravel Hill, CR0 5BB (8654 3061, www. addingtonpalacegolf.co.uk).
Croham Hurst Golf Club Croham Road, CR2 7HJ (8657 5581, www.chgc.co.uk).
Purley Downs Golf Club 106 Purley Downs Road, CR2 0RB (8657 8347 www.purleydowns golfclub.co.uk).
Selsden Park Golf Club 126 Addington Road, CR2 8YA (8657 8811, www.selsdonparkcroydon.co.uk).
Shirley Park Golf Course 194 Addiscombe Road, CR0 7LB (8654 1143, www.shirleyparkgolfclub.co.uk).

Spectator sports

Crystal Palace FC Selhurst Park, SE25 5EX (8768 6000, www.cpfc.co.uk). Premier League football.
Crystal Palace National Sports Centre (www.better.org.uk). Track and field events.

Schools

Primary

The borough has 76 primary schools including 16 church schools. There are also 12 independent primary schools. See www.croydon.gov.uk, www.education.gov.uk/edubase and www.ofsted.gov.uk for more information.

Secondary

Addington High School Fairchildes Avenue, CR0 0AH (01689 842545, www.addington.croydon.sch.uk).

Al Khair School 109-117 Cherry Orchard Road, CR0 6BE (8662 8664, www.alkhairschool.org.uk) Muslim; private.

Archbishop Tenison's Church of England High School Selborne Road, CR0 5JQ (8688 4014, www.archten.croydon.sch.uk). Church of England.

BRIT School for Performing Arts & Technology 60 The Crescent, CR0 2HN (8665 5242, www.brit.croydon.sch.uk). Performing-arts specialist.

Cedars School Coombe Road, Lloyd Park, CR0 5RD (8185 7770, www.thecedarsschool.org.uk). Roman Catholic; boys only; private.

Croydon High School Old Farleigh Road, CR2 8YB (8260 7500, www.croydonhigh.gdst.net). Girls only; private.

Edenham High School Orchard Way, CR0 7NJ (8776 0220, http://edenham.publishpath.com).

Harris Academy South Norwood Cumberlow Avenue, SE25 6AE (8405 5070, www.harris southnorwood.org.uk).

Harris City Academy Crystal Palace Maberley Road, SE19 2JH (8771 2261, www.harriscrystal palace.org.uk).

Harris Invictus Academy Croydon London Road, CR0 2TB (3371 3002, www.harrisinvictus.org.uk).

Oasis Academy Arena Albert Road, SE25 4QL (7921 4263, www.oasis academyarena.org).

Old Palace of John Whitgift School Old Palace Road, CR0 1AX (8688 2027, www.oldpalace.croydon.sch.uk). Girls only; private.

St Andrew's Church of England High School Warrington Road, CR0 4BH (8686 8306, www.standhigh.net). Church of England.

St Joseph's Roman Catholic College Beulah Hill, SE19 3HL (8761 1426, www.stjosephscollege.org.uk). Roman Catholic.

Shirley High Performing Arts College Shirley Church Road, CR0 5EF (8656 9755, www.shirley.croydon.sch.uk).

Virgo Fidelis Roman Catholic Convent Senior School 147 Central Hill, SE19 1RS (8670 6917, www.virgofidelis.org.uk). Roman Catholic.

Property

Local estate agents

Benson & Partners www.bensonpartners.co.uk
Conrad Fox www.conradfox.co.uk
Charles Fox www.charlesfox.net
Choices www.choices.co.uk
Cray & Norton www.crayandnorton.co.uk
James Chiltern www.jameschiltern.com
John Dallas www.johndallas.co.uk

Local knowledge

www.croydonadvertiser.co.uk
www.croydonguardian.co.uk
www.croydonradio.com
www.southnorwood.net
www.thecroydoncitizen.com

USEFUL INFO

Borough size
8,650 hectares

Population
380,900

Ethnic mix
White 55.2%
Black or Black British 23.8%
Mixed 13.7%
Asian or Asian British 6.2%
Chinese or other 1.1%

London Borough of Croydon
Bernard Weatherill House,
8 Mint Walk, CR0 1EA (8726 6000,
www.croydon.gov.uk)

Council run by
Labour

MPs
Croydon Central, Gavin Barwell
(Conservative); Croydon North,
Steve Reed (Labour); Croydon South,
Chris Philp (Conservative)

Main recycling centre
Recycling Centre, Factory Lane, CR0 3RL
(8726 6200, www.croydon.gov.uk)

Council tax
£977.60 to £2,932.78

Ealing

Carved up by canals, road and rail, this borough still has plenty of pleasant leafy corners, with wide-open green spaces and a genteel feel. But the coming of Crossrail is bringing major new developments around key transport hubs that could create the sort of wide-scale regeneration in the west that the Olympics created in the east.

AVERAGE PROPERTY PRICE

Detached £757,645	**Terraced** £482,470
Semi-detached £757,645	**Flat** £482,470

AVERAGE RENTAL PRICE PER WEEK

Room £107	**1 bed** £265
Studio £180	**2 bed** £316
	3 bed £391

Ealing Park Tavern

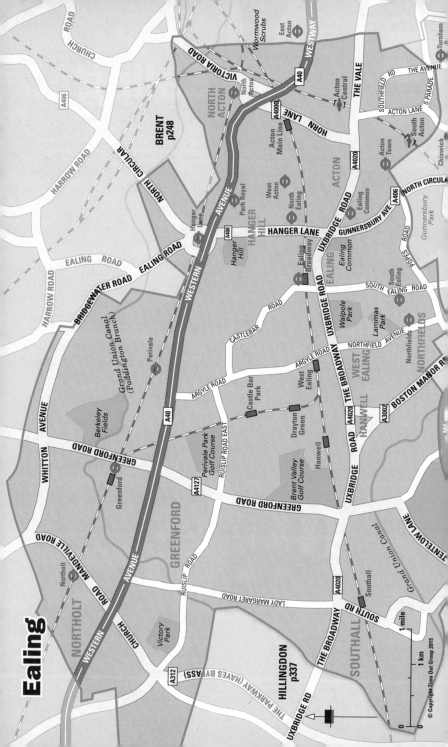

Neighbourhoods

Acton W3

For many, Acton is just a place on the way to Heathrow. But get off the main road and you'll find a thriving neighbourhood – although not all of it is prospering.

North Acton is dominated by the business-park-cum-industrial-estate Park Royal; this is also a road and rail spaghetti junction. The South Acton housing estate, meanwhile, is the largest in west London. But parts of the south and east are profiting from money squeezed in Acton's direction by the prohibitive property prices of Chiswick and Fulham – hence the smart houses, parks, sports fields and upmarket private schools. An area known for its long-established Polish population, Acton has more recently seen the arrival of Somali and Iraqi immigrants and also has a Japanese community in West Acton.

In Acton Town, the High Street, which is a conservation area, has all the usual banks, fast food franchises and supermarkets – plus the old Acton Library and the Town Hall. The former is to become a Curzon cinema, while parts of the latter have been converted into a new leisure centre and library. Meanwhile, the tired Oaks Shopping Centre on the High Street is being redeveloped in phases and is set to house a branch of Waitrose.

The Dragonfly Brewery at the historic half-timbered George & Dragon on the High Street brings a new microbrewery to an old pub, with the shiny tanks in a spectacular space at the back of the premises. The Aeronaut is the other local brewpub but is quirkier, with a circus-style garden and in-house troupe of cabaret performers. Tandoori eateries provide for curry fans – Bombay Bistro is popular – but there's also a good Chinese in the shape of North China. Friendly Acton Market has a decent mix of stalls from Indian street food and artisanal baking to handmade jewellery, and fruit and veg. Novice traders can receive training as part of a local enterprise scheme.

TRANSPORT

Tube lines Central, District, Piccadilly
Rail services into Paddington
Main bus routes into central London
7, 70; night buses N7, N11; 24-hour buses 94

The district is swamped by 1930s mock-Tudor houses, but you can still find some impressive Victorian detached residences and brick terraces, particularly around Creffield Road. Other upmarket areas include South Acton, Acton Green and Bedford Park, which all gain from being near the shops and restaurants of Chiswick High Road over the borough boundary in Hounslow. Further north, the streets around Acton Park are jammed with Clerkenwell-style office conversions, while East Acton has long rows of posh semis and sports grounds.

Pretty Churchfield Road has embraced gentrification and is now lined with enticing cafés, food shops and specialist stores, although there's a high turnover of occupants. Favourites include pubs such as the Rocket and the Station House, the Vindinista! wine bar (an offshoot of the Park + Bridge wine shop), café-bakery Laveli, the Mill Bakery, the Bake Me crêperie and florist Heart & Soul.

The level crossing and tranquil Acton Park, which is overlooked by the quaint Goldsmiths' Almshouses, complete the villagey illusion. The surrounding streets are some of Acton's most desirable, particularly the grand Victorian villas around Perryn Road and the popular terraces in the area known as Poets' Corner.

Further south, Acton Green Common, near Turnham Green tube station, is a nice example of an old village green, though cut in half by a railway line; Chiswick Common is on the other side of the tracks.

The north and west of Acton are the least attractive places to live in the borough. West Acton is dominated by railway lines and industrial estates; North Acton is an unappealing jumble of industrial developments and retail parks, cut off from the rest of the district by the traffic mayhem of Western Avenue, also known as the A40. However, a landscaped station square is being created next to North Acton tube station, which could provide a much-needed public space, and there is a good canalside pub, the Grand Junction Arms, with a large beer garden.

This is one of the most ethnically mixed areas in west London, and also one of the best integrated. There is a panoply of churches and faith centres, all of which seem to pull in large congregations.

The transport links in the borough are already excellent, with numerous tube stops, rail stations, and the A40 and M4 right on the doorstep, but the area will also reap the benefits of HS2 and Crossrail. Major mixed-use developments are already planned around new transport hubs, with work at Old Oak Common, next to Wormwood Scrubs, set to be one of the UK's largest regeneration programmes and expected to have the same sort of enormous, long-term impact that the Olympics is having on east London.

Ealing and Hanger Hill W5

Leafy, suburban with a fast-developing character, this area has come a long way since Ealing Studios produced its famous comedies on the edge of Walpole Park.

It has its share of tower blocks and housing estates – most notably around Argyle Road – but Ealing is overwhelmingly upper middle class, and it shows. The district is ultra-suburban, with tree-lined avenues full of independent faith schools and stately detached homes with gravel drives.

From a resident's perspective, the main attractions apart from the houses are the schools – mostly of the private, opted-out variety – and transport links: half a dozen train and tube stations, plus the A40 leading to the M40, and the M4 providing easy access to Heathrow and all points west.

It's also very green, so you can forget the fast pace of central London if you wish. Lammas Park is a large green lung, complete with playground and tennis courts, while the recently re-landscaped Walpole Park, near the Broadway, is child-friendly and hosts jazz and comedy festivals in summer. Opposite Walpole Park is the Questors, an Ealing gem: Europe's largest community theatre and a great way for children and adults to get involved with the performing arts. There is also a half marathon held in September, for those who are more athletically minded.

Ealing Green rivals Chiswick in terms of genteel affluence although it doesn't have the same yummy-mummy air; the most extravagant houses are north of the Broadway towards Hanger Hill. Pitshanger Village, near Pitshanger Park, does feel villagey but, by contrast, the area beyond the western end of the park is soon dominated by retirement homes and planned housing.

The main civic centre is on Ealing Broadway; the streets around the station (rail and tube) and Haven Green are packed with banks, cafés, restaurants, chain pubs, shops and, of course, more green spaces. South Ealing has huge mock-Tudor houses stretching to the neighbourhoods around

Ealing Common, and also plenty of shops and restaurants along Ealing South Road.

The high concentration of restaurants in Ealing, and oodles of independent coffee shops, reflects the division of disposable income in the borough. As well as the familiar list of chain options on and around the Broadway, a wide spread of independent eateries are in the mix. Café Grove serves Polish specialities, tiny Santa Maria provides excellent, authentic Neapolitan pizza, while other favourites include Farm W5 selling organic produce and tasty lunches; its avocado, date and honey milkshake is a highlight. Next door is All Original, with handmade gifts.

Ealing is not the best neighbourhood for a pub crawl, but there are a handful of good drinking holes. The area's oldest and most attractive pubs tend to be found in South Ealing, in the vicinity of St Mary's Road where the original Ealing village developed. There's the cosy Red Lion, a stone's throw from Ealing Film Studios, and the huge, ever-popular gastropub Ealing Park Tavern in South Ealing with its great back garden. Further north, you'll find the Village Inn in Pitshanger Village.

If you do venture to Ealing Common, try a cocktail at the Common Room, the only place to get a decent espresso martini in the area. Charlotte's Place is an excellent restaurant just off the common too. Go next door to the Grange and you can relax in the pub's summer house and reading room.

The North Star pub is a small gem amid the Broadway chains, with live music on selected nights, while further north, past West Ealing station, is the Drayton Court Hotel, where you can kick back with a drink in the bar area or the large landscaped garden.

Although it's not a focus for destination shopping, Ealing's retail resources meet local needs. The Ealing Broadway Centre houses an array of chain stores, while Rumbles, just outside the centre, is an attractive gift boutique. For more retail nearby, there's the Polish flavour of the Parade Delicatessen, and the organic food store As Nature Intended. New additions to the area are Caribbean chain diner Turtle Bay and Maggie's Vintage Beats & Breakfast, where you get great music, cocktails and an all-day breakfast.

Greenford and Perivale UB6

Greenford is a somewhat overlooked suburb sliced in half by the thundering A40; its main landmarks are the art deco Hoover Building and RAF Northolt. Residents wanting to be near the shops and private schools of Ealing generally prefer West Ealing and Hanwell, where the properties are similar.

In Greenford south of the A40, winding streets of mainly 1930s semis surround the town centre, which has been given a £5 million revamp by the council. Greenford's 'other town centre' and residential stretch, north of the A40, is posher. It's home to Indian and Polish communities.

Ravenor Park, Perivale Park and the 21st-century Northolt and Greenford Countryside Park (a landscaped space of man-made hills and ponds) comprise a real visual and recreational bonus for the area: much-needed green spaces for the many surrounding housing estates. The area is also blessed with low property prices and good transport links but there's not much in the way of restaurants or nightlife. Its best-kept secret is that the Grand Union Canal leads to Horsenden Hill, which feels like open countryside.

Perivale is a kind of satellite to Greenford, an out-of-the-way neighbourhood that doesn't have what you could call a proper town centre. But it's right next door to a Tesco superstore, the Westway Cross shopping park, and is even closer than Greenford to the canal and Horsenden Hill.

Hanwell, Northfields and West Ealing W13

Bounded by Northfield Avenue and Boston Road, Hanwell is the poorer cousin of Ealing. As you travel west along the Uxbridge Road, from West Ealing to Hanwell to Southall, the borough declines in status. Drayton Manor, a much-sought-after secondary school, is here, but it's generally all a bit grotty. Uxbridge Road cuts through the middle, providing the usual high-street amenities and a Bentley and Rolls-Royce showroom.

Hanwell and adjacent Northfields both score highly for green spaces, however; there are recreation grounds and sporting clubs galore, and a decent Fuller's pub, the Plough Inn, serving seasonal dishes. Ealing Farmers' Market is held in Leeland Road every Saturday. Uxbridge Road also passes between two significant cemeteries: the Royal Borough of Kensington & Chelsea Cemetery on the north side of the road and the City of Westminster Cemetery on the south side.

For golfers, it's a short putt to courses in the environs of Osterley Park and the Brent Valley. Back in Hanwell, Brent Lodge Animal Centre is a small zoo, endearingly known locally as Bunny Park.

The most appealing streets are in West Ealing, east of Northfield Avenue. There are some huge detached houses here, notably

HIGHS & LOWS

Unpretentious public golf facilities

Crossrail and HS2 on their way

Huge regeneration plans

Superb transport links

Indian food in Southall

Multicultural mix

▲ ▼

The A40

Not much for culture vultures

Soulless Park Royal industrial estate

Ealing's centre gets busier and blander

Churchfield Road, Acton

around Lammas Park, while the south end of Northfield Avenue boasts an array of restaurants. For travelling to central London, there are tube stops at Boston Manor and Northfields, overland train stations at Hanwell and West Ealing, plus the congested M4.

Southall UB1

Southall is a vibrant town that is also known as 'Little India'. It's been estimated that 55 per cent of its residents are Indian or Pakistani, and there is a large Somali community too.

The Punjabi population is sizeable in its own right, hence the Sri Guru Singh Sabha Southall, the largest Sikh temple outside India; its golden dome can be seen for miles. Other religious centres include St Anselm's Catholic Church, and local mosque the Central Jamia Masjid.

The area has given rise to a number of writers including Kwame Kwei-Armah and Tim Lott, as well as notable bhangra artists such as Jay Sean, Juggy D, H-Dhami and

Stroll along the Grand Union Canal towpath, then pop into the Grand Junction Arms for a pint.

Panjabi Hit Squad. Sadly, Southall's Chinese-style Himalaya Palace cinema, a Grade II-listed art deco landmark built in 1929, closed its doors to Bollywood fans in 2010. It now functions as a budget shopping centre.

The Broadway, running through the centre of Southall, is a boisterous slice of the subcontinent. From wedding caterers to sari shops, wholesale grocers to pavement snack stalls, there's little that you can't get here. There are also lots of restaurants, mainly Punjabi, and even the McDonald's advertises itself as halal. Notable eateries include the New Asian Tandoori Centre (Roxy), purveyor of no-frills north Indian dishes; its sibling restaurants Brilliant and Madhu's specialise in food that is Punjabi by way of Kenya; Giftos Lahore Karahi offers Lahori and handi dishes, among others; Moti Mahal is the home of Punjabi street food and Desi pizza.

Crossrail is coming to Southall, and a new residential quarter is being created on the site of the former gasworks, next to the Crossrail station. This will add 3,750 new homes as well as a school, open public spaces and more over a 30-year period.

Eating

Bake Me 92 Churchfield Road, W3 6DH (07790 793170).
Bombay Bistro 47 High Street, W3 6ND (8992 5131, www.bombay-bistro.co.uk).
Brilliant 72-76 Western Road, UB2 5DZ (8574 1928, www.brilliantrestaurant.com).
Café Grove 65 The Grove, W5 5LL (8810 0365, www.cafegrove.co.uk).
Charlotte's Place 16 St Matthew's Road, W5 3JT (8567 7541, www.charlottes.co.uk).
Farm W5 19 The Green, W5 5DA (8566 1965, www.farmw5.co.uk).
Giftos Lahore Karahi Fort Lahore, 162-164 The Broadway, UB1 1NN (8813 8669, www.gifto.com).
Laveli Bakery 7 Churchfield Road, W3 6HE (8993 6490, www.lavelibakery.com).
Madhu's 39 South Road, UB1 1SW (8574 1897, www.madhus.co.uk).
Maggie's Vintage Beats & Breakfast 39-41 New Broadway, W5 5AH (8840 8308, www.foodandfuel.co.uk).
Moti Mahal 94 The Broadway, UB1 1QF (8571 9443, www.motimahal.co.uk).
New Asian Tandoori Centre (Roxy) 114-118 The Green, UB2 4BQ (8574 2597, www.roxy-restaurant.com).
North China 305 Uxbridge Road, W3 9QU (8992 9183, www.northchina.co.uk).
Santa Maria 15 St Mary's Road, W5 5RA (8579 1462, www.santamariapizzeria.com).
Turtle Bay 16 High Street, W5 5DB (3067 0007, www.turtlebay.co.uk).
Village Inn 122-124 Pitshanger Lane, W5 1QP (8998 6810, www.village-inn.co.uk).

Drinking

Aeronaut 264 High Street, W3 9BH (8993 4242, www.aeronaut.pub).
Common Room 3-4 Grosvenor Parade, Uxbridge Road, W5 3NN (8992 7774, www.thecommonroom.co.uk).
Dragonfly Brewery at the George & Dragon 183 High Street, W3 9DJ (8992 3712, www.dragonflybrewery.co.uk).
Drayton Court Hotel 2 The Avenue, W13 8PH (8997 1019, www.draytoncourtlondon.co.uk).
Ealing Park Tavern 222 South Ealing Road, W5 4RL (8758 1879, www.ealingparktavern.com).
Grand Junction Arms Canal Bridge, Acton Lane, NW10 7AD (8965 5670, www.rampubcompany.co.uk).
Grange Warwick Road, W5 3XH (8567 7617, www.grangeealing.co.uk).

North Star 43 The Broadway, W5 5JN (8579 0863, www.thenorthstarealing.co.uk).
Plough Inn 297 Northfields Avenue, W5 4XB (8567 1416, www.ploughnorthfields.co.uk).
Red Lion 13 St Mary's Road, W5 5RA (8567 2541, www.redlionealing.co.uk).
Rocket 11-13 Churchfield Road, W3 6BD (8993 6123, www.therocketw3.co.uk).
Station House Churchfield Road, W3 6BH (8992 7110, www.thestationhousew3.com).
Vindinista! 74 Churchfield Road, W3 6DH (07703 502520, www.parkandbridge.com/vindinista).

Shopping

Acton Market High Street, W3 9NW (8993 9605, www.actonacton.com).
All Original 20 The Green, W5 5DA (3689 7034, www.alloriginalealing.co.uk).
As Nature Intended 17-21 High Street, W5 5DB (8840 1404, www.asnatureintended.uk.com).
Ealing Broadway Shopping Centre The Broadway, W5 5JY (8567 3453, www.ealing broadwayshopping.co.uk).
Ealing Farmers' Market Leeland Road, W13 9HH (7833 0338, www.lfm.org.uk).
Heart & Soul 65 Churchfield Road, W3 6AX (8896 3331, www.heart-n-soul.co.uk).
Mill Bakery 67 Churchfield Road, W3 6AX (7998 1010).
Parade Delicatessen 8 Central Buildings, The Broadway, W5 2NT (8567 9066).
Park + Bridge 73 Churchfield Road, W3 6AX (8993 0261, www.parkandbridge.com).
Rumbles 3A Oak Road, W5 3SS (8579 6979).
Westway Cross Greenford, UB6 0UW.

Things to do

Cinemas & theatres
Questors 12 Mattock Lane, W5 5BQ (8567 0011, www.questors.org.uk). The largest community theatre in Europe; around 20 shows a year.
Vue Acton Royale Leisure Park, Western Avenue, W3 0PA (0871 224 0240, www.myvue.com).

Galleries & museums
London Motorbike Museum Ravenor Farm, 29 Oldfield Lane South, UB6 9LB (8575 6644, www.london-motorcycle-museum.org).
London Transport Museum Depot 118-120 Gunnersbury Lane, W3 9BQ (7565 7298, www.ltmuseum.co.uk).
Pitzhanger Manor House & Gallery Walpole Park, Mattock Lane, W5 5EQ (8567 1227, www.ealing.gov.uk/pmgalleryandhouse). Closed for refurbishment until spring 2018.

Other attractions
Brent Lodge Park Animal Centre Church Road, W7 3BP (07940 021183, www.ealing.gov.uk). Zoo.

Green spaces
For details, see www.ealing.gov.uk.
Acton Park Uxbridge Road, W3. Sports facilities, playground, café and art centre.
Brent Lodge Park & Churchfields Church Road, W7. Tennis courts, animal centre and maze.
Gunnersbury Park Popes Lane, W3. Ornamental gardens and sports facilities.
Horsenden Hill Horsenden Lane North, UB6. Ancient woodland and grassland bordering the Grand Union Canal.
Lammas Park Northfield Avenue, W5 & W13. Formal park with bowling, croquet and more.
Northolt & Greenford Countryside Park Kensington Road, UB5 (www.ngcps.tripod.com). New landscaped park.
Pitshanger Park Church Road, W7. Golf course, play areas, river walk and allotments.
Ravenor Park Ruislip Road, UB6. Formal parkland, rose garden and sports facilities.
Southall Manor House Grounds The Green, UB2.
Walpole Park Mattock Lane, W5 5BQ. Formal Regency-era park in Pitshanger Manor grounds.

Gyms & leisure centres
Dormers Wells Leisure Centre Dormers Wells Lane, UB1 3HX (8571 7207, www.ealing.gov.uk).
Elthorne Sports Centre Westlea Road, off Boston Road, W7 2AD (8579 3226, www.ealing.gov.uk).
Featherstone Sports Centre 11 Montague Waye, UB2 5HF (8813 9886, www.ealing.gov.uk).
Greenford Sports Centre Lady Margaret Road, UB1 2NP (8575 9157, www.ealing.gov.uk).
Gurnell Leisure Centre Ruislip Road East, W13 0AL (8998 3241, www.ealing.gov.uk).
Twyford Sports Centre Twyford Crescent, W3 9PP (8993 9095, www.ealing.gov.uk).
Virgin Active Ealing Broadway Centre, W5 5JY (3740 8745, www.virginactive.co.uk). Private.

Outdoor pursuits
Brent Valley Golf Club Church Road, W7 3BE (8567 0489, www.bvgc.org). 18 holes.
Ealing Golf Club Perivale Lane, UB6 8TS (8997 0937, www.ealinggolfclub.com). 18 holes.
Hanger Hill Park Pitch & Putt Hanger Hill Park, Hillcrest Road, W5 2JL (8991 5343, www.pitchn putt.co.uk). Nine-hole pitch and putt.
Perivale Park Golf Course Stockdove Way, off Argyle Road, UB6 8TJ (8575 7116, www.everyoneactive.com). Nine-hole parkland course.

West London Golf Centre Ruislip Road, UB5 6QZ (8845 5350, www.westlondongolfcentre.com). Nine-hole course, driving range.

West Middlesex Golf Club Greenford Road, UB1 3EE (8574 3450, www.westmiddlesexgolfclub. co.uk). 18 holes.

Schools

Primary

There are 61 state primary schools in Ealing, including 12 church schools. There are also 13 independent primaries. See www.ealing.gov.uk, www.education.gov.uk/edubase and www.ofsted. gov.uk for more information.

Secondary

Acton High School Gunnersbury Lane, W3 8EY (3110 2400, www.actonhighschool.co.uk).

Alec Reed Academy Bengarth Road, UB5 5LQ (8841 4511, www.alecreedacademy.co.uk).

Brentside High School Greenford Avenue, W7 1JJ (8575 9162, www.brentsidehigh.ealing.sch.uk).

Cardinal Wiseman Catholic School Greenford Road, UB6 9AW (8575 8222, www.wiseman.ealing. sch.uk). Roman Catholic.

Dormers Wells High School Dormers Wells Lane, UB1 3HZ (8566 6446, www.dwhs.co.uk).

Drayton Manor High School Drayton Bridge Road, W7 1EU (8357 1900, www. draytonmanorhighschool.co.uk).

Ellen Wilkinson School for Girls Queen's Drive, W3 0HW (8752 1525, www.ellenwilkinson.ealing. sch.uk). Girls only.

Elthorne Park High School Westlea Road, W7 2AH (8566 1166, www.ephs.ealing.sch.uk).

Featherstone High School 11 Montague Waye, UB2 5HF (8843 0984, www.featherstonehigh. ealing.sch.uk).

Greenford High School Lady Margaret Road, UB1 2GU (8578 9152, www.greenford.ealing.sch.uk).

Northolt High School Eastcote Lane, UB5 4HP (8864 8544, www.northolthigh.org.uk).

Notting Hill & Ealing High School 2 Cleveland Road, W13 8AX (8799 8400, www.nhehs.gdst.net). Girls only; private.

St Benedict's School 54 Eaton Rise, W5 2ES (8862 2000, www.stbenedicts.org.uk). Roman Catholic; private.

Twyford High School Twyford Crescent, W3 9PP (8752 0141, www.twyford.ealing.sch.uk). Church of England.

Villiers High School Boyd Avenue, UB1 3BT (8813 8001, www.villiers.ealing.sch.uk).

William Perkin Church of England High School Oldfield Lane North, UB6 8PR (8832 8950, www. williamperkin.org.uk). Church of England.

Property

Local estate agents

Adams www.adamsproperty.co.uk
Brendons www.brendonsresidential.co.uk
Castle Hill www.castlehillproperties.co.uk
Castle Residential www.castleresidential.co.uk
Churchill www.churchill-estates.co.uk
Gardiner Homes www.gardinerhomes.co.uk
Robertson, Smith & Kempson www. robertsonsmithandkempson.co.uk
Sinton Andrews www.sintonandrews.co.uk

Local knowledge

www.actonw3.com
www.ealingcivicsociety.org
www.ealingtimes.co.uk

USEFUL INFO

Borough size
5,554 hectares

Population
349,800

Ethnic mix
White 62.7%
Black/Black British 8.9%
Asian/Asian British 20.7%
Chinese or other 4%
Mixed 3.8%

London Borough of Ealing
Perceval House, 14-16 Uxbridge Road, W5 2HL (8825 5000, www.ealing.gov.uk)

Council run by
Labour

MPs
Ealing Central & Acton, Rupa Huq (Labour); Ealing North, Stephen Pound (Labour); Ealing Southall, Virendra Sharma (Labour)

Main recycling centres
Stirling Road, off Bollo Lane, W3 8DJ (8993 7580, (www.ealing.gov.uk);); Greenford Road, UB6 9AP (8578 5674)

Council tax
£903.29 to £2,709.86

Enfield

The capital's northernmost borough is now drawing young families from more central locales, who are bringing life, culture and artisanal bakeries to otherwise suburban swathes of generally affluent green belt.

AVERAGE PROPERTY PRICE		AVERAGE RENTAL PRICE PER WEEK	
Detached £718,026	**Terraced** £322,473	**Studio** £167	**2 bed** £276
Semi-detached £433,291	**Flat** £264,443	**1 bed** £207	**3 bed** £334

Broomfield Park

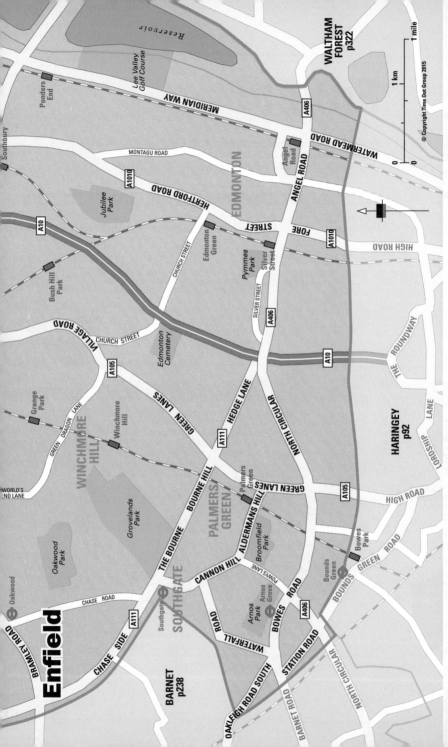

Neighbourhoods

Palmers Green N13

You know a place is on the up when an artisanal bakery opens on the site of a former betting shop. In the last couple of years, this leafy, if slightly rough-around-the-edges, enclave of the borough of Enfield has become a magnet for families priced out of places such as Crouch End, Islington and Muswell Hill.

Located just north of the North Circular along the top end of Green Lanes, N13 has a well-established Greek Cypriot community. It's becoming a draw for young families from outside the area thanks to its good schools, laid-back arty vibe and roomy Edwardian houses. More and more streets in the area are applying to the council to become designated 'play streets', so they can be shut to traffic once a month while children play outside; it's a scheme that seems to be bringing together the whole community.

At the town's heart is the attractive Broomfield Park, opened in 1903 when the area was known as London's 'northern heights' and lured middle-class families from central London with its promise of fresh air and greenery. While not as elegant as it would have been then, it's still pretty and pleasant. Historical Broomfield House remains derelict after fires in 1984 and 1994 although restoration plans are in place, and don't miss the Victorian greenhouse, community orchard and volunteer-run café, the Palmers Greenery (open Wednesdays and weekends), by the popular tennis courts.

Overlooking the park, Aldermans Hill, has an attractive parade of shops and eateries including, the popular Greek seafood restaurant Nissi and thriving Baskervilles Tea Shop, where you can find a local speciality tea named after one of the local streets in the Lakes Estate conservation area. The newest arrival to the area is the quietly hip Yard café-cum-florist, located in the station, where you can buy a mean soya latte, mouthwatering lemon cake and a bunch of peonies.

Head to the high street (Green Lanes) for the brilliant Red Cross bookshop (great for cheap second-hand kids' books) and good independents such as Kiva Coffee House, a new family-friendly café, Skate Attack, specialising in anything skate-related, and the lovely new Le Grand Jour bakery. If it's local Turkish fare you're after, head to Vadi, where you'll find traditional meats cooked on hot coals epitomising the eclectic, friendly spirit of this thriving patch of north London.

Winchmore Hill N21 and Southgate N14

Retaining its village credentials, peaceful Winchmore Hill has a pace of life that suits its family-focused residents down to the ground. Its railway station, also called Winchmore Hill, is handily positioned by the picturesque old village green. A nearby cluster of independent shops is enough to keep residents loyal to the area at the weekends: the House, a decoration specialist selling fabrics, paint and wallpaper; Minsky, a fashion boutique with mid-range labels; and also popular farmers' market the Sidings N21. Locals rate the recently opened Buckle & Vaughan, a slick modern Mediterranean restaurant.

There are a few good pubs in the area, attracting a well-heeled set, including the Kings Head, with a prime position on the green, and the more laid-back Salisbury Arms on Hoppers Road, next to popular Deli on the Green. With its mix of smart Edwardian houses, smattering of Victorian cottages, and lavish modern mansions in Broadwalk – the area's own version of the Bishop's Avenue – this salubrious enclave attracts Enfield's wealthiest residents.

Fresh air is in ample supply, thanks to nearby Grovelands Park, also home to the Priory Hospital. The park itself has a large boating lake, tennis courts and attractive woodland play area for older kids. Sport-lovers are well served by Winchmore Cricket Club – a local institution that also offers tennis, football and hockey – and Enfield Golf Club.

On the west side of Grovelands, you'll find the suburban town of Southgate, home to the late Amy Winehouse, and offering hints of of a medieval and Georgian past. Southgate's well-kept residential streets, busy high street, outstanding schools and good transport connections – served by the Piccadilly line

TRANSPORT

Tube lines Overground, Piccadilly
Rail services into Liverpool Street, Stratford
Main bus routes into central London 29, 141, 259, 279; night buses N29, N91, N279; 24-hour buses 149

and several bus routes – make it a convenient and pleasant place to live. The pivotal hub of the area is the circular art deco tube station, a classic designed by Charles Holden and opened in 1932.

For wide, open green spaces, travel a little further to Trent Country Park for bracing walks through woods and grassland. Near the Bramley Sports Ground (home of Saracens Amateur RFC), the dynamic Chicken Shed Theatre offers true community theatre, running a drama club for able-bodied and disabled children.

Similarly affluent, though much further north, is Hadley Wood. Tucked beside picturesque Monken Hadley Common, this is a small but affluent pocket of Enfield, noted for its high number of aspirant millionaires. This is the place to find your detached ranch-style house, complete with spacious grounds, swimming pool and electronic gates. Key to the area's social life is Hadley Wood Golf Club, with its prestigious course and imposing clubhouse, a mansion built in 1781.

Enfield Town EN1

Church Street is Enfield Town's main thoroughfare, a narrow, down-to-earth shopping street with charity shops aplenty. Just off it, historic Enfield Market (established over 700 years ago) bursts into life three days a week, selling a cheap and cheerful mix of clothing, household goods, fresh fruit and veg. The other side of the road sees local trading in

its 21st-century form: the Palace Gardens and Palace Exchange shopping centres.

These refurbished shopping centres are the place to go for chain stores, especially clothes shops such as H&M, River Island, Monsoon and Next. However , commercial Enfield's claim to fame is that is was the first place in the world to get an ATM. Installed in 1967 at the local branch of Barclays, it was 'opened' by *On the Buses* actor Reg Varney and is commemorated with a blue plaque.

Enfield is rediscovering its sense of community, as many more families decide to settle and small local businesses open up. Avert your eyes from the street-level bargains in Superdrug and New Look and you might notice the Enfield Word Wall, a public art installation that uses extracts from Enfield conversations past and present to create a snapshot of local life: 'You don't know names you just know the faces, but everyone says hello when you go past' or 'I was evacuated during the war but back in time for the doodlebugs and our Anderson shelter'.

Just a short stroll from the Enfield one-way system is Gentleman's Row, probably the area's most desirable address. With its much sought-after large Georgian and Victorian houses backing on to the historic New River, it offers a reminder of the town's prosperous past.

Indian and Greek restaurants dominate and, while destination dining doesn't really exist in Enfield, there are several friendly

Aldermans Hill

HIGHS & LOWS

Pretending you live in the countryside

Historic parkland

Horticulture

Schools

▲ ⋯⋯⋯⋯⋯⋯⋯⋯⋯⋯⋯⋯⋯ ▼

Industrial estates and A roads around Edmonton and Ponders End

Only just inside the M25

Lack of nightlife

Golf bores

locals. Many of Enfield Town's boozers can have a brash element to them, so for a peaceful pint head to the picturesque Old Wheatsheaf, a friendly, old-fashioned Victorian pub with decent beer; the Cricketers in the Chase Sides conservation area is family friendly. For a more rural setting, try the King & Tinker, parts of which date from the 16th century – these days, you'll find decent ales and a large beer garden.

Edmonton N9/N18

Surrounded by huge arterial, traffic-clogged roads and light industrial estates, Edmonton struggles to achieve a distinct identity and suffers from many of the problems traditionally associated with deprived, inner-city areas. Cheap rented housing – much of it in the form of looming twin and triplet towers of council estate flats – is characteristic, rather than owner-occupied houses. On the plus side, there's a huge IKEA.

Edmonton Green, with its railway station and bus terminal, is the public transport hub of the neighbourhood and home to a shopping centre occupied by many household names. At its heart is Market Square with traditional market stalls.

Further east, the underused and vacant industrial sites by the A406 in Upper Edmonton are earmarked for the £1.5 billion Meridian Water development. This will capitalise on its location beside the Lee Valley Regional Park; the plans are to create approximately 8,000 new homes, 3,000 new jobs and attractive public waterfront spaces over the next decade and more.

Eating

Baskervilles Tea Shop 66 Aldermans Hill, N13 4PP (8351 1673, www.baskervillesteashop.co.uk).
Buckle & Vaughan 10-12 The Green, N21 1AY (8886 2981, www.buckleandvaughan.com).
Kiva Coffee House 346 Green Lanes, N13 5TW (8886 4094, www.kivacoffeehouse.co.uk).
Nissi 62 Aldermans Hill, N13 4PP (8882 3170, www.nissirestaurant.co.uk).
Palmers Greenery Café Broomfield Park, Broomfield Lane, N13 4HE (www.friendsofbroomfieldpark.org).
Vadi 430-434 Green Lanes, N13 5XG (8882 2228, www.vadipalmersgreen.co.uk).
Yard Palmers Green rail station, Aldermans Hill, N13 4PN (8886 6884, www.theyardcafe.co.uk).

Drinking

Cricketers Chase Side Place, EN2 6QA (8363 5218, www.mcmullens.co.uk/cricketersenfield).
King & Tinker Whitewebbs Lane, EN2 9HJ (8363 6411, www.kingandtinker.com).
Kings Head 1 The Green, N21 1BB (8886 1988, www.geronimo-inns.co.uk).
Old Wheatsheaf 3 Windmill Hill, EN2 6SE (8363 0516).
Salisbury Arms Hoppers Road, N21 3NP (8882 9103, www.thesalisburyarmswinchmorehill.co.uk).

Shopping

British Red Cross Bookshop 385 Green Lanes, N13 4JG (8886 8364, www.redcross.org.uk).
Crews Hill EN2 9DJ (www.crewshill.com). A cluster of specialist garden centres and nurseries between Enfield and the M25.
Deli on the Green 251 Hoppers Road, N21 3NP (8882 5631).
Edmonton Green Shopping Centre 10 West Mall, N9 0AL (0345 656 4176, www.edmontongreencentre.co.uk).
Enfield Market Church Street, EN2 6AA (8367 8941, www.toect.org.uk).
Le Grand Jour 399 Green Lanes, N13 4JD (8882 6513).
House 19 The Green, N21 3NL (8886 3800).
IKEA 6 Glover Drive, N18 3HF (3645 0000, www.ikea.com).
Minsky 45 Station Road, N21 3NB (8360 4488, www.minskylondon.com).
Palace Exchange Shopping Centre Hatton Walk, EN2 6BP (8362 1934, www.palaceexchange.co.uk).
Palace Gardens Shopping Centre Church Street, EN2 6SN (8367 1210, www.palacegardensenfield.co.uk).
Sidings N21 62 Station Road, N21 3NG (www.thesidingsn21.co.uk).
Skate Attack 397 Green Lanes, N13 4JG (8886 7979, www.skateattack.co.uk).

Things to do

Cinemas & theatres
Artzone 1st floor, Edmonton Green Shopping Centre, 54-56 Market Square, N9 0TZ (8803 9877, www.artzone-facilities.org.uk). Community theatre, gallery, and film and studio space.
Chicken Shed Theatre Chase Side, N14 4PE (8292 9222, www.chickenshed.org.uk).
Cineworld Enfield Southbury Leisure Park, 208 Southbury Road, EN1 1YQ (0871 200 2000, www.cineworld.co.uk).

Millfield Theatre Silver Street, N18 1PJ (8807 6680, www.enfield.gov.uk/millfield).
Odeon Lee Valley Lee Valley Leisure Complex, Picketts Lock Lane, N9 0AS (0871 224 4007, www.odeon.co.uk).

Other attractions

Capel Manor Gardens Bullsmoor Lane, EN1 4RQ (0845 612 2122, www.capelmanorgardens.co.uk). Thirty acres of specialist gardens.
Forty Hall & Estate Forty Hill, EN2 9HA (8363 8196, www.enfield.gov.uk/fortyhall). Grade II-listed Jacobean house and estate. Grounds contain the remains of Elsynge Palace.
Parkside Farm Hadley Road, EN2 8LA (8367 2035, www.parksidefarmpyo.co.uk). Pick your own fruit and veg.

Chicken Shed's inclusive, disability-friendly theatre shows are excellent and the annual panto is a regular sell-out.

Whitewebbs Museum of Transport
Whitewebbs Road, EN2 9HW (8367 1898, www.whitewebbsmuseum.co.uk). Museum housed in an 1898 pumping station.

Green spaces

For more details, see www.enfield.gov.uk.
Broomfield Park Broomfield Lane, N13. Sports pitches, playground, crazy golf and yacht pond.
Bush Hill Park Lincoln Road, EN1. Sports pitches, tennis courts, playground, croquet and skatepark.
Grovelands Park The Bourne, N14. Historic park laid out by Humphry Repton, plus a Grade II-listed house designed by John Nash. Sports pitches, playground, pitch and putt, and ornamental lake.
Jubilee Park Galliard Road, N9. Sports ground, formal gardens and art deco gates.
Oakwood Park Oakwood Park Road, N14. Oak Lodge has a walled garden, orchard and igloo-shaped ice well. Facilities include sports pitches, tennis courts and a playground.
Pymmes Park Victoria Road, N9. Sports pitches, basketball court, playgrounds, bowling green, lake and pond.
Town Park Cecil Road, EN2. Sports pitches, bowling green, water play, rose garden, and riverside walks along the New River.
Trent Country Park Cockfosters Road, EN4. Ancient royal hunting forest. Cycle path, fishing, and a wildlife hospital and animal centre.

Gyms & leisure centres

Albany Leisure Centre 505 Hertford Road, EN3 5XH (8804 4255, www.fusion-lifestyle.com).
Arnos Pool 269 Bowes Road, N11 0BD (8361 9336, www.fusion-lifestyle.com).
David Lloyd Enfield Carterhatch Lane, EN1 4LF (8364 5858, www.davidlloydleisure.co.uk). Private.
Edmonton Leisure Centre 2 The Broadway, N9 0TR (8375 3750, www.fusion-lifestyle.com).
Island Fitness 57 Island Centre Way, EN3 6GF (01992 762107, www.islandfitness.co.uk). Private.
LA Fitness (www.lafitness.co.uk); 18 East Barnet Road, EN4 8RW (8440 2796); Winchmore Hill Road, N14 6AA (8886 8883). Private.
Southbury Leisure Centre 192 Southbury Road, EN1 1YP (8245 3201, www.fusion-lifestyle.com).
Southgate Leisure Centre Winchmore Hill Road, N14 6AD (8882 7963, www.fusion-lifestyle.com).
Virgin Active Enfield Tower Point, Sydney Road, EN2 6SZ (8370 4100, www.virginactive.co.uk). Private.

Outdoor pursuits

Enfield Golf Club Old Park Road South, EN2 7DA (8363 3970, www.enfieldgolfclub.co.uk). 18-hole course.
Hadley Wood Golf Club Beech Hill, EN4 0JJ (8449 4328, www.hadleywoodgc.com). 18-hole course laid out by Alister McKenzie.
Lee Valley Athletics Centre Lee Valley Leisure Complex, 61 Meridian Way, Picketts Lock, N9 0AR (8344 7230, www.leevalleypark.org.uk). Superb athletics centre.
Lee Valley White Water Centre Station Road, EN9 1AB (0845 677 0606, www.leevalleypark.org.uk/whitewaterrafting). The site of the canoe slalom at the 2012 Games.
Rectory Farm Shooting Ground The Ridgeway, EN2 8AA (07971 162048, www.clayshoot.org.uk).
Southgate Hockey Centre Trent Park, Snakes Lane, EN4 0PS (8440 7574, www.southgatehockey centre.co.uk). Home to one of the top hockey clubs in the country.
Trent Park Equestrian Centre East Pole Farmhouse, Bramley Road, N14 4UW (8363 9005, www.trentpark.com). One of the largest riding schools in London.
Winchmore Hill Cricket Club Ford Grove, N21 3ER (8360 1271, www.winchmorehill.org). A large range of sports on offer, not just cricket.

Schools

Primary

There are 59 state primary schools in Enfield, including 16 church schools and one Jewish school. There are also six independent primary schools.

See www.enfield.gov.uk, www.education.
gov.uk/edubase and www.ofsted.gov.uk for
more information.

Secondary

Aylward Academy Windmill Road, N18 1NB
(8803 1738, www.aylwardacademy.org).
Bishop Stopford's School Brick Lane, EN1 3PU
(8804 1906, www.bishopstopfords.enfield.sch.uk).
Broomfield School Wilmer Way, N14 7HY
(8368 4710, www.broomfieldschool.co.uk).
Chace Community School Churchbury Lane,
EN1 3HQ (8363 7321, www.chace.enfield.sch.uk).
Edmonton County School (www.edmonton
county.co.uk); Little Bury Street, N9 9HZ
(8360 3158); Great Cambridge Road, EN1 1HQ
(8360 3158).
Enfield County School (www.enfieldcs.enfield.
sch.uk); Holly Walk, EN2 6QG (8363 3030);
Rosemary Avenue, EN2 0SP (8363 9934). Girls
only; mixed sixth form.
Enfield Grammar School Market Place, EN2
6LN (8363 1095, www.enfieldgrammar.com).
Boys only.
Highlands School 148 Worlds End Lane, N21
1QQ (8370 1100, www.highlands.enfield.sch.uk).
Kingsmead School 196 Southbury Road, EN1
1YQ (8363 3037, www.kingsmeadschool.org).
Latymer School Haselbury Road, N9 9TN (8807
4037, www.latymer.co.uk).
Lea Valley High School Bullsmoor Lane, EN3
6TW (01992 763666, www.lvhs.org.uk).
Nightingale Academy 34 Turin Road, N9 8DQ
(8443 8500, www.nightingaleacademy.org).
Oasis Academy Enfield 9 Kinetic Crescent,
Innova Park, Mollinson Avenue, EN3 7XH (01992
655400, www.oasisacademyenfield.org).
Oasis Academy Hadley Hadley Bell Lane, EN3
4PX (8804 6946, www.oasisacademyhadley.org).
St Anne's Catholic High School for Girls
6 Oakthorpe Road, N13 5TY (8886 2165, www.st-
annes.enfield.sch.uk). Roman Catholic; girls only.
St Ignatius College Turkey Street, EN1 4NP
(01992 717835, www.st-ignatius.enfield.sch.uk).
Roman Catholic; boys only.
Southgate School Sussex Way, EN4 0BL (8449
9583, www.southgate.enfield.sch.uk).
Winchmore School Laburnum Grove, N21 3HS
(8360 7773, www.winchmore.enfield.sch.uk).

Property

Local estate agents

Absolute Property www.absoluteproperty
agents.com
Addison Townends www.addisontownends.co.uk
Anthony Pepe www.anthonypepe.com

Anthony Webb www.anthonywebb.co.uk
Baker & Chase www.bakerandchase.co.uk
Barnfields www.barnfields.co.uk
Bennett Walden www.bennett-walden.co.uk
Brien Firmin www.brienfirmin.com
Castles www.castles-estateagents.co.uk
James Hayward www.james-hayward.com
Lanes www.lanesproperty.co.uk
Peter Barry www.peterbarry.co.uk

Local knowledge

www.enfieldindependent.co.uk
www.enfield-today.co.uk
www.loveyourdoorstep.co.uk
www.n21.net
www.palmersgreencommunity.org.uk
www.palmersgreennn13.com

USEFUL INFO

Borough size
8,083 hectares

Population
329,200

Ethnic mix
White 71.6%
Black or Black British 12.1%
Asian or Asian British 9.7%
Mixed 3.8%
Chinese or other 2.8%

London Borough of Enfield
Civic Centre, Silver Street, EN1 3XA
(8379 1000, www.enfield.gov.uk)

Council run by
Labour

MPs
Edmonton, Kate Osamor (Labour);
Enfield Southgate, David Burrowes
(Conservative); Enfield North, Joan Marie
Ryan (Labour)

Main recycling centre
Barrowell Green Recycling Centre,
Winchmore Hill, N21 3AR (8379 1000,
www.enfield.gov.uk)

Council tax
from £930.23 to £2,790.68

Hounslow

Leafy Chiswick has long been a favourite of affluent, middle-class families, but development in up-and-coming Brentford and culturally diverse Hounslow is bringing a new lease of life to the more mundane parts of the borough.

AVERAGE PROPERTY PRICE			AVERAGE RENTAL PRICE PER WEEK		
Detached £671,172	**Terraced** £349,992		**Room** £113	**1 bed** £247	
Semi-detached £390,537	**Flat** £303,675		**Studio** £161	**2 bed** £282	
				3 bed £344	

Neighbourhoods

Chiswick W4

This swanky part of west London offers easy access to the city centre along with a tranquil, suburban feel. Two main thoroughfares running west to east divide Chiswick: the bustling A315 (Chiswick High Road), which is the main shopping hotspot, and the imposing, six-lane A4 (Great West Road), which runs out to Brentford, Isleworth and Hounslow. At the junction of the two roads, and the start of the M4, is Chiswick Roundabout, flanked by car dealerships and usually gridlocked. Some of the area's most affordable property is nearby. Chiswick Village (www.chiswick villagew4.co.uk), a collection of attractive 1930s flats, is popular and has a good sense of community.

The riverside section of the A4 is anchored by Hogarth Roundabout, named after 18th-century artist and satirist William Hogarth, who lived mere yards away. Also next to the roundabout is Fuller's, London's oldest brewery.

Lined with upmarket shops, landmark restaurants and Parisian-style pavement cafés, Chiswick High Road is bustling day and night. The number of sports cars, 4x4s and all-terrain buggies is testament to the predominance of wealthy, middle-class families. The demographic means Chiswick High Road has also been earmarked for a new Picturehouse cinema, in the former Ballet Rambert building.

At the west end of the road is Chiswick Business Park, a glassy, high-tech office complex designed by Richard Rogers on the site of the old Gunnersbury bus depot. Landscaped public spaces – including a lake, waterfall and cycle paths – host lively events and relaxed alfresco dining. Nearby is a triangular green space called Turnham Green; Chiswick Common, meanwhile, can be found next to Turnham Green tube station. Further west is expansive Gunnersbury Park, site of the hugely popular London Mela.

It's the southern half of Chiswick that is most sought after, however, with notable riverside stretches at Chiswick Mall – whose spectacular Georgian residences have mini-gardens across the road from the Thames, facing Chiswick Eyot – and at Strand on the Green, whose waterside pubs are popular with walkers and cyclists. Tiny Church Street is full of architectural gems, while Corney Reach, just to the south, is a more modern residential complex.

Also in great demand is the Grove Park area. Huge houses from all eras squat on a network of wide, tree-lined streets, with a smattering of shops around Chiswick rail station to break the residential norm. Sutton Court Mansions on Fauconberg Road is popular with renters. To the south lies Dukes Meadows; if you want to mooch around here, it helps if you have an allotment or belong to the upmarket Chiswick Riverside Health Club & Racquet Club. Otherwise, you could always come to the Sunday market: the Food Market Chiswick. Along this stretch of the Thames, you'll also find the Barnes and Chiswick bridges, while the elegant 18th-century Chiswick House is another local treasure; the restored grounds are stunning and there's a striking café too.

As befits such a well-heeled neighbourhood, there's a vibrant restaurant culture. Family-friendly chains abound on the High Road, as well as independents such as the High Road Brasserie in High Road House (sister venue to Soho House), Modern European restaurant and wine bar Carvosso's at 210, upmarket chippie the Catch and – towards Gunnersbury – Napa with its British ingredients and Californian cuisine. Boys Authentic Thai offers Thai, Chinese and Malaysian treats, but for Asian food more generally, you're better off heading east towards Hammersmith or west to Hounslow. For top-notch cheap(ish) eats, there's a branch of Franco Manca pizza, the Vietnamese Ngon and the Iranian Faanoos Chiswick, while the sweet of tooth can indulge at Château Dessert.

The big high-street noise is Michelin-starred Hedone, helmed by Swedish chef-patron Mikael Jonsson. Elsewhere are seriously stylish Michael Nadra and laid-back café the Copper Cow. Chiswickians also have the choice of two of London's best French restaurants: the near-perfect La Trompette – part of the mini-empire of Nigel Platts-Martin and Bruce Poole, which includes Chez Bruce – and classic bistro Le Vacherin.

This is prime gastropub territory too, with the Pilot, the Roebuck and Bollo House. Best of the bunch, and hugely popular with locals, is the Swan, which, along with the sympathetically restored Duke of Sussex, has a large beer garden.

But there's no excuse for wasting your time on a below-par pint in Chiswick. The proximity of the Fuller's brewery means plenty of exemplary drinking establishments. Located on riverside Strand on the Green are

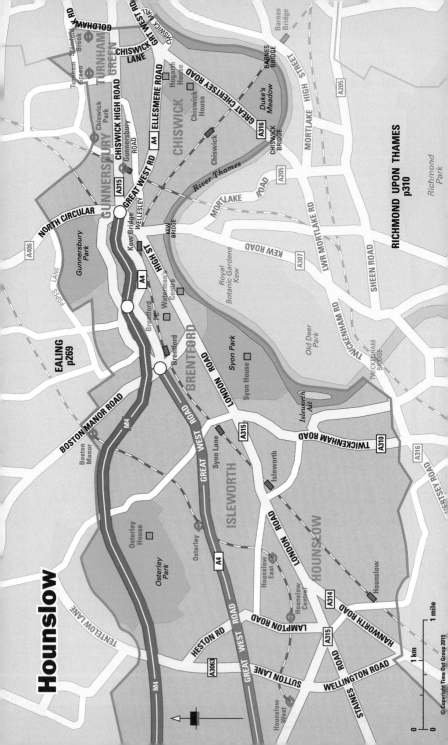

the Bell & Crown and City Barge; both are child-friendly, with decent pub grub, waterside terraces and real ales. Nearby is the Bull's Head, opposite Oliver's Island. Meanwhile, on Devonshire Road, the Italian Job claims to be the UK's first Italian craft beer pub and, near Turnham Green Station, the Tabard retains its beautiful Arts and Crafts tiled friezes.

Chiswick High Road also has plenty of options, albeit without the river views. The recently refurbished George IV hosts the Headliners Comedy Club, while the Old Pack Horse offers open fires, leather sofas and Thai food. But for a pint of Chiswick Bitter within barrel-rolling distance of Fuller's Brewery, head for the Mawson Arms, which is also the starting point for the brewery tour.

Chiswick's shops know their audience: plenty of chichi boutiques, pricey kids' clothes and upmarket interiors shops, mainly along Chiswick High Road again or clustered

Fuller's Brewery has weekday tasting tours for a very reasonable £10.

around Devonshire Road and Turnham Green Terrace. Women fare better than men, with various upmarket chains such as Sweaty Betty and Whistles, designer label outlet RSPV (set up by stylist Pippa Vosper, whose credits include *i-D* and *Harper's Bazaar*) and clothing and jewellery shop Blink. Middle-class surfer wannabes are kept happy thanks to branches of Fat Face and White Stuff.

Among the abundance of interiors chains, the Old Cinema offers three floors of antiques and retro furniture, while Neptune's arrival has brought with it the lure of timeless elegance. There are also good finds to be had at the High Road or Chiswick auction houses.

Foodies are, of course, well catered for with the excellent Covent Garden Fishmongers, lovely continental deli Mortimer & Bennett, Philip Neal Luxury Chocolates and organic supermarket As Nature Intended.

There are also a growing choice of independent cafés and delis: Tamp on Devonshire Road, Hack & Veldt deli on Turnham Green Terrace and Grove Park Deli on Fauconberg Road. Alternatively, the Chiswick Car Boot Sale is a very different shopping experience, held on the first Sunday of the month, with proceeds to Chiswick School.

Brentford TW8

It may still be a little down-at-heel compared to neighbouring Chiswick, but Brentford has undergone significant redevelopment of late. There's certainly potential: a riverside location, old rail and canal infrastructure, a 20-minute train ride to Waterloo, a strong community spirit and relatively affordable housing.

In Old Brentford, south of the A4, Brentford Dock Estate is a 1970s development on the site of former docks and has a fantastic location next to the Thames. Adjacent is Ferry Quays, one of several new housing developments, containing restaurants and small businesses as well as swanky apartments. Closer to Kew Bridge is Kew Bridge West, boasting private communal gardens and penthouses. There are also impressive canalside developments: the Island is an expensive gated community; Heron View is somewhat more affordable. Housing elsewhere consists mainly of Victorian two- and three-bed terraces. There are also two large council estates, while at the other end of the market, the Butts Estate – a Georgian square and associated conservation area – contains several Grade II-listed buildings, some dating back to 1680.

The Grand Union canal and Brent River both join the Thames at Brentford Lock, and all three waterways are home to a friendly community on a variety of barges and houseboats. Casual cruisers should have no trouble finding visitor moorings at Brentford Lock, Brentford Kew Reach or Ferry Quays for about £20/night for a narrowboat, but longer-term moorings are, as elsewhere in London, very hard to come by. Expect residential moorings to cost £7,000 or more per year, if you can find one.

Brentford has strong appeal for families, downsizers and young professionals wanting

TRANSPORT

Tube lines District, Overground, Piccadilly
Rail services into Clapham Junction, Waterloo
Main bus routes into central London night buses N9, N11; 24-hour buses 27, 94
River boat services into central London and Kew Pier

a foot on the property ladder. GlaxoSmithKline has its global headquarters here, and folding-bike maker Brompton still designs and builds all its bikes in Brentford. The area also offers decent amenities. While Chiswick lacks a theatre and cinema, Brentford has both at the trusty riverside Watermans arts centre, which offers everything from comedy to panto. The programme at the small but modestly excellent cinema offers both commercial and arthouse fare.

Well-heeled residents mean Chiswick's charity shops are worth a rummage.

Ferry Quays has a good restaurant in Pappadums and, while the High Street itself has little to offer lovers of fine dining, the Italian La Rosetta is popular – plus there's an outlet of Thai chain Fat Boys. Watermans arts centre has a pleasant café and a decent Indian restaurant, perfect for a quick pre-show bite. If you're more of a home cook, you'll appreciate the Sunday market that is finally up and running on Market Place after a false start or two.

For a drink, try the Old Fire Station – Cuban-themed bar downstairs, Persian restaurant upstairs – or the Weir gastropub with its waterside garden. The Lord Nelson in north Brentford is a friendly, cosy choice, while the boatie-favourite Magpie & Crown offers an astonishing array of beers, plus good home-cooked food. For live music, try the Six Bells.

There's fervent local support for Championship team Brentford FC, currently playing at retro football stadium Griffin Park but in the process of planning themselves a new 20,000-seater in Lionel Road South by the M4, along with mid-rise apartment blocks, a hotel and shops.

Other attractions include Boston Manor Park, which has a restored Jacobean manor house and hosts the annual Brentford Festival; spacious Syon Park; and Kew Gardens, just across the Thames in Richmond. The Kew Bridge Steam Museum is home to the world's largest working beam engine; the Musical Museum has a large collection of pre-modern mechanical musical instruments, such as player pianos and a Mighty Wurlitzer organ.

Isleworth and Osterley TW7

Isleworth and Osterley, separated by the thundering Great West Road, are largely residential, with lots of large 1930s homes – both areas are popular with families who find the prices in Chiswick too steep. Isleworth's shops are clustered near the rail station on London Road, St John's Road and Twickenham Road – though they're not much to shout about: a few restaurants and takeaways, betting shops, convenience stores and florists.

Osterley, home to gorgeous Osterley House and Park, and the headquarters of BSkyB, is quieter than Isleworth and has a low-key, villagey feel. The excellent second-hand Osterley Bookshop is housed in the old tube station and the owners sell free-range eggs – from their own chickens – and home-made jam; for a curry, try Memories of India.

The nicest part of the area, however, is riverside Old Isleworth, where the landscape is dominated by the small, tree-covered island of Isleworth Ait, a nature reserve with very limited access.

Old Isleworth also has some fabulous places to drink. The London Apprentice, just outside Syon Park, opposite Isleworth Ait, was once a favourite of Charles Dickens; it's a fine place to enjoy a drink by the river in summer. For food, Greedies on South Street is much loved – an organic greasy-spoon café-deli, now with a conservatory.

Moving into new Isleworth and Osterley, there's the Coach & Horses, also mentioned in Dickens, and the quaint Hare & Hounds. Also of note is the Red Lion: it offers up to nine real ales at any one time, as well as music, quiz nights and beer festivals.

Hounslow TW3

If excellent transport links are high on your list of priorities, you'll find escape routes galore in Hounslow. Unfortunately, you may well feel the need to use them. What this area lacks in glamour, peace and des res addresses, it makes up for in proximity to Heathrow – the constant roar of planes overhead is an issue – and easy access to central London. Other pluses include cheap houses and a large Asian population that makes this the borough's most diverse corner.

The pedestrianised High Street is run-down, although hints of regeneration are appearing, such as the Blenheim Centre, a huge, glass shopping complex with luxury flats. In general, housing stock is not particularly exciting: 1930s and 1960s semis, and 1980s flats. Green spaces include Hounslow Heath and Hounslow Urban Farm, one of the capital's largest community farms.

Hounslow High Street offers down-at-heel chains as well as the outdated Treaty Centre, which houses a Debenhams, H&M and other chains. A 24-hour Asda has opened in the newer Blenheim Centre, but locals generally prefer to get their groceries from smaller independents such as Ortadogu Supermarket, which offers Greek, Middle Eastern and Turkish goodies.

Hounslow is dominated by big-name chains and fast-food joints, but there are also plenty of Indian restaurants, including the locally admired Heathrow Tandoori and glitzy Mantra.

Planned regeneration of Hounslow town centre will involve making the High Street a focus for shopping, leisure and entertainment, with a new market and performance venue at the western end and landscaped new public spaces.

Eating

Boys Authentic Thai 95 Chiswick High Road, W4 2EF (8995 7991, www.boysauthenticthai.com).
Carvosso's at 210 210 Chiswick High Road, W4 1PD (8995 9121, www.carvossosat210.co.uk).
The Catch 293 Chiswick High Road, W4 4HH (8747 9358, www.the-catch.co.uk).
Château Dessert 213 Chiswick High Road, W4 2DW (8742 2344, www.chateaudessert.com).
Copper Cow 2 Fauconberg Road, W4 3JY (8742 8545, www.thecoppercow.co.uk).
Faanoos Chiswick 472 Chiswick High Road, W4 5TT (8994 4217, www.faanoosrestaurant.com).
Fat Boys 68 High Street, Brentford, TW8 0AH (8569 8481, www.fatboysthai.co.uk).
Franco Manca 144 Chiswick High Road, W4 1PU (8747 4822, www.francomanca.co.uk).
Greedies 49 South Street, TW7 7AA (8560 8562).
Heathrow Tandoori 482 Great West Road, TW5 0TA (8572 1772, www.heathrowtandoori.co.uk).
Hedone 301-303 Chiswick High Road, W4 4HH (8747 0377, www.hedonerestaurant.com).
High Road Brasserie 162-170 Chiswick High Road, W4 1PR (8742 7474, www.highroad brasserie.co.uk).
Mantra 253 Bath Road, TW3 3DA (8572 6000, www.mantradining.com).
Memories of India 160-162 Thornbury Road, TW7 4QE (8847 1548, www.memoriesofindia.co.uk).
Michael Nadra 6-8 Elliott Road, W4 1PE (8742 0766, www.restaurant-michaelnadra.co.uk).

Napa Restaurant 626 Chiswick High Road, W4 5RY (8996 5200, www.claytonhotelchiswick.com).
Ngon 195 Chiswick High Road, W4 2DR (8994 9630, www.ngondeli.com).
Old Fire Station 55 High Street, Brentford, TW8 0AD (5568 5999, www.the-firestation.co.uk).
Pappadums 1&2 Ferry Lane, Ferry Quays, TW8 0BT (8847 1123, www.pappadums.co.uk).
La Rosetta 201 High Street, Brentford, TW8 8AH (8560 3002).
Tamp 1 Devonshire Road, W4 2EU (www.tamp coffee.co.uk).
La Trompette 5-7 Devonshire Road, W4 2EU (8747 1836, www.latrompette.co.uk).
Le Vacherin 76-77 South Parade, W4 5LF (8742 2121, www.levacherin.co.uk).

Drinking

Bell & Crown 11 Thames Road, Strand on the Green, W4 3PL (8994 4164, www.bell-and-crown.co.uk).
Bollo House 13-15 Bollo Lane, W4 5LR (8994 6037, www.thebollohouse.com).
Bull's Head 15 Strand on the Green, W4 3PQ (8994 1204, www.chefandbrewer.com).
City Barge 27 Strand on the Green, W4 3PH (8994 2148, www.metropolitanpubcompany.com).
Coach & Horses 183 London Road, TW7 5BQ (8181 5627, www.coachandhorsesisleworth.co.uk).
Duke of Sussex 75 South Parade, W4 5LF (8742 8801, www.thedukeofsussex.co.uk).
George IV 185 Chiswick High Road, W4 2DR (8994 4624, www.georgeiv.co.uk).
Hare & Hounds Wyke Green, TW7 5PR (8560 5438, www.hareandhoundsosterley.co.uk).
Italian Job 13 Devonshire Road W4 2EU (8994 2852, www.theitalianjobpub.co.uk).
London Apprentice 62 Church Street, TW7 6BG (8560 1915, www.thelondonapprentice.co.uk).
Lord Nelson 9-11 Enfield Road, TW8 9NY (8568 1877, www.thelordnelsonbrentford.co.uk).
Magpie & Crown 128 High Street, Brentford, TW8 8EW (8560 4570).
Mawson Arms Mawson Lane, W4 2QD (8994 2936, www.mawsonarmschiswick.co.uk).
Old Pack Horse 434 Chiswick High Road, W4 5TF (8994 2872, www.oldpackhorsechiswick.co.uk).
Pilot 56 Wellesley Road, W4 4BZ (8994 0828, www.pilot-chiswick.co.uk).
Red Lion 92-94 Linkfield Road, TW7 6QJ (8560 1457, www.red-lion.info).
Roebuck 122 Chiswick High Road, W4 1PU (8995 4392, www.foodandfuel.co.uk).
Six Bells 148 High Street, Brentford, TW8 8EW (3302 4168, www.six-bells-brentford.co.uk).
Swan 1 Evershed Walk, 119 Acton Lane, W4 5HH (8994 8262, www.theswanchiswick.co.uk).

Tabard 2 Bath Road, W4 1LW (8994 3492, www.taylor-walker.co.uk).
Weir 22-24 Market Place, TW8 8EQ (8568 3600, www.theweirbar.co.uk).

Shopping

As Nature Intended 201 Chiswick High Road, W4 2DR (8742 8838, www.asnatureintended.uk.com).
Blink 294 Chiswick High Road, W4 1PA (8742 1313, www.blinkfashion.co.uk).
Brentford Market Market Place, TW8 8AH (8847 3222, www.brentfordmarket.squarespace.com).
Cancer Research UK 392 Chiswick High Road, W4 5TF (8994 4391, www.cancerresearchuk.org).
Chiswick Auctions 1 Colville Road, off Bollo Lane, W3 8BL (8992 4442, www.chiswickauctions.co.uk).
Chiswick Car Boot Sale Chiswick School, Burlington Lane, W4 3UN (www.chiswickcar bootsale.com). First Sun of the month (not Jan).
Covent Garden Fishmongers 37 Turnham Green Terrace, W4 1RG (8995 9273).
Fara www.faracharityshops.org; 40 Turnham Green Terrace, W4 1QP (8994 2287, for children); 78 Turnham Green Terrace, W4 1RG (8994 4724).
Food Market Chiswick Grove Park Farm House, W4 2RX (8742 2225, www.thefoodmarketchiswick.com).
Grove Park Deli 22 Fauconberg Road, W4 3JY (8995 8219, www.groveparkdeli.com).
Hack & Veldt 94 Turnham Green Terrace, W4 1QN (8742 0563, www.hackandveldt.com).
High Road Auctions 30-34 Chiswick High Road, W4 1TE (8400 5225, www.highroadauctions.co.uk).
Mortimer & Bennett 33 Turnham Green Terrace, W4 1RG (8995 4145, www.mortimerandbennett.com).
Neptune 305-307 Chiswick High Road, W4 4HH (www.neptune.com).
Old Cinema 160 Chiswick High Road, W4 1PR (8995 4166, www.theoldcinema.co.uk).
Ortadogu Supermarket 51-53 High Street, Hounslow, TW3 1RB (8814 1928).
Osterley Bookshop 168A Thornbury Road, TW7 4QE (8560 6206).
Oxfam Boutique 190 Chiswick High Road, W4 1PP (8994 4888, www.oxfam.org.uk).
Philip Neal Luxury Chocolates 43 Turnham Green Terrace, W4 1RG (8987 3183, www.philip nealchocolates.co.uk).
RSPV 34 Chiswick Lane, W4 2JQ (www.rspv store.com).

Things to do

Cinemas & theatres

Cineworld London – Feltham Leisure West, Air Park Way, TW13 7LX (0871 200 2000, www.cineworld.co.uk).

Tabard Theatre 2 Bath Road, W4 1LW (8995 6035, www.tabardweb.co.uk). Drama and comedy performances, upstairs from the Tabard pub.
Watermans 40 High Street, Brentford, TW8 0DS (8232 1019, www.watermans.org.uk). Multi-purpose arts centre next to the river.

Galleries & museums

Gunnersbury Park Museum Popes Lane, W3 8LQ (8992 1612, www.hounslow.info). Local history museum. Closed for renovation but scheduled to reopen in 2017.
London Museum of Water & Steam Green Dragon Lane, TW8 0EN (8568 4757, www. waterandsteam.org.uk). Steam-pumping engines, in a Victorian pumping station, the history of London's water supply, outdoors splash zone for kids and more.
Musical Museum 399 High Street, Brentford, TW8 0DU (8560 8108, www.musicalmuseum. co.uk). Self-playing instruments and old-fashioned music rolls; also hosts events, sometimes featuring the giant Mighty Wurlitzer organ.
Redlees Studios Redlees Park, Worton Road, TW7 6DW (www.redlees.org). Council-run artists' studios, set in a former Victorian stable block.

Other attractions

Brentford Festival Blondin Park, W5 (www. brentfordfestival.org.uk). Community festival, held on the first Sun in Sept.
Chiswick House & Gardens Burlington Lane, W4 2RP (8995 0508, www.english-heritage.org.uk). Neo-Palladian villa dating to 1725 with interiors by William Kent. The lovely gardens were the birthplace of the English Landscape Movement.
Hogarth's House Hogarth Lane, Great West Road, W4 2QN (8994 6757, www.hounslow.info). Country home of the great 18th-century painter, engraver and satirist William Hogarth.
Hounslow Urban Farm Faggs Road, TW14 0LZ (8831 9658, www.hounslowurbanfarm.co.uk). Community farm offering family activities.
London Mela Gunnersbury Park, W3 (www. londonmela.org). South Asian cultural festival, with music, dancing, street theatre, food and more; Sun in late summer.
Osterley House & Park Jersey Road, TW7 4RB (8232 5050, www.nationaltrust.org.uk). Former Tudor house utterly transformed, from 1761, into a swish neoclassical villa by Scottish architect Robert Adam; with formal gardens and a summer house.
Syon House & Park London Road, TW8 8JF (8560 0882, www.syonpark.co.uk). Family seat of the Duke of Northumberland, with interiors by Robert Adam. The park includes an arboretum and tidal water meadows.

Green spaces

For more details see www.hounslow.info.

Bedfont Lakes Country Park Clockhouse Lane, TW14. Dedicated nature reserve with bird hides for birdwatching, information centre, lake, play areas, cycling trail and orienteering.

Boston Manor Park Boston Manor Road, TW8. Contains a restored Jacobean manor house, play areas and tennis and basketball courts, and hosts the annual Brentford Festival.

Dukes Meadows Riverside Drive, W4 (www. dukesmeadowspark.com). Riverside park with playground, paddling pool, sports clubs and its own bandstand. Also here is Dukes Hollow, a site of ecological importance.

Gunnersbury Park Popes Lane, W3. Ornamental gardens, golf course, tennis courts, and football and cricket pitches.

Hounslow Heath 450 Staines Road, TW4. Site of Importance for Nature Conservation and part of the London Outer Orbital Path (LOOP), running north, along the River Crane, all the way up to and beyond Cranford Park.

Osterley Park Jersey Road, TW7 (8232 5050, www.nationaltrust.org.uk). National Trust parkland containing Osterley House. There are ancient woodland and meadows through which to stroll.

Syon Park London Road, TW8 (8560 0882, www.syonpark.co.uk). Riverside park comprising a huge diversity of habitats; forms part of Syon House grounds.

Gyms & leisure centres

Brentford Fountain Leisure Centre 658 Chiswick High Road, TW8 0HJ (0845 456 6675, www.fusion-lifestyle.com).

David Lloyd Heston Southall Lane, TW5 9PE (0345 129 6793, www.davidlloydleisure.co.uk). Private.

Hanworth Air Park Leisure Centre Uxbridge Road, TW13 5EG (0845 456 6675, www.fusion-lifestyle.com).

Heston Community Sports Hall Heston Road, TW5 0QZ (8570 6544, www.hestoncommunity school.co.uk). Outside school hours only.

Heston Village Hall New Heston Road, TW5 0LW (0845 456 2828, www.fusion-lifestyle.com).

Hogarth Health Club Airedale Avenue, W4 2NW (8995 4600, www.thehogarth.co.uk). Private.

Isleworth Leisure Centre Twickenham Road, TW7 7EU (0845 456 6675, www.fusion-lifestyle.com).

New Chiswick Pool Edensor Road, W4 2RG (0845 456 6675, www.fusion-lifestyle.com).

Roko Chiswick Chiswick Sports Ground, Hartington Road, W4 3UH (8747 5757, www.roko.co.uk). Private.

Virgin Active (www.virginactive.co.uk); Riverside Drive, Dukes Meadows, W4 2SX (3603 5801); Building 3, 566 Chiswick High Road, W4 5YA (3355 4517). Private.

West 4 Gym Sutton Lane North, W4 4LD (8747 1713, www.west4gym.co.uk). Private.

Outdoor pursuits

Chiswick Tennis Club Burlington Lane, W4 3EU (07503 874006, www.chiswicktennisclub.com). Four all-weather hard courts; other activities on offer.

Dukes Meadows Riverside Drive, W4 2SH (8994 1202, www.dukesmeadows.com). Private club, with tennis courts, golf and a Skiplex ski slope.

Duke of Sussex

HIGHS & LOWS

Historic houses and parkland

Chiswick restaurants

Charming riverside

▲ ....▼

Far-flung neighbourhoods feel disconnected from London

The ugly commercial areas of Brentford and Hounslow

Heathrow flight path

Spectator sports

Brentford FC Griffin Park, Braemar Road, TW8
0NT (0845 345 6442, www.brentfordfc.co.uk).
The club hopes to be playing in its new stadium at
Lionel Road South in time for the 2016/17 season.

Schools

Primary

There are 45 state primary schools in Hounslow,
including eight church schools. There are also six
independents, including one international school
and one Muslim school. See www.hounslow.gov.uk,
www.edubase.gov.uk and www.ofsted.gov.uk for
more information.

Secondary

Brentford School for Girls 5 Boston Manor Road,
TW8 0PG (8847 4281, www.brentford.hounslow.
sch.uk). Girls only.
Chiswick School Burlington Lane, W4 3UN
(8747 0031, www.chiswick.hounslow.sch.uk).
Cranford Community College High Street,
Cranford, TW5 9PD (8897 2001, www.cranford.
hounslow.sch.uk).
Feltham Community College Browell's
Lane, TW13 7EF (8831 3000, www.feltham.
hounslow.sch.uk).
Green School for Girls London Road, Busch
Corner, TW7 5BB (8321 8080, www.thegreen
school.net). Church of England; girls only.
Gumley House RC Convent School St John's
Road, TW7 6XF (8568 8692, www.gumley.
hounslow.sch.uk). Roman Catholic; girls only.
Gunnersbury Catholic School The Ride, TW8
9LB (8568 7281, www.gunnersbury.com). Roman
Catholic; boys only.
Heathland School Wellington Road South, TW4
5JD (8572 4411, www.heathland.hounslow.sch.uk).
Heston Community School Heston Road,
TW5 0QR (8572 1931, www.hestoncommunity
school.co.uk).
Isleworth & Syon School for Boys Ridgeway
Road, TW7 5LJ (8568 5791, www.isleworthsyon.
org). Boys only.
Kingsley Academy Prince Regent Road, TW3
1NE (8572 4461, www.kingsleyacademy.org).
Lampton School Lampton Avenue, TW3 4EP
(8572 1936, www.lampton.org.uk).
Reach Academy Feltham Bridge House,
Hanworth Road, TW13 5AB (3551 9305, www.
reachacademyfeltham.com).
Rivers Academy Tachbrook Road, TW14 9PE
(8890 0245, www.riversacademy.org.uk).
St Mark's Catholic School 106 Bath Road, TW3
3EJ (8577 3600, www.st-marks.hounslow.sch.uk).
Roman Catholic.

Property

Local estate agents

Anderson Knight www.anderson-knight.co.uk
Bridge Property Services www.bridge
propertyservices.co.uk
Chase Buchanan www.chasebuchanan.london
Featherstone Leigh www.featherstoneleigh.co.uk
Fletcher www.fletcherestates.com
Quilliam Property Services www.quilliam.co.uk
River Homes www.riverhomes.co.uk

Local knowledge

www.brentforddockresidents.co.uk
www.brentfordtw8.com
www.chiswickish.co.uk/blog
www.chiswickw4.com
www.getwestlondon.co.uk

USEFUL INFO

Borough size
5,598 hectares

Population
271,800

Ethnic mix
White 64.6%
Asian or Asian British 23.4%
Black or Black British 5.3%
Mixed 3.5%
Chinese or other 3.2%

London Borough of Hounslow
Civic Centre, Lampton Road, TW3 4DN
(8583 2000, www.hounslow.gov.uk)

Council run by
Labour

MPs
Brentford & Isleworth, Ruth Cadbury
(Labour); Feltham & Heston, Seema
Malhotra (Labour)

Main recycling centre
Space Waye Reuse & Recycling Centre,
North Feltham Trading Estate, Pier Road,
TW14 0TH (8890 0917, www.hounslow.
gov.uk)

Council tax
£916.52 to £2,749.54

Kingston upon Thames

The 'secret' side of south-west London, Kingston doesn't have the tube, so it doesn't get the hype that Richmond and Wimbledon do. Yet for shops, schools, security and river views, it's well able to compete with its posher neighbours – and if you live on the right railway line, it's effectively 'closer' to Waterloo than Brixton.

AVERAGE PROPERTY PRICE

Detached £862,955	**Terraced** £395,895
Semi-detached £491,059	**Flat** £337,246

AVERAGE RENTAL PRICE PER WEEK

Room £106	**1 bed** £229
Studio £173	**2 bed** £299
	3 bed £368

Kingston Bridge

Kingston upon Thames

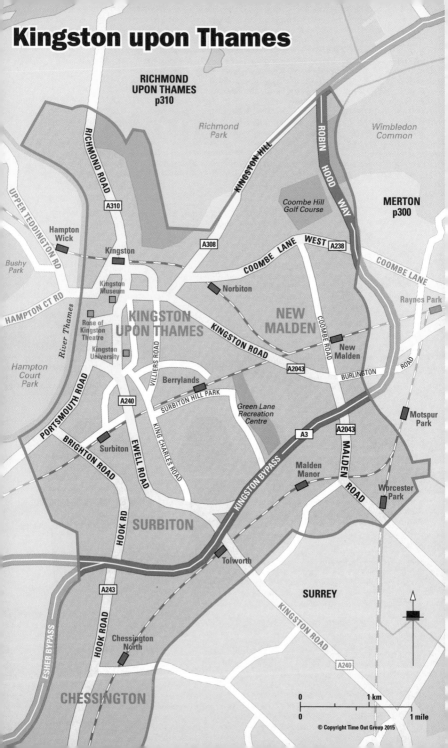

RICHMOND
UPON THAMES
p310

Richmond
Park

Wimbledon
Common

MERTON
p300

Coombe Hill
Golf Course

Bushy
Park

Hampton
Wick

Kingston

Kingston
Museum

Rose of
Kingston
Theatre

Kingston
University

River Thames

Hampton
Court
Park

KINGSTON
UPON THAMES

Norbiton

NEW
MALDEN

Raynes Park

New
Malden

Berrylands

Green Lane
Recreation
Centre

BURLINGTON

Motspur
Park

SURBITON

Surbiton

Malden
Manor

Worcester
Park

Tolworth

SURREY

Chessington
North

CHESSINGTON

RICHMOND ROAD
A310
UPPER TEDDINGTON RD
HAMPTON CT RD
A308
COOMBE LANE WEST
A238
COOMBE LANE
COOMBE ROAD
KINGSTON HILL
ROBIN HOOD WAY
KINGSTON ROAD
A2043
PORTSMOUTH ROAD
A240
VILLIERS ROAD
SURBITON HILL PARK
KING CHARLES ROAD
EWELL ROAD
BRIGHTON ROAD
HOOK RD
A3
A2043
KINGSTON BYPASS
MALDEN ROAD
ROAD
A243
HOOK ROAD
ESHER BYPASS
KINGSTON ROAD
A240

0   1 km
0   1 mile

© Copyright Time Out Group 2015

Neighbourhoods

Kingston Town KT1/KT2

Although geographically one of London's farthest-flung boroughs, Kingston town centre is just 25 minutes from Waterloo on a very regular train service. The pedestrian is king in the compact yet comprehensive shopping district, and you'll barely see a bus or car all day. There's a huge John Lewis, TK Maxx and the well-stocked Bentall Centre. Fife Street and Castle Street are home to smaller brands such as Jo Malone, which is set in a gorgeous Tudor-style building. You'd be hard-pressed to find any high-street favourites missing – and the same goes for big-name chain restaurants.

The recently revamped Ancient Market bustles with life at the weekend, day and evening. It may have been a space for locals to peddle their wares for 800 years (seven Saxon kings are said to have been crowned on the Coronation Stone, which stands beside the Guildhall on the High Street), but there's nothing ancient about the new perforated timber market stalls. At night, when the lights flicker on, the new market stalls resemble futuristic wooden spaceships, but they somehow manage not to look out of place in their Saxon surroundings.

Riverside Edge is the latest addition to Kingston's Thames frontage. From Kingston Bridge, it has the look of a baby Southbank Centre with a wide variety of well-known restaurants, even though the opposite bank is filled with the green expanse of Hampton Court Park rather than the buzz of Charing Cross. For more tasty bites, head to Riverside Edge's Pocket Restaurants, Kingston's street-food hub. Open six days a week, it's home to five pop-up restaurants, from Mexican burritos to a champagne bar, along with outdoor entertainment. Further along, on the High Street, there's idiosyncratic vegetarian restaurant Riverside Vegetaria and friendly Italian Al Forno.

Kingston's predominantly middle-class culture is countered by its thriving student population, which can make evenings a bit loud and lairy, especially during the summer months. Hide away in Bacchus, a small venue more popular with locals than the student crowd. For entertainment, there's the well-respected Rose Theatre, which looks set to receive more funding soon, as well as the annual International Youth Arts Festival throughout July.

The northerly residential streets towards Ham are dominated by Richmond Park, London's biggest enclosed expanse of green. (And with Hampton Court just across the river, there's no shortage of green space.) It's also home to one of London's best-performing state schools, Tiffin Girls' (along with its opposite number, Tiffin for boys, it's one of the main reasons people move here). This is also where you'll find the area's best pubs: the Canbury Arms (good restaurant), the Willoughby Arms, the Wych Elm and the Boaters Inn.

Just up the hill to the east is Coombe, a microcosm of modern, bourgeois gated life. Around the Coombe House conservation area – developed on the estate land of a demolished manor – it's all culs-de-sac, CCTV, three Mercs per garage and preened pampas grass beside the porch. There are also two golf courses. On Coombe Road, you'll find golf emporium American Golf, Japanese food store Atari-Ya, wine merchant Wined Up Here and high-quality fishmonger Jarvis.

Property in Kingston, though more affordable than in central London boroughs, can be pricey (especially the desirable riverside houses), with lots of large Victorian detached and semi-detached homes. There are a few sought-after modern developments too, such as the Royal Quarter. New Malden has become a more popular home for those looking for something less expensive in the same area.

New Malden KT3 and Berrylands KT5

New Malden's centre spreads out across Kingston Road, Malden Road, Burlington Road and New Malden High Street, with the majority of shops and services on the last. Discount stores, charity shops and chains dominate, with the only colour provided by the restaurants and shops that employ and serve the area's large, vibrant Korean community.

This has made New Malden the best place in London for Korean food, with restaurants and grocers mainly clustered on the High

TRANSPORT

Rail services into Clapham Junction, Waterloo
Main bus routes into central London night bus N87
River boat services between Richmond, Kingston and Hampton Court (Apr-Oct)

Street, but with a few gems scattered up Burlington Road and Kingston Road. Try a traditional table-top barbecue at Jee Cee Neh or Korea Garden; noodles and *jeongol* stews at Palace; bustling Sorabol; intimate Yami and Ham Gi Pak; or sophisticated Su La to rub shoulders with Korean businessmen.

Meanwhile, for a great array of British beers, try Woodies – hard to find but worth it.

The word 'Seoul' features in many local business names, but New Malden looks more like Pyongyang, with the grey hulks of the 16-storey Apex and CI Towers looming over the townscape and the A3 throbbing in the background. Developed around the railway station, the area's housing consists mainly of Victorian and Edwardian terraces. Heading north on Coombe Road – later Traps Lane – things get immediately leafier.

Berrylands, the next stop along the train line to Surbiton, is primarily residential. Apart from a smattering of shops – a florist, a launderette, a picture framer – on Chiltern Drive, the neighbourhood is devoted entirely to 19th- and mid 20th-century housing. A good cycle path connects Surbiton, Berrylands and New Malden.

Surbiton

Pity the residents of Surbiton: they still have to put up with tedious ribbing about 1970s sitcom *The Good Life* (filmed in Northwood, but fictionally located here), the notion that it's just a railway junction (it isn't) and the stereotype that it's the definitive suburb (it isn't that, either).

Located to the south of Kingston, Surbiton is 12 miles from central London, but it's closer – in travelling minutes – than many places in Zone 2. Fast trains to Surrey and Hampshire stop here after Clapham Junction. The beautiful, white art deco station is a monument to the suburb's role as a commuter town, but conservation areas off Maple Road and along Claremont Road and the Crescent hint at a leafy graciousness that pre-dates the trains.

Surbiton's more sociable residents are happy with their handful of fine eateries, mainly along Maple Road and Claremont Road. The French Table has long been praised by critics, and is now joined by next-door bakery the French Tarte. But there's also well-priced Italian Da Lucio for a good, low-key bite; Gordon Bennett! for creative menus and craft beer; the Press Room for coffee; and Rubi or Hotel Bosco for cocktails.

Despite its boring reputation, Surbiton is brimming with kooky community-led events. You can take part in the annual Surbiton ski (strapping ice to your feet to slide down St Mark's Hill) or visit the Sardine Festival. Homage de Fromage, Surbiton's monthly cheese club at the Lamb pub, sets ridiculous tasks, including making sculptures out of leftover cheese. Plus there's an award-winning farmers' market every month.

Ancient Market, Kingston

HIGHS & LOWS

Attractive riverside

Huge expanses of green space

Good schools

Brand-name shopping

Korean restaurants

▲ .... ▼

The A3

Deepest suburbia

Cultural desert

Lairy town centres

There's an excellent gym on the riverside, some good charity shops on Victoria Road, popular shoe shop Shoes at Last, and a few decent pubs – but just as people go to London for work, they go to Kingston for shopping and to Thames Ditton for bucolic boozing.

Since its facelift, the Ancient Market is an attractive and vibrant place to spend time, and particularly pretty in the evening.

Eating

Al Forno 1-3 High Street, Kingston, KT1 1LY (8439 7555, www.alfornokingston.co.uk).
Da Lucio 101 Maple Road, KT6 4AW (8399 5113, www.dalucio.co.uk).
Fish! Kitchen 58 Coombe Road, KT2 7AF (8546 2886, www.fishkitchen.co.uk).
French Table 85 Maple Road, KT6 4AW (8399 2365, www.thefrenchtable.co.uk).
Gordon Bennett! 75 Maple Road, KT6 4AG (8390 7222, www.gordonbennetts.co.uk).
Ham Gi Pak 169 High Street, New Malden, KT3 4BH (8942 9588).
Jee Cee Neh 74 Burlington Road, KT3 4NU (8942 0682).
Korea Garden 73 Kingston Road, KT3 3PB (8336 1208).
Palace 189 High Street, New Malden, KT3 4BH (8949 3737).
Press Room 5 Claremont Road, KT6 4QR (8399 8313, www.pressroomcoffee.co.uk).
Riverside Edge Riverside Walk, KT1 1QN (www.riversidewalkkingston.co.uk). Street-food stalls.
Riverside Vegetaria 64 High Street, Kingston, KT1 1HN (8546 7992, www.riversidevegetaria.co.uk).
Sorabol 180 High Street, New Malden, KT3 4ES (8942 2334, www.sorabol.co.uk).
Su La 79-81 Kingston Road, KT3 3PB (8336 0121).
Yami 69 High Street, New Malden, KT3 4BT (8949 0069).

Drinking

Boaters Inn Canbury Gardens, Lower Ham Road, KT2 5AU (8541 4672, www.metropolitan pubcompany.com).
Canbury Arms 49 Canbury Park Road, KT2 6LQ (8255 9129, www.thecanburyarms.com).

Hotel Bosco 9 St Mark's Hill, KT6 4LQ (8339 5720, www.hotelbosco.co.uk).
Lamb 73 Brighton Road, KT6 5NF (8390 9229).
Rubi 97 Maple Road, KT6 4AW (8399 5055, www.rubi-london.com).
Willoughby Arms 47 Willoughby Road, KT2 6LN (8546 4236, www.thewilloughbyarms.com).
Woodies The Sportsground, Thetford Road, KT3 5DX (8949 5824, www.woodiesfreehouse.co.uk).
Wych Elm 93 Elm Road, KT2 6HT (8546 3271, www.thewychelmkingston.co.uk).

Shopping

American Golf 11-13 Coombe Road, KT2 7AB (0844 499 2159, www.americangolf.co.uk).
Ancient Market Market Place, KT1 1JS (www.kingstonmarkets.co.uk). 8am-5pm daily.
Atari-Ya 44 Coombe Road, KT2 7AF (8547 9891, www.atariya.co.uk).
Bentall Centre Wood Street, KT1 1TP (8541 5066, www.bentallcentre.co.uk).
French Tarte 83 Maple Road, KT6 4AW (8399 1123, www.thefrenchtarte.co.uk).
Jarvis 56 Coombe Road, KT2 7AF (8296 0139, www.fishkitchen.co.uk).
Jo Malone Eden Walk Shopping Centre, 48 Union Street, KT1 1RP (0370 192 5281, www.jomalone.co.uk).
Shoes at Last 81 Maple Road, KT6 4AW (8390 5673, www.shoesatlast.com).
Surbiton Farmers Market Maple Road, KT6 4AG (www.surbitonfarmersmarket.co.uk). 3rd Sat of mth.
Wined Up Here 30 Coombe Road, KT2 7AG (8549 6622, www.wineduphere.co.uk).

Things to do

Cinemas & theatres

Cornerhouse 116 Douglas Road, KT6 7SB (8296 9012, www.thech.org). Community arts centre.
Odeon Kingston The Rotunda Centre, Clarence Street, KT1 1QP (0333 006 7777, www.odeon. co.uk). The Rotunda complex (www.therotunda kingston.co.uk) contains this 14-screen cinema, plus a bowling alley, fitness centre and restaurants.
Rose Theatre 24-26 High Street, Kingston, KT1 1HL (8174 0090, www.rosetheatrekingston.org). Purpose-built theatre with a populist programme, from Shakespeare to comedy nights.

Galleries & museums

Dorich House Museum 67 Kingston Vale, SW15 3RN (8417 5515, www.dorichhousemuseum.org. uk). 1930s house with a large collection of Russian art. Guided tours on certain days only.

Riverside Edge, Kingston

Kingston Museum Wheatfield Way, KT1 2PS (8547 6460, www.kingston.gov.uk/museum). Local history museum.
Stanley Picker Gallery Faculty of Art, Design & Architecture, Kingston University, Knights Park, KT1 2QJ (8417 4074, www.stanleypickergallery.org).

Other attractions
Chessington World of Adventures & Zoo Leatherhead Road, KT9 2NE (0871 663 4477, www.chessington.com).
Coombe Conduit Coombe Lane, KT2 7HD (0370 333 1181, www.english-heritage.org.uk). Two Tudor buildings connected by an underground passage that carried water to Hampton Court Palace.
Turks (8546 2434, www.turks.co.uk). Paddle-steamer cruises.

Gigs, clubs & comedy
Bacchus 2 Union Street, KT1 1RP (8546 7798, www.bacchuslatebar.co.uk).
Banquet Records 52 Eden Street, KT1 1EE (8549 5871, www.banquetrecords.com). In-store gigs.
Comedy Store at the Rose Theatre 24-26 High Street, Kingston, KT1 1HL (8174 0090, www.rosetheatrekingston.org).
Fighting Cocks 56 Old London Road, KT2 6QA (8974 6469, www.the-fighting-cocks.co.uk).

Green spaces
For more details see www.kingston.gov.uk.
Elmbridge Meadow Elmbridge Avenue, KT5 9HF. Park along the Hogsmill River Path.
Jubilee Wood Nature Reserve Fairoak Lane, KT9 2NG. Ponds and woodland.
Manor Park Malden Road, KT3 6AU. Sports pitches, green gym and a playground.

Richmond Park TW10 5HS (www.royalparks.org.uk). Though mainly in Richmond, some of this ancient deer park can be claimed as Kingston's.

Gyms & leisure centres
Chessington Sports Centre Garrison Lane, KT9 2JS (8974 2277, www.chessingtonsportscentre.co.uk).
David Lloyd The Rotunda, Clarence Street, KT1 1QJ (0345 129 6798, www.davidlloyd.co.uk). Private.
Kingfisher Leisure Centre Fairfield Road, KT1 2PY (8546 1042, www.placesforpeopleleisure.org).
Kingsmeadow Fitness & Athletic 422A Kingston Road, KT1 3PB (8547 2198, www.placesforpeopleleisure.org).
Malden Centre Blagdon Road, KT3 4AF (8336 7770, www.placesforpeopleleisure.org).
New Malden Sports Club Somerset Close, KT3 5RG (8942 0539, www.newmaldenclub.co.uk).
Nuffield Health Simpson Way, KT6 4ER (8335 2900, www.nuffieldhealth.com). Private.
Surbiton Racket & Fitness Club Berrylands, KT5 8JT (8399 1594, www.surbiton.org).
Tolworth Recreation Centre Fullers Way North, KT6 7LQ (8391 7910, www.placesforpeopleleisure.org).
Virgin Active Richmond Road, KT2 5EN (8481 6000, www.virginactive.co.uk). Private.
YMCA Hawker Centre, Lower Ham Road, KT2 5BH (8296 9747, www.ymcalsw.org).

Outdoor pursuits
Albany Park Canoe & Sailing Centre Albany Mews, KT2 5SL (8549 3066, www.kingston.gov.uk).
Coombe Hill Golf Club Coombe Hill, KT2 7DF (8336 7600, www.coombehillgolfclub.com). 18 holes.
Coombe Wood Golf Club George Road, KT2 7NS (8942 0388, www.coombewoodgolf.com). 18 holes.

Kingston Rowing Club The Boat House, Lower Ham Road, KT2 5AU (8546 8592, www.kingstonrc.co.uk).
Minima Yacht Club 48A High Street, Kingston, KT1 1HN (8546 8241, www.minimayc.co.uk).
Surbiton Golf Club Woodstock Lane South, KT9 1UG (8398 3101, www.surbitongolfclub.com).
Thames Sailing Club Portsmouth Road, KT6 4HH (8399 2164, www.thamessailingclub.co.uk).

Spectator sports

AFC Wimbledon/Kingstonian FC The Cherry Red Records Stadium, Kingsmeadow, Jack Goodchild Way, 422A Kingston Road, KT1 3PB (8547 3528, www.afcwimbledon.co.uk; 8330 6869, www.kingstonian.com). Home to what many fans consider the real Wimbledon FC.

Schools

Primary

There are 35 state primary schools in Kingston (including 14 church schools), plus nine independent primaries. See www.kingston.gov.uk, www.education.gov.uk/edubase and www.ofsted.gov.uk for more information.

Secondary

Chessington Community College Garrison Lane, KT9 2JS (8974 1156, www.chessingtoncommunitycollege.co.uk).
Coombe Boys' School College Gardens, KT3 6NU (8949 1537, www.coombeboysschool.org). Boys only.
Coombe Girls' School Clarence Avenue, KT3 3TU (8942 1242, www.coombegirlsschool.org). Girls only.
Hollyfield School & Sixth Form Centre Surbiton Hill Road, KT6 4TU (8339 4500, www.hollyfield.kingston.sch.uk)
Holy Cross Roman Catholic School 25 Sandal Road, KT3 5AR (8395 4225, www.holycross.kingston.sch.uk). Roman Catholic. Girls only.
Kingston Grammar School 70 London Road, KT2 6PY (8546 5875, www.kgs.org.uk). Private.
Richard Challoner Roman Catholic School Manor Drive North, KT3 5PE (8330 5947, www.richardchalloner.com). Roman Catholic. Boys only.
Southborough High School Hook Road, KT6 5AS (8391 4324, www.southborough.kingston.sch.uk). Boys only.
Tiffin Girls' School Richmond Road, KT2 5PL (8546 0773, www.tiffingirls.kingston.sch.uk). Girls only.
Tiffin School Queen Elizabeth Road, KT2 6RL (8546 4638, www.tiffinschool.co.uk). Boys only.

Tolworth Girls' School Fullers Way North, KT6 7LQ (8397 3854, www.tolworthgirlsschool.co.uk). Girls only.

Property

Local estate agents

Carrington's www.carringtonsproperty.co.uk
Chancellors www.chancellors.co.uk
Cocoon www.mycocoon.co.uk
Curchods www.curchods.com
Dexters www.dexters.co.uk
Gascoigne Pees www.gpees.co.uk
Greenfield www.greenfield-property.co.uk
Hawes & Co www.hawesandco.co.uk

Local knowledge

www.kingstonguardian.co.uk
www.kingstononline.co.uk
www.surreycomet.co.uk

USEFUL INFO

Borough size
3,726 hectares

Population
170,900

Ethnic mix
White 80.7%
Asian or Asian British 9.1%
Black or Black British 3.8%
Chinese or other 3.4%
Mixed 2.9%

Royal Borough of Kingston upon Thames
The Guildhall Complex, 2 High Street, KT1 1EU (8547 5000, www.kingston.gov.uk)

Council run by
Conservatives

MPs
Kingston & Surbiton, James Berry (Conservative); Richmond Park, Zac Goldsmith (Conservative)

Main recycling centre
Villiers Road Recycling Centre, Chapel Mill Road, KT1 3GZ

Council tax
£1,115.98 to £3,347.94

Wimbledon Village

Merton

With excellent transport links both into and out of London, and an abundance of green spaces, shops, restaurants and pubs, Merton offers a retreat from the hustle and bustle of the city centre to those lucky enough to be able to afford to buy or rent a property in this pricey borough.

AVERAGE PROPERTY PRICE

Detached	Terraced
£1,570,224	£435,582
Semi-detached	Flat
£570,135	£355,296

AVERAGE RENTAL PRICE PER WEEK

Room	1 bed
£129	£253
Studio	2 bed
£178	£316
	3 bed
	£368

Neighbourhoods

Wimbledon, Wimbledon Village and Wimbledon Park, SW19

Contrary to popular belief, the Wimbledon tennis grounds are not, in fact, in Wimbledon itself, but easily reached by hopping on the tube for two stops to Southfields. The area blossoms during the tournament, but at any time of year Wimbledon town centre is the buzzing hub of Merton, with mums, thirtysomething couples and innocuous teens filling the piazza in the town centre.

Property is certainly not cheap, and there are plenty of razzle-dazzle houses located around Wimbledon Village and the Common, where prices easily soar into the millions. You'll find interesting architectural variety on the upper reaches of hilly Arthur Road, adjacent Vineyard Hill Road and the parkside stretch of Wimbledon Park Road (which overlooks a golf club) – but it will cost you. However, prices drop across the busy Kingston Road or towards Merton Park tram stop.

Residents are well provided with cultural amenities. There are three theatres on the Broadway alone: plushly restored New Wimbledon Theatre; its intimate Studio space; and the child-friendly Polka Theatre.

The area has also spawned some acclaimed musicians – both Jamie T and MIA grew up around here – and the once uninspired choice of drinking establishments has matured into a reasonable selection of pubs, bars and nightclubs. The Old Frizzle and the Alexandra offer a fabulous selection of beer and wine, and excellent food to match, while the Suburban cocktail bar and the Terrace, beside the station, are perfect for late-night dancing and debauchery.

Wimbledon Village, up the hill from the town centre, is home to sports cars and chinos, with the boutique-lined High Street running through it to Wimbledon Common. A strangely rustic sight for London is the 'horse crossing' in the centre of the village.

TRANSPORT

Tube lines District, Northern
Rail services into Waterloo, Blackfriars
Tram to West Croydon, East Croydon
Main bus routes into central London
no direct service; night buses N44,
N133, N1

Of Merton's many green spaces, Wimbledon Common (the stomping ground of Elisabeth Beresford's loveable eco-warriors the Wombles) offers 1,140 acres of woodland, and its own windmill and golf course. It also hosts popular events such as the annual Wimbledon Village Fair. Less famous, but equally unmissable, are the romantic landscaped gardens of Cannizaro House (now the Hotel du Vin Wimbledon, West Side Common); it's a quaint (if pricey) place to take afternoon tea, while Cannizaro Park features an aviary and sculptures, and hosts various events.

One tube stop along the District line, the compact satellite of Wimbledon Park provides another local green haven, including kids' playgrounds, tennis courts, bowling greens, mini-golf areas, football pitches and a boating lake.

Wimbledon offers pretty much every kind of chain restaurant on a plate but there are a few welcome independent establishments too. Hot Pink is the latest addition, serving healthy fare and offering great value. La Nonna and Al Forno are both popular Italian eateries, and there are some super Indian restaurants too, such as Chutneys and Ahmed Tandoori. Opposite Wimbledon Park tube, Dalchini specialises in Hakka Indo-Chinese cuisine. Further north, Café Nero serves full English breakfasts and fresh smoothies.

Up in the Village and towards the Common, the Lawn Bistro (British) and Aubaine (French) provide fine dining, while Hemingways, the Dog & Fox and Fox & Grapes are great for upmarket pub food and a drink.

Wimbledon town centre is the main retail area, with a wide range of high-street chain stores (plus a handful of independent retailers and charity shops) located on the Broadway. Centre Court shopping mall has plenty of familiar names, while local department store Elys has a wide range of upmarket brands.

Even the Village, once a bastion of high-end boutiques, is now becoming increasingly chain-led, but worth a browse on the High Street are Bayley & Sage (speciality foods), Cath Kidston (colourful retro homewares), and designer boutiques Diane von Furstenberg, Luella's Boudoir (bridal), MaxMara, Matches and Question Air.

The compact Wimbledon Farmers' Market, held every Saturday (9am-1pm) in the playground of Wimbledon Park Primary School, is popular. Wimbledon Stadium's

Fox & Grapes, Wimbledon Village

vast car park provides a more down-to-earth street-market experience: weekend stalls and a popular car boot sale on Saturday and Sunday.

The industrial estates off busy Durnsford Road conceal the marvellous Vallebona Sardinian Gourmet. It's worth a visit for the climate-controlled cheese room alone.

South Wimbledon SW19 and Colliers Wood SW20

History hasn't been as well preserved in these neighbourhoods. Merton's new-build phenomenon is most pronounced in South Wimbledon, traditionally the more rough-and-ready end of the Broadway, but increasingly home to young professionals who've taken advantage of the cheaper property prices. The side streets off Haydons Road, including the so-called 'Poets' Corner' to the east, are worth checking out for Victorian and Edwardian terraces.

Moving towards Colliers Wood, you'll find evidence of the area's cultural mix, from Asian grocers to Irish pubs, plus a few late-night bars and soulless but convenient retail parks. One dubious landmark is the Tower, a 19-storey 1960s concrete office block opposite the tube station; it currently lies empty and its future is the subject of ongoing debate.

The 12th-century Merton Abbey once educated Thomas Becket; its ruins can be seen behind the Savacentre car park. The new apartments here have brought a chain gym and more fast-food outlets – give these a miss and instead head to the former Liberty silk works at Merton Abbey Mills, which hosts a weekend craft and book market. On summer evenings, this is a convivial spot to drink and catch jazz and folk acts beside the River Wandle.

For real-ale fans, the Trafalgar pub in South Wimbledon is scarcely large enough to swing a cat but offers a great selection, and the William Morris, near the Merton Abbey Mills crafts enclave, has a riverside beer garden.

South Wimbledon and Colliers Wood are limited on choice for eating and drinking, but not lacking on quality. Hi Bangkok impresses with its authentic Thai dishes, while Eggs Benedict, near South Wimbledon station, is impossible to pass thanks to its selection of sumptuous cakes displayed in the window. Keep trekking from there along the High Street towards Colliers Wood and you'll find diverse gems Corleone, Istanbul Meze Mangal and Spice of Raj.

Other notable shops include Burge & Gunson (bathrooms) and Architectural Salvage, near South Wimbledon tube, for unusual interior fittings.

Morden SM4, Mitcham CR4 and Raynes Park SW20

Acclaimed young indie rockers the Good Shoes promoted a 2007 song about their home town with the slogan: 'Morden Life Is Rubbish'. Located at the southernmost end of the Northern line, the area has seen little improvement since the 1980s. This is where Merton Council is based, in the grim Crown

House tower block on traffic-clogged London Road. Morden doesn't have a specific town centre – you're better off heading into Wimbledon for shopping and restaurants.

Morden Hall Park, run by the National Trust, is a welcome retreat, with meadows, wetlands, waterways and Deen City Farm (a big hit with kids), not to mention weekend markets, a garden centre and the occasional beer festival.

Like Morden, Mitcham's streets don't seem particularly welcoming after dark. Still, its local shops offer a few treats, including lots of South Asian groceries. Gino's serves traditional-style Italian dishes, and has a very reasonably priced lunchtime menu.

It's hard to believe that this sprawling suburb was once full of lavender fields (expansive Mitcham Common is now the main local green space), or that the remains of a Roman settlement were unearthed near the gasworks. But Mitcham still lays claim to the world's oldest cricket green (dating back to 1730); these days, players have to cross the busy Cricket Green Road to reach the pavilion.

Another local enclave with rural roots is Raynes Park. Taking its name from 19th-century landowners and developed as a garden suburb (like nearby Merton Park), it's clearly more affluent than Morden or Mitcham, with the biggest family homes outside of Wimbledon Village (particularly on Grand Drive), and the lowest crime rates. It is sometimes referred to as 'West Wimbledon' by local estate agents.

Restaurant finds here include Cah Chi, a convivial Korean canteen (reflecting the area's significant South Korean community), several chains and a few independents, including Cocum (lovely and inventive Indian cuisine), Italian restaurant the Olive Garden, and the Great Wall with Chinese cuisine.

Eating

Ahmed Tandoori The Broadway, W19 1RF (8946 6214)

Al Forno 2A Kings Road, SW19 8QN (8540 5710, www.alfornowimbledon.com).

Aubaine 18 High Street, SW19 5DX (3434 1960, www.aubaine.co.uk).

Café 377 377 Durnsford Road, SW19 8EF (8946 7733, www.cafe377.com).

Cah Chi 34 Durham Road, SW20 0TW (8947 1081).

Chutneys 31A Hartfield Road, SW19 3SG (8540 9788, www.go2chutneys.co.uk).

Cocum 9 Approach Road, SW20 8BA (8540 3250, www.cocumrestaurant.co.uk).

Corleone 186 High Street, SW19 2BN (8543 5151, corleonerestaurant.co.uk).

Dalchini 147 Arthur Road, SW19 8AB (8947 5966, www.dalchini.co.uk).

Eggs Benedict 224 Merton High Street, SW19 1AU (7998 1716, www.eggsbenedictcafe.com).

Gino's 6-8 Upper Green East, CR4 2PA (8648 9788, ginosmitcham.co.uk).

Great Wall 24 Coombe Lane, SW20 8ND (8947 4072).

Hi Bangkok 132 Kingston Road, SW19 1LY (8542 3528, www.hibangkok.co.uk).

Wimbledon Car Boot Sale

HIGHS & LOWS

Tennis

Theatre and comedy

Wimbledon Common

Razzle-dazzle houses

▲ ⋯⋯⋯⋯⋯⋯⋯⋯⋯⋯⋯ ▼

Colliers Wood Tower

Mitcham's gritty streets

Characterless newbuilds

The price of the razzle-dazzle houses

Hot Pink 86 The Broadway, SW19 1RQ (8542 6066, www.hotpinkgrill.com).

Hotel du Vin Wimbledon Cannizaro House, West Side Common, SW19 4UE (8879 1464, www.hotelduvin.com).

Istanbul Meze Mangal 222 High Street, SW19 2BH (8543 3123, http://istanbulmezemangal.co.uk).

Lawn Bistro 67 High Street, SW19 5EE (8947 8278, www.thelawnbistro.co.uk).

La Nonna 213-217 The Broadway, SW19 1NL (8542 3060, www.lanonna.co.uk).

Olive Garden 48 Coombe Lane, SW20 0LA (8296 0205, www.theoliveraynespark.co.uk).

Spice of Raj 26 Christchurch Road, SW19 2NX (8542 6545, www.spiceofrajlimited.co.uk).

Vallebona Sardinian Gourmet Unit 14, 59 Weir Road, SW19 8UG (8944 5665, www.vallebona.co.uk).

Drinking

Alexandra 33 Wimbledon Hill Road, SW19 7NE (8947 7691, www.alexandrawimbledon.com).

Dog & Fox 24 High Street, SW19 5EA (8946 6565, www.dogandfoxwimbledon.co.uk).

Fox & Grapes 9 Camp Road, SW19 4UN (8619 1300, www.foxandgrapeswimbledon.co.uk).

Hemingways 57 High Street, SW19 5EE (8944 7722, www.hemingwaysbar.co.uk).

Old Frizzle 74-78 The Broadway, SW19 1RQ (3274 3056, www.theoldfrizzle.co.uk).

Suburban 27 Hartfield Road, SW19 3SG (8543 9788, www.suburbanbar.com).

Terrace Unit 601, Centre Court, Queens Road, SW19 8YA (8944 9970, www.terracewimbledon.co.uk).

Trafalgar 23 High Path, SW19 2JY (8542 5342, trafalgarfreehouse.co.uk).

William Morris 20 Watermill Way, SW19 2RD (8540 0216, www.faucetinn.com).

Shopping

Architectural Salvage 83 Haydons Road, SW19 1HH (8543 4450).

Bayley & Sage 60 High Street, SW19 5EE (8946 9904, www.bayley-sage.co.uk).

Burge & Gunson 13-27 High Street, SW19 2JE (8543 5166, www.burgeandgunson.co.uk).

Cath Kidston 3 High Street, SW19 5DX (8944 1001, www.cathkidston.co.uk).

Centre Court 4 Queens Road, SW19 8YA (8944 8323, www.centrecourtshopping.co.uk).

Diane von Furstenberg 38B High Street, SW19 5DE (8605 9156, www.dvf.com).

Elys of Wimbledon 16 St Georges Road, SW19 4DP (8946 9191, www.elyswimbledon.co.uk).

Luella's Boudoir 78A High Street, SW19 5EG (8879 7744, www.luellasboudoir.co.uk).

Matches 34 High Street, SW19 5BY (8947 8707, www.matchesfashion.com).

MaxMara 37 High Street, SW19 5BY (8944 1494, www.maxmara.com).

Merton Abbey Mills Merantun Way, SW19 2RD (8543 9608, www.mertonabbeymills.org.uk).

Question Air 77 High Street, SW19 5EG (8946 6288, www.question-air.com).

Wimbledon Farmers' Market Wimbledon Park Primary School, Havana Road, SW19 8EJ (7833 0338, www.lfm.org.uk).

Wimbledon Stadium Market Wimbledon Stadium Car Park, Plough Lane, SW17 0BL (07903 919029).

Things to do

Cinemas & theatres

Colour House Theatre Merton Abbey Mills, Watermill Way, SW19 2RD (8542 5511, www. colourhousetheatre.co.uk).

New Wimbledon Theatre & Studio Theatre The Broadway, SW19 1QG (0844 871 7646, www.atgtickets.com).

Odeon Wimbledon 39 The Broadway, SW19 1QB (0333 006 7777, www.odeon.co.uk).

Polka Theatre for Children 240 The Broadway, SW19 1SB (8543 4888, www.polkatheatre.com).

Galleries & museums

Museum of Wimbledon 22 Ridgway, SW19 4QN (8296 9914, www.wimbledonmuseum.org.uk). Charts the 3,000-year history of the area.

Wimbledon Lawn Tennis Museum Church Road, SW19 5AE (8946 6131, www.wimbledon.org/museum). Costumes, memorabilia and film footage.

Wimbledon Windmill Museum Windmill Road, Wimbledon Common, SW19 5NR (8788 7655, www.wimbledonwindmill.org.uk). The windmill, built in 1817, works on high days and holidays.

Other attractions

Buddhapadipa Temple 14 Calonne Road, SW19 5HJ (8946 1357, www.buddhapadipa.org). London's first Buddhist temple.

Deen City Farm 39 Windsor Avenue, SW19 2RR (8543 5300, www.deencityfarm.co.uk). Community farm on the edge of the Morden Hall Park Estate.

Merton Priory Watermill Way, off Merantun Way, SW19 2RD (8946 4141, www.mertonpriory. org). A 12th-century Augustinian priory.

Morden Hall Park Morden Hall Road, SM4 5JD (8545 6850, www.nationaltrust.org.uk).

Southside House 3-4 Woodhayes Road, Wimbledon Common, SW19 4RJ (8946 7643, www.southsidehouse.com). Grand house, open to visitors (Apr-Sept).

Green spaces

Cannizaro Park West Side Common, SW19 4UE (8879 1464, www.cannizaropark.com). Fabulous public gardens.

Cannon Hill Common Cannon Hill Lane, SW20 9DB. Nature conservation site.

Mitcham Common Croydon Road, CR4 1HT (www.merton.gov.uk). Large expanse of grass and woodland, including Seven Islands Pond and Mill House Ecology Centre.

Morden Park London Road, SM4 5HE (www.merton.gov.uk). Bookable sports pitches, paddling pool, and pitch and putt.

Wandle Trail The route of the River Wandle; 14 miles from Croydon to the Thames at Wandsworth.

Gyms & leisure centres

Christopher's Squash & Fitness Club Plough Lane, SW17 0BL (8946 4636, www.christophers squash.co.uk). Private.

King's Club King's College School, Woodhayes Road, SW19 4TT (8255 5401, www.sportkings. org). Private.

Morden Park Pool Morden Park, London Road, SM4 5HE (8640 6727, www.better.org.uk).

Wimbledon Club Church Road, SW19 5AG (8971 8090, www.thewimbledonclub.co.uk). Private multi-sports club.

Wimbledon Leisure Centre Latimer Road, SW19 1EW (8542 1330, www.better.org.uk).

Wimbledon Racquets & Fitness Club Cranbrook Road, SW19 4HD (8947 5806, www.wimbledonclub.co.uk). Private.

YMCA 200 The Broadway, SW19 1RY (8542 9055, www.ymcalsw.org.uk). Private.

Outdoor pursuits

Wimbledon Park Watersports Centre Home Park Road, SW19 7HX (8947 4894, www.merton. gov.uk).

Wimbledon Village Stables 24A/B High Street, SW19 5DX (8946 8579, www.wvstables.com).

Spectator sports

All England Lawn Tennis Club Church Road, SW19 5AE (8944 1066, www.wimbledon.org). Site of the annual Wimbledon tournament.

Wimbledon Stadium Plough Lane, SW17 0BL (0870 840 8905, www.lovethedogs.co.uk). Greyhound and speedway racing.

Schools

Primary

There are 44 state primary schools in Merton, including 12 church schools. There are also eight independent primaries, including one

Norwegian school. See www.merton.gov.uk, www.education.gov.uk/edubase and www.ofsted. gov.uk for more information.

Secondary

Harris Academy Merton Wide Way, CR4 1BP (8623 1000, www.harrismerton.org.uk).

Harris Academy Morden Lilleshall Road, SM4 6DU (8687 1157, www.harrismorden.org.uk).

King's College School Southside, Wimbledon Common, SW19 4TT (8255 5300, www.kcs.org.uk). Boys only; private.

Raynes Park High School Bushey Road, SW20 0JL (8946 4112, www.rphs.org.uk).

Ricards Lodge High School Lake Road, SW19 7HB (8946 2208, www.ricardslodge.merton.sch. uk). Girls only.

Rutlish School Watery Lane, SW20 9AD (8542 1212, www.rutlish.merton.sch.uk). Boys only.

St Mark's Academy Acacia Road, CR4 1SF (8648 6627, www.stmarksacademy.com). Church of England.

Ursuline High School Crescent Road, SW20 8HA (8255 2688, www.ursulinehigh.merton.sch.uk). Roman Catholic; girls only; mixed sixth form with Wimbledon College.

Wimbledon College Edge Hill, SW19 4NS (8946 2533, www.wimbledoncollege.org.uk). Roman Catholic; boys only; mixed sixth form with Ursuline High School.

Wimbledon High School Mansel Road, SW19 4AB (8971 0900, www.wimbledonhigh.gdst.net). Girls only; private.

Property

Local estate agents

Christopher St James www.csj.eu.com

Dicksons www.dicksons-estate.com

Drury and Cole www.drury-cole.co.uk

Eddison White www.eddisonwhite.co.uk

Ellisons www.ellisons.uk.com

Goodfellows www.goodfellows.co.uk

Hawes & Co www.hawesandco.co.uk

Jackson-Stops & Staff www.jackson-stops. co.uk

Lauritson www.lauristons.com

Longbow Property www.longbowproperty. london

Moss & Co www.mosswimbledonhill.co.uk

Local knowledge

www.lovewimbledon.org
www.merton.gov.uk/mymerton.
www.wimbledonguardian.co.uk
www.wimbledonsw19.com

USEFUL INFO

Borough size
3,762 hectares

Population
208,500

Ethnic mix
White 73%
Asian/Asian British 11.2%
Black/Black British 8.4%
Chinese or other 3.8%
Mixed 3.6%

London Borough of Merton
Civic Centre, London Road, SM4 5DX
(8274 4901, www.merton.gov.uk)

Council run by
Labour

MPs
Mitcham & Morden, Siobhain McDonagh
(Labour); Wimbledon, Stephen Hammond
(Conservative)

Main recycling centre
Garth Road Refuse & Recycling Centre,
63-69 Amenity Way, Garth Road, SM4 4AX
(8274 4902)

Council tax
£931.50 to £2,794.50

Wimbledon Common

Richmond upon Thames

Richmond is the only London borough that straddles the Thames. An abundance of private schools, the gorgeous riverside location, spacious parks and attractive housing make it a magnet for the affluent. Only the relentless air traffic in and out of Heathrow spoils this sylvan scene.

Richmond Riverside

AVERAGE PROPERTY PRICE

Detached	Terraced
£1,192,668	£696,450

Semi-detached	Flat
£821,780	£453,527

AVERAGE RENTAL PRICE PER WEEK

Studio	2 bed
£196	£345

1 bed	3 bed
£276	£495

	4+ bed
	£759

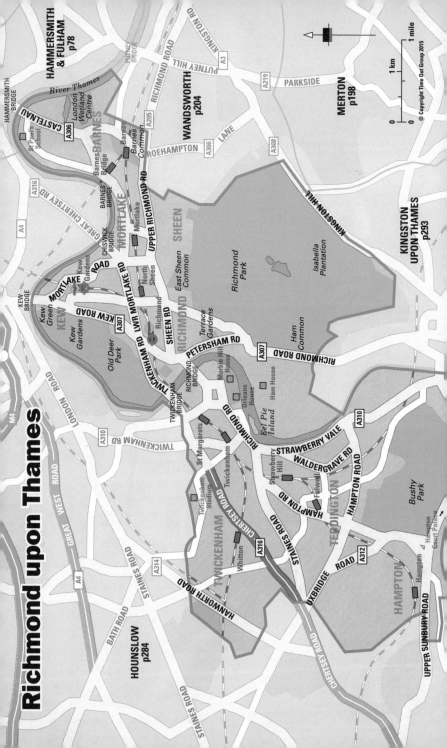

Richmond upon Thames

HAMMERSMITH & FULHAM p78

HAMMERSMITH BRIDGE

River Thames

London Wetland Centre

St Paul's School

CASTELNAU
A306

BARNES

Barnes Bridge

Barnes Common

ROEHAMPTON

A205

WANDSWORTH p204

PUTNEY BRIDGE

PUTNEY HILL

RICHMOND ROAD

KINGSTON ROAD

A3

PARKSIDE

A219

MERTON p198

LANE

A306

A308

BARNES BRIDGE

GREAT CHERTSEY RD

A316

A4

KEW BRIDGE

MORTLAKE

CHISWICK BRIDGE

UPPER RICHMOND RD

North Sheen

Mortlake

SHEEN

East Sheen Common

Richmond Park

Isabella Plantation

KINGSTON HILL

KINGSTON UPON THAMES p293

M4

LONDON ROAD

Kew Green

KEW

Kew Gardens

KEW ROAD

Old Deer Park

TWICKENHAM RD

LWR MORTLAKE RD

Kew Gardens

A307

SHEEN RD

Richmond

RICHMOND

Terrace Gardens

PETERSHAM RD

Marble Hill House

A307

Ham Common

RICHMOND ROAD

RICHMOND BRIDGE

TWICKENHAM BRIDGE

Orleans House

Ham House

A310

A310

GREAT WEST ROAD

TWICKENHAM RD

St Margarets

RICHMOND RD

Eel Pie Island

STRAWBERRY VALE

Strawberry Hill

WALDERGRAVE RD

A4

BATH ROAD

STAINES ROAD

Twickenham Stadium

Twickenham

CHERTSEY ROAD

TWICKENHAM

HAMPTON RD

Fulwell

HAMPTON ROAD

TEDDINGTON

Bushy Park

A310

HOUNSLOW p284

A314

Whitton

HANWORTH ROAD

A316

STAINES ROAD

UXBRIDGE ROAD

A312

HAMPTON

Hampton

Hampton Court Palace

STAINES ROAD

CHERTSEY ROAD

UPPER SUNBURY ROAD

1 mile

1 km

Neighbourhoods

Barnes SW13

Barnes lives up to its semi-rural, villagey reputation. At its centre is a large duck pond and adjoining green – site of a popular annual midsummer fair – surrounded by a mix of independent shops, pubs and restaurants. To the south is the buffer zone of wild and wooded Barnes Common, where Marc Bolan had his fatal crash. The London Wetland Centre, an expansive bird reserve converted from defunct reservoirs, sits to the east of Castelnau, the long spinal road that leads to Hammersmith Bridge. Enclosing it all is a sharp loop of the Thames, offering riverside walks and rowers aplenty. The Oxford and Cambridge boat crews race this stretch each year, finishing at Mortlake; the White Hart gastropub offers a perfect view.

Combine such attractions with some of London's best private schools, the proximity of Hammersmith and its tube station just over the bridge, and a regular service to Waterloo from Barnes and Barnes Bridge stations, and it's clear why affluent families and retirees love the area so much. Consequently, property prices are very high. There are plenty of attractive Victorian and Edwardian houses, and a few grand mansions, including Milbourne House, by the pond, once occupied by writer Henry Fielding.

There's no candlestick-maker in Barnes but it's still got a butcher and a baker, plus a fishmonger, greengrocer, handy hardware shop, the well-run Barnes Bookshop and the lovely Real Cheese Shop. All are located on Barnes High Street and Church Road. There's a smattering of upmarket fashion boutiques such as Question Air, and Nina for tasteful Swedish clothing and knick-knacks.

Barnes has a trio of excellent, long-running restaurants: the Modern European Sonny's Kitchen, the Italian Riva and the less formal riverside brasserie the Depot, which is a perfect spot for sunset-viewing. Orange Pekoe is a gem of a café, with pillowy scones and a sterling selection of loose teas.

Also in Barnes is the Bull's Head, which has been a legendary jazz venue since the late 1950s. It still has gigs every night, alongside Young's ales and a well-priced Thai restaurant in the former stables at the back. More modern – in looks, food and drink, with a global selection of bottled beers and a good wine list – is the Sun Inn, idyllically positioned opposite the duck pond.

Locals are delighted that the Olympic Studios – where legends such as the Rolling Stones, Jimi Hendrix, the Who and Led Zeppelin all recorded – has returned to its roots as a cinema, with an airy café attached.

Mortlake and Sheen SW14

West from Barnes, sandwiched between the Upper Richmond Road and the Thames, is Mortlake, presided over by the mammoth Stag Brewery, which is earmarked for redevelopment. The river is hidden from view here and the area is split in two by the railway line; hanging around at level crossings is a local pastime. Any village atmosphere

Join a Petersham Nurseries' foraging walk.

disappeared long ago – save for the odd nook – and it feels a bit of a no-man's-land, but property prices are significantly lower than in Barnes. There are some handsome Edwardian terraces, and cute cottages and allotments around the railway tracks.

White Hart Lane is the main shopping street, lined with independent boutiques and restaurants, and home to posh deli Gusto & Relish and a couple of swanky interiors shops: Tobias and the Angel, and the Dining Room Shop. A local Swedish school means good Scandi restaurants in the area, such as Stockholm Restaurant & Deli on Sheen Lane.

The residential heart of East Sheen sits between the busy Upper Richmond Road (forming part of the South Circular), East Sheen Common and the northern fringe of Richmond Park. House prices are as astronomical as in many other parts of the borough, with some grand Victorian and Edwardian villas near the park; the Parkside and Palewell Park areas are sought after.

TRANSPORT

Tube lines District, Overground
Rail services into Clapham Junction, Waterloo
Main bus routes into central London night bus N22
River boat services between Richmond, Kingston and Hampton Court, April to October

Retail here tends to involve useful chains, charity shops, and furniture and kitchen suppliers. However, the neighbourhood does have a brace of excellent gastropubs in the shape of the Brown Dog and the Victoria; the latter is also a hotel. Faanoos Richmond, out towards North Sheen, is the destination for Iranian eats.

Kew TW9

Everyone knows Kew Gardens, officially the Royal Botanic Gardens, Kew. This exquisitely planned extravaganza of botanical biodiversity, stretching south along the Thames from Kew Bridge, attracts two million visitors a year. But it's not the only chunk of green in this greenest of London boroughs. Adjoining the Gardens to the south is the Old Deer Park and the exclusive Royal Mid-Surrey Golf Club, while Kew Green abuts the northern end.

Across Kew Road is the main residential area, with assorted restaurants and shops on Sandycombe Road. Property is relatively varied, with houses dating from the era of Queen Anne to that of Queen Victoria, converted flats and modern purpose-built apartments. It makes Kew exceedingly popular with prosperous middle-class families who appreciate the highly rated primary schools and good transport connections: tube and train to get into central London; easy access to the A4 and M4 to get out. A local vibe remains, especially in the characterful cluster of shops and restaurants around Kew Gardens station. Alternatively, for high street brands, visit user-friendly Kew Retail Park, off the A205.

Gastrofication has come to Kew, and visitors to the Botanic Gardens have a trio of handy pubs to choose from. The Inn at Kew Gardens, in the Kew Gardens Hotel on Sandycombe Road, is spacious, airy and big on food. Next to Kew Green are the Coach & Horses, a congenial Young's gastropub-with-rooms offering traditional Sunday roasts, and the Botanist, a more modern affair with its own microbrewery and poshed-up pub grub.

HIGHS & LOWS

Richmond Park – three times the size of Central Park, New York

Attractive riverside path

Protected vistas

Boutiques

Hampton Court Palace

Rugby

River boat trips

The crowds in Richmond Park on a sunny day – cars, cyclists and joggers

Richmond Riverside in summer when it's packed with drinkers

Some of the capital's most expensive housing

Heathrow flightpath

Rugby fans

The Glasshouse, next to Kew Gardens station, is an extremely polished Mod Euro restaurant, while TV chef Antony Worrall Thompson has Kew Grill on Kew Green – visit for steaks and burgers and an unstuffy vibe.

Richmond TW9

Over 100 years ago, an act was passed to protect the view from Richmond Hill back into London, and after making the steady climb it's clear why. Even on a cloudy day you can see Richmond Palace, eight miles from Westminster, surrounded by green. The pretty riverside setting, huge green spaces and stunning period houses have proved an irresistible lure for moneyed professionals.

Richmond is precisely that, a very rich mound. It's one of the most affluent boroughs in England and you're unlikely to find many first-time buyers. (You're looking at half a million on average for a one bed and around £1 million for a three bed.) Prices start to shoot up on Richmond Hill, which local celebrity Ronnie Wood calls home.

The town centre is dominated by upmarket chains (Joules, Reiss, SpaceNK), but tucked away behind George Street – essentially the high street – is Richmond Green, one of the borough's proudest assets. Remnants of Henry VIII's palace still stand in one corner, now converted into lodgings. When the sun's out, the grass is invariably strewn with lounging locals and drinkers from the Cricketers pub or the Prince's Head – except when cricket is being played, in an authentically casual, village-green fashion.

The lanes leading off Richmond Green have a sense of being caught in the Tudor history of the town while being a stone's throw from the high street. Here you'll find small outlets such as Gelateria Danieli and chocolate wizard William Curley. Across George Street, seek out children's bookshop the Alligator's Mouth down Church Court.

The Saturday farmers' market in Heron Square offers 30 food stalls, a bit like a mini Borough Market without too much bustle, and 42 craft stalls on a Sunday. You'll see

Petersham Meadows

everything from South African-style beef jerky to home-made beeswax candles.

Things get classy along Hill Rise and up Richmond Hill with wine merchant Philglas & Swiggot, Italian fashion at Anna Boutique, Bramble & Moss florist, and second-hand designer togs at Vintage Rose. Independent restaurants in the town centre include Don Fernando's for classic Spanish tapas; Breton specialist Chez Lindsay for galettes and cider; Matsuba for Korean and Japanese dishes; and La Buvette for French bistro classics. Fragrant infusions and floral aromas are the order of the day at cosy café Tea Box, and stronger stuff at the Orange Tree pub.

At first glance, the options for eating along the river seem chains-only but a short wander down to the riverside – or what the boat makers under the arches call 'the shore' – there are a few vegan and healthy-eating joints. For riverside drinking, try the White Cross on Water Lane; and for riverside dining, Argentine grill chain Gaucho or, further along the towpath, Stein's beer garden for bratwurst and Bavarian beer (although it opens weekend afternoons only in winter). Boats and bikes can be rented from Richmond Bridge Boathouses or Blazing Saddles at reasonable hourly rates.

Richmond Hill leads steeply up to a dainty cluster – shops, restaurants, a pub – known as Richmond Village and, beyond, the vast expanse of Richmond Park, London's largest royal park. Just over seven miles in circumference, it attracts cyclists, walkers, joggers and riders and can feel busier than Piccadilly Circus at weekends. Deer roam freely over its ancient grasslands, but it's also studded with formal gardens such as the Isabella Plantation – a carefully tended enclosure of azaleas and rhododendrons – and King Henry's Mound, from where the view of St Paul's Cathedral is protected by law and no tall buildings can be built in between.

Transport links from Richmond are excellent, with regular District line, Overground and national rail services into central London.

Ham and Petersham TW10

The famous view from Richmond Hill of cows grazing on Petersham Meadows is preserved by a 1902 Act of Parliament, no less: the culmination of a public campaign to prevent a housing estate being built here. The meadows once formed part of the estate of Ham House, a spectacular Stuart mansion set further along the river – and also visible

from the hill – which is now owned by the National Trust.

Ham and Petersham have maintained their rural character thanks to their secluded location, hemmed in by the Thames on one side, and Ham Common and Richmond Park on the other. There are council estates here, but Petersham also has some particularly fine 17th- and 18th-century mansions – including Rutland Lodge, Montrose House and Petersham House – alongside Victorian cottages and more modern dwellings. Those trying to get into catchment areas for Richmond's schools often move to Ham and Petersham as a more affordable alternative to Richmond itself. Both are becoming more and more popular.

Ham Polo Club is the only club of its kind left in London, so regular polo matches, and events such as the Richmond Regatta in June, add to the countrified vibe – as does the absence of a train station.

More recently, Petersham has become synonymous with its nurseries, an idyllic place of elegant glasshouses and expensive garden ornaments, plus a smart restaurant – an outdoor/indoor venue that serves excellent lunches among the plants and sculptures. There's a separate tea house for tea and cake. Lesser known – but not for long – is the Dysart, which serves an exquisite seasonal menu full of exciting twists, yet still manages to keep a friendly local feel with music nights and provision for dog-walkers.

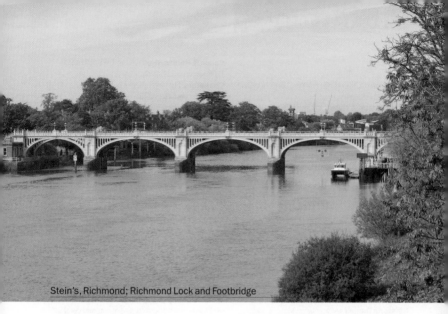
Stein's, Richmond; Richmond Lock and Footbridge

Twickenham TW1

Fans of the oval ball game around the world revere Twickenham for its connection with rugby, but there's no shortage of local rugger-buggers too – evident from the thronged pubs, packed railway station and traffic jams around Twickenham Stadium on match days. South from the stadium lies the town centre, around Heath Road, London Road and King Street. It has none of the grandeur of Richmond across the river, and too many pound shops, but proud residents would assert that they have Church Street instead – a cobbled lane off the main road flanked by restaurants, pubs and independent shops.

Well-kept late Victorian and Edwardian terraces dominate Twickenham's residential districts; compared to Richmond, property prices are certainly more palatable. But it's the riverside that is, and has always been, the area's main attraction. Eminently fashionable in the 17th and 18th centuries, this bank of the Thames was lined by posh countryside retreats built by the likes of Horace Walpole and Alexander Pope. Most of these mansions are long gone, though Marble Hill House, Strawberry Hill House and York House remain, the last in use as council offices. Of the once-numerous ferries, only Hammertons Ferry (www. hammertonsferry.com) still operates; it's the best way to get between Marble Hill House, and Ham House and Petersham Nurseries.

Watery activities have always been big business. Ferry Road retains old watermen's cottages and boatsheds, while Eel Pie Island – connected by a footbridge to the mainland – is home to Twickenham Rowing Club, Richmond Yacht Club and about 50 much-prized houses. The island was also the centre of a thriving music scene in the 1950s and '60s, when George Melly, the Rolling Stones, the Who, Eric Clapton and Rod Stewart all performed here. The Eel Pie Club continues the tradition by hosting gigs at the Cabbage Patch pub on London Road.

Riverside drinking is also a popular pastime – try the historic White Swan next to the river in Twickenham. Towpath flooding is a factor here too – hence the steep steps up to the entrance – as the Thames becomes tidal just upstream at neighbouring Teddington. Alternatively, play it safe at the low-key and very popular Eel Pie on pretty Church Street, serving fine Hall & Woodhouse beers. Twickenham Fine Ales microbrewery is open to drinkers on rugby days, or get a carry-out from the Real Ale Shop (real ales, ciders, perries and beers from British microbreweries).

In St Margarets, north Indian Tangawizi and French brasserie Le Salon Privé keep the locals happy.

Twickenham lacks the tube, but there are train stations at St Margarets, Twickenham and Strawberry Hill, and easy access to the M3 via the busy Chertsey Road (A316).

Eating

La Buvette 6 Church Walk, TW9 1SN (8940 6264, www.labuvette.co.uk).
Chez Lindsay 11 Hill Rise, TW10 6UQ (8948 7473, www.chez-lindsay.co.uk).
Depot Tideway Yard, 125 Mortlake High Street, SW14 8SN (8878 9462, www.depotbrasserie.co.uk).
Don Fernando's 27F The Quadrant, TW9 1DN (8948 6447, www.donfernando.co.uk).

Richmond Theatre's Christmas panto is an annual sell-out.

Dysart 135 Petersham Road, TW10 7AA (8940 8005, www.thedysartpetersham.co.uk).
Faanoos Richmond 481 Upper Richmond Road West, SW14 7PU (8878 5738, www.faanoos restaurant.com).
Gaucho The Towpath, TW10 6UJ (8948 4030).
Gelateria Danieli www.gelateriadanieli.com; 16 Brewers Lane, TW9 1HH (8439 9807); 13 The Green, TW9 1PX (8439 9111).
Glasshouse 14 Station Parade, TW9 3PZ (8940 6777, www.glasshouserestaurant.co.uk).
Kew Grill 10B Kew Green, TW9 3BH (8948 4433, www.awtkewgrill.com).
Matsuba 10 Red Lion Street, TW9 1RW (8605 3513, www.matsuba-restaurant.com).
Olympic Café & Dining Room The Olympic Studios, 117-123 Church Road, SW13 9HL (8912 5161, www.olympiccinema.co.uk).
Orange Pekoe 3 White Hart Lane, SW13 0PX (8876 6070, www.orangepekoeteas.com).
Petersham Nurseries Café Church Lane, off Petersham Road, TW10 7AB (8940 5230, www. petershamnurseries.com). Also has a tea house.
Riva 169 Church Road, SW13 9HR (8748 0434).
Le Salon Privé 43 Crown Road, TW1 3EJ (8892 0602, www.lesalonprive.net).
Sonny's Kitchen 94 Church Road, SW13 0DQ (8748 0393, www.sonnyskitchen.co.uk).
Stockholm Restaurant & Deli 109 Sheen Lane, SW14 8AE (8876 7747, www.stockholmdeli.co.uk).
Tangawizi 406 Richmond Road, TW1 2EB (8891 3737, www.tangawizi.co.uk).
Tea Box 7 Paradise Road, TW9 1RX (8940 3521, www.theteabox.co.uk).

Drinking

Botanist 3-5 Kew Green, TW9 3AA (8948 4838, www.thebotanistkew.com).
Brown Dog 28 Cross Street, SW13 0AP (8392 2200, www.thebrowndog.co.uk).

Coach & Horses 8 Kew Green, TW9 3BH (8940 1208, www.coachhotelkew.co.uk).
Cricketers The Green, TW9 1LX (8940 4372, www.cricketersrichmond.com).
Eel Pie 9-11 Church Street, TW1 3NJ (8891 1717, www.theeelpie.co.uk).
Inn at Kew Gardens 292 Sandycombe Road, TW9 3NG (8940 2220, www.kewgardenshotel.com).
Orange Tree 45 Kew Road, TW9 2NQ (8940 0944, www.orangetreerichmond.co.uk).
Prince's Head 28 The Green, TW9 1LX (8940 1572, www.princeshead.co.uk).
Stein's Richmond Towpath, 55 Petersham Road, TW10 6UT (8948 8189, www.stein-s.com).
Sun Inn 7 Church Road, SW13 9HE (8876 5256, www.thesuninnbarnes.co.uk).
Twickenham Fine Ales 18 Mereway Road, TW2 6RG (8241 1825, www.twickenham-fine-ales.co.uk).
Victoria 10 West Temple Sheen, SW14 7RT (8876 4238, www.thevictoria.net).
White Cross off Water Lane, Riverside, TW9 1TH (8940 6844, www.thewhitecrossrichmond.com).
White Hart The Terrace, Riverside, SW13 0NR (8876 5177, www.whitehartbarnes.co.uk).
White Swan Riverside, TW1 3DN (8744 2951, www.whiteswantwickenham.co.uk).

Shopping

Alligator's Mouth 2A Church Court, TW9 1JL (8948 6775, www.thealligatorsmouth.co.uk).
Anna Boutique 44 Hill Rise, TW16 6UF (8948 0199, www.annaboutique.com).
Barnes Bookshop 60 Church Road, SW13 0DQ (8741 0786, www.barnesbookshop.co.uk).
Bramble & Moss 60 Hill Rise, TW10 6UB (8332 2268, www.brambleandmoss.co.uk).
Dining Room Shop 62 White Hart Lane, SW13 0PZ (8878 1020).
Gusto & Relish 56 White Hart Lane, SW13 0PZ (8878 2005, www.gustoandrelish.co.uk).
Kew Retail Park Bessant Drive, off Mortlake Road, TW9 4AD.
Nina 55 Church Road, SW13 9HH (8240 0414, www.shopnina.co.uk).
Petersham Nurseries Church Lane, off Petersham Road, TW10 7AG (8940 5230, www.petershamnurseries.com).
Philglas & Swiggot 64 Hill Rise, TW10 6UB (8332 6031, www.philglas-swiggot.com).
Question Air 86 Church Road, SW13 0DQ (8741 0816, www.question-air.com).
Real Ale Shop 371 Richmond Road, TW1 2EF (8892 3710, www.realale.com).
Real Cheese Shop 62 Barnes High Street, SW13 9LF (8878 6676).

Richmond Farmers' Market Heron Square, TW9 1EJ (www.reelfarmers.co.uk).
Tobias and the Angel 68 White Hart Lane, SW13 0PZ (8878 8902, www.tobiasandtheangel.com).
Vintage Rose 24 Richmond Hill, TW10 6QX (8940 1222).
William Curley 10 Paved Court, TW9 1LZ (8332 3002, www.williamcurley.co.uk).

Things to do

Cinemas & theatres

Curzon Richmond 3 Water Lane, TW9 1TJ (0330 500 1331, www.curzoncinemas.com).
Odeon Richmond , www.odeon.co.uk; 72 Hill Street, TW9 1TW; 6 Red Lion Street, TW9 6RE (0333 006 7777).
Olympic Cinema Olympic Studios, 117-123 Church Road, SW13 9HL (8912 5161, www. olympiccinema.co.uk).
Orange Tree Theatre 1 Clarence Street, TW9 2SA (8940 3633, www.orangetreetheatre.co.uk).
Richmond Theatre Little Green, TW9 1QJ (0844 871 7651, www.atgtickets.com).
Vue Staines Two Rivers Retail Park, Mustard Mill Road, TW18 4BL (0871 224 0240, www.myvue.com).

Galleries & museums

Museum of Richmond Old Town Hall, Whittaker Avenue, TW9 1TP (8332 1141, www.museumof richmond.com). Richmond's regal history.
Orleans House Gallery Riverside, TW1 3DJ (8831 6000, www.richmond.gov.uk). The borough's main art gallery, located in riverside gardens.
Twickenham Museum 25 The Embankment, TW1 3DU (8408 0070, www.twickenham-museum. org.uk). Local history museum in 18th-century waterman's cottage.

Other attractions

Garrick's Temple to Shakespeare Hampton Court Road, TW12 2EN (07880 790763, www. garrickstemple.org.uk). Riverside folly.
Ham House & Garden Ham Street, TW10 7RS (8940 1950, www.nationaltrust.org.uk). Riverside mansion built in 1610, with fine gardens and a café.
Hampton Court Palace East Molesey, KT8 9AU (0844 482 7777, www.hrp.org.uk). Tudor palace with a famous maze, exhibitions and an ice-rink.
London Wetland Centre Queen Elizabeth's Walk, SW13 9WT (8409 4400, www.wwt.org.uk).
Marble Hill House Richmond Road, TW1 2NL (0370 333 1181, www.english-heritage.org.uk). Elegant Palladian house built in 1724 by George II for his mistress, Henrietta Howard.
National Archives Ruskin Avenue, TW9 4DU (8876 3444, www.nationalarchives.gov.uk).

Accessible archives office in Kew, housing 1,000 years of official government and law records.
Royal Botanic Gardens, Kew TW9 3AB (8332 5655, www.kew.org). Big, famous, lovely.
Strawberry Hill House 268 Waldegrave Road, TW1 4ST (8744 1241, www.strawberryhill house.org.uk). Horace Walpole's Grade I-listed 'little Gothic castle', restored to the tune of £10 million.

Gigs, clubs & comedy

Bull's Head 373 Lonsdale Road, SW13 9PY (8876 5241, www.thebullshead.com). Well-appointed gastropub with nightly jazz gigs.
Cabbage Patch 67 London Road, TW1 3SZ (8892 3874, www.cabbagepatch.co.uk). Family-run pub with regular music nights hosted by the Eel Pie Club (www.eelpieclub.com).

Green spaces

For more details, see www.richmond.gov.uk.
Barn Elms Playing Fields Queen Elizabeth Walk, SW13. Riverside sports pitches plus a small fishing lake and a Scouts and Guides campsite.
Barnes Common Vine Road, SW13. Football and cricket pitches, woodland and nature trail.
Bushy Park Hampton Court Road, TW12 (www.royalparks.org.uk). London's second-largest royal park. Includes a Baroque water garden and the Diana Fountain.
Copse Meadlands Drive, TW10. Conservation site with bridle paths.
Crane Park Crane Park Road, TW2. Wildlife park with marsh frogs and water voles.
Ham Lands Kingfisher Drive, TW10. Nature reserve and horse riding; includes BMX track by Teddington Lock.
Hampton Common Buckingham Road, TW12. Outdoor gym and BMX track.
Hatherop Park Hatherop Road, TW12. Conservation area, sports pitches and a pond.
Kings Field Hampton Court Road, KT1. Includes a skatepark, cricket pitch, football pitch and tennis courts.
Leg O'Mutton Lonsdale Road, SW13. Mile-long nature reserve by a reservoir.
Old Deer Park Old Palace Lane, TW9. Sports pitches, playgrounds and outdoor pools.
Petersham Meadows River Lane, TW10. Historic water meadow painted by Turner.
Radnor Gardens Cross Deep, TW1. Rare trees and historic summerhouse and gazebo.
Richmond Park Holly Lodge, TW10 (www.royalparks.org.uk). Historic deer park and London's biggest enclosed space at 955 hectares.

Gyms & leisure centres

Hampton Sports & Fitness Centre Hanworth Road, TW12 3HB (3772 2999, www.richmond. gov.uk).

Pools on the Park, Springhealth Leisure Old Deer Park, Twickenham Road, TW9 2SF (8940 0561, www.springhealth.net). Private.

Richmond Hill Health Club Lewis Road, TW10 6SA (8948 5523, www.richmondhillhealthclub. co.uk). Private.

Shene Sports & Fitness Centre Richmond Park Academy, Park Avenue, SW14 8AT (3772 2999, www.richmond.gov.uk).

Teddington Pools & Fitness Centre Vicarage Road, TW11 8EZ (3772 2999, www.richmond. gov.uk).

Teddington Sports Centre Teddington School, Broom Road, TW11 9PJ (3772 2999, www. richmond.gov.uk).

Twickenham Fitness & Wellbeing Centre Stoop Memorial Ground, Langhorn Drive, TW2 7SX (8892 2251, www.nuffieldhealth.com). Private.

Whitton Sports & Fitness Centre Twickenham Academy, Percy Road, TW2 6JW (3772 2999, www.richmond.gov.uk).

Outdoor pursuits

Blazing Saddles 2 Bridge Boathouses, TW9 1TH (8948 8240, www.blazingsaddlesbikehire.com). Bike hire by the Thames at Richmond.

Ham Polo Club Petersham Road, TW10 7AH (8940 2020, www.hampoloclub.com).

Hampton Pool High Street, TW12 2ST (8255 1116, www.hamptonpool.co.uk). Open-air, heated pool.

Richmond Bridge Boathouses Bridge Boathouse, Riverside, TW9 1TH (8948 8270, www. richmondbridgeboathouses.co.uk). Boat hire.

Richmond Golf Club Sudbrook Lane, TW10 7AS (8940 4351, www.therichmondgolfclub.com).

Royal Mid-Surrey Golf Club Old Deer Park, Twickenham Road, TW9 2SB (8940 1894, www. rmsgc.co.uk).

Richmond Park Golf Club Norstead Place, SW15 3SA (8876 3205, www.richmondparkgolfclub.org.uk).

Spectator sports

Harlequins Twickenham Stoop, Langhorn Drive, TW2 7SX (8410 6000, www.quins.co.uk). Rugby club.

Kempton Park Racecourse Staines Road East, TW16 5AQ (01932 782292, kempton.thejockey club.co.uk). Just outside the borough.

London Scottish The Athletic Ground, Twickenham Road, TW9 2SF (3397 9551, www.londonscottish.com). Rugby club.

Rosslyn Park Priory Lane, Upper Richmond Road, SW15 5JH (8876 6044, www.rosslynpark. co.uk). Rugby club.

Twickenham Stadium Whitton Road, TW2 7BA (0871 222 2120, www.rfu.com). Home of the England rugby team and the Museum of Rugby.

Schools

Primary

Richmond has 44 primaries, of which 17 are church schools: nine Church of England and eight Roman Catholic. See www.richmond.gov.uk, www.education.gov.uk/edubase and www.ofsted. gov.uk for more information.

Secondary

Christ's School Queens Road, TW10 6HW (8940 6982, www.christs.richmond.sch.uk).

Grey Court School Ham Street, TW10 7HN (8948 1173, www.greycourt.richmond.sch.uk).

Hampton Academy Hanworth Road, TW12 3HB (8979 3399, www.hamptonacademy.org.uk).

Orleans Park School Richmond Road, TW1 3BB (8891 0187, www.orleanspark.richmond.sch.uk).

Richmond Park Academy Park Avenue, SW14 8RG (8876 8891, www.richmondparkacademy.org).

St Richard Reynolds Catholic High School Clifden Road, TW1 4LT (8325 4630, www.st richardreynolds.org.uk). Roman Catholic.

Teddington School Broom Road, TW11 9PJ (8943 0033, www.teddingtonschool.org).

Twickenham Academy Percy Road, TW2 6JW (8894 4503, www.twickenhamacademy.org.uk).

Waldegrave School for Girls Fifth Cross Road, TW2 5LH (8894 3244, www.waldegrave.richmond. sch.uk). Girls only.

Property

Local estate agents

Antony Roberts www.antonyroberts.co.uk
Carter Jonas Boileaus www.boileaus.com
Charles Banks www.charlesbanks.co.uk
Halletts www.hallettsestateagentskew.com
Jardine & Co www.jardineandco.co.uk
John D Wood & Co www.johndwood.co.uk
Major Son & Phipps www.major-estateagents.com
Marquis & Co www.marquisandco.com
Parkgate Estate Agents www.parkgate.info
Philip Hodges www.philip-hodges.co.uk
Richmond Bridge Residential www.rb residential.com
Stuart Mackenzie www.stuart-mackenzie.co.uk

Local knowledge

www.barnesvillage.com
www.richmondandtwickenhamtimes.co.uk
www.totallyrichmond.co.uk

Royal Botanic Gardens, Kew

USEFUL INFO

Borough size
5,741 hectares

Population
196,200

Ethnic mix
White 84.6%
Asian or Asian British 6.8%
Black or Black British 3.1%
Mixed 2.8%
Chinese or other 2.8%

**London Borough of Richmond
upon Thames**
Civic Centre, 44 York Street, TW1 3BZ
(8891 1411, www.richmond.gov.uk)

Council run by
Conservatives

MPs
Richmond Park, Zac Goldsmith
(Conservative); Twickenham, Tania
Mathias (Conservative)

Main recycling centre
Townmead Road Re-use & Recycling Centre,
Townmead Road, TW9 4EL (8876 3281,
www.richmond.gov.uk)

Council tax
£1,054.93 to £3,164.78

Waltham Forest

It's all change for this very east London borough. Investments made for the 2012 Olympics are taking hold, and higher house prices in neighbouring districts are bringing new residents who want to make things happen.

AVERAGE PROPERTY PRICE	
Detached £574,826	Terraced £374,610
Semi-detached £474,765	Flat £281,381

AVERAGE RENTAL PRICE PER WEEK	
Room £104	1 bed £207
Studio £173	2 bed £276
	3 bed £334

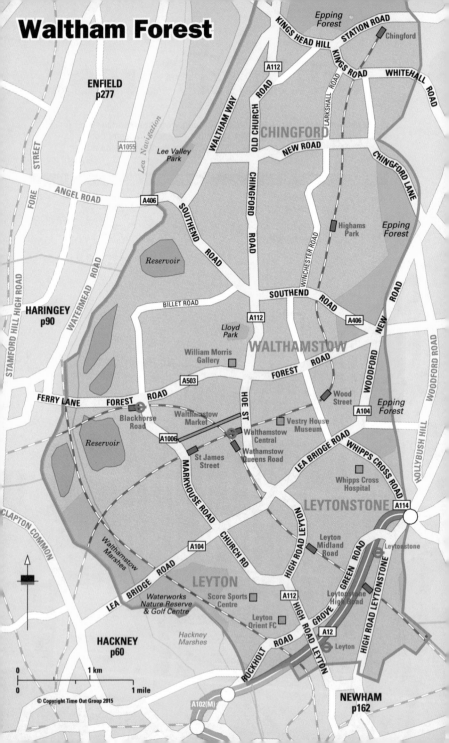

Neighbourhoods

Walthamstow E17

No longer the distant stop at the end of the Victoria line where you wouldn't dare venture, Walthamstow is now another up-and-coming area. Swarms of people are moving here, including hipsters hacked off with Hackney house prices. Particularly popular are the dark brick terraces of Warner maisonettes, home to young professionals and families. More than 5,000 of these were built from the 1880s to the 1930s, a remarkable enterprise by a local landowner, providing homes for the masses.

The High Street is known for its sprawling market, a teeming strip of some 450 stalls and 300 shops. On Sunday mornings, organic and free-range produce comes to the fore at the farmers' market in the Town Square. Here, too, is the Scene development, bringing the borough a much-needed multi-screen cinema, chain restaurants and 71 new apartments.

The High Street is also home to some unreconstructed favourites, such as the Chequers (good pub grub and beer) and Manze's (pie and mash, since 1929), offering a touch of East End authenticity.

The independent shops and middle-class families can be found in Walthamstow Village, where a handful of quiet streets with cute cottages huddle around the attractively overgrown churchyard of St Mary's. On Orford Road, Eat 17 serves excellent, ethically sourced Modern British food and is hugely popular; it's also got a pizzeria in the adjoining and award-winning Spar shop, where you can buy Eat 17's famed bacon jam. There's great tapas at Orford Saloon and Italian eats at Trattoria La Ruga, while the East London Sausage Company is a fine butcher and the newly opened Froth & Rind deals in artisanal cheese and craft beer.

No village is complete without good drinking holes. That means the Castle for gastropub dishes and popular Sunday roasts; the Nag's Head (cats welcome, children less so); and the Village, which is more corporate in feel but with a nice beer garden. Orford House Social Club hosts both the locally run Stow Film Lounge (offering more than multiplex blockbusters) and frequent design fairs run by E17 Designers.

Further west, Ravenswood Industrial Estate has become Walthamstow's centre of hip, home to the Wild Card Brewery and its excellent selection of beers, the retro-neon art haven of God's Own Junkyard with its Rolling Scones Café, and Mother's Ruin (maker of award-winning fruit liqueurs).

East of the Village is the Wood Street area, home to Wood Street Market – a quirky maze of small stalls, artists' workshops and units selling everything from James Bond memorabilia to cake decorations and baby slings. Also hereabouts are yet more cafés: Lot 107 and Hillman's Tearoom are the pick of the bunch.

North from the station along Hoe Street is Hoe Street Central (home to an eclectic mix of frequently changing pop-ups, from independent designers to sweet and savoury food businesses) and Ye Olde Rose & Crown, which remains a real community hub for gigs and comedy – a bit on the grimy side but full of charm and friendly locals. At the south end of Hoe Street is the Hornbeam, a great organic vegetarian café and another community hangout.

Many new establishments are setting up in the Lloyd Park area. The Bell (once a pub you'd only enter for a fight) has been done up and serves great ales and food; Swedish café Bygga Bo seduces with the scent of freshly baked cinnamon buns; Wynwood Art District pulls in the local coffee-drinkers.

Leyton E10

Leyton may be firmly in Zone 3 but it's well served for transport, with the Central line whisking commuters to the heart of the City, and the A12 running down towards the Thames or out towards Essex and the M11. However, these very visible rail and road links leave the area feeling less of a destination and more like somewhere people merely transit.

For now, Leyton remains more inner-city than suburban. There are some pleasant terraces, and the Coronation Gardens beside Leyton Orient's redeveloped Matchroom Stadium are charming thanks to their restoration to Edwardian glory a few years back, but there are almost as many industrial zones and concrete estates.

TRANSPORT

Tube lines Central, Overground, Victoria
Rail services into Liverpool Street
Main bus routes into central London 48, 55, 56; night buses N8, N26, N38, N55, N73

Steadily, things are getting less shabby. The council has given a stretch of Leyton High Road a multicoloured makeover, painting facades in different pastel shades and restoring shop fronts, giving the street a distinctive character – a pleasant place for retail therapy.

Joining the world tour of transient single-room caffs along the High Road are now several foodie faves. The Leyton Technical, originally a 2012 pop-up in the old town hall, has become an established neighbourhood favourite with its seasonal British menu and plenty of community entertainments (comedy, occasional markets and quizzes). Uptown Burger has brought a Shoreditch vibe and Le Petit Robe Rose (French café and vintage shop) has brought Gallic charm, gluten-free cakes and friendly social evenings. Over on Francis Road, there's Marmelo Kitchen (a local caterer serving inventive sharing plates Friday to Sunday) and Albert & Francis (a vintage-styled café that's also home to Leyton's Little Free Library).

The area is next door to the Olympic site in the borough of Newham which means Leyton residents have also benefited from the new sports facilities built there for 2012: the aquatics centre, hockey and tennis centre, the ice centre and the velodrome – all a cut above your average gym. These are in addition to the fabled Hackney Marshes, the world's biggest Sunday league football venue, with 82 pitches.

Leytonstone E11

This corner of the borough is having a moment. With Hackney types now spreading over from the other side of the River Lea, and house-hunters from more genteel Wanstead recognising this as a cheaper place to buy, the area has attained the critical mass of go-getters necessary for things to happen. Residents blog and tweet with gusto about the frequent new openings that are changing the face of the high street, and each July the

Hiring a boat for an hour's row on Hollow Ponds is a popular Sunday outing.

creative community comes together for a local festival (www.leytonstonefestival.org.uk) and arts trail (www.leytonstoneartstrail.org).

The district is a product of mid 19th-century railway expansion; the terraces that sprang up as a result are now occupied by middle-class Asian and British families. (Upper Leytonstone has a Hindu temple, Bushwood bags the mosque.)

New-build flats on the High Road confirm Leytonstone's reputation as a target for local-authority personnel, nurses and teachers, while the 20-minute Central line journey to Liverpool Street is a strong lure for City workers. Nearby are the vast expanses of Epping Forest and Wanstead Flats, straddling the boundary with Redbridge.

There's been excitement about openings such as Wild Goose Bakery (the obligatory artisan bakery and café on the High Road), Vietnamese restaurant Little Saigon, the Northcote pub (drawing crowds with Sunday drag nights) and the revamped Red Lion (now with a huge beer garden, chillout areas and dining areas).

What's Cookin' has moved its celebrated country and bluegrass sessions over to the Leytonstone Ex Servicemen's Club on Harvey Road, a 1950s-'60s-style function room with real ale. Meanwhile Transport for London has turned gallerist by opening Fill the Gap beside Leytonstone tube station. It's dedicated to showcasing local talent and managed by TfL employees who also happen to be artists.

Don't worry, though: Leytonstone isn't yet an identikit middle-class enclave. It still treasures solid boozers such as the North Star (tucked away in the pretty Browning Road conservation area). Locals have also clubbed together to buy the Heathcote Arms and turn it into a family-friendly community pub.

Leytonstone is very proud of one of its most famous sons: film director Alfred Hitchcock. Look out for Hitch-related street art referencing his movies.

Eating

Albert & Francis 153 Francis Road, E10 6NT.
Bygga Bo 8 Chingford Road, E17 4PJ (8527 3652, www.byggabo.com).
Eat 17 28-30 Orford Road, E17 9NJ (8521 5279, www.eat17.co.uk).
Hillman's Tearooms 100 Wood Street, E17 3HX (07742 436995, www.hillmanstearoom.co.uk).
Hornbeam 458 Hoe Street, E17 9AH (8558 6880, www.hornbeam.org.uk).
Leyton Technical 265 High Road Leyton, E10 5QN (8558 4759, www.leytontechnical.com).
Little Saigon 686 High Road Leytonstone, E11 3AA (3581 1490, www.littlesaigonlondon.co.uk).
L Manze 76 Walthamstow High Street, E17 7LD (8520 2855).
Lot 107 107 Wood Street, E17 3LL (8520 5632).

Marmelo Kitchen 169 Francis Road, E10 6NT (3620 7580, www.marmelokitchen.com).
Orford Saloon 32 Orford Road, E17 9NJ (8503 6542, www.orfordtapas.co.uk).
Le Petit Robe Rose 330 High Road Leyton, E10 5PW (07766 704637).
Rolling Scones Café Unit 12, Ravenswood Industrial Estate, Shernhall Street, E17 9HQ (8509 0157, www.godsownjunkyard.co.uk).
Trattoria La Ruga 59 Orford Road, E17 9NJ (8520 5008, www.laruga.co.uk).
Uptown Burger 466 High Road Leyton, E10 6QA (8558 8788, www.uptownburger.co.uk/leyton).
Wynwood Art District 2A Chingford Road, E17 4PJ (www.wynwoodartdistrict.co.uk)

Drinking

Bell 617 Forest Road, E17 4NE (8523 2277, www.belle17.com).
Castle 15 Grosvenor Rise East, E17 9LB (8509 8095, www.thecastlegastropub.co.uk).
Chequers 145 High Street, Walthamstow, E17 7BX (8503 6401, www.chequerse17.com).
Heathcote Arms 344 Grove Green Road, E11 4EA (8558 7713).
Nag's Head 9 Orford Road, E17 9LP (8520 9709, www.thenagshead17.com).
Northcote Arms 110 Grove Green Road, E11 4EL (8518 7516).
North Star 24 Browning Road, E11 3AR (8989 5777).
Red Lion 640 High Road Leytonstone, E11 3AA (8988 2929, www.theredlionleytonstone.com).
Wild Card Brewery Unit 7, Ravenswood Industrial Estate, Shernhall Street, E17 9HQ (www.wildcardbrewery.co.uk). Brewery Tap Bar open at weekends.
Ye Olde Rose & Crown 53 Hoe Street, E17 4SA (8509 3880, www.yeolderoseandcrowntheatrepub.co.uk).

God's Own Junkyard; Wild Card Brewery

On the up

Olympic sports facilities

Community spirit

Dismal shopping

Zone 3

A12

Hornbeam, Walthamstow

Shopping

East London Sausage Company 57 Orford Road, E17 9NJ (8520 4060).
Froth & Rind 37 Orford Road, E17 9NL (www.frothandrind.com). Includes the East London Cheese Board and the E17 Tap Rooms.
God's Own Junkyard Unit 12, Ravenswood Industrial Estate, Shernhall Street, E17 9HQ (8509 0157, www.godsownjunkyard.co.uk).
Hoe Street Central Hoe Street, E17 4RT
Mother's Ruin Unit 18, Ravenswood Industrial Estate, Shernhall Street, E17 9HQ (07905 484711, www.mothersruin.net).
Walthamstow Farmers' Market Town Square, by Selborne Walk shopping centre, E17 (7833 0338, www.lfm.org.uk). Sun.
Walthamstow Market High Street, E17 (Street Trading Section 8496 3000). Tue-Sat.
Wild Goose Bakery 654 High Road, E11 3AA (www.thewildgoosebakery.co.uk).
Wood Street Market 98-100 Wood Street, E17 3HX (8521 0410, www.woodstreetindoor market.co.uk). Tue-Sat.

Things to do

Cinemas & theatres
Empire The Scene, 267 High Street, Walthamstow, E17 7FD (0871 471 4714, www.empirecinemas.co.uk).

Stow Film Lounge Orford House, 73 Orford Road, E17 9QR (07910 643987, www.stowfilmlounge.com). Independent rep cinema.

Galleries & museums
Fill the Gap Church Lane, EH11 1HE (07984 473516). TfL-run community exhibition space.
Stone Space 6 Church Lane, E11 1HG (www.the stonespace.com). Community-run exhibition space.
Tokarska Gallery 163 Forest Road, E17 6HE (8531 5419, www.tokarskagallery.co.uk).
Vestry House Museum Vestry Road, E17 9NH (8496 4391, www.walthamforest.gov.uk). Local history museum.
William Morris Gallery Lloyd Park, Forest Road, E17 4PP (8496 4390, www.wmgallery.org.uk). Celebration of the Arts and Crafts designer in his former home.

Gigs, clubs & comedy
Walthamstow Folk Club 53 Hoe Street, E17 4SA (07740 612607, www.walthamstowfolk.co.uk). Friendly folk club at Ye Olde Rose & Crown pub.
What's Cookin' Leytonstone Ex-Servicemen's Club, 2 Harvey Road, E11 3DB (8539 2584, www.whatscookin.co.uk).

Green spaces
For more details see www.walthamforest.gov.uk.
Coronation Gardens Buckingham Road, E10 5NG. Ornamental gardens, bandstand and maze.

Drapers Field Temple Mills Lane, E15 2DD. Olympic legacy sports park.

Ridgeway Park The Ridgeway, Old Church Road, E4. Putting, pétanque, playgrounds and a miniature railway.

Lee Valley Walk. Footpath and cycle path from Waltham Abbey to the Thames.

Leyton Flats & Hollow Pond Whipps Cross Road, E11 1NJ. Angling, walking and boating.

Leyton Jubilee Park Seymour Road, E10 7BL. Sports pitches and a pirate ship.

Lloyd Park Forest Road, E17 4PP. Playground, skatepark, outdoor gym and sports including free tennis. Home of William Morris Gallery.

Walthamstow Marshes Lea Bridge Road, E10 7QL (www.walthamstow-wetlands.org.uk).

WaterWorks Centre & Middlesex Filter Beds Lammas Road, E10 7QB (8988 7566, www.visitleevalley.org.uk). Disused filter beds, now a nature reserve.

Gyms & leisure centres

More facilities are available in the Queen Elizabeth Olympic Park, Newham.

Chingford Leisure Centre Unit 4, Larkswood Leisure Park, New Road, E4 9EY (8523 8215, www.better.org.uk). With 25m and children's pools.

Community Pool Waltham Forest College, 707 Forest Road, E17 4JB (8501 8172, www.thecommunitypool.org). 30m pool available outside college times.

Lee Valley Hockey & Tennis Centre Eton Manor, Leadmill Lane, E20 3AD (0845 677 0604, www.visitleevalley.org).

Lee Valley Ice Centre Lea Bridge Road, E10 7QL (8533 3154, www.leevalleypark.org.uk).

Leyton Leisure Centre 763 High Road Leyton, E10 5AB (8558 8858, www.better.org.uk). Steam room, pools and flumes.

Leytonstone Leisure Centre Cathall Road, E11 4LA (8539 8343, www.better.org.uk).

Peter May Sports Centre 135 Wadham Road, E17 4HR (8531 9358, www.better.org.uk).

Waltham Forest Pool & Track 170 Chingford Road, E17 5AA. Athletics track, competition pool, diving boards, spa, floodlit pitches, climbing wall, skatebording and BMX. Reopening 2016.

Walthamstow Leisure Centre, 243 Markhouse Road, E17 8RN (8520 7464, www.better.org.uk). Includes Walthamstow Gymnastics Club.

Outdoor pursuits

Epping Forest Mountain Biking (07543 033515, www.eppingforestmtb.co.uk). Guided rides and skills coaching.

Lee Valley Riding Centre Lea Bridge Road, E10 7QL (8556 2629, www.leevalleypark.org.uk).

Lee Valley White Water Centre Station Road, EN9 1AB (0845 677 0606, www.visitleevalley.org.uk/go/whitewater).

Score 100 Oliver Road, E10 5JY (8539 8474, www.walthamforest.gov.uk).

Wanstead Golf Course Overton Drive, E11 2LW (8989 3938, www.wansteadgolf.org.uk).

Spectator sports
Leyton Orient FC Matchroom Stadium, Brisbane Road, E10 5NF (0871 310 1883, www.leytonorient.com).

Schools

Primary
There are 52 state primary schools in Waltham Forest, seven of which are church schools. There are also seven independent primaries, of which six are faith schools and one is a Montessori school. See www.walthamforest.gov.uk, www.education.gov.uk/edubase and www.ofsted.gov.uk for more information.

Secondary
Buxton School Terling Close, E11 3NT (8534 3425, www.buxtonschool.org.uk).
Chingford Foundation School 31 Nevin Drive, E4 7LT (8529 1853, www.chingford-school.co.uk).
Connaught School for Girls 39 Connaught Road, E11 4AB (8539 3029, www.connaught-school. co.uk). Girls only.
Frederick Bremer School Siddeley Road, E17 4EY (8498 3340, www.bremer.org.uk).
George Mitchell School 192 Vicarage Road, E10 5DX (8539 6198, www.georgemitchellschool.co.uk).
Heathcote School 96 Normanton Park, E4 6ES (8498 5110, www.heathcoteschool.com).
Highams Park School 34 Handsworth Avenue, E4 9PJ (8527 4051, www.highamspark. waltham.sch.uk).
Holy Family Technology College 34 Shernhall Street, E17 3EA (8520 0482, www.holyfamily. waltham.sch.uk).
Kelmscott School 245 Markhouse Road, E17 8DN (8521 2115, www.kelmscott.waltham.sch.uk).
Lammas School 150 Seymour Road, E10 7LX (8988 5860, www.lammas.waltham.sch.uk).
Leytonstone School 159 Colworth Road, E11 1JD (8988 7420, www.leytonstoneschool.org).
Norlington Boys' School Norlington Road, E10 6JZ (8539 3055, www.norlington.net). Boys only.
Rushcroft School 57 Rushcroft Road, E4 8SG (8531 9231, www.rushcroft.waltham.sch.uk).
Walthamstow Academy Billet Road, E17 5DP (8527 3750, www.walthamstow-academy.org).
Walthamstow Girls' School 60 Church Hill, E17 9RZ (8509 9446, www.wsfg.waltham.sch.uk). Girls only.
Willowfield School Clifton Avenue, E17 6HL (8527 4065, www.willowfield-school.net).

Property

Estate agents
Allen Davies www.allendavies.co.uk
Central Estate Agents www.central-estates.co.uk
Churchill Estates www.churchill-estates.co.uk
Clarke Hillyer www.clarkehillyer.co.uk
CMC Estates www.cmcestates.co.uk
Estates17 www.estates17.co.uk
Village Estates www.villageestates.org.uk

Local knowledge

www.guardian-series.co.uk
www.leytonstonerlondon.in
www.walthamstownow.org.uk
www.walthamstowscene.org.uk
www.walthamstowvillageguide.com
www.walthamstowvillage.net

USEFUL INFO

Borough size
3,882 hectares

Population
274,100

Ethnic mix
White 62.0%
Asian or Asian British 15.7%
Black or Black British 14.4%
Mixed 4.3%
Chinese or other 3.7%

London Borough of Waltham Forest
Waltham Forest Town Hall, Forest Road, E17 4JF (8496 3000, www.walthamforest.gov.uk)

Council run by
Labour

MPs
Chingford, Iain Duncan Smith; Leyton & Wanstead, John Cryer (Labour); Walthamstow, Stella Creasy (Labour)

Main recycling centre
South Access Road Household Waste & Recycling, Markhouse Avenue, E17 8AX

Council tax
£964.81 to £2,894.42